Michael Armstrong is a management consultant with extensive experience in general, personnel and reward management in the aerospace and food industries and in publishing. He is a well-known author on personnel and management subjects and his books include *A Handbook of Personnel Management Practice, How to be an Even Better Manager, Improving Organizational Effectiveness* and *Performance Management*, all published by Kogan Page.

Helen Murlis is a senior director of Hay Management Consultants, providing practice leadership in performance management and its links with reward strategy. She was previously head of the Top Pay Unit at Incomes Data Services and executive remuneration adviser at the British Institute of Management. She is currently Vice President of Pay and Employment Conditions as well as Chairman of the IPD Compensation Forum.

REWARD MANAGEMENT

A HANDBOOK OF REMUNERATION STRATEGY & PRACTICE

Michael Armstrong
AND
Helen Murlis

Published in association with the
Institute of Personnel and Development

First published in 1988
Second edition 1991
This third edition in 1994
Reprinted 1995, 1996 (twice), 1997

Kogan Page Limited
120 Pentonville Road
London N1 9JN

© Michael Armstrong and Helen Murlis 1988, 1991, 1994

British Library Cataloguing in Publication Data

A CIP record for this book is available from the British Library.

ISBN 0 7494 1009 4

Typeset by DP Photosetting, Aylesbury, Bucks
Printed and bound in Great Britain by Clays Ltd, St Ives plc

Contents

PART 9   MANAGING REWARD PROCESSES

APPENDICES

Acknowledgements

We are indebted to Employment Conditions Abroad and Lucy McGuire of KPMG for assistance in the preparation of the chapter on international remuneration, to Alan Judes of Bacon and Woodrow for Chapter 31 (Tax Considerations) and Appendix K – the UK Share Option Pricing Model and Tony Vernon Harcourt of Monks Partnership for permission to quote from survey findings. We would also like to thank Isabel Bartlett of Howe Associates for contributing Appendix B (Statistical terms used in pay surveys and analysis).

We are grateful to Towers Perrin, the Wyatt Company, KPMG Peat Marwick, PA Consulting, Saville and Holdsworth and Employment Relations Associates, PE-International, the Institute of Administrative Management and Price Water-house for allowing us to summarize their approaches to job evaluation.

We are also grateful to the IPM Library, Incomes Data Services, Industrial Relations Services and the Library of Hay Management Consultants for assistance with sources and material for the bibliography.

We would also like to record our gratitude to Vicky Wright, Cliff Weight, Frank Hartle, Paul West, Derek Pritchard, Tony Richter, Richard Bednarek, Celia Barker and Steve Watson of Hay Management Consultants for their many helpful specialist comments and suggestions on the manuscript for this new edition.

We also owe a considerable debt of gratitude to our families for their unstinting support and encouragement to keep this book 'alive' to reflect the rapidly changing world of reward management in the 1990s.

Preface to the Third Edition

This edition of *Reward Management* incorporates radical revisions to the previous text based upon the many developments in the field which have occurred over the last three years. It also takes into account some significant research findings published recently on performance-related pay, incentives, skill-based pay and performance management. More attention is paid to the Government's profit-related pay scheme which, since changes were made to some of its regulations, has become much more popular.

Specifically, the parts on reward management processes and the evolution, review and development of reward management policies and practices have been largely rewritten. We have also rewritten the chapter on job evaluation in order to explore new concepts of this as a process, and to provide answers to the many criticisms of job evaluation which have been based mainly on the way job evaluation schemes used to operate. We provide examples of the new approaches being developed to fit changing organizational requirements.

We have also enlarged the scope of the book to cover shop floor payment arrangements, including incentive and skill-based schemes and gainsharing.

Our philosophy

In developing and, in some areas, rethinking ideas expressed in earlier editions, we have evolved our own philosophy about reward management, the key points of which are as follows:

- It is neither possible nor desirable to be prescriptive in the sense of providing easy and superficial answers to subtle and far-reaching problems of motivation and reward. We believe absolutely that a contingency approach has to be used when dealing with this subject; ie that the right reward processes are the ones which are right for a particular organization. There is indeed such a thing as good practice, but it is never universally good practice.
- We are not in the business of peddling panaceas. There are no quick fixes or sudden transformations available in this field – no holy grails, only horses for courses.
- We do believe, however, that there are guidelines available when deciding what *is* the most appropriate practice and we have described the various approaches available from which a choice can be made, and their advantages and disadvantages, as they appear to us. We have also included a number of checklists to help in analysing requirements and we have provided examples of good practice for comparison purposes.
- Our approach is empirical. It is based on the experience and observations of colleagues, researchers and ourselves. It is, however, underpinned by theories about motivation, incentives and reward. But we join with Douglas McGregor

in the belief that 'there is nothing so practical as a good theory', ie one which is based on practical research, experimentation and analysis of experience.

- We have come to the view that what we are writing about is a set of processes relating to reward management, which include the design and maintenance of pay structures as well as the fundamental processes of assessing job size (job evaluation) and measuring and rewarding performance (performance management, incentives and performance-related pay). We have rejected the term 'reward system' because it conveys the idea of some sort of mechanism for converting inputs into outputs, and there is nothing mechanical about reward management. Of course reward management involves the application of schemes and procedures within pay structures. But what matters most is not the design of the scheme, procedure or structure, but the way it is applied and used, and these are the process issues which ultimately determine the effectiveness of an organization's reward policies and practices.
- Planned and managed incremental change is easier to design and implement than quantum leaps into unknown territory.
- It is necessary to provide for tactical advances and retreats. We will not get it right all the time.
- Philosophy needs to precede strategy and implementation. We need to be clear about what we are paying for and why before we rush into detailed design. Strategic integrity needs to underpin technical excellence.
- In Voltaire's words: 'The best is the enemy of the good' – sometimes a successful future lies in agreeing what, in the short term, we can only get 'nearly right'. We follow Aristotle's teaching in the *Nichomachean Ethics* that: 'It is the mark of an educated mind to rest satisfied with the degree of precision that the nature of the subject admits, and not to seek a degree of exactness when only an approximation is possible'. Practicality not perfection should be the aim. There will always be time available in the future to make improvements based on experience.
- It is, however, still necessary to set clear short *and* longer term objectives about what is to be achieved by reward management innovations. Some attempt must also be made to define critical success factors and performance measures and it is, of course, essential to monitor and evaluate progress in the light of these success factors and measures.

Introduction

Purpose

In this book we examine all aspects of reward management. We consider how reward processes function within the framework of organization and pay structures and in the context of an organization's reward philosophies, strategies and policies. Our purpose is to define how reward management can become an integral part of the management processes of an organization and make a major contribution to fulfilling its mission and reaching its objectives.

Achieving the purpose

To achieve this purpose, we first consider the basic processes of reward management and what motivation theory can teach us about financial and non-financial rewards. We then review the foundations of reward management – its philosophies, strategies and policies and the guiding principles which govern how reward processes operate.

In part two, we continue with a general analysis of how reward management processes are affected by the position of an organization in its life cycle of birth, maturity, decline and regeneration. Consideration is then given to the points which should be covered when carrying out a diagnostic review of reward policies and practices and the factors which affect the overall development of reward processes and structures.

In part three we move into the fundamental processes of establishing job size and values before examining, in part four, the various forms of reward structures and how they are designed and developed.

One of our recurrent themes is that reward management is about performance: of individuals, teams and the organization as a whole. In parts five and six we therefore examine the philosophy and operation of performance management processes and the various approaches that can be adopted to paying for performance, skill and competence.

The rest of the book covers specific aspects of reward management, including employee benefits, total remuneration, boardroom pay and the management of reward processes. The book concludes with a review of trends in reward management.

The complexity of reward management processes is illustrated by the range of subject matter we are considering. It is enhanced by the extraordinarily rapid developments in reward management over the last decade. These have led to fundamental changes in approaches to reward management and, recently, a surge in iconoclasm as some of the traditional reward beliefs and practices have been challenged by academics and practitioners. There is now a much wider variety of choice than there was even ten years ago about how we tackle any of the fundamental reward processes and practices such as job evaluation, pay structures, performance management or paying for performance. We review these developments below in order to provide a backcloth against which reward management policies and practices will be examined in this book.

A decade of fundamental change

Over the last decade or so the way in which pay is managed and the principles applied to remuneration policy development in the UK have changed fundamentally. The changes involved have been felt across all parts of the UK economy, although they have occurred at varying speeds and to varying degrees, depending on the capability of organizations in the different sectors of the economy to respond to changes in their operating environment. In this introduction we track what was happening to remuneration practice in the UK in the early 1980s; what has changed over the ensuing decade and why; what are the key components of pay among major UK employers and the main influences on current pay and benefit entitlements; how organizations have responded to the pressures of the continuing economic recession; and what the pointers are for remuneration policy developments over the next few years.

Where have we come from?

The remuneration practices prevailing in the UK in the early 1980s were very much the legacy of the previous decade in which a Labour government implemented various forms of incomes policy, and trade unions had more influence than ever before, and which resulted in the increasing centralization of pay decision-making.

The election of a Conservative government in 1979 changed little immediately – it first had to grapple with the economic recession of the early 1980s and begin to put the foundations in place which, over the course of the 1980s, led to a process of accelerating change. It has to be said, too, that at the beginning of the 1980s remuneration professionals saw their role in a very different light from the way they perceive it today. Salary administration was very much seen as a 'back-room' function in which numerate specialists worked out the details of policies that came from elsewhere – from government, from head office or from general management. There was little obvious link between what happened on the remuneration front and overall business strategy, let alone an organization's human resources management strategy – if it had one. There was certainly little line management involvement in, or ownership of, the pay practice that emerged.

So the main characteristics of UK pay practice at the beginning of the 1980s were as follows:

- a relatively homogeneous pay market for much of the economy based on national 'going rates' negotiated centrally with the major trade unions;
- pay structures for white-collar and managerial staff based on 'fine' grades which, while designed to facilitate promotion increases that fell outside the control of incomes policy, were all too frequently built upon increasingly abused and decaying job evaluation schemes;
- compressed differentials at management level resulting from years of incomes policy in which management came off worse;
- few incentive schemes or performance-related salary progression systems for managers, professional, technical or office workers, the norm being fixed service-related pay increments;

- equity sharing restricted to the all-employee provisions of 1978 and 1980;
- an unhealthy emphasis on the provision of tax-effective benefits for senior management (this was the time of leased suits and leased hand-made shirts!) resulting from punitively high levels of marginal taxation; and
- initially, a sense of inertia and unwillingness to move towards a more strategic view of remuneration policy development.

What has changed and why?

Once the 'Thatcher Revolution' took root and created greater business confidence (towards the mid-1980s), major changes in remuneration practice began to appear. In looking at the remuneration policy developments that emerged it is important to remember that their philosophical underpinning was often the 'think tanks', pressure groups and academic market economists (such as Milton Friedman, Madsen Pirie and Alan Walters) who influenced the Prime Minister and the right wing of the Conservative party. As far as influencing opinion was concerned, the pressure groups (eg the Adam Smith Institute, the Institute of Directors and the Institute of Economic Affairs) largely took precedence over the business schools and more academic UK management theorists, who might have been expected to add a dose of 'wet' occupational and motivation psychology as well as organization theory to what emerged largely as a 'dry' economic argument about people, money and motivation. In retrospect, top management, whether they were ministers, senior civil servants or directors of major companies, sought to translate a simplistic motivational view into the way employees were managed and paid.

As a consequence, remuneration moved very rapidly in the mid-1980s from a back-office administration role to a major management lever for change in the creation of the 'enterprise culture'. In particular, there was a strong focus on creating a 'pay-for-performance' environment. Since this time, top managers have continued to recognize that remuneration is an important ingredient of business strategy, but they increasingly acknowledge that simplistic models of pay and output-based performance linkage are not necessarily appropriate or workable. The last few years have therefore been characterized by a whole range of developments.

Recent developments

Pay structures

Competitive pressures, the recession of the early 1990s and the need to respond and adapt rapidly to new challenges have forced organizations to slim down and operate more flexibly. New technology imposes entirely different and much more flexible working patterns and creates roles in which new and wider ranges of skills have to be deployed.

Pay structures have had to respond to these pressures. New broad-banded structures are often replacing the traditional narrow grades. Simpler, integrated pay structures or pay spines are being developed within which special needs can be catered for. Structures for 'families' of related jobs are being created which incorporate 'ladders' defining different levels of work or pay curves along which people progress as they acquire additional expertise and make a greater contribution to the achievement of team or organizational objectives.

Job evaluation

As noted above, organizations increasingly are placing less emphasis on hierarchy, introducing greater role flexibility and operating more fluidly. In these circumstances, job evaluation as traditionally practised has come under attack as being too rigid and unable to respond to the new demands for role flexibility.

It can indeed be said that job evaluation used to be about the control of uniformity, but it can not and should not fulfil that role any more. What it can contribute is help in the management of diversity in the kind of organizations and structures that we are now learning to live with.

In the face of these new organizational imperatives, businesses are now reviewing the appropriateness of their job evaluation schemes and the processes they use to operate them. It is still critical to have a firm and well-understood base for pay differentials, however the organization is structured and whatever its work patterns. But it is recognised that job evaluation has to function in organizations where roles are much more flexible, and its methodology and processes must take account of that fact.

Paying for performance

There has been much more focus on incentives for top management and the implementation of performance-related pay down through organizations. This has happened as a conscious move to change the nature of the debate about performance, and also to reflect a new perception of equity based on the developing view that it is fairer to reward in relation to personal contribution than for length of service in a job.

However, from some, mainly academic, quarters vigorous attacks have been directed at the concept of performance-related pay (PRP) as a nostrum for increasing motivation and performance. And it has become generally recognized that PRP can not be relied upon as a single lever for this purpose. It has also been accepted that PRP has often been introduced naively without sufficient consideration having been given to problems such as that of measuring performance fairly and consistently – 'if you can't measure performance, you can't pay for it'.

Other important developments in pay-for-performance schemes have been the increased emphasis on 'team pay' (team as distinct from individual incentives) in response to new working arrangements, the need for role flexibility, and the greater interest in organization-wide schemes such as gainsharing and profit-related pay.

Performance management

Greater attention has been given to the process of performance management – an imperative born at least in part of the realization that crude cash incentives or merit pay systems rarely, if ever, work without adequate support, and that the best way to produce real performance improvements is to change behaviour. This comes from achieving much greater clarity as to what success in a particular role looks like, what resources need to be devoted to securing success, what skills and competences are required, what training and development is needed to produce these required levels of skill and competence and how rewards can be designed to be consistent with this broader series of processes – not least how they reinforce team and collegiate contributions as well as individual endeavour. Research published recently by the Institute of Personnel Management,[1,2] the Institute of Manpower Studies and the London School of Economics, based on evaluations of performance-related pay practice at the end of the 1980s and in the early 1990s, have strongly reinforced this view.

Skills, careers and flexibility

As the skills shortages of the mid-1980s sharpened, an increasing fragmentation of the pay market occurred. Gaps developed between the sufferers and the survivors of the early 1980s recession and between regions dogged by skills shortages. Skills shortages were particularly evident in London and the south east (where the finance sector, which took off under the deregulation of the City in 1986, stretched the labour market to its limits), in information technology and in the high-technology sector, where the graduate shortage of the late 1980s hit hardest. In contrast, labour supply in the north of England and in Wales and the west presented few problems. The market remained heterogeneous until the early 1990s, putting increased pressure on the quality of market monitoring which was only mitigated by the recession of the early 1990s when labour market pressures largely evaporated.

As a result there was an increasing demand for flexibility in pay structures both in terms of specific market premiums to deal with skills shortages and of regional market responses where 'London rates' were uncalled for in the face of lower local living costs and market pressures. Benefits packages became more closely scrutinized as the Government's progressive moves towards tax neutralization of company cars and other benefits encouraged organizations to review the extent to which they could opt for 'clean cash' in place of a benefits package structured to meet the needs of an often rapidly vanishing 'cradle to grave' career pattern.

A growing focus on pay and performance management processes which reflect the acquisition and use of defined skills and competences is emerging from the need to expand the skills base and create 'learning organizations' able to respond rapidly to changing market conditions and to follow the principles of *kaizen*, or continuous improvement. In tandem with this, organizations are delayering – dispensing with middle-management hierarchies made redundant by a mix of changed management styles and the information revolution. More emphasis is being placed on the value of lateral moves which build needed experience, and on progression through fewer, broader salary bands.

What has also become more evident is that people are tending to develop, in Charles Handy's phrase, a 'portfolio' of careers. As noted above, people are less likely to remain with the same firm for the whole of their career or even a sub-stantial part of it. By choice or perforce they are making many more job and, indeed, career changes. Organizations, especially in the public and voluntary sectors, are turning more towards short-term contracts and there is an increasing tendency to use contract labour and casual employees. Pay structures and employee benefit packages no longer need to cater for long-term careers and career planning has become a much more short-term affair – the questions asked now are not 'where is this individual likely to be in ten years' time?' but 'what's the next move?', and this could well be a horizontal or at least a diagonally upward move rather than a vertical one. The emphasis is turning to flexible roles at broadly the same level and this encourages pay practices which relate a proportion of earnings to demonstrable competence and skill. Job analysis and job evaluation has to take more account of role flexibility and the 'job family' concept – the existence of groups of jobs where the basic role is broadly the same but where role requirements involve the use of different levels of skill and competence and greater degrees of responsibility.

Empowerment and devolution

The pressure for flatter organizations and devolution has been accompanied by the concept of empowerment – the process of giving people more scope or 'power' to exercise control over and take responsibility for their work, thus providing greater 'space' for individuals to use their abilities and encouraging them to take decisions close to the point of impact. The drive for empowerment, however, has to be accompanied by processes which reward people appropriately for the greater contribution they have been enabled to make.

Line management has increasingly become involved in the design and operation of new pay systems as the processes of empowerment and the decentralization of remuneration policy decision-making advance, and as organizations seek to make practice as relevant as possible to local business needs. To work successfully, this process has required a considerable investment in the training and continuing development of line managers.

Role of the human resource function and the remuneration specialist

In spite of, perhaps because of, this process of devolution, there is still a need for the human resource (HR) function to provide guidance in creating and developing reward policies and processes and to ensure that agreed policies are implemented consistently. Remuneration specialists have an important innovatory role based on an understanding of the strategic business needs of the organization and knowledge of good practice elsewhere. They should be in a position to track new reward management concepts and applications and evaluate their relevance to the business. They can also provide for continuity – in our experience, the danger of devolving all responsibility for reward management to line managers is that they spend too much time re-inventing the wheel – reviving, often naively, old ideas which are past their sell-by date.

It should also be recognized that good reward practice is also based on an understanding of the factors which influence motivation and performance. Without this knowledge, there is a real danger of introducing half-baked pay-for-performance and benefit schemes or unworkable pay structures. Remuneration specialists should be in a position to use their knowledge of these factors to influence the design and application of reward practices which take them fully into account.

Finally, remuneration professionals are in the best position to analyze and evaluate the effectiveness of the organization's pay practices. They can take a reasonably detached view and they have access to all the information needed for such analyses, especially when reward management administration has been fully computerised.

The pressure on costs

The forces of world-wide competition and recession have compelled organizations to pay much more attention to managing costs. The emphasis in reward management practice has therefore shifted to getting value for money rather than pouring funds into pay-for-performance and employee benefit schemes, for which thorough cost/benefit analyses have not been undertaken. The objectives of reward initiatives increasingly are spelt out in cost/benefit terms and more care is taken over monitoring their impact and evaluating their cost-effectiveness.

Traditional fine-graded salary structures and payment-for-results schemes have come under attack because they have led to grade or earnings drift – upgradings or pay increases taking place without a commensurate increase in responsibility or performance.

Although pay decisions are being devolved more to line managers, tighter controls have been imposed over their pay budgets, and they are being held more accountable for the productivity of their work forces in the sense of labour costs per unit of output.

Pay increases are much more related to individual and organizational performance and individual market worth. The move away from fixed incremental schemes has already been noted, but some organizations are questioning the validity and cost-effectiveness of permanent increases in base pay within a performance-related pay/salary grade progression environment. They are questioning the assumption that an improvement in performance one year will be maintained in succeeding years and asking why someone should be paid a continuing premium above the rate for the job when performance is declining. There has therefore been a move towards more one-off but re-earnable 'achievement' bonuses. These recognise the reality that in times of low inflation (under 2 per cent in the summer of 1993) such bonuses may have more meaning and impact than smaller increases which may disappoint – however well expectations about market conditions have been managed.

Companies are no longer committing themselves to annual pay reviews linked to the cost of living. They are saying that it is not their business totally to protect their work force against inflation. They are also saying that their first consideration must be what they can afford to pay, although it is often advisable for an organization to consider what it *has* to be able to afford to pay to get and keep high quality employees.

Impact of these developments

The result of these more recent developments has been to cast doubts on a number of cherished assumptions about how people should be rewarded. There has been a pendulum effect, for example a tendency to swing from a naive belief in the transformational nature of performance-related pay to the equally fallacious view that pay should not be related in any way to performance. Panaceas such as skill-based pay are adopted with enthusiasm in some quarters and equally quickly dropped as their costs become apparent.

Iconoclasm prevails, for example dismissing job evaluation because, as Ed Lawler has written: 'it is a poor fit in many business situations'.[3] But the iconoclasts seem unable to suggest anything to put in the place of job evaluation as a means of managing relativities or of performance-related pay as a method of rewarding contribution.

Yesterday's certainties have become today's dilemmas. If one were to take a pessimistic view, it would seem that reward management is in a state of chaos. In the words of Yeats, it appears that: 'Things fall apart, the centre will not hold; mere anarchy is loosed upon the world'.

We are more optimistic. As we intend to demonstrate in this book, we believe that a coherent philosophy on how to manage rewards has emerged in the last few years. We also believe that it is possible to identify clear guide-lines on reward management practices, although these will always have to be interpreted and applied within the context of the organization's culture and strategies and there will always be a choice on what reward policies and practices are best for an organization in the light of its particular circumstances.

References

1. (1992) *Performance Management in the UK – an analysis of the issues*, Institute of Personnel Management, London.
2. Cannell, M and Wood, S (1992) *Incentive Pay: impact and evolution*, Institute of Personnel Management, London
3. Lawler, E (1990) *Strategic Pay*, Jossey-Bass, San Francisco

PART 1

REWARD MANAGEMENT PROCESSES

1

The Basis of Reward Management

What reward management is about

Reward management is about the design, implementation, maintenance, communication and evolution of reward processes which help organizations to improve performance and achieve their objectives.

Reward processes are based on reward philosophies and strategies and contain arrangements in the shape of policies, guiding principles, practices, structures and procedures which are devised and managed to provide and maintain appropriate types and levels of pay, benefits and other forms of reward. This constitutes the financial reward aspect of the process which incorporates processes and procedures for tracking market rates, measuring job values, designing and maintaining pay structures, paying for performance, competence and skill, and providing employee benefits.

Non-financial rewards – intrinsic and extrinsic motivation

However, reward management is not just about money. It is also concerned with those non-financial rewards which provide intrinsic or extrinsic motivation. Intrinsic motivation (motivation from the work itself) is achieved by satisfying individual needs for achievement, responsibility, variety, challenge, influence in decision-making and membership of a supportive team. Extrinsic non-financial motivation (motivation through means other than pay incentives) provided directly by the organization is achieved by recognition, skills development and learning and career opportunities.

We therefore agree with the following views expressed by Michael Beer:[1]

> Organizations must reward employees because, in return, they are looking for certain kinds of behaviour: they need competent individuals who agree to work with a high level of performance and loyalty. Indivi-

23

dual employees, in return for their commitment, expect certain extrinsic rewards in the form of promotion, salary, fringe benefits, perquisites, bonuses or stock options. Individuals also seek intrinsic rewards such as feelings of competence, achievement, responsibility, significance, influence, personal growth, and meaningful contribution. Employees will judge the adequacy of their exchange with the organization by assessing both sets of rewards.

The total reward process

Although most of this book deals with financial rewards, we feel strongly that in developing and operating reward processes just as much attention should be paid to non-financial rewards, and we discuss this in Chapter 2. We take a holistic view of reward management as a process which is integrated with all aspects of human resource management and which provides a number of important levers for improving performance and commitment. This is what we mean when we refer to the total reward process, which contains the elements illustrated in Figure 1.1.

This shows that reward management strategies and policies are driven by corporate and human resource management strategies. These provide guidance on the processes required in four main areas: (1) non-financial rewards, (2) employee benefits, (3) pay structures and (4) the measurement and management of performance. All these contribute as follows to the ultimate aim of improved performance at the business, departmental, team and individual levels:

- non-financial rewards satisfy individual needs for challenge, responsibility, influence in decision making, variety, recognition and career opportunities;
- employee benefits satisfy employees' needs for personal security and provide remuneration in forms other than pay, which meet other needs and may be tax-efficient;
- pay structures which, by combining the results of market surveys (which also contribute to decisions on benefit levels) and job evaluation, define equitable and competitive levels of pay, pay relativities (differentials) and pay progression limits;
- the measurement and management of performance, which measures performance in relation to outputs (contribution and the achievement of objectives and standards of performance) and inputs (the application of skills and competences and the behaviours affecting performance), and leads to the design and operation of pay-for-performance schemes and continuous development and training programmes;
- basic and performance pay and employee benefits combine to form total remuneration.

In the next two sections of this chapter we consider how this approach can be translated into a wide-reaching set of aims and how these aims can be achieved. We continue by summarizing our views on the overall impact reward management can make. To underline our belief in the need for an integrated approach to reward management we then discuss the framework for the development of reward management strategies and policies provided by the processes of strategic management and human resource management (HRM). Finally, we summarize how the total reward system operates, paying particular attention to the significance of the *processes* of reward management, as distinct from the content of the reward management schemes and procedures used by the organization.

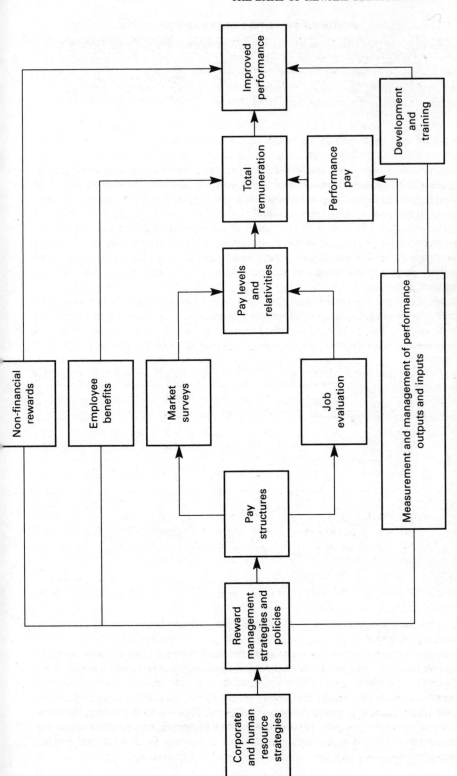

Figure 1.1 *Reward management: strategies and processes*

Aims of reward management

Our contention is that total reward management can have a profound effect on all aspects of the operation of an organization and the ways in which it manages its human resources. Hence the far-reaching nature of the objectives to which we believe organizations should aspire when developing their reward processes.

The aims of reward management should be to:

- *Improve individual and organizational performance* – support the attainment of the organization's mission and strategies and thus help to achieve sustainable competitive advantage and increase shareholder value.
- *Encourage value-added performance* – achieve continuous improvement by focusing attention on areas where the maximum added value can be obtained from improved performance and by getting people to agree demanding goals in those areas that match their capability. This is in accordance with Michael Porter's[2] belief that competitive advantage arises out of a firm creating value for its buyers. His concept of the 'value chain' as a means of identifying those of the firm's activities which are strategically relevant, can be used as a tool to indicate how reward management can help to add value to those primary and support activities.
- *Support culture management* – underpin and, as necessary, provide levers for changing the organization's culture as expressed by its values and norms for performance, innovation, risk-taking, quality, flexibility and teamworking.
- *Achieve integration* – function as an integral part of the management processes of the organization. Reward management should be a key component in a mutually reinforcing and coherent range of human resource management processes.
- *Support managers* – provide them with the authority and skills needed to use rewards to help achieve their goals. It is necessary, however, to ensure that managers have a strong framework of guiding principles and procedures within which they can play their part in managing rewards for their staff with whatever guidance they may need.
- *Empower individuals and teams* – use the total reward system to raise performance and quality through empowered people who have the scope and skills needed to succeed and are rewarded accordingly. Reward processes should help to upgrade competence and encourage personal development.
- *Compete in the labour market* – attract and retain high quality people.
- *Motivate* members of the organization to achieve superior levels of quality performance.
- *Increase commitment* so that members of the organization will develop a strong belief in and acceptance of the organization and will identify with its mission, strategies and values.
- *Achieve fairness and equity* – reward people fairly and consistently according to their contribution.
- *Support new developments* – help in the introduction and effective use of sophisticated management techniques, for example, JIT (just-in-time), FMS (flexible manufacturing systems), cellular manufacturing, CIM (computer-integrated manufacturing) and other applications of information technology such as integrated business systems and point-of-event data capture systems.
- *Enhance quality* – help to achieve continuous improvement in levels of quality and customer service by supporting such processes as TQM (total quality management).

- *Promote teamworking* – assist in improving cooperation and effective team-working at all levels.
- *Encourage flexibility* – help to achieve the most efficient use of human resources through job-based, skills-based, and organization-based flexibility arrangements.
- *Provide value for money* – assess the costs as well as the benefits of reward management practices and ensure that they are operated cost effectively.

Achieving the aims – what reward management can do

The reward management aims set out above are, of course, ambitious. It might, in fact, be more realistic to describe them as aspirations rather than aims. But we do believe that they are worth striving for even if it proves difficult to attain them quickly or in full. We discuss approaches to achieving them below.

Performance improvement
Reward processes can drive and support desired behaviour at all levels in the organization by indicating to its members what types of behaviour will be rewarded, how this will take place and in general, how their expectations on the rewards they can obtain will be met. In particular, reward processes can:

- relate basic pay levels to contribution and value to the organization;
- reward people in accordance with organizational and/or team performance;
- provide incentives which relate pay directly to output;
- relate pay increases or bonuses to performance levels, contribution or increases in competence and skill (performance-related, competence-related and skill-based pay);
- deliver the message through incentive, performance-related pay or bonus schemes (as described in part 6) that performance is important and will be rewarded accordingly;
- develop a performance orientated culture through performance management processes as described in Chapters 14 and 15.

Value-added performance
Attention can be focused on areas where maximum added value can be achieved through performance-related pay and bonus and gainsharing schemes which relate rewards specifically to improved performance in those areas. For this purpose, use can also be made of performance management processes which are based on goal setting, measuring contribution and developing the capability to perform better in specified activities and behaviours.

Culture management
Performance management and pay-for-performance processes can provide for people to be appraised and rewarded on the basis both of the results they achieve and the extent to which what they do supports such values as innovation, quality, teamworking and continual improvement generally. The way in which reward processes are evolved and managed will demonstrate the organization's commitment to those values and other values and norms such as equity, flexibility, risk-taking and quick reaction to opportunities and threats.

Integration
The mutual reinforcement of human resource management practices can be achieved by using performance management processes to achieve a number of

interrelated purposes: clarifying roles, integrating individual and organizational objectives, identifying training needs, providing the basis for continuous development, and measuring performance as a means of deciding on performance-related pay increases. Pay curve systems as described in Chapter 12 can be devised which relate pay to competence and performance but also provide the basis for career planning and development.

Management support
One of the basic tenets of human resource management is that line managers are primarily responsible for all aspects of the management and development of their human resources. HRM is essentially an integrated line management activity. It is managers, therefore, who should manage rewards in their units or departments. But they need a framework within which to exercise this responsibility, and such a framework can and should be based on agreed guiding principles, defined pay structures (although these need not be rigid) and expertise in applying reward management processes in their areas. They will need guidance on how to operate the system – some more than others – and the human resource function will still need to monitor the implementation of reward policies and procedures. Managers will certainly have to work within agreed budgets for expenditure on remuneration.

Empowerment
Empowerment can be defined as the process of giving people control over, and responsibility for, their work, and ensuring that they have the knowledge and skills to do it to the satisfaction of both the organization and themselves. Here again, performance management, as an essential element of reward management, can help. A properly conceived and functioning performance management process will enable individuals to get together with their managers to discuss roles, responsibilities and training needs so that the scope for enlarging or enriching jobs can be identified and action plans agreed to enhance knowledge or skills. The performance management process can also be used to encourage and train managers to include counselling and coaching on performance and development matters as an essential part of their role. An element of upward assessment can be built into the process so that individuals can raise points with their managers concerning how the latter could usefully clarify roles, delegate more responsibility or provide better guidance.

Competitive pay
Levels of pay are by no means the only reasons why people join or stay with organizations, but they can be important factors in these decisions. Reward management policies will define where the organization wants its pay levels to be in relation to market rates (sometimes referred to as its pay stance or posture). Procedures can be set up to track market rates and to analyze recruitment problems and employee turnover rates. The aim will be to establish if pay is uncompetitive in any area and what should be done about it, within the constraint of what the organization can afford to pay.

Motivation

It is widely believed that money is the best motivator. Pay-for-performance schemes will undoubtedly motivate if they meet the stringent conditions set out in Chapter 16, but the degree to which they are effective as motivators will vary from person to person.

Other non-financial aspects of reward such as recognition and opportunities to achieve, learn and develop can be powerful motivators. However, much will depend on the organization culture and the quality of leadership, and this is an area where total reward strategies must be integrated with other aspects of human resource management strategy to develop a positive culture and to emphasise the importance of leadership.

Commitment

Reward processes can increase commitment by linking rewards to organizational performance through gainsharing, profit sharing or profit-related pay plans. A carefully structured and competitive employee benefit package which meets specific needs should help to create more favourable attitudes to the company amongst its employees.

Fairness and equity

Reward processes are more likely to improve motivation, performance and commitment if they are operated fairly and rewards are equitable in the sense that they are commensurate with the value of the job and of the person to the organization. An equitable reward system which is felt to be fair (ie respects the 'felt fair' principle) is most likely to be achieved if a systematic approach is adopted to measuring job or role values (see Chapters 9 and 10), and to assessing and rewarding performance (see Parts 5 and 6).

New developments

The introduction of more sophisticated management techniques and processes and the extended use of new technology may require higher levels of performance, the use of new or a wider range of skills or the acceptance of more responsibility. These techniques and processes include just-in-time systems, total quality management, business process re-engineering, flexible manufacturing systems, cellular manufacturing systems and computer-integrated manufacture. Increased demands on individuals and teams can be rewarded specifically or different pay structures can be introduced which reflect the new systems of work.

Teamworking

Teamworking in JIT systems and manufacturing cells can be supported by team bonuses and skill-based pay schemes which recognize the additional skills and responsibilities required from team members. As a result of flatter organizations, teamworking at management level and in office environments has become more important. This can be furthered by including the ability to manage teamwork as an essential managerial competence which will be appraised and, as appropriate, rewarded.

Flexibility

The requirement to adopt a flexible approach to managing organizations and their human resources arises from the needs to be competitive, adaptive and to manage the impact of new technology with its emphasis on flexible operations. It is also necessary to develop more fluid forms of organization in which complex innovations take place and which require a more flexible approach to structure, the definition of job roles and how job roles interact.

Traditional pay systems have inhibited flexibility in the following ways:

- perpetuating over-rigid demarcations between jobs;
- creating multi- and narrow-banded pay structures;
- using job evaluation schemes to reinforce, indeed ossify, hierarchical approaches to management and tightly controlled grading schemes;
- relating pay to time in the job rather than performance;
- failing to discriminate between good and poor performers;
- not responding quickly to skills shortages;
- failing to recognize that the reward system has to respond to individual needs rather than being imposed monolithically.

Flexibility in reward processes can be achieved by:

- increasing the proportion of variable performance-related pay in the total package;
- avoiding the use of rigid, narrow-banded and hierarchical pay structures by using broad-banded pay structures which allow for more scope to reward for extra skills or responsibilities and improved performance; or by such means as the use of pay curves, where progression is dependent on competence and performance (see Chapter 12);
- not having an over-mechanistic system of relating rewards to performance;
- treating job evaluation as a process which can be adjusted to meet specific needs rather than as a package which has to be applied rigidly – ie using it to help manage diversity rather than control conformity;
- relating pay awards as bonuses entirely to performance (individual, team or organizational) and to market rate movements, thus avoiding an explicit link with increases in the cost of living, and giving scope to award good performers more and poor performers less;
- allowing employees greater choice in the benefits they receive.

Overall impact of reward management

Reward management has an important part to play in the development of cultures in which individuals and teams take responsibility for continuous improvement. It affects organizational performance because of the impact it has on people's expectations as to how they will be rewarded.

However, some words of caution are necessary. Reward management can help to improve organizational, team and individual performance in all the areas discussed above but, essentially, it has a supporting and enabling role. It cannot be relied upon as the sole lever for improving performance. Reward management processes work best if they are part of a mutually supportive and coherent set of people-management activities which are carried out within the context of the organization's processes of strategic and human resource management.

The strategic management framework

The framework for human resource and reward management strategies is provided by the process of strategic management.

Strategic management is concerned with formulating strategies and strategic plans and managing the organization to achieve them. Strategies are declarations of intent. They define what the organization wants to become in the longer term. Human resource strategies which incorporate reward management strategies flow from these corporate or business strategies.

The key concepts used in strategic management are:

- *distinctive competence* – working out what the organization is best at, and what its special or unique capabilities are;
- *focus* – identifying and concentrating on the key strategic issues;
- *sustainable competitive advantage* – creating value for customers and stakeholders by continually improving the position of the organization in relation to its competitors; giving special attention to the three key factors of innovation, quality and cost reduction;
- *synergy* – developing a product-market posture with a combined performance which is greater than the sum of its parts;
- *resource allocation* – understanding the human, financial and material resource requirements of the strategy; ensuring that the resources are made available and that their use is optimized.

All these key concepts impact on human resource and reward management strategies.

Human resource management

Human resource management (HRM) is a strategic, management driven and coherent approach to the management of an organization's most important assets – the people working there who individually and collectively contribute to the achievement of its objectives for sustainable competitive advantage.

The objectives of human resource management are to:

- enable management to achieve organizational objectives through its work force;
- enable employees to fulfil their full capacity and potential and to deliver their maximum contribution to the achievement of organizational goals;
- foster commitment from individuals to the success of the company through a quality orientation in their performance and that of the whole organization;
- integrate human resource policies with business policies and reinforce an appropriate culture or, as necessary, re-shape an inappropriate culture;
- develop a coherent set of personnel and employment policies which jointly reinforce the organization's strategies for matching resources to business needs and improving performance;
- establish an environment in which the latent creativity and energy of employees will be unleashed;
- create conditions in which innovation, teamworking and total quality can flourish;
- encourage willingness to operate flexibly in the interests of the 'adaptive organization' and the pursuit of excellence.

It will be noted that the aims of reward management as set out earlier in this chapter largely coincide with or complement these HRM objectives. This emphasises the need to ensure that reward management strategies, policies and practices are fully integrated with those for all other aspects of human resource management.

How reward management functions

Reward management functions within the context of the organization's environment, its culture, and its business and human resource strategies. Reward management consists of a number of interconnected processes which are concerned with job evaluation, market rate analysis, job analysis, designing and managing pay structures, paying for performance and performance management, together with the procedures required to administer these processes. But we would like to emphasise the significance of *process* as the governing factor in how reward management works. Process is culture in action. It is 'the way things are done around here'. Reward management practices, procedures and structures provide the basic framework but it is the way in which they are used that counts, not the detail of their design.

Basis of reward management

Reward management policies and practices should be based on an understanding of the practical implications of motivation theory and how this affects the provision of both financial and non-financial rewards (see Chapter 2). This provides the foundation for the development of reward philosophies which, as discussed in Chapter 3, influence the formulation of reward strategies and policies and, ultimately, the guiding principles which indicate how the reward system should be designed and managed.

References

1. Beer, M (1984) 'Reward systems'. In *Managing Human Assets* (Beer, M, Spector, B, Lawrence, P and Quin Mills, D) The Free Press, New York
2. Porter, M (1985) *Competitive Advantage: Creating and Sustaining Superior Performance*, The Free Press, New York

2

Motivation and Financial and Non-Financial Rewards

The development of reward management policies, structures and practices will be underpinned by assumptions about how people can best be motivated to deliver high levels of performance. These assumptions may not be articulated but the reward philosophies and policies of an organization can be no better than the motivational theories and beliefs upon which they are based.

In this chapter we therefore examine motivation theory under the following headings:

- the process of motivation;
- types of motivation;
- the six basic concepts of motivation relating to needs, goals, reinforcement, expectations, attribution theory and self-efficacy;
- the implications of motivation theory for those concerned with the design and management of financial and non-financial reward policies and practices.

The process of motivation

Motivation theory is concerned with what determines goal-directed behaviour. It is about:

- how behaviour is initiated by needs and by expectations on the achievement of goals which will satisfy those needs;
- how the achievement of goals and/or feedback on their achievement reinforces successful behaviour;
- how belief in one's ability to carry out a specific task will actuate behaviour which is expected to achieve the successful performance of that task.

The process of motivation can be initiated by someone recognizing an unsatisfied need. A goal is then established which, it is thought, will satisfy the need, and a course of action is determined which is expected to lead towards the attainment of the goal.

Alternatively, someone can be presented with a goal and if it is expected that achieving this goal will meet an unsatisfied need, action is taken to reach the goal and thus satisfy the need.

People can be motivated by rewards and incentives which will enable them to satisfy their needs or will provide them with goals to attain (as long as those goals are worthwhile *and* attainable). But the needs of individuals and the goals associated with them vary so widely that it is difficult if not impossible to predict precisely how a particular reward or incentive will affect individual behaviour.

The social context will also affect the level of motivation. This context will consist of the organization culture generally, but it also includes management style (the way in which individuals are managed) and the influence of the group or team in which the individual works.

Types of motivation

Motivation at work can take place in two ways:

1. *Intrinsic motivation* – this is derived from the content of the job. It can be described as the process of motivation by the work itself in so far as it satisfies people's needs or at least leads them to expect that their goals will be achieved. Intrinsic motivation is self-generated in that people seek the type of work that satisfies them, but management can enhance this process through its empowerment, development and job design policies and practices. The factors affecting intrinsic motivation include responsibility (feeling the work is important and having control over one's own resources), freedom to act, scope to use and develop skills and abilities, interesting and challenging work and opportunities for advancement. The concept of empowerment is strongly influenced by this aspect of motivation.

2. *Extrinsic motivation* – this is what is done to and for people to motivate them. It arises when management provides such rewards as increased pay, praise, or promotion. When the motivating impact of pay-for-performance schemes is discussed, this is the type of motivation to which people are referring.

The extrinsic motivators can have an immediate and powerful effect, but this will not necessarily last for long. The intrinsic motivators, which are concerned with the quality of working life, are likely to have a deeper and longer-term effect because they are inherent in individuals and not imposed from outside, although they may be encouraged by the organization. The effectiveness of pay as an extrinsic motivator is a matter for continuing debate, as discussed below.

Basic concepts of motivation

The framework for non-financial motivators is provided by those concepts of motivation which are concerned with needs, goals, reinforcement, expectations (expectancy theory), attribution theory and self-efficacy.

Needs

Needs theory states that behaviour is motivated by unsatisfied needs. The key needs associated with work are those for achievement, recognition, responsibility, influence and personal growth.

Goals

Goal theory was developed by Latham and Locke[1] on the basis of a 14-year research programme into goal-setting as a motivational technique. They claimed that the level of production in the companies they studied was increased by an average of 19 per cent as a result of goal-setting processes with the following characteristics:

- the goals should be specific;
- they should be challenging but reachable;
- the goals are seen as fair and reasonable;

- individuals participate fully in goal-setting;
- feedback ensures that people get a feeling of pride and satisfaction from the experience of achieving a challenging but fair goal;
- feedback is used to gain commitment to even higher goals.

Reinforcement

Reinforcement theory suggests that successes in achieving goals and rewards act as positive incentives and reinforce the successful behaviour, which is repeated the next time a similar need arises.

Expectancy theory

Expectancy theory as originally developed by Vroom[2] states that for there to be a heightened motivation to perform, individuals have to:

- feel able to change their behaviour;
- feel confident that a change in their behaviour will produce a reward;
- value the reward sufficiently to justify the change in behaviour.

Expectancy theory applies just as much to non-financial as to financial rewards. For example, if people want personal growth, they will only be motivated by the opportunities available to them if they know what they are, if they know what they need to do to benefit from them (and can do it) and if the opportunities are worth striving for.

Expectancy theory explains why extrinsic motivation – for example, an incentive or bonus scheme – works only if the link between effort and reward is clear and the value of the reward is worth the effort. It also explains why intrinsic motivation arising from the work itself can sometimes be more powerful than extrinsic motivation. Intrinsic motivation outcomes are more under the control of individuals, who can place greater reliance on their past experiences to indicate the extent to which positive and advantageous results are likely to be obtained by their behaviour.

Attribution theory

Attribution theory is concerned with how people interpret and explain their success or failure. If they can attribute their achievement or lack of achievement to something over which they have control they are more likely either to repeat their successful behaviour (this is a form of reinforcement) or, alternatively, take steps to behave in ways they believe are more likely to succeed. Managers can do a lot to influence attributions through feedback, communication, appraisal and guidance, thus creating a social context which is more likely to foster high motivation.

Self-efficacy

Self-efficacy is the belief in one's ability to perform a specific task. Those with high self-efficacy will have the capacity to see a link between their own effort and performance and their rewards. They are therefore more likely to take action, to persist in the action and, in the face of failure, to try alternative courses of action rather than give up trying. Self-efficacy is socially learned and developed from personal experience and performance feedback, which creates a sense of competence and reinforces people's belief in themselves.

Implications of motivation theory

Motivation theory conveys two important messages. First, there are no simplistic solutions to increasing motivation. No single lever such as performance-related pay exists which is guaranteed to act as an effective motivator. This is because motivation is a complex process. It depends on:

- *individual needs and aspirations* which are almost infinitely variable;
- both *intrinsic and extrinsic motivating factors*, and it is impossible to generalize on what the best mix of these is likely to be;
- *expectations* about rewards, such expectations will vary greatly amongst individuals according to their previous experiences and perceptions of reward processes;
- *equity and fairness* – the 'felt-fair' principle applies to levels of pay in comparison with others in accordance with what people believe to be the relative size or importance of jobs and their perceptions of relative levels of performance or contribution. Pay-for-performance schemes, for example, will only be accepted as fair and may therefore only act as effective motivators if they are based on acceptable performance measures which are applied consistently.
- *attributions* – the subjective and often distorted explanations people make of their successes or failures;
- *self-efficacy* – the differences in the degree to which people believe in themselves;
- *the social context* where the influences of the organization culture, managers and co-workers can produce a wide variety of motivational forces which are difficult to predict and therefore to manage.

The second key message provided by motivation theory is the significance of expectations, goal setting, feedback and reinforcement as motivating factors. The implications of these two messages are considered below.

Creating the right climate
It is necessary in general to create a climate which will enable high motivation to flourish. This is a matter of managing the organization culture. The aims would be, first, to reinforce values concerning performance and competence; second, to emphasize norms (accepted ways of behaviour) relating to the ways in which people are managed and rewarded; and third, to demonstrate the organization's belief in empowerment – providing people with the scope and 'space' to exercise responsibility and use their abilities to the full. Without the right climate, quick fixes designed to improve motivation such as performance-related pay are unlikely to make much of an impact on overall organizational performance, although they may work with some individuals.

Flexibility
It should be remembered, in the words of McDougall,[3] that:

> 'attempts to apply a standardized, across-the-board system of remuneration, on the assumption of homogeneity of values and motives amongst those it is intended to reward, are unlikely to meet the needs of many of them. There appears to be a strong case for flexibility, both in terms of the mechanisms and administration of remuneration systems and in the form in which individuals receive their remuneration'.

Recognising complexity
Motivation policies should recognize the complexity of the motivation process and not attempt to adopt simplistic solutions to motivational problems. The organi-

zation should provide for a mix of various types of intrinsic and extrinsic motivation and make use of both financial and non-financial incentives. But it should be borne in mind that the social context and the ways in which these incentives are managed for individuals will be key factors influencing their effectiveness.

Goal setting, feedback and reinforcement
Provision should be made for goal setting, feedback and reinforcement to be major features of the management and reward processes. Performance management processes as discussed in Chapters 14 and 15 can fulfil this purpose well.

Managing expectations
It is necessary to manage expectations. No reward offered through an incentive, bonus or performance-related pay scheme will be effective as a motivator unless individuals believe it is worthwhile and can reasonably expect to obtain it through their own efforts.

We discuss these implications as they affect financial and non-financial reward policies and practices below.

Financial rewards

Financial rewards need to be considered from three points of view:

- the effectiveness of money as a motivator;
- the reasons why people are satisfied or dissatisfied with their rewards;
- the criteria which should be used when developing a financial reward system.

Money and motivation

The general theory of motivation described above has produced the following explanations of the relationship between money and motivation: the 'economic man' approach, Herzberg's two factor model, instrumental theory, equity theory and expectancy theory.

The 'economic man' approach
According to this view, which is based on reinforcement theory, people are primarily motivated by economic rewards. It assumes that they will be motivated to work if rewards and penalties are tied directly to the results they achieve. Pay awards are contingent upon effective performance.

Motivation using this approach has been and still is widely adopted and can be successful in some circumstances. But it is based exclusively on a system of external controls and fails to recognize a number of other human needs. It also fails to appreciate the fact that the formal control system can be seriously affected by the informal relationship existing between employees.

Herzberg's two factor model
Herzberg's[4] two factor model of motivation was developed following an analysis of anecdotes of unusually satisfying or unusually dissatisfying job events provided by 200 engineers and accountants. He claimed that money is a so-called 'hygiene factor' which serves as a potential dissatisfier if not present in appropriate amounts, but not as a potential satisfier or positive motivator. A further reason given by Herzberg for regarding salary as a 'hygiene factor', that is, a factor which prevents disease rather than promotes health, was because its impact on favour-

able feeling was largely short-term, while its impact on unfavourable feelings was long-term – extending over periods of several months.

But, as Opsahl and Dunnette[5] point out, Herzberg's argument that money acts as a potential dissatisfier is mystifying.

'In all of the definitions of unusually good job feelings, salary was mentioned as a major reason for the feelings 19 per cent of the time. Of the unusually good feelings that lasted several months, salary was reported as a causal factor 22 per cent of the time; of the short-term feelings, it was a factor 5 per cent of the time. In contrast, salary was named as a major cause of unusually bad job feelings only 13 per cent of the time. Of the unusually bad job feelings lasting several months, it was mentioned only 18 per cent of the time (in contrast with the 22 per cent of long-term good feelings mentioned above).'

They concluded that,

'these data seem inconsistent with the interpretations and lend no substantial support to hypotheses of a so-called differential role for money in leading to job satisfaction or job dissatisfaction'.

Herzberg's two factor model does not therefore provide a reliable basis for developing pay policies.

Instrumental theory

This theory states that money provides the means to achieve ends. It is an instrument for gaining desired outcomes and its force will depend on two factors: first, the strength of the need and, second, the degree to which people are confident that their behaviour will earn the money they want to satisfy the need. The instrumental role of money has been stressed by Gellerman,[6] who suggested that money in itself has no intrinsic meaning and acquires significant motivating power only when it comes to symbolise intangible goals. Money acts as a symbol in different ways for different persons, and for the same person at different times – a man's reaction to money 'summarises his biography to date, his early economic environment, his competence training, the various non-financial motives he has acquired, and his current financial status'.

Money is therefore a powerful force because it is linked directly or indirectly to the satisfaction of all the basic needs. But the effectiveness of money as a motivator depends on a number of circumstances, including the values and needs of individuals and their preferences for different types of financial or non-financial rewards.

Equity theory

Equity theory, as developed by Adams,[7] argues that satisfaction with pay is related to perceptions about the ratio between what one receives from the job (outcomes in the form of pay) to what one puts into it (inputs in the form of effort and skill) compared with the ratios obtained by others.

Equity theory is related to discrepancy theory which, as stated by Lawler,[8] indicates that satisfaction with pay depends on the difference between the pay people receive and what they feel they ought to receive. Equity theory, however, emphasizes that these feelings are based on comparisons.

The significance of equity was also emphasized by Jaques.[9] He stated that (1) there exists 'an unrecognized system of norms of fair payment for any given level of work, unconscious knowledge of these norms being shared among the population engaged in employment', and that (2) an individual 'is unconsciously aware of his own potential capacity for work, as well as the equitable pay level for that work'. Jaques called this the 'felt fair' principle, which states that, to be equitable, pay must be felt to match the level of work and the capacity of the individual to do it.

Application of expectancy theory

Expectancy theory, as described earlier in this chapter, states that motivation will be strong if individuals can reasonably expect that their efforts and contributions will produce worthwhile rewards.

This theory was developed by Porter and Lawler[10] into an expectancy model which suggests that there are two factors determining the effort people put into their jobs:

1. The values of the rewards to individuals in so far as they satisfy their needs for security, social esteem, autonomy, and self actualization.
2. The probability that rewards depend on effort, as perceived by the individual – in other words, his or her expectations about the relationships between effort and reward.

Thus, the greater the value of a set of awards and the higher the probability that receiving each of these rewards depends upon effort, the greater the effort that will be put forth in a given situation.

But mere effort is not enough. It has to be effective effort if it is to produce the desired performance. The two variables additional to effort which affect task achievement are:

■ ability – individual characteristics such as intelligence, manual skills and know-how;
■ role perceptions – what the individual wants to do or thinks he or she is required to do. These are good from the view point of the organization if they correspond with what it thinks the individual ought to be doing. They are poor if the views of the individual and the organization do not coincide.

Conclusions on the role of money as a motivator

Money is important to people because it is instrumental in satisfying a number of their most pressing needs. It is significant not only because of what they can buy with it but also as a highly tangible method of recognizing their worth, thus improving their self-esteem and gaining the esteem of others.

Pay is the key to attracting people to join an organization, although job interest, career opportunities and the reputation of the organization will also be factors. Satisfaction with pay amongst existing employees is mainly related to feelings about equity and fairness. External and internal comparisons will form the basis of these feelings, which will influence their desire to stay with the organization.

Pay can motivate. As a tangible means of recognizing achievement, pay can reinforce desirable behaviour. Pay can also deliver messages on what the organization believes to be important. But to be effective, a pay-for-performance system has to meet very stringent conditions as defined by expectancy theory. To achieve lasting motivation, attention has also to be paid to the non-financial motivators.

Causes of satisfaction or dissatisfaction with pay

Reactions to reward policies and practices will depend largely on the values and needs of individuals and on their employment conditions. It is therefore dangerous to generalise about the causes of satisfaction or dissatisfaction.

However, it seems reasonable to believe that, as mentioned above, feelings about external and internal equity (the 'felt fair' principle) will strongly influence most people. Research by Porter and Lawler[10] and others has also shown that higher paid employees are likely to be more satisfied with their rewards but the satisfaction resulting from a large pay increase may be short-lived. People tend to want more. In this respect, at least, the views of Herzberg have been supported by research.

Other factors which may affect satisfaction or dissatisfaction with pay include the degree to which:

- individuals feel their rate of pay or increase has been determined fairly;
- rewards are commensurate with the perceptions of individuals about their ability, contribution and value to the organization (but this perception is likely to be founded on information or beliefs about what other people, inside and outside the organization, are paid);
- individuals are satisfied with other aspects of their employment – for example, their status, promotion prospects, opportunity to use and develop skills and relationships with their managers.

Financial rewards

The criteria for assessing the effectiveness of financial reward practices as means of motivation are that:

- they are, as far as possible, internally equitable as well as externally competitive (although there will always be a tension between these two criteria – paying market rates may upset internal relativities);
- pay-for-performance systems are created in the light of an understanding that direct motivation only takes place if the rewards are worthwhile, if they are specifically related to fair, objective and appropriate performance measures, if employees understand what they have to achieve, and if their expectations on the likelihood of receiving the reward are high;
- employees understand how the financial reward system operates, how they benefit from it, and how the organization will help them to develop the skills and competences they need to receive the maximum benefit.

Non-financial rewards

Non-financial rewards can be focused on the needs most people have, although to different degrees, for achievement, recognition, responsibility, influence and personal growth.

Achievement

Research carried out by McClelland[11] of the needs of managerial staff resulted in the identification of three major needs, those for achievement, power and affiliation. The need for achievement is defined as the need for competitive success measured against a personal standard of excellence.

Achievement motivation can be increased by organizations through processes such as job design, performance management, and skill or competency-based pay schemes.

Recognition

Recognition is one of the most powerful motivators. People need to know not only how well they have achieved their objectives or carried out their work but also that their achievements are appreciated.

Praise, however, should be given judiciously – it must be related to real achievements. And it is not the only form of recognition. Financial rewards, especially achievement bonuses awarded immediately after the event, are clearly symbols of recognition to which are attached tangible benefits, and this is an important way in which mutually reinforcing processes of financial and non-financial rewards can operate. There are other forms of recognition such as long service awards, status symbols of one kind or another, sabbaticals and work-related trips abroad, all of which can be part of the total reward process.

Recognition is also provided by managers who listen to and act upon the suggestions of their team members and, importantly, acknowledge their contribution. Other actions which provide recognition include promotion, allocation to a high-profile project, enlargement of the job to provide scope for more interesting and rewarding work, and various forms of status or esteem symbols.

The recognition processes in an organization can be integrated with financial rewards through performance management and pay-for-performance schemes. The importance of recognition can be defined as a key part of the value set of the organization and this would be reinforced by education, training and performance appraisals.

Responsibility

People can be motivated by being given more responsibility for their own work. This is essentially what empowerment is about and is in line with the concept of intrinsic motivation based on the content of the job. It is also related to the fundamental concept that individuals are motivated when they are provided with the means to achieve their goals.

The characteristics required in jobs if they are to be intrinsically motivating are that first, individuals must receive meaningful feedback about their performance, preferably by evaluating their own performance and defining the feedback they require, second, the job must be perceived by individuals as requiring them to use abilities they value in order to perform the job effectively and third, individuals must feel that they have a high degree of self-control over setting their own goals and over defining the paths to these goals.

Providing motivation through increased responsibility is a matter of job design and the use of performance management processes. The philosophy behind motivating through responsibility was expressed as follows in McGregor's[12] theory Y: 'The average human being learns, under proper conditions, not only to accept but also to seek responsibility'.

Influence

People can be motivated by the drive to exert influence or to exercise power. McClelland's research established that alongside the need for achievement, the need for power was a prime motivating force for managers, although the need for 'affiliation', ie warm, friendly relationships with others, was always present. The organization, through its policies for involvement, can provide motivation by putting people into situations where their views can be expressed, listened to and acted upon. This is another aspect of empowerment.

Personal growth

In Maslow's[13] hierarchy of needs, self-fulfilment or self-actualization is the highest need of all and is therefore the ultimate motivator. He defines self-fulfilment as 'the need to develop potentialities and skills, to become what one believes one is capable of becoming'.

Ambitious and determined people will seek and find these opportunities for themselves, although the organization needs to clarify the scope for growth and development it can provide (if it does not, they will go away and grow elsewhere).

Increasingly, however, individuals at all levels of organizations, whether or not they are eaten up by ambition, recognize the importance of continually upgrading their skills and of progressively developing their careers. This is the philosophy of continuous development. Many people now regard access to training as a key element in the overall reward package. The availability of learning opportunities, the selection of individuals for high-prestige training courses and programmes and the emphasis placed by the organization on the acquisition of new skills as well as the enhancement of existing ones, can all act as powerful motivators.

Conclusions

Non-financial motivators are powerful in themselves but can work even more effectively if integrated with financial rewards in a total reward process. However, it is important to remember that the needs of individuals vary almost infinitely depending upon their psychological makeup, background, experience, occupation and position in the organization. It is therefore dangerous to generalize about which mix of motivators is likely to be most effective in individual cases. And this is why one cannot rely on nostrums such as performance-related pay, skill-based pay, job enrichment or performance management to work equally well for every person or in every organization. These processes need to be 'customized' to meet the needs of both the organization and the people who work there. But this customization will take place more effectively if judicious use is made of achievement bonuses, pay increases related to the acquisition of specific skills and a performance management and reward process which concentrates on identifying individual needs and gaining the joint commitment of employees and their managers to satisfying them.

References

1. Latham, G and Locke, R (1979) 'Goal setting – a motivational technique that works', *Organizational Dynamics*, 8.
2. Vroom, V (1964) *Work and Motivation*, Wiley, New York
3. McDougall, C (1973) 'How well do you reward your managers?' *Personnel Management*, March
4. Herzberg, F, Mausner, B and Snyderman, B (1957) *The Motivation to Work*, Wiley, New York
5. Opsahl, R and Dunnette, M (1966) 'The role of financial compensation in industrial motivation', *Psychological Bulletin*, 66
6. Gellerman, S (1963) *Motivation and Personality*, American Management Association, New York
7. Adams, J (1965) 'Injustice in social exchange', In L Berkowitz (ed), *Advances in Experimental Psychology*, 69

8. Lawler, E (1971) *Pay and Organizational Effectiveness*, McGraw-Hill, New York
9. Jaques, E (1961) *Equitable Payment*, Heinemann, London
10. Porter, L and Lawler, E (1968) *Management Attitudes and Behaviour*, Irwin-Dorsey, Homewood, Illinois
11. McClelland, D (1975) *Power – the Inner Experience*, Irvington, New York
12. McGregor, D (1960) *The Human Side of Enterprise*, McGraw-Hill, New York
13. Maslow, A (1954) *Motivation and Personality*, Harper & Row, New York

3

Reward Philosophies, Strategies, Policies and Guiding Principles

The design and operation of total reward processes should start from an understanding of the implications of motivation theory and the use of financial and non-financial incentives, but it must focus on the needs of the organization and the people who work in it. These needs are most likely to be met if reward processes are based on an articulated and integrated approach to the development of a framework of reward philosophies, strategies, policies and guiding principles which will support the achievement of the organization's business strategies as well as acting as levers for change.

The framework

The development framework is illustrated in Figure 3.1. It consists of the following elements:

- *The internal and external environments* – the analysis of these provides the information required to help in the formulation of the strategic agenda for the organization and for human resource management strategies. The internal analysis will also influence reward philosophies.
- *The strategic agenda* – this defines the direction in which the organization is going in relation to its environment in order to achieve its objectives.
- *Human resource strategy* – this flows from the corporate strategies and is concerned with the key areas of resourcing, skills acquisition and development, performance and quality management, rewards and employee relations. The aim is to make strategies in each of these areas mutually supportive. It is important, therefore, for the reward strategy to be linked to every other aspect of the human resources strategy.
- *Reward philosophy* – this consists of a set of beliefs which underpin the reward strategies of the organization, govern reward policy and provide the foundation for the guiding principles which determine how the reward processes operate.
- *Reward strategies* - these define the intentions of the organization on the reward policies, processes and systems required to ensure that it continues to obtain, motivate and retain the committed and competent people it needs to accomplish its mission. They will flow from the business and human resource strategies of the organization and, like them, will be affected by environmental factors. They will also be governed by the reward philosophy. Reward strate-

gies strongly influence reward policies and guiding principles and largely determine the form of pay practices, structures and procedures.

- *Reward policies* – these provide guidelines for the implementation of reward strategies and for the development of guiding principles and the operation of reward management processes.
- *Guiding principles* – these summarize the organization's reward philosophies and policies and present them to managers and all other employees as the basis upon which the organization intends to manage rewards.

We examine reward philosophy, strategies, policies and guiding principles in greater detail below.

Reward philosophy

A reward philosophy covers such areas as:

- the importance attached to pay as a motivating force;
- the use of non-financial or intrinsic rewards such as the opportunity to achieve and to learn, the scope for personal growth, responsibility, recognition, challenge and the quality of working life;
- the extent to which the organization believes rewards should be differentiated according to performance, skill or competence;
- the extent to which management believes that pay should be driven by market forces;
- the significance of equity (a just and fair system of payment in relation to position and performance) as a determinant of pay levels;
- the amount of flexibility allowed;
- the degree to which authority for pay decisions should be devolved to line management.

The reward philosophy should be formulated to fit both organizational and individual needs. It is therefore about what the organization will pay for and not pay for and about the time, the place and the conditions for change.

Fitting the reward philosophy to organizational needs

To fit the reward philosophy to organizational needs means that the following issues have to be considered:

- how reward management can in general support the achievement of business strategies;
- how rewards can reinforce good performance and help to achieve improvement;
- how poor performance will be addressed and dealt with constructively;
- how reward management can help to promote cultural change;
- whose performance matters most – a small cadre of key performers or people at all levels in the organization;
- the balance between rewarding individual performance and trying to develop more effective teamworking;
- short term versus long term – pay arrangements which do not reflect immediate past performance lose effectiveness and credibility, and objectives that are focused on the period immediately ahead will have most bite. But reward policies must recognize that the organization needs to develop

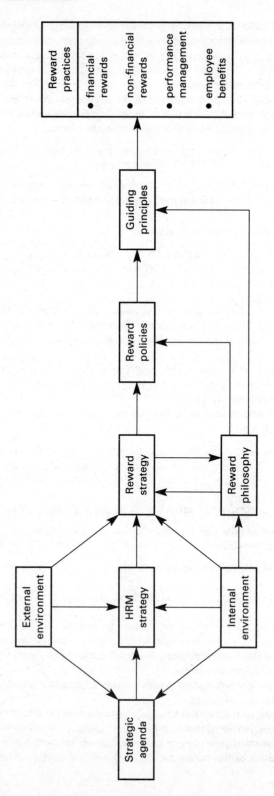

Figure 3.1 *The process of strategic reward management*

employees and their skills over the longer term even if they are not linked to the concept of a life time career.

Fitting the reward philosophy to individual needs

A reward philosophy should take account of individual needs. This means understanding the factors discussed in Chapter 2 which affect motivation, the role of money as a motivator and what influences employee satisfaction with their rewards.

Reward strategy

Reward strategy should be founded on the proposition that the ultimate source of value is people. This means that reward processes must respond creatively to their needs as well as to those of the organization. The basis of the strategy will be the organization's requirements for performance in the short and longer-term as expressed in its corporate strategies. Reward strategy in the private sector should be business driven, responding to the needs of the business to compete, grow, innovate, but it is also a lever for change, reinforcing and validating the thrust of the business. In the public and voluntary sectors, reward strategy is similarly driven by the need of the organization to meet high service delivery standards.

How reward strategy contributes to the achievement of corporate goals

A reward strategy can make an important contribution to the achievement of corporate goals if it:

- provides for the integration of reward policies and processes with key strategies for growth and improved performance;
- underpins the organization's values, especially those concerned with innovation, teamwork, flexibility and quality;
- fits the culture and management style of the organization;
- drives and supports desired behaviour at all levels by indicating to employees what types of behaviour will be rewarded, how this will take place and how their expectations will be satisfied;
- provides the competitive edge required to attract and retain the level of skills the organization needs;
- enables the organization to obtain value for money from its reward practices.

Components of the reward strategy

The reward strategy will mainly be concerned with the direction the organization should follow in developing the right mix and levels of financial and non-financial rewards in order to support the business strategy. The reward strategy will be concerned with:

- the demands of the business strategy, including cost constraints;
- meeting objectives for the attraction and retention of high quality employees;
- how superior performance and performance improvement can be motivated and reinforced;
- the development of pay structures which are competitive in the market place and are performance-driven;
- ensuring that reward policies are used to convey messages about the expectations and values of the organization;

- achieving the right balance between rewards for individual, team and organizational performance;
- evolving total reward processes which incorporate the best mix of financial and non-financial rewards and employee benefits;
- achieving the flexibility required when administering reward processes within fast-changing organizations existing in highly competitive or turbulent environments;
- fitting reward processes to the individual needs and expectations of employees.

The reward strategy should be backed up by a realistic action plan and should incorporate an assessment of risks and contingency plans if things go wrong. Arrangements should also be made to ensure that the results of implementing a reward strategy are evaluated regularly against its objectives and cost budgets.

A framework for developing reward strategy

A framework for developing reward strategy is illustrated in Figure 3.2. The foundation for the strategy will be the business and human resource strategies, the culture, climate and management practices of the organization, the type of people employed and the history and present arrangements for rewards. The reward strategy will be influenced by market considerations and government regulations (including taxation). It leads on to the development of reward policies and practices.

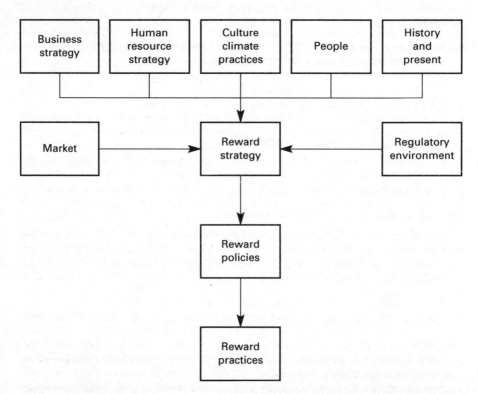

Figure 3.2   *A framework for developing reward strategy*

Reward policies

Reward policies provide guidelines for the implementation of reward strategies and the design and management of reward processes. They will be influenced strongly by the reward philosophy of the organization. The reward policies will be concerned with:

- the level of rewards;
- the relative importance attached to market rates and equity;
- the relationship of rewards to business performance;
- the scope for differentiating rewards according to performance;
- the degree of flexibility required in the system;
- the need to involve employees in the design of the reward system;
- the need to communicate reward policies to employees.

Level of rewards

The policy on the level of rewards indicates whether the company is a high payer, is content to pay median or average rates of pay or even, exceptionally, accepts that it has to pay below the average. Pay policy, which is sometimes referred to as the 'pay stance' or 'pay posture' of a company, will depend on a number of factors. These include the extent to which the company demands high levels of performance from its employees, the degree to which there is competition for good quality people, the traditional stance of the company, the organization culture, and whether or not it can or should afford to be a high payer.

Policy on pay levels will also refer to differentials and the number of steps or grades that should exist in the pay hierarchy. This will be influenced by the structure of the company. In today's flatter organizations an extended or complex pay hierarchy may not be required on the grounds that it will constrain the flexible movement of people in the organization.

Market rate and equity

A policy needs to be formulated on the extent to which rewards are market driven rather than equitable. This policy will be influenced by the culture and reward philosophies of the organization. However, any company which has to attract and retain staff who are much in demand and where market rates are therefore high, may, to a degree, have to sacrifice its ideals of equity to the realism of the market place. The pay management process must cope as best it can when the irresistible force of the market place meets the immovable object of internal equity. There will also be some degree of tension in these circumstances, and while no solution will ever be simple or entirely satisfactory, there is one basic principle which can enhance the likelihood of success. That principle is to make explicit and fully identifiable the compromises with internal equity that are made in response to market pressures.

Relating rewards to business performance

This aspect of reward policy refers to the link between business performance and pay. It will cover the extent to which pay will vary according to results. Ability to pay and value for money will also be important considerations. The policy will include guidelines on how gainsharing or profit-sharing schemes should operate (see Chapters 23 and 24.)

Differential rewards

The policy will need to determine whether or not the organization wants to pay for performance, skill or competence and, if so, how much and under what circumstances. There may, for example, be a policy that bonuses should be paid for exceptional performance but that, to be significant, they should not be less than, say, 10 per cent of basic pay, while their upper limit should be restricted to 30 per cent or so of base pay. The policy may also indicate the approach to be used in relating pay to individual, team or organizational performance.

Flexibility

Reward policies have to take into account the extent to which reward processes should operate flexibly in response to fast-changing conditions, the adoption of a less rigid organization structure and approach to management, and changes or variations in the needs of the company or its employees.

Involving employees

Reward policies and practices are more likely to be accepted and understood and, therefore, more effective if employees are involved in the design and management of reward processes. This particularly applies to job evaluation and methods of measuring and assessing performance and relating rewards to that performance (performance management and paying for performance processes).

Communicating to employees

Reward processes are powerful media for conveying messages to employees about the organization's values and the contribution they are expected to make to upholding those values and achieving the organization's goals. They should not, however, be left to speak for themselves. It is essential to communicate to individuals, teams and representative bodies what reward processes are setting out to do, how they propose to do it, how they affect them, how they will benefit, and the part individuals and teams will be expected to play. It is particularly important to explain the basis of any pay-for-performance scheme and also to convey to employees how their total remuneration package of pay and other benefits is made up.

Guiding principles

Guiding principles are derived from the organization's reward philosophy, strategy and policies and are used to indicate to all concerned how the reward system should be managed. The typical contents of a statement of guiding principles as derived from a number of actual examples are:

Basic principles
Our reward policies and practices are:

- an integral part of an overall human resource strategy geared to business requirements;
- designed to motivate and reinforce superior performance;
- flexible and individually orientated;
- based on the proposition that pay should be related to individual and team contribution;
- based on our philosophy that employees should share in the success of the company;

- founded on policies of involving employees as far as possible in the development of the process, fully communicating its implications to them and providing them with the opportunity to raise with management any concerns they may have about how it affects them.

Basis upon which pay is determined
Individuals will be fairly paid in relation to:

- the work they do and their performance as measured by the results they achieve in relation to agreed objectives;
- their level of skill and competence;
- the value placed on comparable jobs within the company;
- their market value;
- the contribution they make to upholding the values of the organization, especially those concerned with quality, customer service and teamwork;
- the success of the business.

Performance management

- Individuals will be able to agree with their managers the basis upon which their performance will be managed and measured.
- Individuals will be given objective feedback about their performance and will have every opportunity to discuss this feedback with their managers.

Communication of grading or pay decisions

- Individuals have the right to know how decisions about their grade or pay were made.
- Individuals will be entitled to request a review of any decisions on their grade or pay.

Employee benefits

- All employees are entitled to the same range of employee benefits but the scale of such benefits may vary in relation to length of service or the grading given to the job.
- Individuals will have some choice on the benefits they receive.

Management of rewards

- Managers will be given the maximum degree of authority to manage the reward system in their departments in accordance with these guiding principles and within any agreed budgets.

Developing reward processes

Reward processes tend to evolve in response to the needs and demands of the situation in which the organization finds itself. Ideally, of course, they should be developed in line with longer-term strategies, but that is not always possible. While those concerned with the development of reward policies and practices should be thinking ahead, they have also to be alert to immediate requirements so that they can be responsive to new and possibly unforeseen circumstances.

The evolutionary nature of reward processes means that, except in a green field site, their development can become piecemeal, proceeding by incremental steps.

This may be difficult to avoid completely in some circumstances but, wherever possible, we advocate a coherent approach to the development of reward processes which take the interrelationships between the different parts fully into account while recognizing that new approaches may have to be phased in as part of a longer term plan for the implementation of human resource management strategies.

We examine the evolution, evaluation and development of reward management processes in more detail in the next three chapters.

PART 2

THE EVOLUTION, REVIEW AND DEVELOPMENT OF REWARD PROCESSES

4

The Evolution of Reward Processes

Effective total reward processes drive organizational performance. They are founded on the organization's reward philosophy, strategies and policies. These are developed within the context of the organization's environment, culture and business strategies. But they will also be linked to what we term the reward maturity cycle which influences the evolution of reward policies and practices in parallel with the life cycle of the organization.

There are four stages in the reward policy maturity cycle which are linked to the organization life cycle. The way rewards are managed reflects the management style and characteristics of organizations at each stage, although the pace at which elements of reward strategies and policies evolve varies and organizations will not necessarily fit neatly into any one stage during the cycle. Neither will any one organization proceed inevitably and progressively through all four stages. This model does, however, describe the ways in which reward processes can evolve in association with the evolution of the organization. It can therefore be useful as an analytical tool when reviewing reward policies and practices prior to making any changes, and when evaluating their effectiveness as described in the next two chapters. The four stages are:

1. start-up/take off;
2. maturity;
3. old age/stagnation;
4. break-out/regeneration.

Start up/take off

This is the stage at which a new organization is born. It may typically be formed by a group of executives from one or more larger employers fired with the desire to create something new and leave behind the strictures of their old organization. The stage may last for several years until the growth curve begins to flatten. This stage is also found in new, 'stand alone', businesses resulting from diversification, or new ventures in more traditional and mature organizations.

Key elements of reward policy and practice

- Pay is managed by either the finance director or the company secretary who generally has a fairly limited understanding of professional approaches to reward management. Pay is perceived as an overhead cost to be controlled rather than a means of rewarding people and therefore as an asset to be managed.
- A high risk/high reward pay philosophy exists for top management. This means relatively low base salaries, but highly geared incentives and share options are used to deliver exceptional rewards if profit and growth targets are met.
- There are no pay scales. Instead, there are simply 'spot' pay levels for each individual.
- Pay levels are based on a notional view of market rates derived from information provided by job advertisements, recruitment consultants or agencies, the rates needed to recruit people, and hearsay, rather than the systematic analysis of reliable survey data.
- Internal relativities are managed without formal job evaluation or with, at best, notional ranking to determine seniority. The boundaries between jobs tend to be fluid, providing for considerable flexibility in working practices.
- Performance rewards are discretionary and are not underpinned by any formalized or systematic approach to measuring and assessing performance.
- Shop floor workers are probably paid on high day rates. If there is an incentive scheme, it is unlikely to be based on a form of work measurement.
- Employee benefits tend to be an amalgam of the practices most liked in the organizations the new top management team left behind. The benefits tend to be provided inconsistently – a function of the initial contract negotiations with individuals. Decisions on basic elements of the benefits package such as sick pay and overtime payments tend to be *ad hoc*. There are no standard procedures or practices. The benefits made available have not been put together with the concept of a competitive 'total package' in mind.
- The links between skill and competency acquisition and reward are unexplored. Most people are recruited to 'hit the deck running' and training or development policies have yet to take shape.

Typical reward strategies and policy development

The following actions may be taken by organizations when they begin to seek improvements in the way they manage rewards, often in response to growing employee dissatisfaction over inconsistent practice and the need to put their own house in order and obtain greater value for money from the reward system:

- Recruit a personnel professional when the organization reaches a size where this becomes viable (say 80 to 100 employees) who is responsible for developing reward policies and systems and providing services and advice on the operation of the system.

- Regularize the relationship between pay levels and the market by improving the quality of market monitoring and deciding where in the market the company needs to be to recruit and keep the people it wants.
- Develop a more formal approach to job evaluation and the management of relativities. This may mean considering an analytical method of job evaluation, but this would be required to underpin rather than constrain role and operational flexibility. Alternatively, in organizations where functional job families and project ways of working are important, approaches might be developed which focus on the acquisition and use of skills and competences which may or may not be underpinned by job measurement.
- Introduce a more formal approach to performance rewards both at the top of the organization and lower down. This move may be accompanied by the development of a simple appraisal process which places more emphasis on the defensibility of pay decisions than on personal development.
- Develop more sophisticated individual or team incentive or bonus schemes for shop floor workers based on work measurement.
- Rationalize employee benefit entitlements, including pensions and company cars, to provide more consistent practice while containing costs.

Maturity

A mature organization is one which has reached a fairly stable stage. Management, however, is still responsive and flexible, reacting effectively to competitive pressure, proactively seeking new markets and products and developing its management processes and systems to grow and improve performance.

Key elements of reward policy and practice

- Remuneration levels are set competitively and are based on systematic monitoring of surveys and other market data.
- Competitive benefits of which the core (pensions, sick pay, holiday entitlements and subsidized meals) are harmonized among employees as far as possible. Other benefits such as company cars are allocated on as cost effective a basis as possible in relation to market practice while maximizing perceived benefit value.
- The management of internal relativities by the use of a formal approach to job evaluation which minimizes bureaucracy (increasingly by using computer-assisted administration processes), reflects specialist career patterns through the use of job family models, and optimizes on the use of job/role data for other human resource management processes such as organization design and development, recruitment, performance management and training needs analysis.
- A variety of approaches is used to reward performance according to different job categories. Each of these is underpinned by a formal approach to performance management which is used both for individual development and as the decision base for performance-related rewards of various kinds.
- Some mature organizations will have introduced integrated pay structures which cover all employees. Shop floor workers are on salaries and a performance-related pay system is used based on the same principles as those applying to other employees. Where appropriate, the PRP scheme will be used to support processes such as JIT and TQM.

- Company-wide gainsharing schemes may be operating which relate rewards to the generation of added value.
- Innovative responses are made to skill shortages and market pressures which focus on different forms of employment (eg the use of part-timers and various forms of flexible working) rather than throwing money at any problems as they arise.
- More flexible approaches are adopted to reward management where they help to support the organization's aims.
- Continued emphasis is placed on consultation and good communication with employees on reward issues to ensure that the intent and value of remuneration policies are fully appreciated.
- A sensible balance is struck between central and devolved control over pay decisions. The approach increasingly emphasizes line management involvement in and ownership of remuneration policy. This might still mean managing the pay of senior managers centrally so as to reinforce their place as a corporate resource in a multi-site business. However, in a highly diversified business where there is no real inter-company mobility, the responsibility for management remuneration may be largely devolved.

Key reward strategies

The strategic thrust will be to:

- Respond fast to changing business needs which dictate recruitment and career progression patterns with new pay structures.
- Sharpen the focus of performance rewards and improve the supporting processes of reward management.
- Explore increased flexibility and cost effectiveness in benefits practice.
- Where appropriate, develop skill or competence-based pay systems.
- Keep a weather eye out for the unexpected; a prospective merger or takeover or an unforeseen and sometimes rapid change in business circumstances.

Old age/stagnation

This is the stage which organizations reach if they have grown too large and set in their ways to do anything other than trying to maintain their market share and influence. Hierarchy and bureaucracy have become a way of life and the organization becomes progressively more traditionalist in its management style and culture. Such organizations are often characterized by top management teams that have grown up and matured together and which have not sought actively to bring in new blood or to challenge their established assumptions and practices. In the UK, many older, larger organizations and much of the public sector have been through this stage and are in varying stages of emerging from it.

Key elements of reward policy and practice

- Rigid pay structures – these are typically based on fixed service increments with growing numbers of employees reaching the top of the scale as promotion opportunities decline.
- Rigidity and over-emphasis on status and hierarchy in benefits entitlements.
- All elements of pay are subject to comprehensive pay negotiations. Such negotiations cover employees up to senior management levels and therefore prevent any line management involvement with the pay system.
- Long-established and often outdated approaches to job evaluation which

reflect old organizational values in design, application and hierarchies (which may be stratified by level) and may require an army of specialists to maintain. Both managers and employees manipulate the scheme to gain pay increases and grade drift is common.

- Non-existent or timid approach to performance management and rewards exists. The appraisal scheme is viewed with cynicism as an administrative burden and a dishonest annual ritual.
- Shop floor incentive schemes have deteriorated. Lack of management control, loose rates and endless pressure on rate fixers create wage drift (increases in earnings unaccompanied by commensurate increases in output). The emphasis on volume prejudices quality standards and earnings fluctuate wildly and are unpredictable.
- There is complacency in the face of market pressures based on the organization's previous ability to survive.
- Market monitoring is over-systematized and often very costly.
- Policy development is over-centralized, often with too many narrowly focused pay specialists working in an environment where administrative convenience wins over strategy and respect for broader HR management issues.

New reward strategies

This state of stagnation and rigidity can only be tackled by introducing substantial changes to every aspect of reward management along the following lines:

- Carry out radical surgery – often as a result of business process re-engineering and/or a culture change programme designed to revitalize the organization and reform the way it is managed. Devolution and decentralization of power and decision making are high on the agenda.
- Reduce the size of both the personnel and remuneration functions – along with the rest of the organization – and rationalize responsibilities.
- Rationalize and simplify pay structures.
- Review and possibly jettison existing approaches to job evaluation in favour of a process for managing internal relativities which more closely matches the desired culture and carries few of the trappings of the old bureaucracy. This is the stage at which computer-assisted job evaluation processes and skill/competency linked job family models are often implemented.
- Assess the cost effectiveness of market monitoring and rationalize the process.
- Individualize the relationship with senior management by introducing personal contracts, often in tandem with the introduction of management benefits such as company cars.
- Jettison old appraisal systems and associated performance rewards in favour of a new, line management-owned performance management process accompanied by much sharper business-focused rewards.
- Abandon old piece work or time-related shop floor incentive schemes and replace them with measured day work or a high day rate system, possibly with performance-related individual or team bonuses.
- Introduce a gainsharing, profit sharing or profit-related pay scheme to underpin a philosophy of sharing in success.
- Pay much more attention to reward management processes and to communication in order to use remuneration more effectively as a management tool for leveraging performance improvements and flexibility.

- Import fresh blood into the remuneration function to help ensure that pay is managed in accordance with 'best practice for sector' objectives.

Regeneration/renewal

This phase follows the collapse or near collapse of the 'old age' organization. Typically, it starts because a takeover, buyout or the replacement of most of the top management of the organization enables it to pull together what is left, reorganize, and head off in new business directions with renewed vigour. Organizations in this phase often have to operate in a very constrained financial environment in the first years. This phase has much in common with the start-up phase except that the organization is not operating in a green field situation and must still tackle the remnants of the past as well as the future.

Key elements of reward policy and practice

The key elements of remuneration policy in this phase are:

- A questioning attitude to traditional reward practice, often because it is seen as a component in the failure of the old business.
- Policy is decentralized and devolved down to individual business units.
- Old pay structures, incentive schemes and progression systems are abandoned as too costly and too complex to administer.
- Jettisoning of job evaluation as restructuring and downsizing remove many of the old benchmarks and as the organization culture is focused on new values.
- Use of 'spot salaries' in the few areas where recruitment is undertaken and where market pressures exist. This may be for key executives only and may be accompanied by poor cost controls.
- The total revision of benefits policy with a bias towards eliminating all superfluous items in favour of 'clean cash'.
- Market monitoring is very limited and confined to 'hot spots' where turnover is still causing problems.
- Performance awards are paid only for demonstrable added value, often in the form of unconsolidated bonuses which have to be re-earned against new targets each year. Old approaches to performance appraisal may have been abandoned as an unnecessary administrative burden and may not have been replaced.

New reward strategies

In response to these features of the reward management process, new reward strategies will be developed which are linked to the regeneration strategy for the business and are implemented by means of clear steps as a process of managed change. These strategies will be developed with the help of an entirely new remuneration function which brings in fresh ideas from outside. The emphasis is likely to be on involvement and empowerment of line management in the whole reward management process.

The typical strategies evolved in these circumstances are to:

- Develop basic processes such as job evaluation and performance management and new pay structures to support the coherent development of human resource management strategies.
- Apply skill based/technical ladders to reinforce multiskilling and the link to training and development policies in specialist areas.

- Sharpen the focus on performance improvement – concentrating first on the development of performance management skills.
- Introduce both short and long term performance rewards consisting of annual rewards for all plus long term incentives tied to the achievement of key milestones by top executives.
- Explore a much more flexible approach to benefits practice.

In the next chapter we suggest the points to be covered in a diagnostic review of reward policy and practice which, in association with the life cycle analysis contained in this chapter, can form the basis for designing or developing new and revised reward management processes as described in Chapter 6.

5

Evaluation of Reward Processes

The evaluation of reward processes can be carried out by means of a diagnostic review, the purpose of which is to assess their effectiveness in helping the organization to achieve its objectives and provide a basis for the development of new or revised reward policy and practice.

The review should cover reward philosophies, strategies, policies, guiding principles, practices and procedures. It should be carried out by examining any written policies and guiding principles. Any documentation of schemes, structures and procedures should also be examined. It is equally important to find out how the various processes work out in practice by studying reports and records and by interviewing personnel managers, line managers and employees.

There is much to be said for conducting an attitude survey to establish the feelings of employees about their organization's reward policies and practices. An example of such a survey is given in Appendix A. Focus group discussions can also be used to obtain the views of groups of employees about particular issues.

The diagnostic review can form the basis for action in any area of reward management. The following check list sets out the points to be covered.

Philosophy

1. *Is there a well articulated reward philosophy which underpins the reward strategies of the organization, governs reward policies and provides the foundation for the guiding principles which determine the operation of reward processes?*

Reward philosophy should cover such areas as the importance of pay as a motivating force, the use of financial rewards, the relative significance of internal equity and external competitiveness, the amount of flexibility allowed and the extent to which authority for pay decisions is devolved to line managers.

Strategy

2. *Is there a strategy for reward management which clearly states the intentions of the organization on how reward processes will support the needs of the overall business and the achievement of corporate objectives?*

The strategy should be concerned not only with obtaining, retaining and motivating high-quality people but also underpinning the organization's values, conveying to employees the message that the organization will satisfy their reward expectations and indicating the type of behaviour that will be rewarded.

3. *Are reward strategies linked to key business and human resource manage-*
    ment strategies?

The strategies should be concerned with how reward processes can provide levers
for encouraging business strategies such as growth, quality, innovation and
improved performance. They should be integrated with other HRM strategies in
such areas as continuous development.

4. *Do the reward strategies provide a good basis for the development of reward*
    policies, processes and procedures?

The strategies should clearly indicate the direction the organization wants to go in
developing its reward policies and practices.

5. *Are the strategies congruent with the culture of the organization?*

The strategies should not only reflect the culture of the organization but should
also be used as necessary to help change the culture, eg by increasing the degree to
which the organization is performance orientated.

Policies

6. *What is the policy on the levels of reward?*

The policy on the levels of reward should define the pay stance of the company, ie
the relationship between internal and market rates. This should be done for the
whole company and in relation to specialist markets where necessary.

7. *Are reward levels linked to business performance?*

This question should establish how reward management policies and practices will
respond to fluctuations in business performance and will consider the use of one-
off bonus payments in response to business success, rather than basic pay
increases which have a cost commitment for future years.

8. *What is the policy on market rates?*

This question covers the policy on the extent to which special treatment will be
given to jobs whose market rates are high and are critical to the future success of
the business. It will also involve taking a view on whether particular functions
need 'high flyers' or whether more 'mainstream' employees are needed.

9. *What is the policy on equity?*

This policy should define how the company achieves equity in rates of pay
according to levels of responsibility and performance. There is often tension
between market rate and equity policies and this question should seek to establish
how this tension is managed.

10. *What is the policy on performance-related rewards?*

This policy should define the extent to which leverage for growth, innovation and
improved results is to be provided by performance-related pay or incentive
schemes. It should refer to how far rewards are related to individual, team or
corporate performance and what proportion of total remuneration for different
categories of employees should be related to performance.

11. *What is the policy on the pay structure?*

This policy should be concerned with what sort of pay structure is required. It should consider such aspects as:

- the extent to which there should be spot rates or pay brackets;
- whether jobs of a broadly similar size should be grouped into pay grades or whether each job should have its own grade;
- the use of 'broad-banded' structures to enhance flexibility;
- the use of alternative pay structures such as pay curves for job family based progression on technical ladders.

12. *What is the policy on total reward?*

Total reward policy should establish the mix of financial and non-financial reward, the mix of pay and employee benefits and the extent to which employees will be allowed flexibility or choice over their benefits.

Guiding principles

13. *Is there a set of guiding principles on how the reward processes should operate?*

Guiding principles help to define how line managers should apply reward management policies in their areas of responsibility. They also spell out to employees the way in which reward processes are expected to function.

Impact

14. *What impact are the reward practices of the organization making on organizational performance?*

This question addresses the fundamental requirement for reward management practices to give added value by improving organizational performance. It is particularly concerned with the degree to which pay-for-performance schemes do provide real incentives, the effectiveness of performance management processes as means of motivating and developing employees, and the amount of increased commitment generated by employee benefits. Essentially, the question is 'do we get value for money?' It is, however, not an easy question to answer. There are so many internal and external factors which influence organizational performance that it may be difficult to establish cause and effect from any one performance lever. But the question still needs to be asked.

15. *Do employees feel that the pay policies and practices of the organization are fair?*

However carefully and logically pay structures are designed and administered, ultimately, they will be judged by employees according to their perceptions of the degree to which they operate fairly and equitably. This is the 'felt-fair' principle. The problem may simply arise because of a failure to communicate the rationale behind the structure and the remuneration policies and practices of the organization. Alternatively, it may be because there are fundamental flaws in some aspect or aspects of reward processes. In either case, something should be done to address the problem or there could be a serious fall in morale accompanied by higher staff turnover and lower levels of performance.

16. *How effective are reward policies and practices in attracting and retaining high quality people to the organization?*

It is necessary to find out if it is proving difficult to recruit or retain any category of employee, and if so, the extent to which this arises because pay levels are not competitive.

17. *Can the organization afford the pay practices it has installed?*

This question addresses the fundamental requirement of 'affordability'. It is not just a matter of value for money. Businesses have to consider how much of their financial resources they can allocate to employment costs. When times are hard, they may have to look very carefully at existing practices and decide where costs can be reduced.

18. *Is the organization getting value for money from its reward policies and practices?*

This is a fundamental question which can only be answered by assessing the impact of each process. For example:

- Is the performance-related pay scheme simply handing out money to people without any commensurate improvement in individual, team or organizational performance?
- Is wage drift (pay increases unrelated to output or productivity) endemic in incentive schemes?
- Is money being wasted on under-appreciated or unwanted employee benefits?
- Are 'across-the-board' pay increases being awarded to compensate for increases in the cost of living without regard to what the company can afford to pay or the merits of individuals receiving the rewards?
- Are pay increases given automatically to employees simply for 'being there'?
- Is the pay structure getting out of control because of grade drift, performance rating drift or over-reaction to market rate perceptions?

Pay determination

19. *Is information collected systematically on market rates, and is it acted upon?*

The information should be obtained by regularly conducting and/or scrutinizing pay surveys and by analysing other published data (not just job advertisements). There is no point in doing this, however, unless the results are incorporated in an overall review of levels of pay and relativities. There is also the danger of spending too much time and money in chasing information which will not be used.

20. *Is a formal system of job evaluation used to determine the relative size of jobs?*

Some relatively formal process of job evaluation is generally essential to provide reference points against which basic pay levels can be set for jobs and to ensure that the organization meets equal pay for work of equal value requirements. But job evaluation schemes can easily 'work loose', ie erode, if jobs are upgraded without being evaluated properly (a process usually referred to as grade drift) and this needs to be checked. It is also necessary to check that the existing scheme and the way it is administered does provide reliable information on relative job size, especially when structures, roles and relativities within the organization are changing rapidly.

21.   *Is sufficient attention given to paying the same for work of equal value?*

The design and implementation of the job evaluation scheme should not discriminate against individual employees or categories of employees in any way.

Pay structure

22.   *Are pay structures relevant to the needs of the organization as a whole or the parts in the organization or employee categories for which they operate?*

There is a choice of structures from relatively rigid fine-graded structures to flexible broad-banded structures and even more flexible pay curve systems. A structure will be relevant if it:

- fits the circumstances and culture of the organization by, for example, operating flexibly in fast-moving organizations subject to rapid change, or being well defined and rigorously applied where order and predictability are of paramount importance;
- provides a logical framework within which consistent and defensible decisions can be made on levels of pay, salary progression and differentials;
- makes provision for the inevitability of sometimes having to allow external market considerations to prevail over internal equity imperatives, especially in areas of skill shortage.

23.   *If there is a graded pay structure, is it designed and administered properly?*

This question can be answered by reference to the following supplementary questions:

- Are grades clearly defined?
- Is the grade structure logical and acceptable in the sense that it reflects the distinct and 'felt fair' levels in the job size hierarchy?
- Is the width of ranges sufficient (*1*) to enable worthwhile differentials to be maintained between individuals in the range according to their competence and performance and (*2*) to provide for role flexibility?
- Is there a defined reference point in each range which represents the desired position in the market place?
- Is there an adequate differential between grades?
- Are consistent methods used to allocate jobs into grades?

24.   *Is there any evidence of grade drift?*

Grade drift happens when upgradings have taken place without adequate justification in order to increase remuneration or status or acquire extra benefits. This often happens because the job evaluation scheme is being manipulated by managers or employees, especially in situations where there a number of border line cases in a multi-graded structure. The problem may have to be tackled by tightening up job evaluation and regrading procedures and/or by reexamining the pay structure and grade boundaries.

Paying for performance, skill or competence

25.   *Is there a consistent method of progressing pay according to performance, skill or competence?*

This question considers all types of pay progression within a pay structure. The ways in which the rate of progression is determined should be examined to ensure that they are based on fair, consistent and appropriate methods of measuring performance and the levels of skill or competence achieved.

26.   *Are there any performance-related pay or incentive schemes?*

If so, for any scheme:

- Does the organization have clear objectives for the scheme?
- Is the relationship between performance or contribution and reward clearly defined?
- Have appropriate performance measures been established and is performance measured fairly and consistently?
- Have employees a reasonable degree of control over the results which determine reward levels?
- Is the amount receivable under the scheme sufficient to provide a meaningful reward and to act as a motivator?
- Do bonus earnings fluctuate too much?
- Is the scheme easy to understand and administer?
- Is there any evidence of wage drift in shop floor incentive schemes?
- Does an over-emphasis on individual rewards militate against team work?
- Does an over-emphasis on crude output measures militate against quality?
- Has the impact of the scheme on individual, team and organizational performance been properly evaluated?
- Is the operation of the scheme carefully monitored so that remedial action can be taken swiftly when necessary?

Employee benefits

27.   *Is there a balanced and cost-effective approach to the provision of employee benefits?*

This question should be answered by examining the whole benefit package to establish:

- if it provides an appropriate range of benefits at each level;
- the extent to which the benefit package is competitive;
- the scope for giving employees more choice over their benefits, either for each individual benefit or over the 'non-core' elements of the benefit package;
- the scope for moving towards a 'clean cash' policy (providing money instead of a benefit), having taken tax considerations into account;
- if the organization is getting value-for-money from its expenditure on benefits in terms of increased motivation and commitment.

28.   *Is there a consistent and fair basis for allocating benefits?*

It is necessary to examine the criteria which govern the allocation of benefits to ensure that they are both logical and equitable. Whether or not the organization has harmonized its benefits sufficiently should be considered in relation to good market practice.

Pay reviews

29.   *Are individual pay reviews properly controlled to keep within budgets and to be consistent with pay progression guidelines?*

The whole system for setting pay budgets and controlling increases should be examined to ensure that it is well defined and properly administered and controlled.

30. *What is the basis for pay reviews?*

- Is there scope to be more flexible in relating rewards to contribution by not paying separate cost-of-living increases?
- Are there adequate arrangements for tracking market rates and adjusting levels of pay for particular jobs or market groups accordingly?

Communication

31. *Are policies and guiding principles communicated to employees generally?*

There is no point in developing forward-looking reward policies unless employees are fully aware of them and the benefits they will provide. It is particularly important to communicate how pay policies aim to achieve fairness and equity, bearing in mind the need to be competitive.

32. *Are individual employees given full information on how pay policies affect them and the total remuneration, including benefits, they receive?*

Again, it is pointless to have a competitive reward structure, to reward employees fully according to their contribution and to provide them with benefits all or any of which they may take for granted. The organization needs to ensure that the total remuneration package is fully appreciated by employees as a means of improving their motivation and commitment. The quality of communication each time there is a change in reward policy also needs to be reviewed for what it has contributed to employee appreciation of the reward package.

Reward management procedures

33. *Are there established procedures for fixing rates of pay on appointment, promotion or transfer and for regrading jobs?*

The procedures should be well defined and applied consistently.

34. *To what extent has the authority to manage their own pay structures and pay reviews been devolved to line managers?*

Managers should be given the maximum amount of responsibility for this key area of human resource management. It is, after all, a major tool for them to use in raising individual and team levels of performance within their departments. Reward management policies are more likely to be implemented effectively if they are 'owned' by managers. But it is essential to provide them with clear guidelines on how they should exercise this responsibility and it is equally essential to monitor how these guidelines are being applied.

6

The Development of Reward Policies, Processes and Structures

Reward processes sometimes have to be designed from scratch, as in a start-up situation (see Chapter 36). Usually, however, it is a matter of developing existing policies, practices and structures to respond to change, help shape a new culture, deal with problems of performance, recruitment and retention or update a decayed part of the total process.

Conducting the development review

The development review should consist of the following phases:

- *Analyze* the internal and external circumstances of the organization and the present arrangements for reward management – reference can be made to the life cycle model described in Chapter 4.
- *Diagnose* the strengths and weaknesses of the present arrangements in the light of the analysis using the points in the diagnostic review set out in Chapter 5.
- *Reward philosophy* – define the reward philosophy of the organization.
- *Reward strategies* – develop reward strategies and objectives based on the preceding analysis, diagnosis and definition of reward philosophy.
- *Reward policies* – develop any new or revised policies required to implement the strategies.
- *Design and develop processes* in the main areas of reward management: pay structures, job evaluation, financial incentives, non-financial incentives, performance management and employee benefits. This will include defining performance criteria.
- *Implement* the new or revised parts of the total reward management process.
- *Evaluate* the effectiveness of the processes by reference to objectives and performance criteria.

We describe below approaches to identifying areas for development, the various factors which will need to be taken into account and the objectives that might be set for a development review.

Identifying areas for development

Potential areas for development include:

- *pay structures* – reducing the number of grades to promote flexibility and reflect organizational changes; creating a pay curve system based on job families; introducing an integrated pay structure;
- *job evaluation* – updating a decayed evaluation scheme; introducing formal job evaluation, ensuring that job evaluation processes are functioning properly;
- *market positioning* – reviewing external relativities and adjusting rates of pay to reflect market levels and maintain a competitive edge;
- *performance management* – replacing a moribund performance appraisal system; introducing a new and more integrated process of performance management based on objective setting, competence analysis and assessment and the continuous review of performance;
- *performance-related pay* – introducing a performance-related pay system to replace a fixed incremental scale or pay spine;
- *executive bonus scheme* – modifying or introducing an executive bonus scheme;
- *shop floor incentive schemes* – replacing worn out incentive schemes with a high day rate system or measured day work;
- *skill or competence-based schemes* – introducing schemes which relate pay to levels of skills (or replacing over-expensive schemes);
- *gainsharing* – introducing an added-value company-wide scheme;
- *profit-related pay* – introducing a profit-related pay scheme;
- *employee benefits* – developing a more flexible approach to the provision of employee benefits; harmonizing benefits for all categories of staff; moving towards a 'clean cash' system rather than providing a multiplicity of benefits;
- *management of reward processes* – devolving more responsibility for reward management to operating units and line management while still maintaining an appropriate degree of control over the implementation of corporate policies and remuneration costs.

These are examples of specific areas for development but many of them are interrelated. We believe in adopting an approach which takes into account the many factors which affect the development of each process and the pay structure as well as these interrelationships.

Factors to be taken into account

The design and development of reward management processes is a matter of selecting the optimum mix of rewards and benefits within the most appropriate structure and of ensuring that the various processes fit the culture of the organization. A hypothesis developed by Hay Management Consultants on culture/pay/performance management matches in large companies is set out in Tables 6.1 and 6.2.

The problem is that differences between the circumstances and cultures of organizations mean that there is no one right mix or structure and no ideal approach to reward management which suits all organizations. This diversity is why the design and development of reward processes is never straightforward. There is only one universal design principle: analyze and understand the circumstances and culture of the organization and make a choice accordingly. The factors to be taken into account are discussed below.

Table 6.1   *A Hypothesis of Cultural/Pay/Performance Management Matches in Large Companies – I*

	Traditional Bureaucracy	Performance Bureaucracy	Performance Change Organisation
PAY *Base pay*			
Structure	Grades	Grades/spines	Grades/spines
Variability	Fixed increments (service driven)	Increments with limited flexibility	Variable increments and general increases
Bonus			
Individual and	Nil	Nil	Performance bonuses at senior level
Team	Nil	Nil	Nil
Organization	Nil	Profit sharing/all employee equity participation	Profit sharing/all employee equity participation
Performance Pay Philosophy	Promotion is only performance reward	Cultural	Cultural and directional
PROCESS			
Performance Management	Administrative performance appraisal	Administrative performance appraisal	First steps to performance management as a line process
Employee Relations Climate	Collective impersonal	Collective impersonal	Collective and individual

Source: Hay Management Consultants

Type of organization

The following are some examples of how reward processes can vary according to the type of organization:

- *Bureaucracy* – there is likely to be a hierarchical pay structure with fairly narrow salary bands. Rewards will be job rather than person based. Pay progression within salary brackets and the amount of pay at risk will be small.
- *Traditional manufacturing* – the pay system for middle managers and office staff will follow the bureaucratic model. A higher proportion of the pay of senior managers and sales staff will be variable and at risk. Direct production workers may be on individual incentive schemes or measured day work.
- *High-technology companies* – the process is likely to be flexible and based on job families. Total rewards will be related directly to performance, competence, skill and market worth. There will probably be an integrated pay structure covering all employees and benefits will be harmonized.
- *Entrepreneurial firms* – the reward package for people who make a direct impact on results will have a large at-risk element. Pay levels will be market

Table 6.2   *A Hypothesis of Cultural/Pay/Performance Management Matches in Large Companies – II*

	Performance Oriented Organization	Entrepreneurial and Empowering Organization	Professionally Empowered Teams
PAY			
Base pay			
Structure	Pay ranges for grades	Pay ranges for broader grades	Some broader grades/individual arrangements
Variability	Formula approaches to individual performance related pay	Performance related pay within guidelines	Relegated management spend within budget
Bonus			
Individual and Team	Individual performance bonuses cascade to managers, some selected team elements	Flexible bonus arrangements, teams and individuals	Delegated, managerial discretion over bonuses for individuals and teams
Organization	Profit sharing/all employee equity participation	Promotion of employee ownership	Employee ownership/sharing in success
Performance Pay Philosophy	Cultural, directional and motivational	Cultural, directional, motivational and positional	Cultural, directional, motivational and positional
PROCESS			
Performance Management	Performance management as a line process to achieve business objectives	Performance management as an individual development activity linked to business and team objectives	Performance management as a development process within business 'vision'
Employee Relations Climate	Breakdown of collective orientation management of individuals	Individual relationships	Individual and collegiate relationships

Source: Hay Management Consultants

driven. Reward management policies and practices will encourage innovation and recognize success in managing diversity and change.

Company size

Larger companies, especially if they are centralized, will tend to have more formal reward systems and control mechanisms. It is easier for smaller companies to adopt an informal and flexible approach.

Business strategy

The business strategy for growth (or survival) and plans for acquisitions, mergers or diversification will affect both the direction and rate of change of the system.

Occupational characteristics

Within an organization, different methods may be used to reward people according to their occupation or job family. A high proportion of the pay of top managers and sales staff may be at risk. Knowledge workers, especially scientists and design engineers may respond well to competence-based schemes, and the level and range of skills used may determine the pay of workers in manufacturing 'cells'. People on repetitive work may be motivated by a direct incentive scheme, while managers and office staff may be on performance-related pay. Some jobs will be more market-sensitive than others.

Number and diversity of jobs

The complexity of reward management practices will be influenced by the number and diversity of jobs it has to cover. In highly complex organizations job families may be catered for by separate pay curve systems or technical ladders especially when the jobs in these families are market-sensitive.

Individual characteristics

The motivational impact of rewards depends on how far they meet individual needs. To cater for individual differences, reward policies and practice need to broaden the range of motivational approaches as much as possible, relate pay to individual levels of performance and skill, use performance management processes to help people achieve personal growth, and allow them some choice in the benefits they receive.

Employee expectations

The development of reward processes should take account of the expectations of employees and their representatives (if any) on internal equity and external competitiveness.

Organization culture

Organization culture is manifested in values (what is believed to be important), norms (accepted ways of behaviour) and management style (how managers manage their staff). Every organization has its unique culture and reward policies and processes have either to fit that culture or help to shape it in line with a culture change plan.

Organization culture affects rewards in ways such as the following:

- The emphasis will be as much on non-financial as on financial rewards when the value system reflects the belief that people will be well motivated when their work environment provides opportunities for achievement, recognition, responsibility and personal growth, ie empowerment.
- Alternatively, a value system which is based on the belief that money is the only thing that motivates people will concentrate on financial rewards and neglect the non-financial motivators.

- If a more performance-orientated culture is wanted, a significant proportion of financial rewards will be dependent on pay-for-performance schemes which will be expected to deliver powerful messages about the need for high performance.
- When one of the key values is quality, the pay arrangements will be designed to provide rewards for achieving high quality standards and levels of service delivery.
- In a high involvement organization where there exists what Charles Handy calls a 'culture of consent', individuals and groups will participate in designing the system. Peer performance reviews and/or upward feedback may be introduced (although, as yet, these are rarely linked to pay).
- If innovation is a key value, the emphasis will be on rewarding initiative, innovation, risk taking and success in managing change.
- Behavioural norms which support an informal and open management style will encourage the development of equally informal and open reward processes.
- An autocratic management style will tend to concentrate the authority for managing reward at the top of the organization, while a democratic style will encourage the devolution of authority down the line.

Other internal factors

Other internal factors which may have to be taken into account include:

- the financial resources available to introduce new practices – are they affordable?
- the human resources available to introduce new practices – this includes not only specialist personnel staff, supported as necessary by consultants, but also line management; will they support any new approaches and will they be capable of managing the new procedures?
- the organization climate – the working atmosphere of the organization; how people work together;
- employee attitudes – what they feel about the company and its employment and reward policies;
- the organization structure – hierarchical, flat, matrix, homogeneous, diversified, decentralized, formal or informal, flexible or rigid;
- the sharpness with which individual accountabilities and objectives are defined;
- historical practices to do with such matters as how different groups in the organization are paid, the proportion of pay at risk or dependent on performance and the basis upon which pay should be increased (time in job, performance, cost of living or market rate movements);
- organizational processes – teamworking, networking, individualistic, command or consultative;
- technology – use of information technology, use of new operational technology and processes, eg just in time, computer or direct numerical control, group technology, flexible manufacturing systems or computer-integrated manufacturing;
- recruitment and promotion practices – the extent to which posts are filled from inside or outside the organization;
- differentiation – the spread of pay from the top to the bottom of the organization.

External factors

Some of the external factors which may have to be taken into account are:

- business performance – profitability, market share, reputation in the City and elsewhere;
- competition – in the UK and worldwide;
- need to devote financial resources to maintaining or achieving competitive advantage;
- inflationary pressures (or the lack of them);
- economic trends;
- trends in market rates, generally or for specific categories of staff;
- critical skill shortages;
- government policies and regulations;
- fiscal and employment law.

Life cycle
The stage reached by the organization in its life cycle will influence the design of its reward system as described in Chapter 4.

Design and development objectives

Having identified possible areas for development and taken into account the various factors which might affect the design it is useful at this stage to consider the objectives of the development programme.

Clearly, the first objective will be to design or develop reward management processes and structures which as a whole will achieve the overall aims set out in Chapter 1, particularly those concerned with supporting business strategies, improving performance, increasing commitment, being competitive, achieving equity, and attracting, retaining and motivating staff. Other objectives could include:

- *Acceptability* – the system should be acceptable both to management and employees as satisfying organizational and individual needs. The objective of acceptability is achievable through the analysis of these needs, the involvement of individuals and groups in developing the system, and the communication of the aims of the system – how it will operate and how people will benefit from it.
- *Flexibility* – the objective should be to develop a system that can operate flexibly in response to change in so far as the organization is operating in an unstable environment.
- *Manageability* – the system should aim to be easily manageable so that undue burdens are not imposed on managers and members of the personnel function.
- *Affordability* – the total costs of reward management and pay reviews should be affordable by the organization.
- *Value for money* – the costs of running a pay and benefit system are huge. Even if they *are* affordable, organizations need to ensure that they are getting maximum value from their investment in reward. They need to set objectives which will enable them to move from being merely bulk purchasers of employees – paying an undifferentiated going rate – towards becoming discerning buyers and focusing reward on those people who provide a positive benefit to the organization. To achieve value-for-money objectives they must assess the costs as well as the benefits of any reward initiative. Too often, organizations blithely introduce such systems as performance-related or skill-

based pay without establishing what it will cost to run them, without a proper assessment of the impact they are likely to make on performance and motivation and, importantly, without defining criteria at the outset against which the success of the scheme can be measured. The same principle applies to employee benefits.

- *Controllability* – arrangements should be made to ensure that policies can be implemented consistently and costs can be contained within budgets.
- *Integration* – the aim should be to develop reward strategies which are integrated with human resource and business strategies.
- *Matching pay culture to organization culture* – the objective should be to ensure that reward management underpins the existing or desired organization culture and helps the organization respond to change.

The development process

The reward management development process is illustrated in Figure 6.1.

The starting point is provided by agreed reward strategies, philosophy and policies. These will all be derived from the organization's business and human resource strategies and will be influenced by its internal and external environment.

Reward management processes consist of the following strands:

1. *Non-financial rewards:* these consist of all the intrinsic motivators, such as achievement, responsibility and the opportunity to grow within the organization. They also include the extrinsic non-financial motivators such as recognition (very important), job enrichment, praise and status. The provision of training opportunities can be another important element.

These rewards, as discussed in Chapter 2, can have a powerful and long-term effect on motivation and commitment. Their effectiveness depends on the culture of the organization, including its values and management style, and the processes of management it uses.

Developing non-financial reward processes will therefore mean paying attention to culture management. This involves defining or re-defining values relating to how employees should be treated and developed. It is also necessary to ensure through educational and training interventions that managers are fully aware of their role in applying these values and understand the approaches they can use to motivate their staff through the use of non-financial rewards. Performance management will be a particularly effective way of ensuring that managers are aware of the processes they should use to recognize achievement, provide added responsibility and develop their staff.

2. *Performance management:* performance management, as described in Chapters 14 and 15, is a means of getting better results from the organization, teams and individuals by measuring and managing performance within an agreed framework of planned goals. It should impact directly on corporate performance but will also feed into the non-financial reward and payment for performance processes.

3. *Financial rewards:* these are provided in accordance with reward policies and within a basic pay structure which is designed and maintained by reference to job evaluation and market rate analysis processes. To provide additional motivation and directly to influence performance, some form of performance-related pay, incentive scheme or payment for skill or competence may be adopted. A choice may be made on the combination of pay-for-performance arrangements, for

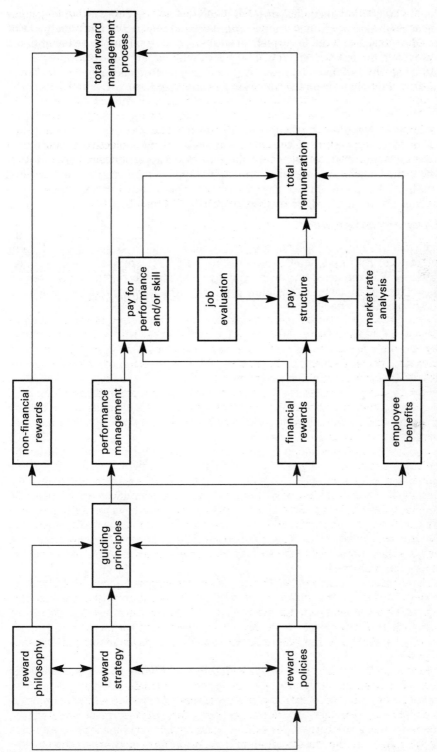

Figure 6.1 *The reward management development process*

example combining individual or team incentives with a company-wide scheme such as gainsharing, profit sharing or profit-related pay to develop what might be termed a total performance pay plan. In addition, a range of employee benefits will be provided, the level of which will be affected by market considerations.

All these types of financial rewards (basic pay, performance pay and employee benefits) combine to form the total remuneration process.

Choice of process

The choice of process is contingent on the reward strategy, philosophy and policies of the organization, its culture and environment and the type of people it employs. There is therefore no such thing as an ideal approach and there is always choice. The choices available in relation to the type of organization are illustrated in Table 6.1. But there will be many variations on this pattern and it is impossible to prescribe the most appropriate arrangement. It all depends.

Achieving coherence

Whatever the choice of system, it is important to achieve coherence by relating each aspect of it to one another and to the overall reward and human resource strategies. This process can be helped by distilling the organization's reward philosophies and policies into guiding principles which will govern the design and operation of the system.

PART 3

ASSESSING JOB VALUES AND RELATIVITIES

7

Factors Affecting Job Values and Relativities

Reward management involves the development of pay structures of varying degrees of formality which define the rates of pay for jobs, the pay relativities between jobs and the basis upon which job holders are paid. Pay structures are designed by reference to judgements about job values as expressed by relativities with other jobs and external (market) rates of pay for comparable jobs. These judgements are made against the background of the factors which influence job values. Bearing these in mind, steps can be taken to establish internal job values by using some form of job evaluation. External values are also established by surveying and analyzing market rates, and the information gained from job evaluation and market rate surveys is combined when developing the pay structure.

This chapter deals with the factors influencing job values and relativities and the basis upon which the rates of pay for individual jobs and job holders are determined. The next chapter in this part examines methods of providing the basic information required for job evaluation, pay surveys and performance management through job, skills and competence analysis. The remaining chapters deal with job evaluation processes and techniques of conducting pay surveys. Reward or pay structures are dealt with in Part 4.

General factors influencing job values

The general factors influencing job values are intrinsic value, internal relativities, external relativities, inflation, the circumstances of the firm and trade union pressures.

Intrinsic value

The concept of intrinsic value is based on the apparently reasonable belief that the rate for a job should be determined by reference to the amount of responsibility involved or the degree of skill or level of competence required to perform it. The responsibilities of a job are the particular obligations that have to be assumed by any person who carries out the job. Responsibility is exercised when job holders are accountable for what they do. The level of responsibility is related to the outputs job holders are expected to achieve and their contribution – the impact they can make on the end results of their section, department or the organization as a whole.

Responsibility involves the exercise of discretion in making decisions which commit the use of the organization's resources. Rates of pay are therefore influenced not only by the scope of the job in terms of its impact on results but also by the size of resources controlled, the amount of authority job holders possess, the degree of freedom they have to make decisions and to act, and the extent to which they receive guidance or instruction on what they should do.

Perceptions about the intrinsic value of jobs will be influenced not only by the outputs of job holders but also by the impact they can make on the results achieved by the organization as a whole. The scope or size of jobs and their rates of pay are therefore related to the accountability of job holders for achieving results.

The intrinsic value of jobs may also be related to the input and process factors of knowledge and skills and competences. Knowledge and skills refer to what job holders need to know and are able to do to meet the requirements of their jobs. Competences are the behavioural characteristics which demonstrably differentiate between levels of performance in a given role.

Internal relativities

The problem with the concept of intrinsic value is that it does not take account of the other factors affecting value. It can be argued that there is no such thing as absolute value. The value of anything is always relative to something else and is affected by external economic factors as well as internal relativities.

Within an organization, job values will be determined by perceptions of the worth of one job compared with others. Internal differentials reflect these perceptions, which may be based on information relating to the inputs made by job holders as reflected by the requirement to use different levels of knowledge or skill. Or more importance may be attached to outputs – the added value they create. Internal differentials will be strongly influenced by differentials established in the external market from which the organization recruits and to which existing employees may be tempted to return.

The organization structure will clearly influence differentials and methods of payment. A hierarchical structure with well-defined layers of responsibility will provide a clear indication of the pattern of differentials and produce a pay structure with fairly narrow bands. A flatter, more flexible, structure will make it hard to establish a rigid rank order and differentials will be more fluid within broader pay bands and will depend more on relative levels of competence and contribution.

External relativities

A salary or wage is a price which, like any other price, represents the value of the service to the buyer and the seller: the employer and the employed. The external value of a job – the market rate – is primarily determined by the laws of supply and demand.

However, all the market does is to allow us to assume that people occupying equal positions tend to be paid equally and as Kanter[1] puts it: 'The process is circular ... we know what people are worth because that's what they cost in the job market, but we also know that what people cost in the job market is just what they're worth'.

The market rate concept is in any case an imprecise one. Market rate surveys always reveal a considerable range of rates which reflect the special circumstances of the organizations, including the level of people they employ and their policies on how they want their levels of pay to relate to market rates – their market stance or pay posture.

There will, however, be trends in market rates to which internal pay structures must respond if they are to remain competitive. Individual rates and differentials have to be adjusted in the light of changing market pressures if the organization needs good quality staff. This will be particularly important at the intake points in a structure and in respect of individuals whose market worth is high and who are therefore vulnerable to the attractions of better paid jobs elsewhere.

It is also important to bear in mind the concept of individual market worth. In effect, this says that any employable individual has a price which is related to what other organizations are prepared to pay for his or her services. Organizations ignore at their peril the individual market worth of any employees they wish to retain whose talents are at a premium in the market place.

Inflation

Inflationary pressures clearly affect general trends in rates of pay and earnings.

Organizations have been accustomed to taking into account inflation when adjusting their pay structures although, if their managements have any sense, they have refused to commit themselves to any semblance of index linking. They have had to be prepared to increase rates by less than inflation in hard times and they have reserved the right to restrict increases to individuals to below the rate of inflation if their performance does not justify the retention of their real level of earnings. Increasingly, however, employers are basing pay reviews on movements in market rates, which are, in any case, responsive to the rate of inflation.

Business performance and/or financial circumstances

The business or strategic aims of the organization and its plans for achieving those aims will provide the basis for developing pay strategies and policies. The resulting business performance and/or the financial circumstances of the organization will influence the amount it can afford to pay and its pay policies on such matters as how it wants to relate pay to performance and market rates.

Trade union pressures

Depending on their bargaining power, trade unions will attempt to pressurize managements into increasing pay by at least the amount of inflation. They will press for higher rates on the grounds of the organization's ability to pay and trends in the going rate, and they may attempt to restore lost differentials.

Factors influencing pay levels for individuals

The pay levels of individual job holders will be influenced by three factors in addition to the rate for their job:

- their market worth as mentioned above;
- the level of skills or competence they possess – their inputs;

■   their level of performance in the job – their outputs and the overall contribution
    they make to organizational success.

The amount of influence these factors exert will depend on the job and the internal
environment of the organization. In a non-bureaucratic and flexible firm, where
the level of technology is high and a large proportion of the staff are knowledge
workers, individual worth will be more important than position in a job hierarchy.
As Kanter[1] has stated:

> 'Major employing organizations are rethinking the meaning of worth
> itself. And as they are doing this, they are gradually changing the basis for
> determining pay from *position* to *performance*, from *status* to
> *contribution*'.

How rates of pay for individual jobs and job holders are determined

The determination of individual rates of pay is a function of a number of factors as
illustrated in Figure 7.1.

Overall levels of pay will be affected by business aims, plans and performance,
external economic and union influences, reward policies and market rates.

These general considerations will, of course, affect individual rates for jobs and
job holders. These rates will be determined by market relativities, the 'size' of the
job within the structure, as measured by job evaluation, and individual levels of
performance. The latter will determine rates of pay above the base rate either by a
performance management process or a pay-for-performance scheme.

This process of individual pay determination takes place within the framework
of job and role analysis and, apart from business and market rate considerations, is
largely influenced by the interrelated processes of job evaluation and performance
management for those in receipt of performance-related pay.

Job evaluation is used to measure relativities and determine where the job
should be placed in a pay structure (the rate for the job). Relative job size is
assessed in terms of inputs (knowledge and skills), process (behavioural
requirements involving the use of competences) and outputs (the level of
responsibility for results and the impact the job makes on team or organizational
performance).

Performance management assesses the individual's performance in the job and,
in a performance-related pay environment, determines the rate of pay for that
individual in the job – where he or she is positioned within a pay range or on a pay
scale. The performance management process will be based on precisely the same
factors used in evaluating the job as recorded in a job description or role definition
derived from job or role analysis: namely skills, competences and results. The
starting point of performance management is an agreement on skill and competence requirements and on the principal accountabilities or main tasks of the job.
This leads to agreements on specific standards of performance, targets and work
plans and personal development plans which form the criteria on which performance is reviewed and assessed.

For those on an incentive or payment by results scheme, pay will be determined
by reference to job evaluation and the quantified results achieved by job holders.

Reference

1.   Kanter, R M (1989) *When Giants Learn to Dance*, Simon and Schuster, London

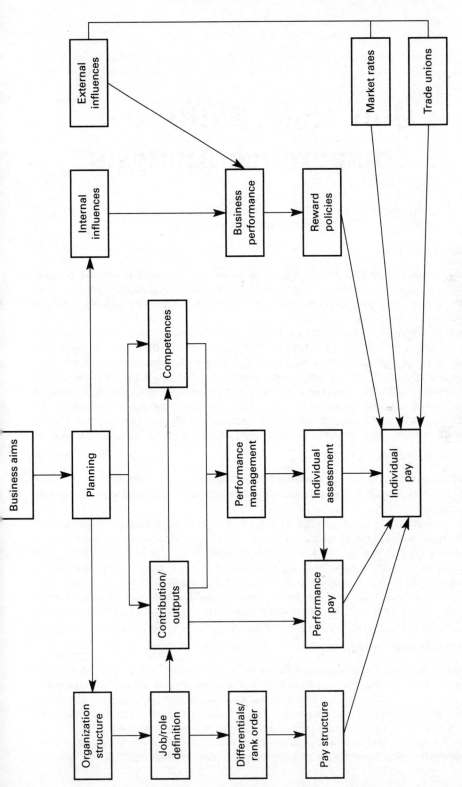

Figure 7.1 *Factors affecting individual pay*

8

Job, Role, Skills and Competence Analysis

Definitions and purpose

Job analysis

Job analysis is the process of collecting, analysing and setting out information about jobs in order to provide the basis for a job description or role definition and data for job evaluation, performance management and other human resource management purposes.

A distinction should be made between a job description and a role definition. A job description sets out the purpose of a job, where it fits in the organization structure, the context within which the job holder functions and the principal accountabilities of job holders, or the main tasks they have to carry out. A role definition additionally describes the part to be played by individuals in fulfilling their job requirements. Role definitions refer to broader aspects of behaviour, for example, working flexibly, working with others, and styles of management. They may incorporate the results of skills or competence analysis, as described below.

Skills analysis

Skills analysis starts with a definition of the tasks job holders are expected to carry out and then describes the particular skills and abilities they need to perform them effectively.

It was originally used mainly as a basis for training manual operatives but, following the rapid development of new technology applications, its use has been extended to the analysis of the more technical skills required by working, for example, in a cellular manufacturing environment. This is particularly important in flexible manufacturing systems where multi-skilling is required.

Skills analysis provides the basic data for skill-based pay as described in Chapter 26. It produces the information needed to define skill blocks for training and skill levels for pay grading purposes.

Competence analysis

Competences are the behavioural dimensions which affect job performance. They describe the capacity that exists in a person and the type of behaviour required to perform a task satisfactorily. Competence definitions may refer specifically to the knowledge, skills and qualities which individuals must apply if they are success-fully to achieve their job objectives and standards of performance.

Competence analysis in its earliest forms concentrated on the definition of competence requirements for management development and assessment centres.

It has since been extended to provide information for performance management (see Chapters 14 and 15) and the design of competence-based pay schemes (see Chapter 27).

Job analysis

Job analysis as defined by Pritchard and Murlis[1] is an analytical process involving gathering facts, analysing and sorting these facts and re-assembling them into whatever consistent format is chosen.

Job analysis gets the facts about a job from job holders, the job holder's manager (preferably both) and the job holder's colleagues or team mates. It is not a matter of obtaining opinions or making judgements. What goes into a job description should be what actually happens and why, not what people would like to think happens, or what they feel people should be like to make it happen. Thus judgemental statements such as 'Carries out the highly skilled work of ...' should be avoided (who is to say that the work is highly skilled and in comparison with what?)

The facts can be obtained by interviews (the best but most time-consuming way) or by asking job holders and/or their managers to write their own job descriptions in a structured format. It is helpful in both cases to be quite clear about the questions to be asked and answered and it is essential in the latter case to provide guidance on how the analysis should be carried out and expressed on paper.

Alternatively, questionnaires can be used – either universal questionnaires or those designed for job families.

Universal questionnaires

Universal questionnaires are designed to cover all the jobs to be analysed. They are typically used in association with computer-assisted job evaluation (see Chapter 9 and Appendix G). They should be tailored to the particular organization and the range and type of jobs to be covered, and they should focus on those aspects of performance and values which are considered to be important in the organization concerned. It is usual to incorporate multiple choice questions, as in the example given in Figure 8.1, but questions may simply ask for a number to be entered to establish the dimensions of the job, for example, number of people supervised or the value of the budget controlled.

Job family questionnaires

Job family questionnaires are designed to establish the main factors which differentiate between jobs at different levels in a job family. A job family consists of jobs in a particular function or discipline such as research scientist, development engineer or personnel specialist which are related in terms of the fundamental activities carried out but are differentiated by the levels of responsibility, skill or competence required (job families and the 'ladders' used to describe changing levels of work are discussed in more detail later in this chapter – pages 93–94). A job family questionnaire is designed with the advice of an expert team of managers from the organization. It is based on definitions of the differentiating factors and the levels at which they may be present in a job. The questions are then structured to establish the levels for each factor in a job, as illustrated in Figure 8.2.

Job analysis interview check lists

Elaborate check lists are not necessary. They only confuse people. The essence of the art of job analysis is to keep it simple. The points to be covered are:

Select the level that best describes the most common way in which the job must liaise with others.

(Internal means within the company and includes remote sites/headquarters, etc)

1. The job involves no need for contact outside the particular work group and its management.

2. The job involves infrequent contact with others, and the contact is for the purpose of exchanging job related information, which needs to be done accurately and effectively.

3. The job requires frequent contact with people outside the department in order to provide or obtain information. There is a need to express oneself clearly. The job requires courteous behaviour in face-to-face dealings with other employees.

4. The need to express oneself clearly is an important part of the job, and jobholders will typically have had specific training in communications skills or will have been selected because they possess these skills. The importance stems from a requirement to create a favourable impression on others as well as communicate information effectively.

5. The job requires you frequently to seek cooperation from, or influence others. The jobholder must develop relationships and persuade others to help resolve problems. The ability to listen to others and to develop a mutual understanding is an important requirement of the job. This level usually includes jobs which allocate, monitor and review work of other employees, or jobs which have regular and significant dealings with colleagues in a variety of different locations.

6. The job requires you to motivate subordinates or colleagues where the degree of motivation and commitment achieved will directly impact upon the result of the department.

7. The job requires highly developed communication skills for dealing with sensitive, or potentially controversial interpersonal situations. The jobholder must create behaviour change in people and/or obtain the cooperation and commitment of subordinates/colleagues. This level is usually required for positions responsible for the development, motivation, assessment and reward of other employees.

Source: Pritchard, D and Murlis, H (1992) *Jobs, Roles and People: The New World of Job Evaluation*, Nicholas Brealey.

Figure 8.1 *Typical question from a universal questionnaire*

QUESTION 4

INFORMATION HANDLING

Please tick the box which best describes the job:

☐ 1. No responsibility for the processing of data.

☐ 2. Responsible for checking data, and referring errors for correction.

☐ 3. Responsible for maintaining, checking, updating and deleting information held in files or systems of predetermined format.

☐ 4. Responsible for extracting information from files or systems and compiling reports in standard format.

☐ 5. Responsible for gathering information from a variety of established sources and compiling reports within an agreed framework.

☐ 6. Responsible for compiling special and one-off reports, using data from a range of sources, involving non-standard information retrieval and report formats.

☐ 7. Responsible for identifying new sources of information and/or the setting up of new administrative procedures, systems and reporting formats.

Source: Pritchard, D and Murlis, H (1992) *Jobs, Roles and People: The New World of Job Evaluation*, Nicholas Brealey.

Figure 8.2 *Extract from a job family questionnaire for a group of clerical and administrative jobs*

- What is your job title?
- To whom are you responsible?
- Who is responsible to you? (an organization chart is helpful)
- What is the main purpose of your job? ie in overall terms, what are you expected to do?
- To achieve that purpose, what are your main areas of responsibility (eg principal accountabilities, key result areas or main tasks)? Describe *what* you have to do, not, in any detail, *how* you do it. Also indicate *why* you have to do it, ie the results you are expected to achieve by carrying out the task.
- What are the dimensions of your job in such terms of output or sales targets, numbers of items processed, numbers of people managed, number of customers?
- Is there any other information you can provide about your job to amplify the above facts such as:
  - how your job fits in with other jobs in your department or elsewhere in the company
  - flexibility requirements in terms of having to carry out a range of different tasks
  - how work is allocated to you and how your work is reviewed and approved
  - your decision-making authority

- the contacts you make with others, inside and outside the company – the equipment, plant and tools you use
- other features of your job such as travelling or unsocial hours or unusual physical conditions
- the major problems you meet in carrying out your work
- the knowledge and skills you need to do your work.

The aim is to structure the job analysis interview or questionnaire in line with these headings.

Analyzing the facts

However carefully the interview or questionnaire is structured, the information is unlikely to come out neatly and succinctly in a way which can readily be translated into a job description or role definition. It is usually necessary to sort out, rearrange and sometimes rewrite the information under the headings and in the manner described below. But writing job descriptions or role definitions is not a literary exercise. All that is required is clear and simple prose.

Job descriptions

The format for job descriptions will depend upon the requirements of the organization. There are many varieties but one which is commonly used consists of the following sections:

Purpose

This is a short statement of why the job exists. It should be expressed in a single sentence. When defining the purpose of a job it is helpful to consider questions like:

- What part of the organization's/unit's total purpose is accomplished by this job?
- What is the unique contribution of this job which distinguishes it from other jobs?
- How would you summarize the overall responsibility of the job holder?

Organization

This section explains where the job fits into the organization. It sets out the job title of the person to whom the job holder is responsible and the job titles of the people who are directly responsible to the job holder.

Principal accountabilities

Principal accountabilities (also known as key result areas, main tasks, main duties, major activities, key responsibilities etc) are statements of the continuing end results or outputs required of the job. They answer the question: 'What are the main areas in which the job must get results to achieve its purpose?'

For most jobs between four and eight accountabilities are sufficient to cover the major result areas. Less than four probably means something is missing; more than eight may mean that individual tasks are being listed.

The main characteristics of principal accountabilities are that:

- taken together, they represent all the major outputs expected of the job;
- they focus on *what* is required (results and outputs) not *how* the job is done (detailed tasks and duties);

- each one is distinct from the others and describes a specific area in which results are to be achieved;
- they suggest (but need not state explicitly) measures or tests which could determine the extent to which the accountabilities are being fulfilled.

An accountability statement is written in the style: 'Do something in order to achieve a stated result or standard'. Each statement is made in one sentence beginning with an active verb such as prepare, produce, plan, schedule, test, maintain, develop, monitor, ensure.

Context

The context section, also called 'nature and scope', is designed to add flavour to the bare list of principal accountabilities by describing aspects of the job and the role of the job within the context of the organization.

It is usually expressed in a structured narrative which follows the questions raised at the analysis stage, namely:

- where the job fits in with other key aspects of the work of the organization or unit;
- decision making authority;
- how work is assigned, reviewed and approved;
- the particular knowledge, skills and experience required;
- the degree of flexibility needed to undertake different tasks or use of different skills;
- the particular demands on the job in such areas as total quality management, leadership, teamworking, interpersonal skills, planning, crisis management etc;
- the major problems job holders are likely to meet in carrying out their work;
- physical conditions;
- the plant, equipment or tools used.

Dimensions

The dimensions (sometimes called the critical dimensions) of a job include any quantitative data which indicate its size and the range of responsibilities involved. For example, output, number of items processed, sales turnover, budgets, costs controlled, numbers supervised, number of cases dealt with over a period.

An example of a job description is given in Appendix I.

Role definitions

A role definition expands the basic information contained in a job description by including more information on the skill and behavioural requirements of a job. Role definitions provide the basis for performance management, recruitment and career planning as well as the information required to develop a skill or competence-based pay structure.

'Role blueprint' is a term used by Pritchard and Murlis for a role definition which results from a comprehensive analysis of a role covering:

- the achievements and outputs required by the organization;
- the skills, knowledge and expertise required in the role;
- the competences which characterize the role.

The achievement and outputs are covered by a conventional job description in terms of purpose and principal accountabilities. Additionally, in order to obtain a full understanding of a role, it is necessary not only to analyze and describe the technical knowledge, skills and experience needed to deliver the required level of output but also the behavioural competences which characterize the role and strongly influence how it should be performed.

It is useful to distinguish between:

- *skills* – learnable skills, knowledge and expertise, and
- *competences* – behavioural characteristics which can be demonstrated to differentiate high performers in a given role under such headings as achievement drive and concern for order.

Skills analysis

Skills analysis extends the basic analysis of the results to be obtained by assessing and describing the abilities and skills job holders need to carry out their tasks and achieve the expected levels of performance.

Skills analysis may take the form of job learning analysis as described by Pearn and Kandola.[2] This concentrates on inputs and processes by analysing the learning skills which contribute to satisfactory performance. A learning skill is one used to increase either skills or knowledge and represents broad categories of job behaviour which need to be learned. The learning skills are the following:

- Physical skills requiring instruction, practice and repetition to get right.
- Operating and maintaining plant, equipment and machines.
- Complex procedures or sequences of activity which are memorized or followed with the aid of written materials or manuals.
- Non-verbal information such as sight, sound, smell, taste and touch which is used to check, assess or discriminate, and which usually takes practice to get right.
- Memorizing facts or information.
- Ordering, prioritizing and planning, which refer to the degree to which a job holder has any responsibility for, and flexibility in, determining the way a task is carried out.
- Looking ahead and anticipating.
- Diagnosing, analysing and problem solving, with or without help.
- Interpreting or using written manuals and other sources of information such as diagrams or charts.
- Adapting to new ideas and systems.

Competence analysis

Competence analysis provides the basis for producing role definitions and competence models for use in performance management, selection and career development.

Competences were defined earlier in this chapter as those behavioural characteristics which can be demonstrated to differentiate high performers in a given role.

A competence analysis is usually carried out by means of a structured interview, although a workshop approach can be adopted in which a number of management experts and/or job holders get together to analyze a job or a job family.

During the interview or workshop, the initial questions establish the overall purpose of the job and what it entails in terms of principal accountabilities. It then goes on to analyze the behavioural characteristics which distinguish performers at different levels of competence.

The basic question is: 'What are the positive or negative indicators of behaviour which are conducive or non-conducive to achieving high levels of performance?' These may be analyzed under such headings as:

- personal drive (achievement motivation)
- impact on results
- analytical power
- strategic thinking
- creative thinking (ability to innovate)
- decisiveness
- commercial judgement
- team management and leadership
- interpersonal relationships
- ability to communicate
- ability to adapt and cope with change and pressure
- ability to plan and control projects.

In each area instances will be sought which illustrate effective or less effective behaviour.

This analysis then leads to an assessment of specific knowledge and skill requirements and what sort of education, training and experience are needed to obtain them.

There are three other more refined techniques of competence analysis:

- critical-incident technique
- repertory grid analysis
- job competency assessment.

Critical-incident technique

The critical-incident technique is a means of eliciting data about effective or less effective behaviour which is related to examples of actual events – critical incidents. The technique is used with groups of job holders and/or their managers or other 'experts' (sometimes, less effectively, with individuals) as follows:

- Explain what the technique is and what it is used for, ie – 'to assess what constitutes good or poor performance by analysing events which have been observed to have a noticeably successful or unsuccessful outcome, thus providing more factual and "real" information than by simply listing tasks and guessing performance requirements'.
- Agree and list the key areas of responsibility – the principal accountabilities – in the job to be analyzed. To save time, the analyst can establish these prior to the meeting but it is necessary to ensure that they are agreed provisionally by the group, which can be told that the list may well be amended in the light of the forthcoming analysis.
- Each area of the job is taken in turn and the group is asked for examples of critical incidents. If, for example, one of the job responsibilities is dealing with customers, the following request could be made:

    I want you to tell me about a particular occasion at work which involved you – or that you observed – in dealing with a customer. Think about what the circumstances were, eg who took part, what the customer asked for, what you or the other member of the staff did and what the outcome was.

■ Collect information about the critical incident under the following headings:

 – what the circumstances were
 – what the individual did
 – the outcome of what the individual did.

This information should be recorded on a flip chart.

■ Continue this process for each area of responsibility.
■ Refer to the flip chart and analyse each incident by obtaining ratings of the recorded behaviour on a scale such as 1 for least effective to 5 for most effective.
■ Discuss these ratings to get initial definitions of effective and ineffective performance for each of the key aspects of the job.
■ Refine these definitions as necessary after the meeting – it can be difficult to get a group to produce finished definitions.
■ Produce the final analysis which can list the competences required and include performance indicators or standards of performance for each principal accountability or main task.

Repertory grid

Like the critical incident technique, the repertory grid can be used to identify the dimensions which distinguish good from poor standards of performance. The technique is based on Kelly's[3] personal construct theory. Personal constructs are the ways in which we view the world. They are personal because they are highly individual and they influence the way we behave or view other people's behaviour. The aspects of the job to which these 'constructs' or judgements apply are called elements.

To elicit judgements, a group of people are asked to concentrate on certain elements, which are the tasks carried out by job holders, and develop constructs about these elements. This enables them to define the qualities which indicate the essential requirements for successful performance.

The procedure followed by the analyst is known as the triadic method of elicitation (a sort of three card trick) and involves the following steps:

1. Identify the tasks or elements of the job to be subjected to repertory grid analysis. This is done by one of the other forms of job analysis, eg interviewing.
2. List the tasks on cards.
3. Draw three cards at random from the pack and ask the members of the group to nominate which of the these tasks is the odd one out from the point of view of the qualities and characteristics needed to perform it.
4. Probe to obtain more specific definitions of these qualities or characteristics in the form of expected behaviour. If, for example, a characteristic has been described as the ability to plan and organize, ask questions such as 'What sort of behaviour or actions indicate that someone is planning effectively?', or 'How can we tell if someone is not organizing his or her work particularly well?'
5. Draw three more cards from the pack and repeat steps 3 and 4.
6. Repeat this process until all the cards have been analysed and there do not appear to be any more constructs to be identified.

7. List the constructs and ask the group members to rate each task on every quality, using a six or seven point scale.
8. Collect and analyze the scores in order to assess their relative importance. This can be done statistically as described by Markham[4].

Like the critical-incident technique, repertory grid analysis helps people to articulate their views by reference to specific examples. An additional advantage is that the repertory grid makes it easier for them to identify the behavioural characteristics or competences required in a job by limiting the area of comparison through the triadic technique.

Although a full statistical analysis of the outcome of a repertory grid exercise is helpful, the most important results that can be obtained are the descriptions of what constitute good or poor performance in each element of the job.

Both the repertory grid and the critical incident techniques require a skilled analyst who can probe and draw out the descriptions of job characteristics. They are quite detailed and time consuming but even if the full process is not followed, much of the methodology is of use in a less elaborate approach to job analysis.

Job competency assessment

The job competency assessment method as described by Spencer, McClelland and Spencer[5] is based on David McClelland's research in what competency variables predict job performance.

He established twenty competences which most often predict success. These are grouped into six clusters, as follows:

Achievement cluster

1. Achievement orientation
2. Concern for quality and order
3. Initiative

Helping/service cluster

4. Interpersonal understanding
5. Customer-service orientation

Influence cluster

6. Impact and influence
7. Organizational awareness
8. Relationship building (networking)

Managerial cluster

 9. Directiveness
10. Teamwork and cooperation
11. Developing others
12. Team leadership

Cognitive thinking/problem solving cluster

13. Technical expertise
14. Information seeking
15. Analytical thinking
16. Conceptual thinking

Personal effectiveness cluster

17. Self control, stress resistance
18. Self-confidence
19. Organizational commitment – 'business-mindedness'
20. Flexibility

McClelland then developed with his colleagues an expert system containing a database of competence definitions under these headings.

The competency assessment method is used to model the competences for a generic job, ie a position occupied by a number of job holders where the basic accountabilities are similar, such as research scientists in a laboratory or areas sales managers. The method (now used by Hay McBer) is based on McClelland's list of competences and uses the expert system developed from his research.

The starting point is to assemble an expert panel of managers to express their vision of the job, its duties and responsibilities, any difficult job components, any likely future changes to the role and the criteria against which the job holder's performance is measured. The members of the panel nominate job holders whom they consider to be outstanding and those whom they consider satisfactory.

The next stage is to conduct a 'behavioural event interview' with the nominated job holders. This interview focuses on the distinction between a person's concepts about what it takes to be successful and what the person actually does to create that success. It employs a structured probe strategy, rather than a standard set of questions, to elicit what the interviewee sees as his or her most critical job experiences. The interview is investigative, not reflective, the object is to gather the most accurate performance data, not to collect a person's ideas about what he or she might have done under similar circumstances. The interviewees are not allowed to draw conclusions about what it takes to do that job, rather, they are pressed for information on their actual behaviour, thoughts and actions by a trained interviewer.

Following this analysis, differentiations can be made between superior and average performers in the form of:

■ the competences that superior performers possess and exhibit which the average performers do not;
■ the activities the average performers undertake which superior performers do not;
■ the competence and performance criteria that both superior and average performers exhibit, but the superior performers exhibit far more frequently.

Generic job descriptions

Generic job descriptions cover groups or families of jobs where the nature of the tasks carried out is basically the same although there may be significant differences in the level of work undertaken.

For example, in a branch organization, the job of all branch managers will fundamentally be the same but the size of the branches, in terms of income and number of customers, and therefore the size of the job, may vary considerably. Or, in the case of design engineers working in a research and development organization, the basic job may be the same but the level at which engineers operate will vary in terms of such factors as undertaking more difficult or complex assignments, carrying out more sophisticated experiments or being involved in a wider range of projects requiring different skills and abilities.

Increasing use is being made of generic job descriptions for two reasons:

- *Process efficiency* – there is no point in carrying out a detailed separate job analysis for every generic job in categories such as those mentioned above. All that is necessary is to produce a generic job description covering the common ground and then identify any variations in the level at which the work is carried out. This variation analysis can be applied generically to produce a ladder of jobs differentiated by the levels at which these distinct factors apply.
- *Job flexibility* – the increasing requirement to build job flexibility into job descriptions has encouraged the growth of generic approaches. If, for example, a group of technicians are carrying out broadly the same kind of work but on different projects, defining the role generically gives greater flexibility as people move from project to project. This avoids having to go through the unnecessary task of re-writing the job description each time, only to arrive at much the same result.

For jobs where there are no significant differences in the levels at which the work is carried out, a conventional job description format is suitable, with only minimal amendments required.

Where, however, there are differences in the level of work, it is necessary to define a series of these levels to form a ladder or family of generic roles. This approach has been used for many years in professional and technical areas, but it is now being extended to other functions as the requirement for flexibility means that jobs have to be more generically defined, while still recognizing the need to distinguish between levels of work.

It is, however, necessary to bear in mind the importance of ensuring that generic job descriptions *are* only used when posts are broadly the same. In most organizations there will always be a proportion of jobs which are individual and which should not be streamlined into generic formats.

Job ladders and families

When defining the different levels at which work is carried out in a generic job, the aim is to distinguish the levels clearly by selecting the factors which differentiate between them and then expressing each level in terms of these factors. An example of such a ladder for a family of scientific jobs is given in Table 8.1. This ladder will, of course, be superimposed on a statement of the common purpose and principal accountabilities of the job family.

To apply this approach it is necessary first to divide the job population into job families of basically similar jobs. At the same time, the jobs that will need to be treated individually should be identified.

The next step is to analyze each family of jobs to establish the extent to which work is carried out at different levels. Where this is the case, the levels within each family are analyzed and described in terms which differentiate them clearly and in the language of the family. Job evaluation as described in Chapters 9 and 10 can then be used to evaluate the levels so as to provide the cross-family relativities which are needed to build the framework for company-wide pay structures.

Some job families are more diverse than others and it may be useful to divide the broad family of, say professional engineers, into homogeneous groups of, for example, design engineers, development engineers, and project engineers. A set of parallel ladders could then be developed representing the different degrees to which factor levels apply between these sub-groups. This broad family approach is more appropriate when career development is not simply up a series of parallel

Table 8.1 *Extract from scientist ladder, expressed in terms of levels and differentiating factors*

	Technical accountability/ leadership	Assignment leadership	Setting objectives
Level 1	Accountable for applying established techniques within a defined area or specialization.	Carries out defined experiments and procedures as part of a research investigation.	Determines day to day procedures within overall experimental design.
Level 2	Accountable for providing specialist expertise in a defined discipline.	Undertakes well defined research investigations in a specialist area, or particular parts of a multi-disciplinary investigation.	Determines experimental programme to meet defined objectives.
Level 3	Accountable for developing the company's body of knowledge within a defined discipline.	Leads significant research investigations in the area of specialization.	Plans and programmes research investigations including inputs from other areas of specialization.

Source:

ladders but includes diagonal moves as people gain experience in a variety of roles. As Pritchard and Murlis[1] put it: 'What is wanted is a wide staircase or scrambling net which can accommodate diversity of roles and career paths between them'.

The significance of job and role analysis

Job analysis can be an exacting and time consuming process. But the effort is worthwhile. In the absence of sound job, skill and competency analysis, the processes of job evaluation, conducting market rate surveys and performance management cannot be carried out effectively. In addition, a database of properly analysed and defined jobs and roles can be an essential part of a human resource expert system used for such key activities as recruitment, training, continuous development, career planning, organization development and job design.

References

1. Pritchard, D and Murlis, H (1992) *Jobs, Roles and People: the New World of Job Evaluation*, Nicholas Brealey Publishing, London
2. Pearn, K and Kandola, R (1986) *Job Analysis*, Institute of Personnel Management, London
3. Kelly, G (1955) *The Psychology of Personal Constructs*, Norton, New York
4. Markham, C (1987) *Practical Consulting*, Institute of Chartered Accountants, London
5. Spencer, L, McClelland, D and Spencer, S (1990) *Competency Assessment Methods*, Hay/McBer Research Press, New York

9

Job Evaluation – Purpose and Methods

Financial reward systems have to provide for the management of internal pay relativities, and this process has to be based on a method of comparing the size or importance of jobs.

Some organizations do this mainly by relating internal rates of pay to market rates on the assumption that 'a job is worth what the market says it is worth', and that therefore market rate relativities should dictate internal relativities. The problem with this approach is that the concept of a market rate is much less precise than most people think. Market rates are also volatile and unpredictable. Relying on market rate comparisons alone will not result in the provision of a sufficiently reliable or stable basis for an equitable pay structure, although market rates will, of course, influence rates of pay within the structure.

To provide a stable framework for financial rewards some method of assessing the relative internal value of jobs is required. This chapter contains an introduction to the principles and methods of job evaluation under the following headings:

- definition of job evaluation;
- the full meaning of job evaluation;
- why job evaluation is necessary;
- the measurement of relative job size;
- methods of job evaluation;
- criticisms of job evaluation and our answers to them.

Definition of job evaluation

Job evaluation is the process of assessing the relative size of jobs within an organization.

In job evaluation terminology, the word 'size' is used to indicate the relative significance or importance of a job to the organization. It is not an absolute term. Size can only be measured by comparing the incidence of various factors in a job such as the knowledge and skills required, level of responsibility, level of decision-making and impact on end results with the incidence of the same factors in other jobs. This may be done 'holistically' by considering the relative size of 'whole jobs' on the basis of what is believed (consciously or unconsciously) to be the key criterion or mix of criteria for comparative purposes. Alternatively it may be done more analytically by identifying a range of factors and assessing the degree to which they are present in different jobs. In either case the basis for measuring job size will be influenced by the values of the organization.

The primary purpose of job evaluation is to provide a rational basis for the determination and management of internal relativities between jobs and for the design of pay structures. However, because job evaluation is based upon an analysis of the relevant facts about a job, the information collected in a job evaluation exercise can be used for a number of other purposes such as organization design, human resource planning, training and continuous development. By emphasising output factors such as impact on end results, job evaluation can support change programmes designed to develop a high performance culture. The use of factors related to skill and competence means that job evaluation can encourage the acquisition of additional skills or the improvement of levels of competence.

The meaning of job evaluation

The meaning of job evaluation is best understood if it is regarded as a comparative, judgemental, analytical and job-centred process.

A comparative process

Job evaluation is a comparative process. It deals with relationships not absolutes. There is no single unit of measurement which will tell us precisely how much a job is worth. All we can do is to compare the size of jobs with one another. And although we can make these comparisons more accurate by factor analysis and the use of scales to help the measurement process, judgement is still required.

A judgemental process

Up to a point, job evaluation could be regarded as a science in that it requires the systematic organization and formulation of a body of knowledge about jobs. But job evaluation can never be fully scientific. This is because first, the concept of a job or role is not a precise one. Second, it is hard to produce a precise and scientific definition of what job 'size' really means since the range and relative weight attached to the different factors which contribute to job size will depend on the values within the organization.

Job evaluation can be described as a systematic process for measuring job size but always requires the exercise of judgement in interpreting facts and situations and in applying these interpretations to decisions on the relative size of jobs. The aim of the job evaluation process is therefore to minimize the subjectivity of these judgements and to maximize the consistency with which they are made.

An analytical process

Job evaluation may be judgemental but it is about making *informed* judgements. These are founded on an analytical process of gathering facts about jobs, sorting these facts out systematically, and re-assembling them into whatever consistent format is being used. All job evaluation methods are based on job analysis, but when measuring size some use the non-analytical method of whole job comparisons or job classification, as described on pages 100–102. The most frequently used methods, however, are analytical (see pages 102–8).

A structured process

Job evaluation is structured in the sense that a framework is provided for helping evaluators make consistent and rational judgements. This framework consists of agreed methods or sets of criteria which are used by all evaluators in the organization, and which represent the values of the organization as a whole. The structure, however, has to avoid rigidity – there must be some scope for exercising informed judgement within the framework because, as we have already noted, total precision in measuring relative job sizes is unattainable.

A job centred process

One of the dogmas of job evaluation is that it is concerned with evaluating the job not the person. This means that evaluators are there to look at the content and context of the jobs people do rather than how well they do them. Job evaluation and performance appraisal or assessment are separate activities. This is an entirely reasonable proposition and indeed it must be emphasized when conducting a job evaluation exercise. Unless this is done people will feel that a back-door method is being used to assess their performance, and this could create suspicion and fear, and seriously damage the credibility of the job evaluation exercise.

There are, however, two caveats which should be made about this proposition. First, although evaluation and assessment are separate processes, they both spring from the same root – an understanding from job analysis of the purpose and content of the jobs and what the job holders are expected to achieve (sometimes referred to as their principal accountabilities). Second, and importantly, it is impossible to separate completely the person from the job in situations where there is scope for responsibilities to be enlarged because of the capability (and sometimes the ambition) of the job holder. A job does not necessarily consist of a finite set of tasks, especially in today's more flexible and fluid organizations and in any innovative, entrepreneurial role.

The process of breaking down traditional (pyramid) hierarchies and relying less on structured definition and more on team and project relationships means that the old concept of a job upon which traditional job evaluation methods were based has to be supplemented if not replaced by the concept of roles. This takes a broader view of how people should work within organizations and emphasizes team work, flexibility and the need to provide job holders with scope to make the best use of their abilities. As Pritchard and Murlis[1] point out: 'Traditional job evaluation practice is often seen as reinforcing the old hierarchical model. How is modern practice responding to these challenges, and how does it relate to pay determination based on skills and competences?' We shall be providing an answer to that question in this chapter.

Why is job evaluation necessary?

As it stands, this is a misleading question for two reasons. First, no employing organizations have any choice. They *have* to make decisions on rates of pay and these decisions must be made on the basis of assumptions about the relative size or value of jobs. The question should be rephrased as: 'To what extent do we need to have a formal process of evaluation rather than relying on subjective judge- ments?' Second, it begs the question of what sort of job evaluation is appropriate for a particular organization. Organizations with different cultures, structures and technologies and operating in different environments may need to adopt different approaches to job evaluation. There is no one system of evaluation which meets all requirements. There is, however, a need for some degree of formality in evaluating jobs for the following reasons:

- a rational basis is required for making defensible decisions on job grades and rates of pay – such decisions are more likely to be accepted if the logic upon which they are based is clear;
- a consistent approach is required to the management of relativities;
- an equitable pay structure is unlikely to be achieved unless a logical method of measuring relative job size exists;
- equal pay for work of equal value issues can ultimately only be resolved by the use of a formal and analytical method of job evaluation;
- a reasonably formal approach to job evaluation provides a strategic framework within which rational decisions can be made in response to changing organization structures and roles and to market rate pressures;
- a logical and consistent approach to measuring the relative size of jobs will not be achieved unless there is an agreed method and set of criteria for doing so which is used by all evaluators and represents the values of the organization as a whole.

How are relative job sizes assessed?

The significance of the last point above becomes even more evident when consideration is given to the basis upon which job size is assessed.

Job evaluators frequently use the concepts of size or importance when comparing job values but it can be difficult to understand exactly what they mean by these words. Does size simply refer to the dimensions of the job in terms either of resources controlled (eg money, people, plant and equipment) or outputs (eg sales turnover, units processed)? Or should size be measured by the contribution the job can make to achieving organizational objectives? But how do you assess contribution? This may be easy in sales or manufacturing jobs where outputs can readily be measured. It is harder in occupations such as basic research and personnel.

The concept of importance also creates difficulties. There is a psychological aspect. To tell people that their jobs are less important than others is hardly likely to increase their self-respect or their motivation. Then there is the problem of what criteria can be used to measure degrees of importance. Is it simply a matter of rank in a hierarchy? Or is it the level of responsibility (however that is defined), the impact of the job on end results (however that is determined), the difficulty of the job (eg, complexity, manual or mental skills – however they are measured), or the qualifications, knowledge, skills and experience required to carry out the job (however these are established)?

This lack of precision in the concepts of size and importance means that in every organization those concerned with introducing and managing job evaluation have to make up their own minds about how job size should be defined (for the rest of this chapter we shall use the term 'job size' to cover the dimensions of the job and its relative value, thus avoiding the psychological difficulty with 'importance' referred to above).

To a large degree the definition of job size will depend on the organization's values – that is, what is considered to be important so far as work is concerned. Some organizations will attach more weight to measurable results. Others will concentrate on responsibility, which may be defined as the size of resources controlled or, more generally, as the particular obligations that have to be assumed by any person who carries out the job. Others will weigh the inputs people make to their job in terms of knowledge, skill and mental or physical effort more heavily;

while others will simply relate job size to the job's position in an established hierarchy.

These values are not often articulated, and one of the virtues of job evaluation is that it forces organizations to be more explicit about how they assess the relative size of jobs or roles. Job evaluation can, in fact, be used as a lever for helping to change such values if they are no longer functional. It is easier to clarify values about jobs and roles if a model can be used, as described below, to categorize sizing criteria and, as required, weigh them in accordance with their perceived significance.

The input-process-output role model

The input-process-output role model as illustrated in figure 9.1 can be used to analyze the essential characteristics of any job or role. The existence of a job is only justified if it has a purpose which can be defined in terms of what is expected from the job holder – his or her *output*. This output is initiated by the job holder's *input* – the skills and knowledge needed to achieve the expected results. All work is essentially about the transformation of inputs into outputs, and this is the *processing* element of a role which involves such activities as mental or physical effort, problem solving, decision making, being creative, dealing with people, handling complex issues or carrying out a diversified range of tasks.

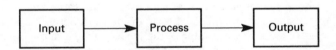

Figure 9.1   *The input-process-output role model*

This model helps first to clarify which features of a role are being analyzed and evaluated, and second, to ensure that sufficient weight is being given to these different aspects of a role. It is of use not only for job evaluation purposes but also as a basis for seeing that every facet in an individual's performance is properly assessed. For assessment purposes, however, a distinction may be made between outputs and outcomes. The former refers to immediate results and the latter to the longer-term contribution of job holders to organizational success.

Job evaluation methods

There are a number of methods of job evaluation available which can provide the basis for making judgements on relative job size, and we describe these in this section of the chapter. It is important to remember, however, that the basic method of job evaluation is only part of the total process of job evaluation which we describe in the next chapter.

Classification of job evaluation methods

Job evaluation methods can be classified into two main types according to the means of comparison used:

- *Non-analytical methods* in which whole jobs are examined and compared, without being analyzed into their constituent parts or elements.

■ *Analytical methods* in which jobs are analyzed by reference to one or more criteria, factors or elements.

In both these means of comparison there are two bases upon which the comparisons are made: *Job-job* where judgements are based on direct comparison between one job and another, and *Job-scale* where the judgements are made by comparing each job with a set scale.

The main types of job evaluation classified according to the means and basis of comparison are set out in Table 9.1 in which each type is described. In addition we describe what might be termed single factor schemes based either on competences or skills. It should be mentioned that all these are generic methods which can form the basis for tailor-made schemes within organizations. There are also a number of what might be called proprietary brands of job evaluation which are based on one or other of these methods and have been developed by management consultants to offer to their clients. These are described in Appendix D.

Job ranking

Job ranking is a non-analytical approach which compares whole jobs and does not attempt to assess separately different aspects of the jobs.

Job ranking determines the position of jobs in a hierarchy by placing them in rank according to perceptions of their relative size.

If a graded pay structure is required (see Chapter 12), decisions are made on how the rank order should be divided into groups of jobs, the values of which are thought to be broadly comparable or at least within the same size range.

Ranking is the simplest and quickest form of job evaluation. It may be claimed that the process of assessing the value of the job as a whole to the organization is, in practice, what people do even when they go through the motions of assessing the different facets of a job in an analytical scheme. Ultimately, it can be argued, people will feel that their grading is fair by noting where their whole job is placed in relation to others.

For this reason, job ranking is sometimes used as a check on the results obtained by using more sophisticated analytical methods for the evaluation of a sample of key or 'benchmark' jobs (the definition and use of benchmark jobs is

Table 9.1   *Categorization of job evaluation methods*

		Means of comparison	
		Whole job (non-analytical)	**By factors (analytical)**
Basis of comparison	**Job-job**	Simple ranking Paired comparisons	Factor comparison
	Job-scale	Classification	Points factor rating

discussed on pages 123–5). The aim of such a check is to assess the extent to which the hierarchy produced by the analytical scheme is 'felt-fair'.

The disadvantages of ranking are:

- There is no rationale to defend the rank order – no defined standards for judging relative size. It is simply a matter of opinion, although it can be argued that analytical methods do no more than channel opinions into specified areas.
- This lack of a rationale makes it difficult to defend evaluations if an equal pay for work of equal value issue arises.
- Judgements become multi-dimensional when a number of jobs have to be placed in order of importance.
- Inconsistencies arise because different evaluators give more weight to some aspects of a job than others.
- It is difficult to rank dissimilar jobs.
- It does not provide for any quantification of the differences between jobs, which makes grading an arbitrary process.
- While it will be easy to establish the extremes in a rank order, it may be difficult to discriminate between the middling jobs. Consensus on the current rank order may therefore be hard to obtain.

These problems can be ameliorated by thorough job analysis, the careful training of evaluators to ensure that they do consider all aspects of the job, and by initially ranking a number of key or benchmark jobs whose relative position is easily recognized. This benchmark ranking can then be used as a framework for ranking other jobs. It may also be possible to overcome the problem of ranking a number of middling jobs by using the pair comparison method as described below. The absence of a rationale for ranking, however, makes it difficult to justify ranking decisions and this problem is particularly acute in equal value cases. For this reason, and because of the other problems mentioned above, ranking tends only to be used as the main method in relatively small and simple organizations where job relativities are well understood and accepted, although some larger organizations have used it as a basis for allocating jobs into a broad-band pay structure (see Chapters 12 and 13).

Paired comparisons

The paired comparison method is a refinement of job ranking. It is non-analytical, comparing whole jobs with one another. The underlying principle of paired comparisons is that a direct comparison between two items is likely to be more sensitive and discerning than attempting to compare a number of items to one another.

Paired comparisons are made as follows:

- Evaluators refer to job analyses, usually for a sample of benchmark jobs – it is difficult to carry out paired comparisons for more than about 50–60 posts, even with the aid of computers to process the data.
- Each job is compared in turn with all the other jobs.
- If it is considered that the size or importance of the job for which comparisons are being made is greater than that of the other job in the pair it scores two points.
- If the size is thought to be the same the job scores one point.
- If the size is considered to be less, it scores nothing.

■ The total score is added for each job and a rank order is produced as illustrated in Table 9.2 below.

By forcing evaluators to confine their comparisons to pairs of jobs rather than trying to make multiple comparisons this method is likely to produce a more accurate rank order, especially when different types of jobs are being considered. But it suffers from the same basic disadvantages as simple ranking in that it lacks a rationale for justifying rank orders, does not measure the differences between jobs and is still non-analytical from an equal value point of view.

Table 9.2   *Example of paired comparison*

Job	A	B	C	D	E	Total score	Rank order
A	–	0	2	0	2	4	2
B	2	–	2	2	2	8	1
C	0	0	–	2	0	2	5
D	2	0	0	–	1	3	3
E	0	0	2	1	–	3	3

Job classification

Job classification is also a non-analytical method which compares whole jobs to a scale, in this case a grade definition.

It is based on an initial decision on the number and characteristics of the grade into which the jobs will be placed. The grade definitions attempt to take into account discernible differences in skill, competence or responsibility and may refer to specific criteria, such as level of decisions, knowledge, equipment used and education and training required to do the work. Jobs are allotted to grades by comparing the whole job description with the grade definition.

Job classification is a simple, quick and easily implemented method of slotting jobs into an established structure. It attempts to provide some standards for judgement in the form of grade definition. Its lack of complexity and the ease with which it can be learned and used means that it is suitable for large populations and for decentralized operations in which more complex systems might be difficult to operate consistently.

The problem with job classification is that it can not cope with complex jobs with features which will not fit neatly into one grade. Like other non-analytical systems it is not being accepted for use in equal value issues and there is a danger of the descriptions becoming so generalized that they provide little help in evaluating borderline cases, especially at higher levels. Job classification also tends to be inflexible in that it is not sensitive to changes in the nature and content of jobs.

Points-factor rating

Points-factor rating is an analytical method of job evaluation using job-scale comparisons.

The method is based on the breaking down of jobs into factors or key elements. It is assumed that each of the factors will contribute to job size and are a part of all the jobs to be evaluated but to different degrees. Using numerical scales, points are allocated to a job under each factor heading according to the degree to which it is present in the job. The separate factor scores are then added together to give a total score which represents job size.

The key features of the points-factor method are:

- the factor plan;
- the factor rating scales;
- factor weighting.

The factor plan

A factor is a characteristic which occurs to a different degree in the jobs to be evaluated and can be used as a basis for assessing the relative value of the jobs. If, in common parlance, a job is said to be more responsible than another, and therefore worth more, responsibility is being used as a factor, however loosely responsibility is defined.

When we evaluate a job, even if there is no formal evaluation scheme, we always have some criterion in mind. It may be some generalized concept of responsibility, or may be more specifically related to the size of resources controlled or the contribution to end results.

Points-factor schemes may have any number of between three and twelve factors. These can broadly be grouped under the three headings of:

- *Inputs* – the knowledge and skills and any other personal characteristics required to do the job. These may include such aspects as technical or professional knowledge, manual and mental skills, interpersonal skills and team-leading skills. The education, training and experience required to develop the knowledge and skills may also be regarded as a factor, as might the academic, technical or professional qualifications which indicate the level of knowledge acquired.
- *Processes* – the characteristics of the work which determine the demands made by the job on job holders. These include such aspects as mental effort, problem solving, complexity, originality, creativity, judgement and initiative, team-working, dealing with people and physical factors such as physical effort, working conditions and dangers or hazards associated with the work.
- *Outputs* – the contribution of impact the job holder can make on end results taking into account such aspects of jobs as responsibility for output, quality, sales, profit etc, responsibility for resources such as people, assets and money, decision-making authority, and the effect of errors.

It is sometimes felt when drawing up a factor plan that a multiplicity of factors will guarantee more accurate judgements by evaluators. This is an illusion. The more factors there are, the greater the likelihood of overlap and duplication. Evaluators therefore find it difficult to make the fine distinctions required when making their judgements. And the extra work involved in using multi-factor schemes is considerable. It is seldom necessary to have more than six factors.

Factor rating scales

Factor rating scales consist of definitions of the levels at which the factor can be present in any of the jobs to be evaluated. Jobs are analyzed in terms of these factors and the result of this analysis is compared with the factor level definitions to establish the factor level. The maximum points score for a factor is determined by factor weighting (see below), and when this has been established, each level can be allocated a points score or a range of scores. Points progression is usually arithmetical (eg 20, 40, 60, 80, 100). But it can be geometric, as in the Hay Guide

Chart-Profile method (see Appendix D). In a geometric scale, each number increases by a percentage over the previous one, which reflects the reality that comparative judgements are related to the relative difference being judged, not its absolute size.

The number of levels or degrees to each factor depends on the range of jobs to be covered and the amount of sensitivity the scheme is attempting to achieve. Most schemes seem to have up to six or seven levels but there is no rule that says all factors must have the same number of levels.

When defining factor levels the aim is to produce a graduated series of definitions which will produce clear guidance on how the factor should be scored. This is difficult to achieve and can become a semantic exercise in the use of comparative adjectives (big, bigger, biggest) to which no precise meaning can be attached. In some cases, however, it is possible to quantify levels in terms of outputs or the size of resources controlled. Successive levels can also be defined by reference to the use of specified skills or the need for particular qualifications, training or experience.

In practice, level definitions become more meaningful to evaluators when they can relate them to benchmark jobs. What happens, in effect, is that the somewhat abstract level definition is brought to life by an example and the comparison is made from job to job as well as from job to scale.

An example of a definition of a factor and its scale is given in Figure 9.2.

Factor weighting

A factor plan involves making decisions on the relative importance of the various factors – ie, their weighting for scoring purposes. It could be decided that all factors should be equally weighted but the great majority of points factor schemes do weight their factors differently.

Clearly, this is a critical decision. A factor which is overweighted in relation to its true significance as one of a number of factors could result in evaluations becoming badly skewed. For example, overweighting a factor which refers to the number of people controlled could unduly favour managers with large numbers of easily controlled staff rather than high-powered specialists. Weighting also has equal value implications. To overweight a factor such as physical effort which mainly applies to male job holders could be seen as discriminatory.

Techniques of weighting factors are described in Appendix E.

Advantages of points-factor schemes

The advantages of points-factor schemes are that:

- Evaluators are forced to consider a range of factors which, as long as they are present in all the jobs and affect them in different ways, will avoid the over-simplified judgements made when using non-analytical schemes.
- Points schemes provide evaluators with defined yardsticks which should help them to achieve some degree of objectivity and consistency in making their judgements.
- They at least appear to be objective, even if they are not, and this quality makes people feel that they are fair.
- They provide a rationale which helps in the design of graded pay structures (see Chapter 13).
- They are acceptable in equal value cases.
- They adapt well to computerization (see page 123).

Factor 6 : contacts

This factor considers the requirement in the job for contacts inside and outside the company.
Contacts may involve giving and receiving information, influencing others, or negotiation.
The nature and frequency of contacts should be considered, as well as their effect on the company.

Level 1 : little or no contacts except with immediate colleagues and supervisor. (10 points)

Level 2 : contacts are mainly internal and involve dealing with factual queries or exchange of information. (20 points)

Level 3 : contacts may be internal or external and typically require tact or discretion to gain cooperation. (30 points)

Level 4 : frequent internal/external contacts, of a sensitive nature requiring persuasive ability to resolve non-routine issues. (40 points)

Level 5 : frequent internal/external contacts at senior level or on highly sensitive issues, requiring advanced negotiating/persuasive skills. (50 points)

Level 6 : constant involvement with internal/external contacts at the highest level or involving negotiation/persuasion on difficult and critical issues. (60 points)

Figure 9.2   *Example of a factor scale from a points factor rating scheme*

Disadvantages of points-factor schemes
Points schemes have these disadvantages:

- They are complex to develop, install and maintain.
- They give a somewhat spurious impression of scientific accuracy – it is still necessary to use judgement in selecting factors, defining levels within factors, deciding on weightings, and interpreting information about the jobs in relation to the definitions of factors and factor levels.
- They assume that it is possible to quantify different aspects of jobs on the same scale of values and then add them together. But skills cannot necessarily be added together in this way.
- They are based on the assumption that the factor weightings in the scheme apply equally to all jobs. But it is possible to argue that each job will have its own pattern of factor weights. In other words, not only will the levels at which factors are present in jobs vary, but within a job the relative weight to be attached to that factor will be different from its weight in other jobs.

Apart from the complexity issue, however, this list of disadvantages simply confirms what we already know about any form of job evaluation: it cannot guarantee total objectivity or absolute accuracy in sizing jobs. It can do no more than provide a broad indication of where jobs should be placed in a pay structure in relation to other jobs. But the analytical nature of points factor rating will at least give a more accurate indication than non-analytical methods. If the process of using this method is carefully managed the results are more likely to be acceptable (to be felt-fair), and a sound basis for dealing with equal value issues will have been established.

In addition, and importantly, points-factor evaluation provides a good basis for designing a graded pay structure as described in Chapter 13.

Approaches to developing and using the points-factor rating method are discussed in the next chapter (pages 121–2).

Graduated factor comparison

Graduated factor comparison is an analytical method which compares jobs factor by factor with a scale. However, the scale is a graduated one in which the descriptive level definitions may be set out under three headings such as low, medium and high. There is no numerical score and no weighting of factors.

This method is frequently used by the independent experts called in by industrial tribunals to report in equal value claims. These experts apply their own analytical approach to the assessment of equal value which is often developed specifically for the requirements of the case. For example, in the leading case of *Bromley and others v HJ Quick* (see Appendix H) this approach was used by the expert with the following factors:

■ knowledge;
■ experience;
■ judgement and decision making;
■ contacts;
■ physical effort;
■ consequence of errors.

This method avoids weighting problems and facilitates job to job comparisons by reference to a defined and graduated scale. It is therefore useful in sorting out job relativities, especially in equal value cases. Its use by an independent expert in such cases may well be appropriate because of the limited area of comparison. However, it would be more difficult to apply in a large population where numerical scales do help when multiple decisions on the relative size of jobs have to be made.

Factor comparison

The factor comparison method is analytical, but compares jobs with jobs against a number of factors rather than using a scale. It was originally developed in the US by Benge and co-workers with the objective of overcoming some of the difficulties associated with points-factor schemes, particularly in the areas of the choice and weighting of factors. The method was based on careful analysis of a wide range of existing points-factor schemes. This identified at least 200 potential elements of job content which were grouped together into a relatively small number of more general and comprehensive factors. In the early examples the factors used were:

■ mental requirements;
■ skill requirements;
■ physical requirements;
■ responsibility;
■ working conditions.

A fundamental difficulty with points-factor schemes, as mentioned above, is the weighting of the factors. This is both a practical difficulty and a conceptual one in that the fixed-scale, fixed-weighting framework of points-factor methods assumes a constant weighting between factors for all jobs, which is unlikely. In factor comparison, explicit judgements are made job-by-job about the relative contribution which each factor makes to the total job size, eliminating the need for blanket weighting, and allowing each job to be considered individually.

The main steps in the process are:

- Each member of an evaluation committee ranks a selection of benchmark or key jobs under each factor to produce separate rankings under each factor heading.
- The evaluators make a separate judgement on how each job's total weight is reflected in each of its chosen factors. These are expressed in numerical scales.
- Numerical factor scales are then drawn up which reflect the relationships established by the two sets of judgements made earlier: one of the ranking of jobs by factor, the second of the relative importance of each factor by job. There is no fixed weighting between these scales and they are not necessarily of the same length or spread. The progression of numbers in the scales is typically geometric. The purpose of these scales is to facilitate comparisons between jobs on a factor-by-factor basis. They are not used for sizing jobs against an absolute scale as in points factor rating.
- Evaluators can then compare other jobs with the key jobs against each factor, to yield a total job size expressed in numerical terms.

Conceptually, factor comparison has a lot to offer because it avoids the universal weighting problem and recognizes that, ultimately, what evaluators are best and most comfortable at doing is comparing real jobs with real jobs rather than using an abstract scale.

The factor comparison method is, however, complex to develop and administer and cannot be described to people as easily as other methods of job evaluation. It is therefore little used, although it has influenced other important developments in job evaluation, especially the Hay Guide Chart Profile method as described in Appendix D.

Single factor analytical methods

Some methods of job evaluation are based on the premise that there is one key factor or factor type which can be used to measure relative job size. Jobs are analyzed in terms of this factor and compared with some form of chart or scale defining the graduated steps which indicate the grade or relative importance of the job. The best known single factor methods are:

- skill-based evaluation;
- competence-based evaluation;
- decision bands;
- time span of discretion.

Skill-based evaluation
Skill-based evaluation grades jobs according to the level of skills or expertise required to perform them. There may be a number of skill factors, each with a rating scale.

This method focuses on individuals and the inputs they are capable of providing. The assumption is made that the process demands made on job holders to deliver the expected outputs can be measured by the level of inputs required. It is therefore a person rather than a job-orientated approach to evaluation.

Skill-based evaluation is flexible and can respond more quickly to demands for new skills, the acquisition or development of which need to be encouraged and rewarded. It is most commonly used for technical and operational jobs in manufacturing and process industries.

The problem with this approach is that the emphasis on inputs seems to imply that skills are rewarded even when they are not delivering results. This does not make sense. Skills should only be valued if they are used productively and the analysis and evaluation process should take account of this.

Skill-based evaluation is associated with skill-based pay (see Chapter 26). Skills analysis techniques were described in Chapter 8.

Competence-based evaluation

Competence-based evaluation measures the size of jobs by reference to the level of competence required for their successful performance.

Competences are the behaviours required to achieve job objectives. These will involve the application of skills, expertise and experience and generally making things happen. Competence is therefore measured not only in relation to the skills people possess but also to how well they are used.

The conceptual basis for this type of job measurement is that the level of competence demanded for the effective performance of different jobs is a measure of the relative value of those jobs.

Like skill-based evaluations, competence-based measurement focuses on people. It concentrates on inputs and process and it can be argued that it fails to assess contribution. This drawback can be tackled by incorporating performance requirements in definitions of competency levels, bearing in mind that competence is not just knowledge and skills but the ability to use those skills effectively.

Decision bands

This method uses decisions as the single factor. There are six bands, each of which refers to a different level of decision making in the job. The rationale for the system, which was developed by T T Paterson in the 1970s, was that the ultimate factor for valuing jobs was the level and quality of decision making involved. The system is now offered by Employment Relations Associates as the Decision Band Method (DBM) and is described in Appendix D.

Time span of discretion

This approach was developed by Elliott Jaques on the basis of his hypothesis that the longest period of time for which job holders can exercise discretion about their work without supervision correlated with the demands of the job and people's perceptions about relativities. It is an appealing concept but, although influential, it has proved difficult to apply in practice and has been little used.

Criticisms of job evaluation

Over the years, job evaluation has come under attack for a multitude of reasons. These attacks have intensified in recent years and we sum up the main criticisms below.

Basic approach

'Whole job' comparisons look wrong because they seem to oversimplify – but analytical schemes are also suspect. Apples and pears cannot be added together.

The quantification of subjective judgements does not make them any more objective.

Reliance on human judgement

The methodology of job evaluation may be logical and it does provide guidelines on the exercise of judgement. But these guidelines are necessarily broad. They are subject to different interpretations and varying standards among evaluators. Subjectivity inevitably creeps in. Averaging a group of subjective judgements made by a job evaluation panel does not increase their objectivity.

A priori judgements

Despite emphasis on objective and balanced decisions based on job analysis assisted by a paraphernalia of points and level definitions, evaluators tend instinctively to pre-judge the level of a job by reference to their own conception of its value. The information presented to them about the job is filtered through these preconceptions and the scheme is used to justify them.

Manipulation

Any job evaluation scheme, however well conceived and managed, can be manipulated by determined people who want the results to fit their own purposes.

Over-emphasis on the job as distinct from the job holder

Conventional job evaluation ignores the fact that individuals in more flexible or project-based organizations, operating in unstable conditions, may modify their role and job content to fit their own skills, or in response to customer/market needs. What is defined in such organizations is the role that an individual performs, not a specific job. Conventional job evaluation approaches are unworkable for jobs which require creativity and imagination and where the level at which people operate is entirely determined by their particular competences. As Lawler[2] has put it: 'Job evaluation tends to depersonalize people by equating them with a set of duties rather than concentrating on what they are and what they can do. It tends to de-emphasize paying people for their skills and for their performance'.

Bureaucratic orientation

Conventional job evaluation is based on the concept of bureaucratic management. It slots people into rigid and hierarchical pay structures and can help to create unnecessary and undesirable pecking orders.

Grayson[3] believes that job evaluation systems have usually been designed on the basis of traditional assumptions about work: 'The result is job evaluation schemes which are seen to be too slow, inflexible, unhelpful in implementing change, and more geared to preserving the status quo'.

An Incomes Data Services[4] report summarized the arguments against job evaluation as follows:

> The most damning charge against job evaluation for employers and employees alike, is that it simply measures the wrong things. The idea that the focus should be measuring the job, not the job holder, runs counter to the way work is increasingly organized. More and more functions and businesses are subject to rapid change and depend on the ability of groups of employees to apply their skills in a flexible way. The

established systems fail to measure what is important in the contribution of these 'knowledge workers'.

Response

In spite of these objections,job evaluation schemes continue to be popular because they are perceived to be logical, systematic, fair and a good basis for handling equal value issues. It is still the case that problems with internal relativities are the most divisive and cause the most pain in organizations. It is critical to have a firm and well-understood base for pay differentials, however the organization is structured and whatever its work patterns.

The important thing to remember, therefore, is that even in the most flexible work environment it is still necessary to have some guidelines on relativities. Job evaluation provides these guidelines. In itself it need not impose rigidity, a bureaucratic approach to management or unnecessarily extended hierarchies. Job evaluation is indeed a tool which can support a bureaucratic/hierarchical approach to management. But it does not have to be used that way. Job evaluation fits perfectly well with pay structures which are specifically designed to provide for flexible roles such as the broad-banded structure described in Chapter 12. In this type of structure, job evaluation is still necessary as a means of adopting a systematic approach to making decisions on where jobs should be placed in the bands. The emphasis may be much more on skill or competency factors in such roles but these are still used as criteria for measuring the size of jobs in terms of the input and process demands they make on job holders.

Moreover, although job evaluation used to be about the control of uniformity it can not and should not fulfil that role any more. What it can contribute is help in the management of diversity in the kind of organizations and structures that we are now learning to live with.

Formal job evaluation schemes do indeed work well in stable, hierarchical organizations. But it has to be recognised that job evaluation methodologies which emphasise place in hierarchy, numbers of people supervised or resources directly controlled, without taking into account technical expertise or complex decision making, have little to contribute. Indeed, in more flexible environments, it is frequently not the scheme itself which is at fault but the way it is applied. The process used to operate the scheme is always more significant than the scheme itself. We examine job evaluation as a process in the next chapter.

References

1. Pritchard, D and Murlis, H (1992) *Jobs, Roles and People*, Nicholas Brealey, London
2. Lawler, E (1986) 'What's wrong with points-factor job evaluation', *Compensation and Benefits Review*, March–April
3. Grayson, D (1987) *Job Evaluation in Transition*, Work Research Unit, London
4. Incomes Data Services (1991) *IDS Focus No. 60*, September

10

The Process of Job Evaluation

None of the job evaluation methods described in Chapter 9 should be regarded as a self-contained package which, having been installed, will inevitably lead to the production of an orderly, equitable and appropriate pay structure. As suggested by Pritchard and Murlis:[1]

> It is much more helpful to see job evaluation as a process which contains a series of separate but connected steps – considerations of why you are doing it in the first place, right through to how you are going to use the results. In this way, each step can be designed and when necessary modified, simply and practically to suit specific needs and the changing pattern of those needs.

In this chapter we therefore examine job evaluation as such a process.

The process summarised

The process of job evaluation is summarized in Figure 10.1. We would like to stress, however, that this is a purely conceptual model. The various steps involved do not necessarily follow one another as sequentially or as logically as the flow chart suggests. The full development and implementation of job evaluation from the initial analysis of needs and setting objectives to the design and introduction of the pay structure is often an iterative process. As one proceeds, new facts or requirements come to light and this may mean returning along the path followed so far and reconsidering earlier decisions. For example, a decision may be made to use points-factor evaluation for individual jobs method but it may emerge later that job-family based classification would be more appropriate. However, the analytical work carried out on the development of points-factor rating may contribute to measuring each 'level' in the family. The process of job evaluation, like all management processes, is a learning process. You will not necessarily get it right first time but you will get better as you go along.

The activities incorporated in Figure 10.1 are described in this chapter.

Analysis

The initial analysis should provide answers to the following questions:

Existing arrangements

- What formal method, if any, is currently used to evaluate jobs?

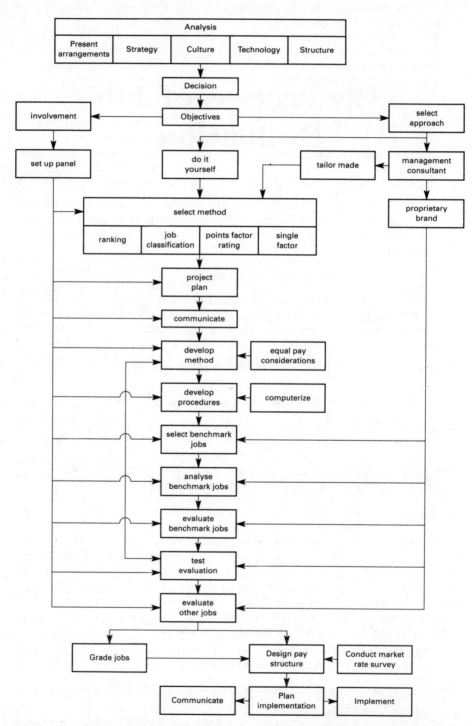

Figure 10.1   *The job evaluation process*

- To what extent are there perceived inequities in the present method (formal or informal) of valuing and grading jobs?
- Can the existing approach cope with the new role requirements emerging in the organizations? (eg increased flexibility, more project/team work, multiskilling).
- Has the existing job evaluation method deteriorated over time so that it can no longer cope with changing organizational and work requirements?
- Are we convinced that the method used and the results achieved meet equal value requirements?
- Is there any evidence that the existing evaluation method is being manipulated?
- Is the existing method time-consuming and expensive to use?
- Are we satisfied with the pay structure which has been produced as a result of job evaluation?
- Does everyone concerned believe that the method is intrinsically fair and is operating fairly? (If not, in what respects is it unfair?)

Strategy

The main question to be asked under this heading is: 'How should our job evaluation strategy fit into and support our reward strategy and, ultimately, our human resource management and corporate strategies?'

Job evaluation strategy can provide support in a number of ways, for example:

- providing a framework within which strategic decisions can be made about rewards;
- concentrating either on output factors to focus on improved performance and contribution, or on input factors to develop and extend the skills base, or, better still, a combination of both;
- helping to manage diversity;
- reinforcing the existing reward system or helping to make it more responsive to organizational needs for flexibility, teamworking, quality, multiskilling etc;
- producing information on roles and relationships which will assist in developing a more effective organization;
- obtaining data on job demands in terms of skills and competences to assist in formulating continuous development and career management strategies and to provide information for performance purposes.

Culture

The questions to be answered concerning culture include:

- What are our values about work? Do we, for example, believe that it is more important for jobs to be designed to allow people to expand rather than to constrain them; and to what extent do we believe that 'people make jobs' rather than the other way round?
- Would we describe ourselves in Charles Handy's[2] terms as having a *role* culture (one which bases its approach around the definition of the role or the job to be done, not around personalities), or a *task* culture (where management is seen as being concerned basically with the continuous and successful solution of problems)?
- Do we want to change our culture in any way? For example, to become more performance-orientated;
- To what extent do we believe that a hierarchical form of organization based upon the exercise of authority at different levels is appropriate?

Technology

This refers to the basic techniques of research, development, manufacturing and distribution in a company. In an organizational context it can also embrace the information system (information technology) and management systems generally (the extent to which they are bureaucratic, flexible and innovative). The questions to be considered when analyzing the technology are:

- To what extent could this organization be described as 'high tech', ie making the maximum use of new technology?
- In manufacturing companies: what is the basic production technology/system (eg mass, batch or process production, just-in-time, computer-integrated manufacture, cellular manufacturing)?
- In other organizations: to what extent can the operational and administrative systems be described as the mass processing of data, the routine provision of services, the delivery of professional services, the innovation and development of new products or services, or the management of research development, constructional or investigatory projects?

Structure

This refers to the way work is organized. The analysis should provide answers to questions on the extent to which the structure is:

- hierarchical, with a number of layers and supporting a bureaucratic type organization;
- flat, with the emphasis on teamworking;
- flexible, involving frequent changes in the composition of project teams or roles. This could take the form of a matrix organization with individuals responsible either for the overall control of a discipline or area of activity, or for the control of projects carried out by interdisciplinary teams (heads of disciplines could also act as project controllers).

Jobs and roles

To what extent:

- does the population include people carrying out managerial, professional, innovatory, complex or routine work?
- are roles structured or flexible at the various levels in the organization?
- does the work involve high degrees of skill or competence or a wide range of skills and competences in the main occupational groups within the organization?
- can the jobs be grouped into job families where the basic responsibilities are similar but there may be significant differences in the level of work undertaken?

Administration

The analysis should cover how job evaluation is administered and answer the following questions:

- Is too much time being spent on administering the system, eg conducting job analyses and evaluations, maintaining records?
- Have we got people with the necessary knowledge and skills to administer the scheme?

- Are we constantly having to hear appeals? (This may be an indication that there is something fundamentally wrong with the job evaluation scheme itself or the way it is managed).
- Is there a need to introduce computer-assisted job evaluation or extend its use?

The analysis areas of culture, technology, structure, jobs and roles and administration are closely interconnected. They all help to explain the shape of the present arrangements and will jointly influence the job evaluation strategy.

Decision points

Following the analysis a decision can be made to:

- retain the present arrangements and take no further action; or
- revise the existing arrangements to a greater or lesser degree, which might necessitate the re-evaluation of some or even all the jobs; or
- introduce completely new arrangements which might involve changing the method or developing an entirely new version of the existing method.

Whichever of the latter two alternatives is chosen, it will be necessary to evaluate or re-evaluate all the jobs.

Before going any further, consideration should be given to the likely costs and time involved. These could include the costs of outside help from consultants and the time required to analyze jobs and evaluate them (even with the assistance of consultants, the amount of time spent on a job evaluation exercise can be considerable).

A further cost, but one which is impossible to predict with any accuracy, is that of implementing the results of a job evaluation exercise. If jobs are upgraded, the job holders will have to be paid more, at the time or later. When jobs are downgraded, it is difficult, indeed highly undesirable, to reduce the pay of incumbents. Some addition to payroll costs is therefore almost inevitable. As a rule of thumb, it often amounts to about three per cent of payroll, but it can be more or less.

Another decision required at this stage is on which jobs should be covered by job evaluation. If there is an integrated pay structure, ie one covering all employees, it is appropriate to use only one scheme. If, however, there is a distinct pay structure for any category of employee, for example shop floor workers, then it may be thought necessary to have a separate scheme, but only if it seems likely that this division will continue for some time. Wherever possible, it is desirable to have one scheme.

Having made these decisions, the next step is to define the objectives of job evaluation (throughout the rest of these sections on the process of job evaluation it is assumed that a new method of evaluation is to be introduced, or that the previous method is being radically changed).

Objectives

The objectives of the job evaluation exercise will be derived from the initial analysis and could include one or more of the following:

- to develop a new pay structure, eg a broad-banded structure (see Chapter 12);
- to remove inequities in the existing structure;
- to improve the objectivity and consistency of existing methods;
- to deal with equal value issues;
- to assist in the integration of different pay structures, eg office and shop floor;

- to provide data on jobs, roles and relationships which will assist in organization design, the design of training and development programmes and the development of improved methods of performance measurement;
- to support a culture change programme where, eg the emphasis is to be on performance;
- to support skills development programmes;
- generally to demonstrate to all staff through processes of involvement and communication that the organization recognizes their contribution and understands their needs.

Involvement

There are four reasons for involving employees in the process of job evaluation:

1. At the design and development stage, participation can increase the acceptability of the process as a fair method of valuing jobs. Involvement is likely to increase ownership.
2. At the evaluation stage, the involvement of a cross section of employees on an evaluation panel means that a wider range of knowledge of jobs and how the organization works can be used in making judgements. This should again help to increase the acceptability of these results as well as their accuracy and consistency, although this must depend upon the collective commitment and expertise of the panel.
3. Involvement in the processes of job analysis and job evaluation is in itself an excellent training ground for panel members.
4. A more participative culture can be fostered in the organization.

These are powerful arguments, but they are only valid if the job evaluation panel is well briefed, trained, guided and led. And the panel must not be too large. If there are more than six to eight members too much time will be wasted in achieving consensus if, indeed, it is ever reached.

Whatever approach is adopted, it must fit the culture of the organization. There is no point in an autocratic 'command culture' type organization suddenly leaping into a 'culture of consent' approach if it is only paying lip service to the idea of participation. Some organizations have successfully introduced job evaluation on a management-led basis without the active participation of employees. But they have usually taken great care to communicate to everyone concerned what they are doing and why and how they are doing it.

If it is decided to set up a job evaluation panel it will be necessary to define its terms of reference with care. This will include the degree to which it is involved in the successive stages of the job evaluation exercise as described below, ie choice of method, selecting benchmark jobs, developing the method, evaluating benchmark and non-benchmark jobs and grading jobs. Panels are not always involved in the choice or development of the method, the selection of benchmark jobs or the grading of jobs. They seldom take part in conducting market rate surveys or developing the pay structure.

If there are active and recognized trade unions in the organization they may want to get involved in the programme, but they may have reservations about the process. For example, one trade union is concerned that job evaluation can emphasize 'the rate for the job' and overlook the importance of 'the rate for the ability to do the job'. A trade union might also refuse to commit itself to the findings of a job evaluation exercise, especially if it feels that it is being used by management as a device to supplant traditional pay negotiation processes.

Briefing employees

The effectiveness of the initial briefing of the people affected by job evaluation will have a major influence on the acceptability and therefore the success of the process. It is best done by means of face-to-face meetings. The key points to be got across at such meetings are that:

- job evaluation is about assessing the relative size of jobs or roles – it is not concerned with the assessment of any individual's performance;
- its aim is to provide a fair, factual and consistent basis for assessing internal relativities and developing an equitable pay structure;
- the facts will be collected in agreed job descriptions which will be prepared after careful analysis;
- the organization and all its members will benefit from having a more rational and defensible basis for valuing and grading jobs;
- job evaluation in itself does not precisely determine rates of pay; it simply provides guidance on where jobs should be fitted into a grade structure or related to one another in some other form of structure;
- job evaluation is not a one-off exercise but a process, with useful spin-offs which will need to be carefully monitored and maintained.

Choice of approach – who does the work?

The choice is between doing it yourself entirely or enlisting the support, to a greater or lesser degree, of outside consultants.

Doing it yourself is cheaper, but it can be time-consuming and it may be difficult to convince staff of the fairness of the exercise. Consultants can bring expertise and independent judgement to bear on the problems of introducing job evaluation schemes.

The simpler the approach, the less the need for outside help. But even if a basic exercise is being carried out, consultants can still provide extra staff and expertise which may not be available internally. Moreover, they may at least appear to be more objective than people already within the organization.

If it is thought that assistance from consultants is desirable, consideration will have to be given as to whether help is wanted in designing a tailor-made scheme to suit particular circumstances, or in the application of their own proprietary brand. In making this decision you should be aware of the possibility that the consultant who offers a tailor-made approach is likely to have a fairly standardized scheme which may be modified with regard to factor definitions and weighting but will not necessarily be designed from scratch with your particular requirements in mind. A consultant who provides a proprietary brand will be making available to you considerable expertise and experience in ensuring that this scheme fits the organization. The factors to be taken into account in using consultants are discussed more fully in Chapter 39.

Choice of method

If it is decided to develop a tailor-made method, with or without the aid of consultants, the initial choice is between a non-analytical approach (ranking, paired comparisons or job classification) or an analytical one (points-factor rating or a skills or competency based single factor method). The essential features of the main methods are summarized in Table 10.1.

Table 10.1   *Choice of evaluation method*

Scheme	Characteristics	Advantages	Disadvantages
Ranking	Whole job comparisons made to place them in order of importance	Easy to apply and understand	No defined standards of judgement: differences between jobs are not measured
Paired comparisons	Panel members individually compare each job in turn with all the others being evaluated. Points are awarded according to whether the job is more, less or equally demanding than each of the jobs with which it is being compared. These points are added to determine the rank order, usually with the help of a computer. The scores are analyzed and discussed in order to achieve consensus among the members of the panel	Ranking is likely to be more valid on the principle that it is always easy to compare a job with one other job rather than with the whole range of disparate jobs	As with ranking, the system neither explains why one job is more important than another nor assesses differences between them
Job classification	Job grades are defined and jobs are slotted into the grades by comparing the whole job description with the grade definition	Simple to operate and standards of judgement are provided in the shape of the grade definitions	Difficult to fit complex jobs into a grade without using elaborate grade definitions
Points-factor rating and factor comparison	Separate factors are scored to produce an overall points score for the job	The analytical process of considering separately defined factors reduces subjectivity and helps assess differences in job size. Consistency in judgement is helped by having defined factor levels. In accord with equal value law	Complex to install and maintain. Objectivity is more apparent than real: subjective judgement is still required to rate jobs against different factors and level definitions

There are no rules which can be applied to decide on which method is best. It will depend entirely on circumstances and the following factors will have to be taken into account:

- the type of organization concerned;
- the organization's culture – what it wants to keep and what it wants to change;
- the number of jobs/roles to be covered;
- the scale and diversity of the employee groups involved;
- the resources available in terms of time, people and budgets;
- the employee relations climate;
- equal value considerations as described below;
- previous experience of job evaluation – it may be necessary to re-position the mapping of internal relativities because an old, decayed or defunct system has lost credibility, was subject to manipulation or has incurred top management disfavour. Perfectly respectable approaches have been dispensed with because 'process' issues such as the above have rendered them inoperable.

The points-factor rating method has been steadily increasing in popularity, partly because it is thought to be the best way of dealing with equal value problems, but also because of its 'face validity'. People *feel* that the process is thorough and delivers a more rigorous result. There are certainly question marks over all other approaches on equal value grounds. The critical issue, whatever scheme is chosen, is to ensure that the processes are well designed, defensible and cost effective, as well as being regularly monitored and maintained.

Consideration should also be given to getting a consultancy to install their own proprietary brand of job evaluation (the main brands are summarized in Appendix D).

Prepare project schedule

A project schedule as illustrated in Figure 10.2 defines the sequence and timing of each job evaluation activity. The time required will obviously depend on the number of jobs to be dealt with and the complexity of the scheme. It is unwise to rush job evaluation. The design of a tailor-made scheme may take a number of weeks, although this could be reduced if a consultant's scheme is used. To analyze a job thoroughly may take several hours; three or four hours is typical – it could take more. Time can be saved by using questionnaires associated with a computerized system of job analysis and evaluation – but the preparation of such questionnaires can take a considerable amount of time.

When it comes to the actual job evaluation process, evaluators or job evaluation panels are unlikely to do justice to more than eight jobs or so a day.

In conducting the job evaluation exercise, the normal rule for managing any type of project should be applied as follows:

- prepare a list of the major activities in sequence;
- break down each major activity into a sequence of subsidiary tasks;
- analyze the relationships and interdependencies of subsidiary tasks;
- estimate the time required to complete each activity and task;
- schedule the whole project in accordance with estimated activity times, using a bar (Gantt) chart or a computerized network system which is used to record progress and generate control reports;
- allocate the required resources for each stage (people, money and systems support) and define and agree cost budgets;
- set up a feedback system to enable progress to be monitored by reference to the satisfactory completion of specified tasks and to ensure that costs are controlled within budget.

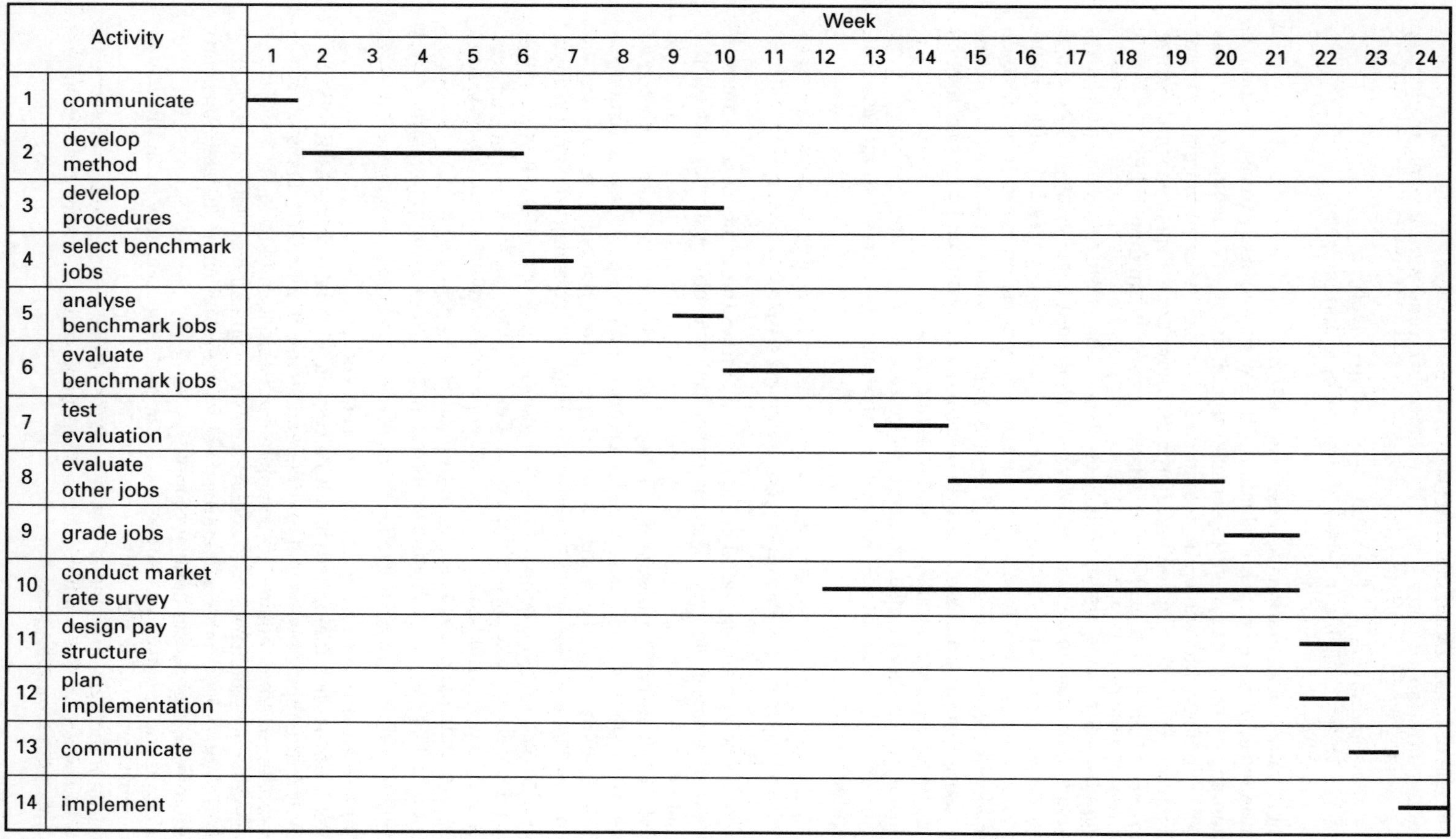

Figure 10.2 *Job evaluation project schedule*

Develop job evaluation method

The development of non-analytical methods of job evaluation is quite straight-forward. Analytical methods are obviously more complex to design. It may be necessary at this stage to select and analyze a number of key or benchmark jobs as described later in this chapter. The approaches used for each method are summarized below.

Job ranking

The design of a job ranking scheme requires no more than an initial decision on the format of the job description (see Chapter 8). It is also necessary to ensure that the job analysis covers all the factors which need to be taken into consideration and does not emphasize any elements disproportionate in different jobs. A decision may have to be made on which factors should be included when analyzing the job (eg skill, effort, responsibility, decisions) and it will also be necessary to determine how jobs should be graded, if that is required (see Chapter 12).

Paired comparisons

A paired comparison system is basically designed in the same way as a ranking scheme. Like ranking, it can include the use of factors. The only additional task is to train evaluators in making paired comparisons.

Job classification

When developing a job classification scheme, the initial decision is on how many grades are required. It is then necessary to decide what factors should be covered when defining a grade level. The factors frequently included are:

- experience, knowledge, skills and qualifications;
- complexity;
- use of judgement and initiative;
- decision making;
- responsibility;
- any other competences established by competence analysis – see Chapter 8.

It is not easy to produce a ladder of grade definitions which clearly and positively identify where jobs should be allocated to grades. Help in producing such definitions can be sought if the grades in the scheme are defined following a ranking or a points factor rating exercise. Reference can then be made to the job analyses or factor evaluations of the jobs placed in each grade. The factor definitions used in a points factor scheme will also provide guidance on grade descriptions.

Some organizations have started the job evaluation process by using a points-factor scheme and then, for ease of administration, have converted this into the appropriate grade in a job classification scheme after the initial benchmark job evaluation. Grading jobs in a job classification scheme will be easier if the system enables evaluators to compare the job to be evaluated with the benchmark jobs to which grades have already been allocated.

Points-factor rating

The critical design decisions to make when developing a points-factor rating scheme are the choice of factors (the factor plan), the definition of factor levels and the weighting of factors.

As mentioned earlier, the choice of factors is a matter of getting the right balance between input, process and output factors without over-complicating the method by having too many factors (not more than, say, six).

The mix of factors must depend on the particular requirements of the organization. A typical factor plan as illustrated in Appendix C might include:

1. Knowledge and skills (input)
2. Decisions (process)
3. Complexity (process)
4. Contacts (process)
5. Responsibility (output)

The next stage is to produce the level definitions, the aim being to produce a graduated series of definitions which will provide clear guidance on how the factor should be scored. Again, this is not easy and what frequently happens is that the initial level definitions have to be refined as experience is gained in using them. The design of job evaluation schemes is often an iterative process. An example of factor and level definitions in a points-factor scheme is given in Appendix C.

Finally, the factors have to be weighted. In the plan given above it would be necessary to decide on the relative importance of each factor. It might be thought, for example, that the input and output factors should be equally weighted and that the total weighting given to the three process factors should be the same as the respective weightings of the input and output factors. This could result in the following weighting:

	%	Score
■ knowledge and skills	33.33	300
■ decisions	11.11	100
■ complexity	11.11	100
■ contacts	11.11	100
■ responsibility	33.33	300

But there could be endless variations to this pattern depending on the type of jobs to be evaluated and the values of the organization on the relative importance of the factors.

A weighting exercise is generally an empirical one. There are no rules, although there are methodologies for helping to produce a weighting pattern which is likely to result in a felt-fair valuation of the job. Further information on weighting is provided in Appendix E.

Skills and competence-based methods

Both these methods are developed by job and role analysis as described in Chapter 8. This establishes different levels of skills or competences and these are translated into pay structures as described in Chapters 12, 26 and 27.

Equal pay considerations

It is essential to ensure that in selecting, developing and administering any method of job evaluation equal pay and value considerations are taken fully into account. This particularly applies to the use of analytical schemes and the selection and weighting of factors in such schemes. This important subject is dealt with fully in Appendix H.

Develop procedures

The procedures to be developed will consist of the methods used by job evaluators or the job evaluation panel to analyze and evaluate jobs. It should also cover arrangements for evaluating new jobs or re-evaluating existing jobs. Provision should be made for employees to appeal against evaluations or gradings.

Attention should also be given at this stage as to how the job evaluation system is to be administered and maintained – who will be responsible and what systems they should use, including computers.

Use of computers

A job evaluation exercise can generate a lot of paper and take considerable time. The use of knowledge-based software systems, usually known as expert systems, can organize the analytical processes in a way which makes the best use of a database of job analyses and evaluations, assists in making consistent judgements and records decisions to be added to the database. An expert system does this by:

- defining the evaluation rules relating to the weighting of factors, the points, levels or degrees attached to each factor and the assessment standards which guide evaluators to the correct weighting of jobs – these may take the form of benchmark jobs and/or level definitions;
- programming the computer to ask appropriate questions concerning each factor in a job to enable it to apply the evaluation rules;
- applying the rules consistently and determining the factor score for the job;
- grading the job;
- sorting the job into position in the rank order;
- storing the information entered in the form of a factor analysis into the computer's memory so that it can be called to the screen or printed at any time.

It should be remembered, however, that computer-assisted job evaluation systems (CAJE) do not replace the need for human judgement in the evaluation process. They simply provide an efficient means of applying the evaluation criteria and values which have been incorporated by the designers into the expert system on the basis of their analysis of the processes and rules used by evaluators to achieve consistent results. Computer-assisted job evaluation is discussed in more detail in Appendix G.

Select benchmark jobs

Benchmark jobs are key jobs selected to cover each level and major function in the organization because they are well structured and representative of those levels and functions. Benchmark jobs should have the following characteristics: they are well known, clearly defined and, ideally, the relativities between them will be well established. They should also be jobs which, as far as possible, can be matched with jobs outside the organization for market rate survey purposes.

The initial evaluation of these jobs provides, as the term implies, reference points or signposts for evaluators when they are evaluating the other jobs in the organization, often the difficult and contentious ones.

The first step is to select benchmark jobs by:

- listing all the discrete jobs to be covered by function or department;
- identifying from this list a sample of well known and easily recognized jobs

which reflect the range of responsibilities in the organization, both vertically and horizontally across functions;
- so far as possible, ensuring that a sufficient proportion of benchmark jobs is identified which can be matched to jobs in other organizations to establish external relativities;
- ensuring that equal value considerations are taken into account – the sample should reflect the distribution of jobs which are primarily carried out by male or female employees, if that is a feature of work in the organization.

The number of benchmarks required will depend on the size of the organization and its complexity in terms of the number of different functions, levels and jobs. Typically, between 10 percent and 30 percent of the total number of jobs may be selected as benchmarks.

Analyze benchmark jobs

In order to evaluate the relative size of the benchmark jobs it is first necessary to gather and analyze the relevant facts about each job and present them in a way which is appropriate to the evaluation process used. The analysis will either be presented in some type of job description format or, if a computer assisted evaluation process is to be used, the vehicle for presenting the information will be a multiple choice questionnaire. Methods of job and role analysis, including the analysis of skills and competences are described in Chapter 8.

Evaluate benchmark jobs

The evaluation of benchmark jobs is a means of pilot testing the job evaluation scheme, training the job evaluation panel and providing a basis for the full analysis of the remaining jobs.
    The steps required are:

1. Apply the job evaluation method to the outcome of the benchmark job analysis.
2. Test the results of the benchmark evaluation to ensure that it has produced felt fair relativities between the benchmark jobs. This may be carried out simply by examination. Alternatively, if an analytical method has been used, the

function job	A	B	C	D	E
a					
b					
c					
d					
e					

Figure 10.3 *Benchmark job matrix*

benchmark jobs may be ranked by the paired comparison method and this ranking compared with the rank order produced by the analysis scheme. This exercise is sometimes called 'sore thumbing' as it identifies the sore thumbs which stand out as being wrongly evaluated on a common sense felt fair basis.

3. Take any action required following the initial analysis. This may include a re-examination of the factor plan and weightings. This is again an aspect of the job evaluation process which is iterative. It could also be decided at this stage to convert the points-factor scheme into a job classification scheme for use in evaluating the remaining jobs. Other possible actions may include re-analysis and re-evaluation of the benchmark jobs or further training for the panel.

Analyze and evaluate remaining jobs

The analysis and evaluation of the remaining non-benchmark jobs can now take place. As evaluators gain experience and can refer to more previous evaluations they will be able to speed up the job evaluation process while still achieving an acceptable level of consistency. For example, factor definitions in analytical schemes become more meaningful if they can be compared with examples of jobs where the factors have been evaluated at the same level. Computerized job evaluation systems can facilitate such comparisons.

Develop pay structure

Pay and grade structures as described in Chapters 12 and 13 are developed on the basis of market rate surveys (see Chapter 11), job analysis and job evaluation.

At this stage it is advisable to assess the cost implications of the proposed structure. It may have to be modified if it appears too high (yet another iterative process) although the impact of costs can be alleviated by phasing increases.

Plan implementation programme

The implementation plan should finalize individual gradings and rates of pay, including how any increases may be phased. A communications plan should also be prepared.

Communicate results

If a new pay or grade structure has been evolved this will have to be communicated generally. Individuals should be told how it affects them, ie how they are graded and what changes this will make, if any, to their present and future salary.

If there is going to be some form of progression through pay brackets on an incremental scale or by means of performance-related pay (see Chapter 17), the system will have to be explained generally and its effect on individuals will also have to be spelt out.

Individuals should, of course, be informed of their grade and pay bracket. If a points-factor rating job evaluation scheme is used they may be told their score but not necessarily in detail how it has been arrived at. Some organizations keep scores secret, especially if the evaluation has been management led. But this approach could raise doubts in the minds of employees about the fairness of the scheme.

However, if individual scores are released when a general graded structure is in operation, it will have to be explained why jobs with different scores are placed in the same bracket. This question should have been anticipated in the original briefing by emphasizing that the purpose of the job evaluation scores is to allocate jobs into grades within which individual rates of pay will be differentiated according to experience or performance. In other words, points do not equal pounds. To anticipate this question it is also worthwhile to stress in any initial briefing that the points-factor approach can do no more than give a broad indication of relativities. It is not accurate enough to fix rates of pay to the nearest pound.

Employees should also be told of their right of appeal against evaluations and gradings and the process involved.

Implementation

The implementation can now proceed. If there has been adequate consultation and good communication there should be no major problems. However, it is impossible to please everyone and the likelihood of appeals has to be anticipated. Experience suggests, however, that if the benchmarking and subsequent evaluation has been both rigorous and consistent, then appeals are likely to be few. It should also be emphasized that a small number of well handled appeals can do much to enhance the credibility and acceptability of any newly implemented job evaluation scheme. Much of the success of implementation does, however, rest on the quality of communication of new or changed pay or grade structures and the way these are related to broader issues of HR management.

Conclusion

The prime purpose of job evaluation is to provide information which will assist in the management of relativities. However, it should be remembered that there are two other equally important bases for managing pay relativities: the external market and the acquisition and use of skills needed to perform jobs or roles. These are interdependent with job evaluation – each has a part to play in measuring job values for pay structure design purposes. We consider the external market aspect in the next chapter.

References

1. Pritchard, D and Murlis H (1992) *Jobs, Roles and People: the New World of Job Evaluation*, Nicholas Brealey, London
2. Handy, C (1974) *Understanding Organizations*, Penguin Books, Harmondsworth

11

Market Rate Surveys

Competitive pay levels and salary structures can only be developed and maintained if the external market is systematically monitored. This can be done using a range of sources from salary and benefits surveys to job advertisements, companies' annual reports, informal confidential contacts and other forms of market intelligence.

This chapter describes:

- The purpose of making market comparisons
- the process of carrying out analyses of market rates
- the sources of comparative remuneration data
- how to conduct a company or club survey
- how survey data should be used.

The purpose of making market comparisons

Market comparisons aim to compare external relativities, ie:

1. The rates and benefits provided for equivalent jobs in other organizations (market rates) with those provided within the organization, in order to ensure that the latter are fully competitive.
2. The rates at which pay is increasing in other organizations (going rates) in order to provide guidance on pay reviews.

The data from market comparisons help organizations to:

- decide on starting rates
- design and modify salary structures
- determine acceptable rates of salary progression in pay structures and pay curve systems
- review pay, incentives, bonuses and other forms of performance-related pay
- decide on the types and levels of benefits to be provided
- assess the level of increases required to salary levels generally and to individual employees.
- identify special cases where market rates have to be paid irrespective of the evaluated position of the job in the grade hierarchy.

The process of carrying out market comparisons

Sources of data

The main sources of data are:

- general published surveys

- specialized occupational, professional, industrial or local surveys
- company surveys – ie those carried out by the company, with or without the help of consultants
- salary survey clubs – ie a group of companies who regularly exchange information
- published data in specialist or other journals, newspapers and the business press
- analyses of job advertisements
- other market intelligence.

We provide a brief description and comparative analysis of each of these later in this chapter, followed by a more detailed examination of company and club surveys. But before looking at these sources, it is necessary to review the basic considerations affecting market comparisons.

Basic considerations

When making market comparisons, the aims as far as possible are to:

- obtain accurate and representative data on market rates
- compare like with like, in terms of data, regional and organizational variations and, importantly, type and size of job or role
- obtain information which is as up to date as possible
- interpret data in the light of the organization's particular needs
- present data in a way which clearly indicates the action required.

The problem of defining the market rate

People often refer to the 'market rate' but it is a much more elusive concept than it seems. There is no such thing as a definitive market rate for any job, even when comparing identically sized organizations in the same industry and location. There are local markets and there are national markets, and none of them is perfect in the economist's sense. Different surveys of the same types of jobs produce different results because of variations in the sample, timing and job matching.

No survey is designed or, indeed, should be designed to show that one salary level is the 'correct' market rate for any given job. It should give as clear an indication as possible of the current operating or going range for establishing salary levels or setting pay structures and define which factors affect the distribution of individual salaries within it.

Despite these points, most pay specialists and survey producers will sometimes have to put up with the reader's expectation that their survey will give a 'correct' salary for a job for any given set of conditions. Some top executives, and others needing to make policy decisions but having restricted understanding of the problems of carrying out surveys, still tend to believe that it is possible to find out exactly what the precise market rate is for any given job, in any industry, at any location, for any given age or experience level – preferably to the nearest pound! But this is not a reality and is unlikely to become one. Because survey participation is voluntary, and because decisions about pay levels tend to be pragmatic rather than strictly logical, actual salaries are less predictable than many people would like to believe. Where there is little data available, salary patterns tend to be fairly anarchic. Most salary decisions made in relation to salary surveys are conformist, which can mean that there are more regular and predictable operating ranges for jobs covered regularly by well-established salary surveys than, for instance, for new or rapidly evolving jobs not yet much subject to survey analysis.

This means that, however hard you work at getting accurate results, all you will obtain is an approximation – a range of possibilities. In spite of yourself you may, where data is hard to come by, be forced into averaging averages to obtain an informed view of the derived market rate. And that is a statistically undesirable process.

It should also be remembered that individuals as well as jobs have market rates. When looking at a range of market rates you have to decide two things – first, what the rate for the job should be, and second, what the range for individuals in the job should be as they enhance their marketability through experience, training and 'track record' or performance. Salary surveys may give some indication of the range of salaries you should offer; for example, you could set the lowest point of the range at the median (the middle point in the distribution of salary rates covered by the survey) and the highest point at the upper quartile (the value above which 25 per cent of the values in the range fall).

The more you can track the actual salaries paid to people in identical jobs in similar areas, the greater the accuracy of the market rate information. But this may require a tremendous amount of effort and you may need to question the cost effectiveness of the process. That is why some people rely on published surveys and other readily available data. Increased accuracy can be provided by company (do-it-yourself) and club surveys, but cost typically limits how far you can go.

However, in spite of these limitations, surveys of market rates are necessary to provide indications, albeit broad ones, of where the company stands in the market-place. Considerable judgement is still required to interpret results, but at least that judgement can be based on data which have been collected and analyzed systematically.

Types of data collected

- *Basic (or base) pay:* gross pay before deducting national insurance, tax and pension contributions. It includes merit increments or incremental payments added into salary but excludes performance-related bonuses, overtime pay, fringe benefits and most allowances. In the latter case, the only exception may be a location allowance (eg, a London allowance) which may or may not be incorporated in the base salary, but whether or not it is included should be made clear
- *Cash bonuses:* any performance-related bonus or payment under an incentive scheme which is not part of basic pay
- *Total earnings* (sometimes called total cash earnings): the sum of the basic annual pay and any cash bonuses received over the previous twelve months. This figure excludes the value of employee benefits
- *Employee benefits:* details of the entitlement to benefits such as pensions, company cars, private petrol, mortgage assistance, loans, permanent health insurance, medical insurance, health screening, relocation packages, holidays, other forms of leave, sick pay, etc
- *Other allowances:* any cash payments made in special circumstances, such as call-outs, shift or night work payments, car mileage allowances
- *Total remuneration:* the total value of all cash payments and benefits received by employees (note that valuing benefits depends on agreed assumptions – these should be scrutinized carefully)

■ *Salary structure information:* the salary scale or range in the structure for particular jobs.

Regional and company variables

Market comparisons should take account of the following variables which affect the comparibility and validity of the data:

■ *location:* whether the jobs involved need to be assessed in relation to national, regional or local markets
■ *industry:* usually analysed on the basis of a simplified version of the Standard Industrial Classification (SIC)
■ *organization size:* because it can affect job size, there is often some correlation between pay levels (especially salaries for managers) and company size. The following variables are typically taken into account:
  – sales turnover derived from the accounts for the annual accounting period preceding the survey date
  – the total number of employees, analyzed as necessary according to location, company, division or group.

Job matching

Market comparisons are most valid when like is compared with like. This means matching jobs as far as possible in the following respects:

■ function, eg general management, marketing, production
■ sector – private or public
■ industry classification
■ location
■ size of organization
■ range of responsibilities – the tasks or duties carried out by job holders
■ level of responsibility – size or weight of the job in terms of its impact on end results, resources controlled, scope for exercising discretion and judgement, and complexity.

The various methods of job matching in ascending order of accuracy are:

■ *job title:* this can be completely misleading. Job titles by themselves give no indication of the range of duties or the level of responsibility and are sometimes even used to convey additional status to employees or their customers unrelated to the real level of work done
■ *brief description of duties and level or zone of responsibility:* national surveys frequently limit their job-matching definitions to a two- or three-line description of duties and an indication of levels of responsibility in rank order. The latter is also often limited to a one-line definition for each level or zone in a hierarchy. This approach provides some guidance on job matching, which reduces major discrepancies, but it still leaves considerable scope for discretion and can therefore provide only generalized comparisons
■ *capsule job description:* club or specialist 'bespoke' surveys frequently use capsule job descriptions which define the job and its duties in approximately 250 words. To increase the refinement of comparisons, modifying statements may be made indicating where responsibilities are higher or lower than the norm.
   Capsule job descriptions considerably increase the accuracy of comparisons as long as they are based on a careful analysis of actual jobs and include

modifying statements. But they are not always capable of dealing with specialist jobs and the accuracy of the comparisons in relation to levels of responsibility may be limited, even when modifiers are used.

■ *full job descriptions:* full job descriptions of individual jobs, sometimes including a factor analysis of the levels of responsibility involved, are sometimes used in special surveys when direct comparisons are made between jobs in different companies. They can be more accurate on a one-for-one basis but their use is limited because of the time and labour involved in preparing job descriptions. A further limitation is that comparator companies may not have available, or be prepared to make available, their own full job descriptions for comparison.

■ *job evaluation:* job evaluation can be used in support of capsule or full job descriptions and provides a more accurate measure of relative job size or weight. A common method of evaluation is necessary. In the UK, surveys are run on this basis by both Hay and Wyatt. This approach will further increase the accuracy of comparisons but the degree of accuracy will depend on the quality of the job evaluation process. Consistency depends on quality assurance of the evaluation process, both within organizations and across survey participants.

Timing of surveys

The competitiveness of current salaries can only be established by finding out what other organizations are offering and paying now. Pay data can easily become stale when the market is moving erratically, and the time-lag between the collection of the data and its publication is commonly three months. To mitigate this problem, salary surveys sometimes update results. They should always indicate the specific date for which the pay information is applicable and explain the assumptions made if updating has been carried out. Wherever possible, they should set out the pattern of the salary review dates of the companies included in the survey.

Increases from one survey to the next – the importance of matched samples

Market comparisons involve not only assessing current market rates but also trends in pay increases in order to indicate the going rate.

The percentage rise in average pay between successive surveys will be misleading because of changes in the sample of companies and losses, gains or replacements in the sample of job holders.

The problem can be alleviated by matching the sample of companies so that comparisons are only made for companies subscribing to both surveys. But this does not cover changes in job holders, and the most refined matching process will isolate increases for individuals who have remained in the same job between the consecutive surveys. This measure, however, may not distinguish between increases arising from general pay reviews and individual incremental, merit or performance-related payments.

Interpreting average, median and quartile increases

Since many employers review all aspects of salaries only once a year, the increase compared with a year earlier in the average earnings of a group of employees in a sample will usually approximate to the weighted average of the increases granted. The same is true of medians, with some qualifications. But rarely is the increase during a survey year in the upper or lower quartiles of an earnings survey the same as the upper or lower quartile of the increases granted. This is because groups which have lower-than-average increases one year may often secure an above-average increase in the following year to restore their position (which may well be below the median of the market). Organizations which implement pay freezes or give below average increases continuously over a period of years tend to end up with salaries going right through the market floor. If a firm chooses to place its salaries in the lower quartile of the market and reaches this position by awarding a lower quartile increase for a year or two, what then? To maintain salary levels at the lower quartile of the market (or indeed at any chosen fixed relativity), it may now need to offer near-to-average increases to keep up with others in the market. Otherwise salary levels will fall below even the reduced targets that have been set and will continue to do so indefinitely.

Presentation of data

Data on pay are presented in two ways:

1. *Measures of central tendency*, ie the point about which the several values cluster. These consist of:
    (a) the arithmetic mean or *average* (A), which is the total of the values of the items in the set divided by the number of individual items in the set. The average can, however, be distorted by extreme values on either side of the centre
    (b) the *median* (M), which is the middle item in the distribution of individual items – 50 per cent of the sample fall above the median, 50 per cent below. This is unaffected by extremes and is generally preferred to the arithmetic mean, as long as there are a sufficient number of individual items (the median of a sample much less than 10 is suspect). Medians are often lower than arithmetic means because of the tendency in the latter case for there to be a number of high values at the top of the range.
2. *Measures of dispersion*, ie the range of values in the set, which provides guidance on the variations in the distribution of the values of items around the median. These consist of:
    (a) *the upper quartile* (UQ): the value above which 25 per cent of the individual values fall
    (b) *the lower quartile* (LQ): the value below which 25 per cent of the individual values fall
    (c) *the interquartile range:* the difference between the upper and lower quartile values; this is a good measure of dispersion
    (d) *upper and lower deciles:* the values above and below which 10 per cent of the individual values fall. This is less frequently used but does provide for greater refinement in the analysis of distribution
    (e) *the total range:* the difference between the highest and lowest values. This can be misleading if there are extreme values at either end, and is less often used than the interquartile range, except where the sample is very small.

Data are usually presented in tabular form but the significance of the information can sometimes be revealed more clearly if the tables are supplemented by graphs.

- *tables* should identify the job, the size of the sample and, where appropriate, may analyze data according to the size and type of organization and its location. For example, see Table 11.1.

Table 11.1   *Sample table*

Job title: Marketing Director

	LQ	M	UQ	Sample
Turnover (£m) 1–10				
Base salary	28,420	31,165	34,255	23
Total earnings	30,150	33,643	37,521	
Turnover (£m) 11–50				
Base salary	31,141	33,620	36,591	41
Total earnings	33,409	37,712	39,916	

An example of a layout of the results of a club survey is given in Table 11.2. This quotes the average gross pay for the job and gives tabulated details by companies of salary ranges and average salaries and bonuses.

- *Graphical presentations* can highlight significant data or trends as in the example in Figure 11.1.

In practice, there are many variations on these forms of presentation. More are emerging as pay specialists become more creative with the graphics packages available on the computers appearing on their desks. Further information on statistical terms used in pay surveys and analysis is given in Appendix B.

Published surveys

There is a wide range of published surveys which either collect general information about salaries, mainly managerial, or refer to more specialist professional or technical jobs. Many, such as those produced by Hay, Computer Economics, Wyatt and Towers Perrin, are available only to participants but some are available 'over

Table 11.2   *Salary survey data*

Job title: Production Manager   *Job No:*

Brief job description: To direct the activities of a production department to achieve agreed delivery targets. Monitor costs and profit margins to ensure that agreed prices are met. Deal with day-to-day disciplinary and personnel problems.

Average Salary (Gross) – Min: £18,250 Max: £26,789 Mean: £23,750
Number of Companies – 25

Company code	Sample size	Salary range (min) £	Salary range (max) £	Actual basic average salary £	Average bonus £	Average (gross) £	Rank
12	21	21,860	32,950	26,789	2,100	28,889	01
06	24	21,350	31,350	26,230	1,800	28,030	02
13	19	21,100	30,500	25,650	1,950	27,600	03
09	17	21,250	30,250	25,480	2,000	27,480	04

134   REWARD MANAGEMENT

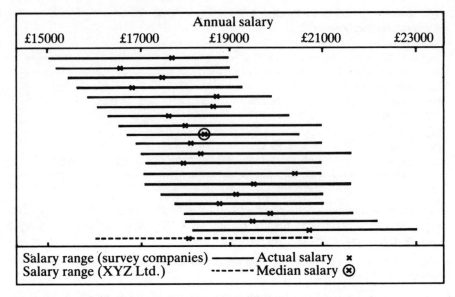

Figure 11.1   *Salary survey data presented graphically*

the counter' (eg Monks/Charterhouse, Remuneration Economics and Reward). In either case, it is advisable to ensure that they will meet your requirements for relevant information. Their potential value as a reliable information source can be evaluated with the help of the following check-list:

1. *Source*
   Who produced the survey?
   (a)   a firm of general/specialist management consultants
   (b)   a recognized organization specializing in salary and benefits surveys
   (c)   recruitment/executive search consultants
   (d)   an employment agency
   (e)   an employers' association
   (f)   a professional body
   (g)   a trade union
   (h)   the Government or one of its agencies
   (i)   a company/employer wishing to exchange salary data
   (j)   a specialist or other journal.
2. *Database*
   What is the survey based on?
   (a)   actual salaries paid to matched jobs or responsibility levels
   (b)   average salaries for jobs/grades/levels
   (c)   estimated market price given by employers where no direct job match has been made
   (d)   recruitment salaries – offered, asked or paid
   (e)   annual company report data based on audited earnings for the previous financial year
   (f)   informed opinion.
3. *Sample composition*
   Who participated in the survey?

(a)   other organizations similar to or competing directly with the user

(b)   individual members of professional bodies or trade unions.

Are there:

(a)   enough participants to provide acceptable comparisons assuming that the methods of collection and analysis are effective?

(b)   matched samples of participants either on the basis of the same individuals doing the same jobs or the same companies from year to year?

4.   *Data collection*

How were the data collected?

(a)   personal collection by survey producer to discuss job matching and current salary issues for the jobs in question

(b)   postal questionnaire – with what response rate?

(c)   from employers or job holders

(d)   on a well-designed, clearly explained questionnaire/computer input sheet.

5.   *Job matching*

How accurately are survey bench-mark jobs or levels of responsibility matched?

(a)   against job titles

(b)   against 'capsule' job descriptions or rank definitions with provisions for separating those with more or less responsibility than the core definition

(c)   against full job descriptions/definitions of responsibility level

(d)   by using an agreed measure of 'job size', eg the same method of job evaluation used by all participants with checks on the consistency of grading an application.

6.   *Timing*

How up to date are the salary data?

(a)   what is the distribution of salary review dates among participants? Are data on this provided?

(b)   are data correct on a given survey date or given over a survey period, eg three months?

(c)   how much time has elapsed between data collection and the publication/circulation of results?

7.   *Presentation*

How well does the survey illustrate current practice and the reliability of data in individual analysis? Are there:

(a)   full details of sample composition and response rate

(b)   tables listing average, median, upper and lower quartiles (or other quantiles such as octiles/deciles)

(c)   lists or bar charts/scattergrams of the raw data from which the summary analyses are calculated; coded by size/type of organization to allow more detailed analysis; giving current scales/ranges/actual salaries where not too commercially sensitive

(d)   analyses by company size, industry, location or other relevant factors

(e)   regression lines to give a 'feel' for market position; if so is the sample or subsample basis clearly explained?

8.   *Increase data*

How valid is the information provided on pay increases (often hard to interpret)?

    (a)   is it based on matched samples of individuals in the same job year on year/organizations participating in the same survey?

    (b)   do the percentage increases quoted include merit awards, bonuses, cost of living adjustments, or a combination of these, and how well is this explained?

    (c)   is the basis for calculation made clear?

9.   *Other data*

What else does the survey contain:

    (a)   details of major benefits/entitlements

    (b)   amounts/types of incentives/profit sharing payments

    (c)   details of salary administration policy

    (d)   a commentary on current developments including special areas of market pressure or other major influences, written by someone able to interpret the data effectively.

10.   *Cost*

Is it worth its price in terms of:

    (a)   savings in company/personnel resources required to obtain equivalent data?

    (b)   the time/effort involved in participation?

11.   *Integrity of survey producers*

Does the producer maintain consistent and professional standards? Does the survey:

    (a)   state when samples are too small to provide useful analysis and define the point at which this is reached?

    (b)   show ability to adapt/improve in response to changing market demands?

    (c)   include the availability of advice on the interpretation of the data, and is this available free/for a fee?

    (d)   give good value for money?

12.   *Purpose*

Why was the survey produced?

    (a)   as the producer's sole business

    (b)   as an occasional/major part of other business/consultancy activities

    (c)   to provide other organizations/individuals with data on a particular sector of the market

    (d)   to put forward a point of view

    (e)   to attract press coverage.

General published surveys

There are many surveys, but the quality of data they provide varies enormously. Both the Management Pay Review of Incomes Data Services and the *Pay and Benefits Bulletin* published by Industrial Relations Services publish regular reviews of these surveys and analyses of the trend data they contain. Incomes Data Services also publishes a *Directory of Salary Surveys* every couple of years which is essentially a consumer's guide to the whole of the salary survey market. It gives full information on the jobs covered, sample data, cost and availability, as well as comment on the quality and reliability of the data.

General surveys, such as those produced by Hay Remuneration Economics, Monks/Charterhouse, PE International, Reward and the Executive Compensation Service (now part of the Wyatt Company) are based on data collected from as large a number of participating organizations as they can attract – typically from clients and mailshots to a large number of employers. They cover base salary and total earnings levels paid on a given date and a certain amount of data on benefits entitlements. Most surveys also provide data on annual salary movement.

Survey data are normally grouped by job title and function, and by job size or level of responsibility in relation to company size and type. The most usual company analyses are by industrial sector and size, in terms of annual sales turnover and/or numbers of employees.

Most surveys include some indication of regional variations and can be expected to add to this, given the interest in regional pay differences for jobs where local market influences are more important than national trends. Clerical and shop-floor jobs that are recruited using local sources need local salary analyses to give an acceptable picture of the market – especially among smaller organizations. National data will always be needed, however, for jobs which are recruited on a national basis. It is important to remember that where, for instance, there appear to be regional differences in management pay, this will almost always turn out on deeper analysis to be related to the size of the job and the nature, age and culture of the industry rather than just the location.

Traditional engineering companies tend to pay less than their high-tech counterparts and they tend to be located in different parts of the country. They may often not demand the same academic background and level of skills from the managers they employ. Nor, sadly, are some of them in a position to afford higher salaries for better qualified managers able to improve profitability through innovation and improved financial management, other than in exceptional cases.

Publishers of general surveys can be asked, at a price, to extract data relating to particular firms who participated in the survey. These data are, of course, anonymous, and are only made available if a reasonable number of firms are involved. They can be very helpful if you want more specific information about your own industry.

Specialized professional, industrial or local surveys

There are three basic types:

- analyses of members' salaries conducted by professional institutions
- local or national market surveys of particular industrial groups produced by employers or trade associations
- local or national market studies carried out regularly or on a one-off basis by consultants, either for a single employer or for a group of organizations who may share the cost (a multi-client study).

Professional institute surveys are usually more concerned with providing salary data in relation to age, qualification and membership status than they are with placing members in their organizational context. They therefore provide useful salary profiles and salary movement data, but are often of little help when it comes to looking at an individual's place in the company reporting structure in relation to particular sizes and types of organization. Some are now including analyses by function and level of responsibility within the organization, but the relevance and clarity of the definitions should be looked at carefully. They should, therefore, mainly be used as an additional check on more specific salary survey data from which real job comparisons should be clearly identifiable.

These professional institute surveys are widely read by their members, who may seek to use them either as individuals or through their unions as a negotiating base for salary improvements. If this occurs, it is essential to be familiar with the particular survey quoted and aware of any limitations in the validity of the data. If it does not correlate well with more specific salary market data, the reasons should be analysed and explained. There may be distortions caused by the inclusion, for example, of members who are high flyers and have reached director status early in their careers, too large a proportion of members working for highly paid consultancies or multinationals, members who have moved on to more highly/ lowly paid areas outside the specialism, or those who are 'blocked' within an organization because performance or an unwillingness to move or take extra responsibility holds them back.

The surveys conducted by employers and trade associations deal mainly with jobs specific to their industry for which reliable outside salary data often does not exist. They cover a limited market and are useful because they can be very specific about job definitions and organization structures for the staff covered. Often they are only available to participating organizations who may then share the cost of data collection and analysis. They may be local or national and by no means all are produced regularly. It may often be worth checking with the trade association appropriate to the company whether surveys of this kind are likely to be produced before special company market surveys are undertaken.

Employers who have neither the time nor in-house expertise to conduct their own market studies are increasingly opting to commission consultants to carry out this task. The approach used is usually very similar to that outlined in the section below on company surveys, and consultants involved in this sort of exercise will need to be briefed accordingly. The choice of appropriate consultants for this type of 'one-off' study should be based on firm evidence of expertise in the field of salary surveys and a good level of understanding of the personnel philosophy and market posture of the commissioning employer.

Company surveys

These are surveys conducted by a company approaching others to exchange comparative salary information on a 'one-off' basis. Company surveys can be held with or without the help of consultants. The use of consultants provides for expertise in the collection and analysis of data and they save time, but they can, of course, be expensive.

Company surveys can be as simple or sophisticated as required. They can be as quick and cheap as simple confidential 'pricings' or exchanges of information over the telephone with established contacts willing to exchange data, or a fully fledged study of pay and benefits which is coded and circulated to all participants.

The principal advantage of the 'one-off' company salary survey is that the company alone decides which jobs it needs to study and which of its local or national competitors should be invited to participate. This should, in theory, produce the best possible comparative data. The main drawback is the time it takes to complete this kind of exercise and the cost and organizational implications of taking staff away from other work while the survey is in progress.

Because of the time, effort and cost of running company surveys, there are advantages in joining or setting up a salary club. The methods used to plan and conduct a company survey are basically similar to those adopted by salary clubs as described below. The sequence of activities is illustrated in Figure 11.2.

Salary club surveys

Clubs may be administered either by management consultants or by companies themselves. Clubs tend to operate in single industries, although some cover a

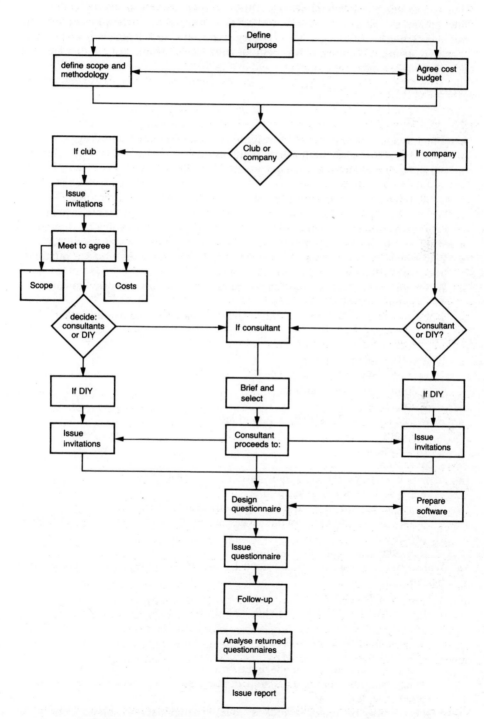

Figure 11.2 *Conducting a club or company survey*

range of industries – a survey of 'blue chip' companies, for instance. Many cover all managerial and professional grades, although there are those which cover only one employee category – graduates or accountants for example, within one industry. When a single employee category is chosen, this will normally be because there is strong competition for people with skills which are in demand, eg accountants or software engineers.

Club surveys – check-list

Membership criteria

- Which types of company will be eligible for membership? Will they:
    - all be in the same business, ie competitors?
    - all be of similar size and type, eg all 'blue chip'?
    - all be in the same area?
    - all have similar parentage, eg all subsidiaries of US multinationals?
- Will separate parts of the same company be allowed to participate or will only aggregate data be accepted? How will decentralized companies be treated?
- Will there be a pre-set minimum and maximum number of participants?
- Who will decide on requests to join the club from companies who are 'qualified' to do so? Will existing members have a veto?
- Will membership be restricted to companies who are able to provide data on a specified minimum number of jobs?
- Will it be possible to expel a club member if they transgress club rules?

Collecting the data

- Who will collect the data?
    - one of the members
    - a combination of members
    - a consultant
- How frequently will a survey be conducted?
    - annually
    - every six months
    - quarterly
- How will accurate job matching (pricing) be ensured? By:
    - using summary job descriptions
    - using an agreed form of job evaluation/sizing (eg Hay or Wyatt)
    - personal visits to participants to discuss differences in job scope and other problems
    - a regular 'audit' of job matching
- Will a postal questionnaire be used to collect the data, or a personal visit/ interview?
- What data will you collect?
    - basic actual salaries of individuals in post
    - salary ranges
    - incentive/bonus payments
    - other cash additions to pay
    - share options and profit sharing payments
    - fringe benefits including pension, death-in-service provisions, cars, medical insurance, loans, etc.
- Will the survey be 'open' or 'closed', ie will participants be able to identify the salary ranges or the salaries paid by other members?

- Will all grades of employee be included in the same survey, or will separate surveys be conducted for manual, non-manual, professional and managerial grades?
- Is a 100 per cent response rate expected? What sanctions will the club impose if members fail to provide data?

Analyzing and presenting the results
- Will a computer be used to process the data or, will they be analyzed by hand?
- Will actual salaries and salary ranges be listed by company (using a simple number code) in rank order?
- What statistical analyses will be produced from the aggregate data?
  - averages
  - medians
  - quartiles (if large enough sample)
  - interquartile ranges (if large enough sample).
- Should these be related to individuals' salaries, company averages/medians, or salary range mid-points?
- Will any significant regression or correlation tests be made on the statistical results?
- How will the results of the club survey be compared with general data on salaries, from commercial surveys etc?
- Will club members be charged a fee to cover the cost of analyzing the results and producing the survey report?

Setting up the salary club

The establishment of a salary club may start from a more informal exchange of salary information between two or more companies who employ similar types of staff. A club may be the result of individual initiatives by one or two compensation specialists within companies. In some industries, the computer industry for example, there is a more regular exchange of salary information than in others. Some consultants specialize in club survey work in certain industrial groups. If the target group is sufficiently finely defined as, for example, in the international banking sector and the pharmaceutical industry, then not only are a homogeneous group of employees being surveyed, but also a very high proportion of the potential number of participants will probably take part.

Approaching companies

The exchange of accurate, up-to-date salary information depends on mutual trust. This will exist among established contacts but has to be carefully built up when individuals are contacted for the first time. This can be done over the telephone but, unless the person responsible for the survey has a particularly confident and persuasive telephone manner, a carefully drafted letter may be a better approach. Letters may in any case be preferable because the recipient then has time to consider carefully whether it is worth participating and is unlikely to make a snap decision based on an understandable dislike of the use of what may be seen as telephone sales techniques. Letters may be ignored, but this problem is reduced if they are worded properly.

In a letter of invitation to an unknown company the messages that have to be communicated are that:

1. A responsible individual/consultant is conducting the survey.
2. The survey will be carried out competently and in confidence.

Table 11.3 *Example of a profile job description used in job matching*

	JOB DESCRIPTION	POSITION CODE E27.
POSITION:	PERSONNEL MANAGER (1)	
ALTERNATIVE TITLE:	Manager Human Resources, Asst. Vice President, Asst. Director (Personnel), Associate Director	
REPORTS TO:	Managing Director, Senior Vice President, Vice President, Branch Manager	
SUPERVISES:	Training Officers, Personnel Officers and Staff (4–8 staff)	
RESPONSIBILITIES:	Under direction, responsible for the implementation of the bank's policy on personnel, recruitment, training, salary administration, welfare, payroll, pensions and management development. Advises senior management on all matters to do with personnel policies such as legal changes, terms and conditions of employment, pay trends, benefits, etc.	
MODIFIER +:	Having more personnel staff or totally responsible for general administration, premises, catering staff, etc.	
MODIFIER –:	Having less specialist staff and/or in a small bank or branch of less than 100 people.	
EXPERIENCE OR LEVEL:	Possibly a graduate with several years' experience in personnel management or, alternatively, a banker with many years experience and at least five years' personnel management experience in banking.	
TYPICAL SITUATION:	Working in his/her own office in close contact with senior management.	
NOTE:	The difference between Personnel Management (1) and (2) is the scope of the job and will be a combination of factors such as reporting, supervision given and received and relative position within the overall management structure. Look at both descriptions and decide which most suits your bank. A Personnel Manager reporting to the Financial Controller, Operations Manager, Administration Manager or Company Secretary is unlikely to fall into this category.	

Source: London Banks Personnel Management Group Management Salary Survey (1991)

3. The information collected and shared will be relevant, up to date and useful.
4. The company will not be put to too much trouble.

Which jobs to include

The major advantage of running a club is that participants to the survey know who the other participants are and that their data are relevant. When members of the same club are in the same industrial sector they may be thought of as competitors for the same type of staff in the same salary market. This is particularly true for managers and specialists whose skills are easily transferable from one company to another in a similar line of business. At managerial level, members of the same club typically employ a rather homogeneous group of staff in terms of the experience required, the demands of the job and their qualifications. Some clubs exchange salary information only on managerial and specialist grades, eg from first line to senior management, while others cover technical and professional grades, clerical or indeed only manual employees.

Job matching and pricing

Club surveys offer a potentially better quality of job matching than industry-wide surveys covering very heterogeneous groups. Most salary clubs take great care over this stage of the research.

A typical approach to assist the matching process is to circulate a profile job description for each job to participants. This will contain the job title, a brief description of the job's responsibilities, reporting level, supervisory responsibility (number of subordinates), together with the typical age and/or experience and qualifications an incumbent of such a job might have. An example of a profile job description for a senior personnel manager is shown opposite (taken from the London Banks Personnel Management Group Survey of International Banks). Participants are asked to match as closely as possible, indicating whether their jobs are slightly more or less responsible than the one described, or are about equal. The modifier mechanism is often used as a shorthand way of describing slight differences in job scope – a plus (+) modifier indicates it is more responsible, a minus (–) modifier is less responsible and an equals (=) modifier is used when the participant's job is equal in responsibility to the profile job.

The key to success in any salary club survey lies in accurate job matching, a process demanding painstaking work and eternal vigilance. The wholesale regrading of a set of jobs in one or two companies could potentially throw the results of an otherwise useful survey. The communication of changes in internal relativities is essential to the reliability of survey results. A regular audit is desirable to keep track of company regradings of jobs and to ensure they are still being matched with similar jobs in other companies.

Where individual jobs cannot be matched, organizations may be asked to price them. This involves assessing the relative worth of a job in relation to other jobs carrying similar responsibilities in areas or grades where reasonable comparisons can be made.

Salary data collection

Survey professionals often find that it is worth printing the questionnaire form on coloured paper so that it is less easily lost among the other white papers in the participants's 'in' tray. Colours selected should be light and in no way interfere with the clarity of the printing. Survey questionnaires should always be sent out with a covering letter further encouraging participation and giving a clear final return date. A week or so will have to be allowed after this date for the stragglers to come in. It is always worth telephoning companies who have not yet returned responses a few days before the deadline to check whether the questionnaire has arrived safely or whether there are any problems with job matching which need to be ironed out. In these circumstances the companies may have to be visited to deliver new questionnaires and to collect the comparative data on the spot. However inconvenient this is, it should greatly improve the scope and quality of the data collected.

Club surveys, unlike many commercial surveys, collect information not only on actual salaries, but also on salary ranges. Questionnaires are used and, typically, there are number codes for each company and for each job category covered.

Company and pay data commonly collected/presented

- company name
- number of employees

- annual sales turnover
- data by job:
  - job title/code
  - number of incumbents
  - modifier (+, =, or −)
  - average actual basic salary/total cash
  - median actual basic salary/total cash
  - highest actual basic salary/total cash
  - lowest actual basic salary/total cash
  - salary ranges – minimum/maximum/mid-point
  - salary review dates

All surveys collect salary data, but the information collected on cash additions to basic pay and fringe benefits is very variable. An example of the company information and the detailed fringe benefit data collected by one club survey are listed below:

- *General company information:* number of employees, annual sales turnover
- *Salary increases:* general increases (timing and last percentage increase), and individual increases (criteria and timing)
- *Graduate starting salaries:* basic salary + bonus, projection for the next year
- *Incentive/bonus schemes:* basis of payment, employees qualifying for payment, frequency and amount (%) payment
- *Overtime premiums:* for managers, monthly and professional staff, and weekly paid staff
- *Shift premiums in relation to shiftwork patterns*
- *Company cars:* for business need or status, engine size (bench-mark car), private petrol paid, and charges for private use
- *Payment for use of employees' own cars:* Mileage allowances by car engine size
- *Regional and occupational allowances:* London allowances, telephone and professional institute expenses
- *Relocation expenses – existing employees:* Disturbance, removal, and temporary housing allowances, plus bridging loan facilities
- *Relocation expenses – new employees:* Disturbance, removal, temporary housing allowances, plus bridging loan facilities
- *Travel and accident insurance:* In the UK and overseas
- *Private medical insurance:* Insurer, category covered, proportion paid by the company and type of cover
- *Redundancy:* Payments in addition to statutory minima
- *Periods of notice:* Both from employer and employee
- *Pension scheme:* employer and employee contribution rates, escalation of pensions in payment and ex-gratia supplements
- *Pension scheme – benefits:* Entitlement per year of service (fraction), definition of salary used for pension calculations, contracted in or out, and life assurance provisions
- *Pension scheme – additional benefits:* Death in service: early retirement provisions

Sick pay entitlements
- *Long-term disability absence:* salary continuation entitlements

- *Call out and stand by payments and premiums*
- *Holiday entitlements:* Standard entitlement and additional service days
- *Subsistence allowances:* For short and long stays on company business
- *Overtime pay for travel:* Differentials between hourly paid and staff
- *Share options:* entitlements by seniority
- *Profit sharing:* basis, annual percentage paid (including profit-related pay under the 1987 Finance Act provisions).

Analysing and presenting the results

As survey returns come in, they should be checked carefully to ensure that acceptable matching or pricing has been given for each job. Any doubtful figures should be referred back to participants and discussed with them. Where comparisons turn out not to be close enough to be acceptable, the data should be rejected – preferably with the agreement of the participant concerned.

Salary club surveys can generally be processed very quickly and participants typically expect a report within a month of sending in their returns. Strict deadlines usually have to be set and enforced (see above) to ensure this is possible. Whoever is responsible for the survey should also ensure that the analysis of results can begin as soon as the first few returns have come in and been checked.

The methods used in the analysis and presentation of survey results will depend on the number of returns received and the degree of sophistication in salary policy of both the survey producer and the participants. It can therefore vary from simple histograms (bar charts), either set out on graph paper or drawn by computer, showing the salary scales or actual ranges paid by participants and coded company by company, to complex statistical analyses producing computer printouts which present the data in relation to a number of different variables. In selecting which forms of analysis will yield the most meaningful results and present the data in a way which helps the salary policy decision making process, it helps to concentrate on what the data are actually based on and who will use the findings. The use of regression analysis looks very sophisticated and is therefore sometimes seductive. For data based on large samples such techniques have their value and can be used to effect. But the application of sophisticated statistical techniques to rather tentative data collected in a small-scale salary survey is not appropriate. What matters most is presenting a limited amount of directly relevant market data in a way which shows what the actual operating salary range is for any given job – and where the extremes of practice lie as well as the mid-point – backed by a brief commentary on the underlying influences affecting the distribution.

A more detailed set of definitions of the statistical terms used in such analyses is given in Appendix B. In many surveys, the salaries for each job category are typically listed by company code, in rank order of the total cash earnings, actual basic salary or salary range mid-points. In addition, the number of employees in that job category within each company may be printed out as well as the modifier, the minimum, maximum and mid-point of the salary range, the highest and lowest actual salaries, average basic salary and bonus, median basic salary and bonus. Other information which might be provided is the 'compa ratio' in each salary range for each company, matching the company average salary to the mid-point of the salary range.

Confidentiality

Although the company compensation specialist or consultant who processes the survey results will have access to the individual company codes, it is necessary for each club to decide whether all club members should have this facility or not. Knowing which code applies to which company would mean that comprehensive information about participants' salary ranges and actual salaries in payment would be available to each participant. Some clubs think this is a good idea, others do not – commercial sensitivity in the pay area is growing in some sectors!

Response rate

Club surveys usually expect a 100 per cent response rate. Failure to provide data normally means expulsion from the club, except in mitigating circumstances. However, it may also be necessary for the club to set a minimum response rate for each job category – there is little point in a company joining a club collecting data on 60 job categories if they only employ one or two of these, as they are going to lower the general response rate for particular jobs.

Published data in journals

Apart from the summaries of published survey findings that appear at various times in the business press, there are two major sources of company and public sector salary data. Both Incomes Data Services and Industrial Relations Review and Report monitor wage and salary settlements and publish details of agreements as soon as they are made. A great deal of staff and management salary information is available because companies have shown willingness to contribute data in order to benefit from the detailed analysis of trends these organizations provide.

Both sources also comment on economic trends and analyze the effects of any government policy affecting pay. An enquiry service is part of the subscription.

Another useful source of trend information is the *Department of Employment Gazette* which also summarizes the findings of the *New Earnings Survey* as it is produced. It is also worth checking specialist information in journals such as *Taxation* to monitor the changing effects of tax on higher earnings where this might affect management remuneration policy. Newspaper coverage of surveys and major pay awards is also worth monitoring. These days few pay and benefits specialists can avoid monitoring the *Financial Times* and the Sunday papers with reputable Business News sections. Where resources permit, it is worth setting up press cuttings files for key jobs or functions and techniques, both to monitor the market and to ensure that those responsible for reward management see the same articles as the executives who may ask questions relating to them and require an immediate response on policy options.

Analysis of job advertisements

Attractive as this approach may be, it is beset with problems. The racily phrased job descriptions used in the hope of attracting high-calibre applicants are not usually precise enough to allow accurate comparisons with real jobs. Salary levels are often 'by negotiation' (often a sign of undeveloped salary policy) or they may be overstated or inflated because the company is desperate. Even where a salary scale is quoted in full this may not be the range within which the vacancy is ultimately filled. A quick check in the main national newspapers will show that the salaries on offer for jobs described as 'finance director' will show an enormous variation. This normally rules out useful application of the data other than as an indication of trends, though it has some value if the prospective employer is named and offers supplementary – if suspect – additions to information derived from more reliable sources.

Similar problems occur in using information provided by employment agencies. Specialist agencies may, however, have a good 'feel' for salaries in the particular areas they cover. They may therefore be worth consulting where the company is already a regular and satisfied client, and when the agencies' expertise in the area is known.

Other market intelligence

Setting salary levels is not, as we have shown, just about the scientific application of survey statistics. Monitoring salary markets also involves gleaning facts and opinions from personal contacts. It means building up a network of reliable people with whom trends and innovations can be discussed and insights shared, and developing a 'nose' for what currently influences pay. Job adverts for salary specialists now often specify that candidates should have a good knowledge of practice in the potential employer's industry. And most effective managers responsible for pay have built up a 'card index' of contacts designed to ensure they know what is going on in their sector and which factors are likely to affect pay levels for all the different types of jobs involved.

Talking to informal contacts, exchanging experience and testing out ideas are valuable supplements to the more formal activities of salary clubs. It happens over the telephone and is a common activity at conferences on pay and related issues, IPM branch meetings and similar gatherings. Over time, the information acquired by this means can considerably sharpen an individual's 'feel' for what is going on in the salary market.

The sort of questions you can ask are:

- what level are you currently paying your junior systems analysts (those with less than two years' experience)?
- what is the increase you believe you will have to pay to your product managers this year to keep pace with the market-place?
- what would you need to offer in the shape of a total remuneration package to attract a really good legal executive?
- what rates of pay are graduate members of your profession getting two years after qualification?
- at what level of salary are you having to offer a company car?
- what do you think the trends in salary levels are likely to be for members of your profession who have executive appointments below board level in industry?
- what is happening to the demand for production managers in your industry sector and what impact is that making on market rates?

One of the reasons why companies employ consultants to carry out salary surveys rather than do the work 'in house' is because a good consultant will have extensive networks of contacts which they will use not just to get a good sample of participants, but to talk to discreetly about market influences. This should enable them to explore, for instance, recruitment pressures, special inducements and incentives, tax strategies and examples of new payment systems which might be of relevance in interpreting survey data and developing remuneration strategy.

Advantages and disadvantages of data sources

The advantages and disadvantages of each source are as follows:

Published general surveys

Advantages: wide coverage, readily available.
Disadvantages: risk of imprecise job matching, quickly out of date.

Published specialist surveys

Advantages: deal with particular categories in depth, quality of job matching better than general surveys.
Disadvantages: job matching not entirely precise, can quickly become out of date.

Club surveys

Advantages: more precise job and company matching, can provide more detail on pay structures and benefits.
Disadvantages: sample size may be too small, relies on goodwill of participants to conduct survey.

Company or 'do-it-yourself' surveys

Advantages: precise job matching
Disadvantages: time and trouble, problem of building a large enough sample.

Published data in journals

Advantages: readily accessible, good background data.
Disadvantages: not necessarily comprehensive, job matching imprecise.

Analysis of job advertisements

Advantages: readily accessible, highly visible indications of market rates and trends, up to date.
Disadvantages: job matching very imprecise, salary data can be misleading.

Other market intelligence

Advantages: good background.
Disadvantages: imprecise.

Selecting data sources

If time and the budget permit, more than one source should be used to extend the rate of data and provide back-up information.

General surveys can be supplemented by specialist surveys covering particular jobs. A company-administered survey or a salary club can provide information on local market rates. If the quality of job matching is important, an individual survey can be conducted or a salary club can be formed. If a salary club already exists it can be joined, if there is room (some clubs are over-subscribed). Published surveys, which are readily accessible and are based on a large sample, can be used to back up individual or club surveys. But the information has to be relevant to the needs of the organization and particular attention should always be paid to the range of data and the quality of job matching.

Market intelligence and published data in journals should always be used as back-up material and for information on going rates and trends. They can provide invaluable help with updating.

Although the analysis of job advertisements has its dangers, it can be used as further back-up, or to give an instant snapshot of current rates, but it is risky to rely on this source alone.

Using survey data

The translation of salary market data into competitive salary levels for individuals, or into an acceptable company salary structure, is a process based on judgement and compromise. The aim is to extract a derived market rate based on informed and effective estimates of the reliability of the data. It means striking a reasonable balance between the competing merits of the different sources used. This is essentially an intuitive process. Once all the data available have been collected and presented in the most accessible manner possible (ie job by job for all the areas the structure is to cover), a proposed scale midpoint or 'spot' salary/rate has to be established for each level based on the place in the market the company wishes to occupy, ie its 'market posture'. The establishment of this midpoint will be based not only on assessment of current and updated salary data, but also on indications of movements in earnings and the cost of living which are likely to affect the life of the whole structure. For organizations needing to stay ahead of the market, this point will often be between the median and the upper quartile (of a significant population). For others, closer alignment with the median is adequate. Once the series of midpoints in relation to the market has been established and assessed the principles of salary structure construction outlined in Chapter 13 can be applied.

It has to be recognized that salary surveys can rapidly become out of date. To ensure that you stay ahead of the market, or at least do not lag behind, it may be advisable to attempt to forecast how rates will increase over the next year. This can be done by extrapolating trends and analyzing economic forecasts. Inevitably, there is an element of guesswork involved and the forecasts have to be treated with caution. But they at least given you some guidance on where salaries are likely to move and what you should do about it.

PART 4

PAY STRUCTURES

12

Types of Pay Structures

In this chapter we define pay structures – their purpose and aims, the criteria for effectiveness, and the different types of structure that can be used in an organization. We examine the process of developing pay structures in the next chapter.

Definition

A pay structure consists of an organization's pay ranges for jobs grouped into grades or for individual jobs, pay curves for job families, or pay scales for jobs slotted into a pay spine. However, a system of individual job rates (spot rates) could also be regarded as a pay structure.

In a typical graded structure, jobs will be allocated to job grades according to their relative size, which in a formal system will have been determined by some type of job evaluation. There will be a pay range for each grade which defines the minimum and maximum rates of pay for all the jobs in the grade. This pay range will take account of market rates for the jobs in the grade.

The term pay band is often used synonymously for pay range. We prefer to reserve the word 'band' to describe the overall size of a job grade or a pay range. Thus a broad-banded structure will have a much wider spread of jobs in terms of job size and a greater range of pay than a narrow-banded structure.

Purpose and aim

The purpose of a pay structure is to provide a fair and consistent basis for motivating and rewarding employees.

The aim is to further the objectives of the organization by having a logically designed framework within which internally equitable and externally competitive reward policies can be implemented, although the difficulty of reconciling often conflicting requirements for equity and competitiveness has to be recognized.

The structure should help in the management of relativities and enable the organization to recognize and reward people appropriately according to their job/role size, performance, contribution, skill and competence. It should be possible to communicate with the aid of the structure the pay opportunities available to all employees.

The pay structure should also help the organization to control the implementation of pay policies and budgets.

Criteria for pay structures

Pay structures should:

- Be appropriate to the characteristics and needs of the organization: its culture, size and complexity, the degree to which it is subjected to change and the type and level of people employed.
- Be flexible in response to internal and external pressures, especially those related to market rates and skills shortages.
- Facilitate operational and role flexibility so that employees can be moved around the organization between jobs of slightly different sizes without the need to reflect that size variation by changing rates of pay.
- Give scope for rewarding high level performance and significant contributions while still providing appropriate rewards and recognition for the effective and reliable core employees who form the majority in most organizations.
- Facilitate rewards for performance and achievement.
- Help to ensure that consistent decisions are made on pay in relation to job size, contribution, skill and competence.
- Clarify pay opportunities, developmental pathways and career ladders.
- Be constructed logically and clearly so that the basis upon which they operate can readily be communicated to employees.
- Enable the organization to exercise control over the implementation of pay policies and budgets.

The basis of pay structures

Pay structures are based on decisions about internal relativities and external comparisons but they must also take account of pay progression policy.

Internal relativities

Internal relativity decisions are usually formed through processes of job evaluation. This normally excludes personal factors, and the relative size of jobs is measured on the basis of what has to be done to achieve a standard and acceptable level of job performance. In an individual job range structure this provides the reference point for the rate within the range which should be paid to a fully competent person. In a conventional graded structure the same assumption is made for all the jobs grouped into the grade although in practice their relative size may differ.

External comparisons

External comparisons are made through market rate surveys, and decisions on external relativities follow the organization's policy on how its pay levels should relate to market rates – its market stance.

Market stance policy depends on the organization's views as to whether it should pay above the market, match the market or pay less than the market. These will be influenced by such factors as the level of people the organization wants to attract and retain, the degree to which it is thought that pay is a major factor affecting attraction and retention rates and, of course, what it can afford to pay.

Some organizations are market driven in the sense that they pay a lot of attention to market rates when designing and maintaining their pay structures. Others take the view that they are not going to allow other companies' business and reward strategies to drive their own structure. They pay people in accordance with their beliefs on what they are worth to them. They will not, because they cannot, ignore the market place and the need to be competitive but they do not allow these needs to dominate their thinking.

It is possible to design pay structures entirely on the basis of external relativities and allow these to determine internal differentials, ignoring internal equity considerations. But this extreme approach is rare except in small or rapidly growing organizations or within sectors such as some parts of the finance sector in the City where it is accepted as the norm. It is more usual to start by assessing the relative size of jobs by some form of job evaluation and then price those jobs on the basis of external comparisons.

Thus the reference point in a pay range may be aligned at the average market rate for jobs in the grade or above or below that rate. This may result in tension between the need for both internal equity and external competitiveness.

This tension creates general problems of market rate differentials between distinct occupational categories and particular problems when the market rate for individual jobs or an individual's market worth are above the level suggested by internal equity considerations.

One approach to dealing with the problem of significant market rate differences between certain occupations is to set up separate market group structures in a job family system as described later in this chapter.

When there is pressure for one job to be paid more because of its market rate, a market premium can be paid, although this should only be done when there is no alternative and the premium should be removed if market rate comparisons no longer justify it. This need not result in a decrease in pay for the individual concerned who might not, however, receive the same general or market-related increase as others, with the result that the premium could be progressively reduced and eventually consolidated into base pay.

Alternatively, in a structure with reasonably wide pay ranges, it may be possible to absorb market rate differentials within the range. But this approach can lead to problems with internal equity unless it is only embarked upon when absolutely necessary and is controlled carefully.

Number of pay structures

There may be different structures according to level or to the category of employee. For example, some organizations still have two structure levels: one for staff and one for manual workers. Other organizations even have three levels of structure – for managerial and professional staff, for junior staff and for manual workers. Top management (directors) may be left out of the main structure altogether and their remuneration agreed individually (considerations affecting board room pay are discussed in Chapter 33). Fully integrated single structures covering all employees except, sometimes, directors, are becoming more common as organizations simplify their approaches and continue to reduce status differentials. They are described later in this chapter.

Organizations sometimes have separate parallel structures for different occupations. For example, there may be technical ladders for scientists or research and development engineers, which recognize that progression can sometimes depend more on professional competence than the assumption of managerial responsibility for people and other resources.

This principle may be extended to setting up separate structures for different job families or market groups as described under the heading of job family structures later in this chapter.

Types of pay structures

The types of pay structures described in this chapter are:

- graded pay structures;
- broad-banded structures (a variant of graded structures);
- individual job ranges;
- job family structures;
- pay or progression/maturity curves;
- spot rates;
- pay spines;
- pay structures for manual workers;
- integrated pay structures;
- rate for age.

Graded pay structures

A graded pay structure consists of a sequence of job grades to each of which is attached a pay range. A typical graded structure with overlapping pay ranges is illustrated in Figure 12.1.

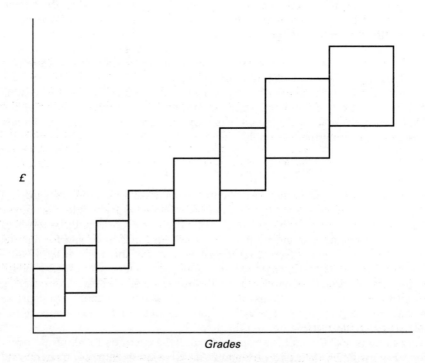

Grades

Figure 12.1 *A typical graded pay structure*

The main features of graded structures are described below under the following headings:

- job grades;
- pay ranges and grades;
- defining a pay range;
- number of pay ranges;
- size of ranges;
- range reference points;
- differentials;
- overlap between ranges;
- pay progression through ranges;
- make up of a pay range;
- progression through the structure;
- adjusting the structure.

Job grades

Jobs are allocated to job grades on the basis of an assessment of their relative size and all jobs allocated to a grade are treated the same for pay purposes.

If a points-factor job evaluation process has been used, all jobs in a grade will be within the same job size range as defined by points scores. If some other method of job evaluation is adopted such as job classification, jobs in each grade are also assumed to be broadly within the same job size range although this range would not be quantified in points terms.

Pay ranges and grades

A pay range is attached to each grade. This defines the minimum and maximum rate payable to any job in the grade and indicates the scope provided for job holders to progress through the range. There is a reference point in the range (see below) which defines the rate of pay for a fully competent individual and which is related to market rates.

Individuals recruited, upgraded or promoted to a grade can be paid above the minimum of the pay range (but not, usually, the reference point) if they have the qualifications and experience to achieve more than the minimum expected from job holders in the grade.

It is important to distinguish between grade width in job size terms and the size of the pay range attached to the grade. Grade width describes the range of job sizes contained within a grade, while the pay range is there to cater for pay progression based upon such criteria as performance, contribution, skill acquisition, competence or length of service. Pay ranges for a grade do not exist to enable differences in job size to be reflected in pay within that grade. The whole point about a grade structure is that for pay purposes, jobs placed in the grade are assumed to be of equal size.

Defining a pay range

A pay range may be defined in terms of the percentage increase between the lowest and highest points in the range, for example:

Table 12.1   *Defining a pay range – I*

£ Minimum	£ Maximum	% Range
20,000	26,000	30
20,000	28,000	40
20,000	30,000	50

Alternatively, the range may be defined as a percentage of the midpoint, for example:

Table 12.2   *Defining a pay range – II*

£ Minimum	£ Midpoint	£ Maximum	% Range
90%	100%	110%	
22,500	25,000	27,500	22
85%	100%	115%	
21,250	25,000	28,750	35
80%	100%	120%	
20,000	25,000	30,000	50

Number of pay ranges

The number of pay ranges will depend on:

- the pay of the highest and lowest paid jobs in the structure, which gives the overall range of pay within which the pay ranges have to be fitted;
- the width of the pay ranges; and
- the differentials between ranges.

Size of ranges

The span of a range from the minimum to the maximum rate allows for pay flexibility. It recognizes that room should be provided for progression because people in jobs placed in the same grade will perform differently and can possess different levels of skill and competence. The size of ranges can vary. In a narrow or fine-banded structure the span may be about 20 per cent above the minimum for each range. In a conventionally banded structure the span of the ranges might be around 30 to 60 per cent above the minimum. A span of 50 per cent above the minimum (ie 20 per cent on either side of the midpoint – an 80 to 120 per cent range) is fairly common and was orthodox practice a decade and more ago. Wide-banded structures as described in the next section of this chapter can have spans as much as 300 per cent above the minimum for a range.

There is no reason why ranges should all be of the same size, although it is advisable to be reasonably consistent throughout the hierarchy. Some organizations vary range sizes at different levels on the assumption that the higher the grade the more scope there is for differences in performance, which should be rewarded accordingly. For example, 30 per cent ranges for junior jobs, 40 per cent for middle managers and 60 per cent for top management.

Range reference points

In each range there will be a reference point that defines what the organization is prepared to pay to job holders whose performance in a job of a particular size over a period of time is fully acceptable and who have reached the full level of competence required.

If an individual were recruited who is qualified and expected to perform at the fully competent level, then that person could be positioned at the reference point of the range.

The reference point is often the midpoint of the range, thus in a symmetrical 80 per cent to 120 per cent range, the reference point would be 100 per cent. It could, however, be higher or lower depending on the organization's pay progression policy. For example, the reference point in a range of £20,000 to £30,000 could be 110 per cent (£27,500). There is no rule which says that a range should be symmetrical around the reference point.

In a fixed incremental system in which people automatically progress to the top of their scale, the reference point is traditionally the maximum scale rate of pay.

The reference point is also related to market rates in accordance with the organization's market stance. This expresses the organization's view on what it needs to pay in order to attract individuals who can perform at the fully competent level now or have the potential to do so, and also what it should pay to retain them when they reach or exceed that level.

The policy on market stance could be, for example, to line up the reference point with median rates. Alternatively, if the organization wishes to attract and retain experienced and above average employees and expects above average performance from them it might adopt a high pay policy, in which case the reference point could be related to a market rate above the median level, say, at the upper quartile or even above. Some organizations are prepared or forced to pay below average market rates.

However, the difficulty of establishing exactly what *the* market rate is, especially when there is a variety of jobs in a range, means that this process of alignment is often an imprecise one. It is frequently only possible to establish in fairly broad terms the relationship between reference points and market rates.

The line drawn between market-related reference points in successive pay ranges can be described as the pay policy line for fully competent job holders. This forms the basis for the graded pay structure (the use of pay policy lines in designing pay structures is discussed in Chapter 13, page 190).

Differentials

A graded structure provides for differentials between adjacent ranges which provide adequate scope for recognizing differences in the value of jobs in the grades concerned. Differentials tend to be between 15 and 20 per cent, but 20 per cent is typical. Again, there are no fixed rules.

Overlap between ranges

An overlap between adjacent pay ranges will exist whenever, in percentage terms, the span of the ranges exceeds the differential between them. Overlap is measured by the proportion of a range which is covered by the next lower range. Table 12.3 shows that when the size or span of a range is the same as the differential between ranges, there is no overlap. The more the range span exceeds the differential, the greater the overlap.

Table 12.3 *Examples of overlaps between pay ranges*

Size of range (span as a % of minimum)	Differential between ranges	Grade A minimum	Grade A maximum	Grade B minimum	Grade B maximum	% Overlap
50	20	12,000	18,000	14,400	21,600	50
35	20	12,000	16,200	14,400	19,440	36
20	20	12,000	14,400	14,400	17,280	0

Overlaps between ranges acknowledge that an experienced person doing a good job can be of more value to the organization than a newcomer to a position in the grade above.

A large overlap of 40 to 50 per cent is typical in organizations with a wide variety of jobs where a reasonable degree of flexibility is required in grading them.

Pay progression through ranges

Pay increases to individual job holders and progression within a range will typically vary according to assessments of performance, contribution, skill or competence and, to some degree, length of service or time in the grade. Progression is basically dependent on a combination of speed through the range and the extent of penetration into the full range.

A diminishing number of pay structures, particularly in the public sector, still have fixed service-related incremental scales, often in the shape of pay spines as described later in this chapter. However, a certain amount of flexibility can be introduced in such structures through variable increments (eg half, one and a half times or double the standard increment depending on performance assessment), or range points, which are spine points above the range maximum available only to consistently good performers. These have been used in government departments and other agencies and local authorities to provide a type of performance-related pay, although many are now moving on from this approach.

Pay progression policies within ranges are required on:

- the criteria for progressing pay;
- the limits, if any, to progression within a range;
- the rates at which pay can progress within a range.

Progression criteria

The criteria for progression may be performance, contribution or overall level of competence (performance-related pay as described in Chapter 17). Progression can, however, be more specifically linked to increases in skill (skill-based pay as described in Chapter 26) or competence (competence-based pay as described in Chapter 27).

Some organizations cater for both performance and skill or competence in a graded structure by providing for increases up to the reference point in the range to be subject to reaching defined levels of skill or competence, and then providing for progression beyond that point to depend on superior performance or contribution.

Limits within a range

A pay progression policy may provide for a movement-through-the-range element which enables individuals to reach the reference point if and when they achieve and sustain the required level of performance, skill and competence. Progression beyond that point (assuming it is not at the top of the range) will depend on achieving levels of performance and contribution which are higher than the fully acceptable level. Within each range, target rates of pay may be defined which employees can reach if they achieve a sustained level of performance, as illustrated in Figure 12.2. This could be represented by incorporating performance bars (sometimes called merit bars) at, say, a reference point of 100 per cent in a 80 to 120 per cent range, above which highly effective individuals could progress to the 110 per cent level. Exceptional employees could move on to the maximum.

Progression policies (or lack of them) may allow everyone to reach the ceiling of a range, but at different rates according to performance, as shown in Figure 12.3.

Rate of progress through the range

The rate of progress to the reference point in a range should be related to the average time it takes individuals who sustain fully competent performance to attain that level. The reference point should represent a competitive rate of pay and it is important to ensure that competent employees reach that level at the right time.

Typically, if the range of tenure of job holders is narrow, a constant rate of progression would be appropriate. However, in high growth organizations the rate of progression through a range may decelerate, giving an initial boost but slowing down as the ceiling is approached. In the latter case many individuals would be

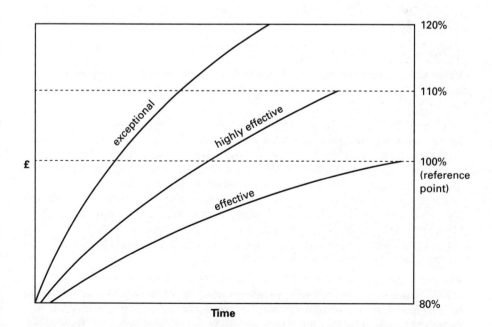

Figure 12.2   *Pay progression to varying target levels according to performance*

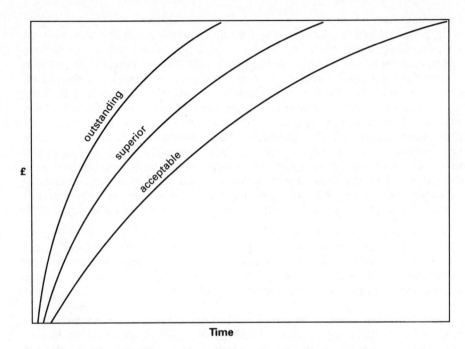

Figure 12.3 *Pay progression to the top of the range varying according to performance*

promoted before the ceiling is reached. These alternatives are illustrated in Figures 12.4 and 12.5.

Make-up of a pay range

There are a number of ways of structuring a pay range as described below.

Semi-structured
Semi-structured pay ranges may simply set out the starting point and ceiling of each range but provide no guidelines on how pay should progress between those limits. Some organizations have what may be described in contradictory terms as 'topless ranges' – only the lower level is specified and there is no defined ceiling, just a generalized understanding that there will be some limit to the level to which any individual's pay may progress, often set by paybill controls.

These approaches have some validity at very senior levels where they enable high level people to be recruited at a premium, but at more junior levels they can create problems of inequity and control and are not favoured by any organization wanting to adopt a systematic, consistent and logical approach to pay determination which it can communicate to employees.

Fully structured
A fully structured pay range will provide for progression to be governed by a fixed or semi-variable incremental system. Progression may be service-related to the range ceiling. This has been the typical, although now less common, fixed increment structure found in the public sector.

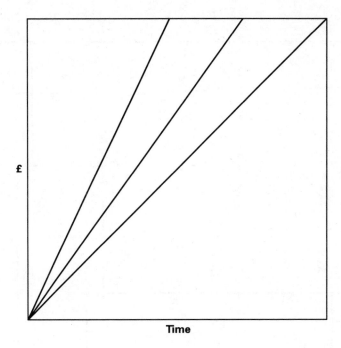

Figure 12.4   *Rate of progression – narrow range of job tenure*

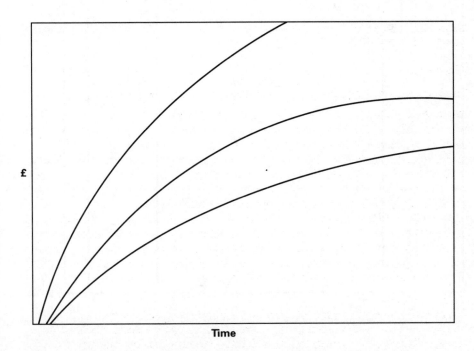

Figure 12.5   *Rate of progression – wide range of job tenure*

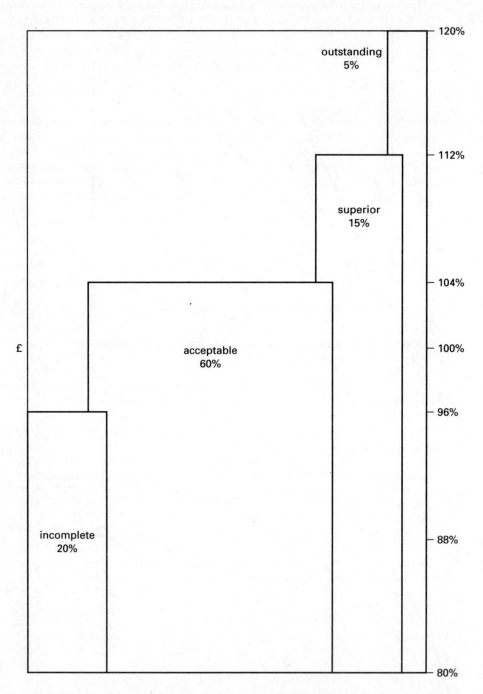

Notes: The range is a function of the job itself. Movement within the range depends upon the individual's performance

Figure 12.6 *Make-up of a performance-zoned pay range*

Performance-zoned

A performance-zoned pay range as shown in Figure 12.6 will set out the basis upon which individuals can move further and faster through the range for various performance levels. The full range at the quickest rate of progression is reserved only for top performers, while only a smaller part of the range at a lower rate of progression is available for less effective individuals. Performance-zoned structures provide for variable progression to target pay levels as described earlier in this chapter (page 159) and illustrated in Figure 12.2.

This approach represents the performance track concept in which individuals can follow a track of pay opportunity based on assessed performance. High achieving people are thus enabled to reach higher pay levels more quickly than those whose rate of achievement is not so high. The latter will progress at a slower rate and reach a lower pay ceiling. The key principle of this type of structure is that rewards are given as a result of sustained performance at a particular level rather than on the basis of one-off performance.

Progression-zoned

A progression-zoned structure as illustrated in Figure 12.7 is a variant of the performance-zoned structure. It defines in a different way the typical stages through which individuals might go, starting from the bottom of the range. These are:

- *The learning zone* which represents the learning curve for inexperienced individuals beginning at the minimum rate of pay for the range. This is where someone may start who has the basic qualifications for the job but lacks the directly relevant experience required to perform at the fully competent level. People with more relevant experience would start at a higher point in the range. In this example of an 80 to 120 per cent range the upper limit of the learning zone is set at 90 per cent. But this figure could be varied according to the average length of the learning curve. Employees who start at the bottom of the zone and make average progress would be expected to reach the top of the zone in a defined period of time.

- *The competent zone* which represents the range of pay for those who are competent in the key areas of their jobs. One approach to handling this zone is to position the range reference point in the middle and relate it to market rates in accordance with the organization's market rate policy – its pay stance. The starting point of the zone would be for employees who have achieved an acceptable level of competence but still have more to learn. Scope is provided for individuals to advance further to the top of the zone on the basis of their performance and contribution. An alternative approach is to align the starting point of the zone to market rates and provide scope above this to reward extra contributions.

- *The premium zone* which is reserved for individuals whose performance is exceptional. It could also be used to accommodate people who have special responsibilities which are higher than those carried out by others in the same zone but are not high enough to justify allocating the job into the next highest grade. Care would have to be taken to ensure that people do not drift into this zone. It should only be available for those whose *sustained* performance or long-term increase in responsibilities justifies payment at this level. Short-term achievements or increases in responsibility for individuals in the competent zone could be rewarded with special lump-sum bonuses which do not perpetuate the increase or add to consolidated cost.

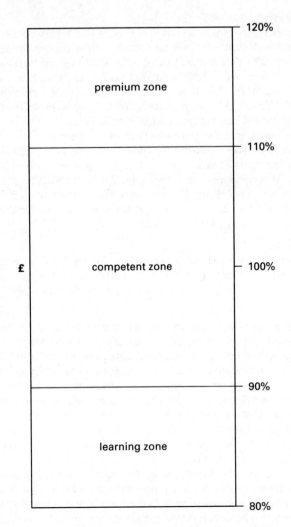

Figure 12.7 *Make-up of a progression-zoned structure*

High performance/high reward structure
This is a variant of the progression-zoned arrangement and takes the form of a fine-banded structure for high pay/high achievement organizations whose policy is to pay above market rates and expect commensurately superior levels of performance. The reference point is set according to the pay stance at, say the upper quartile. Above that point employees are not eligible for any permanent increases to their basic rate but can earn an achievement bonus for meeting specific and challenging objectives. It is accepted that there may be a learning curve that some employees will have to follow to reach the high level of competence required, but the starting point of the learning zone may be aligned to median market rates. The span of this learning curve zone and therefore the whole range may be restricted to 15–20 per cent.

Progression through the structure

Progression through the structure will be based on promotion or on upgrading when the size of a job carried out by a job holder increases sufficiently on a permanent basis to place it in a higher grade.

Upgrading procedures have to be carefully controlled to prevent grade drift – the situation which arises when jobs are upgraded unjustifiably simply to gain higher rates of pay or to respond to what may well be temporary market rate pressures. If this is allowed to happen, the integrity of the internal relativity structure will be damaged if not destroyed. Methods of avoiding grade drift are discussed in Chapter 36.

In typical pay structures with a fair degree of overlap between grades (eg 40–50 per cent), promotions may involve a two grade jump. In other words, the grading sequence in such structures does not necessarily correspond with the promotion ladder.

Adjusting the structure in response to general increases in pay levels

A decision generally to increase pay levels to ensure that the pay structure remains competitive, or following pay negotiations, can be implemented by proportionate increases to the midpoint of each range. If the existing span of the ranges is to be retained a similar increase is given to their maxima and minima. It might be decided, however, that it would be appropriate to alter the size of the ranges by increasing the maxima or the minima less or more than proportionately.

Advantages of graded structures

The advantages of this type of structure are that:

- Grades are easy to explain to employees and help in the communication of pay policies and practices. They clearly indicate the relativities between various job levels, especially when pay ranges are published. This is an important consideration – the management of relativities is perhaps the most onerous task facing those who manage reward practices.
- Consistent methods of grading jobs and managing relativities can be maintained.
- The use of graded structures can be useful in communicating opportunities to progress through a range.
- Grades allow a degree of job flexibility and individuals can be moved round the organization to jobs of slightly different sizes without the need to change pay to reflect that size variation. The wider the grade, the greater the scope for flexibility but the greater is the need to pay close attention to the management of pay differentials.
- A well-defined and comprehensible framework exists for managing reward and career progression.
- Better control can be exercised over pay for new starters, individual performance-related pay increases and promotion increases.
- A grade structure with reasonably wide bands allows a degree of job flexibility and some scope to accommodate differences between the market rates of jobs in the grade.

Disadvantages of graded pay structures

The disadvantages of this type of structure are that:

- The mechanics of designing and managing the grade structure and the processes of grading and regrading can create major problems. The fact that there are grade boundaries dividing groups of jobs into separate entities creates discontinuities. This in turn puts pressure on the evaluation process and the grade boundaries need to be selected with great care. This can not be done scientifically. There is always room for judgement and the design of graded structures is often an empirical and iterative process.
- Inevitably there will be a tendency for grade drift to take place as jobs get pushed into the next grade above as a result of pressure from employees and, frequently, their managers.
- The grouping of jobs into grades means that there are different sizes of jobs within a single grade. As each grade is for pay management purposes a single unit, this inevitably means that smaller jobs in the grade will be over-paid while larger jobs will be under-paid. The wider the grade, the larger the potential scale of this problem. This process inherently abandons some of the precision of quantitative job measurement. Points-factor evaluation, for example, identifies relatively fine differences between jobs. When the jobs are grouped into grades, some of the advantages of differentiating jobs is of necessity eliminated by the aggregation process. This may be difficult to justify. The fact that in a graded structure based on points-factor job evaluation, pounds are *not* paid for points, may be difficult to explain to someone in a job who is in the same grade as someone else with a lower score. This is why some organizations introduce individual job grades based on the principle of paying for points, especially for more senior jobs.
- A graded pay structure can impose a degree of hierarchical rigidity which may be at odds with the fluidity with which some roles develop in an organization. For example, the careers of scientists or development engineers in high-tech organizations do not necessarily progress step by step up a promotion ladder. Some organizations are providing for even more flexibility by introducing broad-banded structures as described in the next section. Others adopt the pay curve approach as discussed later in this chapter.
- The existence of a known pay range generates expectations amongst employees that they will inevitably reach the top. However carefully the company spells out that progression depends on performance and may not go beyond a certain limit, people are still disappointed and aggrieved when their progression is halted. The result is that in many organizations managers tend to allow the pay of their staff to drift to the top of the range irrespective of their performance.
- Graded structures mean that some people will inevitably hit the ceiling of their range and, assuming the size of their jobs has not increased enough to justify regrading, they have nowhere to go unless they are promoted, which in today's flatter organizations may be less likely. Yet they may continue to make a real added value contribution and they are likely to be demotivated if they are not rewarded appropriately. This problem can be alleviated by providing for lump sum, re-earnable achievement or continuing superior level of performance bonuses. These are typically not consolidated for pension purposes.

Conclusions

Historically, the advantage of graded structures was that they eased pay administration problems, especially when there were large numbers of jobs. However, with the advent of sophisticated reward management computer systems this becomes less necessary. Such systems enable organizations to manage and control individual job range, pay curve or spot rate structures more easily and avoid some of the difficulties mentioned above.

Conventional grading structures may be part of the culture and therefore difficult to change to some other form of structure or from a fine-graded structure to a broad-banded one. On the other hand, the introduction of a new type of structure may be a lever for assisting the process of culture change.

Broad-banded pay structures

A broad-banded structure is one in which the range of pay in a band is significantly higher than in a conventional graded structure.

Main features

Broad-banded pay structures as illustrated in Figure 12.8 usually cover the whole workforce from the shop floor to senior management although top management (directors) may be excluded.

At their most extreme, such structures may contain no more than four bands, the span of each of which could be between 200–300 per cent above the minimum. This contrasts with the typical 40–50 per cent ranges in a conventional graded pay structure. Jobs or job families are allocated to bands on the basis of job evaluation (points-factor or job ranking).

Within each of the bands there will usually be a number of pay zones which indicate, broadly, the range of pay for particular jobs or job families. Levels of pay are related to market rates – what the Americans call market anchors. The size of the pay zones is sufficient to allow for appropriate pay progression related to growth in job knowledge and performance and competency growth. It is typically 50–60 per cent. In some broad-banded structures, pay zones can extend beyond the band limits if the market reference points or anchors are high in the band.

The architecture of a broad-banded structure defined in terms of areas and job types covered and incorporating pay zones within bands for the job types in each area is illustrated in Figure 12.9. In this example, the pay ranges for bands are defined by reference to the lower and upper limits of the range of pay for all the zones in the band.

A common feature of a broad-banded structure is that line managers are given freedom to manage the pay of their staff within their budgets and in accordance with pay policy guidelines. The guidelines will indicate what levels and ranges of pay are appropriate in each zone, the rate of progression for different levels of performance and competence and the basis upon which performance should be reviewed.

Organizations with broad-banded pay structures make the maximum use of computerized reward management procedures. These have involved the development of software which enables managers to test alternative distributions of pay increases for members of their departments on a 'what if' basis and establish the impact of any one of these alternatives on their pay budgets.

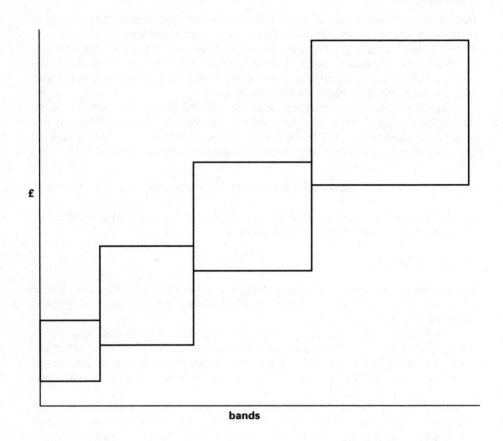

Figure 12.8   *A broad-banded pay structure*

Reasons for introducing broad-banded pay structures

Broad-banded pay structures are being introduced for the following reasons:

- they provide for more flexibility in making and administering pay decisions;
- the structure recognizes that in delayered organizations careers are more likely to develop within broadly homogeneous areas of responsibility rather than progressing up a number of steps in a clearly defined hierarchy;
- the existence of a few broad bands reduces, indeed may eliminate, the problem of grade drift common to conventional more narrowly-banded pay structures;
- if the basis of the structure is carefully explained, employees can recognize the logic of the banding of their jobs more readily and should be less inclined to make the invidious comparisons between their position and those of others which happen in more finely-banded structures;

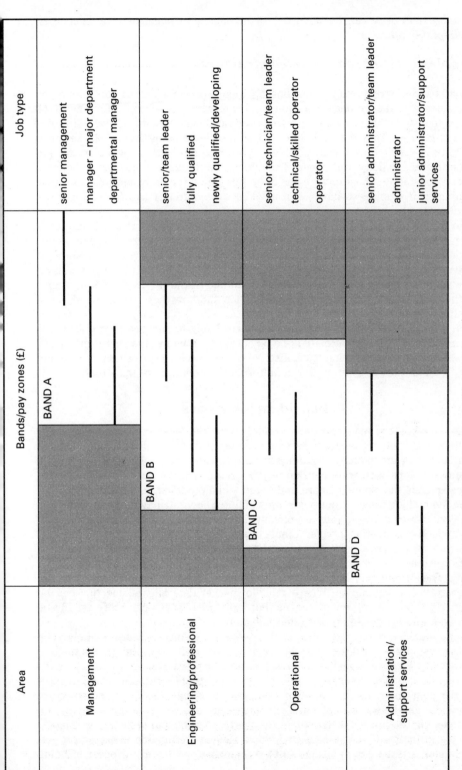

Figure 12.9 *Broad-banded structure by areas, bands, pay zones and job type*

■ more authority can be devolved to managers to manage rewards in their departments.

Problems with broad-banded structures

Broad-banded structures present one obvious problem – that of controlling pay decisions so that a fair degree of equity and consistency is achieved. Care has to be taken to ensure that pay zones are anchored firmly and that the spread allowed is clearly defined. They demand quite a lot of detailed administration. Market rates have to be tracked systematically and rigorously, often from several sources to maximize the validity of the data. The allocation of jobs to zones has to be monitored constantly. The structure has to be fine-tuned regularly and this can cause confusion if employees have been used to the continuity provided by a more traditional structure.

In principle, it is a good idea to give managers more freedom to operate their own reward processes. In practice, some managers will be better at it than others. Broad-banded structures demand an uncommon degree of pay-literacy amongst line managers. Thorough planning, comprehensive training and plenty of hands-on guidance is required from the personnel or human resource (HR) function, at least in the early stages. The impact of broad bands and how they operate needs to be evaluated regularly.

In short, broad-banded structures are most likely to succeed in sophisticated organizations with a tradition of good pay practice, effective managers and an HR function with remuneration specialists who can provide professional advice and play a major part in planning and monitoring the operation of the structure.

Individual job ranges

Where the content and size of jobs is widely different, for example at senior levels, an individual job grade structure may be preferable to a conventionally banded structure. An individual job grade structure avoids the problem of grouping a number of jobs with widely different job sizes into a grade, with the inevitable consequence that some jobs are underpaid while others are overpaid.

Individual job range structures simply define a separate pay range for each job. The relativities between jobs are usually determined by points-factor job evaluation which may in effect convert points to pounds by the application of a formula. There is a reference point in each range, often the midpoint, and the range is expressed as plus or minus a percentage of the reference point, typically 20 per cent. The reference point is aligned to market rates in accordance with the organization's pay stance. Where reliable market data is available this can be carried out job by job which means that individual ranges can more readily be changed in response to market rate movements.

Individual job ranges are often used for senior jobs where there are likely to be considerably greater differences between job sizes. The remaining jobs may be covered by a conventionally graded structure. Individual ranges can also be used in rapidly growing companies where a normal grade structure would restrict recruitment policy too much, or in small organizations where a grade structure would be cumbersome. Individual job ranges are sometimes adopted by organizations who do not want to operate an overtly hierarchical system which labels people in their different grades. Individual ranges are flexible in the sense that dissimilar jobs are not subjected to the somewhat procrustean process of being forced into the rigid confines of a grade. They avoid the inevitable problems which occur when jobs are evaluated just below grade boundaries.

But they can encourage individuals to put pressure on management to have their jobs re-evaluated on the grounds that more points mean more pay. And in this respect, graded structures allow for more flexibility than individual ranges in that, where points-factor job evaluation is used, there is a range of points within which jobs are grouped and which can accommodate small variations in job size.

Individual grade structures can be more difficult to control than a conventional graded structure, although they are easier to manage with the help of a computer-based reward management system.

Benefit grade structure

It may be necessary to superimpose a benefit grade structure on top of a job range system, as illustrated in Figure 12.10, if the organization wants to maintain a hierarchy of benefits for the more senior staff who are given individual salary ranges. Each benefit grade would define the benefits available such as a company car or an improved pension scheme. Jobs may be allocated to benefit grades by means of job evaluation. Alternatively, jobs may be placed more subjectively into benefit grades according to a broad assessment of levels of responsibility (eg senior, middle management and junior management).

The establishment of benefit grades means that an individual job grade structure looks more like a broad-banded structure. In fact, the pay zones in the latter

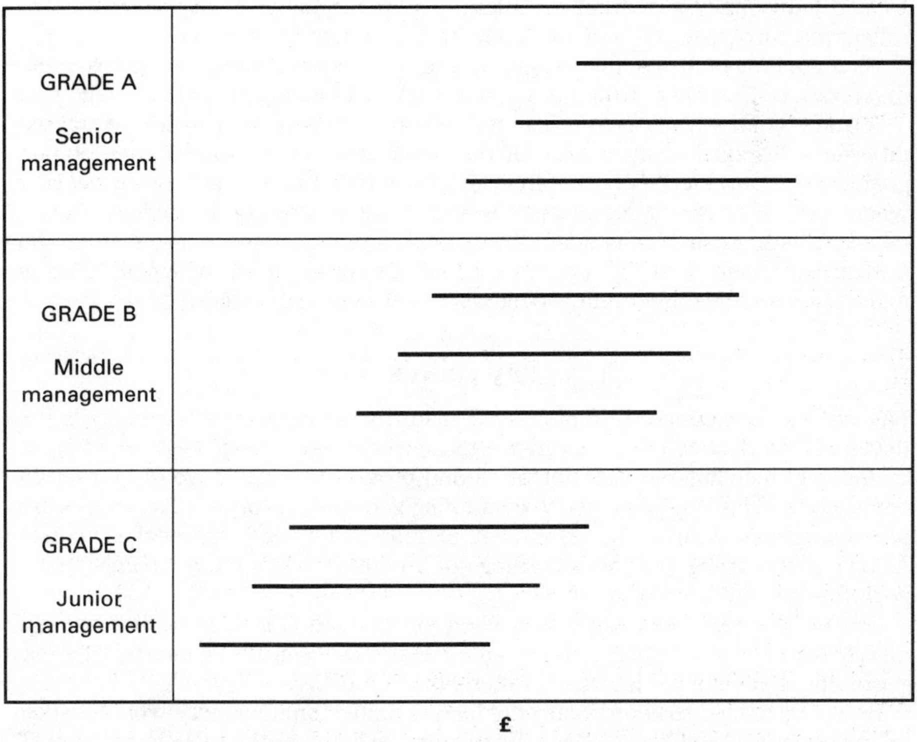

Figure 12.10 *Individual job ranges and benefit grades*

structure may be similar to individual job ranges. The main differences between a broad-banded structure and a benefit grade structure with individual ranges is that in the former *all* employees are graded within the banded structure and the bands are not exclusively concerned with defining the entitlement to differential benefits.

Job family structures

The advantages of operating one pay structure for all jobs in terms of achieving consistency and facilitating control seem to be obvious. But it becomes progressively more difficult to do this in two situations. First, where market rate pressures operate differentially on particular occupations or categories of employees and second, when there are significant variations in the type of work carried out and the competences required by different occupational groups which cannot easily be catered for in a single pay structure.

Job family structures provide a method of dealing with these problems. A job family consists of jobs in a function or discipline such as research scientist, development engineer or personnel specialist. The jobs will be related in terms of the fundamental activities carried out and the basic skills required, but they will be differentiated by the level of responsibility, skill or competence involved. Job families may also be distinguished from one another in terms of the market rates for the occupations within the family. Significant differences in market rates may mean that a family will constitute a separate 'market group'.

A job family structure consists of separate graded pay structures for each of the job families which have been identified for this purpose. These structures are aligned individually to market rates and contain a number of pay ranges which reflect the particular levels of work within the job family.

Separate job families or market groups may only cover some occupations in the organization. The others would be catered for by a common graded pay structure.

Job family structures can be suitable where occupations need to be treated differently because of the nature of the work and/or their special market rate position. But they can be divisive and equity is more difficult to achieve, especially where they are strongly orientated towards market rates and individual competences. Unless great care is taken to justify differences in these terms, it can be difficult to ensure that the principle of equal pay for work of equal value is maintained and this important aspect has so far not been tested.

Pay curves

Pay curves (sometimes referred to as maturity or progression curves) are a development of job family structures. A pay curve system recognises that different methods of handling pay determination and progression may have to be used in some job families, especially those containing knowledge workers. Pay curves are also concerned with the development of more integrated approaches to pay involving rewarding people according to a combination of their competence, performance and market worth.

Graded structures can work well when job evaluation is used to discriminate clearly between job responsibilities, and progression is made in a series of steps representing a distinct hierarchy of increases in job size.

However, graded structures may not be so suitable for knowledge workers such as professional staff, engineers, scientists, technologists, technicians or IT specialists whose skills may be transferable to different locations in a knowledge-based organization. It is often the case that the value of such people increases progressively as they mature in the sense of acquiring additional skills and competences and/or the ability to use an increasing range of skills more flexibly. These are the individuals whose experience over time will equip them to do a bigger job. They are likely to develop continuously as new opportunities and challenges arise. Their advancement will not be a matter of climbing distinct steps in a job hierarchy where job size can be determined by points-factor evaluation scores, although it may be possible to define levels of competence to which they can aspire.

Pay curves, as illustrated in Figure 12.11, provide different pay progression tracks along which people in a family of jobs can move according to their levels of competence and performance. Pay levels are determined by reference to market rates. The assumptions governing pay curves are that first, competence develops progressively through various levels or bands rather than between a number of fixed points; second, individuals will develop at different rates and will therefore deliver different levels of performance which should be rewarded accordingly and third, market rate considerations should be taken into account when determining levels of pay at each point in the curve.

The concept of pay curves is linked to that of competence-based evaluation (see

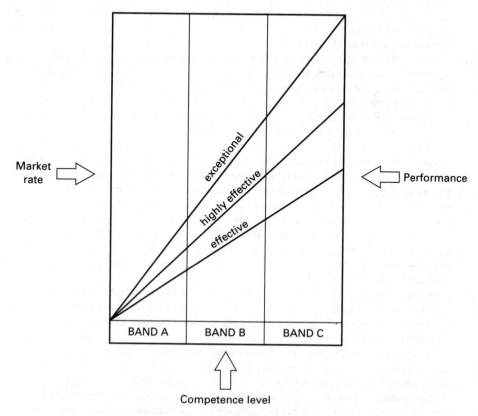

Figure 12.11 *A job family pay curve*

Chapter 9), which, like skill-based evaluation, recognizes that roles may expand to the level of ability or competence of the job holder rather than being constrained within narrowly defined jobs in traditional hierarchies.

A job family pay curve contains a number of competence bands, each of which constitutes a definable level of skill, competence and responsibility. Individuals move through these bands at a rate which is related to their performance and their capacity to develop. They would not move into a new band until they have demonstrated that they have attained the level of competence required. Pay ranges in each band are related to market rates for the job family concerned in line with the organization's pay stance. Pay curves may be introduced for knowledge-workers alongside a more conventional structure for other employees.

Pay increases for individuals are usually determined by line managers by reference to policy guidelines and data provided by the HR department on market rate movements and their pay budgets. Decisions are made by first giving individual consideration to how people are performing, the level of competence they have reached and their existing level of pay and then comparing these factors with the guidelines on progression and position in the pay structure for different levels of competence and contribution. Such decisions are helped when a computerized reward management system produces printouts for managers on where each member of their staff is placed in the structure. Comparisons are then possible between where an individual is situated compared with the pay curve guidelines and the position of other people in the department. Decisions can be made on an immediate movement or a longer-term plan to bring pay into line. The computerized system can also be used to calculate the impact of different pay increase decisions on the pay budget.

Under this system there is usually no common level of movement for all employees. Instead, each set of job family pay curves will be amended as necessary to reflect market rate movements. Even within a job family there may not be a general increase in pay. Reviews take account of how the pay of individuals reflects their market worth (which is, of course, affected by their performance and competence) and their rate will be adjusted accordingly.

Pay curves may be introduced, as at Glaxo Pharmaceuticals, because an existing system has been found unsatisfactory on the following three counts. First, a common grading system which lacks the flexibility to respond to market pressures for particular groups of specialists. Second, the absence of the facility to reward staff who are delivering consistently good performance and who are increasing their competence through a process of continuous development once they have reached the pay ceiling for their grade. Third, incentives are insufficient to reward very good performers, either in terms of accelerated pay progression or progression beyond the normal grade boundaries. These are common problems in conventionally graded structures.

However, pay curves are unsuitable in many organizations, especially when there are clearly defined job hierarchies and where it would be in conflict with the culture to distinguish between employees in separate job families.

A further problem with pay curves is that they are harder to manage and less easy to control than graded pay structures. Although in principle it is right to give the maximum amount of authority to line managers to run their own pay processes, it is still necessary to provide explicit guidelines, up-to-date and comprehensive data on market rate movements and detailed, preferably computerized, information on the distribution of pay in individual departments. All this makes heavy demands on the HR function, members of which may have to spend quite a lot of time educating line managers and 'holding their hands' as the latter learn how to run the system.

Spot rate structures

In its simplest form, a spot or individual job rate structure allocates a specific rate for a job. There is no scope for the basic rate for the job to progress through a defined pay range, although individual rates of pay for job holders for whom the rates have not been negotiated with a trade union may change, possibly at the whim of management. Job holders may be eligible for performance pay through performance-related base pay progression, or an incentive or bonus scheme.

Spot rates can be fixed entirely by reference to market rates in a market driven structure and, unless this is done systematically, a spot rate system can hardly be described as a structure at all. In more structured systems, job evaluation is used to measure relative job size and establish a job hierarchy. The rates may be negotiated with trade unions.

Spot rate structures are typical for manual workers but they are adopted for other types of staff by some organizations who want the maximum degree of scope to pay what they like. Such organizations are very unlikely to use a systematic process of job evaluation.

Modifications can be made to spot rate structures so that they give some room for varying levels of pay other than by means of performance-related pay or incentives. These modifications can produce something akin to an individual job grade structure. There will be provision for paying less than the spot rate for those on a learning curve where they are not fully qualified to do the job, or for paying more for specified skills, job responsibilities or conditions of work.

Pay spines

Pay spines consist of a series of incremental points extending from the lowest to the highest paid jobs covered by the structure. Pay scales or ranges for different job grades may then be superimposed on the pay spine. An example of a pay spine is given in Figure 12.12.

Pay spines are most often found in the public sector or in agencies and voluntary organizations which have adopted a public sector approach to reward management.

If performance-related pay is introduced, individuals can be given accelerated increments. The Civil Service has used this approach to add range points to the top of the normal scale which enable staff who achieve very high or consistently high performance ratings to advance above the scale maximum for the grade. The Civil Service is now, however, moving on to a diversity of approaches at different levels which involve more delegation of pay decisions to departments.

Pay structures for manual workers

A pay structure for manual workers consists of the rates paid to employees who work on the shop floor, in distribution, transport, public services and anywhere else where the work primarily involves manual skills and tasks. The structure will be similar to any other pay structure in that it incorporates pay differentials between jobs which reflect real and assumed differences in skill and responsibility but are influenced by pressures from the local labour market, by custom and practice and by settlements reached between management and trade unions.

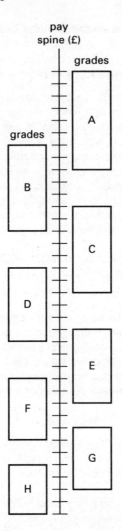

Figure 12.12 *A pay spine*

The pay structure may include a number of spot rates, ie fixed base rates for each job which do not vary according to skill or merit. Alternatively there may be a formal structure in which there are defined job grades into which jobs are slotted according to their levels of skill or responsibility. There may be a fixed rate for each job in the grade, or there may be a pay bracket to allow for other individual skill or merit payments to be made above the minimum time rate. In the latter case the pay structure closely resembles a graded structure as described earlier in this chapter. Some structures are based entirely on levels of skill, as when skill-based pay operates (see Chapter 26).

Pay levels in the structure are determined in a number of ways. They may be imposed by national, local or plant negotiations. Or they may be fixed by management by reference to national minimum rates and the rates paid for similar jobs in the local labour market.

Differentials may be established by tradition, by reference to market rate relativities, by negotiation or by job evaluation. There may in some instances be no formal structure, or it may be limited to a crude division of jobs into skilled, semiskilled and unskilled categories. In these cases, differentials within or between categories may be haphazard, or dictated by custom and practice, or determined by the ways in which payment-by-result schemes reward different classes of employees.

Many structures incorporate various plus rates for particular skills or demands made on employees. These may include shift rates, pay for unsocial working hours, overtime rates, and pay for difficult or unpleasant working conditions.

Unplanned structures may easily result in a mass of overlapping and confused grades without any acceptable pattern of rational differentials between jobs. Such structures offer endless scope for argument and conflict over grading and upgrading issues. They also lead to a failure to fulfil equal pay for work of equal value obligations.

The case for a planned and rational pay structure for manual workers is overwhelming, although achieving order from chaos may be a formidable task. Differentials which have been built into the structure over a number of years are hard to change. This is where a job evaluation programme which involves the full participation of trade unions can be valuable.

One approach which is becoming more common is to develop an integrated pay structure covering all employees with the possible exception of senior management. This is happening in high technology firms which have a preponderance of knowledge workers and highly skilled employees and in firms, especially multinational companies, opening on greenfield sites. Integrated structures are described later in this chapter (pages 179–80).

Basis of the pay structure

The task of management is to assess what level and type of inducements it has to offer in return for the contribution it requires of its workforce.

The worker's aim is to strike a bargain about the relationship between what he or she regards as a reasonable contribution and what the employer is prepared to offer to elicit that contribution. This is termed the effort bargain and is, in effect, an agreement which lays down the amount of work to be done for a rate of pay or wage rate, not just the hours to be worked. Explicitly or implicitly, all employees are in a bargaining situation with regard to pay. A system will not be accepted as effective and workable until it is recognized as fair and equitable by both parties.

Rates of pay may be fixed by negotiation with trade unions, in which case the settlement depends on the relative bargaining strengths of the two parties. But they are also influenced by the going rate (the level of settlements reached by other, similar employers) as well as the company's ability or willingness to pay, the state of the economy and the state of the labour market (shortages or surpluses of skills). Agreement may also have to be reached with a trade union on the introduction of new types of payment-by-result schemes or the amendment of existing ones. There will, for example, be tight rules in an agreement on the circumstances in which rates can be altered by management.

In non-unionized companies (derecognition is becoming increasingly common) the contract is an individual one. Employees have either to accept an offer in accordance with fixed, non-negotiable terms and conditions or to exert whatever bargaining strengths they possess.

Even when a company is not unionized, it still makes sense for management to consult employees on the design and operation of the pay structure, although levels of pay and other terms and conditions of employment may be non-negotiable.

Typical structures

A typical pay structure for manual workers will have the minimum number of grades required to accommodate the clearly differentiated levels of skill and responsibility that exist in the organization. The more straightforward the operational process, the less reason to have numerous grades. A further driver for reducing the number of grades has been to encourage more broadly-defined, flexible roles. Current practice is to have no more than three or four grades covering all manual workers when a separate pay structure exists. It is important to have adequate pay differentials between grades to provide for a significant increase in pay as a result of upgrading and to avoid the disputes about regradings which result if the increases between grades are too small.

The structure will be founded on the basic rates for jobs or time rates as described below. In addition there may be provision for a pay-for-performance or skill element in the shape of piece rates (although piece rate systems are becoming increasingly rare), work measured payment-by-result schemes, measured day work or skill-based pay. Work measured schemes may operate on an individual or group basis and additionally, or alternatively, there may be a group or enterprise-wide bonus scheme or a gainsharing plan (see Chapter 23). The various forms of incentive or bonus schemes for manual workers are described in Chapter 18.

Rates of pay may, therefore, be divided into a basic time rate for the job, which is paid according to the hours worked, and an incentive element which is related to some measure of performance or skill. Traditionally, the ratio of base rate to incentive has been 2:1, but the current trend is to reduce the target proportion of incentive pay to one third or one quarter to minimize fluctuations in earnings and to control wage or earnings drift (increases in incentive based earnings which are higher than the increases in output which generated the incentive payment – wage drift is an undesirable but common phenomenon associated with old and decaying payment-by-result schemes). A further reason for reducing the incentive element is that many organizations find it more difficult to justify highly personalized differentiated pay because it can be counter-productive in terms of the achievement of quality and teamwork.

There might also be a guaranteed or fall-back rate for workers in payment-by-results schemes which would be related to the consolidated time rate for a worker at a similar level.

Time rate

Time rate, also known as day rate or flat rate, is the arrangement under which workers are simply paid a predetermined rate per month, week, day or hour for the actual time worked. Pay only varies with time, never with output, performance or the level of skill attained in a job. In many companies there is constant pressure from trade unions to consolidate average bonus earnings into the base rate. Most firms resist this because they believe it removes the incentive element, but a certain amount of consolidation may be conceded from time to time to reduce the payment-for-results proportion of total earnings.

In some companies, what are termed high time or day rates are paid which are set at a level above the minimum rates. The high day rate may include a consolidated bonus element and is probably greater than the local labour market rate to attract and retain good quality workers. High day rates have been common in industries such as motor manufacturing where above average earnings are expected because of a history of payment-by-results, and where there is a high degree of machine control over output. They are appropriate in machine-paced assembly lines and in some high technology plants where multiskilling and flexibility are important – both these requirements may be inhibited by a traditional payment-by-results scheme.

Time rates are often used when it is believed that it is undesirable or impossible to operate an incentive scheme, eg in maintenance work. But they are being increasingly introduced in situations where a payment-by-result scheme has proved to be unsatisfactory in the sense that it creates wage drift, is costly to run, creates conflict or is clearly not providing value for money in the shape of increased productivity, and where there is a focus on total quality.

From the point of view of many operators, time rates are better because earnings are predictable and steady and they do not have to engage in endless arguments with industrial engineers, rate fixers and supervisors about piecework rates or work measured time allowances.

The obvious argument against time rates is that they do not provide the motivation of a direct financial incentive which clearly relates pay to performance. The point is often made that people want money and will work harder to get it. The argument is a powerful one and is supported by the many successful incentive schemes that are still in operation, although the difficulty of maintaining a successful payment-by-result scheme should never be underestimated.

Integrated pay structures

Integrated pay structures cover groups of employees who have traditionally been paid under separate arrangements. An integrated structure may have one grading system which includes all employees – managers, professional, technical and office staff *and* manual workers, although such structures frequently leave out senior management.

An integrated pay structure may be based on the same system of job evaluation applied to all employees. It will involve the harmonization to some extent of employee benefits and conditions of employment such as holidays, hours of work, sick pay and pensions, although the scale of such benefits may still be related to position in the grade hierarchy.

Reasons for integration

The main reasons for the rapid development of integrated pay structures in recent years are:

- The blurring of the differences between manual and non-manual employment, partly because of the introduction of new technology but also because of a change in the social climate.
- The introduction of new manufacturing technology and processes and the widespread use of information technology has entailed greater flexibility and broader job definitions to incorporate new ranges of skills and to allow for different working practices. Some office jobs have, in effect, been de-skilled, while the skill requirements for many shop floor jobs have been considerably enhanced. Knowledge workers now function widely on the shop floor as well as in the office. The belief is no longer tenable that someone operating, say, a word processor should in any way be treated as being of a higher status than

someone operating, say, a computer numerically controlled machine tool.
- Many American and Japanese companies with subsidiaries in the UK have a company philosophy of offering single-status employment conditions.
- These and other companies opening on greenfield sites have seized the opportunity to introduce an integrated pay structure from the outset.
- There has been a move towards single-table bargaining with trade unions (all negotiations on one site involving all unions, including those traditionally concerned with white collar as well as manual workers). The introduction of this form of bargaining as a means of achieving joint and comprehensive agreements may encourage the integration of the pay structure.
- Equal pay for work of equal value considerations.
- The human resource management concept of integrating all aspects of personnel management – development and training as well as reward – has led to the introduction of more comprehensive employment and pay policies.
- Integrated pay can lead to the simplification of pay administration usually because the number of grades is significantly reduced.

Forms of integration

Integrated pay structures are usually formed round grades, although it is possible to adopt a job family approach. The grades are usually established by job evaluation, generally a points-factor scheme, although ranking has been used. The tendency, as at Perkin Elmer and Motorola, is to have a broad-banded structure which allows for a fair degree of operational flexibility.

The introduction of integrated pay has frequently been accompanied by the abolition of old payment-by-result schemes and their replacement by one consolidated rate of pay. Some schemes, however, have introduced performance-related pay for all categories of staff, including those manual workers who were previously receiving incentive pay. A gainsharing plan is also sometimes introduced as part of the integrated pay structure.

An integrated structure will not necessarily lead to the abolition of all plus payments. Allowances may be paid for shift or unsocial hours, and separate overtime payments up to a certain level in the structure may be made.

Some companies with integrated pay structures such as Continental Can, Hydro Fertilisers and Yorkshire Television operate an annual hours system in which the annual hours totals are the same for all employees. An annual hours system involves scheduling employee hours on the basis of the number of hours to be worked over the year, with provision for the increase or reduction of hours in any given period, according to the demand for goods or services.

Rate for age scales

Rate for age scales provide for a specific rate of pay or a pay bracket to be linked to age for staff in certain jobs. They are relatively uncommon nowadays because of changing patterns of work. The rationale for rate for age scales used to be the learning curve principle, but that can be catered for in a graded pay structure. They are, however, still in use for employees below the age of 21 on formal training schemes extending over two or three years.

Choice of structure

The choice of structure depends partly on the type of organization – its size, complexity, culture, and traditions – and partly on the people it employs – the existence and proportion of managers, knowledge workers, sales staff, office workers and skilled or unskilled manual workers.

Larger enterprises and institutions with formal, hierarchical organization structures will tend to prefer conventional graded structures which provide for orderly administration and ease in managing internal relativities. High technology organizations who want to achieve rather more flexibility but within a defined framework may opt for a broad-banded structure.

Individual job ranges may be favoured by organizations who want a degree of formality, for example in progressing people through a range, but do not wish to put one-off jobs into what they may perceive as the strait-jacket of a graded structure.

Organizations who are particularly concerned with maintaining competitive pay levels and have a number of different market groups among their employees may prefer a job family structure which they may also introduce if there are a number of distinctive job families which need different grade structures. If they employ a large proportion of knowledge workers who are continually developing in their jobs, especially in their formative years, they may go further and introduce a pay curve system for certain categories of staff.

Smaller organizations, those whose environment induces a more flexible, less formalized approach to administration, companies which are market rate driven and fast-moving entrepreneurial companies who demand very high performance may prefer a spot rate structure, coupled, especially in the latter category, with a powerful pay-for-performance system.

13

Developing Pay Structures

Methodology

The process of developing a new or modified pay structure consists of the following steps:

1. Analyse present arrangements – the type of organization and its employees, the organization's reward strategies and policies, the existing pay structure and how effectively it operates, and any specific objectives which the new or revised structure is expected to achieve. The check list contained in Chapter 5 can be used for this purpose.
2. Set objectives and a timetable for the review.
3. Consider who is going to conduct the review, including the possibility of seeking help from management consultants (the use of consultants is discussed in Chapter 39).
4. Estimate the likely costs of conducting and implementing the review and agree a budget.
5. Decide on the extent to which employees should be involved in the review. This is highly desirable, especially for job evaluation. And there is everything to be said for getting them involved as far as practicable with other aspects of the design. If there are trade unions, processes of consultation and negotiation will have to be followed.
6. Brief employees on the objectives of the review, how it is going to be conducted and how they will be involved. Care must be taken in this briefing to avoid creating expectations of a pay bonanza for all concerned.
7. In the light of the analysis of present arrangements, make preliminary decisions on what type of structure or structures are required. Criteria to assist in making this choice are given in Chapter 12.
8. Analyse and evaluate bench mark and related jobs.
9. Obtain market rate information.
10. Make a final decision on the type of structure or structures required and the main design and operational features.
11. Prepare a detailed design for the structure and how it will be managed and maintained.
12. Communicate to all staff the details of the structure and how it will affect them.
13. Train managers in how to operate the structure.
14. Monitor the implementation of the structure.
15. Evaluate the application and impact of the structure.

Principles of pay structure design

The objective is to be as systematic as possible in basing the design on analysis and the information produced by job evaluation and market surveys. But pay structure design is not a scientific process. Judgement is required at every stage to interpret findings. This is especially the case when deciding on grade boundaries in a graded pay structure and in balancing the respective demands of internal equity and external competitiveness.

Pay structure design is, therefore, often an empirical process. There is no one right way of doing it. The data assembled in the development programme seldom point to an inevitable design conclusion. Iteration may be unavoidable. An initial, apparently satisfactory, structure may be designed but when presented for consideration, many different views may be expressed about its suitability. Alternative designs may have to be tried, tested and, often, reconsidered until a result is at last obtained with which, on balance, everyone is reasonably happy.

The aim should be to produce a structure which:

- is in accordance with the organization's pay philosophy and policies concerning differentials, relationships with market rates and the scope for and methods of progressing pay in jobs;
- is designed on a logical basis and helps in the application of equitable and consistent reward management processes;
- assists in the management and maintenance of appropriate internal and external relativities;
- is flexible enough to enable the organization to respond to change and reward properly improvements in competence and performance;
- can be implemented with the minimum amount of disruption and cost;
- is likely to be acceptable to management and every other member of the organization.

These criteria are not easy to satisfy. We examine in the rest of this chapter the approaches that can be adopted to the design of graded, individual job range, job family, pay curve, pay spine and manual workers' structures. We concentrate on graded structures as these are the most typical and the principles used in their design can be extended to most other structures.

Graded pay structure design

Areas for consideration

Decisions have to be made on each of the following major grade structure variables:

- the basis on which jobs should be graded;
- the number of grades;
- the width of grades;
- the size of pay ranges;
- the positioning of range reference points;
- how levels of pay in ranges should be related to market rates;
- the size of the differentials between pay ranges;
- the amount of overlap between ranges;

Basis for job grading
The purpose of job grading is to group together those jobs which are of a similar

size and separate those which are significantly different. So far as possible, the range of pay for the grade should accommodate the range of market rates for the jobs in the grade, although this is an ideal arrangement which may be very difficult to put into practice, not least because of the often imprecise and incomplete nature of market rate data.

The aim should be to mirror the perceptions of people in the organization about different levels, so that jobs which are generally perceived as being about the same size should not be placed in different grades and *vice versa*. A structure which does not reflect the majority view of the *status quo* is unlikely to prove acceptable in the long term. The position of the grade boundaries needs to be handled with particular sensitivity. Failure to do so can result in considerable pressure on job evaluation processes by employees whose sense of equity has been offended.

Grading jobs is easiest when jobs and their evaluated sizes fall into clear natural groupings. Within each group, jobs would then be perceived as similar in level, and the differences between groups would be generally recognized. Conversely, if such natural groupings do not exist, a grade structure is by no means precluded, but it is more difficult to design and the sharp steps which it introduces may be difficult to justify.

Number of job grades
The number of grades will be related to the number of distinct levels of responsibility in the hierarchy. The number of grades, however, does not necessarily equate to the number of levels in a reporting structure. A reporting structure of, say, five levels may need to be represented by a grade structure of as many as 8 or 10 grades. In such a case, one department may have jobs at grades 1, 3, 5, 7 and 9 while another may have jobs at grades 2, 4, 6, 8 and 10. Grade structures should not be designed on the assumption that a grade 1 job has to report to a grade 2, which has to report to a grade 3 and so on. If this happens, the result would be a series of overlayered reporting structures, simply to use all the grades available.

In the past, grade structures were characterized by a large number of relatively narrow grades. In such structures the emphasis was on separating clusters of jobs from one another rather than grouping clusters together. Currently, there is a growing tendency to develop grade structures with fewer, wider grades which can accommodate a number of job clusters, cater for higher role flexibility and emphasize pay progression based on performance, skill and competence rather than on climbing a promotion ladder. Increasingly, reward is by performance rather than by promotion.

Grade width
The width of a grade is determined by the variation in the size of the jobs placed in it. If a points-factor scheme is used which is based on arithmetical progression, grade widths can be defined in job scores. If geometrical progression is used, as in the Hay evaluation methodology, then grade widths are defined as percentages of the minimum job unit score for the grade.

Clearly the width of individual grades will depend on the range of job sizes to be included in the structure and policy decisions on the number of grades required to accommodate those jobs.

Given these overall structural considerations, the key factor in grade design is to minimize the disruption caused by the inherent discontinuities built into the structure through defining grade boundaries. The width of the grade, ie the range of job sizes incorporated into a grade, should allow for differentiation between the perceived key levels of responsibility in an organization. This differentiation may need to be very fine for fast growing and relatively young organizations but can be quite wide for mature and stable organizations.

Pay range size

The size of a pay range will be affected by the following factors:

- policy on the scope which should be allowed for pay progression within a range – this is perhaps the most important factor. The policy may vary at different levels in the organization – the ranges for more senior and innovative jobs may be larger because it is assumed that there is more scope for the contribution and competence of individual job holders to affect their results. Policy decisions in this area are clearly linked with pay progression policy as discussed below;
- assumptions on the average time people will take to achieve the fully competent level in the jobs within the grade;
- the time that employees normally spend in jobs – the shorter the stay the smaller the range;
- the amount of flexibility needed to fix pay for new or promoted employees – if the rate of pay has to be higher than the minimum because of the amount required to attract a new employee or to provide a reasonable increase in pay on promotion, then a larger range will still provide more room for pay progression in the grade;
- the amount of flexibility required to accommodate differences in the market rates of jobs in the grades. However, as mentioned above, when allocating jobs into grades the aim should be to group jobs together which are within a reasonably compact range of market rates. Where this is not possible, consideration has to be given to set up job family ranges for separate market groups.

Larger ranges emphasize the performance of individuals within the grade, while narrower ranges place more emphasis on job size and promotion. In practice, the concept of moving through a single large range or through a hierarchy of smaller ranges can be applied so as to produce similar effects for the organization and the individuals concerned. But more controls are required to prevent grade drift in a narrowly graded structure.

Pay range sizes vary considerably between organizations. For organizations with performance-related pay, range sizes are typically between 35–50 per cent above the range minima (spans of 85–115 per cent and 80–120 per cent respectively). Some organizations vary the size according to the level of job, for example, 15–25 per cent for the more routine operational and support jobs, 25–40 per cent for more demanding managerial, professional, scientific and technical jobs and 40–60 per cent for senior managerial jobs.

Organizations with fixed incremental systems or pay spines tend to have smaller ranges – about 20 per cent is typical – which allow for seven or eight increments of between about two and a half and three per cent (again, fairly common).

Range reference points

Reference points indicating the level of pay for a fully competent individual and the relationship of a pay range to market rates are frequently located at the mid-point of a pay range. It may be appropriate to provide for more or less space to progress to or beyond this point in a range, in which case the reference point would be placed, as required, above or below the midpoint, usually within the quartile range, ie between the lower and upper quartile.

Alignment with market rates

A critical design factor is how the pay structure should be aligned to market rates. The usual approach is to relate market rates to the reference point of the range in accordance with the organization's stance on how its pay levels should relate to market rates taking into account any variations between the market rates of jobs in the range.

The policy decision on market stance will be affected by the market information available and it may be expressed as a desire on the part of the organization to pay at the median, upper quartile or lower quartile of the range of pay established by pay surveys for the relevant population.

There is no reason why the same market stance policy should be adopted for all jobs. It may be thought that some grades should be treated differently. But care must be taken not to depart too far from the need to achieve a reasonable degree of equity.

Differentials

The pay structure has to provide for appropriate differentials between pay ranges for adjacent grades to reward the significant increase in job size achieved by moving to a job in a higher grade. It is also necessary to ensure in a reporting structure that a meaningful rise in pay is achievable on promotion. The amount clearly depends on the increase in job size resulting from the upgrading or promotion but it should never be less than 10–15 per cent and may well be considerably more at higher levels in the organization. It should be remembered that promotion in a conventional grade structure with overlapping pay ranges may often mean jumping one or more grades.

If differentials between ranges are too close – less than 10 per cent – many jobs become borderline cases and frequent reassessments are required. There may be endless arguments about gradings which cannot always be resolved by job evaluation.

If differentials between pay ranges covering jobs below senior management level are too high – more than 25 per cent – injustices may be done when jobs are considered to be on the borderline between grades, and it would not be easy to allow for the finer gradations that exist between job sizes in most organizations, except at the highest levels.

Experience has shown that in most organizations a differential of from 15–20 per cent is appropriate between all grades except at the highest level. Some companies leave top management out of the pay structure altogether – salaries at this level and therefore differentials are often a matter of individual negotiation and there may be a much larger proportion of total remuneration related to performance and therefore at risk.

A 15–20 per cent differential is large enough to provide an adequate increase to individuals who are promoted or upgraded. It also avoids an excessive number of grades and reduces endless arguments about marginal cases which too often result in grade drift when the differential is unduly small.

Differentials can be designed to widen progressively at higher levels where increases in job size between grades and on promotion are likely to be more significant. A structure can start with differentials of 15 per cent, which can increase to 20–25 per cent between ranges in the middle of the structure and to 30–40 per cent or more at the top end.

Overlap

Overlap between adjacent grades is a function of design decisions on ranges and differentials. It occurs when the size of the ranges in percentage terms is greater than the differential between them. Some overlap is generally desirable in the interests of flexibility but if it is 50 per cent or more, a double overlap will result which could cause confusion because people in one grade could be paid more than people in grades two steps higher.

It is therefore best to keep overlaps below 50 per cent – 30–40 per cent is a typical figure. This can be achieved by adjusting range size and/or differentials.

Pay progression

Pay progression policy decisions are necessary on the method of progression, progression criteria, the rate of progression and the extent to which individuals can penetrate into the range.

The method of progression can be by:

- fixed increments;
- semi-fixed increments (ie a service-related incremental scale which allows for higher, lower or additional increments depending on performance); or
- variable increments related to progression criteria.

Progression criteria can be length of service for fixed or semi-variable systems, or performance, contribution, skill or competence for variable systems. They can vary for different categories of employees. For example, a skill-based progression system as described in Chapter 26 could be used for skilled workers and technicians, and all other employees would be covered by a performance-based system as described in Chapter 17. Within one range, it is possible to have a progression system that provides for skills or competence-related increments to be paid up to the reference point and variable performance-related progression thereafter.

Policy on the rate at which individuals can progress through the range in relation to progression criteria will obviously be closely associated with decisions on range size. The decision will be affected by policies either on the size of increments in a fixed or semi-fixed incremental system, or on the range of pay increases that need to be catered for in a variable system for different categories of staff. This aspect of policy may be governed by tradition and culture, but it may also be influenced by the market place – the rate of progression provided by other organizations for comparable jobs.

The decision on the rate of progression required adequately to reward and motivate employees performing at different levels will be largely subjective. As a rule of thumb (if market movement is 6–7 per cent), people whose performance is outstanding may deserve and expect rewards of at least 10 per cent of their base rate. Above average performers (superior) may deserve increases of between 8–10 per cent, individuals who are progressing well in accordance with normal expectations (standard performance) may get from 5–7 per cent, while those who are making progress but not at the expected rate (developing) may be eligible for increases of between 3–4 per cent (performance-related increases of less than 3 per cent are probably not worth having). But these amounts vary considerably between different organizations and within an organization, depending on circumstances such as the rate of growth, the demands placed on people and, of course, ability to pay.

Policy on range penetration will determine whether or not there should be target rates of pay for different levels of performance (highly desirable in any performance-related pay system) and if so, where they should be positioned in the range.

Further consideration is given to pay progression systems in Chapter 17.

Grade structure design methods

There are two basic methods of pay structure design; the points-factor evaluation scheme method and the ranking/market rate method. Both of these have the same basic aim – to integrate data on internal and external relativities within a logical framework. The points-factor method is more analytical and can provide better guidance on the difficult task of fixing grade boundaries, but if that type of job evaluation is not used, the ranking/market rate method can produce acceptable results, although it is a more empirical process.

Points-factor evaluation scheme method

This method consists of six steps as described below.

Step 1
Plot the evaluation job scores against the current rates of pay for every job holder to produce a scattergram as shown in Figure 13.1. This provides a picture of the pay practices of the organization regarding the relationships between job size and pay. It enables the dispersal of pay for individual job holders to be analyzed to establish the extent to which larger rates of pay are attached to larger jobs and smaller rates to smaller jobs, ie the degree to which pay is commensurate with job size.

Step 2
Draw a line of central tendency or 'best fit', ie whatever line will minimize variations from it, as shown in Figure 13.2. This trend line can be drawn on the basis of

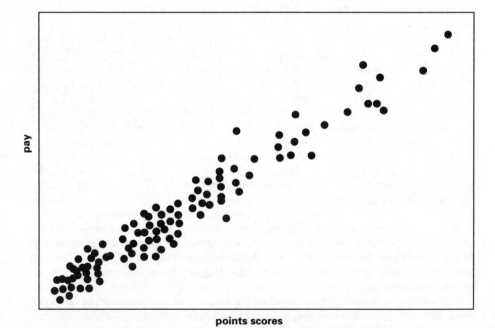

points scores

Figure 13.1 *Scattergram of pay and job evaluation scores*

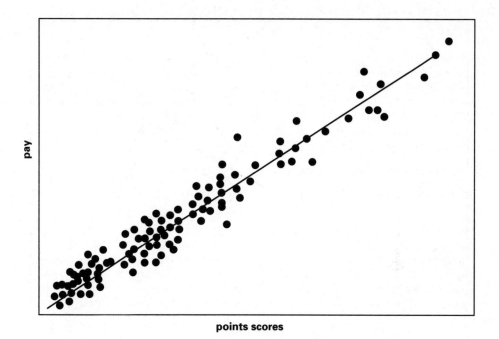

pay

points scores

Figure 13.2   *Trend line through scattergram to produce pay practice line*

visual judgement, the objective being to have roughly the same number of points above and below the line. Alternatively, it can be computed statistically by the method of least squares regression, but the latter method produces a degree of accuracy which is unnecessary in most situations.

This trend line is the pay practice line. It can be inspected to establish whether or not there is a reasonably smooth progression related to job size and pay. If there are marked deviations from the trend, this means that the groups or individuals concerned are being paid significantly more or less than is appropriate for their job size. Assuming the jobs have been evaluated properly – without regard to pay or anything other than job content – the only dependent variable is pay, as this is not a factor in allocating scores.

It may be established that high or low rates of pay related to job size are deliberate and justified. But if they are not, those paid well above the line can be 'red circled' and those well below can be 'green circled'. A decision can then be made either to live with these anomalies or to take steps to reduce them, possibly over a period of time.

Step 3
Obtain whatever information is available on market rates for bench mark jobs and plot the upper and lower quartile and median trend lines. Figure 13.3 illustrates this process, omitting the quartile lines for the sake of clarity. It shows the relationship between actual pay as pictured by the trend line and market rates. The pay practice line in this example is falling below the median market rates for larger sized jobs and this could be an unsatisfactory state of affairs. The value of this exercise depends on the number of accurate comparisons that can be made between actual and market rates of pay. Hay Management Consultant's surveys

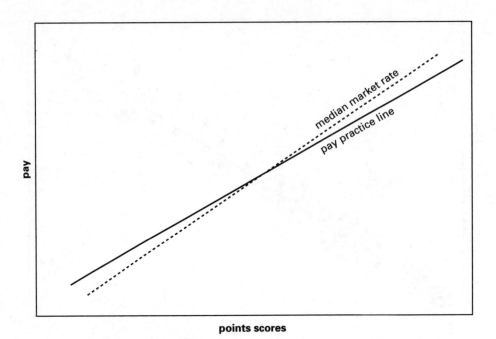

Figure 13.3 *Comparison of pay practice line and median market rate*

can provide a valuable basis for comparison because they use a common method of points evaluation to ensure that consistent comparisons are made between jobs of equivalent size.

Step 4
Decide the desired pay policy line on the basis of the organization's pay policy or pay stance and plot this as shown in Figure 13.4. The slope of the pay policy line represents the organization's policy on the rate at which it wants pay to progress through the job hierarchy. The relationship between policy and practice is also shown and this indicates any gaps which might indicate the need for remedial action, as in the Figure 13.4 example.

Step 5
Decide on the overall shape of the pay structure in relation to the policy line. This is the critical design stage when key decisions are made on the number of grades, the differentials between the pay ranges for adjacent grades, and the width of each grade in terms of points scores. Because of the number of interacting policy variables, an empirical approach is necessary, testing out alternatives against the general principles which underlay graded structures. The key principles are:

■ group together those jobs which are of similar size and separate those which are significantly different;
■ relate the number of grades to the number of distinct levels of responsibility in the hierarchy, bearing in mind the advantage of having grades which are wide enough to allow for role flexibility and career/pay progression based on performance, skill and competence rather than simply a promotion ladder;

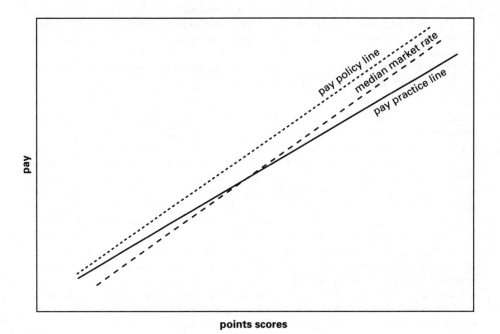

Figure 13.4 *Comparison of pay policy and practice lines with median market rates*

■ when deciding grade boundaries or cut-off points, aim to minimize the disruption which may be caused if there are too many borderline cases.

This step can be broken down into the following interconnected sub-stages:

1. Make an initial decision on the number of grades which may be appropriate, bearing in mind the range of jobs to be covered and taking a view on the desirable width of grades at each level. A start could be made with grade widths of, say, 15–20 per cent of the total points range depending on grade width policy.

2. Study how this arrangement accommodates the various job clusters taking note of any instances where the provisional grade boundaries or demarcation lines create discontinuities by cutting through clusters of related jobs.

3. Where there are boundary problems of this nature, adjust grade boundaries by such means as drawing demarcation lines between clusters where there is gap in the scores so that the discontinuities are minimized as far as possible. This may have to be done by trial and error, or on a 'what if' basis if computer assistance is available (computer programmes exist which assist in the development of a number of options to provide guidance on appropriate grade boundaries). It is inevitable that some jobs which are not significantly different in size will be separated by a grade boundary. It is always worthwhile re-examining the evaluation of these jobs to ensure that the demarcation line is justified.

4. Test the grade boundaries against the pay policy line to establish the implications on pay differentials. If these are not acceptable, further options may

have to be tested until a structure emerges which is on balance satisfactory. This is a process of optimization which should aim to produce a workable structure rather than a structure which corresponds to some unattainable ideal.

5. Draw the final grade demarcation lines established in this way on the pay scattergram as shown in Figure 13.5.

Step 6

Define the pay ranges for each grade as in Figure 13.6, taking into account the considerations affecting the size or span of pay ranges and the provision to be made for pay progression as discussed earlier in this chapter (pages 187–8). Account should also be taken of how the pay range structure relates to market rates as shown by the pay policy line. The reference point of each range would normally be where the pay policy line cuts through the midpoint of the span of points which define the width of the grade. This might have to be adjusted empirically depending on the distribution of jobs in the grade. Attention would have to be paid to the grade overlaps which emerge from this process. If the size of the overlaps causes problems, further adjustments may have to be made to range size and/or grade width. These are all interacting variables, and again, a trial and error or 'what if' process might have to be followed.

An example is given in Table 13.1 of the graded pay structure covering jobs paid between £10,000–£27,250 (individual job ranges might be used above this level) which this procedure might produce. This structure has pay differentials of around 15 per cent and pay ranges of around 30 per cent. By superimposing this structure on the scattergram of actual pay as illustrated in Figure 13.7, a visual check can be made to identify anomalies and potential boundary problems.

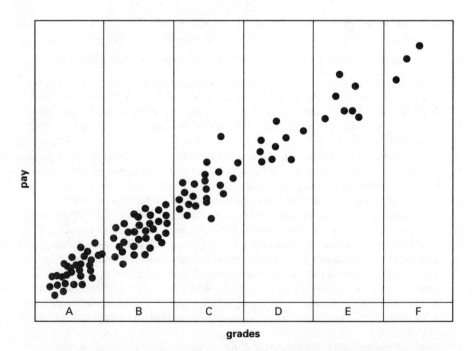

Figure 13.5 *Grade boundaries superimposed on scattergram*

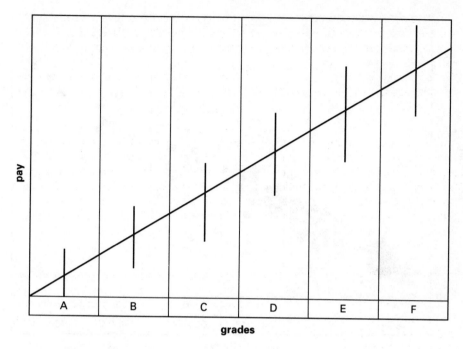

Figure 13.6 *Pay ranges superimposed on a grade structure*

Ranking/market rate method

If a points-factor job evaluation scheme has not been used, the ranking/market rate method provides an alternative. It consists of the following five steps:

Step 1
Rank bench mark jobs and plot their actual rates of pay to give the pay practice line as shown in Figure 13.8.

Step 2
Plot market rate information on the bench mark jobs on the chart and derive a 'best fit' pay policy line as shown in Figure 13.9. In this example the pay policy line passes through the median market rates for each bench mark job.

Table 13.1 *A graded pay structure based on points-factor job evaluation*

Grade	Pay range (£)		Points range	
	minimum	*maximum*	*minimum*	*maximum*
A	10,000	13,000	250	349
B	11,500	15,250	350	449
C	13,250	17,500	450	549
D	16,000	21,250	550	649
E	18,250	24,250	650	749
F	21,250	27,250	750	849

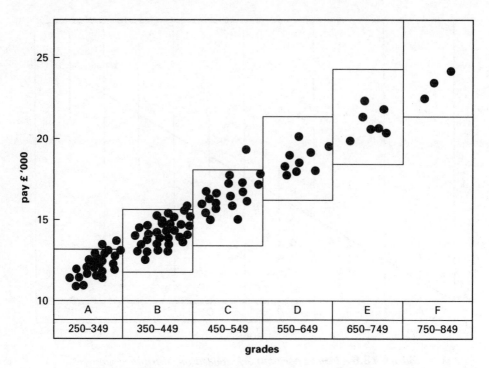

Figure 13.7   *Distribution of pay in a graded structure*

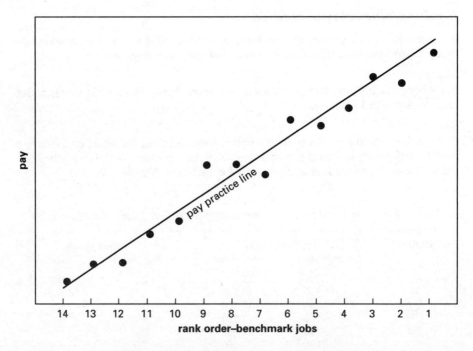

Figure 13.8   *Ranking pay practice line*

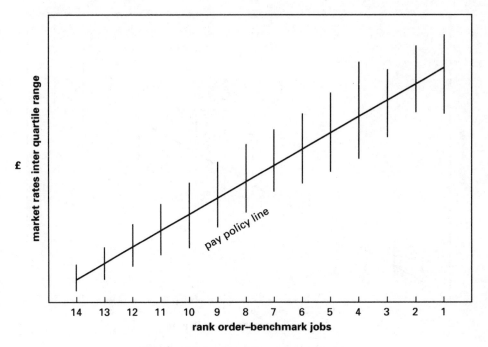

Figure 13.9 *Ranking pay policy line*

Step 3
Using the pay policy line as the midpoint guideline, plot the upper and lower limits of the pay range for each bench mark job in accordance with range size policy, eg plus and minus 15 per cent of the midpoint as shown in Figure 13.10.

Step 4
Develop the grade structure as shown in Figure 13.11, bearing in mind the principles set out above (page 188). This means deciding on the number of grades and grouping jobs within them by placing a dividing line between adjacent jobs in the rank order. This division can be invidious if, as is often the case, the difference between the size of the jobs on either side of the boundary is insignificant. An attempt can be made to fix the cut-off points in the rank order for each grade by identifying clusters of jobs at successive levels in the rank order which are thought to be of a similar size. But this is a largely subjective process. There are no rules on how to do it. Guidance may be sought from any natural promotion ladders in the organization although this has to be done with caution – it is undesirable simply to reproduce an existing hierarchy.

As illustrated in Figure 13.11, it is only possible to show the distribution of actual rates of pay along the line of the pay range because ranking gives no indication of relative job size. Grade boundary problems cannot therefore be detected and analysed except by subjective judgement.

The aim is to allocate jobs into grades on a felt-fair basis, so that job gradings conform to people's perceptions about the broad levels of responsibility in the organization. Experimentation to obtain a reasonably acceptable allocation of jobs into grades will probably have to take place at this stage. Adjustments may have to

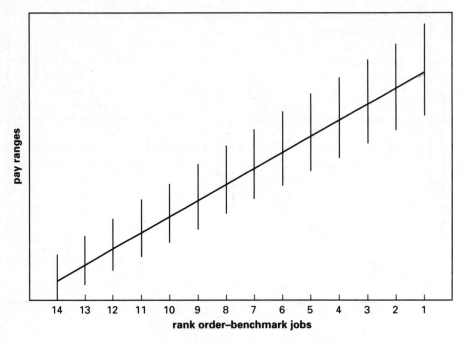

Figure 13.10   *Ranked bench mark job pay ranges*

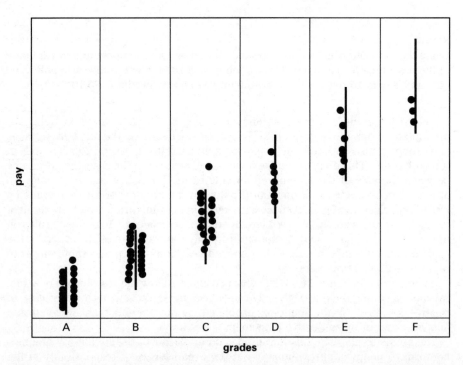

Figure 13.11   *Graded pay structure following ranking exercise and showing
actual pay against pay ranges for grades*

be made to the number of grades to produce what on balance is likely to be considered a satisfactory result.

Account will, however, have to be taken of market rate indicators. If a felt-fair grade and pay range structure produce any serious external relativity anomalies these may have to be dealt with as separate cases. It is difficult sometimes to avoid having to compromise between the principles of internal equity and external competitiveness. But if, for good reason, internal equity principles cannot be adhered to in full, then such modifications should be carefully explained to those concerned.

Grade definitions can be drawn up which broadly indicate the characteristics of jobs eligible for allocation to a particular grade, as in the job classification system of job evaluation described in Chapter 9.

If an acceptable grade structure can not be devised, consideration should be given to adopting an individual job grade structure, especially at higher levels, although these are normally associated with points-factor schemes. The difficulty of basing individual ranges or, indeed, grades on a ranking exercise is an argument in favour of points-factor evaluation.

Step 5
Define the pay ranges for each grade. This is done by referring to the midpoints of the market rate range for bench mark jobs in the grade as recorded by the pay policy line.

Individual job range structure design

The design of an individual job range structure is essentially a matter of establishing internal relativities through job evaluation, usually a points-factor scheme, and then pricing jobs by reference to market rates. This establishes the spot rate or pay reference point for the jobs in accordance with the organization's pay stance. Where reliable market rate data are not available for a job its rate can be determined by comparing its evaluation with jobs for which such data do exist and positioning it accordingly.

Some individual job range structures are influenced more by the results of job evaluation than by market comparisons. Others are market-led in the sense that the market-related pricing takes place first and the relative position of jobs determined in this way is checked against the results of job evaluation. Strongly market-led organizations may ignore disparities between the internal size and external value of the job. Others deal with this situation by the use of market premiums.

When the job has been priced, a pay range is built round the reference point. The considerations discussed earlier in this chapter will determine the size of the range, which could vary between different jobs.

Job family structure design

Designing a job family structure is a matter of identifying the distinct job families which constitute either a market group or a discrete area of activity such as systems analysis or accounting. In each of such areas job holders need distinctive skills or competences which increase at successive levels of responsibility.

The number of families will depend on the complexity, size and structure of the organization. Judgement is required in deciding on the number to be created – too many could lead to administrative complications and difficulties in distinguishing between categories. The key factor in making the selection is that there should be a marked and measurable difference between job families in terms of market rates and/or the range of activities carried out and skill requirements.

A grade structure is then developed for each job family in the same way as a normal graded structure.

Pay curve structure design

The design of a pay curve structure involves the following steps:

1. Identify the job families to be catered for by pay curves. These will probably not cover all the jobs in the organization as pay curves are most suitable for scientific, engineering, technical and professional jobs where the jobs are associated with the same area of activity or function and use the same basic skills, but operate at different levels of skill, competence and responsibility.
2. Define the competence levels or bands for each job family. This requires the following actions:
    - decide what different levels of competence are appropriate for the job family. The number of bands will obviously be related to the range of distinct competence levels but it is usually three or four. More than four or five bands can create an undesirably complex structure;
    - name each band, eg development engineer, senior development engineer, principal development engineer;
    - analyse and define in detail the competence levels in each band as described in Chapter 8;
    - as necessary, reconsider the number of bands and their nomenclature – it may sometimes be necessary to divide too broad a competence band into two or three sub-bands.
3. Obtain market rate data and plot the market rates of progression for jobs in the family through the bands as shown in Figure 13.12.
4. Decide on the basis of the organization's market stance how pay progression through the bands for individuals who achieve the required level of competence at each stage should be related to market rates as shown in Figure 13.13.
5. Define the progression rates and pay ranges for each competence band according to a performance and/or competence rating. There could, for example, be four rating levels depending on the rate at which competence develops:
    - *basic* for those at the beginning of their career in the job family;
    - *developing* for those progressing at a reasonably satisfactory rate but not as fast or as well as might be expected;
    - *effective* for those who are progressing at the expected rate;
    - *highly effective* for those who are progressing at a significantly higher rate than the expected rate.

A job family pay curve matrix could then be drawn up as in Table 13.2.

Spot rate structure design

In a spot rate structure the individual rates for each job are determined by reference to market rates and in accordance with the organization's pay stance. When reliable market rate data are not available for a job its rate is fixed by comparison with the market priced jobs. This comparison may be carried out by job evaluation but smaller high-growth companies may dispense with this formality.

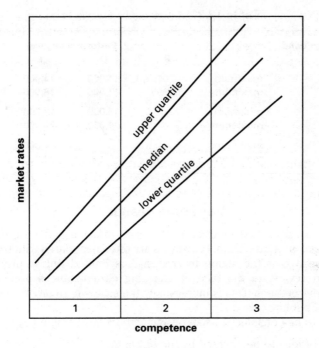

Figure 13.12   *Pay curve – competence related market rates*

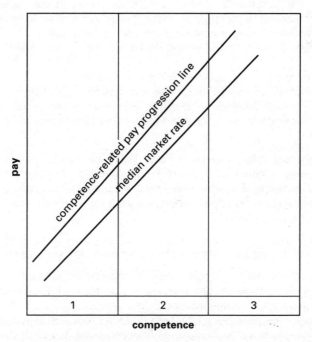

Figure 13.13   *Competence-related pay progression line for pay curve*

Table 13.2 *A pay curve matrix*

Competence band		Performance level			
		B	D	E	HE
1	minimum	14,000	14,000	14,000	14,000
	maximum	16,000	17,000	18,000	19,000
2	minimum		17,000	18,000	19,000
	maximum		21,000	24,000	27,000
3	minimum			24,000	27,000
	maximum			32,000	36,000

Pay spine design

A pay spine, as described in Chapter 12, is in effect a series of overlapping incremental scales stood on end. Pay spines are often negotiated with trade unions which can mean that the scope for redesign is limited unless provisions for flexibility and review in the face of changing circumstances are part of the negotiating environment. This is increasingly the case where pay spines are used within the UK public service.

The points to be considered when designing or redesigning a pay spine are:

- the range of jobs to be covered by the pay spine;
- the number of grades to be incorporated into the pay spine and the allocation of jobs into those grades – this is usually carried out by job evaluation (points-factor or, frequently, job classification);
- the size of the increments needed at different points in the spine – there is typically a standard percentage increase throughout the scale of the order of two and a half to three per cent between each spine point;
- the pay ranges for each grade as defined by the spine points allocated to each grade;
- the extent of any overlap between job grade scales;
- whether or not there should be an element of performance-related pay in the system, eg extra or withheld increments, part increments, or 'range points' at the top of each job scale to enable highly rated individuals to receive extra increments.

An example of a pay spine is given in Table 13.3. This has 11 grades with either seven or eight spine points to each grade. Grades overlap by between two and five spine points. The value of a spine point ranges from £255 in grade A to £897 in grade K. In percentage terms, progression is at an even rate (either 2.67 or 2.77 per cent in a grade).

Designing pay structures for manual workers

Where there are trade unions, pay structures for manual workers are usually not so much designed as negotiated, although each side may well have an optimum design built into its negotiating strategy.

In non-unionized organizations or where there is scope for negotiation, design decisions will be made on the choice of between what is in effect a spot rate structure (fixed base or day rates) and some form of graded structure. Con-

Table 13.3 *A pay spine*

Grade	Spine points	Pay (£)
A	1–8	9,208–11,248
B	5–12	10,323–12,611
C	8–14	11,248–13,353
D	11–17	12,255–14,548
E	14–20	13,353–15,851
F	18–25	14,970–18,287
G	24–31	17,771–21,708
H	30–37	21,097–25,770
I	36–43	25,044–30,592
J	41–48	28,892–35,293
K	45–52	32,392–39,568

sideration may also be given to the merits of an integrated structure, which is normally graded.

Decisions also have to be made on any payment-by-results element in the pay package (see Chapter 18) and on plus rates for special skills, working conditions and overtime. The possibility of skill-based pay (see Chapter 26) could also be considered.

Pay levels and relativities are determined by negotiation and/or market rate surveys and job evaluation. Design decisions on a spot rate or graded structure are based on the same principles and procedures as were described earlier in this chapter.

Implementation

The outcome of a pay structure design or redesign exercise should be presented in the form of:

- an analysis of the job evaluation results;
- an analysis of the market survey results;
- a statement of the policies and principles governing the design of the structure. This will cover such design considerations as market stance policy, reasons for proposing a particular type of structure, size and width of grades, size of differentials and pay progression policies;
- proposals on the grade and pay structure – as there is always some choice, it may be desirable to list alternatives and their pros and cons;
- an analysis of the implications of the proposed structure covering costs, the existence of anomalies and any problems in repositioning employees in the new or amended structure;
- a programme for implementing the structure covering repositioning, the treatment of anomalies and phasing increases in pay to control costs;
- proposals on how employees should be informed about the proposed structure and how it will affect them.

Treating anomalies

The repositioning of employees in the new structure will reveal anomalies in the shape of individuals who are either over or undergraded. It has to be accepted that a structure design programme is likely to be costly because, while undergraded employees must be upgraded with an increase in their pay, overgraded employees do not usually suffer a reduction in pay, although future pay increases may be restricted.

When dealing with undergraded employees, steps may have to be taken to mitigate the costs of bringing employees up to the new rate in one jump. This could take the form of restricted increases to, say, 5 per cent of present pay in one year and, if this increase does not overcome an anomaly, phasing the balance of the increases over a number of years, limiting any single increase to 5 per cent. There may be limits to adopting this approach in times of acute market pressure or skills shortage.

It can be argued, especially if fixed incremental scales still exist, that employees should be placed in the same position in their new grade as they were in the old one, thus retaining the benefit of the increments or performance-related pay they earned in their old grade. There is some logic to this argument, which is often advanced by trade unions when pay structures are negotiated. But if it is accepted, the costs could be considerable even though the employee relations payback may also be high.

Overgraded employees could have their pay frozen or red circled at their present levels until the anomaly is eliminated, although they might still be eligible for across-the-board structural increases. But this approach could be considered inequitable if employees were denied the performance-related increases to which they were previously entitled. One method of dealing with this problem is to make such employees eligible for achievement bonuses, which would not permanently increase their base pay. Another method adopted by some organizations is to create a 'personal-to-job holder' grade which allows valued individuals to progress to the maximum allowed for in their old grade.

Informing employees – a critical success factor

It is important to plan communications to employees about the new structure carefully. If the structure is fully disclosed, as is increasingly the case, its rationale should be explained in full. Individuals should be told how the new arrangements will affect them irrespective of whether or not pay policies and structures are communicated generally.

When communicating the results it should be remembered that any job evaluation and restructuring exercise will create expectations among some employees of massive pay increases. These expectations can be managed if not eliminated by careful briefing before the start of the review which should play down the possibility of general increases and emphasize that, although the result should be a more rational and equitable structure which will benefit all concerned, cost considerations will have to be taken into account when implementing the structure and these might restrict any increases. It could also be pointed out that experience has shown that previous structures are unlikely to have got the whole rank order wrong – only a small proportion usually need to be changed.

After the exercise the communication should present the new arrangements and explain:

- why the exercise was undertaken (reinforcing the original briefing);
- the benefits to all concerned;
- how it will be implemented, including the way in which special cases (anomalies) will be treated;

- to whom people should talk to find out more or to clarify the arrangements and implications.

Major changes should be supported by an information pack which explains them in clear and simple language and is backed up by graphics.

PART 5

PERFORMANCE MANAGEMENT

14

Performance Management – Philosophy

The concept of performance management has been one of the most important and positive developments in the sphere of reward management in the last five years. It began to take shape in the late 1980s, growing out of the realization that a more continuous and integrated approach was needed to manage and reward performance. All too often, crudely developed and hastily implemented performance-related pay and appraisal systems were not delivering the results that, somewhat naively, people were expecting from them.

Performance management emerged as a key business process and a major lever for achieving culture change in the early 1990s, when it became increasingly evident that it could play an important part in an integrated system of human resource management as one of a number of mutually reinforcing processes. The overall architecture of this approach is illustrated in Figure 14.1

As a process for managing and rewarding people, performance management is underpinned by a philosophy. It is important to understand what this is before introducing performance management, and in this chapter we analyze the underlying philosophy in some detail, having first defined performance management and discussed its aims and main features. We describe the basic methods of implementing performance management in the next chapter.

Definition

Performance management is a means of getting better results from the organization, teams and individuals by understanding and managing performance within an agreed framework of planned goals, objectives and standards.

It can be defined as a process or set of processes for establishing shared understanding about what *is* to be achieved, and of managing and developing

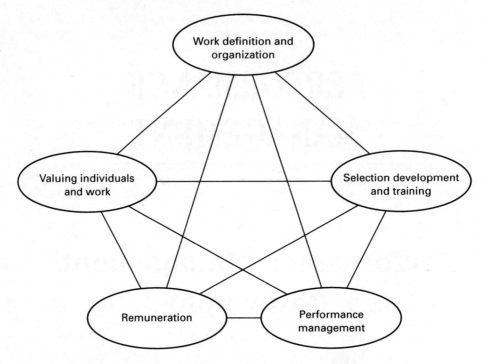

Figure 14.1 *Integrated Human Resource Management*

people in a way which increases the probability that it *will* be achieved in the short and longer term.

Overall aim

The overall aim of performance management is to establish a culture in which managers, individuals and groups take responsibility for the continuous improvement of business processes and of their own skills, competencies and contributions.

Features of performance management

Performance management is concerned with the interrelated processes of work, management, personal development and reward. It acts as a powerful integrating force, ensuring that these processes are linked together. It should be regarded as a process (or series of processes) rather than a management system or set of procedures. This process takes the form of a systematic approach to the management of people, using qualitative as well as quantitative goals, measurement, constructive feedback and recognition as a means of motivating them to realize their maximum potential. It embraces all formal or informal methods adopted by an organization and its managers to increase commitment and individual and corporate effectiveness. It is a much broader concept than performance appraisal or performance-related pay (PRP). These can indeed be important elements in the performance management process, but they will be part of an integrated approach, which consists of an interlocking series of processes, attitudes and behaviours which together produce a coherent strategy for adding value and improving results. We therefore believe that the term performance appraisal is outdated, implying as it often does a 'top down' process associated with what has all too often become a dishonest annual ritual designed to deliver a performance rating to fulfil the demands of a PRP scheme. We also believe that the chequered history of the last five years or so indicates clearly that without effective performance management, performance-related pay can not deliver acceptable performance driven pay differentials. The most positive benefits from PRP initiatives come from the clarity about performance expectations achieved, sometimes for the first time, with the implementation of performance management. This is clear from the research evidence quoted later in this chapter as well as from our own empirical experience.

Perhaps the most important thing to remember about performance management is that it is a *continuous* process shared between managers and the people for whom they are responsible. It is about improving both results and the quality of working relationships. Good performance management means that people are clearer about what their priorities are, what they should be doing currently, what they should be aiming for and how well this contributes to both team and organizational performance. It grows from open, positive and constructive discussion between managers, individuals and teams to produce agreement on how to focus on doing the job better.

How effective performance management works

The way in which effective performance management works is illustrated in Figure 14.2. It starts at corporate level with the definition of the organization's mission, strategy and objectives. These lead to the definitions of functional or departmental missions, plans and objectives.

Performance agreements (sometimes also called performance contracts) are then made between individuals and their managers which set out principal accountabilities or main tasks, the objectives (which will typically include task and personal development objectives) and standards of performance associated with these accountabilities and work and personal development plans.

The competences or behaviours required to fulfil job requirements may also be agreed. These may be generic competences developed within the organization for particular jobs or job families. Alternatively or additionally, they may be individually determined behavioural competences defined by an agreement between the manager and the individual of what sort of behaviour is expected from the latter to meet job requirements.

A combination of definitions of what has to be achieved in terms of objectives or targets linked to outputs and/or tasks and how they are to be achieved in terms of behavioural competences has proved very powerful and is perhaps the most important development in performance management practices in recent years. Indeed in some jobs, eg lawyers, airline cabin crew, hotel receptionists, the 'how' element is by far the dominant determinant of performance. For these and similar jobs, as well as for mainstream roles, the inclusion of properly researched and defined competences has made a major contribution to the management of total performance. Experience in a growing number of organizations has shown that if people are given descriptions and behavioural models of what constitutes successful performance in their immediate environment, as well as the developmental steps they need to take to achieve this, then they will have been given the best possible opportunity to deliver performance improvements.

In an effective performance management process, the performance of individuals and their development is reviewed continuously as part of the normal process of management. It is certainly not deferred to a formal performance review at the end of the year when it will have lost its immediacy and where the relative formality of the proceedings may militate against a constructive discussion. In this process there is a strong foundation of positive reinforcement and constructive problem solving. Effective performance is reinforced with praise, recognition and the opportunity to take on more responsible work. Less effective performance is dealt with as it happens by reiterating the standards and competences required, indicating areas for improvement, and jointly agreeing the actions required to produce improvements. Coaching and counselling are defined as core management skills and used as required to enable continuing performance competence.

There is typically a periodic formal review which, in effect, is a stocktaking exercise, but its emphasis is on looking forward to the next period and jointly redefining the performance agreement rather than raking over past events. The review is concerned with three aspects of the individual's performance (the three C's):

- *contribution* – what the individual has achieved in relation to the objectives, performance standards and work plans contained in the performance agreement and the contribution the individual has made to achieving team, departmental and organizational objectives;
- *competence* – the level of competence reached by the individual in each area of job behaviour as specified in the performance agreement;
- *continuous development* – the progress the individual is making in developing skills and competence and in improving performance on a continuing basis.

The review leads to a jointly revised performance agreement and, if a performance-related pay scheme is in operation, to a decision on a pay increase.

One of the key beneficial features of a fully developed performance management process is the communication of strategies, plans and objectives throughout the organization and the opportunity this gives for upward contributions to the formulation of objectives. Another key positive feature is the means it provides for clarifying roles, performance standards, objectives and competence requirements leading to the joint agreement of work and personal development and training plans.

Philosophy

The philosophy of performance management is based upon the following concepts:

- the need for a process of management which supports the achievement of the business strategy by integrating corporate, functional, departmental, team and individual objectives;
- the need for this process to be based on values which enable it to support other organizational initiatives such as total quality, customer service and business process re-engineering;
- the importance of communicating the organization's mission and goals to all employees and the need to provide for an upward process of contributing to the formulation of the corporate objectives;

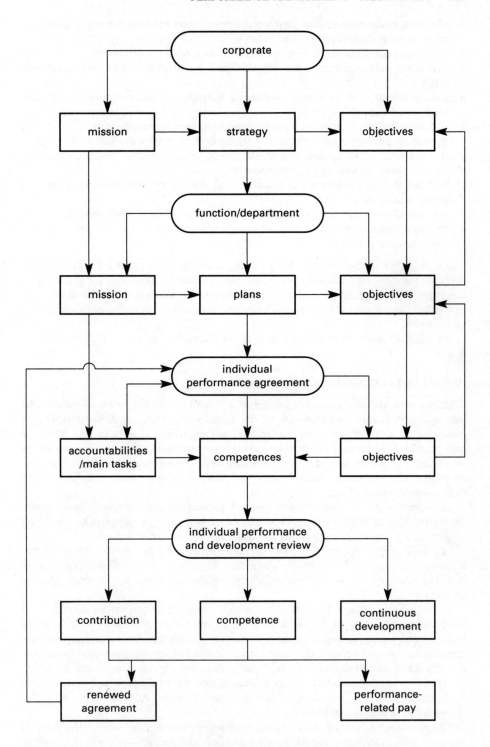

Figure 14.2 *Performance management*

- the need to develop and maintain a process which enables the organization to fulfil its responsibility for its members;
- the need to enable employees to manage their own performance;
- the importance of managing expectations – clarifying roles and responsibilities;
- the significance of the input, processes, output, outcomes sequence in managing performance;
- the importance of creating a partnership between managers and their staff in managing performance – managing by agreement rather than by command;
- the importance of measurement, feedback, reinforcement and 'contingency management' in managing performance;
- the belief that performance management should be regarded as a natural process of management;
- the use of performance management to develop a 'learning organization';
- the significant concept of empowering employees through the performance management processes.

Taken together we believe that they enable individuals and teams to work better because they are clear about where the organization is going and what part they are expected to play, they receive the support and feedback they need and they are rewarded for their achievements across the whole spectrum of personal motivation.

We discuss each of these aspects of performance management philosophy below.

Achieving the business strategy

Clarity about overall business strategy and values lies at the heart of successful management. Businesses that lack clarity about where they are going and why (a besetting problem in parts of the public service where this is at the whim of politicians and sometimes very short-term) rarely prove fertile ground in which to implement durable performance management processes. Although, in our experience, attempting to do this may well force a debate on strategy that might not otherwise take place.

An effective performance management process should develop employees' understanding of what needs to be achieved, help them to improve organizational performance and reward them on the basis of their contribution.

The role of performance management in supporting the achievement of the business strategy is fulfilled by providing a means of integrating objectives downwards, upwards and laterally throughout the organization. This operates as follows.

The top-down process provides for the objectives agreed for senior managers to be directly related to what they need to achieve to contribute fully to the attainment of corporate strategies. Senior managers in turn agree objectives with the members of their management team, spelling out the contribution the latter are expected to make in enabling their division, function etc. to meet its targets. This provides a valuable opportunity to look laterally, discuss interdependencies and how these can be managed positively. An example of a matrix of interdependencies is given in Figure 14.3.

The process of integration continues with less senior jobs where the overall purpose, main tasks and performance standards and targets are defined in a way that is consistent with higher level objectives. Again, such staff have the oppor-

A business targets/senior jobs matrix

Business targets \ names	Deryk Smith	John Craig	Christine Lutyens	Colin Groom	Emma Jones	John Evans	Stuart Philby	John Home	Steve Foster
1. Net trading profit	P	P	P-C		S	S	S	S	S
2. Sales		S	P-C		S		P		
3. Manufacturing / Marketing		S	S		S	P	S	S	P
4. Output		S		S		P		P	
5. Airborne pollution equipment		S (pre-sanction)		P		S		S (post-sanction)	
6. Liquid gas plant			S	P					
7. Manpower productivity	P	S	S	S	S	S	S		S
8. Safety	S	S	S	S	S	P	S	S	P
9. ISO 9000		S	S	S	S	P	S		P
10. Quality	P	S	S		S	S	S	S	S

Key: P = Personal accountability   S = Shared responsibility   C = Policy / facilitating contribution

Figure 14.3   *An example of a matrix of interdependencies*

tunity to make their views known about their role and how they can best contribute to the achievement of departmental and team objectives.

This process is repeated at each level of the organization so that the objectives agreed are consistent with those agreed for the next higher layer and based on the same values. This provides for a link between the objectives set for office and shop floor workers and other employees who are responsible for basic organizational activities and those set at corporate level.

Clearly, the fewer levels there are the greater the chance of achieving consistency throughout the organization; and this combined with speed of decision-making and response is one of the most powerful arguments for flatter organization structures.

Accompanying this process of delayering organizations there is a general trend towards pushing more accountability downwards. This is forcing line managers to introduce better ways of planning and budgeting, and in this environment they have to take objective setting more seriously.

Performance management also enables people to contribute to the formulation of objectives and get closer to the core of the business planning process within the business planning cycle. This is an upward process which provides employees at different levels with the opportunity to contribute to the development, not only of their own objectives, but also of those for their team, department, function, division or the organization as a whole.

Communications

Effective performance management provides a basis for the communication to all employees of the organization's mission, values and objectives. The mission statement provides the framework for the organization's strategies and goals and these can be transmitted and discussed with employees through the processes described above. The organization's values can be built into output and behaviourally-based objectives at all levels and one of the key factors in assessing performance will be the extent to which the individual's behaviour upholds these values.

As mentioned earlier, performance management also provides a very helpful vehicle for upward and lateral communication. Individuals and teams can be encouraged to formulate their own objectives and to discuss how they relate to higher level goals as well as those in related areas of activity and how they can best be achieved.

Increasingly, performance management provides scope for upward assessment; individuals can comment on the leadership, guidance and support provided by their managers, and on any organizational constraints which prevent them from achieving their objectives. This is typically done through the medium of confidential questionnaires whose aggregated results are fed back to individual managers as part of their own personal development process. Leading employers such as BP have found that this is a powerful tool for achieving culture change and in the development of a more enabling rather than 'command and control' management style. In the case of BP, assessment is against its 'OPEN' generic management competences – shown in Figure 14.4.

The implementation of performance management can provide a valuable opportunity to communicate new organizational values signalling a change in culture. In Figure 15.3 we give the 'Vision and Guiding Principles' used by an organization in the finance sector to signal a move away from a traditional

OPEN THINKING

PERSONAL IMPACT

- Bias for action
- Knows what makes others tick
- Concern for impact
- Self confidence

EMPOWERING

- Coaching and developing
- Building team success
- Motivating

NETWORKING

- Influencing others
- Reaching others
- Sharing achievement

Source: Proceedings of 'The Competent Organization' Conference 1993

Figure 14.4   *The BP OPEN generic management competencies*

appraisal process and a considered move away from a traditional hierarchy to a more open culture founded on higher levels of trust.

THE PERFORMANCE MANAGEMENT PROCESS IN XYZ GROUP

Vision

- To underpin and support the group's business vision and strategy and promote flexible responses to changing business circumstances.
- To deliver a series of processes that produces measurable/observable profit and other business related performance improvements.
- To help develop a culture based on joint understanding over what is expected and commitment to achieve it, where good performance is recognized and rewarded and poor performance is addressed fairly, constructively and speedily.
- To provide a sound basis for performance assessments, career moves, promotions and pay decisions in which staff can have confidence.

Guiding principles

- To exist as a continuing dialogue through the year between managers and staff supported by a minimum of documentation. This dialogue will take account of changing circumstances through the year as they occur.

- To help reinforce understanding of the business and the need for good teamwork as well as individual performance improvement.
- To focus effort/skill/competency where it is most needed.
- To help build the skill base of the group to empower staff, to improve their performance and so encourage and deliver flexibility.
- To help build an open, honest debate about continuing performance improvement at all levels.
- To be capable of being monitored, adapted and changed to run with the grain of the business as it evolves.

Fulfilling organizational responsibilities

The organization has the corporate responsibility for enabling its employees to contribute to the satisfaction of both their own needs and those of the organization. Besides setting clear corporate objectives and individual or team targets, this requires the implementation of a policy of human resource development which provides for coaching, counselling and training on a continuing basis.

Enabling employees to manage their own performance and development

Performance management is not just a system driven by managements to manage the performance of their employees. Rather it is a process which enables employees to manage their own performance and development within the framework of clear objectives and standards which have been agreed jointly with their managers. This does not absolve management from their responsibility to develop employees through counselling and training. But it does place people in a situation where they are more in control of the consequences of their actions. This can increase their sense of responsibility. It also helps them to achieve what Maslow[1] refers to as 'self-actualization' which he defined as 'the need to develop potentialities and skills; to become what one believes one is capable of becoming'.

Performance management can therefore help people to develop themselves and this accords with Drucker's[2] view that:

'Development is always self development. Nothing could be more absurd than for the enterprise to assume responsibility for the development of a man. The responsibility rests with the individual, his abilities, his efforts'.

But he goes on to say:

'Every manager in a business has the opportunity to encourage individual self-development or to stifle it, to direct it or to misdirect it. He should be specifically assigned the responsibility for helping all people working with him to focus, direct and apply their self-development efforts productively.'

Managing expectations

Performance management is based on agreed definitions of the contribution employees are expected to make in achieving the purpose of their team, department or function and the organization as a whole. This involves the clarification of accountabilities, main tasks and objectives. It also means spelling out the competences required to carry out the role effectively. Expectations about required performance levels and competences are therefore defined and a basis is provided for managing those expectations so that they are fulfilled. The management of expectations is a joint process requiring managers and individuals to act in partnership.

The input, process, output, outcome model

Performance management is concerned with:

- *Inputs:* the skills, knowledge and personal characteristics individuals apply to their jobs.
- *Process:* how individuals behave in carrying out their work – the behavioural competences they bring to fulfilling their accountabilities.
- *Outputs:* the measurable results achieved by individuals according to the level of performance they achieve in carrying out their tasks.
- *Outcomes:* the impact of what has been achieved by the performance of individuals on the results of their team, department, unit or function and, ultimately, the organization. This is their *contribution*, which is the ultimate measure of their effectiveness in their jobs.

The distinction between inputs, process, outputs and outcomes can be illustrated by reference to the job of a training manager, one of whose objectives is to plan and deliver a new training programme. Performance on this task would be measured by reviewing:

- *inputs:* the knowledge and skill deployed by the training manager in planning the course;
- *process:* the effectiveness with which training skills are used in conducting and evaluating the course;
- *outputs:* the quality of the courses themselves in terms of their content, presentation and administration;
- *outcomes:* the impact made by the training on the performance of participants.

Performance appraisal systems traditionally concentrated on inputs and, to a certain degree, process. They asked managers to assess personality traits and behaviour under such headings as initiative, willingness and relationships with people. The problem was that the ratings were highly subjective – the personality traits identified had never been validated for their relevance to performance competence and there were no standards for exercising judgements on these characteristics. Managers were asked to 'play at being God' and they were not good at it.

In contrast, the management by objectives (M by O) approach developed in the 1960s by John Humble and others concentrated purely on outputs. The philosophical basis of M by O was immaculate within its limits, but it tended to become a mechanistic system which bogged managers down in paper work. It was also introduced at a time when business planning processes were often rudimentary, budgeting procedures at best, and when there were no corporate vision and values to communicate. It was therefore largely discredited and was replaced by the concept of 'results orientated appraisal' which avoided the elaborate procedures associated with M by O. However, the effectiveness of both these systems suffered because they concentrated on outputs. They tended to expect managers to quantify the unquantifiable, so that targets became artificial and short-term – at worst *anything* to provide some comfort to top management that the idea had been taken on board. They neglected the longer-term outcomes (which were often difficult to quantify) and, worse, they deflected the assessors from considering the inputs and processes which produced the result. Thus insufficient attention was paid to what is sometimes referred to as 'behaviour modification', ie analyzing the behavioural factors or competences contributing to outcomes and associated with excellent performance and deciding what needs to be done to get better results by changing that behaviour.

Performance management processes emphasize the importance of outcomes (contribution), which the individual influences, as well as immediate outputs. They analyze inputs and processes to determine development and training needs and provide the basis for performance improvement plans. They will be concerned with diagnosing correctly whether differential performance is a function of the individual's motivation or is a result of his or her ability. The way in which people are managed, the resources they are given and the external factors beyond their control are also taken into account.

The analysis and diagnosis will be closely linked to specifications of behavioral requirements. These will be focused on the competence required to achieve the objectives associated with the individual's role but they will also deal with wider organizational objectives, especially those concerned with the support of values such as quality, customer service, teamworking and flexibility.

The philosophy of performance management is therefore holistic. It takes an all-embracing view of the constituents of good performance; how this contributes to desired outcomes at the departmental and organizational level, and what needs to be done to improve these outcomes. This is entirely consistent with the HRM philosophy of treating employees as valued assets and investing in their management and development in order to enhance their value.

Management by agreement

The essence of the performance management process is that it is a partnership between managers and the individuals who are members of their teams. This means that at every stage the aim is to obtain joint agreement on roles, account-abilities, tasks, objectives and competence requirements, on the means of measuring performance, on the assessment of results and the factors affecting them, and on development and performance improvement plans.

This is management by agreement or contract rather than management by command. It is in line with McGregor's[3] principle of management by integration and self-control. And it implies that there is shared accountability between managers and individuals for improving performance.

The importance of objectives

As Williams[4] has written:

> The setting of objectives is the management process which ensures that every individual employee knows what role they need to play and what results they need to achieve to maximise their contribution to the overall business. In essence it enables employees to know what is required of them and on what basis their performance and contribution will be assessed.

It is also suggested by Williams that objectives should:

- be jointly agreed in advance between the manager and the individual as both realistic and challenging and, as such, they are 'owned';
- measure the actual level of achievement so that the basis on which perfor-mance is assessed can be understood in advance and is as clear as possible;

■ support the overall business strategies of the company so that the objectives, taken together, are mutually supportive and consistent throughout the organization.

At ICL, managers use three types of objectives:

1. Objectives which contribute to the achievement of the business objectives – *key result areas.*
2. Objectives which contribute to an improvement in the performance of the individual – *performance standards.*
3. Objectives which contribute to the development of the individual – *performance development.*

Objectives can be agreed following discussions between managers and the individuals or teams responsible to them. Teams may have joint objectives, and individuals who work together can agree common or overlapping objectives. Some organizations are now developing systems for internal customers to set objectives for internal suppliers of services.

Objectives provide the base for four key areas of performance management philosophy: measurement, feedback, positive reinforcement and contingency management.

Measurement

Measurement requires the collection of performance data to establish a starting point or base line. To improve performance you must know what current performance is.

It is often said that anything which can be managed can be measured. But there is an element of truth in the adage that, in some jobs, what is meaningful is not measurable and what is measurable is not meaningful.

Measurement is obviously easier when financial, sales or production targets can be set. Subjectivity clearly increases when qualitative objectives are used. But it is still possible to agree firm standards of performance which define the conditions under which a job can be said to have been well done, and there have been many developments in recent years in, eg measurement of service quality and customer satisfaction. The notion that employee performance should be measured, at least in part, on the basis of customer satisfaction returns, reports of 'mystery shoppers' in stores, or telephone customer surveys, is well established in many organizations in the retail, leisure and services sectors. In the UK, BT, Grand Metropolitan and Whitbread are examples of prominent organizations taking this approach. Performance management is now supporting total quality management and customer service initiatives with firm performance measures. This is a long way from the view expressed by the TQM guru, W Edwards Deming, that performance appraisal is a 'dread disease' and the enemy of effective quality initiatives. But this view was based on an outdated and mechanistic concept of performance appraisal.

Measuring competences is achieved by the use of behaviourally anchored rating scales which define in some detail the behaviours that indicate success in a given role. These need to be based on a research process (see Chapter 8, pages 82–92) covering the people involved. An example of such a scale is given in Figure 14.5.

Feedback

Measurement is followed by feedback so that people can monitor their performance and, as necessary, take corrective action. As much feedback as possible should be self-generated. The philosophy of performance management empha-

Controlling Work Systems

The ability to follow laid-down systems and to maintain and improve performance by adapting them or developing new systems.

Underdeveloped

Seldom contributes new ideas or new approaches. Doesn't understand or follow company policies, procedures etc. Allows stock levels/resources to fall below required levels. Seeks to avoid responsibility for problem-solving. Applies policies or procedures rigidly in cases where the use of discretion would produce a better outcome.

Developing

Ensures that all work methods and health and safety systems comply with company policies, procedures and codes of practice. Uses appropriate systems to measure productivity or output. Maintains adequate stock levels of basic materials used by the team.

Well developed

Actively seeks improvement and change. Constantly challenges existing methods. Removes or resolves problems by anticipating, taking the initiative, considering alternatives and making logical decisions. Always anticipates stock/resources levels required. Works within the system but will make exceptions when it is necessary to do so.

Figure 14.5 *A differentiating competency definition – Controlling Work Systems – used in a performance management process for supervisory staff*

sizes the importance of employees planning how they are going to achieve their objectives and then obtaining feedback data themselves. The rapid development of management information systems in recent years has increased the capacity to provide quantitative and timely feedback. This applies in all areas. For example cellular manufacturing systems using computer numerically-controlled machines can generate instant feedback to the autonomous working groups in each unit of the system.

Reinforcement

Positive reinforcement is provided when behaviour which leads to improved performance is recognized. The object is to recognize specific performance improvements as soon as possible after the event. This is why performance management should be regarded as a continuing process. Recognition and therefore reinforcement takes place whenever appropriate throughout the year. It is not deferred to an annual performance review session.

Similarly, if someone makes a mistake or fails to deliver the agreed standard of performance this should be discussed immediately and constructively so that learning can take place and improvement plans can be agreed. There should be no surprises in the formal annual performance review meeting. If anything has gone wrong it should be pointed out at the time so that coaching can be given and immediate corrective action can be taken – often based on an agreed performance improvement plan to be reviewed at relevant intervals.

As Handy[5] puts it, reinforcement theory is about 'applauding success and forgiving failure'. He suggests that mistakes should be used as an opportunity for learning: 'something only possible if the mistake is *truly* forgiven because otherwise the lesson is heard as a reprimand and not as an offer of help'.

Contingency management

The concept of contingency management refers to the belief that every behaviour has a consequence. When someone knows that desirable consequences are contingent upon good performance, they are more likely to improve.

The philosophy of performance management is largely based on this theory. The agreement or contract between managers and individuals spells out expectations of what is to be achieved and the sort of behaviour required to achieve it. Implicitly or explicitly, there is an understanding either of the reward that will follow if the expected outcome is attained, or of the penalty that will be exacted if it is not. Rewards or penalties are contingent upon certain behaviours resulting in certain outcomes.

Performance management as a process of management

The philosophy of performance management is strongly influenced by the belief that it is a natural and core process of management. Its emphasis on analysis, measurement, monitoring performance and planning and coaching for performance improvements means that it is concerned with basic aspects of good practice with regard to the management of people. It is a system which should be driven by management so that it becomes a valued part of their everyday working life and not an annual bureaucratic chore imposed upon them by the personnel department.

Performance management systems can help managers, in Handy's[5] words, to:

- be teachers, counsellors and friends, as much or more than they are commanders, counsellors and judges;

- trust people to use their own methods to achieve the manager's own ends;
- delegate on the basis of a positive will to trust and to enable, and a willingness to be trusted and enabled;
- become 'post-heroic' leaders who know that every problem can be solved in such a way as to develop other people's capacity to handle it.

However, the skills required by managers to carry out a performance management process are often underestimated. They need to know how to set clear, measurable and achievable objectives. They need to know how to define and assess competence requirements. They have to be able to handle performance review meetings in which they not only commend staff on their achievements (which is not too difficult) but also coach them and help them to recognize where their performance has been sub-standard and needs to be improved (which can be much harder).

Performance management implies a marked shift in the relationship between managers and their staff. The manager is faced with a new and more challenging situation: counselling skills, effective listening, good communication and the ability to handle and encourage upward appraisal all come to the fore. In essence, the development of performance management leads directly on to the need for a more systematic approach to skills-based management development. For this reason a growing number of organizations have found that implementation of performance management has been achieved as part of major management development initiatives.

Developing a learning organization

A learning organization has been defined by Pedlar et al[6] as 'an organization which facilitates the learning of all its members and continually transforms itself'.

The process of performance management is, or should be, as much about developing people as rewarding them. The development of people's skills and competence and the provision of opportunities for growth are important parts of the total reward process.

Performance management philosophy emphasizes that it is a continuous process not only of assessment but also of development. It sees each aspect of it as a means of providing learning opportunities starting with a performance agreement, continuing with regular reviews, and completing the cycle with a general review of performance and development needs before starting the next cycle with a reward performance agreement.

Empowerment

The concept of empowerment can be described as giving people more scope to exercise control over and take responsibility for their work. It also implies helping them to develop the skills and knowledge they need to maximize their contribution to the satisfaction of both the organization and themselves.

A performance management process with its emphasis on dialogue about work and roles, and on agreement and development, enables an organization to do this.

The reality of performance management

Performance management promises much but it is a process which takes time, effort and determination to introduce and even more dedication to manage well. We discuss the application of performance management in the next chapter.

References

1. Maslow, A (1954) *Motivation and Personality*, Harper & Row, New York
2. Drucker, P (1955) *The Practice of Management*, Heinemann, London
3. McGregor, D (1956) *The Human Side of Enterprise*, McGraw-Hill, New York
4. Williams, S (1991) 'Strategy and objectives', In F. Neale, (ed.), *The Handbook of Performance Management*, Institute of Personnel Management, London
5. Handy, C (1989) *The Age of Unreason*, Business Books, London
6. Pedlar, M, Boydell, T and Burgoyne, J (1989) 'Towards the learning company', *Management Education and Development* 20, 1

15

Performance Management – Applications

The role of performance management

The significant role played by performance management was described by Vicky Wright,[1] Director of Hay Management Consultants, as follows:

> Performance management addresses both outputs and inputs, skills and behaviours. It ceases to be a once or twice a year event. For many it becomes the principal system or set of processes for managing individuals and organization performance while keeping focus on delivery of the business vision.

In this chapter we consider how this role can be applied. We start from what may be termed the basic model of performance management and examine how this operates. We continue with an assessment of the implications of performance management for performance-related pay (PRP) and then discuss integrated approaches to performance management with particular reference to how it fits in with human resource management (HRM), continuous development, teamworking and total quality management. We then give some examples of performance management in practice, bearing in mind that it has become something of a portmanteau term embracing a number of approaches, ranging from what are essentially performance appraisal schemes, to those concerned mainly with performance-related pay, to those which are primarily developmental in character. We conclude with an outline methodology for evaluating the effectiveness of performance management as an essential basis for keeping its processes alive and responsive to changing organizational needs.

The basic model

Following their in-depth, case-study research into what they termed performance management systems (PMS) on behalf of the Institute of Personnel Management[2] Fletcher and Williams[3] came to the conclusion that the majority of organizations they looked at were a long way from operating sophisticated PMS. For most of them, PMS was synonymous with appraisal, or with performance related pay, or both. But as Fletcher commented:

> 'There is, of course, much more to it than that. The real concept of performance management is associated with an approach to creating a shared vision of the purpose and aims of the organization, helping each individual employee understand and recognize their part in contributing

to them, and in so doing manage and enhance the performance of both individuals and the organization.'

Their research suggested four underlying principles of effective performance management:

1. That it is owned and driven by line management and not by the HR department.
2. That there is an emphasis on shared corporate goals and values.
3. That performance management is not a package solution, it is something that has to be developed specifically and individually for the particular organization.
4. That it should apply to all staff, not just part of the managerial group.

We would add to this from our own empirical experience that it may prove beneficial to apply different processes to different parts of an organization and that this is acceptable, provided all processes are seen to exist within the same overall framework and are linked by explicit and common values.

In the first stage of the Institute of Personnel Management research project into performance management, Stephen Bevan and Marc Thompson of the Institute of Manpower Studies came to the conclusion that a 'textbook' performance management system exhibits the following features:

- the organization has a shared vision of its objectives, or a mission statement, which it communicates to all its employees;
- the organization sets individual performance management targets which are related both to operating unit and wider organizational objectives;
- it conducts a regular, formal review of progress towards these targets;
- it uses the review process to identify training, development and reward outcomes;
- it evaluates the effectiveness of the whole process and its contribution to overall performance to allow changes and improvements to be made.

Bevan and Thompson[4] suggested that this textbook definition placed too much emphasis on a top-down approach (particularly in objective setting) which can underplay the extent to which training and development and reward systems are driven from the bottom up:

> 'This in turn, raises questions about how easily corporate objectives can be integrated with individual goals, and the extent to which reward systems which are introduced to support a PMS can frustrate the training and development objectives of the process'.

They also criticized the belief that the PMS model can fit all situations and the fact that many process issues involved in making performance management work were underemphasized.

Applying performance management

These criticisms were, of course, based on research into performance management as a *system* – the very term implies a top-down, imposed and rigid approach which seeks easy solutions to complex problems. We much prefer to regard performance management as a flexible process which involves managers and those whom they manage operating as partners, but within a framework which sets out how they can best work together. This framework has to reduce the degree to which performance management is a top-down process and it needs to encourage a balanced approach with the following features, as described by Wright and Brading[5]:

- Less focus on retrospective performance assessment and more concentration on future performance planning and improvement.
- Identification and recognition of the skills and competences associated with higher levels of performance.
- Identification and recognition of outputs which are defined in qualitative terms and not just quantitative ones.
- A freer, upwardly managed process.
- A more coaching and counselling style of appraisal with less emphasis on criticism.
- More focus on the individual's contribution to the success of the team as a whole, with some objectives defined in these terms.
- Equally concerned with improving performance as assessing it.
- No forced distribution of performance ratings (so no win-lose scenarios).
- Possibly no formal ratings given.

A framework for performance management

Although every organization wanting to introduce performance management should develop its own version to suit its needs, it is useful to have a framework within which appropriate processes can be developed and operated. This framework will help in deciding the approach to be adopted and, when the decision has been made, will provide guidance to managers and the individuals and the teams they manage on what performance management activities they will be expected to carry out.

We described how performance management works in some detail in Chapter 14 (pages 207–8). This is summarized in Figure 15.1 which illustrates the framework for a full performance management process. It consists of the following activities:

- preparation of mission and value statements linked to business strategy;
- definition of corporate and functional or departmental objectives;
- agreement of accountabilities, tasks, objectives, competences and performance measures – the performance agreement or contract;
- agreement of work plans and personal development and performance improvement action plans (this can form part of a performance agreement);
- continuous management of performance throughout the year;
- preparation by the manager and the individual for the formal review;
- the annual performance review, which leads to a new performance agreement;
- formal development and training programmes prompted by the performance review (but throughout the year less formal training will be taking place in the shape of coaching, counselling, on-the-job training and self-development activities);
- rating or ranking performance – although usual, this is not an inevitable performance management activity;
- performance-related pay – again, this is not always associated with performance management, but because an increasing number of organizations are introducing PRP, the link between performance as measured by a performance

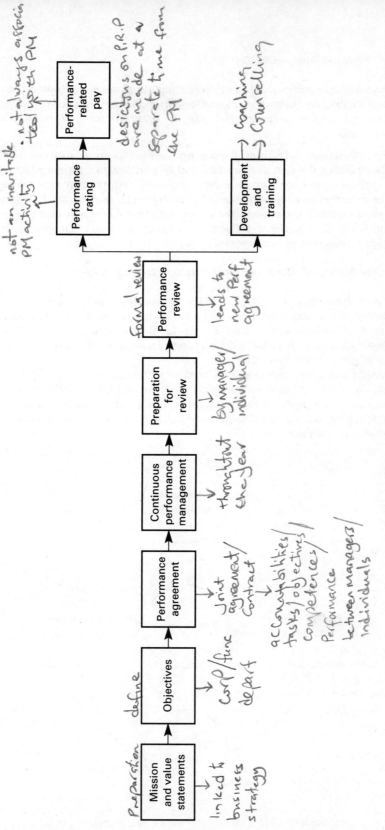

Figure 15.1 *The performance management process*

Handwritten annotations:

Mission and value statements — Preparation → linked to business strategy

Objectives — define → corp/func/ dept

Performance agreement — Joint agreement/ contract → accountabilities/ tasks/ objectives/ competences/ Performance between managers/ individuals

Continuous performance management → throughout the year

Preparation for review → by manager/ individual

Performance review — Formal review → leads to new Perf agreement

Performance rating → not an inevitable PM activity

Performance-related pay → decisions on P.R.P are made at a separate time from the PM · not always associated with PM

Development and training → Coaching, Counselling

management process and pay is becoming more common. However, decisions on PRP may be made at a separate time from the performance review so as not to prejudice the essential developmental nature of the performance management process.

These activities are broadly sequential, but they can overlap and there is scope for feedback during the year and from the formal performance review which can lead to a revised or new performance agreement. Indeed, performance management can be regarded as a continuous self-renewing cycle, as illustrated in Figure 15.2. The most effective processes have a clear link to the business planning cycle – a factor which has a major influence on their successful integration into the everyday processes of management.

Preparation of mission and value statements

These define broadly the purpose of the organization and what it believes to be important in the way it operates and how work is carried out. They provide the essential link to business strategy and the basis for defining corporate, functional and individual objectives and guidance on the standards of behaviour expected of all members of the organization.

Mission and value statements are useless if they are not owned and respected within the organization, communicated to all concerned and maintained as living principles which guide the way organizations go about their business. Recent experience has shown that performance management provides a powerful means of making this happen.

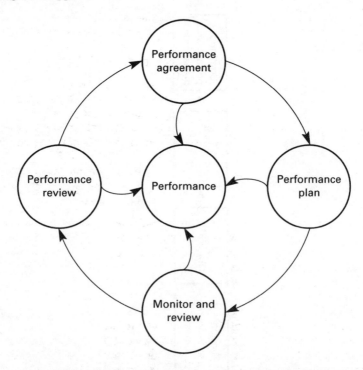

Figure 15.2   *The performance management cycle*

Performance management can operate without formal mission and value statements, but they do help to make the process more coherent by providing a foundation on which all the other activities can be built.

Definition of corporate and functional or departmental objectives

Corporate objectives define in terms of targets, budgets and projects what the organization is setting out to achieve. They translate strategic and business plans into specific goals.

Functional, divisional and departmental objectives flow from corporate objectives. Ideally, however, the planning process which formulates objectives operates on both a top-down and bottom-up basis. In other words, although the organization will want to achieve certain targets for profitability or growth, the constituent parts of the organization should be able to comment on these targets and to contribute their own views on their dimensions and fitness for purpose as well as how they should be achieved.

Performance agreement

A performance agreement defines the work to be done, the results to be attained and the measures used to assess performance. It is sometimes described as a performance contract, a work planning session, or an objective setting meeting (which might form part of a performance review meeting), but it does not matter what it is called as long as it is agreed jointly between managers and their staff and understood to be a normal process of management, not just a component in a performance management 'system'.

Concluding a performance agreement is a separate process from reviewing performance, but much of the content of the performance agreement will be derived from the review.

The work to be done is described by reference to the purpose and content of the job in the form of outputs and outcomes. This is achieved by defining:

- *principal accountabilities* – mainly for more senior or innovative jobs; or
- *main tasks and duties* for less senior and more routine jobs;
- *objectives* which are related to the principal accountabilities and specify outputs in the shape of the achievement of targets and performance standards and the completion of tasks or projects;
- *contribution* which defines the outcomes which individuals are expected to deliver and so support the achievement of the purpose of their team or department and, ultimately, the organization as a whole.

A performance agreement can, and indeed should, be concerned with inputs and process. Inputs refer to the knowledge and skills job holders have to use to achieve the purpose of their jobs. Process is the behaviour expected of them in order to carry out their role satisfactorily. Inputs and process or behavioural requirements can be described as *skills and competences* – the areas of basic accomplishment required in a job.

When defining the role of job holders, reference can also be made to the *core values* they are expected to uphold in carrying out their work.

A performance agreement will additionally set out the performance measures which will indicate the level of achievement reached by job holders. The agreement should enable employees to monitor and review their own performance (self-assessment) as well as providing the basis for more formal review processes.

XYZ Financial Services Group

The performance management process

Objectives

I Vision

1. To underpin and support Itec Group's business vision and strategy and promote flexibile responses to changing business circumstances.
2. To deliver a series of processes that produce measurable/observable profit and other business related performance improvements.
3. To help develop a culture based on joint understanding over what is expected and commitment to achieve it, where good performance is recognized and rewarded and poor performance is addressed fairly, constructively and speedily.
4. To provide a sound basis for performance assessments, career moves, promotions and pay decisions in which staff can have confidence.

II Guiding principles

1. To exist as a continuing dialogue through the year between managers and staff supported by a minimum of documentation. This dialogue will take account of changing circumstances through the year as they occur.
2. To help reinforce understanding of the business and the need for good teamwork as well as individual performance improvement.
3. To focus effort / skill/ competency where it is most needed.
4. To help build the skill base of the Group to empower staff to improve their performance and so encourage and deliver flexibility.
5. To help build an open, honest debate about continuing performance improvement at all levels.
6. To be capable of being monitored, adapted and changed to run with the grain of the business as it evolves.

Figure 15.3 *Example of a company statement on the vision and guiding principles for performance management*

Principal accountabilities

Principal accountabilities (sometimes referred to as key result areas) define what job holders will be held to account for. They spell out responsibilities *and* the results to be obtained to meet the purpose of the job. A principal accountability may indicate the standard of performance required in a particular area of responsibility, thus describing the conditions that will exist when the job can be said to have been well done. Wherever possible, quantified and time-related objectives will be agreed for each principal accountability.

A typical managerial or professional job will probably not have more than seven or eight principal accountabilities. At more senior levels, principal accountabilities are likely to change frequently and therefore need to be subjected to regular review.

Guidance on how to define principal accountabilities is provided in Chapter 11. An example of a statement of principal accountabilities is given in Appendix H.

Main tasks and duties

Some organizations prefer to use the terms main tasks or duties rather than principal accountabilities, especially for less senior or more routine jobs. Main task is a simple and easily recognized term – the expression principal account-ability can be somewhat overpowering because of the emphasis it seems to place on the weight of responsibility involved.

However, the principle remains the same – no more than seven or eight main tasks need to be identified (elaborate and wordy job descriptions are not necessary) and each task is defined in a way that indicates the outputs expected from the job holder.

Objectives

Objectives can be expressed in the form of quantified targets and/or as projects or tasks to be completed satisfactorily within a defined period of time.

Some organizations use the acronym SMART as a guide to setting objectives. They are required to be Stretching, Measurable, Agreed, Realistic and Time-bounded.

Objectives attach quantifiable, measurable and time-related dimensions to the job requirements set out in a statement of principal accountabilities. They may change frequently over the years. Objectives are defined or redefined in a performance agreement but may need to be revised from time to time during the year – as we have stressed throughout this and the previous chapter, a redefinition should not wait until the next formal performance agreement.

Many organizations use the term objective setting to wrap up the processes of defining the performance standards contained in statements of accountability or lists of main tasks, agreeing work plans and setting targets. This is a perfectly valid approach but it can lead to difficulties in practice where it is hard to attach quantified or project/time related objectives to principal accountabilities or main tasks. This may lead to attempts to quantify the unquantifiable – something which bedeviled the original concept of management-by-objectives.

This problem can be acute in more routine jobs where it may be easier to sit down with job holders and agree what they have to do and the standards they have to achieve (which can often be quantified) than to go through what could appear to them an artificial process of setting and resetting objectives in the shape of targets every year for each aspect of their job, however routine it may be.

This is why some organizations wishing to apply performance management at all levels distinguish between the more senior jobs, for which principal accountabilities and quantified objectives are defined, and the more junior jobs, for which the main tasks are listed to which performance standards are attached.

Another way of defining outputs/outcomes, which is adopted by such organizations as IBM, is to use the general term 'contribution' to refer to the overall impact that the job holder can make on end results. Contribution is defined in terms of the results obtained for each of the main accountabilities or tasks and of achievements against objectives.

It is also possible to distinguish between the work-related objectives referred to above and personal objectives. The latter are concerned with personal development aims: gaining knowledge, enhancing skills or improving performance in specified ways. They will be identified during the performance agreement and review stages and will be put into effect following the action planning stage.

Competences

As more and more organizations adopt the language of competences, so they incorporate this concept in their performance management processes. This has been the most powerful addition to this area over the last few years and has given a whole new language to the understanding, management and development of performance improvements.

The competences may be general or generic ones applied to all staff or they may be focused more specifically on a job family or category of employees such as managers, scientists, professional staff such as accountants, customer service staff or office/administrative staff. They can also be either basic proficiencies or areas of skill, or the fully researched differentiating competences such as those developed using Hay/McBer and other methodologies and described elsewhere in this book (see Chapter 8).

For example, Standard Chartered use the following list of competences in their performance management scheme:

- job and professional knowledge;
- commercial/customer awareness;
- communication;
- interpersonal skills;
- teamwork;
- initiative/adaptability/creativity;
- analytical skills/decision making;
- productivity;
- quality;
- management/supervision;
- leadership.

General lists such as these form the basis for agreeing competence requirements for particular jobs. At the performance agreement stage the aim is to ensure that individuals know and accept the competency levels which they are expected to achieve in their job.

Core values

There is no point in defining the core values of the organization unless a deliberate attempt is made to communicate them and to take steps to ensure that they are a reality, not just a string of pious platitudes. The process of performance management enables this to happen, starting with the performance agreement at which the values can be spelt out.

One example we encountered in a major multinational organization set out the following core values in terms of management behaviour for the year in question:

- contribution to the job beyond normal expectations;
- contribution to the work of others (this organization had problems with teamwork);
- contribution to change (the organization was trying to create a more flexible culture).

This organization was making a concerted effort to build a more performance focused, flexible and collegiate management culture and move away from the traditional, individualistic and hierarchical approach to activity that it perceived as a brake to future success. These values were communicated to managers as the main determinants for performance ratings and linked performance rewards.

Other values which can be expressed in a performance agreement include quality, customer service (internal and external), employee development, flexibility, innovation and even, within reason, risk-taking.

Core values are sometimes incorporated in a list of competences, as in the example given above.

Performance measures

Performance measures should be defined at the performance agreement stage so that people understand the basis upon which they will be assessed and, importantly, can monitor their own performance.

Performance measures may refer to such matters as income generation, sales, output, units processed, productivity, costs, delivery-to-time, 'take up' of a service, speed of reaction or turnround, achievement of quality standards or customer/client reactions.

Sun Life, for example, uses the three criteria of work quality, output and 'timeliness' (eg how many cases are dealt with over a given period of time). These output levels are measured by a management information system. Cambridgeshire County Council has identified four distinct types of measurement: money, time, effect and reaction. Money measures include maximizing income and improving rates of return; time measures express performance against work timetables or backlogs; measures of effect look at the original task as a whole and judge the physical completion of the work or the level of take up of a service; reaction indicates how others judge the job holder and is therefore a less objective measure.

Action planning

Action planning covers agreements on whatever steps are required to achieve performance standards and objectives. It embraces work plans and whatever steps individuals need to take to develop their competences and potential or to improve their performance in specified areas. The need for performance improvement plans will be identified during interim and final performance reviews in the year.

Action planning follows the performance standard and objective setting activities leading to a basic performance agreement, but the agreed plans may be incorporated in a final, extended agreement.

Action plans are not simply concerned with what individuals or teams are expected to do. They also indicate the support that the organization and the manager will be providing.

Managing performance throughout the year

As we have stressed from the outset, effective performance management is a continuous process, not an annual event. Conventional performance appraisal schemes have tended to function by means of an annual confrontation between managers and individuals where the former tells the latter what they think about them. Performance management requires managers to manage, and individuals and teams to perform, in accordance with their performance agreement. Progress is continually measured against performance standards, objectives and work plans so that corrective actions can be taken in good time or aspects of the performance agreement changed in the light of new circumstances.

This, of course, is nothing more nor less than good management practice. Performance management does not pretend to provide a unique formula for improving performance; it is simply applied common sense. What it does offer is guidance on what good management practice should be. Some managers will practise performance management instinctively and well – and they do not need to dignify what comes naturally to them with the term performance management. Others will not do it as well and they, and the organization, need all the help a systematic performance management process can provide.

In a continuing performance management process employees will be encouraged to monitor their own performance. Interim progress meetings can take place throughout the year to discuss progress and agree any actions required. These progress meetings can be arranged at fixed intervals or convened when the need arises. At their best, the emphasis in these meetings is on joint review and on coaching to achieve planned performance improvement. Social service departments and charities concerned with service provision, for example, will have regular supervisory meetings at which teams discuss how they are progressing with their work plans.

Preparation for the formal review

The formal review is always more effective if managers and the individuals reporting to them prepare in advance. The points to be considered are those which will be covered in the performance review, namely, how the individual has performed over the review period (typically a year) in meeting the requirements of the performance agreement, the factors that have affected performance and, importantly, what needs to be done next year to improve performance and develop competences. Consideration can also be given to any changes in principal accountabilities or tasks and to new objectives for the coming period. A formal performance review meeting also provides an opportunity for individuals to raise questions about their work and future and about how they are managed.

This part of the process is not always formalized and, indeed, formalization is not essential. But there are advantages to be gained in setting out as check-lists the questions that can be asked so that individuals know what questions they have the right to put and managers know what questions to expect. Examples of such check-lists (the manager's list being a mirror image of the individual's) are given in Appendix I. .

The performance review meeting

The performance review meeting is the basis for assessing the three key elements of performance (the three C's) defined in Chapter 14, namely; contribution, competence and continuous development.

Such meetings are the means through which the five primary performance management elements of measurement, feedback, positive reinforcement, exchange of views and agreement as described in Chapter 14 can be put to good use.

The review should be rooted in the reality of the employee's performance. It is concrete, not abstract, and it allows managers and individuals to take a positive look together at how performance can become even better in the future and how any problems in meeting performance standards and achieving objectives can be resolved. Individuals should be encouraged to assess their own performance and become active agents in improving their results. Managers should be encouraged to adopt their proper enabling role.

There should be no surprises in a formal review if performance issues have been dealt with as they should have been – during the year, as they arise. In one sense the review is a stock-taking exercise, but this is no more than an analysis of where those involved are now, and where they have come from. This static and historical process is not what performance management is about. The true role of performance management is to look forward to what needs to be done by people to achieve the overall purpose of the job, to meet new challenges, to make even better use of their knowledge, skills and abilities and to help them to develop their competences and improve their performance. This process also helps managers to improve their ability to lead, guide and develop their staff, as individuals or as a team.

Typically, there is one annual review which leads directly into the conclusion of a performance agreement (at the same meeting or later). Some organizations require formal reviews to be held more frequently, but it is probably best not to over-emphasize the formality of the continuing review process. It should be treated as part of normal good management practice to be carried out as and when required. But there is much to be said for an annual or half-yearly review which sums up the conclusions reached at earlier reviews and provides a firm foundation for a new performance agreement.

Formal training and development programmes

One of the most important outputs of performance is the information it generates which enables training needs to be identified. Many of these needs can and should be catered for by on-the-job coaching, counselling, guidance and training, but some may only be satisfied by means of formal training. For individuals, this helps to ensure that such training is relevant and can be used to improve performance in specific ways. The identification of a number of common needs will indicate the need for some form of general training.

For some organizations the personal development planning process has fared better if separated from the review of performance against objectives. The two processes remain linked but each is given the time it deserves and some quite sensitive developmental issues can better be handled away from post mortems on shortcomings – however expected and constructive.

In dealing with this area, it is also important to be realistic about groups of staff for whom there is unlikely to be any further development available. People close to retirement, those in jobs from which there is little or no career potential and those who, while content with their lot, have turned their face on further development, should probably not be put through an unnecessary ritual of personal development planning. In practical terms there is every reason to give such individuals the dignity of some form of continuing performance management and an annual review. But we believe that it is wise to follow the example of organizations which cater for such staff with a much simpler and shorter process which is better fitted to the needs, of, say, a 58-year-old part-time clerical assistant.

Rating

Old merit rating schemes and many current performance appraisal systems linked to performance-related pay schemes require managers to rate their staff. These ratings were often made on personality traits such as energy, willingness and determination which were not linked to actual behaviour or any clear definitions based on analysis and research on their relevance to job performance. Performance management reviews, however, seldom include such headings. The argument against assessing personal qualities is that managers are thereby asked to measure abstract personality traits, which have never been properly validated and which they are seldom qualified to do. Such approaches mean that individuals are in danger of becoming passive objects, receiving judgements from on high. It is greatly preferable to use competence analysis techniques as described in Chapter 8. These can provide definitions of behavioural requirements which are related to behaviours which it has been established lead to high levels of performance and which can be identified and defined by managers and individuals in terms of what the latter actually do.

The number of ratings to be used to define performance levels is often a matter for debate. There are many options available in the search to find meaningful definitions that managers and staff find motivational and can use. There is also a well established need, where ratings are linked to pay, to produce definitions which mean that the good, reliable core performers attracting a middle score feel that proper recognition has been given to the contribution they have made. It is increasingly being argued that successful management of the middle scores in performance rating is a key determinant of success for performance-related pay schemes. This is especially the case for middle and junior management and for technical and support roles for whom base pay progression based on performance rating of some kind is the major form of recognition available.

Few organizations manage to do without ratings entirely, since this lack makes consistent and comparable performance judgements difficult. In practice the number of ratings commonly used varies from three to six and there are fairly clear pros and cons for each of these approaches. We outline these below.

Three ratings

What may be called performance management systems or management by contract systems in some organizations ask for ratings either on the overall achievement of objectives, eg 'exceeded', 'achieved', 'failed to achieve', or against each of a list of objectives and competences where the ratings may be 'exceed', 'meet' or 'falls below' for each item. The main argument for this approach is that it is both realistic and straightforward to understand. Outstanding performers will get the recognition they deserve from the 'exceeded' rating while the majority will inevitably fall into the 'met contract' category, which is right and fair. The few performance problems that arise in a well managed organization can be catered for by use of the 'failed to meet contract' category.

The problems that arise with this approach arise from the lack of 'fine' performance definition. Making defensible pay links calls for some care, and careful attention has also to be given to training managers in how to distribute their ratings. Particular difficulties have arisen where pay increase (performance) matrices have been used, as described in Chapter 17, and where three performance levels have meant that promotion increases sit uncomfortably with base pay progression within pay ranges.

Five ratings

Probably the most typical arrangement is for there to be five specified performance levels; for example:

A Outstanding performance in all respects.
B Superior performance, significantly above normal job requirements.
C Good all round performance which meets the normal requirements of the job.
D Performance not fully up to requirements. Clear weaknesses requiring improvement have been identified.
E Unacceptable; constant guidance is required and performance of many aspects of the job is well below a reasonable standard.

This approach provides for two superior performance levels, a fully satisfactory level and two shades of less than competent performance. It is based on a view of the required fineness of performance definition and the extent to which managers can in fact make sensible distinctions. It is usually supported by guidelines – the temptation to have quotas or forced choice performance rating distributions should be resisted.

This approach can easily lead to 'rating drift' – a tendency to push ratings into higher categories (we have come across examples in large departments of two thirds or more of the staff being rated in the top two categories and few being placed in the lower two without any indication that departmental performance is at all out of the ordinary) and avoid the lowest level. The tendency to skew ratings upwards found with this approach seems to emerge as much from the terminology used as from the actual number of performance levels. In considering this terminology, it pays to remember that the words satisfactory or competent can feel like damning an entirely acceptable performance with faint praise, and that awarding a C or even a B can stir up memories of a rather mediocre school report. In these circumstances both managers and individual employees seek to move up the scale, sometimes without any realistic basis in terms of performance delivered.

Six levels

For the reasons just outlined there is quite a strong case for having six performance levels on the grounds that this gives a wider range and eliminates the inevitable tendency in five-level schemes either to pick mainly the central rating or give in to the temptation of drift upwards from it. In the following example from a multinational organization, the six levels are defined as:

XC Exceptional performance: meeting all objectives and requirements and contributing outstanding achievements which significantly extend the impact and influence of the total job.
EX Excellent performance: meeting all objectives and requirements and contributing some notable achievements beyond normal expectations for the job.
W A well-balanced performance: meeting objectives and requirements of the job, consistently performing in a thoroughly proficient manner.
R Reasonable performance: a contribution which is stronger in some aspects of the job than others and where most objectives are met, but with varying degrees of effectiveness.

BE Barely effective performance: meeting few objectives or requirements of the job – significant performance improvements are needed.

U   Unacceptable performance: failing to meet most objectives or requirements of the job and demonstrating a lack of commitment to performance improvement, or a lack of ability which has been discussed prior to the performance review.

This approach means that the core of competent performers who are given a third level W rating are aware that there are three levels below them. This will have a greater motivational value than being placed in the third of five grades with only two lower categories. In this system, A–F or 1–6 ratings have deliberately been avoided – to dispel associations with old systems (which, as we have said, often go back as far as school reports!)

Four positive ratings
Another approach which is increasingly being adopted in organizations working hard on improving their culture is to design a rating scale which provides positive reinforcement at every level. This means that employees cannot be damned out of hand and the stress is on a culture of continuing improvement. If performance from any individual is totally unacceptable, this fact should have been identified during the continuous process of assessing results and corrective action initiated at the time. This is not an action that can be delayed for several months until the next review when a low formal rating is given which may be demotivating or too late. The example given below emphasises the positive and improvable nature of individual performance.

- *Very effective:* meets all the objectives of the job. Exceeds required standards and consistently performs in a thoroughly proficient manner beyond normal expectations.
- *Effective:* achieves required objectives and standards of performance and meets the normal expectations of the job.
- *Developing:* a contribution which is stronger in some aspects of the job than others, where most objectives are met but where performance improvements should still take place.
- *Basic:* a contribution which on the whole meets the basic standards required although a number of objectives are not met and there is clearly room for improvement in several definable areas.

Other organizations use the term 'improvable' for the 'basic' category in this list. Yet others have created 'learner/achiever' or 'unproven/too soon to tell' categories for new entrants to a grade for whom it is too early to give a realistic assessment. The main problem with the four level approach is that some organizations may not be capable of providing a fine enough basis for differentiating performance levels. This is often a cultural issue.

Although there certainly are organizations, notably in the public service, which, as the result of greater delegation of pay decision making, have adopted eight or more performance ratings, we doubt whether such fine definitions will stay in place for long. These tend either to be three or four level approaches which have been split to give more freedom to manage subtleties in the middle range, or they will be based on some pseudo-scientific concept of performance hierarchies. In practice we have found that the full range of ratings are not used as intended because those responsible for rating find the options too hard to manage consistently.

The issue of consistency

The problem with rating scales is that it is very difficult, if not impossible without very careful management, to ensure that a consistent approach is adopted by managers responsible for rating. It is almost inevitable that some people will be more generous than others (the swan effect), while others will be harder on their staff (the goose effect). Ratings can, of course, be monitored and challenged if their distribution is significantly out of line, and computer-based systems have been introduced for this purpose in some organizations. But many managers want to do the best for their staff, either because they genuinely believe that they are better or because they are trying to curry favour. It can be difficult in these circumstances to challenge them.

The best way to deal with this issue is as part of the developmental process associated with performance management. This involves running regular consistency workshops with managers from across departments to discuss how ratings are perceived, explore differences, test out fair rating on 'case study' performance reviews and, over time, build up a better common understanding and level of comfort with the rating process. This can be extended to bringing managers together after their performance ratings have been made and getting them to exchange information and, where necessary, justify their distribution of assessments.

Another, and effective, support to the development of improved consistency is to provide for a 'grandparent' or boss's boss check on both the quality of formal performance reviews and the consistency of performance ratings. Again this needs to be supported by training workshops, but it can and does prove a useful integrating influence on the ownership of performance in a given part of the organization. This approach was, of course, used for many years with annual appraisal schemes. What is different in terms of its application in current approaches to performance management is the continuing support for the management of consistency and the use of workshops and discussion groups further to embed the language of performance improvement.

The HR department can play a useful part in helping to achieve fairly distributed and consistent ratings. Not by taking on a policing role and compelling managers to accept a forced distribution, but by providing guidance and by encouraging managers to reconsider their ratings if they seem to be misjudged.

Ranking systems

An alternative approach is to rank staff in order of merit and then distribute performance ratings through the rank order. Shell UK, for example, gets managers together to rank groups of up to 100 employees and allocate them according to a forced distribution into four performance bands.

A typical forced distribution in a ranking system would be to give the top 10 per cent an A rating, the next 15 per cent a B rating, the next 60 per cent a C rating and the remaining 15 per cent a D rating. Such forced distribution systems do ensure a consistent distribution of ratings but still depend on the relative objectivity and accuracy of the rankings.

Forced distribution

The forced distribution of ratings requires managers to conform to a pattern which quite often corresponds with the normal curve of distribution on the assumption that performance levels are distributed normally. A typical distribution would be:

Rating	%
A	5
B	15
C	60
D	15
E	5

But the assumption that performance and consequential reward is distributed normally is questionable. It tends to produce what Vicky Wright called win-lose situations. It has also to be said that in the many evaluations of performance management and performance-related pay that have been conducted over the last few years, forced choice distributions and quotas have come in for particular criticism. There is no proof that performance is normally distributed or indeed that it should be. There are many examples of high-performance organizations where key departments such as marketing are well staffed with above average people who are delivering a new business strategy, and others where to fill departments such as finance with super-achieving accountants would be quite inappropriate and in any case would result in them withering away from boredom. There is also the view that the level of fully acceptable performance needs to be ratcheted up every year – so what was defined as a good contribution in one year is less than acceptable in the next. This is one of the arguments that can be used to contain rating drift.

Performance management documentation

As a natural process of management, performance management does not rely on forms. It should always aim to avoid the elaborate form filling and box ticking activities which convert it into a bureaucratic exercise imposed by the personnel function on managers who feel, often quite rightly, that they have better things to do with their time.

But for reference and guidance purposes there is a need to provide some basic documentation to record decisions made in performance review and agreement meetings. It is usually necessary to write down the overall purpose of the job, its principal accountabilities or main tasks and agreed objectives. It is also necessary to record any agreement on competence requirements as well as agreements on areas for improvement or development for future reference. Although not essential, check-lists for the points to be raised at review meetings against which notes can be made can provide a useful *aide mémoire* and an agenda for the meeting.

Many organizations are therefore providing basic forms for the use of managers and individuals which can be retained by them and may also allow for the manager's manager (the so-called grandparent) to review the outcome, thus increasing the degree to which, from the individual's point of view, the assessment is felt fair and providing a measure of quality control. An example of a set of forms and pre-review meeting check-lists is given in Appendix I.

Although we believe that documentation should be kept to a minimum, we do believe that what is produced should be well designed and appealing to use. Employees should be given performance management support documents of a similar standard to the kind of documents commonly given to the organization's customers, not something hurriedly produced by personnel and untested before being launched on all employees and their managers. In organizations which are moving from appraisals to performance management and where there is already a set of forms which may be much disliked, there is much to be gained from getting together a working group of managers and staff to say what they most liked and disliked about the old documents and what they would prefer the new ones to look like to support the performance management process. This may need a little guidance, but it will certainly help build ownership – especially if the members of this working group consult a sample of line managers and other colleagues.

It is common practice for review forms to be held by the personnel department for the record and to note training recommendations. The personnel department is often regarded as the custodian of the performance management scheme and, it is felt, should monitor the process to ensure that it is carried out conscientiously and well. It is important to warn here, that if an employer faces an industrial tribunal case for unfair dismissal from an individual who claims previously to have attracted favourable performance ratings, then much will turn on the quality of the record keeping as well as the honesty of the performance review process.

Other organizations understandably believe that, if this is truly a management process, then it is the line managers and their staff who should own it. The completed forms are for their use, not the personnel department's. We favour the sentiments behind this point of view but our experience has shown that performance management is more likely to succeed if the HR function monitors its implementation and provides training and guidance in performance management skills (eg setting objectives, conducting performance review meetings) as required.

A further point that needs to be made about performance management is that it is the process which counts, not the elegance with which forms have been completed. Their purpose is no more than that of recording views and decisions – they are not ends in themselves.

Performance management and performance-related pay

Some people, typically top management with little exposure to the realities of human resource management, regard performance-related pay coupled with performance or merit rating as the be all and end all of performance management. But, as we hope we have demonstrated, performance management goes much further. However, research has shown that to be acceptable at all, performance-related pay has to be based on some defensible system of performance rating so that when it is decided to relate pay to performance it clearly forms part of the performance management process.

A debate has gone on for years about whether linking pay decisions to performance management or appraisal contaminates the developmental and intrinsic motivational purpose of such schemes. Those who dislike the linkage believe that performance assessments and review meetings will be so bound up with their financial implications that it will not be possible to have an open and constructive discussion about areas for development and improvement. Those in favour take the down-to-earth view that once you decide to have performance-related pay you must have a rating system.

A compromise position adopted by many organizations is to communicate ratings as part of the performance review process and make pay decisions separately. This is possible where there is no direct and immediate link between rating and pay increase or bonus. Where there is a direct link then the practice typically is to communicate the pay increase after the rating has been agreed, countersigned and fed into the pay administration system – still providing a measure of separation – and another opportunity to get across some performance messages. This means that the performance agreement and review processes can, apart from a discussion on rating, concentrate on clarifying expectations, measuring outcome and planning for improvements in the future.

Some organizations separate entirely performance pay ratings from the performance management review. But there will, of course, inevitably be a read-across from the performance management review to the pay-for-performance rating.

Integrated performance management

Performance management can play an important part in business development by helping to integrate corporate and individual objectives. It can also act as an integrating process in the areas discussed below.

Performance management and HRM

Performance management can satisfy a number of the fundamental aims of HRM, namely:

■ to achieve sustained high levels of performance from the organization's human resources;
■ to develop people to their full capacity;
■ to establish an environment in which the latent potential of employees can be realized;
■ to reinforce or change the organization's culture.

It can help to deliver a more coherent approach to linking the financial and non-financial aspects of reward and, importantly, it provides a basis for career planning and continuous development.

Continuous development

The concept of continuous development is based on the belief that learning within organizations should be a continuous process associated with everyday work. Continuous development is largely self-development but it is up to the organization to create an environment in which such learning can take place. This is what performance management does when it emphasizes individual and career development and the importance of treating any discussions between managers and their staff about work as learning opportunities. The analysis of competences can indicate to employees not only the areas in which they can develop their abilities to do their present job better but also the levels of competence they need to reach if they want to progress their careers within the organization.

Teamworking

Performance management is often treated as if it were just a matter between managers and the individuals reporting to them. But it can also enhance teamwork by asking teams to identify interdependencies and set team objectives and by getting their members jointly to review progress in achieving them. Teamwork can also be enhanced by setting overlapping objectives for different members of a team.

Some organizations such as Motorola (as described at the IPM Compensation Forum's 1993 Conference) have peer reviews – members of a team appraising each other's performance. This is most likely to work when a high-involvement team approach is well established in which interdependent and multi-skilled team members share the responsibility for setting goals, problem solving and monitoring performance. Motorola's experience is that peer reviews are:

- more stable than supervisor rating;
- focus on results rather than effort;
- reliable and potentially more accurate;
- good predictors of future performance.

But it has been pointed out by Wright and Brading[5] that the difficulties of managing the performance of individuals within a team cannot be ignored:

> 'Indeed, leaving team dynamics to manage performance by such things as team pressure can be dangerous and unfair. Managing team performance is important, but it is not a substitute for managing individual performance.'

Total quality management

The importance of individuals working together in teams and the focus on the continuous improvement of the efficiency and effectiveness of the team is at the heart of the philosophy underpinning TQM and, as indicated above, performance management can enhance teamwork.

The significance of quality as a core value can be emphasised in the performance management process. But the fundamental reason for introducing TQM, or any quality initiative, is to increase stakeholder value – value to shareholders, customers, employees and the community. This adds a critical financial dimension to quality and it can be argued, as do Wright and Brading, that there is a strong case for linking financial rewards to organizational success in a quality environment.

Variations on a theme – different approaches to integrated performance management

In their extensive research into the operation of performance management systems Bevan and Thompson[4] noted the emergence of their use as an integrating process which meshes various human resource management activities with the business objectives of the organization. They identified two broad thrusts towards integration.

Reward-driven integration

Reward-driven integration emphasises the role of performance payment systems in changing organizational behaviour and tends to undervalue the part played by other human resource development (HRD) activities. This appears to be the dominant mode of integration being pursued in the UK, notably in the public sector where there has been a strong political imperative based on faith in the transformational effect of pay on motivation and performance.

Bevan and Thompson[4] suggest that the more limited reward-driven approach may reinforce 'a disposition to short-termism and set back organizational effectiveness in the long term'.

Moreover, we note, and warn, that this belief has not been borne out in recent evaluations of performance-related pay in the public sector. These have revealed that the process of performance management has been valued for the clarity it has provided on performance expectations and for its contribution to improvements in the quality of working relationships, but that the principal virtue of the performance pay has been in terms of the recognition it has provided for past performance in an environment where such rewards have typically been kept on a very tight rein.

Development-driven integration

Development-driven integration stresses the importance of ensuring that appropriate HRD activities are in place to meet the long-term objectives of the organization and, furthermore, to ensure business needs and HRD are coordinated. Although performance pay may operate in these organizations, it is perceived to be complementary to HRD activities rather than dominating or driving them.

Examples of the approaches adopted by different organizations are given below.

ICL

ICL follows an integrated approach to performance management by linking a number of different processes within a performance management framework. Individual objectives are set which support the achievement of business strategies. Formal assessment of performance against these objectives leads to personal job improvement and training plans and a performance rating which influences the pay review. The output of these processes leads to periodical organizational management reviews which are concerned with developing the organizational capability of ICL. These impact directly on business strategies.

Royal Society for Mentally Handicapped Children and Adults (MENCAP)

In contrast, the performance and development management scheme introduced recently by MENCAP emphasizes, as its title implies, both the performance improvement and developmental aspects of the process. It too is based on individual objectives related to the Society's mission and strategic plans, but these lead exclusively to performance improvement and development plans; there is no performance rating or performance related pay.

A multi-national corporation

Performance management in this corporation is defined as a continuous process shared between managers and the people for whom they are responsible. The aim is to build performance management into the everyday management process and to focus on performance: 'how to do everything we do better'. The system is based on a performance agreement which sets out what individuals agree to work towards in the coming year and a performance review meeting where agreement is reached on how well the individual has done – the level of achievement. The system includes the use of a review preparation form, a performance review document summarizing the results of the review and the performance agreement and a performance planner – a working document which individuals and their managers can use to make sure that the performance agreement is achieved and evolved where necessary during the year.

The importance of providing recognition and rewards to people who have performed well is emphasized. It is stated that recognition and rewards come, for instance, in the form of praise for good performance, career and promotion opportunities and in the chance to move into particularly interesting work. Additionally, they come in the form of extra pay and the firm is prepared to pay significant rewards for outstanding contribution and competitive rewards for good, reliable performance.

It is also stated that one of the many goals of the performance management process is to help ensure that decisions on performance-related pay are closely related to balanced reviews of how well individuals have contributed over the year. Great importance is attached to the fair and consistent use of rating to assess levels of achievement as these are fed into the pay review process.

Cambridgeshire County Council

The performance management philosophy adopted by Cambridgeshire County Council is based on the belief that a well planned and implemented performance management system:

- creates a disciplined framework for linking policies and priorities to jobs;
- provides greater clarity of job requirements to job-holders;
- offers regular feedback to individuals for their encouragement, improvement and personal recognition;
- recognises the strengths and weaknesses of job-holders, enabling them to be adequately developed through appropriate training, experience and counselling;
- establishes a proper basis for making promotion decisions and for giving references to other employers;
- enables poor performance to be identified and remedied where possible and, where not possible, to facilitate appropriate action;
- is a means of keeping the relationships between jobs under review;
- makes the task of demonstrating a job holder's effectiveness easier;
- develops in managers the ability to deal with people as individuals on a systematic basis;
- improves the working climate of the organization.

The main features of the system are as follows:

- *Accountabilities* for senior staff which define the purpose of the job and the results to be attained. These accountabilities are directly linked to the job holder's role in achieving the organization's objectives. For lower-graded staff, accountabilities have been replaced with a more flexible and simple system of tasks and duties that is felt to be more appropriate and measurable for assessing performance.
- *Performance measures* relating to money, time, effect and reaction are used to assess the achievement of accountabilities.
- *Performance standards* are used to set acceptable levels of performance.
- *Goals* are used to help staff concentrate on special results which need to be achieved from within their accountabilities.
- *Action plans* are prepared to assist staff in meeting their accountabilities or goals.
- *Progress reviews* – annual reviews are held to assess what has been accomplished in the previous year, to agree what is to be achieved in the following year, to help staff improve performance, and to clarify the job holder's career prospects, aspirations and intentions. Following the review the job holder is given a rating which has to be accepted by both sides as fair. Each of the job holder's accountabilities is also rated on a five point scale. A confirming appraiser has a dual role as a quality controller of performance standards and

as an arbiter to act between the job-holder and manager in any disagreement.

- *Performance-related pay.* Some job-holders, if budget limits allow, are awarded a non-consolidated cash payment if their performance rating exceeds 3-5 points.

Standard Chartered Bank

At Standard Chartered performance is assessed by reference to individual capability against job competences, and to individual achievement against personal objectives. Competences are defined as the skills staff need to develop if they are to perform to a fully satisfactory standard in their work. They can be weighted according to the demands of particular jobs. Both competences and objectives must be set in line with the company's business strategies and aims. Staff who are rated as having exceeded requirements normally receive a performance payment. Those who meet the requirement do not necessarily receive a payment and there is a further selection process within this category.

IBM

IBM has recently introduced a new contribution review system to replace their long-established appraisal/counselling programme. The overall aim of the contribution review system is to achieve market driven quality. The system is based on an assessment of the contribution that it has been agreed employees should make to achieving the mission of their business unit or function. The emphasis is on self-assessment. An assessment is also made of performance in meeting continuing responsibilities – the basic ones all employees have for such matters as health and safety and BS 5750. Contributions are rated and these ratings influence pay decisions.

Managers also meet to agree contribution rankings within groups of employees. The mandatory criteria used in ranking contribution are delivery, customer satisfaction and use of expertise (innovation and acquisition of skills). Others could include teamwork or prudent risk taking. Contribution ranking is a means of calibrating and validating ratings and identifying the top and bottom 10 per cent of employees in the group for developmental and performance improvement purposes.

Introducing performance management successfully: pitfalls to avoid

Performance management systems can promise more than they achieve. They may fail for four main reasons: (*1*) top management is not fully behind the scheme in actions as well as words, (*2*) line management has not been involved in the development of the process and therefore feels it is a waste of time and/or mishandles the objective-setting and review processes, (*3*) staff feel the scheme is having a detrimental and divisive rather than a beneficial effect, and (*4*) quality control and continuing maintenance are not exercised over the operation of the scheme. These issues must be addressed through careful planning and pilot testing, thorough briefing, comprehensive training to managers *and* their staff, and the systematic monitoring and evaluation of the scheme in operation. We cannot stress too strongly the need to keep performance management alive and well-maintained rather that putting everything into the launch and then failing to provide continuing training and support and keeping the values alive and developing.

The criteria for success are exacting and include:

- clarity about what success looks like for and within the organization;
- top management commitment;
- line management ownership and commitment;
- staff believe that the process is consistent and fair in relation to contribution and ability;
- cultural fit – appropriate processes and the development of an enabling management style;
- a shared process of strategic management;
- high levels of skill by both managers and individuals in defining account-abilities and competences, objective setting and measuring performance and contributions;
- a head of HR who plays a major and innovative role in ensuring that these conditions are satisfied and maintained.

Evaluating performance management and related pay systems

The key lesson emerging from the growing number of evaluations in this field can be summed up in the statement 'if you want to find out whether a system or process is working or not, and what to do with it, go and ask representative groups of the people involved'. All of the evaluations in which we have taken part or looked at have yielded useful findings and insights on which organizations have been able to act. From our knowledge of these we believe that the following evaluation methodology will provide a robust understanding of what is going well and the issues to be addressed.

- For credibility and acceptability to all parties (management, employees, unions) the evaluation should be carried out by a working group of people of integrity from within the organization, assisted if need be by a reputable independent body – either consultants or academics with a practical as well as a theoretical understanding of performance management and rewards.
- All concerned in the evaluation should be thoroughly briefed to ensure that they understand the philosophy behind the scheme and its constituent processes, the sources of information likely to yield evidence and the significance of the scheme within the organization's human resource strategy.
- Both individual interviews and group discussions with a cross section of the population involved should be conducted. Some of these will be needed at the attitude survey design stage (see below) and others towards the end of the process to broaden understanding of the issues emerging.
- A confidential postal attitude survey should be conducted which tests not just employees' views on performance management and rewards, but also their views on what they value in their work, basic pay levels and the management environment, and provides the opportunity to comment on changes they believe would be helpful. Wording and design should be neutral, but reflect the existing culture. Such a survey could be based on the relevant sections of the example of an attitude survey given in Appendix A.
- A scrutiny should be made of what the current scheme is delivering in terms of:
  - an assessment of the quality of the performance management processes and the supporting documentation based on a review of a reasonably representative sample of completed forms and scrutiny of the written communication processes for clarity and emphasis;

- – the distribution of performance ratings and any associated payments – preferably over more than one year in the context of the scheme's stated objectives and the pay policy and operating environment;
- A synthesis of findings into a report which provides a detailed and balanced review of practice, outcomes and employee responses, accompanied by conclusions and practical recommendations for necessary change. Recommendations will need to take account of the art of the possible in terms of both cost and timing as well as cultural acceptability.

Inevitably, the detail of any approach to evaluation used will need to vary according to the characteristics of individual organizations and employee groups.

We also believe that it is helpful to provide for evaluation of the organizational climate, attitudes to performance management, reward practice and the time a new initiative is launched, when major changes are made. It is of critical importance to management credibility for the findings of the evaluation to be communicated to employees together with intentions as to how any issues emerging are to be tackled. We observe that a positive culture, centred upon performance improvement, is more likely to emerge when employees are involved in developing policy change – this has its own value as an educative process for all concerned in the realities of working at the detail of new approaches to get them right.

References

1. Wright, V (1992) 'Organization, performance, competency and pay: Integration for success', paper delivered at Hay Annual Client Issues Conference.
2. Institute of Personnel Management (1992) *Performance Management in the UK: an analysis of the issues*, IPM, London
3. Fletcher, C and Williams, R (1992) 'The route to performance management', *Personnel Management* October
4. Bevan, S and Thompson, M (1991) 'Performance management at the cross roads', *Personnel Management* November
5. Wright, V and Brading, L (1992) 'A balanced performance'. *Total Quality Magazine.* October

PART 6

PAYING FOR PERFORMANCE, SKILL AND COMPETENCE

16

Paying for Performance – General Considerations

In this chapter we define the process of paying for performance and discuss:

- the objectives of paying for performance;
- the differences between incentives and rewards and between incentive and bonus schemes;
- the rationale for performance pay – advantages, impact and disadvantages;
- the considerations to be taken into account when introducing performance pay – criteria for individual and organizational effectiveness;
- the main varieties of performance pay schemes.

Paying for performance – a definition

Paying for performance is the process of providing a financial or financially measurable reward to an individual which is linked directly to individual, group or organizational performance.

The principle types of performance pay are performance-related pay (PRP) sometimes called performance-related base salary progression or merit pay, individual and team incentive and bonus schemes, organization-wide profit or added value related plans, skill-based schemes (often referred to as knowledge-based schemes) and competence-based schemes.

Objective of paying for performance

The objective of paying for performance is to improve individual, team and organizational performance by:

- focusing for employees the elements of their performance which deliver organizational success thus directing their attention and effort where it is most needed;

- motivating employees;
- increasing commitment and identification;
- reinforcing or helping to change cultures and values – typically towards a more performance, quality and customer service orientated culture;
- recognizing and rewarding contribution, not just effort;
- differentiating consistently and equitably in the distribution of rewards in relation to contribution;
- delivering positive messages about performance expectations;
- improving the recruitment and retention of high quality employees;
- flexing pay costs in line with organizational performance.

Paying for performance – incentive or reward?

When defining the objectives of their pay-for-performance schemes, many people treat the terms incentive and reward as interchangeable. But there are significant differences, and when defining objectives and evaluating results it is necessary to distinguish between them.

The essential distinction is that incentives are forward-looking while rewards are retrospective.

- *Financial incentives* are designed to motivate people to improve their performance – to make a greater contribution by increasing effort and output and by producing better results expressed in such terms as objectives and targets for profit, sales turnover, productivity, cost reduction, quality, customer service and delivery on time.
- *Financial rewards* provide extra money for achievement in terms of contribution or output. The emphasis is on recognition and on equity, in the sense of paying people according to their just deserts (the labourer is worthy of his hire). Recognition is, of course, an important form of motivation and therefore may provide an incentive, but the relationship between pay and future performance is not always as clear as some people would like to believe.

This difference is important because it highlights the fact that schemes which are designed to provide motivation and incentives may in practice fail to do this directly, although they will be a useful means of recognizing contribution.

This distinction between incentives and rewards points the way to another aspect of reward processes about which there is often confusion – the difference between incentives and bonuses.

The difference between incentives and bonuses

The terms incentive and bonus are often juxtaposed. In this book, the terms are used with special meaning. They resemble each other in that they are both payments which are linked in some defined way to performance. But there the similarity ends.

- *Incentives:* are payments linked to the achievement of previously set and agreed targets. They aim to motivate people to achieve higher levels of performance and then reward it, usually in fixed proportion to the extent to which a target has been achieved, or the amount of time saved in a work-measured incentive scheme for manual workers. Incentive schemes are found from the shop floor to the boardroom and can be applied to individuals or groups. They vary principally in the types of measures used and the time scales involved in payment. Incentive pay is usually provided in addition to basic pay as part of the normal earnings package.

■ *Bonuses:* are essentially rewards for success and are paid out as a lump sum. This happens when the individual, team or organization has achieved something outstanding or, in the case of enterprise-wide schemes such as gain-sharing, when organizational performance has exceeded its target. The typical individual or team bonus tends to be discretionary. The amount paid out depends on the recommendations or decisions of the employee's boss, the chief executive or the board, and is constrained only by budgetary limits. Such bonus schemes are therefore often less structured than incentive schemes. Many companies are now using achievement bonuses as the major form of reward above basic pay on the grounds that as long as the basic rate is competitive the best and most controllable form of reward is one which is only paid in recognition of a specific, easily recognizable and notable achievement. Bonus schemes can be useful in smaller, cyclical and rapidly growing businesses (especially when they are in a startup situation) to focus rewards on results and help to control fixed costs.

The rationale for performance pay

All organizations are engaged in a search for increased added value from their workforce and many see paying for performance as a critical element in achieving that goal. The rationale for the view is often quite simple: the belief that money motivates. This deterministic view has its roots in the scientific management methods of F.W. Taylor[1]. He wrote:

It is impossible through any long period of time, to get workmen to work much harder than the average men around them unless they are assured a large and permanent increase in their pay.

The assumption is made that workers have the power to control the amount of effort they put into the job and that they adjust their effort solely or mainly in relation to the monetary return they get from it.

A more sophisticated rationale for the motivating power of money is instrumental theory. This suggests that, while money in itself is not necessarily a powerful motivator, it does acquire significant motivating power when it comes to symbolize intangible goals. The impact of money on motivation is discussed in detail in Chapter 2.

A further argument in favour of paying for performance is that it maintains earnings at a competitive level compared with other companies which do pay for performance. To which can be added the argument that if people are not paid in accordance with their performance they will be demotivated and may well leave (if they can) or remain as less than effective employees.

But what is perhaps one of the most powerful arguments for performance pay is that it is right and proper for people to be rewarded in accordance with their contribution. It is equitable to differentiate rewards between employees performing at different levels in the same job. Employees should not be paid simply for being there, irrespective of how well they do.

Paying for performance enables an organization to:

■ establish a clear relationship between performance and pay;
■ provide the most direct and meaningful form of financial motivation available by linking rewards to achievements;

- follow through the benefits of performance management by recognising achievement through the pay system;
- reinforce a performance-orientated corporate culture by delivering a clear message that high performance brings about commensurate rewards;
- reinforce team as well as individual contribution by incorporating this in the values of the scheme;
- concentrate effort in priority areas;
- clarify the key issues with which employees should be concerned;
- attract and retain people who are confident in their ability to deliver results but expect to be rewarded accordingly;
- improve pay competitiveness;
- enable employees to share in the success of the organization.

Incentive schemes can work well on the shop floor. Studies made in the US by Lawler,[2] Guzzo et al,[3] Nalbantian[4] and Binder[5] have shown productivity increases of between 15–35 per cent when incentive schemes have been put into place. Our experience of installing a group bonus scheme in a large distribution centre in the UK produced, in work measurement terms, an increase in productivity from 67–102 (35 points) where 100 is regarded as the norm for a fully effective worker.

Reservations about paying for performance

Of course almost everyone wants and needs money, but reservations about the rationale behind paying for improved performance have been expressed by a number of people over the years. McGregor,[6] writing about shop floor incentive schemes, stated that:

> The practical logic of incentives is that people want money, and they will work harder to get more of it. Incentive plans do not, however, take account of several other well-demonstrated characteristics of behaviour in the organizational setting: (1) that most people want the approval of their fellow workers and if necessary they will forego increased pay to obtain this approval; (2) that no managerial assurances can persuade workers that incentive rates will remain inviolate regardless of how much they produce; (3) that the ingenuity of the average worker is sufficient to outwit any system of controls devised by management.

Brown[7] launched a strong attack on piecework systems as being counter-productive and the cause of considerable shop floor conflict and wage drift (pay increasing without any commensurate increase in productivity). And the Office of Manpower and Economics accepted the conclusion of the National Board for Prices and Incomes that:

> 'Our evidence has shown that some degree of wage drift will accompany any conventional payments by results system, no matter how good the managerial or joint controls.'

A more general criticism of the concept of using pay to motivate better performance has been made by Beer[8] who wrote:

> Tying pay and other intrinsic rewards to performance may actually _reduce_ the intrinsic motivation that comes when individuals are spontaneously involved in work because they are given freedom to manage and control their jobs. By making pay contingent upon performance (as

judged by management), management is signalling that it is they – not the individual – who are in control, thus lowering the individual's feeling of competence and self-determination.

Recent research on motivation has confirmed that intrinsic interest in a task – the sense that something is worth doing for its own sake – typically declines when someone is only given external reasons for doing it. Getting people to chase money can produce nothing except people chasing money. It can be argued, for example, that paying commission to sales representatives will encourage them to concentrate on increasing sales turnover at the expense of achieving sustained customer satisfaction and loyalty.

The impact of paying for performance

A number of recent research projects have cast doubts about the impact of paying for performance.

Research conducted by Bevan and Thompson[9] of the Institute of Manpower Studies found no link between improved company performance and performance-related pay. It showed that companies whose financial performance was poor were as likely as good performers to have performance-related pay.

A recent survey of BT executives[10] carried out by the Society of Telecom Executives (the BT management/professional trade union) revealed that only 6 per cent of those responding to the survey thought that performance-related pay improved their performance compared with an overwhelming 70 per cent who thought it had not.

Research conducted for the Inland Revenue Staff Federation by Marsden and Richardson[11] of the London School of Economics among 2,500 Inland Revenue staff produced the finding that:

> 'Revenue staff generally support the principle of performance-related pay but a significant minority feels hostile to it ... The positive motivational effects of performance pay have been, at most, very modest among Inland Revenue staff. It is hard to see that they have been felt to any degree by more than a small minority of staff'.

Since that research, the Inland Revenue scheme has been changed and it is understood that it is now more acceptable.

The research conducted on behalf of the Institute of Personnel Management and the National Economic Development Office into incentive payment schemes, Cannell and Wood,[12] did not confirm that performance-related pay was a motivator. Face-to-face interviews were conducted with 40 personnel directors and managers from large and medium-sized organizations. The conclusions were that:

> The personnel managers interviewed for this report were by no means certain that PRP schemes succeeded in motivating people. Most were not convinced they could unequivocally identify that PRP was increasing either individual or overall organizational performance. Some put it in words such as "it's an article of faith". Or, as a public sector manager put it: "We have no clear evidence either way on whether our schemes improve motivation and morale by rewarding good performance, or whether they serve to demotivate employees who are not motivated".

It was also noted that 'there was widespread uncertainty about the precise role of money'.

An even more recent (1993) research study conducted by Thompson of the Institute of Manpower Studies[13] produced the conclusion that performance-related pay fails to improve staff achievement and often leads to a 'downward spiral of demotivation'. The research examined the attitudes of 1000 employees in a county council, a building society and a food retailer. The report found that pay based on assessments of individual performance was seen as unfair by both union members and by workers with no union affiliations. It failed to improve staff motivation and exposed the poor skills of managers. Thompson believes that the reasons for this reaction included the organizations' failure to involve employees sufficiently in the design and implementation of the scheme, and once implemented, the poor people skills of managers. He has suggested that:

'Although the Government is very keen on individual-based performance pay schemes, the private sector experience has shown they often fail to live up to the claims made for them'.

In the US, *Business Week*[14] cited a 1987 study by Jensen and Murphy of the University of Rochester which examined the relationship between pay and performance. After looking at nearly 2000 executives in 1200 companies, they rejected statistically the pay-for-performance hypothesis and concluded that 'executives tend to be overpaid for bad performance and underpaid for good performance'.

A study by Berlet and Cravens[15] of the pay-for-performance record of 163 US companies from 1987 to 1989 revealed that the relationship between executive pay and company financial performance was virtually random.

Disadvantages of paying for performance

To summarize, the potential disadvantages of paying for performance are that incentive and bonus schemes can:

- if over-individualistic in focus and values be divisive, prejudicing teamwork;
- be inequitable and unfair if they do not clearly and properly relate reward to performance, which they often fail to do;
- encourage 'short-termism' – for example, executives concentrating on short-term issues linked to annual targets rather than the achievement of longer-term plans;
- encourage shop floor workers to go for output at the expense of quality and sales staff to go for sales turnover rather than customer service;
- often be all too easy to manipulate;
- be demotivating if they are linked to corporate performance which is adversely affected by outside influences such as exchange rate fluctuations;
- often be difficult to keep under control – earnings can increase to absurdly high limits (especially in some executive bonus schemes) without any commensurate improvement in performance;
- appear to conflict with the belief that executive – and other – staff should be rewarded by competitive basic salaries because they are expected to give their utmost as professionals;
- add to remuneration costs without delivering real performance improvements.

These disadvantages can be formidable and should be weighed very carefully against the advantages set out earlier before introducing a new scheme or reviewing an existing one. Account should also be taken of the reservations expressed above about the effectiveness of performance pay. Wright[16] has emphasized that: 'Even the most ardent supporters of performance-related pay recognize that it is extraordinarily difficult to manage well'.

The philosophical argument that it is equitable to relate pay to performance is overwhelming, and it does work well in many circumstances especially on the shop floor, in sales jobs, and in managerial or other jobs where there is a visible and direct relationship between focused effort and reward. It can also be argued strongly than performance pay schemes are an effective means of conveying the messages that performance matters and channelling effort in the right direction.

To understand when performance pay might or might not work it is necessary to consider the individual and organizational criteria for effectiveness as set out below.

Criteria for individual and group schemes

The five golden rules for successful pay-for-performance schemes were defined by Mike Langley, past Vice-President of the Institute of Personnel Management's National Committee for Pay and Employment Conditions and first Chairman of the IPM Compensation Forum. These are:

1. Individuals and teams need to be clear about the targets and standards of performance required, whatever they may be.
2. They should be able to track performance against those targets and standards throughout the period over which performance is being assessed.
3. They must be in a position to influence the performance by changing their behaviour or decisions.
4. They should be clear about the rewards they will receive for achieving the required end results.
5. The rewards should be meaningful enough to make the efforts required worthwhile – and the communication of the rewards should be positively handled.

In addition to these basic requirements, performance pay is more likely to work as a motivator if:

■ fair and consistent means are available for measuring performance – it can be said that 'you can't pay for performance unless you can measure performance';
■ it is appropriate to the type of work carried out and the people employed on it and fits the culture of the organization;
■ the reward is clearly and closely linked to the effort of the individual or team;
■ the reward follows as closely as possible the accomplishment which generated it;
■ the reward is clearly and closely linked and proportionate to the effort of the individual or team;
■ employees expect that effective performance (or specified behaviour) will certainly lead to worthwhile rewards;
■ the incentive or performance-related pay scheme operates by means of a defined and easily understood formula;
■ provisions are made in the scheme for amending the formula in specified circumstances;
■ there is a reasonable amount of stability in work methods and flows;
■ constraints are built into individual schemes which ensure that employees

cannot receive inflated rewards which are not related to their own performance;

- the scheme is properly designed, installed, maintained and adapted to meet
changing circumstances;
- employees covered by the scheme are involved in its development and
operation and in making needed modifications;
- managers have the people skills required to obtain the maximum benefit from
the scheme;
- determined and continuing efforts are made by the organization to communicate to employees the rationale of the scheme and how they can benefit from
it.

These are demanding criteria, and it is no wonder that performance pay schemes
often fail to meet expectations. But there is no evidence that some forms of performance pay such as PRP are in decline; quite the reverse, although many first
generation schemes such as that installed by the Inland Revenue are being
extensively revised or revitalized because they are unpopular, or ineffective, or
both. There has, however, been a decline in the number of payment-by-result
schemes for manual workers. A number of PRP schemes at local authority chief
officer level have also been withdrawn for cost/political reasons, leaving the
performance management processes, which were valued, intact.

Organizational criteria

The fundamental organizational criterion is that the performance pay system
should fit business needs (in the private sector) or corporate objectives (in the
public and voluntary sectors). It should also be congruent with the organization's
culture and values, although it can help to shape the culture by, for example,
emphasizing the need for high levels of performance. The following specific points
need to be considered:

- the corporate culture;
- corporate strategy;
- technology and administrative processes;
- opportunity versus risk;
- whose performance matters most?
- individual performance versus teamwork;
- how should performance improvements be shared?

Corporate culture

Performance pay is more likely to succeed in an entrepreneurial and performance-
orientated culture where the values support individualism, hard work, risk-taking
and the acquisition of money and status symbols. A participative culture can also
help by involving employees in the design of pay and performance management
systems, by ensuring that objectives are mutually agreed between managers and
their staff and by the joint analysis of performance issues identified in a gainsharing plan.

The problem is that it is hard for organizations successfully to maintain a culture
which satisfies both these requirements (ie, is entrepreneurial, individualistic etc,
as well as being participative). This is one of the reasons why performance pay can
be difficult to operate effectively.

Corporate strategy

Corporate strategies for growth, innovation, improved quality and customer service should provide the foundation for the design and development processes. They will influence the performance measures and criteria used in the scheme and indicate the targets to be set and how the reasons for and objectives of performance pay should be communicated to employees.

Technology and administrative processes

The technology and administrative processes will largely determine the form of performance pay used. For example:

- Process plants where individuals have little or no control over output will not benefit from individual incentive schemes. But overall performance in terms of output, cost and quality is important and may be rewarded by some form of plant-wide bonus scheme such as gainsharing.
- Mass production and assembly line plants where work is machine-paced are more likely to have line or unit bonus schemes or some form of measured day work rather than individual incentive schemes.
- Batch or jobbing production plants may have individual or group bonus schemes based on work measurement.
- Workshops such as those in the clothing industry where output is largely determined by individual effort may rely on traditional piecework incentive schemes.
- A factory where production uses just-in-time (JIT) principles will base rewards on success in minimizing inventory and work in progress, maintaining throughput and delivery targets, and being 'right first time'. Such a factory may also install a gainsharing plan.
- A plant where the emphasis is on total quality management (TQM) will give priority to the achievement of consistently high levels of quality as a basis for reward as well as productivity.
- A highly automated plant using direct numerical controlled (DNC) or computer numerical controlled (CNC) machine tools in manufacturing cells may wish to reward people for flexibility in the use of a number of skills (multi-skilling) and may therefore institute skill-based pay. Incentive schemes are more likely to be related to team than individual performance.
- A high technology company employing scientists and research or development engineers on largely innovative projects may have a variety of team or organization-wide bonus systems, but could relate pay to the acquisition and use of required competences as well as output.
- A bureaucratic organization may retain some form of incremental system relating rewards mainly to time in the job. Increasingly, however, such organizations are introducing performance-related pay systems which link pay to assessed contribution and competence.
- An organization with an activity-based costing (ABC) system may relate part of the reward package to the achievement of specific cost management and reduction targets as identified by the process of linking costs specifically to department activities.

Opportunity versus risk

Pay-for-performance schemes provide the opportunity to obtain increased financial rewards. Opportunity may, however, involve risk. A key design question will be how much of total remuneration should be set at risk. The risk element may be greatest in entrepreneurial or selling jobs, but the opportunities for increased earnings must be proportionately high. Risk will be minimal in production-paced or routine office jobs and the opportunity for gain will be proportionately reduced. There is also the view that the least well paid employees in an organization should not be asked to have such a high proportion of pay at risk that it might have too much impact on fairly basic living standards.

Whose performance matters most?

In some organizations the overall results achieved depend crucially on the effective performance of a small number of people who are directing the enterprise or who are responsible for innovation, marketing and sales. In such cases it makes business sense to reward these people highly and put a large proportion of pay at risk. Most organizations, however, depend on the efficient performance of employees at all levels. In these circumstances a pay system that syphons off resources to a few star performers would be at best irrelevant and at worst counter-productive.

The good, reliable core performers should be rewarded according to their market worth and this should increase as they gain experience. Even if they can not be given large performance-related increases, they should at least be eligible for an achievement bonus if they make a special contribution, or for a special sustained performance bonus if they consistently deliver a fully competent level of performance. There may be scope for including them in team bonus schemes and there is certainly much merit in their participating in organization-wide gain-sharing, profit sharing or profit-related pay schemes.

Individual performance and teamwork

On the one hand it is necessary to avoid defining individual performance in a way which is so internally competitive that it disrupts teamwork. On the other hand, the situation should be avoided in which poor individual performance can be hidden within the team. This suggests the use of group or team incentive and bonus schemes – team pay – where appropriate, although performance pay for individuals can be, and increasingly is being, influenced by the degree to which they contribute to team results and work well as team members. The scope for using this approach has improved greatly with the increased use of competences, including collaborative behaviour, in performance management and assessment.

How should performance improvements be shared?

There are three basic pay-for-performance models as illustrated in Figure 16.1.

1. *The regressive payment or decelerated model* in which employees are paid incrementally more for initial improvements in performance which taper off as higher levels of performance are reached. In other words, pay progresses proportionately less than output. The rationale for this approach is (*a*) learning theory, which suggests that learning progresses most rapidly when information and expertise are first absorbed and then tapers off gradually as more information is gained, (*b*) competitive pay practices for individual jobs, which often show that pay tends to progress in a similar pattern to the learning curve, and (*c*) to pay more at a similar or greater rate of increase would incur

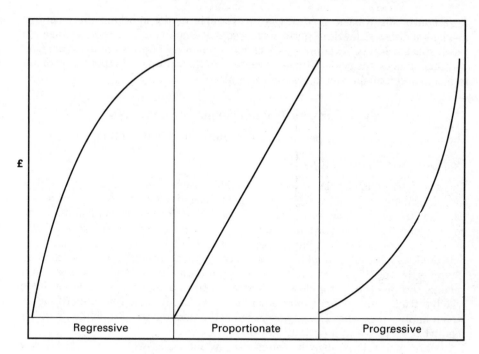

Figure 16.1 *Pay-for-performance models*

unnecessary cost in relation to the extra contribution and time an employee can make.

This system provides less incentive to strive for higher output, possibly at the expense of quality. The spread of earnings is also limited which may reduce the likelihood of discontent because of high variations in pay. But the obvious disadvantage is that the incentive to perform better is reduced.

Most performance-related pay schemes and many shop floor incentive plans follow this pattern.

2. *The proportionate payment or shared model* in which bonus payments increase in direct proportion to output or contribution. A fixed percentage of gain is allocated to employees which is held constant irrespective of performance. This approach is simple to explain and understand and appears to be equitable.

    But employees may be encouraged to go for quantity rather than quality and costs can escalate. Piecework, straight commission and traditional gain-sharing schemes tend to follow this pattern.

3. *The progressive payment or accelerated model* in which the bonus increases proportionately more than contribution or output. The organization is willing to take a smaller percentage of the gain as employees increasingly exceed performance expectations. This provides a high incentive for extra effort or improved results but the employer may incur considerable costs, while employees may skimp on quality and safety. There is also a much wider divide between high and low bonus earners which may be difficult to justify. This approach is relatively uncommon and is usually reserved for high risk/high reward jobs.

A variant of these basic methods is the variable model in which the incentive changes at different levels of performance so that employees can be encouraged to reach specific levels of output by receiving a relatively large boost in earnings at certain points on the scale. The disadvantage of this approach is that it is difficult to install and explain such a system to employees.

Types of pay-for-performance schemes

The main types of pay-for-performance schemes are described briefly below.

Performance-related pay

The term performance-related pay is sometimes used to describe any type of pay-for-performance scheme. We are restricting its use in this book to schemes which base additional financial rewards on ratings of performance, contribution and competence. The ratings are derived from performance reviews and assessments of overall contribution, achievements against objectives, and competence delivered as part of the performance management process, as described in Chapters 14 and 15. We prefer not to use the term performance appraisal as it smacks too much of a top-down relationship from a superior to a subordinate which is what performance management is *not* about. We also reject 'merit rating' which implies that what is being assessed is the personality of individuals rather than what they do and how well they do it.

Performance ratings usually determine pay increases which provide for pay progression through all or part of a pay range, along a pay curve or up a pay spine. However, in some schemes ratings can lead to lump sum bonus payments as an alternative or addition to an increase in pay. Detailed consideration is given to performance-related pay in Chapter 17.

Incentive and bonus schemes

Incentive and bonus schemes offer and provide rewards which are directly related to the measured achievements and results of individuals, teams or the organization as a whole. Different arrangements can be made according to the type of employees concerned. Shop floor and manual workers generally (see Chapter 18) may be involved in some form of payment-by-results scheme based on work measurement. Executives (see Chapter 20) may be rewarded through incentive and bonus schemes based on the achievement of targeted performance levels as may be the case with other levels of staff (Chapter 19) and sales representatives (Chapter 22).

Executive share ownership schemes

Executive share option schemes (see Chapter 21) provide managers with a stake in the company and a longer-term reward by giving them the option to buy shares at a future date for their current market price. Provided that the share price appreciates, the individual makes a profit when the option is exercised and the shares sold.

Gainsharing

Gainsharing (see Chapter 23) is a formula-based company or factory-wide bonus plan which provides for employees to share in the financial gains resulting from increases in added value or another measure of productivity.

Profit sharing

Profit sharing (see Chapter 24) is the payment to eligible employees of sums in the form of cash or shares related to the profits of the business. The amount shared may be determined by a published or unpublished formula or entirely at the discretion of management. Profit sharing differs from gainsharing in that the former is based on more than improved productivity. A number of factors outside the individual employee's control contribute to profit. Gainsharing aims to relate its payouts much more specifically to productivity and performance improvements within the control of employees.

Profit-related pay

Profit-related pay (see Chapter 25) is a Government-sponsored and regulated scheme for linking pay to profits in accordance with a pre-determined formula. The scheme offers significant tax advantages over traditional profit sharing schemes but is governed by statutory criteria and its use is growing.

Skill and competence-based pay

Skill and competence-based pay schemes (see Chapters 26 and 27) relate rewards to the achievement of defined levels of skill or competence.

Choice of scheme

When developing a total remuneration package for all employees or for particular categories of staff, decisions have first to be made on whether there should be any element of reward based on individual, team or organizational performance. The considerations affecting this choice are discussed in succeeding chapters of this book.

If a decision is made that there should be some form of performance pay for all employees or for certain categories, the choice of scheme will, of course, depend on the type of organization, the type of employees who will be involved, the time scale required and the impact it is hoped the scheme will make on performance.

Performance-related pay and other types of bonus and incentive schemes can operate on an individual, team or organization-wide basis. Individual schemes are more appropriate when performance or contribution can be attributed directly to the efforts and abilities of individuals and the individual nature of the scheme will not prejudice teamwork. Group or team pay may be more appropriate when results depend on team rather than individual effort and roles have generally to be more flexible. New working arrangements such as just-in-time, flexible manufacturing systems and cellular manufacturing are driving the move towards more team pay systems.

In general, incentive and bonus schemes in which there is a clear target-related incentive and the reward closely follows the performance are likely to make the most immediate impact on motivation. Performance-related pay where awards are usually made some time after the event will have a medium-term effect and will not impact so directly on motivation. Schemes relating the reward to organizational performance are also likely to have a medium-term effect and will impact on commitment and retention rather than serving as direct motivators. Share option schemes operate on a long-term basis and are more likely to increase commitment than make an immediate impact on motivation.

Pay-for-performance plans such as profit sharing and profit-related pay based

Type of scheme / Time scale	Instrumental schemes affecting motivation		Schemes affecting commitment and retention
	individual	team	
immediate	individual incentive or bonus	group incentive or bonus	
medium-term	performance-related pay		gainsharing profit-related pay profit sharing
long-term			share option

Figure 16.2 *Performance pay choice matrix*

on organizational rather than individual or team performance aim to share the organization's achievements with employees and increase their identification with and commitment to the organization. Gainsharing plans emphasise the involvement of employees as well as their financial rewards.

The matrix illustrated in Figure 16.2 is designed to help in the choice of the scheme or mix of schemes by summarizing the impact of different schemes in terms of motivation, commitment, retention and time scale.

A total performance reward approach

The total performance reward approach uses a range of individual, team and organizational performance rewards. This recognizes the different facets and layers of performance and emphasizes the messages that can be delivered through reward management processes to reinforce success.

Consideration should be given to how a total performance reward approach can be developed which incorporates, as required, both individual and/or team pay-for-performance schemes as well as an organization-wide plan (but only one of the latter at a time). This combines specific incentives and rewards and enables employees to share in the success of the company.

References

1. Taylor, F W (1911) *Principles of Scientific Management.* Harper, New York
2. Lawler, E (1971) *Pay and Organizational Effectiveness*, McGraw-Hill, New York

3. Guzzo, R, Jelle, R and Katsell, R (1985) 'The effect of psychology-based intervention programmes on worker productivity: a meta analysis', *Personnel Psychology* 38.
4. Nalbantian, H (1987) *Incentives, Cooperation and Risk Sharing*, Rowan and Littlefield, Totowa, New Jersey
5. Binder, A (1990) *Paying for Productivity*, Brookings Institute, Washington, DC
6. McGregor, D *The Human Side of Enterprise*, McGraw-Hill, New York
7. Brown, W (1962) *Piecework Abandoned*, Heinemann, London
8. Beer, M (1984) 'Reward systems', In M. Beer, B. Spector, P. Lawrence and D. Quin Mills, *Managing Human Assets*, The Free Press, New York
9. Bevan, S and Thompson, M (1991) 'Performance management at the cross roads', *Personnel Management*, November
10. Society of Telecom Executives (1991) 'Rewarding in secret – a survey of bonuses and PRP in BT', *The Review Journal of the STE*, July
11. Marsden, D and Richardson, R (1991) *Does Performance Pay Motivate? A Study of Inland Revenue Staff*, London School of Economics, London
12. Cannell, M and Wood, S (1992) *Incentive Pay: Impact and Evolution*. Institute of Personnel Management, London
13. Thompson, M (1993) *Pay and Performance: The Employee Experience*. Institute of Manpower Studies, Brighton
14. *Business Week* (1987) 'Executive compensation scoreboard', 4 May
15. Berlet, K and Cravens, D (1991) *Performance Pay as a Competitive Weapon*, Wiley, New York
16. Wright, V (1991) 'Performance-related pay', in F. Neale, (Ed.), *The Handbook of Performance Management*, Institute of Personnel Management, London

17

Performance-Related Pay

Performance-related pay (PRP) links pay progression to a performance and/or competence rating. The rating could be carried out during a performance review, or it could be conducted at a different time exclusively for PRP purposes. PRP is sometimes said to be based on merit rating, but this term is less used nowadays.

PRP is associated with graded pay structures, individual job range structures and pay curves, as described in Chapter 12. It normally provides for an increase in base pay which is governed by a rating against such criteria as performance and contribution outputs and skill and competence inputs. There may, however, be provision in some schemes for achievement bonuses to be paid in certain circumstances which are also determined on the basis of ratings carried out by managers on the individual's performance etc.

We distinguish in this chapter between PRP as described above, which is based on ratings carried out by managers, and other types of pay-for-performance bonus and incentive schemes as covered in subsequent chapters, which pay out lump sums or commission on the basis of the achievement of predetermined targets (often controlled by a formula).

PRP as discussed in this chapter is generally applied to individuals. But the increasing attention being paid to developing good teamwork is encouraging some organizations to concentrate more on team pay, usually through some form of group bonus scheme. And individual PRP schemes are paying more attention to performance criteria related to teamwork.

In this chapter we:

- define the objectives of PRP;
- examine the reasons for the growth of PRP;
- review the arguments for and against PRP;
- describe how individual PRP operates;
- describe the conditions required for a successful PRP scheme and the considerations to be taken into account when introducing PRP;
- consider how the impact of PRP can be monitored and evaluated.

Objectives of PRP

The overall objective of PRP is to provide incentives and rewards which will improve the performance of the organization by improving individual performance. To achieve this objective the aims of PRP are to:

- motivate all employees, not only the high performers but also the core on whom the organization depends;
- deliver a positive message about the performance expectations of the organization;

- focus attention and endeavour on the key performance issues;
- differentiate rewards to people consistently and equitably according to their contribution and competence;
- help to change cultures where they need to become more performance and results orientated or where the development of other key values such as quality and customer service needs to be encouraged;
- reinforce existing cultures and values which foster high levels of performance, innovation, quality and teamwork;
- emphasize the importance of teamwork as well as individual contributions;
- improve the recruitment and retention of high quality employees who will expect PRP as part of a well-managed working environment;
- flex pay costs in line with organizational performance.

Reasons for the growth of PRP

It was established by the IPM/NEDO 1992 study, Cannell and Wood,[1] that PRP has become the main method of determining pay progression for non-manual workers, but it is also being extended to shop floor employees. PRP has now largely replaced the fixed incremental systems introduced in the private sector during the incomes policy era of the 1970s. It is also making inroads within the public sector, where traditional incremental pay spines are being modified to allow some flexibility for performance-related pay.

A large proportion (40 per cent) of the organizations covered by the IPM/NEDO research introduced PRP within the ten years prior to 1991. And it is being extended more rapidly in the public sector. In July 1991 the Government announced that as part of its Citizen's Charter initiative, PRP was to be extended further; there should, it said, be a 'regular and direct link between remuneration and standards of service'.

PRP schemes grew rapidly in the entrepreneurial eighties. A commitment to the market economy was easily extended to a widespread belief that money is the best, indeed, as some extremists hold, the only, motivator although there is no hard evidence to support that belief as a universal proposition.

However, in many organizations there is, rightly, a strong feeling that, even if the effectiveness of money as a motivator can be questioned, it is fair to pay people according to their contribution. The drive against incremental systems has taken place because managements do not see why they should pay people more simply for being there. Incremental systems are explicitly associated by many people with unmotivated performance. At least, so the argument goes, if we reward people more flexibly according to their performance they are more likely to be motivated than if they are sitting around waiting for their next automatic increment.

Another powerful argument advanced for PRP is that it is a lever for cultural change in the direction of accountability for results and orientation towards high performance. One of the most often quoted reasons for introducing PRP given by the personnel managers interviewed during the IPM/NEDO study was that it delivers a strong message about the expectations of the organization. As one personnel manager in a manufacturing firm said:

> Introducing PRP was a key event really. It was a break from the past which said: "You will always get an increase every year; you will always get a minimum increase and on top of that you will always get something else and it doesn't matter how you perform". Now what we are saying is:

"Nobody owes anybody a thing; nobody gets a pay rise unless they earn a pay rise". So it is a total break.

Arguments for PRP

The strongest argument in favour of PRP is that it is right and equitable to reward people according to their contribution. PRP provides a tangible means of recognizing achievement. PRP is also a means of ensuring that everyone understands the performance imperatives of the organization. It is also argued, of course, that PRP works as an incentive because money is the best motivator.

Arguments against PRP

The arguments most frequently levelled against PRP are that:

- Its effectiveness as a motivator can be questioned – there is little firm evidence that people are motivated by their expectations of the rewards they will get from PRP, especially as these are often quite small.
- Financial incentives may work for some people because their expectations that they will be rewarded well are high. But such individuals will tend to be well-motivated anyway. Less confident employees will not respond so well to the possibility of rewards which they do not expect to receive.
- It can be difficult to measure individual performance objectively, especially in demand-led or process jobs – unfair assessments may be made in these circumstances because ratings tend to be both subjective and inconsistent.
- It can encourage people to focus narrowly on the tasks that will earn them brownie points and to be less concerned about innovation, longer-term issues and quality.
- If there is undue emphasis on individual performance, teamwork will suffer.
- It can lead to pay rising faster than performance if proper control is not exercised – there is often a tendency for performance-related pay to drift upwards without any commensurate improvement in performance.

Counter-arguments

The following counter-arguments can be made to these criticisms.

PRP not a guaranteed motivator

While it may not have been proved that PRP guarantees better motivation, neither has it been disproved. The concept that people react positively to financial incentives has considerable face validity – as long as it is not simplistically argued that money is *all* they work for and as long as the financial rewards are worthwhile and attainable.

The impact of PRP as a direct motivator may be arguable and the prospect of a small reward might not provide a powerful incentive. But the achievement of a reward is a tangible means of recognition and can therefore provide for less direct but possibly longer-term motivation.

Even if it is conceded that PRP may have a limited effect as a motivator, it can still play an important part in defining the performance expectations of the organization and focusing effort.

Limited impact of financial incentives

PRP need not be regarded as the only motivator. Attention should also be given to the non-financial approaches to motivation and recognition as described in Chapter 2. An integrated approach to performance management can motivate all types of employees (not just the high-flyers) by providing the basis for a mix of financial and non-financial rewards. The essence of the process of performance management is that it encourages the prior agreement of acceptable targets and performance measures. This can establish realistic expectations about the rewards that can be achieved if the performance agreement is fulfilled.

Measurement problems

It is true that PRP will not work unless fair and realistic performance measures are established. But it can be argued that anything that can be managed can be measured. The trap to avoid is the belief that only quantifiable performance measures are valid. It is possible to measure performance by reference to agreed standards of behaviour by adopting a competency approach which involves the definition and agreement of the levels of competence required and an assessment of performance in relation to that definition. The use of differentiating competences, ie those which separate and distinguish between the excellent and the average as identified in the Hay/McBer and other methodologies, is particularly powerful in this context.

It has to be admitted, however, that this is not an easy answer. The definition and measurement of performance standards and competence levels requires considerable skill and the organization must be prepared to invest in the time and training required to develop these skills.

Narrow focus

The danger of PRP encouraging people to focus narrowly on short-term quantifiable results and quantity rather than quality is a real one. But it is avoidable if care is taken to widen the criteria for rewards to include behaviour which satisfies requirements for innovation, contribution to the achievement of longer-term results and quality.

Prejudicial to teamwork

The potentially harmful effect on teamwork of individual PRP can be mitigated by including the achievement of good teamwork and collaborative behaviour as performance measures. Performance agreements can specify the specific contributions employees are expected to make to teamwork and ratings can take account of levels of performance in this area. Generic and differentiating competence definitions which are used as a basis for assessment can also include teamwork as a key competence area.

Where teamwork is all-important, some form of team pay – pay related to the performance of the team – can be considered in addition to or instead of individual performance-related pay.

Control problems

PRP schemes can fail to provide value-for-money unless they are properly controlled to avoid payments unrelated to performance improvements. This is partly a matter of setting up the scheme in a way which spells out the parameters clearly and specifies how control will be exercised. The careful and continuing training and support of managers in operating the scheme responsibly is also important. And, of course, the implementation of the scheme must be monitored and evaluated. Cost iterations on computerized reward management systems can greatly assist in the pay monitoring and control process.

PRP decisions

Decisions on whether or not to introduce or continue with PRP depend on an evaluation of its pros and cons in the light of the particular culture, environment and objectives of the organization. We discuss the considerations to be taken into account when introducing and evaluating PRP later in this chapter (pages 271–7). But it is first necessary to provide a basis for such considerations by describing how PRP operates.

The operation of performance-related pay

PRP can operate in a pay structure by providing for different rates of progression within the pay range for a grade or a job according to performance, as described in Chapter 12. It can also be used within such a structure to provide some variation in reward when a fixed service-related incremental system is used or in a pay spine. This will take the form of part, extra or withheld increments or additional increments for those at the top of their range (range points) if they consistently receive high ratings. In a pay curve system PRP determines the rate of progression through the competence bands, as also described in Chapter 12.

The most typical PRP system uses variable progression within a pay range. The main operational features of such a system are considered below under the following headings:

- basic characteristics;
- rating arrangements;
- size of increases;
- progression rates and limits;
- progression guidelines;
- use of performance matrices;
- control arrangements.

Basic characteristics

A PRP scheme provides for variable performance-related payments in a pay range. This type of scheme, also known as a pay range scheme, provides for progression within the range to be determined by performance ratings. The size of increases and the rates and limits of progression will vary in accordance with a number of factors as discussed below. The basis for deciding on performance-related pay increases may be governed by guidelines on the allocation and distribution of ratings and how rewards should be related to ratings in accordance with the individual's position in a pay range. These guidelines may be formalized in a performance matrix.

Rating

The size of performance-related increases is governed by ratings. Examples of rating scales are given in Chapter 15. As explained, rating scales need to be defined with great care and managers should be given explicit guidance on how they should decide on ratings. The whole purpose of performance-related pay could be undermined if such ratings were biased or unduly subjective. Ratings should be based on hard evidence, understood and trusted by those under review.

A few organizations are not in favour of including ratings in the performance review process. They believe that this would prejudice the open and cooperative nature of the relationship between managers and individuals, which is an essential feature of a developmental approach to performance management. If such organizations want to use performance-related pay they will separate the PRP review from the performance management review. The PRP rating may simply indicate whether an individual should have, say, a very high, an above average, an average or a below average increase, or no increase at all. Naturally, there is a 'read across' from the performance review to the pay increase decision although the latter will be influenced by other considerations besides performance such as the position of the individual in the range, the need to deal with anomalies and a need to ensure that an individual is paid according to his or her market worth.

The pay dimensions to be attached to these decisions are determined by policy guidelines and controlled within overall and departmental budgets.

Some organizations attempt to ensure fair and consistent ratings across departments by providing a forum in which managers who have carried out performance ratings cross-check and validate their judgements. They do this by comparing their decisions with those of their colleagues and testing them by jointly examining the supporting evidence. Others run 'consistency workshops' each year to help build a common view of ratings and their application between managers.

Others take a directive line and adopt a more rigid, even mechanistic approach to control ratings so that they conform to what the organization believes is the right pattern of distribution. This process of forced distribution has often surfaced as a problem in PRP evaluations and it can create understandable feelings of resentment amongst managers as it takes away most of their authority for managing rewards. It implies that managers are not to be trusted to act responsibly, although it may be thought that if you never trust anyone to be responsible, how can they be responsible? Low-trust organizations can be unpleasant and demotivating to work in.

Size of performance-related increases

The size of performance-related increases is determined by ratings within the framework of policies on pay progression rates and limits and the limits of pay review budgets.

There are no firm guidelines on the desirable relationship between different levels of performance and the size of an increase. Research conducted by Lawler[2] in the US indicates that a pay increase of 3–4 per cent, while noticeable, is not sufficient to improve performance. He suggests that a pay rise of 10–15 per cent is probably required to increase motivation significantly.

As a rule of thumb, those whose performance is outstanding may deserve and expect rewards of at least 10 per cent and more in their earlier period in a job. People whose level of performance and rate of development is well above the average may merit increases of between 8–10 per cent, while those who are progressing well at the expected rate towards the fully competent level may warrant an increase of between 5–7 per cent. Increases of between 3–5 per cent may be justified for those who are not making such good progress but who are still developing steadily. Performance-related increases of less than 3 per cent are hardly worth giving. Much also depends on current market movement.

At a time of low inflation, employers may take the view that they should not be contributing to pay drift and that there is no obligation to do more than maintain the purchasing power of competent performers, although, presumably, if they believe in performance-related pay at all, they must be prepared to provide higher awards to outstanding performers. Such a view could take the average increase in current (1993) conditions to 2 per cent or less. One issue under discussion in late 1993 was how to make rewards meaningful for those who deserve them even if the overall approach is justified.

The amount largely depends on the type of organization, its culture and what it is prepared and able to pay. A performance-orientated, high-achieving organization will offer high rewards in line with its high expectations consistent with what it can afford. If the organization wants to retain good quality employees whose skills are much in demand it will have to take account of the market rates of progression for those people. A meaningful increase in one organization for a particular individual may be significantly higher or lower than what other organizations would be prepared to pay. One organization may feel that it has to pay its top performers 15–20 per cent plus, while another would be content with 8–10 per cent or even less – much less in parts of the public service.

The size of performance-related increases may be constrained by ability-to-pay considerations. If a lot has to be spent on increases to keep pace with market rates, less may be left in the pool for performance pay. But it would be a pity to restrict PRP increases too much. Such 'fire-fighting' can undo months or even years of work in getting the performance-related pay message across.

Performance-related pay increases may be affected not only by performance ratings but also by the individual's position in the pay range. This can be expressed as a comparison ratio or 'compa-ratio' which shows the relationship between an individual's actual rate of pay and the policy pay range reference point for his or her grade as follows:

$$\text{compa-ratio} = \frac{\text{actual pay}}{\text{reference point of pay policy for grade}} \times 100$$

A compa-ratio of 100 per cent means that actual pay is the same as the reference point policy level. A ratio of more or less than 100 per cent means that actual pay is above or below the reference point as the case may be.

Increases may vary according to the compa-ratio. For example, the policy may be to provide for higher increases where the compa-ratio is below 100 per cent in order to reward people more in the earlier part of their period in the job. In this case the assumption might be that in this period there is more scope for achieving higher levels of performance and more significant rewards are justifiable to keep pace with the higher rate of progress. This policy would be in line with the regressive or decelerated payment model as discussed in Chapter 16.

In a fixed incremental system or pay spine the size of the increments is, of course, pre-determined.

Detailed consideration is given in Chapter 37 on how performance-related pay reviews can be carried out and controlled and how they can be linked to more general structural increases in response to external trends in the job market.

Progression rates and limits

As described in Chapter 13, the design of the pay structure will be based on assumptions about the rate at which individuals can progress in a range and how far they can penetrate into the range depending on performance.

A pay progression policy may provide for a movement-through-the-range element which enables individuals to reach the range reference point if and when they achieve the required level of performance, skill and competence. The size of the range below the reference point will be determined on the basis of assumptions about how long it should take the average employee to reach this level. This also involves making assumptions about the size of the increases up to the reference point which such employees could earn if they progress steadily. For example, in a £20,000 to £30,000 range (80–120 per cent) where the reference point is at the midpoint (£25,000) it might be assumed that the average rate of progression to the reference point should be 5 per cent of the minimum of the range (£1000). This would mean that individuals who are rated consistently as achieving a satisfactory rate of progress would take five years to reach the reference point if they started at the minimum rate. The time to reach the reference point can, of course, be varied either by positioning it elsewhere in the range, eg at £20,000 to make the progression period four years at 5 per cent, and/or by selecting different rates of increase. These parameters may only be used as guidelines in order to achieve a reasonable degree of flexibility, and it may be necessary to flex the progression policy in response to changing financial circumstances or other factors.

Above the reference point the policy may be to increase pay only for significantly higher levels of contribution and more flexibility in the rate of progression could be allowed. Target rates of pay may be set for particular levels of performance as illustrated in Figure 12.2.

Progression policy and the associated guidelines may be the same throughout the organization for those in an integrated pay structure. In an individual range, job family or pay curve structure, progression policies may vary between different jobs or occupations in a job family. Some organizations flex progression policies according to the grade level.

All graded pay systems create the problem of what happens to able employees who have reached the top of the range and have no immediate prospects of promotion. It can be argued that if they are at their range maximum they will have been rewarded for exceptional performance and will be paid on a continuing basis well above market rate. But the absence of any financial recognition for exceptional and sustained contribution in such cases can be highly demotivating. Some organizations do allow pay to drift above the range maximum but if this becomes a frequent occurrence where allowance has already been made in the scale for rewarding high-performers, the integrity of the pay structure could be damaged. A better approach is to award unconsolidated special achievement or sustained high performance lump sum bonuses. The size of such bonuses could be linked to performance ratings and they could be re-earnable, as is currently the case for those at the top of their range in the Civil Service. Some organizations, however, limit such bonuses to those who have sustained a high level of contribution over a period of two or three years.

Performance-related pay guidelines

The guidelines for managers on conducting PRP reviews may simply consist of a statement of progression policy and the way in which it should be implemented. This might be accompanied by illustrations on how employees can progress through a range, advice on how to rate performance, the budget for increases and the range of increases within that budget appropriate for different ratings (eg A = 10–12%, B = 6–9%, C = 3–5%). A more comprehensive approach to providing guidance is to use a performance matrix as described below.

Performance matrices

A performance matrix as illustrated in Figure 17.1 provides guidance on how increases should be related to different levels of performance according to the individual's position in the pay range (the individual compa-ratio). The rates will be based on the organization's progression policies and will need to be flexed at the time of the pay review (or annually if pay reviews are conducted on a rolling basis). Matrices can be used flexibly and are helpful in large organizations.

The following factors need to be taken into account when devising or updating a performance matrix:

- The structure of the pay range, ie its dimensions and the position of the reference point. Different matrices will have to be drawn up in accordance with these dimensions.
- The basis of progression, eg decelerating – individuals are paid more for initial improvements in performance but payments are proportionately less as higher levels of performance are reached. This is the most typical pattern. Its rationale was discussed in Chapter 16.
- Market rates of progression.
- The size of the increases. This will be related to the factors listed above and, of course, the pay review budget.
- The likelihood that the majority of employees will be covered by the central group of increases. Particular care would therefore have to be taken in deciding on the rates of increase in this area and they may have to be flexed more often.
- The limits to progression depending on performance.

Position in pay range / Performance assessment	80–89%	90–99%	100%	101–110%	111–120%
Outstanding	15	14	13	11	10
Superior	10	10	9	9	8
Standard	7	6	5	5	0
Developing	4	4	3	0	0

Figure 17.1 *Performance matrix*

Introducing performance-related pay

The decision to introduce PRP

Whether or not an organization introduces PRP will depend on its culture and the extent to which it believes that a scheme can be developed and maintained which will meet the objectives set out at the beginning of this chapter and overcome the reservations about PRP mentioned earlier. PRP may be introduced because of a fundamental belief in the virtues of rewarding people according to their contribution even if it can not be proved that it will make a striking impact on organizational performance. It then becomes almost an article of faith justified by the belief that it conveys a clear message of the performance values of the organization. Its perceived prime importance – giving a clear statement of what is required – ultimately becomes its prime effect.

The *process* of PRP in the sense of its basis in performance management, its capacity to clarify performance and development priorities and its use in providing a tangible form of recognition, can become more important than the amount it pays out.

In some organizations, PRP may be considered necessary simply because of market pressures and employee expectations that it will be part of competitive practice.

Key considerations

Overall the design and development process should take account of the rules for successful pay-for-performance schemes set out in Chapter 16. In general, perhaps the most important ones to bear in mind are that the PRP scheme should provide:

- a clear and strong link between performance and contribution and subsequent reward;
- a fair and consistent basis for measuring performance and contribution;
- a worthwhile reward in line with employee expectations;
- value-for-money (cost-effectiveness) – the gains to the company in terms of improved organizational performance should exceed the cost of the scheme.

The problems of introducing a successful PRP scheme can easily be under-estimated. Before launching a design programme it is necessary to be quite clear about objectives to help guide the development process and to provide a basis for evaluating the scheme. The list of objectives given earlier in this chapter can be used for this purpose.

Readiness for PRP

Assuming a decision is made in principle that PRP is desirable, the degree to which the organization is ready for PRP should be assessed initially under the following five headings: ˙

Culture

- Will PRP fit and support the culture of the organization now or as needed in the future?
- Can PRP act as a lever for changing the culture?
- Is there clarity about what success looks like in the organization? Is a will to increase this understanding already part of the culture?

Process

- Is it possible to devise fair and consistent methods of measuring performance for those who may be in receipt of PRP?
- Is there an effective process of performance management in place which is based on measuring and assessing performance against agreed targets and standards?
- To what extent is there an understanding on the part of managers and members of the HR function of the language of behavioural competences and how they are used as part of a performance management and reward process?
- Is this process of performance management and, therefore, PRP fully integrated into the business planning and objective setting processes?
- Will the communication systems of the organization support the introduction and maintenance of PRP?
- Will it be possible to develop clear guidelines on how pay should progress within the pay structure?
- Will it be possible to exercise control over PRP so that it is cost-effective?

Attitudes

- To what extent is there a shared sense of direction in the organization?
- Is there unequivocal commitment to PRP on the part of top management and are they prepared to work with its processes?
- Will line managers support and 'own' PRP?
- Will employees generally accept that they will benefit from PRP?
- Is management and the HR function determined to make PRP work?

Skills and resources

- To what extent are managers capable of planning and agreeing objectives?
- To what extent are managers capable of assessing levels of competence?
- How good are managers at measuring and rating performance?
- How effective are managers likely to be at using PRP as part of a total performance management process which will involve joint assessments and agreements of performance and individual development needs?
- Will managers be able to manage PRP within their departments without having to rely too much on the support and guidance of members of the HR function?
- Are members of the HR function capable of giving the support and guidance required and have they the resources (eg computerized systems) and time to do so? This will include defining generic competences and training in PRP procedures.

Impact

- Is it likely, taking all the above factors into account, that PRP will work as a means of improving organizational performance?
- Are the likely costs of PRP going to be justified by its contribution to performance improvement?

The answers to these questions will give a general indication of the feasibility of introducing PRP and should suggest areas to which particular attention should be given such as communications to managers and employees, and skills training.

Factors to be taken into account when introducing PRP

Performance-related pay is not an easy option. Before embarking on its introduction the following factors should be taken into account.

- *Matching the culture:* PRP schemes can not be taken off the shelf. There is no magic set of performance measures or simple set of rules waiting for adoption on a universal basis. Successful PRP schemes need to match the culture and core values of the organization. It is only by understanding and working with the culture that it is possible to develop schemes which underpin a bias to action.
- *Linking PRP to the performance management process:* if PRP is to be an effective management tool it must be based on an effective performance management process which is integrated with the business strategy. The focus when relating pay to performance needs to be on issues which emerge from the business planning process such as profitability, productivity, cost-control, research initiatives, product and market development and generally increasing shareholder value.
- *Balancing performance measures:* the performance measures used as a basis for rating must include a balanced mix of both input and process factors (skills and competences) and output factors (performance and contribution). The assessment upon which pay decisions are made should be based not only on performance in achieving objectives, contribution to organizational success and the levels of skill and competence achieved, but also on the degree to which the behaviour of individuals supports corporate values in such areas as teamwork, total quality management, customer service and innovation.
- *Flexibility:* PRP arrangements should allow for some flexibility in the criteria for reward and the method of payment. There may be occasions, for example, when it would be more appropriate to pay a lump sum achievement bonus rather than to increase the basic rate of pay.
- *Teamwork:* poor PRP schemes can produce a lot of single-minded individualists. The importance of teamwork should be recognized in structuring the scheme and in defining critical success factors and performance indicators. Individuals should be aware that achieving their targets at the expense of others is not considered competent performance.
- *Avoiding short-termism:* to avoid the danger of PRP focusing attention on short-term results at the expense of more important longer-term objectives, long-term as well as short-term goals should be set wherever appropriate and short-term objectives should be discussed in their overall context.
- *Involvement in the design process:* the design of PRP schemes is usually an iterative process – trying and testing ideas on measures and structure with those who will eventually be involved in the scheme. It is also a valuable learning process which can throw up fundamental strategic and business issues. Those due to participate in the scheme should have an input into agreeing critical success factors and performance indicators both for themselves and the organization.
- *Getting the message across:* PRP provides a very powerful form of communication. To get the right messages across, the following questions will have to be dealt with:
  - how can the scheme achieve the best possible launch?
  - is it better to give no payout than low payout?
  - what is the best psychological moment for payout?

    – what communications should be used to ensure that all concerned appreciate the aims of the scheme, understand how it will work, and appreciate how they will benefit from it?

Development programme

Performance-related pay schemes need careful implementation over a period of time to achieve maximum effectiveness and acceptability. Many managements do not appreciate this when they first decide to introduce PRP. Boards of directors sometimes appear to believe that all they have to do is wave the magic wand of PRP and, miraculously, all their motivational and performance problems will be over. There is a tendency for some managers to think that people at work do not want to do a good job and must therefore be bribed to increase their efforts through the offer of extra cash. It is certainly true that a lot of managers expect too much too soon.

Top managers need to be carefully briefed about what PRP can and can not do. They must appreciate the significance of the questions set out earlier about readiness for PRP and the factors listed above for consideration before introducing PRP. They need to be persuaded that undue haste will prejudice the introduction of a process which has to be managed with great sensitivity and which can make a significant impact on the culture, for better or, if not handled well, for worse.

The sequence of activities in a PRP development programme is illustrated in Figure 17.2 and described below, together with the questions which our experience of introducing a number of PRP schemes during the last few years has shown need to be answered.

Assess reasons for PRP

■ Why do we want to introduce PRP?
■ What, realistically, do we expect to get out of it?

Assess readiness for PRP

The questions to be answered were set out on pages 271–2 and the main headings are summarized below.

■ Is PRP right for our culture, and is our culture right for PRP?
■ Do we have the performance management and other processes in place required for successful PRP?
■ Are the attitudes of management and other employees in favour of PRP? (An attitude survey can be conducted to establish opinions – see Appendix A).
■ Have the people concerned with managing PRP the required skills and resources?
■ Is PRP likely to make a significant enough impact on performance to justify the costs of developing, introducing and operating the scheme?

Decide whether or not to introduce PRP

■ Does the result of the above assessment indicate that PRP is right for this organization?
■ If so, what are the objectives of PRP? Consider under the headings of improving performance, delivering messages about performance expectations, focusing attention on key issues, culture change, and maintaining a competitive pay position.
■ If not, what are the alternatives? (There are many of them.) Consider perfor-

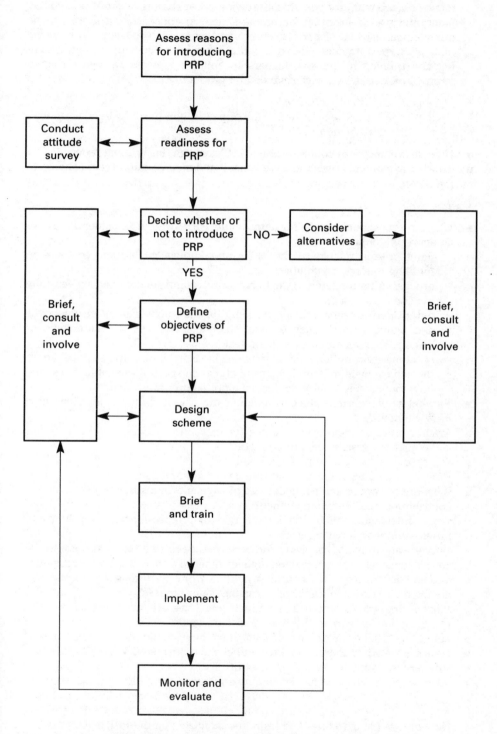

Figure 17.2 *Introducing performance-related pay*

mance-related team pay, organization-wide profit sharing or profit-related pay plans, the use of incentive or bonus schemes, concentrating more on the motivational aspects of performance management, job re-design to increase motivation, performance-related training, more intensive management coaching and training to improve leadership abilities, process re-engineering to improve organizational performance and productivity.

Brief, consult and involve employees

How should employees be informed of the organization's objectives and intentions concerning the introduction of PRP?

- How do we minimize concerns about PRP through this briefing process?
- To what extent and how should we consult and involve employees? (The more the better.)

Design scheme

- What criteria should we use for determining PRP awards? Consider the use of an appropriate mix of:
  - input criteria related to the skills and knowledge brought to bear on fulfilling role responsibilities;
  - process criteria related to the behavioural competences used successfully in achieving results;
  - output performance indicators related to the achievement of objectives and meeting performance requirements as set out in statements of principal accountabilities or main tasks;
  - outcome contribution indicators which measure how outputs contribute to the achievement of team, departmental and organizational objectives and how the behaviour of individuals supports corporate values.
- To what extent will it be possible to define the criteria in the key jobs for which PRP will operate?
- Are performance measures available for these criteria which will enable fair and consistent assessments to be made?
- What form of rating system should be used?
- How are we going to ensure that ratings are fair and consistent?
- What are our policies to be on the size of payments in relation to performance, contribution, skill and competence?
- What should our policies be on the rate of progression and any limits to progression within pay ranges?
- Do we want to make provision for performance-related lump sum bonus for special achievement or sustained high-level performance at the top of a range?
- Should PRP reviews be separated in time from performance reviews conducted as part of the performance management process?
- What rating, pay increase and budget guidelines are we going to issue to managers implementing PRP in their departments?
- Should we use performance matrices? If so, how should they be constructed?
- How are we going to monitor PRP and evaluate its effectiveness?
- How are we going to control the cost of PRP?
- What is the programme for developing and introducing PRP?

Brief and train

- How are we going to brief and train line managers on the PRP scheme?
- How are we going to brief employees in general on PRP in a way which ensures

as far as possible that they understand how it will operate and how they will benefit?

Implement

- How do we start the process off? It is necessary to introduce the scheme with great care. However carefully it has been planned, some unforeseeable problems will inevitably arise. It is often advisable to start with a pilot scheme, probably at management level so that they understand the principles, benefits and problems before applying PRP to the people for whom they are responsible.
- How do we monitor the introductory stages? It is essential to keep closely in touch with how things are going so that problems can be anticipated or dealt with swiftly when they arise.

Evaluate

- Have clear objectives been established for the scheme the progress towards which we can measure and evaluate?
- How do we carry out a continuing monitoring and evaluation process?
- Who is responsible for evaluation and taking any corrective action that may be required?
- What points should be covered? These are listed below.

Evaluating performance-related pay

It is essential to evaluate the acceptability and cost-effectiveness of PRP. The following questions should be answered:

- To what extent have the defined objectives of PRP been achieved?
- How much have we paid out under the scheme?
- What measurable benefits has PRP produced in the shape of improved organizational, team and individual performance?
- How do managers regard PRP? Do they, for example, believe that it is cost-effective and actually helps them to achieve their objectives?
- How do staff regard PRP? Do they, for example, believe that it is operating fairly?
- To what extent have rewards been linked to key and measurable areas of performance?
- Do performance management processes provide adequate support for PRP?
- Are rewards meeting people's expectations?
- Are there any modifications needed to the scheme?
- Do we want to retain PRP in its present form? If not, what are the alternatives?

An approach to evaluating PRP in the context of performance management is given in Chapter 15.

Conclusions

Performance-related pay systems can work for the organization, but the first wave of enthusiasm revealed the following weaknesses in their application:

- too much was expected from the system as the sole lever for improving performance;

- failure to make explicit the business mission to be supported by improved performance;
- reluctance to address the considerable changes in management behaviour and attitudes required to achieve better employee performance;
- too great a focus on one-off, short term improvements in performance;
- a tendency to imitate other organizations, practice or seek (largely non-existent), off the shelf systems rather than to design home-grown schemes rooted in the organizations's own requirements.

The problems arising from these weaknesses can be overcome if the requirements listed earlier in this chapter are met. But this is often difficult and it takes a lot of effort. Performance-related pay is not a panacea. It can work, but not equally well in every organization or for every category of employee. Other forms of reward such as those discussed in later chapters of this part of the book should also be considered.

References

1. Cannell, M and Wood, S (1992) *Incentive Pay: Impact and Evolution,* Institute of Personnel Management, London
2. Lawler, E (1988) 'Pay for performance: making it work', *Personnel,* October

18

Shop Floor Incentive and Bonus Schemes

Incentive or bonus schemes relate the pay or part of the pay received by employees to the number of items they produce or process, the time they take to do a certain amount of work and/or some other aspect of their performance. They usually provide for pay to fluctuate with performance in the short term, but they can, as in measured daywork, provide for a long-term relationship. They are often referred to as payment-by-result schemes.

We examine in this chapter:

- the main types of incentive schemes – individual piecework, work-measured individual schemes, measured day work and group incentive schemes;
- alternative approaches – high day rates, performance-related pay, productivity bonuses and the use of other criteria in bonus schemes;
- bonus schemes in different environments;
- the considerations affecting the design of incentive schemes;
- the process of selecting an incentive scheme;
- how to introduce an incentive scheme.

Individual piecework

In individual or straight piecework a uniform price is paid per unit of production. Operators are therefore rewarded according to the number of pieces they produce or process, so pay is directly proportioned to results.

Most piecework schemes provide a fall-back rate or minimum earnings level. It is common for the minimum rate to be set at 70–80 per cent of average earnings, although some companies set it as low as 30 per cent and others set it equal to the minimum time rate. Companies may also provide guaranteed payments for downtime due to machine failure, maintenance work or waiting for materials.

Advantages of piecework

The advantage to employers of piecework is that the system is easy to operate, simple to understand and can be left to run by itself, provided there is adequate supervision to ensure that quality does not suffer. Piecework can also enable employers to estimate and control manufacturing costs effectively.

The advantage to employees is that they can predict their earnings in the short term and regulate their pace of work in accordance with the level of pay they want to attain.

Disadvantages

Employers can find that they lose control over the level of production, which depends largely on the self-motivation of the workforce. Quality can suffer if close supervision is not exercised and the negotiation of piecerates for new work can be time consuming and fractious.

For employees, it may be difficult to predict longer-term earnings as work fluctuates from week to week. The intensity of work required in this system may cause undue stress or lead to repetitive strain injury (RSI).

Piecework has become more inappropriate as an incentive method as new technology has changed work arrangements. In larger scale manufacturing it has largely been replaced by work-measured schemes or some other form of incentive or bonus payment.

Work-measured schemes

In a work-measured scheme, the job, or its component tasks, is timed and the incentive payment is related to performance above the standard time allowed for the job. The amount of incentive pay received depends on the difference between the actual time taken to perform the task and the standard time allowed. If a task is done in less than the standard time, then there is a time saving, which means that the operator's output will increase.

Methods of measurement

Work measurement involves working out standard values or times for a complete task, which can, however, be broken down into components requiring simple human motions, to each of which standard minute values can be allocated. Work study or industrial engineers can measure the time taken for each component with the help of a stop-watch. A large number of timings will be made in each task to ensure that the variety of conditions under which an operator works are included so as to minimize distortions. Measurements may therefore be taken at different times of the day, and a number of operators may be timed on the same task to extend the range of timings and reduce the risk of errors.

The work study engineer who measures the job will be entirely objective about the stop-watch timing but a subjective assessment will also have to be made of the operator's speed, or effectiveness. This is known as the operator's effort rating. The performance of a qualified worker, if motivated, without over-exertion, is known as standard performance. Industrial engineers sometimes relate this to walking at a reasonably brisk pace, say four miles an hour. All operators who have been timed are given an effort rating relative to this standard and this is taken into account when deciding on standard times.

A refinement of individual work measurement is to adopt a predetermined motion time system such as methods time measurement (MTM). Such a system can be used when a mass of data has been assembled over a period of time which can lead to the production of 'synthetics' – standard times which can be applied to a particular task or operation. If these synthetics are based on reliable data they can eliminate the need for expensive and time-consuming work measurement and avoid disagreements about the accuracy of standards (especially when individual standards have involved the use of subjective effort rating).

When calculating standard values or times, allowances can be made to cover a reasonable amount of relaxation, personal needs, fatigue, and contingencies associated with the work, such as machine adjustments and maintenance.

Performance scales

When standard values have been calculated, a performance scale can be drawn up against which an operator's performance can be rated. Common scales include the British Standard Institution 100/133, on which 100 represents the performance of an average operator working conscientiously without financial motivation, and 133 represents the same worker's performance with financial motivation. Other scales are the BSI 75/100 or the 60/80 scale, which all work on the same principle, ie that the performance for a motivated worker will be set at one-third more than the performance of an operator working without an incentive.

Payment scales

Incentive payments are made when performance exceeds the standard. The relationship between pay and performance usually follows either the proportional or regressive pattern as explained in Chapter 16.

When proportional payments are made, the incentive payment increases in direct proportion to performance. Thus on the BSI 100/133 scale the incentive may be 1 per cent of basic pay for every point above BSI 100. If, for example, the operator works at BSI 110, the incentive payment is 10 per cent of base pay.

In a regressive payment system (the old Halsey/Weir or Rowan schemes) the incentive payment increases proportionately less than output. For example, a performance of BSI 110 may produce a payment of 8 per cent of basic pay, while one of BSI 120 may result in a payment of 14 per cent.

The proportionate payment method is the most equitable one, but a regressive system has the advantage for employers of making mistakes in rate-fixing less costly and lowering unit wage costs for output above standard performance. For obvious reasons, however, the latter approach is viewed with suspicion by trade unions and workers.

It is usual, and advisable, to establish a ceiling to the amount of incentive pay which can be earned to avoid excessive amounts being paid out because of loose rates, or some other form of degeneration (this is sometimes called capping). Typically, the upper limit is set at 133 points in a BSI 100/133 scheme, resulting in a maximum payment of 33 per cent of base pay in a proportional payment system or less – for example, 20 per cent – in a regressive system.

The problem of degeneration

Incentive schemes degenerate. The consultants and work study engineers who install them say they should not degenerate but they do. In an ideal world they would not: managers and supervisors would be able to exercise the degree of control the consultants advise. But the latter do not always live in the real world where there are numerous opportunities for workers to gain more from an incentive scheme than they have earned. Both individual and group incentive schemes are prone to this type of degeneration, which is often called wage or earnings drift.

The main causes of degeneration are:

- *Special allowances.* All schemes have allowances for the payment of shop-average earnings or some other figure which includes a premium over the base rate in certain circumstances. The most common are for unmeasured work or waiting time. Clearly, the higher the proportion of the time when pay is unrelated to effort, the more the scheme degenerates. Allowances are in theory controllable by management, but supervisors closer to the shop floor have been known to make their life easier by granting allowances too readily. This can be done on an hour-to-hour basis and in small increments which can all too easily be missed by more senior managers. Allowances can also be manipulated by, for example, workers booking in waiting time rather than time on a more difficult job which earns a less than average bonus.

■ *Erosion of standards.* The type of work or the work mix can change almost imperceptibly over a period of time. It may not be possible to point to a change in method sufficient enough to justify a retiming of the job under the rules of the scheme. The original ratings, although not slack, may not have been particularly tight; the workers and their representatives will have seen to that. As time goes on, workers learn how to take short cuts, sometimes risky ones, which increase or maintain earnings for less effort.

■ *Cross-booking.* Workers may cross-book from difficult tasks on which it is hard to earn a good bonus to easier ones. Work measurement is not an exact science, whatever work-study engineers may say, and some ratings are easier than others. The ability of work people to get round a scheme should never be underestimated. For example, if there is a reasonably generous fall-back rate, as there often is, employees may work more slowly on the more difficult jobs, thus saving their effort but still earning a reasonable standard rate, while working hard and fast on the easier jobs to achieve the bonus earnings they want. Research studies have frequently shown that workers set the level of bonus earnings they want to achieve and adjust their efforts accordingly. They can sometimes be under pressure from their fellow workers not to work too hard and thus 'bust' the rate, or at least inspire management to launch a rate-cutting exercise.

To prevent management from becoming aware that some jobs are easier than others, workers may not record all their time on these jobs, thus keeping earnings down. Workers then allocate their time to other jobs to raise them into the bonus-earning range, or simply take it easy. They operate, as it were, on borrowed time.

Preventing degeneration

To avoid degeneration, it is advisable only to introduce a payment-by-result scheme when the following conditions apply:

■ short-cycle, repetitive work;
■ changes in work mix, tasks or methods are infrequent;
■ shop-floor hold-ups are rare and not prolonged;
■ management and supervision are capable of controlling the scheme, not only technically, but also to prevent manipulation;
■ productivity is so low that the stimulus of a bonus scheme, even when it might cause problems later, is still worth while.

It is also necessary when introducing a scheme to use the best work study engineers available to ensure that accurate and even standards are obtained.

Recording systems and rules for booking time on non-bonus earning activities should be instituted which minimize the risk of allowance manipulation and cross-booking. Incentive earnings and performance rates should be monitored continuously and immediate action should be taken to crack down on drift. New jobs need to be timed properly and the implications of any changes in methods or work mix should be understood and reflected in altered standards – it is essential to agree initially with trade unions that changes can be made in these circumstances and when there has been an error in the original bonus calculation.

Importantly, managers, supervisors and industrial engineers should be trained in how to manage and control the scheme. It should be impressed upon them that they will be held accountable for productivity and ensuring that the scheme will not degenerate.

Measured daywork

Measured daywork schemes became popular in large batch or mass production factories in the 1950s and 1960s when it became evident that, in spite of all efforts, it was impossible to control wage drift.

In measured daywork, the pay of employees is fixed on the understanding that they will maintain a specified level of performance, but pay does not fluctuate in the short term with their performance. The arrangement depends on work measurement to define the required level of performance and to monitor the actual level. The fundamental principles of measured daywork are that there is an incentive level of performance and that the incentive payment is guaranteed in advance, thereby putting employees under an obligation to perform at the effort level required. In contrast, a conventional work measured incentive scheme allows employees discretion on their effort level but relates their pay directly to the results they achieve. Between these two extremes there is a variety of alternatives, including banded incentives, stepped schemes and various forms of high day rate.

Measured daywork seeks to produce an effort-reward bargain in which enhanced and stable earnings are exchanged for an incentive level of performance. Its disadvantage is that the set performance target can become an easily attainable norm and may be difficult to change, even after extensive renegotiation.

The criteria for success in operating measured daywork are:

- total commitment of management, employees and trade unions, which can only be achieved by careful planning, joint consultation and a staged introduction of the scheme;
- effective work measurement and efficient production planning and control and inventory control systems;
- the establishment of a logical pay structure with appropriate differentials from the beginning of the scheme's operation – the structure should be developed by job evaluation and in consultation with employees;
- the maintenance of good control systems so that swift action can be taken to correct any shortfalls on targets.

These are exacting requirements and this is one reason why measured daywork is relatively rare and has been abandoned by a number of organizations in favour of a high day rate system topped up with team or factory-wide bonuses.

Group or team incentive schemes

Group or team incentive schemes provide for the payment of a bonus either equally or proportionately to individuals within a group or team. The bonus is related to the output achieved by the group in relation to defined targets or to the time saved on jobs – the difference between allowed time and actual time.

Group bonus schemes are in a sense individual incentive schemes writ large – they have the same advantages and disadvantages as any payment-by-results system. The particular advantages of a group scheme are that it develops team working, breaks down demarcation lines and encourages the group to monitor its own performance and discipline itself in achieving targets – an essential characteristic of a high performance work group. In addition, job satisfaction may be enhanced by relating the team more closely to the complete operation. Group bonuses may be particularly appropriate when teams of workers are carrying out interdependent tasks and have to operate flexibly in a just-in-time or cellular manufacturing environment. These requirements may be prejudiced by incentive schemes which emphasize the link between individual pay and performance. Individual schemes might also be invidious because workers have only limited scope to control the level of their own output and are expected to support others, to the detriment of their personal bonus.

The potential disadvantage of a group incentive scheme is that in some manufacturing or operational systems, management is less in control of production – the group can decide what earnings are to be achieved and can restrict output. Thus the scheme fails to provide an incentive. Some opponents of group schemes object to the elimination of individual incentive, but this objection is only valid if it were always possible to operate a satisfactory individual payment-by-results scheme.

Group or team incentive schemes are most appropriate where people have to work together and teamwork has to be encouraged. They are most effective if they are based on a system of measured work where targets and standards are agreed by the team, which is provided with the control information it needs to monitor its own performance. A variety of measured daywork or a high day rate system topped up with achievement bonuses related to quality, delivery-to-time or cost targets may function well.

Alternative approaches

Piecework and other forms of traditional incentive schemes are in decline. In 1983 the proportion of male manual workers receiving incentive payments was 47 per cent. In 1990 the proportion was 37 per cent. There are a number of reasons for this. Traditional doubts about the unfairness and ineffectiveness of incentive schemes have come to the fore over the last decade as the manufacturing sector in the UK declined and the need to control pay costs became more crucial in the recession of the early 1990s. Incentive schemes were perceived by many organizations as being difficult to control (they seemed inevitably to create wage drift) and costly to maintain.

The other reasons for this decline have been:

■ *The nature of the work* – individual incentive schemes can function well when workers are engaged on simple, repetitive tasks and/or can control the pace of the work themselves. However, they are inappropriate in process industries and in assembly line production where the pace is controlled by the machine. More jobs now involve the operation of complex machines or the delivery of services requiring the integrated work of many individuals. Cellular manufacture places more emphasis on teamworking than individual effort. Knowledge work in high technology plants is not amenable to direct payment for results. Rapid changes in technology militate against the stability which is necessary for the successful operation of an incentive scheme.

■ *Increased emphasis on quality* – incentive schemes emphasize speed, often at the expense of quality.

■ *Shorter runs penalize workers* – because of the shorter runs required in much of today's manufacturing, operatives may lose incentive pay because they have less opportunity to maintain top speed on one job before being switched to another.

- *Health and safety problems* – there is growing evidence that in the types of short cycle and repetitive operations associated with piecework, workers who perform a single operation for most of the time are susceptible to repetitive strain injuries.

The alternative approaches include the use of high day rates, performance-related pay and schemes designed to increase productivity as described below. There are also a number of new developments in bonus schemes in different work environments as discussed in the next section of this chapter.

High day rates

In the face of these pressures, managements have often reverted to the payment of time rates, although in many cases the policy has been deliberately to adopt a 'high day rate' policy which involves paying above the going rate but requires workers to meet specified standards of output and quality. This high day rate policy has often been accompanied by the introduction of a bonus scheme which is related to some general measure of productivity or quality and is paid out on a group or a factory-wide basis.

Performance-related pay

Performance-related pay (PRP) schemes for manual workers relate a proportion of pay to indicators of performance such as quality, flexibility, contribution to teamwork and ability to hit targets. They are, in fact, based on the same principles as the PRP schemes for managerial, professional, technical and office staff described in Chapter 17 – namely, a system of assessment which leads to pay progression through a range.

PRP for manual workers has been in existence for a long time but its popularity has increased over the last decade because of the general pressure to introduce performance-related pay, increased disenchantment with traditional incentive schemes and the belief that PRP is more appropriate in high technology, multi-skilled environments where payment-by-result systems are likely to be ineffective.

Companies introducing PRP for manual workers claim that they increase the commitment and capability of their employees. As Kinnie and Lowe[1] comment on the basis of their research into PRP on the shop-floor, the firms they contacted wanted to get 'better value' from their employees but not necessarily in a way that resulted in an immediate reduction in costs or increases in profits. Their objective, more broadly, was to bring about a longer-term improvement in the motivation and performance of the work force as a whole, rather than simply paying a chosen few more.

It was established by Kinnie and Lowe that PRP in these firms often formed part of an overall approach aimed at focusing attention on their individual employees. It could be used as a key component in a wide-ranging attempt to change the management style or even the whole culture of an organization. The specific benefits achieved by the firms contacted were considered to be:

- Improvement in the quality of relationships between team leaders and the members of their teams – this arose because of the need to clarify performance requirements and discuss results against agreed expectations.

- Employees gained increased awareness of critical factors affecting performance such as quality, delivery and costs.
- Employees gained more information about their company and what it was trying to achieve.
- The commitment and capability of employees were improved.

But PRP for manual workers suffers from the same problems as in the office, namely, subjectivity, lack of ability or commitment on the part of supervisors to review performance, and the difficulty of translating assessments fairly and consistently into pay awards. In addition, it can arouse the hostility of trade unions, who object to what they believe to be a potentially unfair dependence on the judgement of supervisors on pay increases for their subordinates. These problems have to be considered carefully before introducing PRP for manual workers, and it should always be remembered that performance-related pay is only one of the factors affecting performance.

Productivity-based schemes

Productivity payments fell into disrepute during the 1960s and 1970s when an outbreak of 'productivity bargaining' took place which aimed to counter pay freezes by producing self-financing bonus schemes. Sadly, many of these schemes depended on specious measures. They were therefore not self-financed and melted away when the pay thaw arrived in 1979.

But productivity, if it is correctly measured, is a perfectly proper basis for the payment of a bonus, usually for a department or a factory. Productivity can broadly be defined as the ratio of inputs to outputs, for example, direct hours worked to units produced, cost per unit of output or, in a more general sense, an added value ratio (employment or direct labour costs as a proportion of total sales value less the cost of bought-in parts and materials). One of the best ways of paying for productivity is to develop a gainsharing plan, as described in Chapter 23. Such a plan is not just about bonus payouts. It also focuses on employee involvement in improving productivity through work teams, improvement groups or quality circles.

Use of other criteria in bonus schemes

The other criteria for use in bonus schemes are quality (in terms of meeting quality standards, delivery-to-time and waste control), cost reduction, and service delivery (the level of service generally to customers). These are discussed in more detail below when we consider bonus payments systems in a number of different environments, including that of total quality management.

Bonus schemes in different environments

Traditional incentive schemes tend to be concerned only with output and unit costs. However, significant changes have been taking place in the working environment in recent years. To maintain competitive advantage in the face of global competition organizations have had to introduce new systems of work and technology. These have led to the development of alternative approaches to paying for performance, particularly in total quality management, just-in-time and cellular manufacturing environments. These approaches generally take the form of bonus rather than incentive schemes.

Total quality management

Total quality management (TQM) is a systematic way of guaranteeing that all activities within an organization happen the way they have been planned in order to meet the defined needs of customers and clients. The emphasis is on involving everyone in the organization in activities which provide for continuous improvement and for achieving sustained high levels of quality performance.

The TQM approach is about gaining commitment to quality. Everyone at every level in the organization has genuinely to believe in quality and to act on that belief. Total quality can be described as an attitude of mind which leads to appropriate behaviour and actions.

For manual workers, a quality bonus can be paid on a plant-wide basis as a specific part of a bonus scheme, or it may be incorporated in a gainsharing plan. One approach is to set a standard of quality (this could be zero defects) and pay a quarterly bonus of, say, 10 per cent of pay, if this standard is achieved. The bonus would be reduced on a sliding scale related to any decline from the zero defects target.

Alternative bases for measuring quality can be used, as at British Steel, Strip Products, where in some works, the quality measure is the amount of prime (top quality) product produced as a percentage of the liquid steel used in the manufacturing process. The higher percentage of prime product, the less non-prime product has been made and the less liquid steel has been wasted in the various stages of production. As the prime percentage increases, so does the bonus.

Quality in manufacturing companies can also be measured simply in terms of waste – the percentage of output rejected or downgraded. As the volume or proportion of wastage falls, the quality bonus rises.

Another quality measure is delivery-to-time – the bonus increases on a sliding scale as the percentage of deliveries made on time increases. For example, at the Llanwern plant of British Steel, Strip Mills, a 1 per cent bonus is paid for every 2 per cent increase in deliveries-to-time above 80 per cent.

A delivery-to-time criterion is, of course, an important element in setting customer service levels and 3M includes this factor (the percentage of deliveries completed on time) as one of the elements in its West Midlands plant bonus scheme – the other elements are productivity (goods packed output per attendant hour) and waste improvements (waste being defined as the percentage of waste on all product lines).

Just-in-time

Just-in-time (JIT) is a programme designed to enable the right quantities to be purchased or manufactured at the right time without waste. It provides for the required flow of production to be maintained with zero inventory (no buffer stocks) at each stage of the supply/manufacturing chain.

The overriding feature of JIT is that materials or parts are generated in the exact quantity required and just at the time they are needed. A classic JIT system consists of a series of manufacturing units each delivering to one another in successive stages of production. The amount delivered by each unit to the next unit is exactly what the latter needs for the next production period (usually one day). There are no safety margins in the form of buffer stocks, live storage or work-in-progress.

Bonus payments in a JIT environment can be based on performance in relation to the critical success factors for JIT. These are:

- *Productivity* – output in relation to the cost of producing it.
- *Inventory and work-in-progress* – the aim of JIT is to minimize inventory and work-in-progress. A bonus can be related to inventory and WIP targets.
- *Delivery* – JIT demands the achievement of high levels of delivery standards, to internal as well as external customers. Delivery-on-time standards can be set for different stages in the manufacturing process and for despatch to customers.
- *Quality* – JIT is based on a zero-defects philosophy. Bonuses can therefore be related to quality performance as described earlier.
- *Set-up times* – JIT depends on speed in setting and re-setting machine tools and manufacturing systems. Set-up targets can be fixed and bonuses paid on achievements in relation to target.
- *Flexibility* – JIT requires flexibility in the use of plant, machinery and, it follows, people. The ability to apply a number of skills (multiskilling) in setting up, operating and maintaining plant and machinery is needed by employees in a JIT environment. A skill-based pay system as described in Chapter 26 can reward employees for enlarging their range of skills to cope with the variety of tasks they may be required to carry out.
- *Teamwork* – JIT systems are often based on cellular manufacturing processes. These require teamwork as described below, and the bonus payment system will almost inevitably have to be related to group or factory-wide performance rather than to individual output.

Cellular manufacturing

A manufacturing cell consists of a small number of closely cooperating machines. Within a manufacturing system a cell can be regarded as the smallest autonomous unit capable of sustained production.

Cellular manufacturing involves the logical arrangement of numerically-controlled equipment into groups or clusters of machines to process families of parts. By definition, processing parts in a manufacturing cell includes completing as much of the workplace processing as possible within the cell before moving it to the next sequential processing, assembly or stock holding station. Cells are staffed by teams of interdependent and multiskilled workers.

Cellular manufacturing systems demand teamwork and flexibility. Within the system, high performance work groups will be functioning that are to a large extent responsible for their own planning, operations, quality and production control. Cellular manufacturing systems require multiskilled people and are therefore possible environments for skill-based pay systems, although such systems are not always cost effective.

It will, however, be important to ensure that a team incentive or bonus system operates in which team members are given the maximum opportunity to monitor their own performance and take action to improve it, and are rewarded accordingly.

Considerations affecting the design of incentive schemes

As Bowey and Thorpe[2] have commented: 'Many managers still believe that as long as an incentive scheme is designed, maintained and operated correctly, higher performances will follow automatically'. But managers often admit that decay is inevitable and seem prepared to live with that uncomfortable fact.

Both these assumptions can be challenged. A payment-by-results scheme will only work if it fits the requirements and situation of the organization and if full consultation has taken place during its introduction. Degeneration *can* be controlled, as described earlier in this chapter, but it is hard work.

When considering the introduction of a new scheme or the revision of an existing one, it is first necessary to understand the criteria for success.

Criteria for success

The criteria for the success of an incentive scheme are that:

- it should be appropriate to the type of work carried out and the workers employed;
- the reward should be clearly linked to the efforts of the individual or team;
- individuals or teams should be able to calculate the reward they get at each of the levels of output they are capable of achieving;
- individuals or teams should have a reasonable amount of control over their efforts and therefore their rewards;
- the scheme should operate by means of a defined and easily understood formula;
- the scheme must be carefully installed and maintained;
- provision should be made for controlling the amounts paid to ensure that they are commensurate with effort;
- provision should be made for amending rates in defined circumstances.

These are demanding criteria and they need to be kept in mind throughout the selection process as described below.

Selecting an incentive scheme

The steps required to select an incentive scheme are:

- define objectives and assumptions;
- analyse the existing situation;
- evaluate alternative systems.

Define objectives and assumptions

Everyone takes for granted that the prime purpose of an incentive scheme is to provide a means of motivating employees which will improve their performance and levels of productivity in the organization. Other objectives which need to be considered when reviewing existing schemes or considering introducing a new scheme are to:

- obtain consistency in performance;
- reduce or at least contain labour costs per unit of output;
- improve product quality and the level of customer service;
- reduce waste;
- obtain a lower level of rejects;
- improve delivery times;
- gain better control over pay to eliminate wage drift, and thereby get value for money;
- reduce the levels of inventory and work in progress;
- improve labour flexibility;
- improve equipment utilization;
- reduce pay disputes;

- expand the skill base;
- generally convince all employees that the incentive pay arrangements are fair and equitable.

The definition of objectives should lead to an assessment of the extent to which they are being achieved by existing incentive schemes. But it is also necessary to examine and if necessary challenge the assumptions held by management about pay and rewards. These can include assertions such as: 'the workers in this plant are only interested in money', 'the existing system is the best one we've got so why change it?', 'all we need to do is to tighten up the loose rates' (rather than find out why the rates were loose in the first place), 'that's the way the workers want it', 'you can't rely on the so and so's to work without a fairly juicy carrot' (as well as a big stick), and so on and so forth.

Analyse the existing situation

The existing system should be analysed by obtaining answers to the following questions:

- What is the system of work – batch, mass production or process?
- What manufacturing, operational and quality control processes are in operation (eg FMS, CIM, cellular manufacturing, TQM)?
- How much new technology is involved in the shape of computerized production control and scheduling systems (eg MRPII), robotics and numerical control (CNC or DNC)?
- To what extent does the work require highly developed technical skills?
- To what extent is multiskilling an important feature of the work?
- To what extent can the work be described as skilled, semi-skilled, unskilled, repetitive or varied?
- Is the work flow or cycle steady or intermittent and are the work methods constant or varied?
- How long are the typical work runs?
- What is the average lot size?
- How frequently are operators required to reset their machines?
- How often are methods changed?
- Does the work mix change much?
- Are product designs and specifications frequently modified?
- How tight are the tolerances to which operators have to work?
- What is the underlying attitude to product quality? To what extent is this of real concern or is only lip service being paid to it?
- What is the incidence of waste and rejects?
- How much waiting time is there?
- To what extent is the work machine paced? How much control do workers have over their output levels?
- What level of productivity is being achieved? Is that high enough?
- What is the scope for increasing work rates?
- To what extent is the work carried out on an individual, team or production line basis?
- What proportion of workers are able to participate individually or in teams in a payment-by-results scheme?
- If productivity needs to be increased, to what extent is that a matter of improving work organization, systems of work (including computerization and

automation) or the quality of management and supervision rather than relying on an incentive scheme to work miracles?

■ What is the climate of employee relations?
■ To what extent have employees been involved in the design and operation of incentive schemes?
■ What is the union's attitude to incentive schemes?
■ How likely are employees to respond positively to a new or revised incentive scheme?
■ Are managers and supervisors capable of controlling an incentive scheme?
■ Has the firm the industrial engineering resources required to install and maintain an incentive scheme?
■ Is there adequate management information available to enable the scheme to be monitored and controlled?

Evaluate alternatives

The alternative arrangements should be evaluated against the criteria listed above and the following points concerning each approach:

Time rates
The first point to consider is whether or not an incentive scheme of any type is suitable. The alternative of using time or day rates may be preferable where:

■ individual or team effort does not determine output;
■ achieving a fair and consistent relationship between performance or skill levels and reward is difficult;
■ it is not easy to establish accurate standards by means of work measurement;
■ there are numerous product or product mix changes;
■ design changes or modifications are frequent;
■ work runs are short, and new setups for machines are frequent;
■ quality is a prime consideration;
■ job stoppages are numerous and downtime is considerable;
■ there is a history of unsatisfactory shop floor relations;
■ it is believed that the time and cost involved in operating an incentive scheme outweigh its (dubious) benefits;
■ the company is confident that performance can be improved and high levels of productivity maintained better by other means, including more effective operational systems, better management and supervision, non-financial incentives and job design.

Work measured individual incentive scheme
This type of scheme may be appropriate when individual effort clearly determines output and:

■ the work requires purely manual skills and/or only single/purpose hand tools or simple machine tools are used;
■ a high proportion of task content is specified;
■ work measurement can readily be applied to the tasks and an effective system of work measurement is in use;
■ product changes or modifications are limited;
■ job stoppages are small;
■ a stable climate of employee relations exists.

Measured daywork

Measured daywork may be appropriate when individual effort largely determines output and:

- conditions are unsuitable for a work measured scheme;
- operations are of the process type or assembly line;
- accurate work measurement of operations is possible so that acceptable standards can be achieved;
- the unions are responsive to the benefits of the system;
- high calibre management negotiators are available.

Group incentive schemes

These may be suitable if collective effort clearly determines output and the other features necessary for individual incentive schemes are present.

Performance-related pay

Performance-related pay may be considered when:

- the company wants to focus the attention of employees on such critical success factors as quality, delivery and costs, as well as output;
- it is believed that team leaders and supervisors are fully committed to the system and can learn new performance appraisal skills;
- a consistent and fair relationship between performance and reward can be achieved;
- the company has PRP for non-manual staff and wants to move towards an integrated pay structure;
- employees and trade unions are likely to support the scheme.

Introducing an incentive scheme

Prerequisites

Following research into payments systems and productivity, the Pay and Rewards Research Centre of Strathclyde University concluded that the three essential prerequisites for introducing a successful scheme were as follows:

- the top of the organization is committed to a programme of change;
- a team of managers is developed which knows what is required of them and has the enthusiasm to make it work;
- the rest of the workforce is convinced that the project is worthy of their support and is shown how to make it work.

The importance of the last of these prerequisites – a participative approach – was emphasised by Bowey and Thorpe.[2] There is no point in introducing a scheme which aims to increase productivity without involving employees in discussing how to obtain improvements and how they will benefit financially from them. It is equally necessary to discuss at each development stage the design of the scheme and how it will operate.

In a work-measured scheme, work measurement techniques should be demonstrated; many companies train selected employee representatives in these techniques so that they can agree timings and, importantly, retimings. Any agreement should spell out the circumstances in which retiming will take place and how such retimings will be conducted in consultation with employees and their representatives. Management must be completely open about the scheme while making it clear that it will not be allowed to deteriorate.

References

1. Kinnie, N and Lowe, D (1990) 'Performance related pay on the shop floor', *Personnel Management*, September
2. Bowey, A and Thorpe, R (1986) *Payment Systems and Productivity*, Macmillan, London

19

Staff Incentive and Bonus Schemes

The performance-related pay schemes described in Chapter 17 are the most frequently used pay-for-performance methods applied to staff other than directors and senior executives. There are, however, other approaches available, as described below.

Individual bonus payments

Definition

Individual performance or achievement bonuses are payments made in addition to base salary which are related to the achievement of specified targets, the completion of a project or a stage of a project to a specified standard, the receipt of an appropriate performance rating, or a combination of any of these.

An individual bonus for those at the top of their part scale could be the normal performance-related payment, according to performance, converted into a lump sum.

Bonuses can, however, be more explicitly linked to performance if they are related to the degree to which targets have been achieved. For example, three levels of bonus may be paid according to whether individuals have:

- only just achieved the target – the threshold bonus
- completely achieved the target – the full bonus
- significantly exceeded the target – the exceptional bonus.

Some schemes pay 'sustained good performance bonuses' for exceptional performance in any one year or for good performance which has been sustained over two or three years. Bonuses should only be paid to people in that position in subsequent years if they achieved or sustained a high level of performance. In other words, they would have to re-earn their bonus – it should not be regarded as an automatic handout.

Individual bonuses were at one time only paid to senior management and sales representatives and others whose performance could be targeted with precision. Their use is now spreading generally to more junior levels and jobs where targets are more difficult to quantify as organizations seek to contain consolidated payroll costs and benefit from the reality that bonuses can, if well implemented, give very strong performance messages. One reason for the effectiveness of bonuses as part of a reward system is the simple fact that people often spend bonus money differently from a 'drip feed' pay increase. They remember and appreciate the extra luxury or weekend in Paris on which they spent the award.

Executive incentive and bonus schemes can differ in a number of ways and are considered separately in Chapter 20.

Advantages of individual bonus payments

The advantages of bonuses related to individual targets or ratings are that:

- the reward is immediately payable for work well done
- the bonus can be linked to specific achievements and future targets, and this constitutes both a reward and an incentive
- the payment is not perpetuated as part of base salary irrespective of future performance
- lump sum payments appeal to some people
- additional rewards can be given to people at the top of their salary scale without damaging the integrity of the salary structure
- the arrangements can be flexible
- the system can be designed for easy administration.

Disadvantages of individual bonus payments

The disadvantages of bonuses related to individual targets are that:

- they are more difficult to apply to people whose jobs have less tangible outputs
- an individualistic rather than a team approach may be encouraged
- people may be diverted away from the innovative and developmental aspects of their work because they are concentrating on the task in hand
- it could be difficult to establish a fair and consistent relationship between the results achieved and the level of the reward, which could be seen as arbitrary and inequitable
- it might be hard to discriminate fairly between those on long-term projects, who could wait for some time before they are rewarded, and those with shorter-term and more visible objectives, who could be rewarded more rapidly.

Design of individual bonus schemes

The points to be considered are:

- the constituents of the bonus in terms of the mix of the payments related to target achievement, ratings or company results
- the method of defining targets and standards of performance for tasks to be completed; and/or
- the basis upon which performance ratings could be translated into bonus payments (including the range of payments that can be made)
- how agreement should be reached with individuals on their targets or tasks
- how performance should be measured and who measures it
- the amount of money to be made available for bonuses, and how and when bonuses should be paid
- how to make the scheme differentiate rewards in relation to performance in a fair, consistent and relevant way, having regard to the disadvantages listed above.

Group bonus schemes

Definition

Group of team bonus schemes relate the reward to the satisfactory completion of a project or stage of a project, or the achievement of a group target.

Advantages of group bonus schemes

Group bonuses are increasingly being used by organizations who want to underpin and reward collective effort. They are particularly helpful in areas such as research and development and information technology where work is strongly project based. Group bonuses can:

- promote the value and successful operation of team-work
- facilitate the setting of group targets where results depend on joint effort
- be less invidious than individual payments, especially when these are affected by the work of other people in the team which is outside the employee's control.

Disadvantages of group bonus schemes

Group bonuses:

- are only feasible where it is possible to identify teams who are working together to achieve defined tasks
- can diffuse individual motivation because the relationship between individual effort and reward may be remote
- can cause ill-directed peer group pressure which effectively punishes weaker performers.

Design of group bonus schemes

The points to be covered are:

- the identification and definition of the groups to be included in the scheme
- methods of defining targets
- how agreement should be reached with groups on their targets
- how the performance of groups should be measured
- the formula for deciding on bonus payments (including minima and maxima) and the extent to which a discretionary element is required
- the amount of money available for group bonus payments and how and when bonuses should be paid
- the procedure for monitoring the scheme.

Target-based incentives

Target-based incentive schemes link the reward to the achievement of agreed targets within the employee's department over which the individual has real control: for example, completing a systems design project, achieving a quality improvement target, test launching a new product, developing a new product or service, finalizing a company training needs analysis. Incentives would only be paid if defined quality standards are achieved within a laid-down timescale.

Target-based incentive schemes may be applied to teams or individuals. The choice depends on whether the need is to promote and reward effective team-work or whether the emphasis in the firm is on motivating individual achievement.

An example of a target-based incentive plan for middle-managers is given in Appendix J.

Branch incentive schemes

A growing number of retailers, banks and building societies have introduced branch incentive schemes. These organizations can have several hundred or even thousands of similar outlets, which all exist to deliver roughly the same organizational objectives and strategies.

Branch schemes should focus on the key measures that branch managers and staff can really influence and that relate to overall organization objectives, both short and long term. They should reinforce team/individual roles; they can also support interdependencies between service outlets and support centres. Many organizations are finding these schemes a useful tool through which to communicate the direction in which the organization is moving.

It is imperative that schemes are consistent with all the other performance messages at branch level, eg appraisal processes, promotion criteria, training. This is necessary to support clarity about what performance is in the branch.

To work effectively, schemes need targets that are realistic and accurate measurement systems. The timescale to implementation must accommodate the necessary changes to Management Information Systems and branch budgeting processes.

Schemes that capture real interest and motivate participants tend to have short time frames, for providing information about performances against target and for making payments, ie quarterly or half-yearly (not annual). They typically pay out to around 75 per cent of branches if the total organization has performed.

20

Executive Incentive and Bonus Schemes

Executive incentive and bonus schemes for directors and senior executives provide additional and often substantial sums in addition to base salary (the distinction between incentives and bonuses was made in Chapter 16). These payments generally reward the attainment of company growth and profitability targets although in some schemes they may be related to the achievement of individual objectives linked to specific accountabilities.

Executive incentives and bonuses incorporate an element of risk money into the remuneration package. Their use has extended rapidly because companies believe that this risk element is appropriate for their executives. It also allows for considerable rewards to be made for success. Some people, however, think that excessively high payments can be made which are not justified by the individual contribution of the chief executive or director.

Another important reason for the spread of executive incentive and bonus schemes is that they are necessary to maintain a competitive overall level of remuneration for key people.

In this chapter we deal with the following aspects of executive incentive and bonus schemes:

- the basis of the strategic decision to have executive incentives
- the aims of executive incentive schemes
- their relationship with other components of the reward package
- their main features
- financial performance measures
- non-financial targets
- the target mix
- discretionary element
- link with performance assessment
- level of payments
- treatment of windfall profits
- relationship between performance improvements and payments
- frequency of payments
- tax planning
- administering an incentive plan
- executive bonus schemes
- long-term incentives.

A strategic decision

The introduction of an executive incentive scheme should be closely tied to a searching review of corporate plans and objectives. It is essential to know where the enterprise is planning to go and what constitutes success before deciding how executives should be rewarded for their performance. The main question to be answered when making this strategic decision is – what do executives have to do and achieve for the company to be more successful? A good scheme will ensure that executives concentrate on business priorities.

Aims

The primary aim of an executive incentive scheme is to increase executive motivation in order to improve company performance. The other aims are to:

- make executives more aware of the key measures of company performances;
- provide executives with a share in the company's prosperity;
- reward personal commitment and success;
- ensure competitive, total compensation linked to company performance and so help to recruit and retain good calibre executives.

Relationship with other components of the reward package

It is essential to relate the incentive scheme to other elements of the reward package. This means reviewing basic salary and benefit packages to ensure that they are competitive. It also means deciding what the incentive scheme is expected to contribute in addition to existing merit payment systems, share option schemes and profit sharing arrangements.

Defining the target group

Only executives who can exert personal control over the selected performance measures as individuals or members of a team should be included in the scheme. These will certainly consist of members of the board, who may need different criteria with individual performance triggers, although incentive schemes for directors often incorporate a common measure based on overall company profitability.

Incentives for executives below this level are often more difficult to design.

The main features of executive incentive schemes

When designing an incentive scheme the following features of it will need to be considered:

1. The choice of performance measures, which lies between financial or non-financial measures or a combination of the two.
2. The extent to which the scheme should be tied down to a formula or should allow an element of discretion when making awards.
3. The link that should exist between the scheme and performance management at executive level.
4. The level of payments that should be made according to performance, which will take account of the target level, the starting point and any limits or 'caps' that will be placed on incentive earnings.

5. The action that should be taken over any 'windfall' profits.
6. The frequency with which payments should be made.

These considerations are dealt with in the following sections of this chapter. Examples of incentive schemes are given in Appendix J.

Financial performance measures

The principal financial performance measures are:

■ profit before tax (pre-tax profit)
■ profit after tax (post-tax profit)
■ earnings per share
■ return on capital or assets employed
■ cash flow
■ others specific to individual businesses.

The factors governing the choice between these measures are discussed below. The main criteria are first, relevance to organization requirements, second, the extent to which the individual or group can influence results, and, third, the existence of reliable methods of measurement – a credible and sophisticated management information system is a prerequisite for any scheme using financial measures.

Profit before tax

This is the key indicator of corporate success and is therefore frequently used as the sole criterion.

Incentives are based on a percentage of profit, typically paid after the achievement of a threshold figure, the level of which is set to protect the interests of shareholders. The threshold may need adjustment after an acquisition or change in the capital structure. Both interest and management charges are taken into account if they are within management control. This, however, may not be the case when interest rates are fluctuating widely or where the situation is complicated by overseas activities.

Profit after tax

This measure aligns more closely with shareholders' interests because it gives a clearer indication of the funds available for re-investment and for payment of dividends. However, it can be significantly affected by changes in national and international tax laws and by the way in which those laws are interpreted. Profit after tax is rarely used as the chief measure in executive incentive schemes below main Board level, although it is sometimes included as one of a set of criteria. The criteria for choosing before or after tax depends upon the degree to which managers are expected to take account of tax considerations when making business decisions.

Earnings per share

This measure relates post-tax profits to the average weighted number of ordinary shares in issue during the financial year. It is used by the City to judge company performance, and is being increasingly adopted as the main measure in directors' incentive schemes. It is, however, subject to changes in corporate taxation in the same way as post-tax profits. It can also be difficult to measure within the year.

Before selecting this measure, the possible impact of mergers, takeovers and changes in accounting policy should be considered.

Return on capital or assets employed

This is another key measure of company performance. It can, however, be manipulated by management who could improve the ratio dramatically by the sale of assets. This criterion is, therefore, generally used in conjunction with others.

Cash flow

This measure is also focused on by the City, who will value the company by estimating the Net Present Value of future cash flow. Shareholder Value techniques also put a greater emphasis on cash flow.

The importance of managing cash can be emphasized by using this criterion as one of the factors in an incentive scheme, but it is not really suitable as the sole measure of performance because it only relates to one aspect of management responsibility.

Use of criteria

The measures used for incentives vary by job level. The 1993 Monks Guide to incentives for management shows how these are used for directors and senior managers:

Table 20.1 *Choice of criteria*

Measure	Board Directors %	Senior Managers %
Pre-tax profit	62	52
Post-tax profit	4	17
Earnings per share	39	11
Return on capital	18	12
Cash flow	15	8
Job-related targets		
– quantifiable	20	46
– qualitative	19	39

Non-financial targets

Although it is always desirable to relate incentives to financial targets they may not be applicable to all aspects of an executive's job, especially in service departments such as personnel. To cover each key result area it may be necessary to set job-related targets which indicate what needs to be achieved to earn a specified level of reward. For example, the target may be to complete a project which meets agreed objectives within a time limit. The objectives would be defined in such terms as cost reduction, increase in productivity, or improvement in quality or customer service levels. Some schemes set a 100 per cent level for full achievement of the objectives, but provide for a partial payment if the results are less than 100 per cent.

The target mix

The mix of performance criteria between financial and non-financial measures will depend on the requirements of the business and the particular demands made on the executives in the scheme. At board level, the mix may be dominated by measures of corporate performance such as earnings per share, to which all directors contribute. But a proportion of the incentive payment may be related to individual targets, which could be defined in financial or non-financial terms and would cover each of the key result areas of the job in accordance with the contribution of job holders to overall performance. To concentrate the minds of executives on these areas and to avoid over-complicating the scheme, it is best not to have more than three or four factors.

Discretionary element

Many schemes which have a mixture of targets also allow for a discretionary element in incentive payments. This may be used by the chief executive or the remuneration committee of the board to reward a manager for exceptional performance 'beyond the line of duty', which would not be adequately recognized by the normal measures.

Link with performance assessment

Discussion on the setting and achievement of targets should take place as part of the normal performance assessment procedure. An important feature of this appraisal will be the review of all aspects of the results achieved by the executive so that those factors not covered specifically by the incentive scheme are also dealt with. There is always the risk in any incentive scheme that an important aspect of the job such as development, leadership or teambuilding is neglected because the executive concentrates only on those areas where short-term rewards can be achieved. Discussions during reviews can help to put these matters into perspective.

At board level it is advisable to have special meetings to discuss the operation of the incentive scheme. The compensation/remuneration committee of the main board, consisting wholly or mainly of non-executive directors, is often used for this purpose.

Level of payments

The value of bonuses by company size and post as revealed by the 1993 Monks survey of incentives for management is shown in Table 20.2.

In the period covered by the study (1992–93) parent board directors were the least likely to receive a bonus payment, reflecting the effects of the recession. The smaller the turnover of the company, the less likely that a bonus would be paid. For subsidiary board directors and senior management, where bonuses are more dependent on personal objectives, non-payment falls to well below 40 per cent for almost all posts.

Three decisions are required on the level of incentive payments:

1. The target level expressed as a percentage of base salary.
2. The starting point for incentive payments.
3. The limit, if any, to the maximum payment that can be made.

Table 20.2   *Value of executive bonuses by company size and post*

	Value of Bonus as % of Salary				
	Nil %	Under 10%	10% – 20%	20% – 30%	Over 30%
I Parent Board Director					
Company Turnover (£m)					
Over 1000	40	14	30	9	7
300–1000	47	18	13	6	16
150–300	43	11	12	17	17
40–150	69	7	9	6	9
Under 40	67	15	6	6	6
II Subsidiary Board Director					
Company Turnover (£m)					
Over 1000	28	19	45	0	8
300–1000	20	11	39	20	10
150–300	23	15	27	11	24
40–150	23	24	32	15	6
Under 40	31	16	30	12	11
III Senior Management					
Company Turnover (£m)					
Over 1000	36	35	22	4	3
300–1000	34	32	15	13	6
150–300	43	20	19	2	16
40–150	29	39	18	6	8
Under 40	34	37	13	12	4

(*Source:* Monks Guide to incentives for management 1993)

Target level: The level of incentive which is paid if the performance targets are reached must be meaningful. As mentioned earlier, payments of less than 10 per cent can have little motivational effect. In the case of senior executives, target figures of 20–30 per cent are typical. For this level of incentive payment, however, the target, although achievable, should be tough.

The payment for reaching the target level of performance should also be self-financing. It should be based on the assumption that the company as well as the individual will benefit. Payments should be regarded as serious money, not to be handed over lightly.

Starting point: The starting point will depend upon the extent to which demanding levels of target performance are set. If the target is reasonably difficult to attain, as it should be, then a trigger point of 90 per cent achievement of the target level of performance would be appropriate.

It is necessary, however, to provide a significant incentive to achieve the target. This can be done by gearing the incentive payment as a percentage of base salary so that its increase between the starting point and the target figure is greater than the percentage improvement in performance needed to reach the target. For example:

	Performance level as a percentage of target	Incentive payment as a percentage of base salary
Start	90%	10%
Target	100%	30%

Upper limit: Many schemes 'cap' incentives by setting an upper limit to payments to avoid them getting out of hand and in the belief, which may or may not be correct, that above a certain level, executives are unlikely to be able to achieve anything more by their own efforts. Some companies are also wary about offering glittering prizes that are over-enticing and therefore misdirect executives into concentrating so much on exceeding their personal targets that the needs of the business are neglected. This happened quite often in the City in the heady days before 'Black Monday' (18 October 1987). Other companies worry, perhaps unnecessarily, about the detrimental effects on executives of wide fluctuations in earnings if there is no upper limit.

A further factor which has led to capping is the incidence of high rates of taxation. The 1988 budget, however, largely removed this factor and companies are becoming more willing to de-limit their incentive schemes.

Where the limit, if any, is fixed depends on the circumstances, especially the level of performance that an executive could achieve. The gap between the target level and the limit may be the same as the difference between the target and the starting point, say 10 per cent on either side of the target. In some schemes, however, the range from the target to the limit is wider at, say, 15 per cent, than the range from the starting point to the target of, say, 10 per cent. This very much depends on the nature of the business and the ability of the management to lever results. Examples of alternative approaches are given in Table 20.3.

Some companies would regard the upper limits shown in Table 20.3 as being rather modest and limits as high as 200 per cent can be found.

Table 20.3 *Incentive payment levels – alternative approaches*

			Payment as a % of base salary	
Scheme	Performance range	levels %	Alternative A	Alternative B
1	Start	90	10	15
	Target	100	20	30
	Upper limit	110	30	45
2	Start	90	10	15
	Target	100	20	30
	Upper limit	120	40	60

The 1993 Monks Survey showed that the maximum payment made to board directors in the parent companies covered by the survey varied as follows over page.

It is interesting to note that 25 per cent of these companies have no upper limit, and aggressive commercial organizations which set demanding performance targets for their executives are increasingly taking the view that incentive payments should not be capped. This is based on the conviction that the benefits to

Table 20.4   *Maximum bonus payments for board directors in parent companies*

	%
Under 20% of salary	7
20% and under 30%	19
30% and under 50%	28
50% or more	21
No formal limit	25

(*Source:* Monks Guide to incentives for management 1993)

shareholders more than compensate for the high payments made, which would not in any case be given unless they were deserved. What, they ask, is the justification for an arbitrary limit on rewards for real achievements? But, in these circumstances, what has to be made absolutely clear to the executives concerned is that what they can earn from the scheme is risk money. The credibility of any scheme where payments are potentially high to shareholders, the public and other employees, depends on the strict application of the no profit–no payout principle.

Treatment of windfall profits

Even when a 'no limit' approach is adopted it may still be necessary to make provisos in the scheme for the treatment of any windfall profits arising from circumstances outside the control of executives, such as the sale of company assets or favourable changes in foreign exchange or interest rates. The decision on whether or not these 'acts of God' should generate incentive payments depends on the nature of the business and the likelihood of such windfalls occurring. This is a matter upon which a remuneration sub-committee of the board may be expected to adjudicate. The perceived need to curb excessive gains in these circumstances should be balanced against the demotivating effect of denying executives the incentive payment they believe they have earned. And it can be argued that extra payments for windfall gains are entirely justified if the system works both ways and executives have their payments reduced in line with unexpected or uncontrollable profit losses. Another argument is that if the circumstance was not covered in the original plans when the incentive targets were set, then they deserve their 'windfall' for making it happen.

If it is decided that earnings should be 'capped' when windfall profits arise, steps should be taken to reduce possible demotivating effects by spelling out in the rules of the scheme the circumstances in which this could happen.

Relationship between performance improvements and payments

The choice is between a straight line relationship between performance improvements and incentive payments, as shown in scheme 1 in Table 20.3, or an arrangement in which payments accelerate over a given threshold. Clearly, if targets become even more demanding above the level that executives can reasonably be expected to reach, then incentive payments should accelerate. Thus, if achieving 10 per cent above the target performance level were twice as difficult as raising performance from 90 per cent to 100 per cent, the gap between the target payment and the maximum should be twice the size of that between the target and the starting point so long as the shareholders benefit to the same extent.

Frequency of payments

Most executive incentive schemes pay out annually, after the annual results have been published. There are an increasing number of long-term incentives in the UK. Most of these (see page 308) are three-year plans, designed to reflect the reality that one year is often too short to reflect the success or not of a business strategy.

Tax planning

The main choices of payment vehicle are shares, share options and cash. Since 1988 – when highest rates of capital gains and income tax were set at 40 per cent – the scope for tax planning has reduced.

The timing of incentive or bonus payments can affect how much tax is paid on them. To minimize (but not avoid, which is, of course, illegal) the tax liabilities of executives who are in the higher tax bracket, tax advice should be sought (see also Chapter 31 which deals more fully with tax considerations).

Administering an incentive plan

The incentive plan should be set up by the Board. To ensure its integrity, its operation should be supervised by a remuneration committee which should be composed of non-executive directors, if they exist. They are there to ensure that the plan is run properly and that the shareholders' interests are protected.

The rules and procedures governing the plan should be set out in a short document given to all participants. From this they should be able to work out how their incentives are calculated and what they have to do to achieve certain payment levels.

The following points should be covered in the rule book:

- scheme objectives in relation to the corporate plan
- eligibility to join the scheme
- timing of payments
- treatment of leavers, voluntary and otherwise
- accounting standards used, indicating whether the scheme is related to the audited or to the management accounts
- a caveat which states that the scheme will be reviewed at regular intervals by the Board and/or the remuneration committee to ensure that it is operating effectively and achieving its objectives.

(Examples of executive incentive schemes are given in Appendix J.)

Executive bonus schemes

As an alternative to a formal, highly structured and complicated incentive plan many companies, especially smaller ones, prefer to use the more flexible approach of an executive bonus scheme. The three main types of scheme are:

1. Profit pool.
2. Discretionary.
3. Personal target.

Profit pool bonus schemes

A profit pool plan sets a given percentage of pre-tax profit over an annually defined threshold. This is distributed pro-rata as a percentage of salary, as in the following example:

1. *Bonus pool:* set at 5 per cent of pre-tax profits over a 1988/9 threshold of £6m. Its total pre-tax profits are £8.8m, the pool is therefore £140,000.
2. *Salary cost:* the total cost of the basic salaries paid to executives in the scheme is £500,000
3. *Basis for distribution:* the proportion of the bonus pool to total salary cost applied as a percentage of basic salary.
4. *Calculations:* Bonus pool (£140,000) $\times$ 100 $\div$ Total salary cost (£500,000) = 28 per cent of salary for each participant.

This approach has the merit of simplicity. It can also be controlled from year to year by adjusting the threshold. But agreement on the formula or process to adjust the threshold can be difficult to achieve.

Discretionary bonus scheme

Some companies, especially private ones, prefer to adopt a completely discretionary approach. This involves awarding bonuses simply on the basis of the opinion of the chief executive or the Board, which may or may not be related to objective criteria. If there are no such criteria, there is a danger of favouritism creeping in – the link between achievement and reward is no longer clear and the scheme can have a positively demotivating effect, particularly in an autocratic culture. It can be difficult to justify large payments in such a scheme, and the danger is that the total pay package becomes uncompetitive. On the other hand, large payments for unclear reasons tend to be discounted by employees when they calculate the total value of their package.

Personal targets

Discretionary bonuses are often paid where companies do not want to be tied to an overall criteria and prefer an individual approach. To avoid the dangers of an entirely subjective scheme, some companies relate bonuses, especially for executives below Board level, to the achievement of agreed personal targets.

Some schemes may operate on a purely individual basis with the overall limits of a bonus pool determined by the Board, the size of which would be determined by the results obtained by the company. Guidelines are produced on how bonuses should be distributed, for example, to no more than X percentage of executives, and on a scale from Y to Z percentage depending on performance. These guidelines would be worked out by reference to the total fund available and control would be exercised to ensure that the guidelines were adhered to and that the total pay-out was not above the limit.

A more structured approach is to allocate units to executives which reflect performance in relation to targets or, in some schemes, in relation to age, service and seniority as well as 'value' to the firm. The total number of units allocated is divided into a bonus pool to give a unit value which is then distributed according to the number of units allocated to each individual. For example:

1. Size of bonus fund – £850,000.
2. Total number of units allocated – 1000 between 250 executives.
3. Value of unit – £850.

4. Allocation – an individual who earns three units for, say, achieving sales targets, would receive a bonus payment of $3 \times £850 = £2550$.

Long-term incentives

Incentives over periods of greater than one year were relatively rare but are becoming much more common. Salary surveys show that about 10 per cent of companies have cash long-term incentive schemes, but the incidence among the *Financial Times* 'Top 100' companies was 40 per cent according to a 1993 survey by Towers Perrin. The pressure for developing such schemes is the concern that annual schemes overfocus on the short term.

The traditional long-term incentive was the executive share option, but there has been increasing questioning of the incentive value these really have. The new long-term schemes are usually cash based, paying out over three years or longer. There are two main types:

■ schemes for main Board directors and possibly a limited number of top executives where direct measures of performance are felt to be more motivational than use of the share price
■ schemes for subsidiary directors, who only have a limited impact on the group share price. Here schemes can be designed which reward long-term performance of the subsidiary. Schemes can be designed to mimic what an option scheme in the subsidiary would look like. This type of scheme can be highly motivational as the executives see the opportunity of significant capital accumulation based on the part of the business they impact upon.

The design process of long-term incentives follows a similar process to that of executive incentives discussed earlier in this chapter. The major additional decision is the choice between a one-off scheme or rolling cycles of schemes. Concern must also be given to the size of payment. This should be larger than – or at least comparable to – the annual scheme. The emphasis of the payment size and the incentive package must be on the long term, not short term. An example of a long-term incentive plan is given in Appendix J.

21

Employee and Executive Share Schemes

Employee and executive share schemes

A favourable climate for employee and executive share schemes has been created as a result of the generous tax treatment of share schemes, the growth of capitalism and share ownership, privatization, the success of the wider share ownership movement and the bull stock market of the 1980s.

Institutional shareholders, whose interests are represented by the Investment Committees (ICs) of the British Insurance Association (BIA) and the National Association of Pension Funds (NAPF), have issued guidelines for share schemes to operate within. They allow up to 5 per cent dilution (ie 5 per cent of the number of existing shares can be issued as new shares) through all employee schemes and a further 5 per cent dilution through executive share option schemes. Both limits apply over any ten-year period. Using unissued shares hides the real cost of share options, and the lack of any change to profits makes them appear 'free' and this has also helped the growth of schemes.

Since the inception of all employee schemes, it is estimated that a total of about 2.9 million employees received shares or options over shares worth, at the outset, about £10.3 billion. In the year to March 1992, nearly 1.3 million directors and employees are estimated to have received shares or options over shares worth about £3 billion. The figures for the years 1989 to 1992 are shown in Table 21.1.

Why share schemes?

The rationale for share schemes is different for executives and for the all-employee schemes. Executives can be viewed as the agents of the shareholders. In order to establish a commonality of interest, it is right that they either own substantial amounts of shares themselves or that their remuneration is closely tied to movements in the company's share price. Share options are the predominant form of executive share schemes.

The rationale for share schemes covering all employees is less clear. There are significant pros and cons. Also there are alternative ways to satisfy the often quoted goals of employee involvement, participation and motivation.

Executive share schemes – a stake in the company

One of the major ways of increasing executive identification with the aims of a business is to give executives shares or share options. As shareholders or potential shareholders, with the chance to benefit from the organization's success and

Table 21.1 *Approved employee share schemes*

Profit sharing schemes (approved under Finance Act 1978)

Year	Number of employees to whom shares allocated during year	Initial value of shares allocated £m	Average per employee £
1989–90	900,000	430	480
1990–91	880,000	410	470
1991–92	720,000	330	460

Total number of schemes approved up to 31/3/92:   1,012

Savings-related share option schemes (approved under Finance Act 1980)

Year	Number of employees to whom options granted during year	Initial value of shares over which options granted during year £m	Average per employee £
1989–90	460,000	1000	2200
1990–91	550,000	1430	2600
1991–92	470,000	1370	2900

Total number of schemes approved up to 31/3/92:   1,058

Executive share option schemes (approved under Finance Act 1984)

Year	Number of employees to whom options granted during year	Initial value of shares over which options granted during year £m	Average per employee £
1989–90	105,000	1900	18,000
1990–91	65,000	1450	22,000
1991–92	80,000	1300	16,000

Total number of schemes approved up to 31/3/92:   5,038

Source: Inland Revenue

achieve capital accrual beyond the scope of pay alone, their perception of their role can change. They can become 'owners' rather than just paid employees and this can have a beneficial effect on their commitment to the long-term future of the business. So goes the argument for executive share schemes, backed by the experience of the many organizations who have adopted this approach as a key element in executive remuneration.

Executive share schemes normally take the form of share options. Essentially the rules of these schemes provide for executives to be given an option to buy shares at a future date for their market price at the time the option was granted. Provided that the share price appreciates, the individual makes a profit when the option is exercised and the shares sold. The profit is the difference between the purchase price when the option was granted and the new market price for which shares can be sold at the end of the option period less any tax due on the capital gain. The prevailing tax regime can have a major effect on the attractiveness of share options.

Taxation of executive share options

Prior to the 1984 Finance Act, executive share option gains were taxed as income. The 1984 Finance Act removed the income tax liability and made gains subject to capital gains tax at the date of sale. From 1984 to 1989 option gains were taxed at 30 per cent, whereas the income tax highest rate was 60 per cent. This huge tax bias drove the growth of executive share option schemes. Before 1984 only one-third of companies had schemes. By 1993 over 5000 schemes have been approved by the Inland Revenue. Nearly all large plcs have schemes.

In the 1989 Finance Act, capital gains tax was raised to 40 per cent and income tax highest rate to 40 per cent, thus removing the major tax advantages of share options (some minor tax advantages still exist, eg tax is not due until sale of shares; the first £5800 of capital gains are tax free). However, executive share options have continued to be popular.

It is important to recognize that tax considerations have been a major influence on the choice of long-term incentive vehicles in the USA and in the UK, and that companies need to review their arrangements when the taxation regime changes.

Why entitlements have grown

The years that have passed since the 1984 Finance Act provided a favourable tax climate for Inland Revenue approved executive share option schemes, and an overwhelming majority of major UK public companies have introduced such schemes. They have done so because, like the Chancellor of the Exchequer who introduced the legislation, they believe in the value of these schemes as motivators. In his budget speech in 1984, the Chancellor said: 'I am convinced that we need to do more to attract top calibre company management and to increase the incentives and motivation of existing executives and key personnel by linking their reward to performance.' Boards of directors are, not unnaturally, attracted by the prospect of doing well personally out of their company's success; but they have also gone for share options because they saw their competitors introducing them and felt that these should also be part of their company's remuneration package. For those few who got in early after the legislation and exercised their options ahead of 'Black Monday' in October 1987, substantial capital gains have been possible, and widely reported in the press.

In the bear market that followed 'Black Monday', views on share options were more mixed and perhaps more realistic about the ups and downs in the system. There is, however, no sign of option schemes going out of favour or being abandoned and new forms of share option are being developed based mainly on US models to meet particular needs. Tax-approved share options have been available in the US since 1945 and in the UK since 1984. With the widespread operation of these plans, a number of serious shortcomings have emerged. These shortcomings have been identified by compensation experts on both sides of the Atlantic, and variations are emerging that attempt to match shareholder requirements more closely to the extensive reward package.

Building executive commitment and loyalty

Most companies coming to the market for the first time include details of an executive share option scheme in their prospectus, usually alongside an all-employee share scheme. This is a sign to potential shareholders that the organization is a well-managed company where executives have a stake in the future success of the business with a remuneration package structured accordingly. It also shows that the top management team should be 'locked in' by the handcuffs of the share scheme as the company goes for growth. Directors are also, it is thought, more likely to stay loyal to a company in which they have options in difficult times in the hope that things will come right by the time they come to exercise their options. Share schemes should make beneficiaries less vulnerable to approaches from executive search consultants – or at least make them very expensive to lure away. Potential employers may baulk at having to buy out existing share options by paying substantial 'golden hellos' to compensate for the lost benefit – probably in addition to granting new options to the executive in question who will negotiate for them as an expected part of the remuneration package.

Types of executive share ownership scheme

In many organizations, directors have shares as part-owners of the business. The Sainsbury family, Lord Weinstock, Lord Hanson, and 'Tiny' Rowland, to name but a few high-profile UK businessmen at the top of public companies, all gain far more income from their dividends as shareholders than they do from the earnings figures which appear in their companies' annual reports. This is also true of many smaller organizations where the income deriving from ownership merges with income from employment. Apart from executive shareholdings which exist as the result of part-ownership, directors and senior managers may also be granted shares under various forms of option scheme.

There are four principal forms of executive share schemes in the UK:

1. *Inland Revenue approved share option schemes* – taking full advantage of the 1984 Finance Act provisions and making up the vast majority of current UK schemes (see also Chapter 31 on tax considerations).
2. *Unapproved share options* – either those introduced prior to 1984 or running in addition to an approved scheme to provide additional potential shareholdings.
3. *Phantom share plans* – set up in organizations where no shares or no further shares are available for distribution, now or in the future. These are essentially a form of deferred incentive based on a notional share issue and linked to the share price or notional share price of the company.
4. *Restricted share plans* – these grant shares to executives which vest (typically in three or five years) depending upon restrictions such as continued employment and achievement of performance targets.

The shortcomings that have been identified with option plans are that:

- share options can provide the same upside as owning shares; however there has been growing criticism of their effectiveness as an incentive as they provide no downside risk. This criticism has been more prevalent in the USA than the UK, but as with many other things it may become so here too.
- the options as currently issued are not true long-term incentives
- the options pay no regard to long-term interests rates or inflation
- the options are not affected by dividends or demergers and therefore do not reflect total shareholder return.

To deal effectively with these shortcomings and to produce plans that reward executives in line with long-term shareholder returns, is a challenge that has been taken up by US and UK compensation experts. An example of the belief in the value of executive share ownership and an attempt to establish a very direct link between company and boardroom performance has recently been provided by Kodak in the US. There, executives are required to invest their own money in the company. Within five years all top forty managers will have at least one year's pay invested in Kodak shares. If Kodak does well, share values rise and executives gain and, of course, vice versa.

The Prudential and BP have recently implemented new share plans based upon restricted shares in place of share options. In the Prudential plan an executive can choose to take his annual incentive payout in restricted shares rather than cash. These restricted shares are then held in trust for five years. To encourage the executive to take shares the Prudential matches each share with a further share. In the BP scheme each senior manager must invest in shares in the company for a five-year period and then the shares are held in trust for a further five years, thus providing a real linkage of reward and share price performance over a ten-year period.

If this seems somewhat drastic, it is interesting to note that there is some evidence from the US which suggests that companies whose executives own significant numbers of shares perform better than companies where executive ownership is low. (Table 21.2 below shows the results of a study conducted in Chicago.) An equivalent analysis of the UK is not yet available but would make an interesting comparison.

These approaches are specially designed to overcome the shortcomings of conventional option plans.

Apart from the technicalities of tax management, for which specialist advice is usually necessary, the administration of all forms of executive share schemes tends to run along similar lines.

External controls

The final entitlements granted under approved executive share option schemes are closely affected by Inland Revenue requirements for tax relief and, in the case of quoted Public Limited Companies (PLCs) with institutional shareholders, by the

Table 21.2 *Performance of companies with stock ownership*

Company type	No of companies	Stock ownership as a multiple of total annual compensation	Three-year return on equity
Industrial:			
High ownership	11	14.6	27.4%
Low ownership	12	6.4	1.4%
Non-industrial:			
High ownership	8	19.8	22.7%
Low ownership	8	12.6	0.2%
Total	**39**		

Source: The Hay Group

guidelines of the Investment Committees (ICs). All share schemes for directors and employees, other than phantom stock plans (which are, as we have explained, really deferred incentives) must, in the UK, be approved by shareholders in accordance with Stock Exchange rules for listed and USM companies. The ICs represent the institutional shareholders, but also speak for the interests of shareholders as a whole. Their shareholding is normally sufficient in most PLCs to secure observance of their guidelines. The two main ICs are the British Insurance Association and the National Association of Pension Funds. Their guidelines apply to both approved and unapproved schemes, and the principal objective is to limit the extent to which the shareholders' equity is diluted. The guidelines have not always been welcomed and have been modified several times since 1984 to reflect changing company practice. It is also clear that individual companies, usually with the help of specialist advisers, have successfully negotiated modifications to suit special circumstances – as long as they could convince the ICs that this remained in the shareholders' interests.

Factors to be taken into account when introducing a scheme

Employers considering the introduction of an executive share option scheme will therefore need to be sure they obtain a full understanding of:

1. the tax position and requirements for gaining Inland Revenue approval
2. Stock Exchange rules
3. the effect of current IC guidelines on potential entitlements
4. market practice in their industry or sector
5. which issues they will need to monitor to ensure that practice remains competitive.

Executive share options – key policy decisions on entitlements

The place of options in the remuneration package

For as long as share options are given to executives because they have reached the Board rather than on a performance-related basis, there will always be a difference of opinion as to whether they are a benefit or an incentive. Like company cars provided on the basis of status rather than job need, share options can create a major distortion in remuneration differentials. The total earnings potential of those with options is substantially greater – and therefore results in a higher differential than a simple difference in salary scale would produce.

Options are certainly perceived by executives as a sign of success – in the same way as a luxurious company car. Share options are thus also a form of recognition for achievement, and well worth having if such recognition breeds commitment.

Deciding entitlements

For approved schemes, the Inland Revenue rules set a maximum multiple of earnings that can be granted in the form of share options; unapproved or phantom stock plans are, of course, free of these rules. But the Investment Committee rules also affect potential entitlements by limiting the amount of the organization's share capital that can be allocated to options. These will, of course, not just affect the first grant of options under a new scheme, but will have to be complied with when schemes are extended. Companies need to ensure that they will have shares available to grant under option when new top executives are appointed.

Within these constraints companies therefore have to decide:

1. whether to give the same entitlement to all directors
2. whether to differentiate on the basis of status, the need to retain key individuals or to recognize particular achievements or, indeed, length of service
3. how large a differential to make between the chief executive and the rest of the board or others picked out for special recognition
4. whether to grant options or permit their exercise only when agreed individual or corporate performance targets have been met
5. whether to extend the scheme to other key executives outside the board whose services are highly valued and whose long-term commitment to the company ought to be secured in some way
6. the policy on death of scheme participants or severance by redundancy, retirement, take-over, liquidation or misconduct
7. whether the new approaches, such as those being developed in the US and UK initiatives, should be used instead of conventional option plans.

These decisions will normally be the task of the non-executive remuneration committee of the Board – part of its role in supervising share option arrangements and safeguarding shareholders' interests. This committee will need to take advice from the organization's financial, legal and tax advisers to ensure that scheme rules comply with any regulations affecting them, are tax-efficient, and reflect best practice in this complex area.

An outline of the main rules to be covered by an approved share option scheme is given in Figure 21.1.

It was always the intention of the 1984 Finance Act that share options be used on a discretionary basis. There is nothing in its provisions which prevent the grant of options to, say, a brilliant research and development manager, a key sales executive or other specialists making a major contribution to company success. In reality, however, survey evidence from a number of reputable sources (Monks Publications, Hay, IDS) shows that the first post-1984 options were granted by boards of directors to themselves on a non-performance-related basis. This pattern continues today in most companies, as options have been extended to lower levels of management. A typical share option policy might be:

	Options as multiple of salary
Directors	4 × salary
Senior Managers	2 or 3 × salary
Other Eligible Managers	1 × salary

Communicating the benefits

In common with other remuneration policies, the motivational effect of share options can be strongly affected by the way in which the new policy is communicated. Bear in mind that any share options granted to directors will be shown in the company accounts so that secrecy is impossible. This could cause problems if any directors are excluded, so steps should be taken in advance to ensure that there are no unpleasant surprises.

Options are valuable to executives, even though they may incur no costs in the books of the employing company. Current practice in the US is to quantify the value of options using the well-known 'Black–Scholes' option pricing model, and to treat this as part of remuneration together with basic pay and bonus. This approach has not been adopted in the UK, but many companies want to com-

Outline of Executive Share Option Scheme

SCOPE	Non-transferable options to acquire shares, granted and exercised within ten years.
GRANT OF OPTIONS	
Whom Invited	Full-time directors and executives selected by board.
When	Within N weeks of announcing annual or half-yearly results.
Option Price	Middle market price at date of grant (or nominal value, if higher) – not payable until option is exercised – subject to adjustment on fair and reasonable terms if capital is varied, eg by a scrip issue.
Fee For Grant	Nominal (£1) or nil.
Individual Limit	Aggregated share values, at market price at time of grant, not to exceed four times the individual's annual emoluments. (The individual's quota of options under this scheme to be reduced if options exercised under an earlier scheme and vice versa).
Company limited	The aggregated value of shares as above, for all options granted under this and earlier executive schemes not to exceed five per cent of the company's total equity, or, together with company-wide share schemes, ten per cent.
EXERCISE OF OPTION **General Rule**[1]	Not before three years or after ten years from date of grant.
Death[1]	Within a year of death by deceased's nominated representative but not after ten years of grant.
Severance[1] (a) Redundancy, incapacity, retirement, take-over, liquidation	Within X months (normally less than a year) and before ten years.
(b) Otherwise	At board's discretion. In the event of option lapsing on loss of office, no compensation payable for loss of option rights.

SHARES
Company to keep available unissued shares to permit exercise of options. These shares to rank *pari passu* with other shares issued by company at time of allotment. Adjustments to be made as necessary on variation of company's capital.

ADMINISTRATION
The main features of the scheme cannot be amended in main outlines without shareholders' approval. Administration in hands of board (aided by Compensation Committee in some cases).

[1] Options exercised outside these time limits would not attract tax relief under the Finance Act, 1984.

Source: Incomes Data Services

Figure 21.1   *A typical Public Limited Company approved scheme*

municate the value of options to employees so that they appreciate the worth of the grant. The 'Judes' option pricing model was published in *Accountancy Age* in August 1990, taking account of tax rates and option granting practice (something that Black–Scholes ignores). Organizations can use the Judes model or similar approaches as a basis for communicating with employees (see Appendix K).

All-employee share schemes

Executive share option schemes are selective in the choice of participant. Other share schemes must apply to 'all' employees in the company. All-employee schemes are similar to executive share schemes in that they also allow employees to have a stake in the company. However the amounts are more modest and the motivational impact is different from executive share schemes. All-employee schemes are a form of financial participation commonly implemented when executive share options are introduced and, perhaps for this reason, their use is widespread.

Types of all-employee share schemes

1. *Inland Revenue approved save as you earn share options* – which take advantage of the 1980 Finance Act and are sometimes called 'Sharesave' schemes. They enable employees to save money through a bank or building society, within defined limits. At the end of either five or seven years, if the share option is exercised, the savings are used to purchase the shares. Since it is an option there is no downside risk for employees and, even if the option is not exercised, employees still receive their savings plus accumulated interest.
2. *Inland Revenue approved profit sharing share schemes* – which take advantage of the 1978 Finance Act and enable companies to distribute shares to employees which are free of tax if kept in trust for five years. These schemes are also known as approved deferred share trusts and are explained in more detail in Chapter 24 on Profit Sharing (pages 340–6).
3. *Inland Revenue approved matching contribution share schemes* – whereby the company matches the shares that employees purchase. These are often called BOGOF schemes (Buy One Get One Free). The schemes use the same 1978 Finance Act legislation as the profit sharing share schemes.
4. *Corporate PEPs* – which enable anyone (not only employees) to purchase shares. For shares in PEPs, capital gains and dividend income are free of tax. In a single company PEP, the annual savings limit is currently £3000 pa. PEPs provide a tax efficient way for employees to increase a shareholding in the company. The original purchase of shares can be marginally cheaper than the normal route through a stockbroker.

Taxation of all-employee share schemes

Successive governments have introduced and amended (usually favourably) the taxation of employee share schemes. They have done this because they believe that employee share ownership should be encouraged and that it is therefore appropriate to have a tax break on these schemes.

The main tax breaks are:

1. Save as you earn share options:
    –   no tax on the interest paid on the savings
    –   options can be granted at up to 20 per cent discount

- no income tax charge on the gain upon exercise; but these gains are subject to capital gains, where the shares are sold
- limit of savings of £250 per month.

2. Profit sharing share schemes:
   - no tax if shares kept for five years in trust
   - maximum of £3000 pa can be paid tax free (or, if pay is more than £30,000, 10 per cent of pay, up to a maximum of £8000 pa of shares)
   - shares transferred into a PEP after the five years in trust have capital gains tax deferred until the shares are actually sold. In the PEP future dividends are received tax free. (This facility also applies to save as you earn share options.)

3. Matching contribution share schemes:
   - the same rules apply as for profit sharing schemes
   - there is no tax break on the matching shares purchased by employees.

4. Corporate PEPs:
   - there is no tax break on the shares purchased by employees
   - dividends are tax free
   - there is no capital gains tax on gains.

Pros and cons of all-employee share schemes

The rationale for executive share schemes is clear in that executives directly impact on the business, so it is correct to have a part of their reward linked to shareholder returns. For all-employee schemes the rationale is less clear. There is an argument that all employees should share in the success of the company. However, there are other ways in which employees can share in this success and they may feel these are more relevant and motivating (eg team incentives, productivity schemes and profit-related pay). This logic tends to suggest that share schemes would be less motivational in large companies; however, the evidence is that the largest companies have been the keenest on these schemes, eg all the high street banks, Tesco, Sainsbury, Marks & Spencer and many other retailers and all the privatized companies have schemes.

The pros and cons for all-employee share schemes are laid out in Table 21.3.

External controls

The Inland Revenue requirements for tax relief are laid out in the 1978 and 1980 Finance Acts. The key condition is that the scheme must apply to all employees on similar terms. It is not possible to discriminate in favour of a particular group of employees.

The ICs have also published guidelines for all-employee share schemes. The key guideline concerns dilution of not more than 5 per cent in any 10-year period (this is in addition to the 5 per cent allowed for executive share option schemes).

Costs

The most expensive scheme from the employers' point of view is the profit sharing share scheme since this involves giving all eligible employees an amount of shares. If unissued shares are used there is no cash flow cost, but nevertheless there is a charge to profits which must be shown in the companies' accounts.

Save as you earn share options provide a cash inflow to the company when the options are exercised. There is no accounting charge to profits. However the

Table 21.3 *Reasons for all-employee share schemes*

For	Against
A stake in the company	Employees should diversify their investment portfolio. Overemphasis on one share is not appropriate.
Provides means for employees to share in success of the company	Share in success of team or business or division may be more appropriate than linkage to a whole company.
Tax effective	Profit-related pay is equally tax effective and can use local profit centre.
	Further complicates the remuneration package; adds one extra component of reward to communicate.
	Expensive. Usually implementation adds cost to the reward package.
	Cost/benefit is poor if employees perceive the value of cash is higher than that of shares.

'Judes' option pricing model (see Appendix K) can be used to estimate the cost of the option.

The relative costs of the four employee share schemes is shown in Table 21.4. In share schemes nothing is straightforward – this is highlighted by the three costs shown which are significantly different. Profit sharing is the most expensive way to transfer shares to employees. However, it does have the benefit that all employees participate, whereas in the other schemes only willing employees choose to join. SAYE share options and matching contribution schemes have broadly the same cost, but in the matching scheme, employees become shareholders immediately and receive dividends but also share the risk if share prices decrease.

A company PEP is the cheapest way to provide the facility for employee share ownership. However, the marginal benefit may not be sufficient to encourage employees to purchase shares.

Key policy decisions

Companies considering all-employee share schemes must decide:

1. why they want employees to own shares
2. whether they want employees to own the shares, receive dividends and vote shares immediately
3. how much subsidy the company is willing to provide
4. whether all employees receive shares or only those who elect to join
5. whether to set the length of service requirement at the Inland Revenue maximum of five years service or a lower figure
6. whether to exclude part timers working less than 20 hours per week, or to set a lower limit

7. whether to have one scheme or two or more schemes
8. If profit sharing share scheme:
   - whether to have a formula to calculate the profit share amount. If yes, then what formula
   - whether to have a cash alternative.
9. If SAYE share scheme:
   - what discount to set
   - whether to have five years or seven years option period
   - what maximum savings to allow
   - if over-subscribed how to scale down applications.
10. If matching contribution scheme:
    - whether to have a match of less than one company share for each employee share subscribed
    - whether to have a maximum lower than the Inland Revenue limit.

Table 21.4 *Cost of providing £1000 of shares to employees[1]*

	1 Profit sharing share scheme	2 Matching contribution	3 SAYE share option	4 Company PEP
Company provides	£1000 of shares	£500 of shares	–	–
Corporation Tax Relief (at 35%)	£350	£175	–	–
Net cost after tax shown in profit and loss account	£650	£325	nil	nil
Employee buys:	nil	£500 of shares	£1000 of shares	£900 of shares[2]
Economic cost	£650	£325	£350[3]	nil
Cashflow to company	nil	nil	+£800[4]	nil

Notes:
1. The table is indicative. There are a number of assumptions that may not apply in all cases. Timing of payments impacts on the figures shown. Assumes company uses unissued shares, except for employee purchased shares.
2. Assumes dividends of c£100 reinvested by PEP manager, so that employee accumulates £1000 of shares after five years.
3. Judes option pricing model indicates value of option granted at 20 per cent discount to market price at date of grant is worth approximately 35 per cent of market price.
4. Received at end of five years.

Communicating the benefits

In common with other remuneration policies, the motivational impact of all employee share schemes can be strongly affected by the way the new policy is communicated.

The savings authority involved in the SAYE share option scheme will be able to provide help in the form of videos, booklets and employee presentations. For other schemes the company must use its own resources or external consultants.

Experience has shown that the communication of employee schemes greatly affects the employees' perception of the scheme and its value.

Corporate PEPs

Personal Equity Plans (PEPs) were first introduced in 1986 to foster wider shareholding by small investors on a tax-effective basis. Sold by high street banks, building societies, insurance companies and other financial institutions, they were not initially a great success. They have, however, grown in popularity as the permitted investment in them has increased (to £6000 pa in 1990) and the rules surrounding them have simplified and relaxed. PEPs are based on the following principles:

- contributions to a plan can be monthly or annual within the current prescribed limits;
- contributions are invested by the plan managers in shares in listed companies held for members;
- dividends are exempt from income tax and can either be reinvested to buy more shares or paid out;
- share disposals are exempt from capital gains tax – gains can be used to buy more shares or paid out;
- there is no minimum holding period other than the 'Plan Year' for obtaining tax benefits.

Corporate PEPs confine shareholdings to a single specified share and can be used to offer both employees and outside shareholders the tax-effective benefits of such plans. Within the organization, corporate PEPs are effectively employee share purchase plans. By 1993 many major UK-listed companies had plans: typically those with a firm belief in the value of wider employee share ownership as well as an eye to providing extra tax-effective components to the remuneration package – albeit a component to which employees contribute themselves. Plan managers such as CC&P Trustees (who were first in the field), Bradford and Bingley and a growing number of others have been able to offer real savings over the administration cost of PEPs available to individual shareholders from high street sources.

Corporate PEPs cannot be introduced without professional advice from a reputable source. If they are to create the increased identification with shareholders' interests, which must be a major motivation for introducing them, the timing and communication of implementation will be critical to success.

ESOPs

An ESOP (Employee Share Ownership Plan) is an employee benefit trust linked to a share participation scheme. The trust receives contributions from the company or borrows money, and then buys shares in the company which are allocated to employees. In 1989 the UK government introduced legislation which gave statutory recognition to ESOPs, and in 1990 a rollover relief for capital gains tax was added. Statutory ESOPs are subject to quite onerous conditions and so far most UK ESOPs have been set up on a non-statutory basis. Again, ESOPs are an area where professional advice is needed for implementation.

A major benefit of using an ESOP, combined with employee share schemes, is that it avoids dilution. Companies which are close to the IC limits on dilution may find an ESOP offers scope to make further grants of share options than would otherwise be possible.

In many management buy-outs the use of an ESOP has enabled the management to temporarily park a percentage of the equity which can then be subsequently released to employees, either through subscription or through an employee share

Table 21.5 *How share purchases add up over the years*

Annual income	Per cent of income used to buy stock
Below $50K	0
$50K–$75K	5
$75K–$100K	7
$100K–$150K	9
$150K–$300K	10
Above $300K	15

Year	Compensation	Stock purchase this year	Number of shares purchased	Stock price	Total number of shares owned	Value of total shares at current price
1	$ 50,000	$ 2,500 (5%)	50	$ 50	50	$ 2,500
2	54,500	2,725 (5%)	52	53	102	5,350
3	59,405	2,970 (5%)	54	55	156	8,588
4	64,751	3,238 (5%)	56	58	212	12,255
5	70,579	3,529 (5%)	58	61	270	16,396
6	76,931	5,385 (7%)	84	64	354	22,601
7	83,855	5,870 (7%)	88	67	442	29,601
8	91,402	6,398 (7%)	91	70	533	37,480
9	99,628	6,974 (7%)	94	74	627	46,327
10	108,595	8,967 (9%)	116	78	743	57,610
11	118,368	9,774 (9%)	120	81	863	70,264
12	129,021	10,653 (9%)	125	86	987	84,431
13	140,633	11,612 (9%)	129	90	1,117	100,264
14	153,290	15,329 (10%)	163	94	1,279	120,606
15	167,086	16,709 (10%)	169	99	1,448	143,345
16	182,124	18,212 (10%)	175	104	1,623	168,725
17	198,515	19,852 (10%)	182	109	1,805	197,013
18	216,382	21,638 (10%)	189	115	1,994	228,502
19	235,856	23,586 (10%)	196	120	2,190	263,512
20	257,083	25,708 (10%)	203	126	2,393	302,396
21	280,221	28,022 (10%)	211	133	2,605	345,538
22	305,440	45,816 (15%)	329	139	2,934	408,631
23	332,930	49,940 (15%)	341	146	3,275	479,002
24	362,894	54,434 (15%)	354	154	3,629	557,386
25	395,554	59,333 (15%)	368	161	3,997	644,589
26 becomes CEO						
Total/average	$169,402	$459,172	3,997	$ 95	3,997	$644,589

Assumptions:
1. 9 per cent increase in compensation each year (reflects increases and promotions).
2. 25-year tenure when promoted to top executive.
3. Initial stock price of $50 increases by 5 per cent per year.

scheme or schemes. This mechanism enables all employees to share in the benefits of the buy-out.

How share purchases add up over the years

Purchasing quite small amounts of shares each year can produce quite a large shareholding for a successful employee in a successful company.

The prototypical plan shown in Table 21.5 has been based on an example in Ira Kay's book *Value at the Top: Solutions to the Executive Compensation Crisis.* Kay argues that executives must own significant amounts of shares in their company. He describes the plan thus:

> The plan requires employees to buy stock annually and hold it. The results are dramatic. By the time an employee rises through the ranks to become CEO he or she will own stock worth $644,589, almost twice the cash compensation. This could be in addition to any stock purchased through stock option plans. While that total remains below the level sophisticated shareholders would like their CEO to own, it is well above typical levels, and it puts the employee into a good position to participate in a CEO-level stock-based incentive programme.

22

Salesforce Incentives

Payment systems for sales staff often differ fundamentally from other staff because of the behavioural assumptions about salesforce motivation. This is the area of 'ego-driven' individuals who, conventional wisdom has it, will only deliver acceptable performance if offered the 'carrot and stick' of substantial financial involvement. Research in the 1980s by the IPM's National Committee for Pay and Employment Conditions (to which one of the authors was a contributor – see bibliography) questioned some of these assumptions. It admitted, however, that, dubious as the stereotypes of the salesforce are, they are believed implicitly by most of the sales managers who devise sales incentive schemes, by the salesforce, and often by the salary administrators responsible for remuneration practice in this area.

Not surprisingly, this research found that this is one area where the top sales executive will have far more power over incentive scheme design and operation than the personnel department. Often the latter is forced, because it is less powerful in corporate terms, to accept and administer schemes which sit ill with remuneration policy for the rest of the staff and which have to be kept separate from them.

Basic design issues

In designing a suitable sales incentive scheme the following questions have to be answered:

- Are the performance measures appropriate?
- Are the territories or targets properly equalized so that staff with 'easy' sales patches or product lines do not have an unfair advantage over those working in areas or with merchandise where the going is tougher?
- Is the plan equitable between people performing at the same level and managed consistently?

Links with remuneration policy for other employees

For many employers it makes more sense to have a separate salary structure for sales staff. This should be designed to be competitive in relation to salesforce remuneration in the industry or sector. It will need to reflect the local, regional and hierarchical breakdowns required to run the sales operation effectively. These may or may not fit sensibly into existing company grading and pay structures. It is often difficult to match sales jobs with job evaluation schemes which have value factors that are irrelevant to the sales function. Where analysis of this relationship with the company job evaluation scheme shows a poor fit, as for example in areas such as data processing, it is better to establish a notional relationship or accept that there need not be one at all.

Merit reviews and annual progression may also need to be on a different basis. The organization may feel it is paying twice for the same performance if it operates both a merit payment scheme and a sales incentive plan. Or, it may decide that the incentive covers only the sales performance and that the merit review looks at wider issues than the bottom line. Whichever way this decision is determined, annual or, in a tight market, more frequent market-related adjustments should be made to keep basic salary levels competitive.

Types of salesforce remuneration plan

There are seven basic forms of salesforce remuneration:

1. *Salary only:* generally used where the product being sold does not lend itself to incentive payments. For example, in some forms of capital equipment sales where identifying the 'seller' can be difficult; or where the use of incentives could be construed as unethical (eg pharmaceuticals); or where the company makes a decision that it will recruit and pay high basic salaries to exceptional salespeople, whose performance is subject to regular scrutiny and reward through the merit payment system. Where the 'salary only' approach is used, organizations may, nevertheless, award non-cash incentives to reward success in short-term sales campaigns. They may also have other rewards such as all-employee profit sharing schemes to reinforce the messages of success.

2. *Salary and standard bonus:* this is basic salary plus a target-related bonus to be paid out at set levels in relation to the achievement of company sales targets. Bonus targets can be based on a formula related to sales or a range of agreed objectives and they might contain a discretionary element.

3. *Salary and individual bonus:* as above, but geared to the achievement of individual targets. They can be a mixture of sales and other factors such as retaining customers, achieving a given percentage of new business, numbers of sales visits made in relation to a plan etc.

4. *Salary with standard bonus and commission:* where there is a bonus in relation to overall sales levels and other targets plus commission paid as a percentage of sales revenue. As with executive and other incentives, commission payments can be subject to 'accelerators'. That is, higher percentage payments are made once a given sales threshold has been met or 'decelerators' to control maximum earnings levels.

5. *Salary with individual bonus and commission:* as above, but where the bonus element is related to the achievement of individual targets – sales and non-sales.

6. *Salary plus commission:* where basic salary is set in relation to the market, and commission as a percentage of sales is paid in addition. In some cases basic salary can be set very low as an incentive to stay on the road and generate sales. As with the commission only approach described below, these schemes tend rapidly to sort out good sales staff from poor sales staff and cause the latter to resign and leave this type of work.

7. *Commission only:* the really tough end of the sales remuneration spectrum. This means that, typically, after a brief training and induction phase, the individual is out on his or her own – dependent on maintaining a high level of sales for survival. This approach has been commonly used in the selling of

insurance and double glazing for example, but organizations who use it expect, and get, a very high drop-out rate with new sales people. A salesforce paid commission only is typically self-employed.

Sales bonus or commission schemes – advantages and disadvantages

Bonus schemes related to targets, or commission schemes where the payment is calculated as a percentage of sales, each have their advantages and disadvantages as described below.

Bonus schemes

Advantages
According to the IPM's research, the main advantages of bonuses over commission schemes are that they:

- permit flexible design – so enabling management to encourage and reward various types of individual or group behaviour
- provide for a basic salary element to cover basic needs thus, in accordance with Maslow's theory of motivation, freeing the representative to attain higher recognition needs through the bonus scheme
- enable payments to be timed to suit the business and its need to retain good staff
- provide some protection against fluctuations in third-party demand levels
- make the equalization of reward easier.

Disadvantages
The main disadvantages of bonus schemes are:

- the link between effort and reward can be weakened
- objectives may be unattainable or difficult to appraise
- where a group bonus pays at the average, it rewards good and poor performers equally
- they can be more complicated than commission schemes
- there can be a confusion between bonus and merit payments
- replacing one with the other can be demotivating unless the rationale of the change is properly communicated.

Many of these problems can be removed by careful planning and monitoring of whichever type of scheme is chosen.

Commission schemes

Advantages
The IPM research also found that commission schemes had certain advantages:

- pay is linked solely to sales volumes or profitability
- there is the maximum financial incentive
- only successful sales representatives will stay
- sales costs related to salaries vary with the measure of performance chosen
- where there is more than one product, they can offer greater flexibility by paying different commission rates to promote different products
- they are generally easy to understand and monitor

- payments can be closely linked to income received and so avoid the problem of tying up money in salaries in advance of receipts
- from the sales representative's point of view, commission schemes keep up with inflation because payments generally increase in line with product price rises
- they can allow the salesforce to be truly self-employed.

Disadvantages
Despite these advantages, the IPM researchers go on to point out some quite severe disadvantages:

- uncertain and fluctuating earnings can be a demotivator
- sales representatives can be tempted to act unethically by overloading customers with stock and pushing goods they may not need – this is potentially damaging to customer relations and the long-term stability of the business
- management has little financial control over earnings
- management has little disciplinary control
- loyalty to the organization can easily take second place to individual self-interest. Self-employed representatives have been known to use the sales area set out by one company to sell the products of another to supplement their income
- schemes may emphasize sales at any price rather than profitable sales
- non-selling services (merchandizing, stocking-up, maintenance, etc) are discouraged because they cost the individual money in terms of lost sales time
- incomes from commission schemes can exceed those of other, higher graded employees – if income exceeds that of sales managers, the problem can be compounded by promotion difficulties
- the greater the commission element, the more likely are sales representatives to be inflexible about sales territory divisions, calls to be made, non-selling services, etc
- lack of pay security can cause recruitment and retention problems, especially during an economic downturn when, ironically, companies need a high calibre sales team
- where commission is linked to sales turnover, price rises are automatically built into salesforce remuneration – internal relativity problems can ensue where price increases exceed pay rises.

The use of decelerators

Although, as we have shown, accelerators are used in commission schemes to reward additional sales, decelerators are also used. These produce a 'regressive' commission line, ie one which pays out a lower percentage once a given sales threshold is reached. The reasons are as follows:

- to avoid 'windfall' pay-outs;
- in circumstances where high sales are not directly attributable to extra sales effort;
- where the correlation between 'selling' the product to the customer and the size of the eventual order is low;
- if a maximum earnings level is thought necessary;
- to encourage new orders by reducing the commission value of repeat business;
- where there is a danger of sales exceeding productive capacity.

Administering sales incentives

Policy in the following areas needs to be set up at the start of a sales incentive scheme to ensure that it has the best chance of working effectively. Once the type of scheme has been selected it is necessary to:

1. Allocate sales territories and product lines carefully and formulate a policy on inter-area crediting.
2. Decide on the timing of payments which are designed to maximize staff retention by only paying out if staff are still in employment after a given period, say, six months.
3. Communicate the objectives of the scheme – with provision for regular reinforcement of these through meetings, newsletters, etc.
4. Establish a system for monitoring the scheme's operation and reviewing the rules if they are not meeting business needs.
5. Develop a policy on short-term incentives designed to reward achievement at the end of seasonal or other sales campaigns.

Non-cash incentives

The provision of various kinds of non-cash incentives to meet the needs of sales campaigns and other reward policies is now a multimillion pound business operation in the UK. It delivers everything from specially produced lapel badges and pens to holidays in the Bahamas.

The principal types of non-cash incentives available are:

1. *Luxury consumer goods:* available either directly or through catalogues catering for tastes from windsurfing to cut glass.
2. *Holidays:* of varying length and location depending on the size of reward required, so that employees can find somewhere that suits them.
3. *Car schemes:* recognizing exceptional performance by allowing top sales representatives to have, say, a more prestigious car such as a white BMW.
4. *Premium clubs:* set up to provide special rewards for top sales representatives or a given number of high achievers at the end of a sales contest. Membership can be marked by anything from a special tie to a 'conference' on the Riviera.

Use of non-cash incentives for other staff

Severe market pressure and the search to find new reward systems for staff outside the salesforce now means that non-cash incentives are finding a wider use. They can, for instance, be used to reward project completion in the data-processing area, meeting a very tough production schedule, or, in the personnel area, to reward staff who have ensured that a sensitive redundancy exercise went according to plan.

When and how to use non-cash incentives

To get the maximum benefit from non-cash incentives, the following points may be useful:

1. *Beneficiaries:* decide whether it is better in terms of company practice and business needs to reward just the top performers or distribute rewards more evenly to recognize general achievement and reinforce the message that everyone is in with a chance.

2. *Publicity:* right from the outset, publicize the rewards and the means of achieving them and, at the end, give wide publicity to the 'winners'.
3. *The award ceremony:* make an occasion of it, say, a formal occasion where the chairman or managing director makes the presentation in front of the winners' colleagues. Local press coverage can be helpful as well as coverage in company magazines. The prize winners should be given as much personal recognition as possible and be made to feel the centre of things.

Problems

Where non-cash incentives reward short-term effort, care is needed to ensure that the 'prize-hunters' do not pursue the rewards to the detriment of longer-term objectives. Research in this area also suggests that it is unwise to let this approach overshadow the continuing need to have competitive basic salaries and cash incentives. Consumer goods should not replace pay to any serious extent. Their role should be just to provide additional recognition – a 'fillip' in the hope that this will increase performance. Poor administration of schemes and unwise selection of prizes and options can also cause problems, as can tactless handling of those unable to reach the standards required to get a prize. Finally, and more importantly, the tax implications of all non-cash incentives should be considered. There is little motivation to be had from being awarded, say, a video machine and then finding that tax is due on its purchase value with no company provision to cover the liability – see Chapter 31 (tax considerations).

23

Gainsharing

Definition

Gainsharing is a formula-based company or factory-wide bonus plan which provides for employees to share in the financial gains made by a company as a result of its improved performance.

The formula determines the share by reference to a performance indicator such as added value or another measure of productivity. In some schemes, the formula also incorporates performance measures relating to quality, customer service, delivery or cost reduction.

Gainsharing differs from profit-sharing in that the latter is based on more than improved productivity. A number of factors outside the individual employee's control, such as depreciation procedures, bad debt expenses, taxation and economic changes, contribute to profit. Gainsharing aims to relate its payouts much more specifically to productivity and performance improvements within the control of employees.

Gainsharing is well established in the US, the first schemes having been introduced in the mid-1930s. They have not made such an impact in the UK – a survey in 1991[1] established that plant or enterprise-wide schemes were operating in just 12 per cent of the participating organizations, but in only 4 per cent of those organizations were all employees included. However, interest is increasing in gainsharing as a method of paying for performance which can be related to more reliable measures, encourages teamwork and provides a basis for participation and empowerment.

We examine gainsharing in this chapter under the headings of:

- aims;
- features;
- formulae;
- benefits;
- ingredients for success;
- why companies introduce gainsharing;
- introducing gainsharing;
- conclusions.

Aims

Fundamentally, the aim of gainsharing is to improve organizational performance by creating a motivated and committed work force who want to be part of a successful company.

More specifically, the aims of gainsharing are to:

- establish and communicate clear performance and productivity targets;

- encourage more objective and effective means of measuring organizational or factory performance;
- increase focus on performance improvement in the areas of productivity, quality, customer service, delivery and costs;
- encourage employees to participate with management in the improvement of operating methods;
- share a significant proportion of performance gains with the employees who have collectively contributed to improvements.

Main features

Gainsharing plans are based on a formula for sharing rewards in relation to measured performance. There are a number of different formulae and these are described in the next section of this chapter.

However, although the financial element is obviously a key feature of gainsharing, its strength as a process for improving performance lies equally in its other important features – ownership, involvement and communication. As Masternak and Ross[2] put it, gainsharing is 'an involvement system with teeth in it'.

Ownership

The success of a gainsharing plan depends on creating a feeling of ownership that first applies to the plan and then extends to the operation. When implementing gainsharing a company must enlist the involvement of all employees so that it can increase their identity with, and their commitment to, the plan, and build a large core of enthusiastic supporters.

Involvement

The involvement aspect of gainsharing means that the information generated on company results is used as a basis for giving employees the opportunity to make suggestions on ways to improve performance, and by empowering them to make decisions concerning their implementation.

Communication

Gainsharing plans are always based on key performance measures such as added value. The company has therefore to ensure that everyone involved knows exactly what is happening in these performance areas, why it is happening and what can be done about it. The communication process is two way: management communicates performance information to employees, who in turn communicate their proposals for improvement back to management. The financial basis of gainsharing (its 'teeth') provides extra focus for the processes of communication and involvement.

Formulae

The traditional forms of gainsharing are the Scanlon Plan, the Rucker Plan and Improshare. There are however many variations on these plans based on added value and other performance measures. There is no such thing as a standard formula – there is always plenty of choice.

The Scanlon Plan

The Scanlon formula measures labour costs as a proportion of total sales. A standard ratio, say 50 per cent, is determined and if labour costs fall below this proportion, the savings are distributed between employees and the company on the basis of a pre-established formula.

The Rucker Plan

The Rucker Plan is also based on labour costs but they are calculated as a proportion of sales less the costs of materials and supplies (ie valued added). Allen Rucker contended that the pay proportion of value added remains a near-constant share unless the organization suffers from severe mismanagement or a drastic change of policy. On the basis of this assumption, the Rucker Plan determines a constant share of whatever added value is created by the joint efforts of management and employees.

Improshare

Improshare is a proprietary plan which is based on an established standard which defines the expected hours required to produce an acceptable level of output. The standard is derived from work measurement. Any savings resulting from an increase in output in fewer than expected hours are shared between the organization and employees by means of a pre-established formula.

Value added

Many versions of gainsharing are based on value added as the key performance measure. Value added is calculated by deducting expenditure on materials and other purchased services from the income derived from sales of the product. It is, in effect, the wealth created by the people in the business.

A manufacturing business buys materials, components, fuel and various services. The combined contribution of management and employees converts these into products which can be sold for more than the cost of the materials. In doing so, the business 'adds value' by the process of production.

In a value added gainsharing plan, increases in value added are shared between employees and the company. Typically, the employees' share is between 40–50 per cent. A value added statement is set out as follows:

Table 23.1   *A value added statement*

	£m	%
Sales income	10.0	100
Deduct: cost of goods, consumerables & energy	4.0	40
Value added	6.0	60
Disposal of value added	6.0	100
Employees' share	2.4	40
Company's share: allocated to	3.6	60
Operating expenses	3.0	50
Operating profit	0.6	10

Determining a value added formula

Decisions have to be made on the following points when determining a value added formula:

- *How should value added be calculated?* This usually accords with the accounting standards and principles upon which the value added statement incorporated in a company's annual report would be based.
- *What reference point or threshold should be used to trigger off payments?* This can be selected by analyzing value added figures over a period of from three to five years. The value added figure chosen must cover current payroll costs, operating expenses and operating profit targets. The reference point is usually maintained for a period of twelve months – the gainsharing year – and will then be revised to take account of changes in payroll costs and operating expenses and revised operating profit targets.

  If value added rises above the threshold this surplus will be shared between employees and the company on the basis that normal payroll and operating costs have been covered and the profit target has been met. If value added falls below the threshold, payroll and other costs already incurred will not be covered and, clearly, there will be no shareout. In effect, the value added gainsharing fund has gone into deficit.
- *How should gains be shared between employees and the company?* This decision is based on the proportion of added value which is represented by normal payroll costs – normally between 40–50 per cent. Extensive research going back to that conducted by Allen Rucker in the 1930s has shown that the pay proportion of added value in a company tends to remain fairly constant. A typical share is 40 per cent of added value gains for employees and 60 for the company.
- *How should the bonus relate to improved performance?* As noted in Chapter 16 there are three pay-for-performance models: deaccelerated (bonuses taper off), shared (bonus is maintained as a fixed percentage) and accelerated (bonus percentages increase with improved performance). Most gainsharing plans use the shared model on the basis that employees should continue to share equally in the company's success.
- *What happens if value added falls below the reference point?* This means that the employees' share is less than the value of the pay they have already received. No shareout is therefore made and the company bears the loss. However, to cater for this eventuality, many value added gainsharing schemes incorporate an arrangement for setting up a buffer in the form of a reserve fund. A proportion of the employees' share, typically 25 per cent, is allocated every period to this fund and any surplus remaining at the end of the year is distributed as a terminal bonus. An end-year deficit would be absorbed by the company so that a new reserve fund is also started with the next financial year.
- *What should be the target for bonus levels?* To make any impact, a gainsharing plan should provide employees with a reasonable chance of earning at least 10 per cent bonus for the whole year. Many schemes in successful companies average 20 per cent.
- *Should there be any limit to the amount shared out?* To allow for the possibility of there being an exceptional 'windfall' increase in added value, some schemes cap the bonus payment to a maximum of, say, 25 per cent in a period. Any residual bonus is placed in the reserve fund for distribution at the end of the year. Clearly, if there has been a fundamental change in the added value situation during the year a company will wish to set up a new reference point for the coming year. It is essential for the rules of the plan to allow this to happen.
- *What should be the basis of distribution to employees?* The usual arrangement

is for the added value bonus to be distributed in proportion to base pay.

■ *How often should shares be distributed?* Distribution is normally at least every quarter. Some schemes distribute every other month and a few distribute monthly on the grounds that this creates a more immediate link between performance and reward. Frequent distributions will, of course, add to the administration involved in the scheme, although the design and administration of a typical plan can be handled fairly easily with a micro-computer incorporating spreadsheet, database management, statistics and desktop publishing applications.

An example of an added value gainsharing plan is illustrated in Figure 23.1. This provides for a bonus to be paid as added value increases beyond a reference point. The fund is in deficit if added value falls below that point. There is an even slope to the bonus curve until it reaches a bonus cap. A proportion of the value added share is allocated to a reserve fund.

For example:

■ A company has 200 employees.
■ Average base pay per employee is £10,000 a year.
■ Average employment cost per employee (pension etc) is £2000 a year.
■ Total pay bill is therefore £2.4m a year (£2.0m base pay plus 0.4m employment cost).
■ Value added in a quarter increases by £200,000 from £6.0m to £6.2m.
■ The increase of £200,000 is shared in the ratio of 40 per cent to employees (£80,000) and 60 per cent to the company (£120,000).

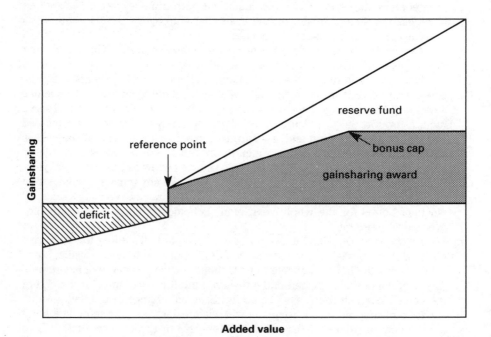

Figure 23.1 *Gainsharing plan*

- Of the employees' share of £80,000, 25 per cent (£20,000) is placed in a reserve fund, leaving £60,000 available for distribution as a bonus for the quarter.
- The £60,000 bonus is distributed to the 200 employees in proportion to their base pay.
- The average bonus is therefore £300 for the quarter, or 12 per cent of the average base pay for the quarter of £2,500.

Other formulae

Formulae relying entirely on value added have been criticized because they do not highlight key performance factors which can be influenced by employees – changes in value added may happen for reasons outside their control. Attempts have therefore been made in some plans, as illustrated in Figure 23.2, to introduce measures such as quality, customer service and cost as well as productivity (expressed as the ratio of employment costs to value added or output).

The problem with this approach is that it may be difficult to establish measures of these factors in a way which will be meaningful to individual employees, and unless this happens the gainsharing plan will be ineffective either as a motivator or as a medium for involvement and communication. There is also the danger of over-complication. A basic value added formula can be complicated enough without additional factors.

Choice of formula

There is no such thing as a standard gainsharing formula which can be applied in any organization. Every gainsharing plan is unique because it has to fit the particular needs and characteristics of the company and its employees. There is always a choice and companies will inevitably be faced with a dilemma – should they select a relatively simple but crude value added plan or go for a more sensitive but complex set of criteria? The answer to this question can only be found by an analysis of the circumstances of the company and the benefits it hopes to obtain from gainsharing.

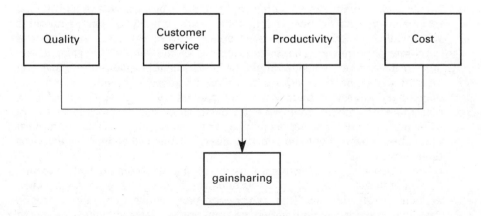

Figure 23.2 *Multi-factor gainsharing plan*

Benefits of gainsharing

The potential benefits of gainsharing are that it:

- focuses the attention of all employees on the key issues affecting performance;
- enlists the support of all employees to proposals for improving performance, not just a selected group;
- supports programmes for empowering employees – decision taking can be pushed down the organization hierarchy and employees can be given more control over their work;
- encourages teamwork and co-operation at all levels;
- promotes better two-way communication about issues concerning work and productivity;
- encourages trust between employees and the company;
- creates a win-win environment in which everyone gains as productivity rises.

Ingredients for success

The potential benefits of gainsharing are considerable, but it is not an easy option. There are a number of demanding requirements for success. The main ingredients are:

- *Management commitment* – the management team must be committed to the concept of gainsharing and all it involves, including sharing performance information with employees.
- *Management style* – the management team must believe in shared decision-making. They must be willing to go out and talk to employees and to listen to and act on their suggestions. A 'command' organization is not likely to succeed with gainsharing.
- *Culture* – the norms and values of the organization should support the thrust for performance improvement, teamworking and cooperation. Gainsharing can be a lever for developing a more performance orientated and cooperative culture but it will not work if it has to start from scratch.
- *Climate* – employee relations should be reasonably stable and there generally should be a working atmosphere of mutual trust between management and employees. Again, gainsharing can help to develop trust, but it can not do it alone.
- *Involvement* – the underlying philosophy of gainsharing is that organizational members want to be involved in their work, employees have something worthwhile to say, employee suggestions can save money and improve corporate performance, and all contributors should share in the gains generated by these improvements. Employee involvement in a gainsharing plan can be said to be the most critical factor in its success. Employees must be encouraged to assume their new and expanded role because no gainsharing plan will work without employee enthusiasm, support and trust. It is necessary to believe not only that people actually carrying out the work have the best ideas about how it should be done but also that they will be most receptive to their own ideas.
- *Communications* – management must be prepared to communicate information on organizational goals, projects and problems which has previously been in their private domain. This information can include news about orders, customer reactions, quality initiatives, new market developments, changes in product mix and plans for introducing new technology. Management must also

be prepared to listen to the reactions and comments of employees about the information. Gainsharing is more likely to be successful if effective systems for communication are already in place, but its introduction can stimulate all-round improvements – an important benefit.

- *Corporate strategy* – one of the most important criteria for the successful implementation of gainsharing is that it should be an integral part of corporate strategy. It must therefore be congruent not only with corporate culture but also the organization's goals and objectives. It may have to be recognized that developments in corporate strategy may influence the way in which gain-sharing operates.

- *Scope for improvement* – there must be scope for improvement in performance by means of the joint efforts of management and employees. Clearly, there is no point in introducing gainsharing if the chances of increasing value added are slim. It is dangerous to make any promises on financial outcomes, but there should be some basis for a shared belief that performance can be improved and that, as a result, there will be financial gains.

- *Nature of the organization and its technology* – a delayered organization relying largely on teamwork will be more likely to benefit from gainsharing. The size of the organization or plant should not be so huge that employees can not understand the work going on elsewhere and how the efforts of each area interrelate. Gainsharing can work well when jobs are highly interdependent, as in flexible manufacturing systems, when just-in-time is in operation, and in cellular manufacturing operations. A full computer-integrated-manufacturing (CIM) system would be an ideal environment for gainsharing.

- *Resources* – the company must have the resources to administer gainsharing. As mentioned earlier, this does not require elaborate systems, but it may be necessary to acquire or develop specialized software and train people to use it. The company must also have the financial resources required to pay for productivity improvement. Venture capitalists financing a start-up high technology company may be unwilling to allow gainsharing bonuses to be paid until the firm has realized a profit.

Why companies introduce gainsharing

Companies introduce gainsharing for a number of reasons. Perhaps the most powerful is the feeling that it is right to link pay to organizational performance, coupled with a belief in the desirability of communicating organizational objectives, creating team spirit, breaking down organizational barriers, increasing the flow of innovative ideas from employees and improving commitment.

Gainsharing can be introduced as a change agent, probably and desirably, in association with other structural and process initiatives designed to achieve cultural change.

Increased competition – national or global – or declining productivity are reasons for introducing gainsharing. They have spurred managements to devise more creative pay arrangements which will stimulate both productivity and quality and keep employment costs under control.

A further reason for introducing gainsharing in some companies is that they have become disillusioned with traditional incentive and bonus schemes. As noted in Chapter 18 some organizations have abandoned piecework or individual work-measured incentive schemes and are paying their manual workers a high basic or day rate, adding to that rate a group or enterprise-wide incentive plan.

Introducing gainsharing

The initial steps to take when considering the introduction of gainsharing are to:

- define as clearly as possible the reasons for introducing the scheme and its objectives;
- conduct a cost/benefit analysis – establishing how much it will cost to introduce and maintain the scheme compared with the financial benefits it is likely to produce;
- review all the criteria, listed earlier in this chapter, to determine whether or not the organization's culture, climate, structure, processes, technology, strategies for growth and resources are likely to be conducive to success;
- draw up some preliminary proposals on the type of gainsharing plan the organization would like to develop and the formula it would wish to use – reference should be made to the questions on this subject set out in this chapter;
- sound out the views of line managers, other employees and, if appropriate, union representatives, on their attitudes to gainsharing – an attitude survey may usefully be conducted for this purpose, or 'focus group' discussions can be held.

It is highly desirable for the next steps to be taken in consultation with line managers and employees. Gainsharing is about involvement and those concerned should participate as fully as possible in the design of the plan and in discussing the arrangements for future communication and involvement. A project team may be set up consisting of management and employee representatives but it is also essential during the design phase to communicate to all employees what is happening, and why.

Once the initial design of the plan has been completed, it should be communicated to all employees by a team briefing process. The brief should explain the philosophy of the scheme, the basis upon which the formula will operate and be revised, how they will be involved and how they may benefit. There should be no doubt in anyone's mind at this stage about the purpose and components of the plan.

There is no point in phasing-in gainsharing – it is an all or nothing process in that it must cover the whole enterprise or plant and be related to corporate performance measures. But it is advisable to build in a review stage after, say, six months' operation, rather than wait for a whole year. The briefing should have emphasized that the reference point in the basic formula will be amended as necessary at the end of each financial year and it may be desirable to make provision for such an amendment at an earlier stage in the first year.

It is essential to validate the scheme. The organization should have a clear idea of the intended results and track the programme's performance against those expectations.

Conclusions

Gainsharing is a potentially valuable component in an organization's overall reward strategy. It has, however, to be developed and maintained as part of an integrated process of reward management – it can not work in isolation. It should also be remembered that gainsharing is essentially a participative process. It is not, like most profit sharing schemes, simply a method of handing out money for reasons which are beyond the ken and control of employees. The success of gainsharing depends largely on the opportunities it presents for involvement so that employees can establish a clear link between their performance and their rewards – an essential requirement for success in any pay-for-performance scheme.

References

1. Cannell, M and Wood, S (1991) *Incentive Pay: Impact and Evolution,* Institute of Personnel Management, London
2. Masternak, R and Ross, T (1992) 'Gainsharing: bonus plan or employee involvement?', *Compensation & Benefits Review* January-February, pp 46–54.

24

Profit Sharing

Profit sharing is a plan under which an employer pays to eligible employees, as an addition to their normal remuneration, special sums in the form of cash or shares in the company related to the profits of the business. The amount shared is determined either by an established formula, which may be published, or entirely at the discretion of management. Profit sharing schemes are generally extended to all employees of the company.

Objectives of profit sharing

Most companies which operate profit sharing schemes have one or more of the following objectives in mind:

- to encourage employees to identify themselves more closely with the company by developing a common concern for its progress
- to stimulate a greater interest among employees in the affairs of the company as a whole
- to encourage better co-operation between management and employees
- to recognize that employees of the company have a moral right to share in the profits they have helped to produce
- to demonstrate in practical terms the goodwill of the company towards its employees
- to reward success in businesses where profitability is cyclical.

It is generally recognized that schemes which share profits according to some universal formula among all or most employees will not provide any real incentive because they fail to satisfy the three basic requirements of an incentive scheme, namely:

(a) that the reward should bear a direct relation to the effort
(b) that the payment should follow immediately or soon after the effort
(c) that the method of calculation should be simple and easily understood.

Types of schemes

The main types of profit sharing schemes are:

1. *Cash* – a proportion of profits is paid in cash direct to employees. This is the traditional and still the most popular approach.
2. *Stock* – a proportion of profits is paid in shares. This is much less popular, especially since the advent of the approved deferred share trust scheme with its considerable tax advantages.
3. *Approved deferred share trust (ADST)* – the company allocates profit to a trust fund which acquires shares in the company on behalf of employees.

4. *Mixed schemes* – an ADST scheme is sometimes offered in addition to a cash scheme, or the latter is made available to staff before they are eligible for ADST shares, or as an alternative to ADST shares.

In addition, the British government introduced in 1987 its profit-related pay (PRP) scheme which provides income tax relief for approved schemes (details of this are given in Chapter 25).

A survey of profit sharing in 356 firms published by the Glasgow University Centre for Research into Industrial Democracy and Participation revealed that in two-thirds of the survey firms which operated profit sharing, the most popular scheme, especially among the smaller firms, was the simple cash-based option. The ADST type scheme is, however, gaining in popularity. Profit sharing was much more common among US-based companies (64 per cent) than their European counterparts (29 per cent), and the schemes were more prevalent in London and the South than in the Midlands and the North.

Cash schemes

The main characteristics of typical cash schemes can be analyzed under the following headings, which are discussed below:

- eligibility;
- formula for calculating profit shares;
- method of distributing profit shares;
- amount distributed;
- timing of distribution.

Eligibility

In most schemes all employees except directors are eligible. The normal practice is to require one year's service to be completed before a share in profits can be received. Profit shares are then usually paid in relation to the pay earned or the time served between the date on which one year's service was completed and the date on which the profit shares are paid.

Formulae for calculating profit shares

There are three basic approaches to calculating profit shares. The first is to use a predetermined formula for distributing a fixed percentage of profits. This formula may be published to staff so that the company is committed to using it. The advantages of this approach are that it clarifies the relationship between company profits and the amount distributed and demonstrates the good faith of management. The disadvantages are that it lacks flexibility and the amount paid out may fluctuate widely in response to temporary changes in profitability.

The second approach is for the board to determine profit shares entirely at its own discretion without the use of any predetermined or published formula. The decision is based on a number of considerations, including the profitability of the company, the proportion of profits that it is felt should reasonably be distributed to employees, estimates of the expectations of employees about the amount of cash they are going to receive and the general climate of industrial relations in the company. This is the more common approach and its advantages are that it allows the Board some flexibility in deciding the amount to be distributed and does not commit it to expenditure over which it has no control. Random fluctuations can be smoothed out and the profit sharing element of remuneration can be adjusted easily in relation to other movements in pay within the company. The disadvantage is that a secret formula or the absence of a formula appears to contradict one of the basic reasons for profit sharing: the development among employees of a firmer commitment to the company because they can identify themselves more clearly with its successes and appreciate the reasons for its set-backs. The scheme is no longer a completely realistic profit sharing device if employees feel that they are insufficiently rewarded for improved performance or insulated from reverses. These arguments against flexibility are powerful ones but, on balance, a flexible approach is to be preferred because it does not commit the company to distributing unrealistically high sums when profits are shared out.

The third approach is a combination of the first and second methods. A formula exists in the sense that a company profit threshold is set, below which no profits will be distributed. A maximum limit is set on the proportion of profits that will be distributed, for example, 5 per cent and/or that percentage of salary that will be distributed as a profit share, for example, 10 per cent.

Methods of distributing profit shares

The main ways of distributing profit shares in cash schemes are to:

- distribute profits as a percentage of basic pay with no increments for service. This is a fairly common arrangement and those who adopt it do so because they feel that profit shares should be related to the individual contribution of the employee, which is best measured to pay. Service increments are rejected because the level of pay received by an individual should already take into account the experience he or she has gained in the company;
- distribute profits as a percentage of earnings with payments related to length of service. This approach is also frequently used and its advocates argue that it will ensure that loyalty to the company will be suitably encouraged and rewarded. They claim that to rely on pay as the sole arbiter of profit shares would be unjust because many valuable employees have, through no fault of their own, limited opportunities to move out of their present occupation or grade;
- distribute profits in proportion to pay and some measure of individual performance. This approach is rare below Board level because of the difficulty of measuring the relationship between profits and performance and because it is considered that individual effort should be rewarded directly by performance-related pay or promotion;
- distribute profits as a fixed sum irrespective of earnings or service. This is completely egalitarian but rare.

The choice of approach is usually between distributing profit shares either in relation to pay or in relation to pay and service. The arguments for and against each approach are finely balanced but there is a good case for providing some uplift for longer service staff in any situation where a company relies on its experienced staff to contribute their specialized skills and knowledge to its success, and cannot ensure that its normal policies for paying merit increments or promoting staff will adequately reward their loyalty to the organization.

Amount distributed

A survey conducted by Incomes Data Services in 1986 revealed that rather more than half of the companies surveyed leave the amount to be distributed to 'directors' discretion'. Others provide limits within which the directors decide. A maximum of 5 per cent of profits is typical, but this may only be paid if it is triggered by profits reaching a defined level.

Other surveys into the amounts distributed in British profit sharing schemes have indicated that the proportion of pay shared out can vary from as little as 2 per cent to 20 per cent or more. The Glasgow University survey showed that in 60 per cent of the firms surveyed which had profit sharing schemes, the share amounted to less than 6 per cent of pay. Ideally, however, the share should be somewhere between 5 and 10 per cent of pay in order to be meaningful without building up too much reliance on the amount to be distributed.

Timing of distribution
Most schemes distribute profits annually, although a few share out profits twice a year. Distribution is usually arranged to fall in good time for either the summer holidays or Christmas.

Approved deferred share trust (ADST) schemes

The basic rules for an ADST scheme, which must be followed to obtain the tax concessions in the 1978 (as amended) Finance Act, are as follows:

1. Schemes must operate through a trust set up for this purpose, and trustees must be appointed to run it. Where there is a group of companies, a single scheme can be set up by the controlling company to cover all the employees of the group.
2. The company must make cash payments to the trustees, who use this money to buy shares in the company. The shares are held by the trustees but are set aside for the individual employees taking part in the scheme.
3. The shares must be part of the ordinary share capital of the company which has set up the scheme, or of its controlling company. They must have the same rights to dividends and bonus issues and so on as other ordinary shares, but the company is allowed to make its own arrangements about voting rights.
4. Employees must agree to leave their shares in the scheme with the trustees for at least two years.
5. The value of the shares set aside for any employee in any one tax year must not exceed a certain limit. At present the limit is £2000 or 10 per cent of an employee's earnings, whichever is the greater, subject to a ceiling of £6000.
6. Anyone who has been a full-time employee of the company for five years must be allowed to join the scheme. In addition the company can allow part-time employees and those with less than five years' service to join the scheme.
7. All employees within a scheme must take part on similar terms – the scheme cannot exclude or favour particular individuals or certain groups of employees.
8. Shares cannot be set aside for an employee more than 18 months after he or she has left the company. There are also restrictions on employees taking part in more than one scheme.
9. Employees receive the dividends from shares which are held on their behalf. The dividends are taxed in the normal way, the final amount of tax depending on the employee's total income.
10. Employees cannot normally sell their shares during the first two years they are held in trust. Subsequently, if the rules of the particular scheme permit, they can be sold, but there may be income tax payable on the proceeds.
11. If the shares are held for over five years, there is no tax to pay. If the shares

are sold early, tax is payable on either their value at the date they were set aside, or on the proceeds of the sale, whichever is lower.

12.   When an employee sells shares he or she may be liable to capital gains tax on the difference between the sale of proceeds and the value of the shares at the time they were set aside for him. But tax will not be payable unless net gains in any year exceed the exempt amount for that year.

13.   If an employee dies, the shares may be sold and there will be no income tax payable, irrespective of how long the shares have been held.

14.   If employees lose their jobs because of injury, disability or redundancy, or if they reach state pensionable age, their shares may be sold immediately, however long they have been held. If the shares have been held for less than five years, income tax is paid as if the five-year period had been completed.

15.   If employees leave for any other reason, their shares cannot be sold until they have been held for two years. Whatever the reason for the employees' departure, they can choose to leave their shares within the scheme.

16.   The scheme has to be cleared with the Inland Revenue and the company's shareholders in advance.

Employees' attitudes

The Involvement and Participation Association (IPA) questioned 2700 employees in 12 companies about their attitudes to profit sharing. The following are extracts from the survey:

Table 24.1   *Attitudes to profit sharing – Industrial Participation Association*

	Agree strongly	Agree	Don't know	Disagree	Disagree strongly
	%	%	%	%	%
1 Profit sharing created a better attitude in the firm	10	55	16	18	1
2 It is popular because people like to have the bonus	24	69	4	3	–
3 It strengthens people's loyalty to the firm	6	41	12	34	2
4 It makes people try to work more effectively so as to help the firm to be more successful	6	45	15	31	3
5 It is good for the company and its employees	14	72	11	3	–

The IPA believes that the survey 'suggests that profit sharing does significantly improve employee attitudes and employee views of their company'. They reach this view essentially by adding together the percentages recorded under 'Agree Strongly' and 'Agree'.

However, in the Incomes Data Services 1986 study of profit sharing, the comment was made that:

another interpretation would be to add up all the responses except those under 'Agree Strongly', the one clear positive statement. This would suggest that most employees do not have a particularly positive attitude.

Of course, employees like the cash but their gratitude to the company is probably short-lived. Company profits are remote figures to people in the offices and on the shop-floor. They will express some interest in their size, because it affects the hand-out, but the idea of working harder to generate more profit for someone else will not necessarily appeal to them.

Benefits of profit sharing

Profit sharing and profitability

A survey carried out by Wallace Bell and Charles Hanson in 1985–86 sought to establish a correlation between profit sharing and profitability. 113 profit sharing companies and 301 non-profit sharing companies were surveyed and their performance compared on the basis of nine economic ratios over a period of eight years. Taking the composite results of all 414 companies, the average performance of the profit sharers over the eight years was better than that of the non-profit sharers in every one of the nine economic ratios used. And taking an average of averages, the average of ratios of the profit sharers was 27 per cent higher than those of the non-profit sharers. Of course, as Bell and Hanson say, the profit sharing companies were not better just because they had profit sharing. It was because they were good companies that they introduced profit sharing.

The particular features of how these companies achieved success were that managers:

- had clear and defined objectives and the ability to harness the resources needed to achieve them
- recognized that their most important resource is people
- saw employees not in terms of 'them and us', as adversaries, but as part of a team that should be working together for the success of the enterprise and sharing in its success
- were able to generate a reciprocal attitude among the employees and thus overcome the 'them and us' feelings that are found equally and sometimes more strongly, among employees towards management
- were able to generate a commitment to success.

Profit sharing and industrial relations

The Glasgow University survey referred to earlier expressed the more pessimistic view that the influence of profit sharing on industrial relations is marginal. The researchers concluded that profit sharing was used by employers as an effort–reward operation and not as an attempt to involve employees more closely in the decision-making apparatus. Yet, the evidence that profit sharing does increase effort hardly exists at all and that is simply because, as was mentioned earlier, the link between effort and reward is so tenuous. What, therefore, is the point of having a profit sharing scheme if it is not used to increase productivity by means of involving employees and mounting a communications campaign pointing out how *they* benefit from increased output and profitability?

Conclusions

It is worth noting that a number of companies have introduced profit sharing primarily because they feel that it is their duty to share their prosperity with their employees. If this view is held, then any uncertainty about the benefits arising from profit sharing is not an argument against its introduction. It is, of course, possible to take the opposite view: that profits are the wages of capital and that a company is not under any moral obligation to share profits with its employees, although it has the duty of treating them fairly and providing them with the rewards, benefits and conditions of employment that are appropriate to the contribution they make.

For anyone contemplating the introduction of profit sharing, or wondering whether to continue an existing scheme, the fundamental question is, 'do you consider that, in addition to all the benefits already provided by the company to its employees, it has a moral obligation to share its prosperity with them?' If the answer to this question is 'yes', a profit sharing scheme is what you want. If the answer is 'no', there may still be good reasons for considering profit sharing. But alternative means of rewarding employees and increasing their identification with the company (as described elsewhere in this book) may well deserve attention.

25

Profit-related Pay

Introduction

Companies and employees have much to learn and little to lose from tying pay to profits. Inland Revenue approved profit-related pay schemes allow up to £4000 or 20 per cent of pay (whichever is the lower) to be paid tax free. From a slow start when the government introduced the profit-related pay scheme legislation in 1987, there has been a dramatic increase recently in the number of schemes – in March 1993 there were over one million people in 4615 schemes, and the numbers are rising.

Profit-related pay schemes are often referred to as PRP schemes, which confuses them with performance-related pay, also referred to commonly as PRP. In this book we are reserving the acronym PRP for individual performance-related pay schemes as described in Chapter 17.

Main features of profit-related pay

The main features of profit-related pay as approved by the Government are as follows:

1. In a profit-related pay scheme, a part of pay moves up and down with profits so that employees' pay reflects the profit which has been earned by their work.
2. All profit-related pay will be free of income tax up to the point when profit-related pay is 20 per cent of pay or £4000 a year, whichever is lower. For a married man on average earnings of £300 a week the relief could add about £15 a week to take home pay which is equivalent to a gross pay increase of 7 per cent.
3. Profit-related pay is subject, like other earnings, to National Insurance Contributions (NIC) unless it is part of total earnings below the lower earnings limit for employer's NIC. However, profit-related pay which is exempt from employer's NIC (eg because it is paid through a trust) cannot also qualify for the income tax relief.
4. The relief will be available to all private sector employees paying income tax through PAYE, with the exception of controlling directors.
5. Employers will be free to design their own schemes. They have to be registered by the employer with the Inland Revenue in advance of coming into operation. A scheme must relate to an employment unit which is either a complete incorporated or unincorporated business in the private sector, or a sub-unit of the business.
6. The main qualifying features for a scheme are:

     (a)   schemes must establish a clear relationship between the profit-related pay of the specified employment unit and the audited profits generated by it (see 7 below);

     (b)   new recruits and part-timers may be excluded, but at least 80 per cent of the other employees in the employment unit must be covered by the scheme;

     (c)   a scheme must last for at least one year.

7. The two main choices are the *employment unit* and the *formula* linking profits and profit-related pay for which, of course, a definition of profit is required. It must be possible to produce audited profit figures for the employment unit chosen. Subject to that, the employer can choose whatever unit makes sense in the circumstances of the business. Employers also have a choice between two ways of linking profits and profit-related pay:

     (a)   total profit-related pay, or the 'profit-related pay pool', can be a simple proportion of profits

     (b)   the profit-related pay pool can be a sum of money which varies in line with year-on-year changes in profits.

In either case, there will be scope for modifying the effect of large changes in profits in order to avoid big fluctuations in profit-related pay or to safeguard a minimum level of profit.

8. The basis for calculating the size of a scheme's profit-related pay pool will be the level of profits of the employment unit after taxation as defined in the Companies Act 1985. Schemes will, however, be able to provide for a number of adjustments in the production of these profit figures, such as for tax, interest costs and R&D costs. The chosen definition of profit must be used consistently throughout a scheme's life.

9. The profit-related pay distributed to employees must be determined and paid at least once a year on the basis of audited profits. But it can be on an interim basis (ie on account) as frequently as desired, for example, in monthly or weekly pay packets.

10. Tax relief is, in effect, administered by a 'self-assessment' system. The employer is responsible for:

     (a)   ensuring that the scheme complies with the statutory requirements;

     (b)   calculating profit-related pay profits and the amount of profit-related pay due to each employee;

     (c)   giving the tax relief due to each employee as part of the normal operation of PAYE.

11. An independent auditor's report must accompany an employer's application for registration of a scheme (to confirm that it meets statutory requirements) and the employer's return at the end of each profit-related period (to confirm that the scheme and the tax relief have been operated properly).

12. New recruits may be excluded from a scheme for up to three years and employers can decide for themselves how to deal with employees who leave before profit-related pay for a particular year can be calculated and paid. The rules provide flexibility for employers to make special arrangements to deal with reorganizations etc.

13. Part-timers working less than 20 hours a week may be excluded.

14. Profit-related pay can be introduced or increased in amount in place of a conventional increase in pay, and this might be coupled with a conversion of some existing pay to profit-related pay. This type of scheme is becoming popular and is often referred to as a salary sacrifice scheme.

15. Existing profit-sharing schemes can qualify if they meet the criteria and are registered.

It will be seen that the most significant differences between a profit-related pay scheme and a traditional gainsharing or profit sharing scheme are that profit-related schemes:

■ provide for sizeable tax relief;
■ are governed by statutory criteria, although there is a measure of choice within the regulations;
■ can involve a measure of 'salary sacrifice' – this implies that employees in such a scheme have to accept that their pay may go up *or* down as profits rise or fall;
■ can involve regular monthly or weekly payouts on account as part of the normal pay packet.

Tax relief

The tax relief available from profit-related pay is illustrated in Tables 25.1 and 25.2. These tables assume that there is no other income, allowances or tax relief.

Why introduce profit-related pay?

For a higher rate tax payer, the maximum £4000 of profit-related pay saves £1600 of income tax. For the average employee, the maximum 20 per cent of profit-related pay produces tax savings equivalent to a seven per cent pay rise. The Government's logic in introducing these tax breaks was that tying pay to profits would lead to greater employee participation and motivation and act as a brake on wage costs, since when profits dropped so would the profit-related element of pay.

Profit-related pay is intended to be an incentive. However, it should be remembered that a true incentive gives a specific reward for a given level of achievement of an objective on which the incentive can make a direct and sig-nificant impact. In most profit-related pay schemes the employee has little direct impact on profits – usually external and accounting factors have a much greater effect. Profit-related pay is a useful add-on in terms of motivation but it is not a substitute for the real thing, ie some form of direct individual or team incentive scheme. But there is no reason why organizations cannot have both so that rewards are related to both individual or team performance and the overall per-formance of the company.

Many companies are introducing profit-related pay in place of a pay rise, par-ticularly when costs have to be tightly controlled, there is no chance of price

Table 25.1 *Illustrative values of tax relief at 1992–1993 tax rates and allowances related to weekly earnings*

Proportion of pay that is profit-related pay	Value of tax relief (tax at 25%)		
%	£ per year	£ per month	£ per week
5	197.99	16.50	3.81
10	395.98	33.00	7.62
20	791.96	66.00	15.23

Note: (Average earnings estimated at £304.60 a week in 1992)

Table 25.2 *Illustrative values of tax relief at 1992–1993 tax rates and allowances related to annual pay*

Annual pay £	Proportion of pay that is profit-related pay	Value of tax relief	
	%	£ per year	£ per week
5,000 (1)	5	50.00	0.96
	10	100.00	1.92
	20	200.00	3.85
10,000 (2)	5	125.00	2.40
	10	250.00	4.81
	20	500.00	9.62
15,000 (2)	5	187.50	3.61
	10	375.00	7.21
	20	750.00	14.42
20,000 (2)	5	250.00	4.81
	10	500.00	9.62
	20	1000.00	19.23
40,000 (3)	5	800.00	15.38
	10	1600.00	30.77
	20	1600.00	30.77

(1) 20 per cent marginal tax rate (2) 25 per cent marginal tax rate (3) 40 per cent marginal tax rate

increases and there is great pressure to meet their profit targets. If unionized, such companies are in a strong position to argue with shop stewards and officials that they can not afford a pay rise.

For example, an engineering company in the Midlands used a salary sacrifice scheme which enabled the average fitter to see his pay packet rise from £200 to £207 a week, ie by 3.5 per cent. In this scheme, gross pay decreased and such a reduction was referred to as 'banking' £4 a week. However, if profit targets are hit, the fitter will receive the added bonus of £208 of banked pay at the end of the year. The scheme required careful explanation. Employees voted to accept it, although some felt it was too good to be true – 'there must be some trick somewhere'. What finally won the workforce over was when they started to receive their pay cheques with the higher net pay. The subsequent goodwill has enabled negotiations to start on further changes in working practices, job design and individual worker appraisal.

Introducing profit-related pay

There are two ways of introducing profit-related pay. The simplest way is to convert an existing bonus scheme.

The other way is by salary sacrifice. Here part of pay is converted to profit-related pay and this part is then paid monthly or weekly on account with a final payment at year end when profits are shown. Profit-related pay goes up and down with profits, so there is always a risk that employees may be worse off. Such schemes therefore need careful design and communication to employees. This is now the most popular form of profit-related pay, 60–70 per cent of schemes of this type currently being registered.

Rules and pitfalls

The Inland Revenue has produced detailed guidance notes and draft scheme rules to help companies design their own profit-related pay schemes. However, large companies, where circumstances are inevitably more complicated, would be well advised to seek the help of professional advisers who know the potential pitfalls and can advise on how to avoid them.

Some pitfalls are:

- performance measures must be profits and must be calculated to satisfy Schedule 4 accounting rules;
- distribution of the bonus pool has to be on similar terms to all participants;
- the organization must be run with a view to profit and must not be a Government department or local authority or be controlled by one of them;
- HQ and R&D people may need to be considered separately. It is unfair to exclude them simply because they are not in a profit centre. The Finance Act 1989 allows them to participate in a special group scheme as long as certain rules are met;
- there is always the risk in poor years that the scheme will pay out less than expected; it all depends on how good the company is at budgeting;
- if no profits are made than no profit-related pay can be distributed;
- employees can not be guaranteed profit-related pay if profits do not achieve a certain level. If the Inland Revenue believe that such a guarantee has been made, they will revoke the scheme's registration and claim back any tax relief given;
- schemes have to be registered with the Inland Revenue before the start of the scheme year. If the Inland Revenue question the application, then the deadline may be missed. It is best to apply one month before the start of the scheme year.

Perhaps the biggest pitfall is to attempt to treat profit-related pay in isolation from other aspects of human resource and reward management. The organization must be certain of how it wants to share success and how performance should be linked to the individual, team and company elements of pay. If this is not clear at the design stage the communications on the profit-related pay scheme and how it fits into the wider picture will fail.

Design choices

Once the reward philosophy is clear the following design choices have to be made:

- which profit centres to use;
- which employees to include and exclude (the rules allow 20 per cent to be excluded);
- how much to pay;
- how to phase payments through the year;
- the formula for the profit-related pay distribution pool;
- whether or not to link the profit-related pay scheme with the next pay settlement.

Registration and declaration

The Inland Revenue have made the formal process of registration commendably straightforward. It is done by means of a simple form which is countersigned by the company's auditors. At the end of the year the company has to submit another form in which it declares that the scheme has been operated in accordance with the rules, that all the profit-related pay pool was paid out and that the correct amount of tax was deducted. This form is countersigned by the company's auditors who check that the declaration is correct when the main audit is undertaken.

Schemes can be registered for one year or longer. Re-registering each year gives the company the opportunity to reset the target profit-related pay to be distributed in the next year. This helps to reduce the possibility of profit-related pay decreasing and employees suffering decreases in pay.

Communicating profit-related pay

The important task of communicating details of the scheme and its benefits to employees is best carried out by line managers with support from personnel specialists – although the finance function is heavily involved in the scheme's design, it is line mangers who have to live with it. It is therefore essential to ensure that they are briefed carefully in advance.

A salary sacrifice scheme involves a contractual change so it is preferable to get positive approval from employees. Usually 95–99 per cent agree and the rest are easily persuadable. In the case of such schemes, it is advisable to use a team of briefers to inform all employees at approximately the same time. The briefing materials should be of high quality but not lavish.

26

Skill-based Pay

Skill-based pay is a payment method in which pay progression is linked to the number, kind and depth of skills which individuals develop and use. It involves paying for the horizontal acquisition of the skills required to undertake a wider range of tasks, and/or for the vertical development of the skills needed to operate at a higher level, or the development in depth of existing skills.

Skill-based pay systems are people rather than job orientated. Individuals are paid for the skills they are capable of using (as long as those skills are necessary) not for the job they happen to be doing at the time. There may be a basic job rate for individuals with the minimum level of skills, but above that level they will be paid for what they can do themselves and as members of teams. Skill-based pay, however, is not concerned with how well people use their skills. This is the role of performance-related pay, although it is possible to add a performance pay dimension to a skill-based pay system.

Reasons for skill-based pay

There is nothing new about paying for skill. In the engineering industry, for example, there has traditionally been a basic three-tiered structure for manual workers: unskilled, semi-skilled and skilled. And there has often been a hierarchy in the skilled rate category, depending on the type of machines or tools used and the degree of skill required. The main difference between these traditional structures and skill-based pay is that the latter places more emphasis on the horizontal acquisition of a greater range of skills – multi-skilling – and on the ability to use these skills flexibly. It is also linked to planned education and training programmes and the accreditation of the skills acquired through the NVQ (National Vocational Qualification) system or some other method.

This emphasis on range and flexibility has arisen from the rapid developments in technology and the changes in manufacturing methods which have required individuals to exercise a wider range of skills. The rise over the last decade of the 'knowledge worker', on the shop floor as well as in offices and laboratories, has accentuated the need to extend not only the range but also the depth of skills. The specific reasons for the emergence of skill-based pay as an alternative to more traditional payment systems are discussed below.

Raising the skills base

The extension and development of the skills base of an organization is perhaps the most important reason for introducing skill-based pay. There is considerable competitive pressure for skills. Competitive edge is achieved by learning faster than the competition.

Within organizations it is necessary to reduce the time taken to introduce new products or services and to respond to customer requirements. Just-in-time systems impose considerable demands on skill and the ability to respond quickly.

Changes in technology have meant reductions in the volume of routine, predictable work for which employees could be trained quickly when they started work in the organization (if they were trained at all). They could then be left to carry on without any further training until, in many cases, they became redundant because technology moved faster than they could.

Employees have had to become more adaptable. As new technologies and new products are introduced they must be able to respond quickly to demands for new skills.

The emphasis on total quality and customer service has also led to the demand for increased skill and greater capacity to achieve rigorous service delivery standards.

Finally, there is the impact of European and global competition. The UK has undoubtedly lagged behind many European and international competitors in developing skills. It cannot afford to neglect any means of bridging this skills gap. Skill-based pay, which encourages the acquisition of skills and has to be associated with planned and specific training, is a good way of doing this.

The creation of National Vocational Qualifications (NVQs) as a means of defining and assessing skill levels and a basis for training programmes has arisen from this need to extend the skills base and has encouraged the growth of skill-based pay schemes.

The need for flexibility

Fast-changing technologies and competitive pressures require organizations to operate more flexibly. Skill-based pay systems support this process. A multiskilled workforce is a flexible workforce.

Flexibility allows organizations to move people quickly in response to new demands – peak-loads, the removal of a bottleneck in production or the elimination of temporary parts shortages when a just-in-time system is in operation. Absentees can be replaced quickly. Flexibility can reduce downtime and waiting time because operatives carry out their own routine maintenance and basic repairs without having to wait for a maintenance worker.

Cellular manufacturing systems and the emphasis on teamworking in traditional industries like clothing, have also created greater interest in skill-based pay systems.

Increased pressure for efficiency and effectiveness

Increased competition pressurizes companies to improve their efficiency and overall effectiveness, and skill-based pay systems are seen by those companies who have introduced them as a means of helping to achieve these aims. Research conducted by Incomes Data Services[1] in 1992 into the operation of skill-based schemes in six British companies indicated that they were all able to operate with a leaner and more efficient workforce than would have been possible with more traditional job-based systems incorporating strict demarcation lines.

The quest for commitment

Ever since Walton[2] wrote his seminal Harvard Business Review article 'From control to commitment in the workplace' in 1985, organizations have been seeking ways of increasing the commitment of their employees. Skill-based pay systems are seen as means of achieving more commitment because they offer employees the opportunity to enhance their skills and develop their careers within the organization.

Culture change

The belief engendered by Peters and Waterman[3] that corporate excellence can be achieved through culture change has encouraged the introduction of skill-based pay systems as a means of reinforcing culture management initiatives. As Lawler[4] has said, they back up the commitment of organizations to such otherwise glib statements as 'people are our most important assets' by delivering a tangible reward to individuals for doing what the organization says it believes they can do: grow, learn and develop. Organizations with skill-based pay typically have cultures which value human development and are optimistic about the capability and potential of people who work there.

The drive towards self-management

The drive towards the creation of self-managing teams in some organizations has encouraged the introduction of skill-based pay systems. These can empower people to work more effectively with others, to control their own behaviour and to exercise the managerial and quality assurance skills required.

Incidence of skill-based pay

Skill-based pay schemes are well established in the US. A study carried out by Lawler and Ledford[5] found that 40 per cent of the RDM 1000 *Fortune* service and manufacturing companies had skill-based pay somewhere in their organization. This was applied mainly to production workers who were often only a small proportion of those employed.

In the UK, skill-based pay schemes are not so common, but research sponsored by the Institute of Personnel Management and conducted by Cross[6] covering over 400 sites established that 144 of them had installed some form of skill-based pay, mainly for technical and operator jobs, although some schemes are operating in service industries.

How skill-based pay functions

There are many varieties of skill-based pay, but a typical scheme for operatives is likely to have the following features:

- the scheme is based on defined skill blocks or modules – clusters or sets of skills which the organization is willing to reward with extra pay;
- the type and number of skill blocks which individuals need to learn and can learn are defined;
- the successful acquisition of the skills contained in a skills block or module results in an increment to base pay – the Incomes Data Services research established that in their case studies, payments per module ranged from about £200 to £700, the average being about £300. Rates of pay for each skill level are aligned as far as possible to the market rates for those skills and the base rate will be adjusted to take account of general movements in market rates for people with the range of skills covered by the scheme;
- the incremental skills payments will be limited to a defined hierarchy or range of skills;
- the order in which the skills must be acquired in a skills hierarchy may be

defined or more freedom is allowed to build up a range of skills blocks (this freedom may however be restricted by defining the basic skills which have to be acquired first);

■ training modules and programmes are defined for each skill block to provide the necessary 'cross-training';

■ the training and/or the acquisition of the skills within a module is usually accredited by organizations such as the National Council for Vocational Qualifications, the Engineering Training Authority or the City and Guilds Institute. Alternatively or additionally, the training may be certified by the company and/or an education and training institution.

Introducing skill-based pay

Before introducing skill-based pay it is essential to establish that it is right for the organization and that the organization is ready for it. Skill-based pay is most appropriate in organizations where the following conditions apply:

■ the level and range of skills needed is high;

■ flexible working arrangements are required;

■ the technology is appropriate – skill-based pay is likely to work best in continuous process technologies or cellular manufacturing systems, although they have been introduced successfully in customer service operations where employees need a wide range of skills if they are to serve people properly;

■ the organization is capital equipment intensive rather than labour intensive and direct labour therefore accounts for a fairly low proportion of product costs – in this situation, priority has to be given to efficient resource utilization;

■ there is a high-involvement management culture which encourages the participation of all concerned in the design and operation of the system – without such involvement success is much less likely;

■ the trade unions (if any) are likely to be cooperative.

It is also essential at this stage to be quite clear about the objectives of introducing skill-based pay.

Finally, it is necessary to carry out an initial analysis of skills requirements, training resources and the availability of accreditation and certification processes.

If this analysis indicates that the conditions are favourable to the introduction of skill-based pay, the following steps should be taken:

1. Identify jobs to be covered by the scheme.
2. Define job families – group individual jobs into job families where the basic skill requirements are similar.
3. Analyze skills within job families.
4. Define skill levels or blocks by reference to the skills analysis – a skill level is a pay grade related to the ability to use certain skills and a skill block is a training input which has to be successfully completed to warrant extra pay. It is common for skill levels to consist of a number of skill blocks, each of which represents a distinct role which can be developed by training.
5. Devise skill training modules.
6. Design 'cross training' programmes for each module to extend skills.
7. Decide on methods of testing and assessment.
8. Establish base rates for job families.
9. Define range of payments for skill in terms of progressing through skill bands or meeting the requirements of a skill block;

10. Establish procedures for making skill-based payments – these set out the testing and training arrangements and indicate that extra skill payments would be made only if they can be used operationally when required (but it may be stipulated that they do not need to be used all the time).

The importance of developing well thought-out training plans should not be underestimated. The IPM report noted that significant resources have to be devoted to training – typically, organizations with skill-based pay provide 80–120 training hours per year per person. Such training involves open and distance learning as well as traditional techniques.

This is a considerable investment and rewards need to be linked not only to the acquisition of skills but also their application and the resulting performance, otherwise the training investment will not pay off.

Advantages of skill-based pay

Skill-based pay can:

- improve the degree of flexibility of operators, engineering craftsmen and others within a teamworking environment and/or work situations where the priorities are maximum plant utilization and speed of response;
- extend the skills base of the organization especially in the direction of multiskilling – encouraging them progressively to develop their skills at their own rate and in line with the needs of the business;
- encourage and support the progressive breakdown of demarcations between jobs – eg, collaboration between process operators and maintenance craftsmen in carrying out repairs;
- help to eliminate gross inefficiencies created by the multiple manning of jobs as a result of narrowly defined job descriptions;
- provide employees with the encouragement and help to enlarge their skills and develop broader, more challenging roles which open up new career paths and enhance their employability; portfolios rather than continuing employment in the same role.

Problems with skill-based pay

Skill-based pay systems are expensive to introduce and maintain. They require a considerable investment in skills analysis, training and testing. Although a skill-based scheme will only in theory pay for necessary skills, in practice, individuals will not be using them all at the same time and some may be used infrequently, if at all. Inevitably, therefore, payroll costs will increase. If this is added to the cost of training and certification, the total of additional costs may be considerable. The advocates of skill-based pay claim that their schemes are self-financing because of the resulting increases in productivity and operational efficiency. But there is little evidence that this is the case, and there is some indication from the IPM research that companies introducing skill-based pay schemes have underestimated the costs involved and are finding it difficult to quantify the benefits.

To summarize, the disadvantages of skill-based pay are that:

- employees may be encouraged to develop skills which they will not use in their jobs and for which organizations are unwilling to pay;
- payment for skills may therefore be inflationary because productivity does not increase in line with skill payments:

- it can create the need for the delivery of a lot of training without receiving benefits which are commensurate with training costs;
- skill-based pay schemes demand extensive administration, not only of the training but also the accreditation process and the payment system;
- it may be difficult to control the acquisition by employees of redundant and unusable skills;
- there is a tendency for pay to drift to the top rate with employees in jobs where the level and range of skills they have acquired are under-utilized;
- the 'topping out' situation when employees acquire the full range of skills can lead to frustration because there is nowhere else to go and no more prospects of an increase in pay apart from a general increase.

Skill-based pay may in many ways be a good idea, but its potential costs as well as its benefits need to be evaluated rigorously before its introduction.

References

1. Incomes Data Services (1992) *IDS Focus No. 500* February
2. Walton, R (1985) 'From control to commitment in the workplace', *Harvard Business Review* March–April
3. Peters, T and Waterman, R (1982) *In Search of Excellence*, Harper and Row, New York
4. Lawler, E (1990) *Strategic Pay*, Jossey-Bass, San Francisco
5. Lawler, E and Ledford, G (1987) 'Skill-based pay: an idea that's catching on', *Management Review* February
6. Cross, M (1992) *Skill-based Pay: a Guide for Practitioners*, Institute of Personnel Management, London

27

Competence-based Pay

Basing pay on the level of competence required in a job or demonstrated by an individual implies that pay is related to the process aspects of a job – the behaviour required to convert inputs into outputs and outcomes.

As we indicated in Chapter 8 it is possible to represent the performance requirements of a job in terms of an input-process-output-outcomes model.

The level of pay for the job or an individual should be related to all these factors. We are not in favour of any system which concentrates on only one aspect, eg inputs (skill-based pay), process (competence-based pay in its crudest form) or outputs and outcomes (short and longer term results and contribution).

We do believe, however, that it is important to incorporate the concept of competence into pay processes. We have already referred to this in earlier chapters on skill and competence analysis (Chapter 8), job evaluation (Chapters 9 and 10), reward structures (Chapter 12) and performance management (Chapters 14 and 15). Our aim in this chapter is to present an integrated view of competency pay summarized under the headings of competence-based pay structures and competence-based performance management.

Competence-based pay structures

Theoretically, it is possible to develop a competence-based pay structure for any job family. A job family ladder can be produced as described in Chapter 9 in which each level or grade is defined in terms of the competences required. The competences are then used as sizing factors.

In practice, the approach works best when used for relatively narrowly defined populations (eg scientists, engineers, designers and visualizers, copy writers, computer analysts/programmers) where it is possible to define competences clearly and to differentiate the levels at which they are applied. For larger, more diverse populations in large organizations, a number of different frameworks may be needed, related to each other by a common sizing system which uses factors such as those used in the Hay method: knowhow, problem solving and accountability.

However, as Fitt[1] points out, the problem is that even in fairly narrowly defined populations, the types of capability described can usually be expressed equally well in terms of 'required to' (role) or 'capable of' (person). But these are not true competences in the sense of deep-seated qualities. On the basis of the consultancy experience of Hay Management Consultants, he comments that:

'It is difficult either to generalise about levels of competence (except in special cases such as research scientists), or to find the behavioural indicators, critical for the successful operation of any competency assessment process, which apply universally'.

In making this point he distinguishes between the two meanings of competence, (*1*) referring to the skills and knowledge which can be acquired through study, training and experience, and (*2*) referring to the deeper-seated traits and personal qualities developed by individuals, which are harder to develop and change. He suggests that in the latter case, competences are fundamentally indicators of performance or potential that are dependent variables. But, he asserts, they can not be used as skill factors for sizing and pay structure design purposes.

A competence-based structure may therefore have to be developed more superficially. In effect, it could simply turn job evaluation factors which define job requirements into competence factors which define the capabilities needed to meet job requirements. Thus the job evaluation factor for integration might refer to the *requirement* to integrate directly technologies, skills or knowledge (and define the factor levels accordingly), while the competence factor might refer to the *ability* to integrate directly technologies, skills or knowledge.

There are three main types of competence-based pay structures – narrow-banded, broad-banded and competence and performance pay curves. All of these are associated with job families.

Narrow-banded structure

A narrow-banded structure is, in effect, a conventional graded structure, as described in Chapter 12. A ladder of competence levels is developed and each grade is defined accordingly. Alternatively, a skill matrix job evaluation scheme is used as described by Fitt, and an example of a skill matrix factor is given in Table 27.1.

Table 27.1   *Example of skill matrix factor and definitions*

Engineering job family

Factors	Factor definition
Knowledge Application of knowledge Integration Autonomy People management Management of relationships Creativity Project management	*Integration* 'Your ability to integrate directly technologies, skills or knowledge'

Factor levels
1. Capable of working within own speciality
2. Capable of co-ordinating some elements within a speciality
3. Capable of integrating all elements within a speciality
4. Capable of integrating a group of specialities within a discipline, or a number of relevant disciplines on a project, component, process or system
5. Capable of the integration of all specialities within a discipline, or the integration of all relevant disciplines on a major project, component, process or system

Broad-banded structure

A broad-banded structure, as described in Chapter 12, may incorporate only three or four grades each of which can have a pay range extending to as much as 300 per cent above the minimum. This leaves much more scope for rewarding people according to their competence and contribution.

An example quoted by Fitt is the pay structure recently introduced by a major UK general insurance company. A core job evaluation process allocates jobs to broad grades. Within these grades, line managers have discretion to progress individuals on the basis of demonstrated competences and performance. Competence frameworks are well defined and assessments are made regularly. Managers make all decisions subject only to overall budget constraints. 'Role size' is still the core variable in differentiating levels, but its impact relative to the variations of performance and competence is considerably reduced.

Competence and performance pay curves

Competence and performance pay curves, as described in Chapter 12, provide different pay progression tracks along which people in a family of jobs can move according to their levels of competence and performance. A job family pay curve contains a number of competence bands each of which constitutes a definable level of skill, competence and responsibility. Individuals move through these bands at a rate which is related to their performance and their capacity to develop.

The assumptions governing competence/performance pay curves are that first, competence develops progressively through various levels or bands rather than between a number of fixed points and second, that individuals will develop at different rates and will therefore deliver different levels of performance which should be rewarded accordingly.

The concept of pay curves recognizes that roles may expand to the level of ability or competence of the job holder rather than being constrained within narrowly defined jobs in traditional hierarchies. This particularly applies to scientific, engineering, professional and other types of knowledge workers.

Competence-based performance management

The original approach to performance management was to base it entirely on the agreement of objectives and the review of achievement against them, ie on outputs. Modern thinking and practice in this area now recognizes that for most jobs, simply using achievement against target is an incomplete view. In many jobs it may be difficult to identify sensible targets, yet there are clearly different levels of performance between individuals.

The best current approaches to performance management add a competence (ie input/process) dimension to assessment. This may make use of generic competences for a job family and/or involve an initial agreement between the manager and the individual on the level of competency that should be achieved in each of the key aspects of the latter's job. The aim of this agreement would be to ensure that individuals understand the sort of behaviours expected of them and appreciate that if they fulfill these expectations they will be regarded as having performed well and will be rewarded accordingly. This is followed by a review of performance which, by referring to specific examples of behaviour, assesses performance in respect of each competence area.

Reference

1. Fitt, D (1992) 'Paying for competency – what does it mean?' In A Mitrani, M Dalziel and D Fitt (Eds), *Competency Based Human Resource Management*, Kogan Page, London

28

Other Cash Payments

To ensure a balanced set of remuneration policies, organizations often have to use one or more of a number of different additional payments to meet market needs. These can be divided into two categories:

1. Payments in response to market pressure.
2. Payments to reward special circumstances or working practices.

In times when there is a formal incomes policy, or to get special, subtle market advantage, payments in the latter category can be, and certainly have been, used as responses to the market.

Market pressure responses

These are essentially lump sum payments or continuing allowances used to obtain competitive advantage in a tight labour market. They are used on recruitment and as 'top-ups', often called 'market premia', to basic salary – paid only to employees in scarce categories, whose basic salary will otherwise be contained within the organization's normal salary structure. They are now in widespread use in the UK both in the private and the public sector, but most of the thinking behind them has come from the United States.

The following are the most common forms of payment in this category:

1. *Golden hellos:* also called recruitment bonuses, 'up-front' or 'front-end' bonuses. These are payments to entice sought after individuals to join a particular employer. They can be paid as a lump sum on joining or as a phased bonus, sometimes over as much as a couple of years. Such payments have been used for graduates with rare specialisms: computer specialists, researchers, financial specialists and top executives likely to make an exceptional contribution to the business.

   There are no set formulae for determining these payments – they can run from quite large amounts, say, a year's salary, down to a few hundred pounds. At senior executive level, the offer of shares, usually using a 1984 Finance Act share option scheme to obtain maximum tax benefits, is also common.

   Market premium payments can also be given as benefits: perhaps a larger or more exotic company car than is normal for the grade, a second car, special pension arrangements, housing assistance, additional relocation assistance etc. In conceding to demands for additional benefits, organizations need to think hard about the effects this may have on others who have the same rare specialisms, but have been in the job well before market pressure built up. Some adjustment to their reward package may have to be considered, therefore, to keep the team together. In addition, the tax implications of golden hellos should always be explored.

2. *Golden handcuffs:* these are payments given to staff to lock them in to the organization and prevent them being 'attracted away' by the competition. Again, they are being used in both the public and the private sector in the UK. They are used both as 'retention payments' for staff subject to severe market pressure and, more rarely, for keeping staff in departments that have been cut back by redundancy – to ensure that a core of the best people stays. 'Golden handcuffs' can take the form of phased lump sum payments, sometimes in the form of guaranteed bonuses, which may then be phased out if the market eases or circumstances change. They also commonly take the form of shares – especially at executive level – on the basis that equity participation breeds additional commitment to the business. Again, the tax implications of these provisions should be fully explored.

3. *London and large town allowances:* these are paid because of housing and other cost-of-living differentials. Most London employers either have a separate London allowance which is reviewed annually and paid as an addition to basic salary or, alternatively, they expect to pay extra on basic salary in response to local market pressure. Both Incomes Data Services and Industrial Relations Services report regularly on changing company practice in this area. Reward Regional Surveys report in detail – through local cost-of-living surveys – on the effects of changes in living costs including house prices.

Rewards for special circumstances or working practices

Golden handshakes

Golden handshakes are also discussed in the context of redundancy (see Chapter 30), and are essentially termination payments – usually substantial ones – paid typically to top executives to ensure that they leave with a financial cushion and without making any fuss. In size they tend to bear some notional relation to the unexpired period of the executive's contract where there is one. But for tax reasons this has traditionally not been stated in the contract. Where there is no fixed term contract, or where the company feels that, in addition to its statutory redundancy obligations it only needs to tide the individual over until a new job is found (enshrined in the legal concept of obligation to mitigate loss) – then a year's salary tends to be the maximum. But again there are no set rules. Lawyers are quite often involved in top executive 'separations' and the good ones are familiar with current practice as it is likely to apply to the case in question. Such payments are generally, for tax purposes, defined as compensation for loss of office. Payments to directors show up eventually in the accounts of public companies – something in which the press usually takes great interest. This should be borne in mind at the time the details of a separation are negotiated – a case for making any large payment should be prepared and it should be one that holds water for shareholders as well as curious journalists. Part of the separation 'handshake' package may also involve outplacement counselling to enable executives to decide what to do next with professional assistance and support.

Overtime payments

Overtime payments are made wherever the standard working week is exceeded on a regular basis for employees at supervisory level and below. In some union negotiated environments and in other special circumstances it may be extended to the lower levels of management. But it is usually implicit if not explicit in most management contracts that managers will work whatever hours can be reasonably required to ensure the fulfilment of their responsibilities. Sometimes exceptional management overtime (eg in business start-ups or during special projects) is rewarded by one-off bonuses.

For staff working overtime and being paid for it, the levels of payment vary in relation to whether the work is done on weekdays, at the weekends or on National Holidays. Payments currently vary from time to time-and-a-half (sometimes after a minimum threshold of overtime working, say, eight hours a month) on weekdays to time-and-a-half on Saturdays and higher multiples for Sundays and National Holidays. People who maintain essential services on Christmas Day expect very high rewards – as high as four times the normal rate – as compensation for being away from their families and sometimes in addition to time off in lieu.

The payment of overtime pay is generally held to be reasonable as long as the nature and amount of overtime working is strictly controlled. People do not work well and consistently if excessive overtime is worked and they should never be allowed to take on too much to supplement what may be, or perceived to be, an inadequate basic salary.

Shift pay and unsocial hours payments

These are given where the pattern of working hours differs from the typical working day. They are typically given to computer staff, production employees, various medical staff, broadcasting employees and others where 24-hour cover for services is essential. Payments relate to the shift patterns worked, to associated time-off arrangements and to market practice in the sector in question. As with overtime, care should be taken to ensure that working practices are sensible and not geared to propping up otherwise uncompetitive pay rates. Buying out practices that have got out of hand is both difficult and expensive.

Attendance bonuses

Attendance bonuses are generally paid to categories of staff where absenteeism is a problem and the organization wishes to encourage more consistent attendance. They can be useful where the work itself or the environment is unpleasant and it is not within the employer's power to improve this. Many employers reject the idea because they consider it is a payment for what is already a contractual obligation which merely gives employees the opportunity to earn a bit more 'by getting out of bed earlier'. Such employers have not always been so scathing however, in the face of severe market pressure during times of national incomes policy; or indeed in the face of a very tight local market where they need to resort to payments of this kind to get the edge.

Clothing allowances

Clothing allowances are paid to staff who need to buy special clothing for work where the company does not provide uniforms. Such payments are market-related and should be reviewed for tax implications. Dry cleaning vouchers are sometimes also provided as part of the policy.

Christmas bonuses and thirteenth-month payments

These are normally paid as a matter of tradition in some sectors. Christmas bonuses tend to be relatively small unless they contain a performance element. The essential purpose is generally to reward loyalty and recognize this by helping with the extra costs of the season. Thirteenth- or even fourteenth-month payments have come to the UK from Europe. They are found among organizations with European parents where home country policy has been translated into local practice. Such payments tend to be given as 'double month' salaries paid either at Christmas or in the summer or sometimes divided between the two. A UK variation is the payment of an annual salary on a four-weekly basis, giving thirteen equal payments in the year.

Payments for qualifications

These are used by companies to reward success such as passing accounting, actuarial, legal, managerial or other professional and technical examinations to recognize their added value to the organization. Such payments are generally given as lump sum payments, but can be given as pay increases – sometimes as part of a reward system linked to competency development. Where these payments are made to people who have recently left full-time education, they can fill a useful motivational 'gap'. The wait between annual reviews can seem a long time to someone in their teens (which is one of the reasons why increases for junior staff are often paid on a six-monthly basis).

PART 7

EMPLOYEE BENEFITS AND TOTAL REMUNERATION

29

Employee Benefits

Definition

Employee benefits are elements of remuneration given in addition to the various forms of cash pay. They provide a quantifiable value for individual employees, which may be deferred or contingent like a pension scheme, insurance cover or sick pay, or may provide an immediate benefit like a company car. Employee benefits also include elements which are not strictly remuneration, such as annual holidays.

The terms 'fringe benefits' and 'perks' (perquisites) are sometimes used derogatively, but should be reserved for those employee benefits which are not fundamentally catering for personal security and personal needs.

Objectives

The objectives of the employee benefits policies and practices of an organization should be:

■ to increase the commitment of employees to the organization
■ to provide for the actual or perceived personal needs of employees, including those concerning security, financial assistance and the provision of assets in addition to pay, such as company cars and petrol
■ to demonstrate that the company cares for the needs of its employees
■ to ensure that an attractive and competitive total remuneration package is provided which both attracts and retains high-quality staff
■ to provide a tax-efficient method of remuneration which reduces tax liabilities compared with those related to equivalent cash payments.

Note that these objectives do not include 'to motivate employees'. This is because benefits seldom have a direct and immediate effect on performance unless they are awarded as an incentive; for example, presenting a sales representative with a superior car (eg a BMW) for a year if he or she meets a particularly demanding target. Benefits can, however, create more favourable attitudes toward the company leading to increased long-term commitment and better performance.

Benefits policies

Policies on employee benefits need to be formulated in the following areas:

- *range of benefits provided:* some benefits, such as pensions and holidays, are expected, others, such as permanent health insurance, are optional extras
- *scale of benefits provided:* the size of each benefit, taking into account its cost to the company and its perceived value to employees. Note that the perceived value of some benefits such as company cars, or pension schemes (particularly in the case of older employees), can be very different from their actual cash value
- *proportion of benefits to total remuneration:* in cash terms, a benefit such as a pension scheme can cost the company between approximately 5 and 15 per cent of an employee's salary. A decision has to be made on the proportion of total remuneration to be allocated to other benefits which incur expenditure of cash by the company. This policy decision is, of course, related to decisions on the range and scale of benefits provided, and it can be affected by decisions on allowing choice of benefits and on the distribution of benefits. Many companies are trying to move towards a 'clean cash' policy which minimizes the number and scale of fringe benefits. It is a policy supported by the UK Government, through its stated objective of tax neutral treatment of benefits, but not one that has yet found much favour in terms of competitive practice although there is increasing interest in this approach
- *allowing choice:* benefits will be most effective in the process of attracting and retaining employees if they satisfy individual needs. But individual needs vary so much that no benefits package or single item within the package will satisfy all employees equally. Younger employees may be more interested in housing assistance than a company pension plan. Some employees have ethical or political objections to medical insurance schemes. Not everyone wants a company car – especially if they live in an Inner City area and have a spouse with a better car entitlement. Many people may prefer cash to an automatic benefit which is not precisely what they want. Methods of providing employees with choice are discussed in Chapter 32.
- *allocation of benefits:* policy on the allocation of benefits determines the extent to which it is decided that a single status organization should be created. If the policy is to have a hierarchy of benefits, then the allocation of these at different levels has to be determined, usually in terms of broad bands of entitlements – typically called benefit grades
- *harmonization:* in the new flatter organizations, where multi-skilling is prevalent and new technology is eliminating the old distinction between white- and blue-collared workers, harmonization of benefit packages is increasingly taking place. The objective is to increase unity of purpose and improve team-work by abolishing invidious distinctions between benefits, rewarding different levels of responsibility and contribution by pay alone. Single status companies are becoming much more common. Full harmonization means that there are no distinctions at any level in the hierarchy between the benefits provided, which may vary only with length of service.

  Partial harmonization may provide the same basic benefits in some areas such as pensions, holidays, sick pay and redundancy for white- and blue-collared staff, but have a hierarchy of benefits above this base according to job grades. These benefits could include company cars, topped-up pension schemes or medical treatment insurance
- *market considerations:* whatever degree of choice or harmonization is decided

upon, the precise arrangements will always be affected by market considerations. It may only be possible to attract and retain some key staff by, for example, offering a company car in line with what other organizations are doing for similar jobs. To attract a senior executive, it may be necessary to offer him or her a special pension arrangement – especially if they are earning over the Finance Act 1989 'earnings cap' (£75,000 for the 1993/94 tax year). As in all aspects of pay, market considerations and the need to offer competitive packages may have to override the principle of equity

■ *government policy:* the main current impact made by government policy is in the field of personal taxation, but changes are afoot. It is essential, when reviewing benefit policies, to monitor tax legislation in order to assess the relative tax efficiency of benefits and to keep employees informed of the implications for them. As we move into the projected skills shortage of the mid to late 1990s we can expect the development of policies enabling the more effective recruitment and retention of women returners, older workers and the like who will be needed in the UK labour force

■ *trade unions:* trade unions are increasingly concerned with the whole remuneration package and therefore may be involved or ask to be involved in negotiating the provision and level of benefits. Many companies, however, resist negotiating such items as pensions although they will be prepared to consult unions or staff associations on benefit arrangements and do sometimes have trade unionists as trustees of the pension scheme.

Benefits practice

All employers provide benefits in some form or another to employees, but practice varies according to:

■ *employee status:* typically, the more senior the employee, the more benefits provided. But this is not always the picture. A growing number of organizations, especially in high technology and other sectors requiring rapid growth and employee flexibility, have opted for harmonized benefits and conditions for core benefits

■ *local 'national' sector practice:* there are marked differences in benefits entitlements between the finance sector and the rest of the private sector, between organizations where manpower costs form a small part of corporate expenditure and those which are labour intensive, and between profitable and progressive organizations and those which have to keep a tight control on manpower costs to survive. Differences by job function may also exist

■ *private or public sector status:* differences were much greater in the early 1980s than by the mid 1990s. Apart from generous, index-linked pension schemes and longer holidays, the public sector enjoyed comparatively few fringe benefits and they certainly did not have company cars – market competition for scarce skills has changed that for many public servants, notably in local authorities, non-departmental public bodies and the new agencies being hived off from the core of the Civil Service

■ *employers' views on the advisability of providing benefits:* the extent to which they wish to use benefits to attract and retain staff – some organizations take a much more generous line than others or simply prefer to pay more in 'clean cash' than in benefits.

So the emphasis now in the UK is on cash payments rather than benefits. Most employers have therefore concentrated on providing a competitive set of 'core' benefits to supplement cash remuneration. The wilder extremes of tax-efficient 'beyond the fringe' benefits only exist in areas where extremely high pay is given in response to severe market pressure and for directors/owners of private companies where shareholder pressure is not an issue.

A balanced approach

Benefit entitlements are an area which employees watch closely and where perceived injustice can rapidly cause problems. They are also a major component of employee costs, particularly at management level where keeping up with 'best practice' can add 40 per cent or more to basic salary costs for a fairly average group of executives. The costs can rise sharply above that level where special pension provisions have to be made for older directors, eg those who are earning over the pensions 'cap', and who have been newly recruited with little by way of preserved pension entitlements and expectations of retiring on two-thirds salary in line with Inland Revenue limits. Luxury cars are also a major cost item and other benefit costs can sometimes rise rapidly and unpredictably such as medical insurance in the US.

In this chapter we look first at all the major benefits currently provided by UK employers to give an overview of the options available. We then discuss:

- intangible benefits as an important part of the total benefits package
- the development of employee benefit strategies
- how to recognize the need to review benefits
- the steps to take when modifying the benefits package
- the important subject of communications.

Principal types of benefits

Benefits can be divided into the following categories:

1. *Pension schemes:* these are generally regarded as the most important employee benefit. In the UK they are typically financed during the employee's working lifetime to provide a guaranteed income for employees or their dependants on retirement or death. Pension schemes are so important that they are dealt with separately in Chapter 30.
2. *Personal security:* these are benefits which enhance the individual's personal and family security with regard to illness, health, accident, redundancy or life assurance.
3. *Financial assistance:* loans, house purchase assistance, relocation assistance, discounts, etc.
4. *Personal needs:* entitlements which recognize the interface between work and domestic needs or responsibilities, eg holidays and other forms of leave, child care, career breaks, retirement, counselling, financial counselling, personal counselling in time of crisis, fitness and recreational facilities.
5. *Company cars and petrol.*
6. *Other benefits* which improve the standard of living of employees such as subsidized meals, clothing allowances, refund of telephone costs and credit card facilities.
7. *Intangible benefits:* characteristics of the organization which make it an attractive and worthwhile place in which to work.

Personal security

Death-in-service benefits

Provided either as part of the pension scheme or as a separate life assurance cover, this benefit provides for a multiple of salary to be paid to an employee's dependants should he or she die before retirement. The range of multiples of salary payable, generally ranges from one to four times (currently the limit set by the Inland Revenue). Entitlements may be dependent on employee status or they may be the same for all employees in organizations with harmonized or single status benefit provisions. This is not a particularly expensive benefit to provide and is usually appreciated by employees because it saves on the personal life insurance cover needed to provide for their liabilities if they die prematurely and benefits can generally be paid free of income or inheritance tax. Death-in-service benefits are also discussed on pages 392–3.

Personal accident cover

This insurance cover provides for compensation should an employee be involved in an accident causing serious injury or death. It is a very common benefit, particularly where there is a great deal of travel involved or where the work can be hazardous for environmental and sometimes political reasons.

Permanent health insurance

Also called long-term disability cover, this form of insurance provides for continued income once the provisions of the company sick pay scheme are exhausted. It is therefore used to provide security of income for those struck down with chronic or terminal illnesses, normally payable after the first six months of sick leave and continuing until death or retirement, when the employee's pension becomes payable. Cover can be provided either through a separate insurance or through the ill-health early retirement provisions in the pension scheme. The income provided under permanent health insurance schemes typically ranges from between one-half to two-thirds of salary at the time illness occurred, usually with some provision for escalating payments in relation to rises in the cost of living and a deduction to allow for State benefits. This benefit is not particularly expensive to provide as a percentage of payroll for a group of employees. It is certainly much cheaper than any cover available to individuals. The cost will vary in relation to the age profile of employees and any special health risks involved in employment. It is a much appreciated benefit – the dependants of an employee with terminal cancer or multiple sclerosis can be saved from financial hardship by the scheme's payments. This is a common benefit for employees at all levels among major employers. Employees are only taxed on benefits which are paid and not on the insurance premiums paid by the employer.

Business travel insurance

Arguably a benefit, business travel insurance is normally provided as a matter of course for all employees who have to travel extensively on company business. The insurance cover may be more generous than that obtainable by individuals and it will be offered at advantageous rates.

Given the generosity of some provisions it is not surprising that benefits experts occasionally amuse themselves by working out how much an employee would be worth dead if he or she died in service (4 times salary), in a plane crash (personal accident cover pays out in full), while travelling abroad on company business (business travel insurance pays out too), with an entitlement to dependants' pensions (typically due for the spouse and children under the age of 18).

Medical insurance

There are two basic forms of medical insurance available in the UK:

1. Schemes which cover the costs of private hospital treatment at rates which vary with the location and status of hospital selected by the employer (BUPA, PPP, WPA etc).
2. Schemes which pay out cash to those being treated under the National Health Service, eg Hospital Savings Association (HSA).

The former type of scheme may also pay out if the employee chooses to be treated under the National Health Service. Cover for private medical insurance may be taken out by employers either:

■   on a group discount basis, so that employees can obtain cover more cheaply for themselves and their families than they could as individuals; or
■   at no cost to employees. In this case free cover may only be extended to employees with the possibility of covering families under group discount arrangements – or it may cover spouses and often dependant children too; or
■   somewhere in between the above.

Apart from the obvious comforts of private health care, the real benefit to employers of medical insurance is the freedom it provides for employees to be treated at times that suit their work commitments. For as long as the National Health Service has to run long waiting lists for non-emergency surgery, then medical insurance is a desirable benefit. It can prevent months of performance below par. Private medical treatment also has connotations of status which can increase premium costs. If employees go for minor surgery in unforeseen numbers, partly at least to say they have received private treatment, such costs can escalate rapidly. Some organizations have had to resort to requiring employees to pay, for instance, the first £50 of any treatment costs to keep their schemes within reasonable limits. Medical insurance is an increasingly competitive market. Apart from the three main organizations providing private medical cover mentioned earlier, there is a growing number of other insurers competing for business. It is always worth negotiating with insurance companies and provident associations to see if they can come up with a more appealing quote – or getting brokers or advisers to do this for you.

Health screening

Looking after employee health by providing screening can mean anything from providing for mass X-Rays to screen for chest ailments, to cervical smears for female employees to the full panoply of total health checks. Full screening is often provided for executives, especially for those over 40 or subject to particular stresses and hazards. At its most sophisticated, screening will look not just at an employee's current state of health but analyze their lifestyle and diet to provide advice on the prevention of future problems and the management of stress. Such screening may be far more appreciated than more expensive benefits, particularly if it picks up a health problem early and facilitates immediate treatment before the condition has got out of hand.

Extra-statutory sick pay

Although all employees are covered by statutory sick pay provisions, most major employers supplement these provisions by continuing sick pay for longer than the statutory period. Typically they provide for a given period at full pay and then a further period at half pay until the scheme's provisions are exhausted, sometimes after six months or more. Sick pay entitlements are generally service related. Entitlements may vary with status or be harmonized depending on the employment philosophy prevailing in particular sectors. Generous sick pay provisions are usually much appreciated, but absenteeism often needs to be strictly monitored and controlled to prevent abuse of the system.

Extra-statutory redundancy pay

Although the statutory redundancy payments available in the UK provide some cushion for longer-serving employees losing their jobs, they are not very helpful to shorter service and indeed higher paid employees made redundant through no fault of their own. Trade union agreements therefore frequently cover both redundancy policy and extra-statutory redundancy entitlements to provide additional job security or at least compensation for those covered by them. Many organizations too, faced with a redundancy arising from restructuring or a change of business direction, are more generous with redundancy provisions. This normally takes one or more of the following forms:

- extra notice compensation
- additional service-related payments – these vary considerably, two weeks per year of service being fairly common and one month per year of service not being uncommon and many ignore the statutory weekly pay limit
- *ex-gratia* payments given as compensation for loss of office (golden handshakes).

Policy on redundancy is obviously influenced by what the organization can afford, but account should be taken of the fact that the relative generosity of treatment may well affect the morale of those whose jobs are safe. Redundancy exercises are very unsettling for everyone concerned. They need very careful planning and handling to ensure that the minimum disruption and hardship are caused.

Information on the severance package

When employees are told that they are to be made redundant, they should also be given precise details of the severance package. Preparing this is a major task for company pay specialists – one which often has to be performed in secret and at great speed. The information to be given to newly redundant employees typically comprises the following:

- actual date of redundancy
- notice payments and additional notice payments due
- statutory and extra-statutory service-related redundancy payments
- any *ex-gratia* payments included in the package
- accrued pension rights and any augmented rights given on redundancy (eg early retirement provisions where it is technically possible to turn redundancy into compulsory or voluntary early retirement)
- the position on other benefits eg continued medical insurance or retention of the company car for a limited period to provide protection and continued mobility while a new job is found

- when and how payments of all kinds are to be made
- provisions to deal with special cases of hardship
- sources of information and advice both within the organization and outside.

The humanity and consideration for individuals shown when the package is explained can do much to ease their shock and sense of loss on being made redundant. This is always a situation that needs to be dealt with on a one-to-one basis and for which training in counselling skills is helpful.

It is probably worth emphasizing – even in a chapter such as this – that redundancies should never be announced on Fridays – an early or mid-week breaking of the news provides time for advice to be given and for personal adjustment to the trauma before employees have to face the weekend, and often their social life, without any form of support.

Outplacement advice (career counselling)

One of the benefits which an increasing number of employers are offering to redundant employees is professional help in sorting out what it is they really want to do next and in learning how to apply effectively for the jobs they want. This service can be called outplacement, career counselling or one of a variety of other names dreamed up by the consultants who provide it. It can be given on a one-to-one basis for managerial staff leaving in mid/late career or as a series of lectures and advisory sessions for more junior employees. Good outplacement consultants or career counsellors have a high success rate in helping people replan their lives, build on their strengths and present themselves effectively to potential employers. The provision of career counselling does of course have wider spin-off benefits and a positive effect on the morale of those still in post in the organization who see their ex-colleague learning to survive the trauma of redundancy.

As with any consultancy work, it is always wise to see several outplacement consultants or career counsellors, review their track record and see who provides the most appropriate service for the employees in question.

Financial assistance

Company loans

Loan schemes either provide for modest sums to be lent interest-free or for more substantial sums to be loaned at favourable interest rates. Small sums tend only to be loaned on a compassionate basis where there is personal hardship. Larger loans tend to be for defined purposes such as home improvements or car purchase, but may come without any strings attached at all. Repayments are normally made by regular deductions from salary on a basis specified or agreed between employer and employee. The benefit is more common in the finance sector. The taxable threshold for loan benefits should be monitored (see Chapter 31).

Season ticket loans

The high cost of commuting into London and other major conurbations has led many employers to offer interest-free loans for annual season tickets. Such loans normally fall below the taxable threshold for loan benefits (see Chapter 31) and are repaid in instalments over the year.

Mortgage assistance

Subsidized mortgages are a very substantial benefit, especially for those who have to buy property in high-cost housing areas. The benefit is mainly confined to the finance sector and is usually provided by subsidizing interest payments (down to roughly 4 per cent in 1993) on mortgages up to a given price threshold – often a multiple of salary. Where given, this benefit tends to be provided for all employees subject to set age, grade and service requirements. Service requirements may, however, have to be dispensed with if they cause recruitment difficulties for staff categories already likely to have subsidized mortgages with other employers. The amounts available for subsidy normally rise either with seniority or salary level.

Housing assistance can also be given in the form of bridging loans and guaranteed selling price (usually based on averaging of current valuations), especially for employees who move at company request and who cannot sell one house before they have to move into the house they buy near their new place of work.

Relocation packages

Companies recruiting managers and specialists from other parts of the country, or requiring employees to move, normally expect to pay the costs of removal. They also expect to compensate to some extent for the personal upheaval involved as well as paying for legal and agents fees and the costs of moving their possessions, buying new carpets and curtains and even school uniforms. Following the March 1993 Budget, the Inland Revenue limits tax free relocation assistance to £8000. Companies can use this to the full or exceed it on a taxable basis if they believe this is necessary to induce an employee to make a move essential to business needs to an area not of their choice. Packages can either be drawn up individually or be controlled by set guidelines. Several specialist consultants offer assistance with the property side of relocation.

Company discounts

Where a company has products or services which can be offered to employees at a favourable discount, this is normally much appreciated. Such schemes can run from free sweets or a fixed weekly allowance to employees in sweet factories, to low-cost second and third cars for people working in car manufacturing. Some organizations, unable to give discounts on their own products, negotiate discounts for their employees from suppliers. British trade unions are also active in the area of negotiating discounts as a means of attracting and retaining membership.

Fees to professional bodies

Fees for recognized professional bodies such as the Institute of Chartered Accountants or the Institute of Personnel Management may be refunded.

Personal needs

Holidays

Annual leave entitlements are a major benefit. Very few UK companies give less than four weeks to employees at any level and basic holiday entitlements are often five weeks. The maximum seems to have stopped at six weeks for most people. This is granted either to senior executives (who in practice may rarely have time to take full benefit of the provision) or on a service-related basis to more junior staff. Long entitlements may also be given in recognition of working unsociable hours or agreeing to flexible working practices. Some organizations specify minimum as well as maximum holidays, requiring employees to take one break of two weeks from their entitlement to ensure that they get away from work for at least one reasonably lengthy period a year. Many employers also need to specify when holidays can be taken, either to ensure that everybody is not off work at the same time when continuous working has to be maintained, or to ensure that everybody is off during the annual shutdown.

Compassionate leave

Granted when close relatives are ill, or die, or to deal with other unforeseen events, compassionate leave is normally the subject of formal policy in larger employers. It is usually paid leave for a limited period and unpaid for longer periods. This provision gives the opportunity for the organization to show concern for the individual and recognition of the importance of family responsibilities at times of personal hardship. Sensitivity in dealing with requests for compassionate leave, or offering it when it is clearly necessary, can do much for employee morale – not just for the employee concerned, but for the immediate work group who see that a colleague has been well treated at a time of personal crisis.

Maternity leave and maternity pay

A growing number of women choose to or have to return to work after their babies are born. This reflects changing demographic patterns: the requirement for both partners to work to make ends meet where housing costs are high, the growing number of single-parent families, and the fact that professional women are starting families later with no intention of breaking their career. The nuclear family with a wife at home is a reality for only a small proportion of the population and, for better or worse, a diminishing one.

UK employment law provides for six months' maternity leave after the birth of a child with a right to return to work at the end of this period. Some companies however, often as a result of union negotiations, provide for longer maternity leave with a right to return to the old job. They may also provide additional maternity pay on top of statutory provision. Where employers find that they employ large numbers of women and are dependent on their skills, generous maternity provisions can help with long-term recruitment and retention. It can also be a very useful and cost-effective policy in areas of professional skill shortage, enabling employers to attract qualified women, provided this is achieved without infringing the sex discrimination legislation.

The management of maternity leave and pay requires care. It is not helped currently because women have to make firm statements about their intention to return to work after childbirth, whether or not they know what they want to do and in order to protect themselves in the event of stillbirth. Many of the potential difficulties can be avoided by ensuring that employees have a clear idea of the legislation and that their employer respects this and will make sensible and reasonable provisions for them. Poor treatment of a woman taking maternity leave will affect morale for all her immediate colleagues.

Paternity leave

Outside those who make provisions as the result of union negotiations, few UK employers yet make formal provisions for paternity leave. Where they do, it is for a few days either while the partner is in hospital or when she returns home.

Otherwise, compassionate leave may be granted or the employee is expected to use part of his annual leave entitlement. Some other European countries tend to be more generous, recognizing perhaps that most families stop at two children and the amount of leave involved for most men in a lifetime is less than some need to take as sick leave in a year. In deciding policy in this area, employers need to take account not just of the cost, but of the benefit obtained from recognizing and encouraging involvement in family responsibilities.

Career breaks

A growing number of UK employers are providing for employees (both men *and* women) to take up to five years off to rear children. People taking breaks are usually brought in regularly to keep up to date with developments both in their skills area and the organization in general and are entitled to return full or part-time to work with no loss of job status.

Sabbaticals

Although sabbaticals are a comparatively rare benefit in the UK, they can be a useful retention factor for professionals able to use the time to travel and update their knowledge. They may also be granted to long-serving employees either as straight leave or as time to get involved in something of value to the community. There is no set pattern to the length of leave given – it varies from a few weeks up to a year.

Other leave

Policies also need to be developed by most organizations to cover leave for territorial army training, jury service, civic duties and other special requirements.

Child care

In order to attract or retain employees with young dependant children, employers can offer financial or practical child care provisions. For example, companies such as the Midland Bank are providing workplace nurseries or crèches. Although expensive to provide, such arrangements work well where travel with a child to the workplace is relatively easy. They can pose problems where parents reject the idea of commuting with a toddler in the rush hour. Cash payments or child care vouchers are also now being offered by a growing number of organizations to offset employee costs for childminders, nannies, or after-school baby-sitters.

Practical or financial help in finding, recruiting or retaining child care providers may be welcomed. For instance, arranging a 'nanny-share' for two or three employees; retainer payments for child-minders for part-time workers.

Other types of provision, such as flexible hours, or help with transport can ease practical problems for employee and employer, and be perceived as a benefit.

Pre-retirement counselling

Many larger employers now provide a series of lectures and an information pack for employees nearing retirement. The areas typically covered are:

- personal financial planning
- managing increased leisure time
- health in retirement
- local sources of information and advice.

Personal financial counselling

Top executives and other higher rate tax payers are not always as effective as they might be in organizing their own personal financial planning. Even finance directors able to work wonders with corporate financial policy may have little time or inclination to deal properly with family financial matters. To help with this problem and provide the necessary specialist advice, many major employers offer senior executives the chance to go to independent advisors for personal financial counselling. This should be provided by fee charging advisors who are not going to benefit from the sale of particular financial products, ie those who typically return commissions to either the company or the individual executive where commission-earning products are bought on recommendation. The advice given usually covers areas such as:

- making a will
- inheritance and other planning
- required insurance cover
- provisions for dependants
- savings and investment strategy
- finance and property
- planning for school fees
- trusts and covenants
- tax planning.

Advice is generally provided on a one-to-one basis once the executive has produced an inventory of his or her personal financial situation under guidance. The position is usually reviewed regularly to take account of changed personal circumstances. Companies may also offer this service to widows and widowers of employees to help them plan how best to make use of death-in-service benefits and take stock of the financial situation in which they have been left. Given that many widows of an older generation may have little idea about financial management, this can be a valuable and much-needed benefit.

Personal counselling

Traditionally provided as part of company 'welfare' services, a new generation of personal counselling services (EAPs or Employee Assistance Programmes) is growing up among major employers. Their purpose is to help employees deal with the traumas of bereavement, divorce, alcoholism and the spectre of AIDS. Larger employers typically provide specially trained 'in-house' counsellors on a confidential basis. Others provide a referral service to counsellors in the community, eg to Relate, Alcoholics Anonymous, etc.

Sports and social facilities

Most employers recognize that work is also a social institution. They therefore try to provide at least some leisure activities so that colleagues can meet together outside working hours. Depending on the size, location and culture of the organization, provisions vary considerably. It may be entirely appropriate to negotiate favourable membership terms at nearby health and sports clubs. Whatever the circumstances, providing a social focus can have beneficial effects on the organization's culture (eg assisting team building) and should therefore be regularly reviewed as part of the remuneration package. It can certainly be a retention factor where staff are difficult to find and keep.

Company cars

Few other countries in the world provide company cars to the same extent as the UK. Foreign parent companies setting up in the UK often experience difficulty in persuading head office that such generous provisions are necessary to compete in the salary market. Employees seldom move from a job where they have a car to a non-car job, even if it carries a much higher basic salary. This is because in the private sector, and now in parts of the public sector too, cars are a mark of managerial status. Company cars are normally taxed, insured and maintained at company expense. They are, therefore, a large benefit and create a major differential and, some would say, distortion at the point in a salary structure where they are given on the basis of status alone.

The cash value to an employee of a company car can be as much as £5,000 to £10,000 a year (or more) depending on the model. The gap in a reward structure between the 'haves' and 'have nots' in company car terms is therefore considerable and can and does frequently cause heartache.

Historically, company cars were a tax efficient benefit. This is no longer universally the case following a series of tax increases. The tax regime proposed from April 1994 will be broadly tax neutral on average, ie the taxable value of cars will be similar to their cash value. However, the position will vary significantly from one individual to another depending on the level of their business and private mileage.

Company car policies are often a benefit 'trouble spot' and can take an inordinate amount of top executive time to get right. Car fleet management is not an area for amateurs. Most large organizations have a fleet manager in charge of the acquisition and maintenance of the company car fleet, leaving the details of allocation policy and the way in which cars fit into remuneration policy as the main problems of the compensation and benefits specialists. Here a number of problems arise. People who are not entitled to them often try to get cars on the basis of business need, or to get their jobs regraded to a level where car provision is automatic. When they eventually get cars there may still be problems about the model, the permitted extras or the replacement cycle. In devising the remuneration policy element of company car policies, the following areas have to be dealt with in relation to what the company can afford in the face of competitive practice:

1. *Allocation policy:* this deals with who is to get cars on the basis of status, and what the annual mileage threshold is, before cars are given in response to business need (somewhere between 5,000 and 10,000 miles is common – dependent on the type of journeys made).
2. *Car model entitlements:* when deciding car model entitlements the choice is between setting them rigidly in relation to a small number of models at each status level or, as is now more common, in relation to a bench-mark price or lease cost, allowing varying degrees of freedom of voice. Few companies allow open sports cars, while others restrict the choice to models manufactured in EC or Scandinavian countries or even to British manufacturers' models (although the latter policy becomes confused when cars manufactured in Europe are sold by British-based firms). The market trend is to allow as wide a choice as possible within a given cost framework.

    Organizations may also choose to allow some flexibility either on the additional extras that may be added to the car at employees' expense or, indeed, over whether they can make a contribution out of salary to either the lease cost or the purchase price of a more expensive car if they want one. In either of these cases, strict limits must be set because there is a strong tendency to stretch allowances to their limits and indeed beyond! A typical example of the problem is the organization which leases cars and sets an absolute price limit of, say, £300 a month, and finds that a remarkably high proportion of employees will passionately want metallic paint on this model, which takes the leasing cost to £324. If they are then told that the limit is £300, they may complain bitterly that the company can surely afford an extra £24 a month.

An increasingly common response is to let employees pay the extra – typically with a cost ceiling that might be 20 per cent above the monthly lease cost or purchase price. Some organizations set no ceilings on additions, typically those with a high proportion of young professionals who can then at least try having a Porsche for three years before moving on to a less personally costly family Volvo. If ceilings are imposed it is critical to stick to them *without exception*.

Most car fleet managers know that if they allow themselves to be swayed by these specious arguments, the level will creep up incrementally and the allocation policy will be in tatters. It can however be very hard to hold the line in times of severe market pressure. Chief executives can, and sometimes do, intervene to ensure a favoured candidate gets the car he or she wants. As we have already said, car policy demands far more boardroom time than it should. Getting top executive commitment to the imposition of firm limits each time they are reviewed can help contain abuse of policy by directors with 'special cases'.

3. *Replacement cycles:* cars are commonly replaced every two to four years, or 50,000 to 80,000 miles, but this varies with the use and durability of the cars involved. Three years is the most common replacement period. Salesforce cars suffer more wear and tear and therefore tend to be replaced more frequently than top executive cars, especially where annual mileages for the latter are relatively low.

4. *Eligibility to drive:* the policy on who may drive the car, eg employees/spouse/family/named drivers, is usually determined by the provisions agreed under the insurance cover negotiated. Flexibility in this area is often appreciated – especially in dual career families where the nanny or au pair needs to be insured to drive the car to get children to school and ferry them around.

5. *Permitted fuel* ('Green' issues): the majority of UK employers now specify that all new company cars should run on unleaded petrol – for both environmental and (as the UK Government intended when it reduced the tax) cost reasons. The use of all-diesel fleets is also growing – again encouraged by the Government via the diesel price differential. Buying cars with catalytic converters is also a major contribution to pollution abatement.

6. *Fleet management:* the management of the car fleet involves not only selecting, purchasing and disposing of cars, but also encouraging drivers to treat their cars properly so that their resale value holds up when they fall due for replacement.

Company car policies are normally set out in a manual for drivers which is regularly updated.

Company cars – the future

The Government has progressively increased the income tax liability for the benefit of a company car, both to implement its policy of encouraging clean cash pay and, more recently, in response to a strengthening 'Green' lobby to restrict the number of cars on the road – cars being a major source of 'greenhouse gases', notably carbon dioxide, in the atmosphere. It can be argued that this is a good thing. Company cars are an all too visible status symbol and in these days of single status organizations (following the example of many US and Japanese-owned companies), should something as divisive as this be allowed to continue? Company car policies can effectively demotivate as well as motivate. They cause a lot of pain as well as pleasure. Now that cars are no longer tax effective in general, an increasingly common solution is to offer employees a cash alternative to their car entitlement. Employees can then choose the combination of cash and car which best meets their personal and business needs and which is most sensible from a tax point of view. Cash alternatives also go some of the way to removing status differences and irregular jumps in employees' packages between the 'haves' and the 'have nots'.

The 1993 Hay Benefits survey indicates that 13 per cent of organizations had already introduced cash alternatives and 15 per cent more were planning to introduce them. If this trend continues, the 1980s 'yuppy Porsche' era could be over. The 1990s will be all about choice and flexibility.

Private petrol

Free petrol for private mileage remains a predominantly top and senior management benefit. It is taxable and care should be taken where annual mileage is low that the tax charge does not exceed the cost of petrol for the occasional driver. Employers will also have to decide whether to give private petrol provision for holidays and overseas trips. A return journey to Athens can add significantly to an individual's annual employment cost! Not surprisingly, therefore, most employers restrict the benefit to UK travel.

Car allowances

Where cars are not provided but are used regularly for business purposes, many employers pay car allowances. These should be designed to make a sensible contribution to the cost of depreciation, maintenance and other running costs. A car used on business will inevitably need replacement earlier than one used more occasionally. Organizations such as the Automobile Association provide guidelines on running costs as a basis for settling allowances.

Mileage allowances

The cost of fuel used on business journeys is normally reimbursed. For company cars this will be on a mileage rate which reflects the actual cost of petrol or diesel. For employees' own cars, there will be an addition to compensate for wear and tear. These rates vary both in relation to the price of fuel and market practice. They may also vary in relation to total annual business mileage. The full allowance may be payable for short journeys, but a lower allowance can apply for much longer journeys. Again, the Automobile Association figures are often used in setting the level of allowances.

Other benefits

Other benefits include:

■ subsidized meals in staff restaurants

- luncheon vouchers – especially where employers are cited in large towns/cities
- clothing allowances/cleaning tokens for employees who have to wear company uniforms
- the refund of telephone rentals and the whole or part of the cost of calls – for those required to work at home or from home on occasions
- educational allowances for expatriates – to ensure continuity of education for their children
- credit card facilities for petrol or other purchases – especially for those who do a lot of travelling
- mobile telephone/fax machines – typically job-need related but perceived as a reward too
- funding of non-job related evening classes/training to encourage employees to broaden their interests and skills – an area where 'leading edge' employers such as Ford and Mars have taken major initiatives.

Intangible benefits

It should already be clear from much of this book that the authors do not believe that people work for money alone. There are in fact many determinants of the decision to work for, and stay with, a particular employer. Throwing money at recruitment and retention problems may be the worst possible strategy because this only deals with one aspect of what may be a complex problem. It is also, of course, self-limiting, because there has to be an ultimate ceiling on employment costs. The role of money as a motivator was discussed in Chapter 2. What we want to emphasize here is the simple fact that employees weigh up a number of tangible and intangible factors when looking at what employers have on offer. The list below sets out in more detail the main items involved. Most of them are strongly related to the need for personal recognition and the desire to go on learning and developing as a career goes through different stages. Recognition of the overlap between private and working life is also important. Most people prefer to work for an employer who is caring and supportive as well as challenging and successful.

The principal items are:

- status – recognition of seniority and professional excellence
- power – the opportunity to influence the course of the business and take responsibility for a growing number of functions and people
- recognition for achievement – a culture in which managers praise and reinforce individual success
- training opportunities – the chance to acquire a wider range of skills in preparation for promotion and to function more effectively and confidently
- career progression – the prospect of promotion, preferably in relation to a properly designed succession plan to ensure that the right experience is acquired at the right time to enable new responsibilities to be taken on when the individual has been properly prepared for them.
- good working conditions – pleasant, spacious and well-designed offices and other work environments which facilitate effective working both for individuals and teams
- a well-managed organization – an appropriate organization structure infused with a sense of purpose and commitment. The reputation for running a 'rough shop' spreads quickly and prevents successful recruitment of all but those who believe they can change it – until they give up!
- recognition of the need to balance work and family responsibilities –

employees knowing that they are treated as responsible individuals whose family commitments are important to them. This means not developing a culture where becoming a workaholic and risking family breakdown is a key means to promotion. It also means taking a reasonable view on attendance, for instance, at school functions and other family occasions. Organizations seeking to recruit women returners are finding that they have to pay greater heed to the family responsibilities of their men to enable women to feel free to take up employment with adequate partner support. One is mindful of Rosabeth Moss Kanter's paradox – 'succeed, succeed, succeed and raise terrific children' (*When Giants Learn to Dance*, p21)

- flexibility – a willingness to tailor conditions to the particular needs of individuals. Companies can rapidly develop this when they have to attract staff in great demand, but there may also be benefits to be gained, in terms of commitment and stability, from using the principle in other areas.

Developing employee benefit strategies – key factors

The key factors to be taken into account in developing employee benefit strategies are that they should:

- be an integral part of the total reward management strategy of the organization, which in turn should specifically support the achievement of its business objectives
- add value to basic remuneration and performance-related pay policies by extending the purely financial provisions of these policies into areas where the company will benefit from providing additional rewards and which will support the achievement of employees' specific needs.
- be in line and supportive of the culture of the organization and its value system
- demonstrate to employees that they are members of a caring and enabling organization which is concerned in highly practical terms with meeting their needs for security, support and other forms of help so that they are able really to give their best
- meet the needs of the organization to increase the commitment of its members, to develop their identification with its objectives and to increase unity of purpose
- meet the real needs of individual employees rather than those needs which management believes they should have
- help the organization to recruit and retain high-quality and well-motivated staff by being competitive in the market-place
- ensure that benefits are cost effective in the sense that the increase they produce in commitment and improvement in recruitment and retention rates justify their cost
- take account of relative tax efficiencies in structuring the package
- establish an appropriate degree of flexibility in operating the benefit package
- provide a measure of individual choice to employees
- aim to avoid an over-divisive approach which places employees into clearly defined 'have' and 'have not' categories
- bear in mind the importance of the non-tangible benefits as well as those which provide extra remuneration or financial assistance
- be creative – not simply offering what competitors offer but devising new approaches to structuring the package and to providing individual benefits which are tailored to the strategic needs of the organization (like giving

secretaries having to cope in poor, if temporary, office conditions, fresh flowers on their desk every week in recognition of their commitment and tolerance of the environment).

Recognizing the need to review benefits

The impact and effectiveness of the benefits package should be kept under constant review to identify its impact and effectiveness. The symptoms that might indicate the need for attention include:

- problems in managing the expectations of prospective employees on their benefits package (the 'every other employer I'm talking to provides mobile phones' syndrome)
- problems in retaining staff because of dissatisfaction with the package (as established at leaving interviews)
- discontent expressed by management on the extent to which the benefits package provides value for money
- general information on trends in the provision of benefits which indicates that the level of benefits provided by the company is out of line with good practice elsewhere
- discontent expressed by staff on the scale of benefits provided by the company or the basis upon which they are allocated
- pressure from staff to be allowed more choice in the benefits they get
- changes in fiscal law which reduce the tax efficiency of individual benefits
- problems in administering benefit policies, for example company cars.

Modifying the benefits package

The steps required to modify or re-design the benefits package are as follows:

1. Analyze trends in the market-place using survey and other data for the provision of benefits, and assess what is regarded as the best practice in each area.
2. Analyze trends in the recruitment and retention of staff to assess, in the light of the market survey, any areas where it is believed that improvements in the benefits package and/or the way it is applied might improve the ability of the organization to attract and retain staff.
3. Assess in discussions with management what it wants the employee benefits, strategies and policies of the organization to achieve and the extent to which the present arrangements satisfy these objectives.
4. Consult employees on their needs (consider using an attitude survey for this purpose).
5. Obtain the views of relevant trade unions or staff associations.
6. Assess the tax implications of current and projected government policies.
7. In the light of these processes of analysis and consultation:
   (a) conduct an overall review of employee benefits strategies under the headings listed above
   (b) review each of the main policy areas as set out in the key dimensions part of this section
   (c) decide, on the basis of these reviews, any changes required to strategies and policies and the steps required to get these changes formulated, agreed and introduced.
8. In the light of revised strategies and policies and by reference to the analytical and consultative steps taken earlier (stages 1 to 5):

(a) subject each benefit to careful scrutiny to determine any changes required to content or application

(b) examine the costs of each benefit and assess whether it is providing value for money (this involves comparing the cost of providing and administering the benefit with an assessment of the extent to which it is meeting the needs of the company and its employees – clearly low cost to employer/high value employee items will be the most attractive)

(c) decide if any additional items should be included in the package and assess their likely contributions to meeting organizational and individual needs and their overall cost effectiveness

(d) decide if any items should be eliminated on cost effectiveness grounds – but beware of taking away traditional benefits if the timing is poor and the change is the wrong symbolic act

(e) plan the steps required to make the changes, including the design of the benefit, consultation with staff and methods of communicating information on the changes to all those affected (including tax implications).

9. Introduce the changes, ensuring that the supporting administrative systems are properly installed and that the communication programme takes place as planned.

Communicating the benefits package

Employee benefits can easily be taken for granted by staff, and it is therefore important to tell them about what they are getting and its value. This can be done in company newsletters or, better still, by means of employee benefits statements which set out in full the scale and cost of the benefits for each individual employee.

Trends in employee benefits policy

To summarize, the main trends in benefits policy are:

- less attention being paid to tax avoidance
- greater simplification of benefit packages
- more attention to individual needs
- greater emphasis on individual choice (see also Chapter 32)
- a move towards clean cash rather than benefits in kind
- greater concentration on assessing the cost/effectiveness of the total benefits package and planning a strategy for benefits which is integrated with an overall reward management policy, which is in turn linked to the business strategy of the organization
- more attention paid to communicating the benefits policy.

30

Pensions

Approved pension schemes

Pensions are generally regarded as the most important employee benefit. They are typically financed from contributions which build up rights to a guaranteed income for employees or their dependants on retirement or death. Companies frequently aim to provide adequate or generous pension arrangements because:

1. There is often a perceived moral obligation to provide a reasonable level of security for employees, especially those with long service.
2. A good pension scheme demonstrates that the company has the long-term interests of employees at heart.
3. A good scheme helps attract and retain high-quality staff.
4. Pensions can be a tax efficient form of remuneration.

The area of pension scheme administration is increasingly dominated by highly skilled in-company specialists and external suppliers of software or administration services. Nevertheless, it is essential for the general salary administrator to understand the major policy considerations in order to contribute effectively to pension policy development. The check-list at the end of this section lists the main questions that should be asked when assessing current or proposed pension scheme practice.

Apart from their internal complexity, pension schemes are subject to a number of legal and fiscal regulations, and in recent years the volume of legislation on pensions has increased dramatically. The process of balancing the requirements of the legislation against the optimum benefits levels and funding arrangements invariably requires expert independent advice from actuaries or benefits consultants before final details of a new or revised scheme can be decided.

The most significant changes in recent times are:

1. The requirement that from April 1988 membership of a company pension scheme can no longer be compulsory. Employees can opt out of the company scheme and are then free to choose whether or not to make their own personal pension arrangements or rely solely on the State pension scheme. The employer is less able to adopt a paternalistic approach in deciding what is 'best' for his employees, and new attitudes range from 'this is the company pension scheme, take it or leave it' to a concerted effort to provide good benefits and to sell the advantages of the company scheme over the personal pension or 'State pension only' routes.
2. The ruling of the European Court of Justice on 17 May 1990 (the 'Barber' and related cases) which requires the equal treatment of men and women in pension schemes. Traditionally, UK pension schemes were discriminatory and this ruling has caused serious problems and often incurred substantial costs

for many organizations. The issues involved are highly complex; specialist advice should be sought in order to have any hope of successfully navigating the legislative maze which exists at present (mid 1993).

3. The Social Security Act 1990 requirement to guarantee a level of pension increases. This could ultimately increase some organizations' pension costs by up to 40 per cent.

Inland Revenue approval

All company pension arrangements other than those of a purely voluntary nature require the approval of the Inland Revenue, if the director or employee concerned is not to be liable to income tax on the cost of providing the pension benefit. Inland Revenue approval also confers significant tax advantages on the scheme. The 1989 Finance Act introduced the facility for companies to provide benefits under unapproved pension schemes in addition to those under approved schemes. These unapproved schemes are discussed later in this chapter.

The current code of approval was introduced in the 1970 Finance Act, which has been incorporated into the Income and Corporation Taxes Act 1988, and became mandatory on 6 April 1980. This Act sets out the conditions under which the Inland Revenue will automatically approve a pension scheme for advantageous tax status. In addition it confers discretionary powers on the Inland Revenue to approve schemes which do not fully conform to stated conditions. Most schemes are approved under this discretionary power because the stated conditions are too restrictive.

The Inland Revenue issues guidance as to how it will exercise its discretionary powers in a booklet entitled *Occupational Pension Schemes: Notes on approval under Chapter I Part XIV Income and Corporation Taxes Act 1988*, commonly known as the 'Practice Notes' or 'IR12'. The main conditions of Inland Revenue approval are in the form of restrictions on the maximum benefits that can be provided. The main maxima are summarized below.

1. *Normal retirement pension:* one-sixtieth of final remuneration at normal retirement date for each year of service up to 40. The 1989 Finance Act introduced an 'earnings cap' for new schemes established on or after 14 March 1989 or new entrants to existing schemes on or after 1 June 1989. This cap restricted the amount of final remuneration used in the calculation of maximum benefits to £75,000 in the year ending 5 April 1994. The Act provided for the cap to be increased each year in line with the increase in the Retail Prices Index (suitably rounded). However, in the Budget of March 1993, the Chancellor surprised everyone by freezing the cap at last year's level. Whether this is just a 'slip' in Government policy or the start of a longer trend, remains to be seen. A higher pension fraction under an 'uplifted scale' may be permitted for late entrants to the scheme, who are unable to complete a full 40 years. This uplifted scale rises to two-thirds of final remuneration after only 10 years for members who joined their scheme prior to 17 March 1987, or after 20 years for those who joined on or after that date.

2. *Lump sum option on retirement:* three-eightieths of final remuneration at normal retirement date for each year of service up to 40. As for the pension, a higher fraction under an uplifted scale may be permitted for late entrants to the scheme, who are unable to complete a full 40 years. This scale produces the maximum 120/80ths, or 1.5 times final remuneration after only 20 years, but those who joined their scheme on or after 17 March 1987 are permitted

uplifted cash only if their pension benefits are uplifted, and are also subject to a limit of £100,000 on final remuneration in the calculation of the tax-free cash. For new schemes established on or after 14 March 1989 or new entrants to existing schemes on or after 1 June 1989 the earnings cap introduced by the 1989 Finance Act also applies to final remuneration in the calculation of the tax-free cash.

3. *Spouse's benefits on death in service:* two-thirds of the member's pension achievable at normal retirement date (based on current earnings), plus a cash sum equal to four times current earnings plus a refund of all the members' own contributions with interest.
4. *Spouse's pension on death after retirement:* two-thirds of member's pension.
5. *Inflationary provisions:* benefits may be escalated in line with the increase in the Retail Prices Index.

State pensions and contracting out

State earnings related pension scheme (SERPS)

The Social Security Pensions Act 1975 (the 1975 Act) changed the whole face of UK pensions practice and introduced the new State Earnings Related Pension Scheme (SERPS) on top of the State Basic Pension. SERPS started on 6 April 1978 and originally provided a pension of 1.25 per cent of a person's average annual 'revalued band earnings' for each year completed after April 1978, up to a maximum percentage of 25 per cent by 1998.

Revalued band earnings are earnings between the lower and upper earnings limits for National Insurance Contribution, which are increased in line with earnings inflation for the period up to retirement. The lower earnings limit is approximately equal to a quarter of national average earnings and the upper earnings limit is about one and three-quarters times national average earnings.

Subsequently, the Government considered that the cost of SERPS would be too high in the next century, and introduced changes in the Social Security Act 1986 which became effective from 6 April 1988. The changes should not affect the SERPS pension of anyone reaching state pension age before the end of this century. The SERPS pension for anyone retiring after that will be gradually reduced to an ultimate level of 20 per cent, rather than 25 per cent, of average revalued band earnings. Furthermore, this average will be based on all earnings rather than the best 20 years as originally provided.

Contracting out

The 1975 Act empowered good occupational pension schemes to contract out of SERPS. This meant that the occupational pension scheme undertook to provide benefits at least equal to a guaranteed minimum pension (GMP) in place of the SERPS pension, in return for a reduction in employer and employee National Insurance contributions. A person's GMP is calculated in a similar way to the SERPS pension.

Until April 1988, only final salary schemes which guarantee a minimum level of earnings-related pension could contract out of SERPS. The Social Security Act 1986, however, allowed schemes to contract out of SERPS from April 1988 without having to guarantee any level of minimum benefits. Such schemes are Contracted Out Money Purchase schemes, or COMP schemes, and will provide benefits equal to whatever the contributions accumulated for a member will buy at the time of retirement.

The Government further favoured its pet project – personal pensions – by allowing them to contract out on even more favourable terms than occupational pension schemes. For younger employees in particular, the financial advantages of a contracted out personal pension over SERPS can be substantial. However, if the choice is between a personal pension and a good company scheme, the latter normally wins hands down – or should do – were it not for the exuberance of some insurance company salespeople.

Main features of company pension schemes

The main sources of more detailed information on UK pensions practice are the regular surveys conducted *inter alia* by the National Association of Pension Funds (NAPF), the government actuary and Hay. In addition, there are a number of loose leaf works on pensions and several specialist pensions periodicals. Most leading firms of pension consultants and actuaries produce their own newsletters and other information aids for employers. Guidance on the statutory requirements is published by the Superannuation Funds Office and the Occupational Pensions Board.

The short sections below are not exhaustive and merely summarize the main aspects of current pensions provisions.

Eligibility

Membership of any company pension scheme must be on a voluntary basis. Before 6 April 1968 companies could, and usually did, make joining the company pension scheme a condition of employment.

Eligibility conditions for membership of a pension scheme often express a minimum age and/or length of service before an employee can join, although there is usually a power to waive these conditions in any particular case.

The 1975 Act introduced equal access requirements. These meant that admission to membership of an occupational pension scheme should be on terms which are the same in respect of age and length of service for both men and women.

Pensionable age

The Sex Discrimination Act 1986, which applies to new employees joining a company after 7 November 1987, prohibits employers from forcing women to retire at a different age from men in similar circumstances. This Act does not require pension schemes to adopt a common normal *pensionable* age.

However, various EC directives and judgments handed down by the European Court of Justice have systematically removed elements of sex discrimination from company pension schemes. In particular, the judgment by the European Court in the case of Barber vs Guardian Royal Exchange, which was handed down on 17 May 1990, ruled that pension benefits count as pay under Article 119 of the Treaty of Rome, which requires equal pay for work of equal value. The Court also determined that contracted-out company pension schemes could not impose age conditions which differ according to sex, even if the difference between the pensionable ages for men and women is based on that provided for by the national statutory scheme. Thus this single judgment has the effect of requiring all pension schemes in future to adopt common pensionable ages for men and women and common eligibility conditions for benefits. Unfortunately the wording of the judgment left in doubt the extent of its applicability to benefits earned before 17 May 1990. Some of the uncertainties created are now a step closer to resolution. On 28 April 1993, the Advocate General of the European Court delivered his opinion on four cases, turning on the detailed requirements of the Barber judgment. The opinion is not binding but is normally followed by the European Court. The key points emerging from this are:

1. Only benefits accrued after 17 May 1990 need to be equalized.
2. The factors determining benefits must be unisex.
3. The judgment binds both employers and pension scheme trustees.

A number of schemes have already adopted a common normal pensionable age, or alternatively, have introduced a system of flexible retirement, whereby members can retire at any time between 60 and 65 without any early retirement deduction from their pension. The 1993 Hay Benefits Survey found that most schemes now have equal retirement ages with 65 being the most common choice.

Retirement formulae and pension on retirement

There are three kinds of pension scheme in general: final salary, money purchase and hybrid.

Final salary

The principal method for determining the benefit formula of retirement income is final salary. Pension is calculated as a fraction of either the salary at retirement or an average of salary over the closing years of service multiplied by the length of pensionable service. The most common fraction is sixtieths, giving the full pension allowed by the Inland Revenue after 40 years' service of 40/60ths or two-thirds of final salary. The maximum scheme pension will be subject to the Inland Revenue maximum referred to earlier.

Money purchase

The main alternative to a final salary pension scheme is a money purchase scheme. Under a money purchase approach, the company fixes the contribution it wants to pay in respect of each member. This may be a sterling amount eg £2,000 per annum, or, more commonly, a percentage of the member's salary, eg 10 per cent. The pension payable to a member on retirement is then whatever annual payment can be purchased with the money accumulated in the fund for him.

The company may pay the same rate of contribution for all members, or it may vary its contribution according to status, age, length of service, and the level of the employee's contribution. Alternatively, the company can adjust the contribution paid each year in respect of a member, to home in on a target level of benefit, perhaps determined by reference to a final salary formula.

Hybrid schemes

In order to meet the pension aspirations of different types of employee, some schemes have adopted benefit structures which combined both final salary and money purchase principles. This may take the form of a money purchase 'underpin' to a final salary benefit, whereby a member gets a pension based on a money purchase formula if this gives a higher pension than the final salary formula. Other forms of hybrid might be a final salary benefit based on a fairly low fraction with a money purchase benefit on top, or a money purchase formula below a certain age with a final salary formula above that age.

Other formulae

Other possible pension formulae are:

1. *Average salary:* fixed amounts of pension are given for each year spent in a salary bracket and these are added up and paid at retirement.
2. *Flat rate:* a given rate paid for each year of service.

These methods are rarely used nowadays, the state pension arrangements being a notable exception.

Lump sum on retirement

The Inland Revenue allows up to 3/80ths of final salary for each year of service up to a maximum of 40 years to be paid as a lump sum on retirement. This gives a maximum lump sum of 120/80ths or 1.5 times final salary. Under a final salary scheme, the lump sum is usually obtained by the member exchanging, or commuting, part of his pension entitlement for the lump sum, although some schemes provide a (smaller) pension *plus* a lump sum. With a money purchase scheme, the lump sum will usually be paid from the fund available at retirement, before applying the balance of the fund to buy pension benefits. A lump sum provision of some kind is almost universal in modern schemes.

The 'uplifted scales' and Inland Revenue limits referred to earlier will apply to employees who complete less than 40 years and to those who joined their company pension scheme on or after 17 March 1987.

No tax is payable on the lump sum whereas the pension is subject to income tax. This usually means that a member is better off taking the lump sum and most members do so, whether for this reason, or because the capital is required for immediate material needs such as the purchase of a retirement home, or repayment of a mortgage.

Late retirement

Money purchase pension schemes automatically provide for an enhanced pension for members who continue to work after normal retirement date, through the continued growth of the money purchase fund. The rules of final salary pension schemes will also usually provide for an enhanced pension on late retirement. If contributions continue to the final salary scheme during the period after normal pensionable age, the employee will normally earn additional benefits on the scheme's normal scale, based on the extra years of service completed.

For somebody who has already completed 40 years by their normal retirement date and earned the maximum pension of 40/60ths of final salary, the Inland Revenue permits a further 1/60th of final salary for each year of additional service up to a maximum total pension of 45/60ths. The normal maximum lump sum option of 120/80ths of final salary is similarly increased by an additional 3/80ths for each year, up to an overall maximum of 135/80ths.

If contributions cease at normal retirement age, it is usual for an actuarially increased pension to be paid when retirement takes place, although employees whose benefits are subject to the earnings cap introduced by the 1989 Finance Act may be ineligible for such increase because there is no corresponding limit in the Inland Revenue maximum benefits.

Post-retirement pension increases

Increases to cushion pensioners against at least some of the inroads of inflation are now considered an essential part of most company pension schemes.

Under a contracted out final salary scheme, the part of a member's pension forming the guaranteed minimum pension (GMP) is already inflation proofed by the state, although the company scheme must pay the first 3 per cent per annum of that inflation proofing. Similar increases will be payable to pensioners of contracted out money purchase schemes.

In addition to these statutory increases, most employers will provide for annual escalation by a fixed, funded percentage, commonly three to five per cent of the member's pension, to which the scheme is committed in the trust deed and rules. The 1993 Hay Benefits Survey found that roughly two thirds of schemes guaranteed some level of increases. Alternatively, *ad hoc* or discretionary pension increases may be granted. Some employers give both types of increase. Pension schemes in the public sector go further on pension increases by formally linking the whole of the employees' pensions to the Retail Price Index.

In the 1980s and early 1990s, low rates of inflation, together with good investment returns on pension fund investments, have meant many good pension schemes in the private sector giving discretionary pension increases as good as, or better than, RPI increases, although these have, in part, represented a catching up from previous years. The 1990 Social Security Act has introduced a provision whereby, from an appointed day, all final salary pension schemes will be required to provide annual increases to pensions earned after that day in line with the RPI up to a maximum of 5 per cent per annum. In addition, any surplus revealed by an actuarial valuation of the scheme after that day will have to be used to provide this level of pension increase on pensions already earned before any part of it can be returned to the company, either in cash or by means of a contribution holiday.

The extent to which schemes can continue to afford pension increases which compare well with inflation will depend largely on the government's success in keeping inflation under control. The successful performance of pension fund investments, and the willingness of companies to fund for future increases are equally important factors.

Death in service benefits

Most employees are concerned about the effect their untimely death would have on the financial security of their dependants. It is therefore usual for this problem to be catered for by the pension scheme in one or, usually, a combination of the following ways:

1. By providing a lump sum, usually calculated as a multiple of salary at the time of death.
2. By providing a spouse's pension, normally a proportion of pension due at normal retirement date.
3. By providing a child's pension in order to assist with family costs until the children have reached, say, 18.

Lump sum payments typically vary between one and four times annual salary; a good staff entitlement would currently be three or four times salary. This payment needs to be a significant amount if it is to fulfil its purpose of meeting short-term financial commitments and provide a financial cushion for dependants during the immediate period after bereavement. Most employers provide this cover for all staff regardless of service and make special provisions to allow at least some degree of cover prior to entry to the pension scheme. The earnings cap introduced by the 1989 Finance Act also affects the maximum level of lump sum death benefits for those employees who are subject to it.

Spouses' pensions are commonly one-half of the pension due on the employee's retirement based on his salary at death, although some more generous schemes provide the maximum permitted of up to two-thirds of the prospective pension (up to 4/9ths of pay at the date of death).

Child pensions are also increasingly common but normally cease when the children reach 18 or finish full-time education.

Death in retirement benefits

As with death in service benefits, the principal objective is to ensure that the surviving spouse retains an acceptable level of income until her/his death. For this reason, the most common entitlement is a spouse's pension of one-half of the member's pension. The maximum permitted pension is two-thirds of the member's maximum pension entitlement before death, ignoring any pension reduction as a result of taking a lump sum at retirement.

In addition, pension payments are often 'guaranteed' for five years – irrespective of whether the employee is alive or dead!

Early retirement

Most final salary schemes allow employees to retire before normal pensionable age (but after age 50), and receive an immediate early retirement pension, but at a reduced rate. This is the most realistic approach in terms of costs to the company where early retirement is voluntary. Retirement through ill-health, which may be at any age, is usually given more sympathetic treatment under long-term disability provisions, which either allow for payment of the full pension earned up to the date of early retirement or even give credit for the years between the actual and normal retiring age.

Leaving service

For many employees, career progression depends on the ability to gain experience and promotion with several employers. Fewer and fewer staff stay with one employer for life. But older employees who might otherwise move, and benefit in career terms by doing so, often tend to stay on in companies they have outgrown or jobs where they are not particularly happy, because they feel themselves locked in by the pension rights they cannot afford to lose. Unless they gain substantial pay increases, or are very senior and able to negotiate 'top hat' arrangements, most employees lose out on the final value of their pension by changing jobs.

The loss arises from the way pensions are calculated in final salary schemes. The pension at retirement is a fraction, typically 1/60th, of final salary at retirement for each year of service. On leaving service, however, the pension is based on salary at the date of leaving. Statutory and discretionary increases on the leaving service pension now go some way in making up the difference, but are unlikely to match the rate of increase in salary.

By contrast, a money purchase scheme will not distinguish between a leaver and a stayer. On leaving a money purchase scheme, a member's entitlement is usually the full amount accumulated for him in his individual account to the date of leaving. Thus members do not suffer the reduction in benefits that takes place on leaving service under a final salary scheme.

This does not mean that leaving service benefits are always better under a money purchase scheme. This will depend on such factors as the rate of contribution paid under the money purchase scheme, the success of the scheme's investment performance for the relevant period, the scale of benefits under an alternative final salary scheme, the level of pension increases under the final salary scheme, and the age of the member at the date of leaving.

'Top hat' arrangements

The tax efficiency of approved pension arrangements encourages many employers to provide benefits for senior executives and directors of the company up to the maximum levels permitted by the Inland Revenue. This can be done by exercising powers under the company pension scheme to augment individual members' benefits, or by effecting additional individual pension policies for the members concerned. Some companies operate a separate pension scheme for senior executives and directors.

The 1973 Finance Act removed the restriction on controlling directors joining occupational pension schemes, and this eventually led to the establishment of separate schemes, typically for just one or two controlling directors, and operated on a self-administered basis. This gave the directors the opportunity to decide on the investment of their pension contributions themselves rather than pay them to an insurance company. These schemes, known as 'small self-administered pension schemes', are subject to special additional conditions imposed by the Super- annuation Funds Office to prevent abuse of the tax privileges.

Financing of approved pension schemes

Employee contributions

The 1993 Hay Benefits Survey found that 71 per cent of schemes required contributions from members and 29 per cent were non-contributory. The arguments usually given in favour of contributory schemes are that sharing the cost between employer and employee often enables better benefits to be purchased and that employees appreciate benefits more – and see the schemes as their own – when they have had to pay for them. This can create an area of joint interest and co-operation which may help to improve the industrial relations climate. Employees in contributory schemes are also able to obtain tax relief on contributions – as well as refunds if they leave – after a short period of member- ship.

Non-contributory schemes generally allow the employer greater flexibility, while providing an attractive benefit at no obvious cost to the employee. The administrative costs are less and the total costs may not necessarily be more than those of contributory schemes, because the type of pension scheme can be taken into account in salary-market comparisons which affect the level at which salary scales are set.

Additional voluntary contributions

All schemes must provide a facility for members to pay contributions on a voluntary basis. Such Additional Voluntary Contributions, or AVCs, may be invested in the main scheme, or through a separate contract with a building society or insurance company. AVCs may operate on a cash accumulation principle, whereby the AVCs earn interest, or on a with profits basis whereby they earn bonuses, or they may be unit linked. In a final salary scheme they may be used to buy additional years of service.

The Finance (No 2) Act 1987 removed the requirement that, once started, AVCs could only be stopped after 5 years or in cases of financial hardship, and thus allowed for AVCs to be paid on a one-off basis. However, the same Act also required that AVC arrangements commencing after 8 April 1987 must eventually be taken in pension rather than lump sum form on retirement.

Since November 1987, members have been able to take out a free-standing AVC contract with an insurance company (or other free-standing AVC provider) of their own choice instead of the company's AVC arrangements.

Employer's contributions

Under a final salary scheme, the employer is usually responsible for paying the 'balance of the cost of the benefits'. This will usually result in the employer paying more, often considerably more, than the employees, perhaps between one and three times the employees' contribution rate.

The employer's rate of contribution to a final salary scheme will vary from time to time. If pension costs escalate, eg through high-pay inflation, the employer may need to increase his contribution or pay special additional contributions. Conversely, if the experience goes well, eg investments perform better than expected, the employer may be able to reduce, or temporarily suspend, his contributions.

With a money purchase scheme, the employer simply decides what contribution he wishes to pay. Hence the term 'defined contribution' for a money purchase scheme, and 'defined benefit' for a final salary scheme.

Pension scheme surpluses

At periodic intervals, usually every three years, although sometimes more frequently, a final salary scheme will be valued by an actuary. One of the purposes of the valuation is to compare the value of the investments in the fund against the estimated value of pensions earned up to the date of the valuation. If the investments are worth more than the pension the difference is described as surplus.

The Finance Act 1986 attempted to limit the extent to which surpluses could build up in tax exempt funds. Excessive surpluses must now be reduced by a combination of benefit improvements and contribution reductions or holidays, or repaid to the employer less a 40 per cent tax charge. If no such action is taken to eliminate an excessive surplus, part of the investment income and capital gains of the fund will lose their tax exemption.

Investment medium

A pension scheme will invest the current contributions received from the employer and employees to build up funds from which to provide the benefits when they fall due in the future. The trustees of the scheme, using the services of professional investment managers such as stockbrokers and merchant banks, can invest in their own portfolio of stocks and shares. These schemes are usually referred to as directly invested or self-administered pension schemes. For smaller and medium-sized pension schemes, investment in managed funds operated by insurance companies and other fund managers offers the opportunity to indirectly invest in stockmarkets and property without the costs of individual portfolio management.

Alternatively, the pension contributions can be paid as premiums under an insurance contract. The insurance company will then invest the premiums in stocks and shares, and channel the investment earnings to the pension scheme in the form of interest or bonuses on the insurance contract. The insurance company will generally hold back part of the investment earnings to smooth out market value fluctuations.

The choice of funding arrangements is a complex process and it is usually necessary to obtain independent advice on the approach to be adopted.

Communication

The Social Security Act 1985 provided for greater disclosure of information about company pension schemes to their members. This includes access to scheme trust deeds and rules, annual benefit statements, and annual reports containing a copy of the scheme's audited accounts, actuarial statement and other general information about the scheme.

Apart from the statutory requirement to give information to members, the prohibition of compulsory membership of company pension schemes from April 1988 – and the introduction of personal pensions from July 1988 – has led many employers to make greater efforts to 'sell' their schemes to employees.

The advice which pension scheme managers and administrators give to employees can, in some cases, be subject to the Financial Services Act 1986. The Act covers advising on investments and arranging deals in investments, and only persons authorized under the Act may engage in such investment business. Advising employees about joining the company scheme is not investment advice, but advice on the relative merits of particular insurance policies might be.

Unapproved schemes

In addition to introducing the earnings cap for approved schemes, the 1989 Finance Act made changes to the tax laws governing unapproved pension arrangements so as to make it possible for companies to provide additional benefits through unapproved schemes for employees who are subject to the earnings cap. Two types of unapproved scheme are possible, funded or unfunded.

A funded unapproved scheme operates in the same way as an approved scheme except that:

- the employer's contributions paid are taxable on the employee as earned income
- the employee's contributions, if any, are paid from taxed income
- the fund is taxed at the basic rate of income tax on its income and capital gains
- retirement benefits can be taken entirely in the form of a tax-free lump sum (although any benefits paid as pension are taxed as earned income).

Under an unfunded unapproved scheme the employer makes no contributions in advance, but undertakes to provide benefits at retirement. All benefits received are taxable on the employee.

At present few companies have established unapproved pension schemes. However, the number is likely to grow as more employees become subject to the earnings cap.

An alternative way of compensating employees for loss of pension right is simply to offer them a higher salary.

Pensions check-lists

A. *Information about the present arrangements*

Information about the present arrangements can be obtained from the following documents:

- Trust Deed and Rules, plus subsequent deeds of amendment, variation, etc.
- Insurance policies if the scheme is fully or partly insured.
- Member's booklet and any announcements issued to members.
- Annual reports to members, incorporating trustees' report, audited accounts and actuarial statement. An individual statement of benefits will usually be issued to each member with the report.
- Actuarial reports (usually every three years) on the financial position of the scheme.

From these documents, it should be possible to discover basic information about the scheme as follows:

Administration
- Who are the scheme's trustees?
- Who is responsible for the scheme's administration?
- What external advisers does the scheme have?

Inland Revenue approval
Has the Superannuation Funds Office of the Inland Revenue confirmed that the scheme is fully approved under Chapter I, Part XIV of the Income and Corporation Taxes Act 1988, or does the scheme only have interim approval?

State pensions
Is the scheme contracted out of the State Earnings Related Pension Scheme (SERPS)?

Eligibility
- What categories of employee are eligible to join the scheme?
- What are the minimum and maximum entry ages, if any?
- Is there a minimum service requirement?

Pensionable age
What are the normal pensionable ages for men and women?

Benefits on retirement
- Is the scheme final salary or money purchase, or some other basis?
- If final salary, what is the rate of pension for each year of service? What definition of earnings is used to calculate the pension?
- If money purchase, how is the pension determined?
- Is there an option to take a lump sum at retirement, or does the scheme provide a lump sum as well as pension?
- Can employees who work beyond normal pensionable age remain in the scheme? How are their benefits affected?
- What provisions are there for early retirement? How are early retirement benefits calculated? Do these distinguish between early retirement on ill health grounds, redundancy, and voluntary early retirement?
- Is there any provision to increase pensions in payment? Are increases guaranteed or discretionary? What increases have been awarded in recent years?

Benefits on death
- What lump sums and/or spouse's pensions are payable on death in service or after retirement?
- Are children's benefits payable on death? Are these increased if there is no surviving spouse?
- Are death in service benefits limited to pension scheme members?

Benefits on leaving service
- What benefits are payable on leaving service? Does the scheme treat leavers with less than a minimum number of years' service differently from longer servers?
- What increases does the scheme give to any deferred pensions left in the scheme by early leavers?
- What interest does the scheme pay on refunds of members' contributions?

Financing and investment
- Are members required to contribute, and at what rates?
- What are the facilities for paying Additional Voluntary Contributions (AVCs)?
- What is the company's rate of contribution, currently and historically? How is the company's contribution determined?
- How are the contributions invested; in a self-administered fund, managed fund, or other insurance contract? Who are the investment managers?
- Is the investment return linked directly to the performance of investment markets, indirectly linked, or related to interest rates?
- What have the investment rates of return been historically, or rates of bonus, if applicable?

B. Analysis of present arrangements

State Pensions
Has the right contracting out decision been taken? Should the company operate both contracted out and contracted in arrangements?

Eligibility
- Are the conditions for joining the scheme unnecessarily restrictive? Should coverage be extended?
- Should members who opt out of the company scheme in favour of personal pensions be re-admitted on request? More than once?

Pensionable age
- Is the company's policy on pensionable age equally fair to men and women?
- Should a policy of flexible pensionable ages be adopted, whereby retirement is permitted within a range of ages without reducing a member's pension?

Benefits on retirement
- How does the benefit formula compare with other schemes? Does it result it worthwhile pensions?
- Is the definition of final salary appropriate? Can it be simplified or improved on?
- Does the scheme permit lump sum commutation up to the maximum permitted by the Inland Revenue? Are the rates for commuting pension for cash fair?
- Are the benefits for working beyond pensionable age reasonable?
- Are pensions on early retirement reasonable? Are they consistent with the company's personnel policies (see also Pensionable age)?

- How have past pension increases compared with inflation over the same period? Are pensions reviewed frequently enough?

Benefits on death
- Are the benefits on death adequate for the needs of dependants left behind?
- Are widowers' pensions provided in respect of female members on the same terms as widows' pensions?
- Should death in service benefits be provided for all employees regardless of scheme membership?

Benefits on leaving service
- To what extent are early leavers from the scheme penalized, compared with the benefits they would have received for their past service if they had stayed in the scheme?
- If final salary, does the scheme offer a money purchase underpin, or some other method of limiting the early leaver's loss?
- On leaving service, what assistance does the scheme offer in helping members choose between a deferred pension, transfer value to another scheme, or buy-out policy?

Financing and investment
- If contributory, does the scheme provide good value to members in respect of their own contributions?
- Are the AVC arrangements competitive?
- Is the company getting good value for its contributions?
- If final salary, how well funded are the benefits? Are the benefits in respect of past service, after allowing for projected salaries, fully covered by the current assets?
- What allowance is built into the funding rate for discretionary pension increases?
- Under what circumstances can the scheme be wound up? What are members' entitlements in this event?
- How well have the investments been managed? Is the performance independently monitored and reported on?
- Are the investments appropriate for the liabilities of the scheme?

Communications and administration
- Does the scheme produce attractive and intelligible literature about the scheme? Do they get individual statements of benefits which illustrate their entitlements clearly?
- Do members have sufficient access to scheme managers to obtain advice?
- Do the administration systems allow membership data to be readily accessed and processed? Are benefits calculated promptly and accurately?

C. Introducing or amending a pension scheme

The steps a company will need to take when introducing or amending a pension scheme are as follows:

1. Analyze present arrangements.
2. Consult member representatives for members' views on present arrangements.
3. Make a preliminary assessment of the need to change present arrangements and select advisers to help in developing new or revised scheme.

4. In conjunction with advisers, identify and evaluate the alternatives for each aspect of the pension scheme design from the point of view of:
   - corporate objectives
   - market practice of similar companies
   - employee appreciation
   - costs
   - administration.
5. Make decisions on type of scheme, ie insured or self-administered, final salary or money purchase, contracted out, etc.
6. Decide on benefit and contribution levels. Consider special provisions for certain individuals or categories of staff.
7. If a scheme is new, appoint scheme trustees and an administrator, and engage services of any external advisers as required, eg consultants, actuaries, investment managers, insurers, etc. If the scheme is in place, consider any changes to present advisers. Scheme advisers would be responsible for the remaining tasks, or would assist with them.
8. Notify members of new or revised pension provisions. If appropriate, advance notice of intentions may be given to allow for employee representations. Presentations and discussions may be held to explain pension provisions, and allow for queries.
9. Notify relevant authorities in prescribed forms.
10. Establish new or revised administration procedures.

Note: At the time this book went to press the findings of the Goode Report on Occupational Pensions, commissioned following the debacle of the Maxwell Communications pension fund provisions, were published. This made recommendations providing additional protection for pensioners. The findings should be reviewed and taken account of in any further development of organizational pension arrangements.

31

Tax Considerations

Why tax efficiency matters

There are many messages that can be given by an employer to an employee in the design and implementation of sophisticated remuneration packages, especially for senior management and other highly paid employees. To the extent that taxation reduces the amount of salary, bonus or benefit given by an employer to an employee, it reduces the strength of the message that the latter receives. It follows therefore that a tax-efficient package can benefit both employer and employee. From the employer's perspective it can reduce costs, from the employee's perspective it can enhance the benefits of working for that employer. Unfortunately the government has a monopoly on devising tax-free remuneration products. However those that do exist should be used to the full provided that they support the corporate objectives of the employer.

Tax efficiency

A tax-efficient benefit is one for which the tax payable on the cost of providing the benefit is less than the tax that would be payable by the employer and employee on the equivalent cash sum. In the past, tax efficiency was one of the main reasons for the proliferation of benefits, but it has become progressively less important as governments have tightened up the fiscal rules relating to employee benefits. Pension schemes, however, are still highly tax efficient, as are company cars although, in the latter case, this is being steadily eroded by government legislation.

Although the pursuit of tax efficiency is not of such paramount importance as formerly, it is still necessary to understand the principles and practice of tax law on benefits, and the law as it stands in 1993 (post Budget Statement 1 March 1993) is summarized later in this chapter. But because fiscal regulations are constantly changing, it is essential to update these after every Budget or other piece of fiscal legislation or court decision. It is also necessary to remember that tax legislation, like any form of legislation, can be interpreted in many different ways. It is therefore always advisable to obtain advice from a tax specialist and/or the Inland Revenue before introducing or changing a benefit. It is also advisable to review benefits after each Budget to assess the implications of any changes.

The tax considerations affecting benefits are the most important ones from the point of view of reward management policies and practices. But they need to be considered within the context of the general provisions of tax law, which are summarized below.

The basics of tax law

For most employers, the tax considerations affecting their employees' rewards are

401

contained in that body of law and practice known to taxation practitioners as Schedule E. Income tax was introduced in the UK as a temporary measure to finance the war against Napoleon, and to this day it remains a 'temporary' tax that must be re-enacted each year or lapse. The schedular system of taxation in the UK has its roots in the earliest days of income tax, when the notion was introduced that, before you could compute the income of a taxpayer, it was first necessary to allocate each specific source of income received to a particular schedule. Specific rules were drawn up to deal with the income of each schedule. For example, rents from land were assessed under Schedule A; income from woodlands was assessed under Schedule B; income from Government Securities under Schedule C and so on. This schedular anachronism was reintroduced in 1842 and it and its anomalies have been with us ever since. Its practical effects are to complicate simple matters and to puzzle taxpayers as to why a simple tax computation can lead to three different demands for tax all payable on three different dates! However, what is important for employers to know is that the schedules are mutually exclusive and employees who are taxable under Schedule E will not have their employment income taxed under any other schedule.

Schedule E

Schedule E is found in the Taxes Acts, but in a sense it transcends those Acts and carries with it its very own charging paragraphs:

- Paragraph 1 of Schedule E provides that tax under the schedule shall be charged in respect of any office or employment on the emoluments therefrom, and provides that tax shall not be chargeable in respect of emoluments of an office or employment under any other paragraph of Schedule E. It is divided into three cases: Case I where the employee is resident – and ordinarily resident – in the UK, Case II where the employee is not ordinarily resident in the UK, and Case III where the employee is resident in the UK.
- Paragraph 2 taxes under Schedule E certain annuities and pensions paid by the Crown.
- Paragraph 3 taxes pensions paid in the UK.
- Paragraph 4 charges pensions paid by government departments to public servants who have been employed abroad; and last of all,
- Paragraph 5 states that the preceding provisions of the Schedule are without prejudice to any other provision in the Tax Acts, directing tax to be charged under the Schedule, and tax so directed to be charged shall be charged accordingly.

Defining emoluments

It follows, therefore, that any *emoluments* will be taxed under Paragraph 1 and that *emoluments* may not be taxed under any other paragraph. Paragraph 5 by contrast provides that, notwithstanding Paragraph 1, if any section in any Tax Act states that tax shall be charged under Schedule E, Paragraph 5 enables such a charge to be made. The obvious conclusion which is to be drawn is that Paragraph 1 taxes emoluments but Paragraph 5 brings within the range to income tax under Schedule E items which are not emoluments.

Two categories of income therefore fall within the potential scope of Schedule E – emoluments and other items which are not emoluments, but which are specifically legislated to be taxed under Schedule E.

The scope of Paragraph 1, commonly known as the general rules of Schedule E, is extremely broad. The definition given by the Taxes Acts is that the expression emoluments shall include all 'salaries, fees, wages, perquisites and profits whatsoever'. One advantage of having an antiquated tax system is that we have the benefit of many years of litigation between the Crown and taxpayers and by the time we come to consider the precise meaning of words such as 'perquisites and profits whatsoever', we have the benefit of generations of judicial thought giving us their learned opinions. The 1990 edition of *Tolleys Tax Cases* reported 115 cases dealing with the simple matter of interpreting whether or not certain benefits or payment constituted 'perquisites and profits whatsoever'. Generally it is fair to say that a consensus of tax advisers would be that any payment of money by an employer to an employee on account of services rendered, or to be rendered, be they in the past, present or future, will constitute emoluments.

If assets are provided to employees rather than cash payments made to them, then the value which, in the first instance, would be assessable on the employee is the value of the cash into which they could convert that asset. However, special rules have been introduced for the taxation of directors and other employees earning more than £8,500 a year, and the basis of the taxation liability was shifted to the cost to the employer rather than the second-hand value of any asset. The level of remuneration at which an employee is caught by these benefit rules has not been lifted since 1979 and anyone earning the now modest sum of £8,500 per annum, including all benefits and expenses, will be treated as a director for these purposes. This is called the P11D limit from the designation of the return that has to be submitted to the Inland Revenue, listing the benefits and expenses received by an employee. The erosion of this P11D limit is a deliberate Government policy.

The scope of Paragraph 5 of Schedule E, which charges to income tax items which are not emoluments, encompasses many types of transaction that would not fall within the general rules of Schedule E. For example, restrictive covenants, golden handshakes, share transactions, vouchers, expenses and benefits of directors and higher paid employees, and living accommodation all have their own legislation specifically creating a tax charge under Schedule E.

The PAYE obligations

The Inland Revenue relies on the employer to provide them with details of transactions between the employer and employee. In the first instance, the PAYE system requires the deduction by the employer of tax at source from emoluments paid to the employee and the accounting for that tax direct to the Inland Revenue. For items where a PAYE deduction cannot be made, there are a number of reporting obligations and deadlines which place onerous responsibilities on the employer. For example, all expenses and benefits for higher paid employees have to be reported to the Inland Revenue (on form P11D) by 5 May each year in respect of the tax year ended on 5 April, unless specific dispensation for certain types of expenses has been granted by the Inland Revenue. Similarly, when an employer grants share options to an employee, a return showing full details must be made to the Inland Revenue within 30 days of the end of the tax year.

A table of income tax rates for 1993/94 is set out below.

The table shows how the rate of tax increases from the lower rate of 20 per cent through the basic rate of 25 per cent to the higher rate band of 40 per cent as taxable income grows. From £23,700 (which will be taxed at an effective rate of 24.5 per cent), each pound will be taxed at 40 per cent. It should be noted that taxable income is the income of the individual after deduction of all reliefs and

Table 31.1   *Income tax rates, 1993/94*

Rate %	Slice £	Tax payable £
20	1–2500	500
25	2501–23700	5300
40	23701 upwards	

other tax-deductible expenses or payments. From the employer's perspective, the reliefs and taxable benefits will usually be reflected in the PAYE notice of coding given by the Inland Revenue to the employer and approximately the correct rate of tax will be withheld from the individual's earnings by operation of the PAYE system.

The PAYE system may not, however, fully match up with the tax liabilities of the individual employees and a tax assessment may be issued by the Inspector of Taxes to charge any shortfall. Prior to Finance Act 1989 the taxable amount was based on amounts *earned* by the employee in a tax year irrespective of whether payment was made of the emoluments. Post Finance Act 1989 the taxable amount is now based on sums *received* in a tax year rather than the amount earned.

For the majority of employees on a monthly salary this change will be of little practical effect, but for directors and those paid bonuses there will be some changes. This is a very important change for deferred bonus plans and it makes their introduction and implementation easier from a tax perspective since only when the incentives are paid are they taxable. The main problem area is the definition of when amounts are deemed to be received and when PAYE must be accounted for.

For non-directors this is defined as when payment is made or when the employee becomes entitled to payment, whichever date falls earlier. Thus, if payment of, for example, a bonus is deferred, PAYE should still be accounted for on the date when the employee becomes entitled to payment. For directors, however, the position is more complex in that payment is regarded as being made on the earliest of:

(a)   when payment is actually made;
(b)   when the director is entitled to be paid;
(c)   when earnings of the director are credited in the company's accounts or records (even if they cannot immediately be drawn);
(d)   if the amount of the director's earnings for a particular period is determined before the end of that period, when the period ends; and
(e)   if the amount is determined after the period ends, when the earnings are determined.

The Revenue's guidance note is somewhat confusing in relation to (c) above as it states that an entry for remuneration in accounts being proposed for the company's AGM would not normally constitute the crediting of remuneration to a director, although if the directors are also the controlling shareholders this may not necessarily be the case. It also suggests that a general accounting provision for remuneration not relating to any specific directors will not fall within (c).

An amount will be treated as credited in the company's accounts, even if there is a legal block which prevents the director drawing on the sums, or even if the credit is to an account not specifically in that director's name. However, if the director only becomes entitled to an amount when certain conditions are met, the amount is not 'paid' until the conditions are satisfied.

Taxation of benefits

A benefit in kind is defined as accommodation (other than living accommodation), entertainment, domestic or other services, and other benefits and facilities of whatever nature. This definition is provided by section 154, Taxes Act 1988 and is intended to cover all benefits where no other specific section sets out a charging mechanism such as is stated for company cars, free petrol and cheap-rate loans. The law relating to the taxation of benefits is summarized below.

Benefits for directors and employees paid over £8500 a year

Special rules have been introduced for the taxation of directors and employees paid over £8500 a year which provide for the basis of the tax liability to be shifted to the cost to the employer rather than the second-hand value of the asset.

This level is called the P11D limit from the designation of the return that has to be submitted to the Inland Revenue listing the benefits and expenses by an employee. The threshold of £8500 includes the value of benefits and expenses. The low level of this threshold, which has been maintained deliberately over a number of years, means that the great majority of full-time staff in organizations are above the limit.

Non-taxable benefits

The following benefits are at present (1993) not taxed:

- *Approved Pension Scheme:* in Inland Revenue approved pension schemes no tax charge arises on employees in respect of the contributions made to the pension scheme by the employer; the contributions made by the employees to pension schemes are deductible from earnings for tax purposes; the income accruing to the pension fund does so on a tax-free basis and tax-free lump sums can be given to employees when they retire. To be Inland Revenue approved, the scheme must, amongst other things, limit the pension to two-thirds of final remuneration. There is, however, a pensionable earnings limit on new tax-approved schemes of £75,000, which means that the maximum pension which will attract tax relief is £50,000 (final salary). These limits were introduced in Finance Act 1989 and will increase each year in accordance with the increase in the retail prices index rounded up to the next full percentage point of £60,000 so that no increase will ever be less than £600. In 1992/3 the limit was £75,000 and in the budget of 1993, this amount was frozen and not increased in line with the index.
- *accommodation:* where this is used solely in performing the duties of the appointment. Apart from exemptions for the Prime Minister and Chancellor of the Exchequer, this is unlikely to affect any employer
- *meals:* as long as they are served to employees generally
- *car-parking space:* if this is at or near to the place of work
- *subscriptions:* to approved professional institutions or learned societies.

Benefits for which special taxation rules apply

- *company cars:* where a car is made available to a director or an employee paid over £8500 a year or to his or her family for private use, the employee will be liable to income tax on the cash equivalent, otherwise known as the scale benefit or scale rate. Tax is paid at the highest rate of the employee. For example, the scales applicable in 1993/94 provided for a car of 1401–2000cc, under four years old and costing up to £19,250, to have a scale rate of £1990. If the employee's business mileage for the tax year was between 2500 and 18,000 miles and if his or her marginal tax rate was 25 per cent, the tax cost to the employee would be £747.50. From 1994/95 onwards, the scale charge will be based on the list price of the car rather than on its engine size.

The cash equivalent is increased by half if business travel is less than 2500 miles in the tax year and is reduced by half if business travel in the year exceeds 18,000 miles.

- *petrol:* petrol or other car fuels provided by the company are chargeable to income tax on the basis of the cash equivalent of the benefit in accordance with a car fuel benefit scale or cash equivalent. For example, the scale applicable to higher paid employees in 1993/94 for a car between 1401–2000cc was £760. Thus employees on a marginal tax rate of 25 per cent would pay £190 tax. There will therefore be a benefit as long as they consume more than about 75 gallons a year on private motoring.

The cash equivalent for car fuel is reduced proportionately if the motor car is not available to the employee for the complete tax year (in the same way that the cash equivalent for the motor car is reduced). Similarly, if the motor car is used predominantly for business purposes then the cash equivalent for car fuel is reduced by half. However, there is no provision for increasing the cash equivalent for car fuel by half if the motor car is not used substantially or is a second or subsequent motor car.

If the employee is required to make good the entire expense incurred in providing fuel for his/her private use and he/she does so, or if car fuel is provided only for business travel, then the cash equivalent is reduced to nil. Journeys between the employee's home and normal place of work are regarded as private motoring. If the employee makes good only part of the expenses incurred in providing fuel for his/her private use, the cash equivalent will not be reduced by the amount contributed and the full amount of the cash equivalent will remain taxable. This can be contrasted with payments for the private use of a company car where even a part payment will serve to reduce the cash equivalent.

The cash equivalent for car fuel is only chargeable in respect of motor cars provided by the employer where there is a private use by the employee. It does not apply to fuel provided for an employee's privately-owned motor car where there are different tax considerations.

Employees who use their own car for business purposes can claim a deduction for the business proportion of the running costs, eg insurance, road tax, petrol etc and, in certain limited circumstances, can also claim capital allowances and a deduction for loan interest paid. Mileage allowances paid are taxable if they exceed costs for which relief is due. The Finance Act 1990 has extended the circumstances in which capital allowances and loan interest deductions may be claimed; these are now available (on a pro-rata basis for business use) to any employee who uses his or her car for work. Previously, these were only available if the car was 'necessarily provided' for use in the employment.

The current Voluntary Fixed Profit Car Scheme (FPCS) for 1993/94 is as follows:

Car engine size	Up to 4000 miles	Over 4000 miles
Up to 1000cc	26	15
1001–1500cc	32	18
1501–2000cc	40	22
2001cc upwards	54	30

It is worth pointing out that the FPCS is a voluntary scheme, and any employee is free to 'opt out' of the scheme and have his liability calculated by reference to actual costs incurred. This will require detailed records of business and private mileage and costs incurred to be kept, but it may mean a lower tax liability in some cases

- *relocation allowances:* these can be tax free within limits allowed by the Inland Revenue, but only up to £8000. Disturbance allowances, however, are taxable
- *payments given as compensation for loss of office* (golden handshakes): these are taxable if they amount to more than £30,000
- *uniforms provided by the employer* (within strictly defined limits) are tax free
- *luncheon vouchers:* up to the value of 15p a day are tax free
- *loans:* the benefit from interest-free or low-interest loans is not taxable if the cash equivalent – the difference between the interest charged to the employee, if any – is less than £300. If the cash equivalent is more than £300, then the whole benefit is taxable (including the first £300)
- *workshop nurseries:* are not counted as benefits in kind as long as they are registered nurseries and playgroups for children under five and are provided by the employer at a workplace or elsewhere, or are similar facilities provided for the care of older children after school hours or during holiday periods. Note, however, that a subsidy provided by an employer for a private nursery is treated as a benefit in kind.

Share schemes for directors and employees

A company normally introduces an employee share scheme for the following reasons:

- to provide an incentive for certain key members of the management team by rewarding them according to the performance of the company
- to encourage employees generally to identify with the success or failure of their company by giving them a financial interest in its results.

A simple share scheme might involve giving shares to employees or allowing them to subscribe the shares at less than their market value. However, many employees will not wish both their savings and their jobs to be dependent on the continuing success of the company and therefore may quickly dispose of their shares. If this happens the scheme will achieve its objective only to a limited extent.

More commonly, an employee share scheme is designed to give the individual an equity interest which does not involve any immediate capital outlay and which cannot immediately be sold or realized. One way of achieving this is to grant the employee an option to buy shares at or below their current value, the option to be exercisable only after a period of years. In the past, partly-paid share schemes, where the major part of the issue price is left outstanding, have also been used.

It should be remembered that the incentive effect of employee share schemes may be limited in larger enterprises, since the return which they provide is linked to the performance of the company as a whole measured in terms of the share price and not to the performance of the particular division or section in which the individual is employed. Such schemes will not necessarily lead to employees retaining a long-term equity interest in the company since, if the scheme is to provide any incentive, there must be a date when the participant is freely entitled to dispose of his or her shares and to realize his or her profit in cash.

The basic tax legislation does not permit artificial manipulation to provide remuneration in a disguised form through increase in share values.

Since 1978 however, three types of approved schemes have been introduced which, if certain conditions are met, avoid the tax penalties imposed by the basic legislation and may provide additional tax benefits:

1. Approved profit sharing schemes introduced in the Finance Act 1978.
2. Approved savings-related share option schemes introduced in the Finance Act 1980.
3. Approved share option schemes introduced in the Finance Act 1984.

Although the rules applying to each of the three schemes are similar in many areas, the schemes are very different in concept.

The main contrasting features are as follows:

- shares or options – under an approved profit sharing scheme participants are given shares in the company, whereas under the other two schemes they are given options to subscribe for shares
- eligibility for participation – an approved share option scheme may be applied to selected personnel only, the other two approved schemes must allow all full-time directors and employees to participate on similar terms
- limits on benefits – the maximum which can be provided to an individual under an approved savings-related share option scheme or under an approved profit sharing scheme is much lower than the limit under an approved share option scheme
- cost of shares – shares are provided to participants at no cost under an approved profit sharing scheme, at up to a maximum discount of 20 per cent under an approved savings-related share option scheme, and at up to a maximum discount of 15 per cent under an approved share option scheme
- tax benefits – an approved profit sharing scheme can provide a tax-free benefit since the initial value of the shares which the participant is given is free of all taxes if the shares are held for at least five years. The other two schemes do not provide tax-free benefits but ensure that the benefits obtained are subject to capital gains tax rather than to income tax. Now that the rates of income tax and capital gains tax are equal, this advantage is diminished
- tax deduction – in the case of an approved profit sharing scheme the company may obtain a tax deduction for the cost of providing the shares to the participants, but a deduction is not available for new shares issued when options are exercised under the other two approved schemes.

Taxable benefits

The following cash benefits or benefits in kind are taxable (1993/94) for employees above the earnings limit, apart from certain exceptions noted below:

- payments for expenses which have not been wholly, exclusively and necessarily incurred in the performance of the relevant duties of the employee

- entertaining non-employees of the company
- the cost of medical insurance subscriptions
- the cost of luncheon vouchers above 15p a day.
  (N B this ruling applies to staff earning *below* the earnings limit of £8500 – it is an archaic practice which persists from the time when 3 shillings bought a reasonable three-course meal!)
- the cost of accommodation if not used solely in performing the duties of the appointment
- the cash equivalent of loans or mortgage subsidies (the difference between the interest paid by the employee and the official rate)
- payment of telephone rental charges and private telephone calls (also applies to *all* employees)

It is necessary to re-emphasize, however, that the application of the basic principles of benefit taxation is by no means clear-cut, and it is always advisable to get a ruling from the Inland Revenue on any benefit, for example relocation allowances, where there may be some doubts about tax liabilities. It is particularly important to ensure that employees are warned of potential tax liabilities and the fact that they will be reported on their P11D *before* a benefit is offered to them so that they do not receive any unpleasant surprises when they receive their tax assessment.

Tax and the self-employed

The income tax position for individuals will depend significantly on whether they are liable to income tax as employees under the rules of Schedule E or as self-employed traders under the rules of Schedule D. The tax legislation determining the basis of taxing income either under Schedule D or E has not changed substantially since 1842. Although it is very difficult to state with any certainty whether a particular activity will constitute a trade or an employment because of the great number of conflicting legal decisions there are on the subject, generally speaking companies are aware of whether they are making payments to employees or to independent traders. However, it is not always a clear-cut matter and there is the possibility that, if taken to the Commissioners of Inland Revenue or to the courts, the tax status could be altered with consequent taxation implications. The Inland Revenue has published a leaflet (called IR56 – obtainable from local tax offices) which attempts to help individuals decide if they are employees or self-employed traders.

Using outside advisers

The changing nature of taxation makes it vital to keep up to date with developments in law and Inland Revenue practice. Most personnel departments use a number of publications and from time to time consult outside experts in taxation. These experts will be either tax specialists within the finance function or their external advisers. Or the remuneration function may need to seek independent advice.

One of the difficulties often found after such an encounter is that the tax advice, although sound, is not capable of implementation. Because taxation experts tend to have a narrow perspective, it is essential that the personnel department briefs the expert well and explains the business objectives and context that have created the need to seek advice. It will also need to give an indication of the solutions that will and will not be acceptable, stressing that 'artificial constructions' which run counter to the general direction of salary policy are unlikely to be worth considering.

32

Total Remuneration – Putting the Package Together

Application of the total remuneration or 'remuneration package' concept involves treating all aspects of pay and benefits policy as a whole. It gives valuable discipline and perspective to the overall process of salary and benefits planning and creates a framework within which the different elements of remuneration can be adjusted according to the needs of the organization and the individual. The cost to the company and the value to the individual of each element is assessed with the aim of achieving an appropriate balance between the various components of remuneration for each employee grade or category. The concept applies to all levels of staff, but it is usually of more importance at senior levels because competitive practice and tax considerations have led to the development of a much wider range of benefits in addition to salary for senior executives.

It is generally agreed that senior executives should be paid salaries and be provided with benefits which give enough 'headroom' for the establishment of a series of properly graduated differentials between each level of responsibility below them. At the top level, as indeed elsewhere in most organizations, motivation is not just a matter of money: success, power and influence have substantial incentive value (see Chapter 2). Nevertheless, companies are often judged by their competitors on the salaries paid to directors, whose level of annual remuneration has to be stated by law in the annual report. Despite this, top executive remuneration is not generally as high in cash terms in the UK as it is in the USA and some of Europe although with the internationalization of company operations and executive recruitment this picture is beginning to change. In many cases, however, the benefit provisions are greater, reflecting the tax and other pressures of the last three decades. The distribution of directors' and senior management salaries within this general pattern still varies enormously and is often more unpredictable than one might expect in terms of company size and type (see Chapter 11).

As we have said many times in this book, the approach adopted to remuneration is a matter of individual organization philosophy about the acceptability for each employee level or category of different forms of reward. Practice varies enormously by industrial sector: the pressures imposed by a heavily unionized manufacturing base are very different from those current in the financial sector or from a newly constituted Government Agency.

Assessing and managing the total remuneration package

In assessing the best mix of possible components of remuneration at each level, both from its own and from the employees' point of view, the organization should have a clear idea of the climate and attitudes and culture it wants to achieve and how these meet business needs as well as individual aspirations. Apart from the statutory contributions to state insurance and pension schemes the main elements of total remuneration are:

1. Basic salary, pensions, sick pay, holidays, all-employee profit shares or SAYE share options and other entitlements normally provided for all staff.
2. Benefits or additional remuneration that are available only to staff in limited employee categories: eg incentives and bonuses, executive share options, company cars.
3. Benefits available to all or some staff categories which are only used according to individual need: housing and removal assistance, medical insurance, permanent disability cover, etc.

These will need to be considered in terms of policy on differentials and comparisons with other competing organizations.

All the major salary survey producers give at least an outline of current practice and trends. Consultants with major databases such as Hay and Towers Perrin, Mercer Frazer and Hewitts provide much more detailed analyses of total remuneration packages. As the quality of benefits data improves, especially in club surveys, reasonably reliable information on the components of total remuneration for each job should be available to assist decision making.

It is still, however, not easy to assess the total value of all benefits in addition to pay and to evaluate the pattern of total remuneration against cost parameters for each employee category, because items such as sick pay are always variable and the age and requirements of employees in competing organizations will often be different and so give misleading comparisons. It may be helpful, therefore, just to list the items involved by employee category (see Table 32.1) and check the balance to see if any policy adjustments seem necessary. At the same time the fundamental reason for providing each item and its cost to the organization should be analyzed.

In reviewing policy in this way the following questions which lead on from those in Chapter 29 covering benefits strategy (see p 383) should be asked:

1. Are basic salary levels set at an acceptable and competitive place in relation to the market?
2. Are merit payments, incentives, or bonuses and other performance rewards achieving the results intended?
3. Are basic benefit entitlements of a satisfactory standard?
4. Are status-related differences in benefit entitlements set at the right level? If problems exist what solutions are possible:
   (a) Extension of the benefit to more employee categories if not ruled out by cost considerations?
   (b) Revision of the rules to restrict future entitlement to business need only, phased in at some appropriate time – such as a general salary review – and bought out on an acceptable basis?
5. Are the current entitlements which are based on status differences acceptable in terms of any incentive value that may be gained?
6. What improvements would increase the effectiveness and competitiveness of the package within the organization's remuneration budget limits?
7. Does the remuneration budget need to be amended or enlarged to take

account of measures that may produce long-term benefits in terms of attracting and retaining employees?

8. Is the communication of remuneration entitlements effective and up to date? Is it putting the right message across?

This kind of review really needs to be conducted annually as part of overall compensation policy planning. Proposals for change will need to be considered in the following terms.

1. For which employee categories is the new measure most appropriate?
2. What are the short- and long-term costs?
3. What are the likely effects in terms of employee attitudes? Is the proposed change high in perceived value and low in cost to provide – or the reverse?
4. Is government intervention likely to affect the value or tax effectiveness of new benefits or approaches to salary policy?
5. If this happens could they be bought out without undue resistance?
6. What are the administrative implications of any of the above? Will additional time and/or manpower be involved within the salary function or elsewhere?
7. Is the company verging on the creation of a 'welfare state' within its own walls, so cushioning employees excessively against the realities of the world outside?
8. Would it be more effective to pay higher salaries, provide a limited range of benefits and concentrate on providing a challenging and stimulating work environment in which employees stay and commit themselves to the company's success?
9. How can communication be improved?

Choice – the 'cafeteria' remuneration concept

One way of giving employees a measure of choice on their benefits is to introduce a 'cafeteria' or flexible remuneration system. This allows employees to exercise choice over a range of benefit options within the constraint of total remuneration. Employees, particularly executives with a wider range of benefits, can alter the balance between the range of benefits by cutting back the level of benefits that have less value to them and using the surplus this generates for redistribution to other benefits. For example, an allowance of £500 a month for the contract hire of a car could be reduced to £300 a month, freeing £200 to be allocated to other benefits or, possibly, to be paid as additional salary. The approach is widely used in the USA and now in Australia where the tax regimes encourage the use of this approach, and the range of benefits available – particularly in health care – is wider. In the USA, such systems are used as much to control benefit costs (by having a restricted benefits core and allowing employees to buy 'add-ons') as to meet the requirement for greater choice.

A cafeteria system can enable companies to:

- discover which benefits are popular and which are not, leading to more effective concentration of resources on those benefits welcomed by employees
- develop mechanisms to manage benefit costs more effectively
- inform employees about the real cost of benefits
- make use of a single strategic concept to meet diverse employee needs.

A typical way of managing flexibility in a cafeteria system is to establish a core package of benefits topped up by a percentage of gross pay available for additional

Table 32.1 *An example of total remuneration for a medium-sized employer*

Employee category	Directors	Senior and middle management	Junior management and clerical staff	Manual employees
Salary levels	Ungraded	Grades 1–4	Grades 5–9	Grades 7–12 Union-negotiated in relation to skill
Range (£)	65,000–120,000	25,000–65,000	8,500–25,000	9,000–18,000
Benefits/Entitlements — Pension	Contributory, contracted out of state scheme and 'top hat' pension and provisions for new entrants over the pensions cap	Contributory, contracted out of state scheme	Contributory, contracted out of state scheme	Contributory, contracted in to state scheme
Life assurance	Annual salary × 4	Annual salary × 4	Annual salary × 3	Annual salary × 1
Sick pay	Full pay for 6 months, then permanent disability insurance benefits at $\frac{2}{3}$ salary	Full pay for 13 weeks and half pay for 13 weeks then permanent disability insurance	Full pay for 13 weeks and half pay for 13 weeks then permanent disability insurance	Statutory sick pay entitlements
Medical insurance	Free for directors, spouses and children	Free for managers and spouses	Group scheme discount	Savings scheme to provide income when in hospital
Annual holiday	25 days	25 days	23 days	23 days

Incentive	Target-related—based on profit before tax	Performance-related merit bonus	Merit payment system	Team-based performance rewards
Profit Share		1987 Finance Act Profit Related Pay Scheme	1987 Finance Act Profit Related Pay Scheme	1987 Finance Act Profit Related Pay Scheme
Loan facilities (interest-free)	Season tickets in excess of £250 pa	Season tickets in excess of £250 pa	Season tickets in excess of £250 pa	Season tickets in excess of £250 pa
Company car	Value £25,000,	Value £20,000 senior management and £12,000 for middle management with some flexibility to 'top up' from salary	Salesforce—plus others on a 'job need' basis—value £11,500	On a job need basis only eg. service engineers
Private petrol	Free			
Payment of fees to professional associations	Paid in full	Paid in full—for 2 bodies	Paid in full—for 2 bodies	—
Discount facilities	15% on company products	15% on company products	15% on company products	15% on company products
Subsidized meals	In management dining room	In staff/works restaurants	In staff/works restaurants	In staff/works restaurants
Early/late retirement option	Available	Available	Available	Available
Sports and social facilities	Open to all	Open to all	Open to all	Open to all

(row group label: Benefits/Entitlements)

*This does not in any way present an ideal distribution of pay and benefits, but it does illustrate a framework for assessing acceptability and the necessity for change.

components. But a cafeteria system can be an elaborate affair because of the need to produce comparative valuations of different parts of the package and construct methods of transferring the cash released by foregoing the whole or part of a benefit to another benefit or aspect of remuneration. This is far more difficult to do than it sounds and specialists disagree over approaches to benefits valuation.

Some companies are trying to move away from a complex benefit package to a 'clean cash' system, which provides basic core benefits such as pensions, sick pay and holidays but translates all other items into cash. This may conflict with a policy of maximizing tax efficiency, especially in the case of company cars, but it does give freedom of choice and also reduces administrative costs in the longer term.

The downside of the cafeteria approach

On paper the policy has many attractions for the freedom of choice and improved level of satisfaction with employment conditions it offers. In practice, however, UK experience of the cafeteria approach has been beset with problems, administrative and otherwise, and full applications are therefore still very rare. It is not just a question of devising the alternatives, costing them and working out the possible combinations of options available. There is concern that in the absence of specific legislation to allow flexible benefits, giving choices could adversely affect the tax position of those content with current benefits. Changes in an employee's domestic arrangements can also have a dramatic effect on remuneration options. A manager may have a mid-life crisis and divorce his wife, for instance, and want to exchange a family sized car and high dependants' benefits for a sports saloon and higher cash earnings to pay for exotic holidays. With a UK divorce rate of 1 in 3 this poses very real problems. Such an occurrence is not only inconvenient and costly for the employer; it can also involve making moral judgements on the employee's private life which are best avoided.

The cafeteria approach is still relatively rare and occurs principally as the negotiation of individual packages on recruitment or flexibility between individual benefit entitlements. But the idea of 'menu-driven' remuneration lives on especially for highly paid employees (such as those in the City) with widely varying ideas of how they want their package structured.

Experience indicates that cafeteria arrangements are likely to be most successful when devised by experienced specialist management or employee benefits consultants, and when personal financial counselling is an integral part of the package. There will always need to be a basic level of pay and benefits and the practical reality is that the options available are normally limited in the UK to additional pension provisions, extra life or other insurance cover, variations in the value and model of car supplied, the availability of loans, share purchase or profit sharing, additional leave entitlements and a small collection of more fringe items.

Without specific enabling legislation it remains unlikely that 'cafeteria' schemes will become widespread although at top executive level and where executive search consultants are involved and individual service contracts are negotiated, there is usually some flexibility over the balance of pay and benefits finally agreed. What certainly *is* happening is that flexibilities in individual benefit provisions (especially pensions and cars) continue to grow.

Communicating total remuneration (see Chapter 38)

Informing employees about pay and benefits policy in a clear, appealing and carefully presented manner can have a tangible effect on the level of their satis-

Items typically covered in an employee benefits statement

- The assumptions and basis on which the statement has been drawn up to provide background on reward policies:
  - individual employment status
  - type of pension arrangements including spouse's/children's pensions
- Employee's personal details – taken from payroll records;
- Current remuneration and benefits – typically:
  - basic salary
  - allowances (eg London allowance)
  - profit sharing/share scheme entitlements
  - annual leave entitlements
  - discount entitlements
  - sick pay entitlements
  - permanent disability cover/ill health, early retirement
  - personal accident insurance
  - private medical insurance cover
  - dependant's benefits actually payable for death before or after retirement (including current statutory entitlements)
  - personal retirement benefits actually payable including additional voluntary contribution possibilities/scheme details
  - the basis for reviewing/increasing pensions in payment
  - provisions for early retirement
  - pension entitlements if the employee leaves
  - a total valuation for current benefits.

Such statements can also usefully give summary advice on personal financial planning, eg making a will and reviewing personal assets and liabilities. They may also contain brief details of the pension fund trustees' report to show its financial status.

faction with employment conditions. Appreciation of the value and cost of the elements involved is instructive and ensures that employees are fully aware of what their total remuneration package includes. An approach to this which is increasingly used by major employers is the annual benefits statement. The list above shows what a statement of this kind typically contains, to illustrate how these statements can improve employees' understanding of the policies that affect them. These statements can be produced on an in-house basis provided the payroll and all the necessary associated data are available (preferably computerized). They are usually printed out annually and sent to employees' home addresses as a document to be kept for reference.

PART 8

SPECIAL ASPECTS OF REWARD MANAGEMENT

33

Boardroom Pay

Setting the style of remuneration policy

The principles affecting boardroom pay are generally the same as those described elsewhere in this book for all employees. What is often different is the public visibility of pay decisions and the fact that salary policy for directors can be a determinant of corporate culture. Statements in many company annual reports confirm this, especially when an organization decides to change, and usually sharpen, rewards at the top. The press has always reacted badly to major pay hikes – playing on the politics of envy and the so-called 'bosses' bonanza' syndrome. More recently, major institutional shareholders have taken considerable interest in the link between executive rewards and corporate success and the press in the UK has been increasingly prepared to make adverse comments on what are perceived to be excessive pay increases for chief executives, when increases for the rank and file have been kept at a minimum in times of recession and low inflation.

In the USA the profit/payout link is coming under increasing scrutiny. Minority shareholders are now suing US corporations for excessive executive remuneration, where they believe this prejudices their long-term interests. A particular target is incentive plans, which pay out regardless of profitability as part of the institutionalization of executive capital accrual. Regular articles in *Fortune* and *Business Week* in the US bear witness to growing impatience with unjustifiably high levels of reward.

The way in which boards of directors are paid, or choose to pay themselves, tends to affect the pay philosophy of the organization as a whole. Boards who have adopted and believe in the value of incentives for instance, will push the concept of performance-related pay down through the whole organization. Those who choose to reinforce other values such as loyalty and commitment may place more emphasis on these – but they may, of course, offer performance rewards too.

Critical to the success of the remuneration policies for more junior staff is the level at which boardroom pay is set in relation to the competition. Boards, especially in family companies where remuneration does not come from basic salary alone, do not always appreciate that the level of their basic pay sets the ceiling below which all other salaries generally have to fit. Failing to recognize this can create 'headroom' problems which have an impact on both recruitment and retention. Also potentially damaging are salary levels which employees perceive as excessive in relation to their own rewards. High boardroom pay can and often should be an outward sign of corporate achievement. But the taste can go sour if employees perceive that their pay is 'just a cost to be controlled' and that there is no potential share for them in the organization's success. It is no coincidence that many companies that have gone for generous bonus or incentive schemes or executive share options have also opted to introduce performance-related pay further down, often in addition to some form of all-employee profit sharing or share scheme. Such actions have not just tempered possible accusations of executive greed but have given everyone a potential share in success. They have also of course, in public companies, reassured shareholders that good and competitive remuneration practice has been introduced at all levels. It is, after all, in the interests of shareholders that an effective board be properly remunerated and so be free to get on with the work of running the business.

The Cadbury Report

The report of the Cadbury Committee in 1993 on the Financial Aspects of Corporate Governance made the following important recommendations concerning the remuneration of directors:

- Directors' service contracts should not exceed three years without shareholder approval.
- There should be full and clear disclosure of directors' total emoluments and those of the chairman and the highest paid UK director, including pension contributions and stock options. Separate figures should be given for salary and performance-related elements and the basis upon which performance is measured should be explained.
- Executive directors' pay should be subject to the recommendations of a remuneration committee made up of non-executive directors.

The Cadbury Committee also made the following recommendations on non-executive directors:

- Non-executive directors should bring an independent judgement to bear on issues of strategy, performance and resources, including key appointments and standards of conduct.
- Their fees should reflect the time which they commit to the company.
- Non-executive directors should be appointed for specific terms and their re-appointment should not be automatic.
- They should be selected through a formal process and both this process and their appointment should be a matter for the board as a whole.

Board remuneration committees

In larger public companies and indeed in a growing number of organizations as a whole, directors' remuneration is determined by a non-executive committee of the board. This committee is comprised typically of directors of other organizations and sometimes 'public figures' in the industry sector, and acts on the behalf of shareholders to ensure that:

- basic salaries are maintained at a level which allows the organization to compete effectively for good calibre executives
- annual pay increases are awarded both in relation to performance and to an assessment of market movement based on data from one or more reputable sources
- the basis, targets and payments of executive incentive schemes serve the needs of the business and are satisfactory to shareholders in both the short and the longer term
- the balance of pay and benefits is maintained on a sensible, competitive and defensible basis
- contractual obligations to individual directors are honoured and the contracts themselves are reviewed from time to time to ensure they remain up to date and defensible
- the relationship between boardroom remuneration and policy for employees below this level remains consistent and sensible
- proper and professional advice is sought when policy changes are envisaged either from the organization's own remuneration specialists or, where appropriate, from reputable outside advisers on remuneration, tax and especially on the complexities of the new executive pensions environment.

Composition

As we said earlier, board remuneration committees are normally composed of a group of non-executive directors plus the company chairman or chief executive. The personnel director may well sit in the committee or act as official adviser (often briefed by the company's remuneration specialists). The use of non-executive directors can act as a valuable source of independent experience in reviewing policy as well as a useful brake on enthusiasm for major change until it has been properly considered. Sometimes it may also have to provide a check on excessive boardroom greed – a desire to come top of the salary market can still be a problem at the more aggressive end of some sectors, and this is not always wise for the company. Directors who sit as non-executives on a number of company boards often get a very good idea about which approaches to, say, incentives will or will not work in a particular environment – and why.

Guidelines on the role of board remuneration committees

Pro-Ned (Promotion of Non-Executive Directors) and the Institutional Shareholder's Committee (ISC) have published the following advice for board remuneration committees:

- Companies listed on the London Stock Exchange should have a remuneration committee, the purpose of which is to ensure that the company's directors and senior executives are fairly rewarded for their individual contribution to the company's overall performance.
- Members of the remuneration committee should be independent, non-executive directors and the chairman should be a non-executive director. Decisions on remuneration should be made by those who do not benefit personally from any of their decisions on pay.
- The remuneration committee should have an official remit, recognizing its authority as a committee of the Board; and that all Board members should be clear as to who are committee members and what their remit is.
- The remuneration committee should not only consider the range of executive

directors to be considered, but should also have a thorough knowledge of policies and practices applied below this level. This is desirable so that internal relativities are seen to be sensible and that a fair differential is maintained between the remuneration of Board members and other levels of management.

■ Remuneration should reflect performance properly – 'an objective judgement of appropriate remuneration levels for directors must involve members of the committee in the assessment of individual directors so that remuneration is directly related to performance over time'.

■ Remuneration committees should make their judgements in the light of the competitiveness of directors' remuneration. The committee needs to make external comparisons with directors of other committees of a similar size in a comparable industry sector in the UK and, if relevant, internationally.

■ Clear communication of the decisions for directors' remuneration are critical. Much more information should be included on pay and incentives in the annual report. Salary and performance-related pay should be separated and incentive schemes should be explained.

Method of operation

Board remuneration committees normally review and authorize pay recommendations put by the Chief Executive for subsequent Board approval. This provides the basis for the annual pay review. Such reports will also include revisions to incentive targets, policy on share options and payment structures, reviews of differentials between different directors and, where necessary, changes to pension provisions, car entitlements and other benefits. It cannot be emphasized too strongly that all policy reviews and pay recommendations made by non-executive remuneration committees should be based on well researched fact, as well as the anecdotal experience of the members, however valuable that may be.

Paying non-executive directors

There are two fundamental considerations to be taken into account when setting fees for non-executive directors:

(a) providing reasonable recompense for the time and commitment they contribute to board meetings;

(b) not paying them so much or tying them down with perquisites of various kinds so that they are afraid to be independent and speak their mind when their judgement and experience tells them that the executive directors are wrong about something.

'Reasonable recompense' depends on the following factors:

1. How many board meetings per year the non-executive director is required to attend.

2. Whether he or she also sits on a board committee such as the audit committee or the remuneration committee which involve extra duties and an additional time commitment.

3. How eminent the director is. If he or she is a well-known figure, much sought after for their particular wisdom and expertise, then the fees will have to be greater than they might be for someone with less 'star quality'.

4. Company size – research from sources such as Hay and Monks/Charterhouse shows a fairly clear relationship between the size of non-executive directors' fees and the size of the organization in terms of annual sales turnover. This is

of course also related to the relative eminence of the directors in question – major employers seek non-executives from other major employers or the City who expect, and get, a higher consideration for their services than those from smaller or less prominent organizations.

5.   Position – non-executive chair people are normally paid substantially more than ordinary non-executive directors. This differential partly reflects the additional time input involved and partly the additional responsibility and public exposure that goes with this role. It is also a reality that some non-executive chair people are appointed at milestones in an organization's history when there can be a high risk of failure as well as success. 'High risk' factors usually raise the rewards on offer because a public reputation is at stake.

Maintaining objectivity and independence by not paying too much remains critical to the effectiveness of non-executive directors. If they become dependent on their fees from a company on whose board they sit, they will not perform the independent role required of them by shareholders. For this reason the provision of company cars, pensions etc is generally to be avoided. Most non-executives will in any case already have adequate benefit provisions from their full-time employment and will expect nothing but fees in the form of cash. They should therefore feel free to ask the difficult and searching questions that need to be asked when companies experience problems, when directors make mistakes or when enthusiasm for change needs dispassionate review before the go ahead is given. If non-executives really feel that the organization is taking a wrong turn, they should be in a position to resign, often very publicly, to make their point. Dependence on fees could prevent this.

Fees for non-executive directors should be reviewed regularly in the same way as directors' remuneration as a whole. An annual review is sensible, although in times of low inflation an adjustment is not always carried out. Trends in this area should be monitored from reputable sources to ensure that practice is kept competitive.

The balance between basic salary and incentives for full-time directors

Basic salary differentials

Differentials in basic salary exist in the UK between directors in different functions and between the board as a whole and the chief executive. Differences between directors by function are normally market related – based on survey and other evidence of competitive remuneration practice.

To set the basic salary differential between the managing director or chief executive and other directors, survey evidence should also be sought. In the early 1990s, evidence from a number of sources suggests that board salaries are, on average, some 70–80 per cent of chief executive's pay. The earnings differential with sales directors may sometimes be lower, or even the reverse (ie higher than the chief executive), where special commission arrangements exist. It may also be narrower for other directors in response to market forces or where recent recruitment has dictated a higher basic salary that has not, as it often does, yet triggered a general review of boardroom pay.

As we have already shown in Chapter 20, the majority of major UK employers operate executive incentive schemes and the payments involved continue to grow as a proportion of basic salary. In more aggressive and performance orientated organizations, incentive payments which exceed 100 per cent of basic salary are being made, sometimes with no 'cap' when profits rise unexpectedly. In good times such payments are, as we have already said, an outward visible sign of company and indeed executive success – the 'applause' given to those who perform well.

The credibility of this approach, however, probably depends in the long-term on whether the beneficiaries are prepared to take the decline in payments as inevitable under the current rules of their schemes when profits fall, or when the country faces an economic recession from which even they cannot escape. Warnings about this have come over the last couple of years from all the major remuneration consultants active in helping companies install sharper rewards for performance.

Such considerations inevitably affect the decision on where to set basic, pensionable salary and what to provide as performance reward. If basic salaries are set competitively, there will be less temptation to 'fudge' the incentive payments in lean years because executives have become more dependent than they should on 'risk' payments. Provision of the benefit of independent personal financial counselling, to help directors plan their incentive payments sensibly in 'good' years, is worth considering (see Chapter 30). People who are creative with the company's money may not always be as shrewd with their own. Professional and confidential assistance from a reputable, independent, outside adviser (check the provisions of the Financial Services Act to see what this now means) should help executives plan their investments and personal financial strategy. It may also help prevent them from giving in to the temptation of overstretching themselves on the back of high incentive payments with an unwise, 'rosy' view of the future.

Before a board decides to implement change in its current salary and incentive arrangements, it needs to consider how this will affect salary policy for staff lower down. A particular concern should be the differential within the level of management just below. The basic salary differential should provide for sensible progression and a reasonable jump on promotion to the legal responsibilities of a full-time directorship.

Ensuring long-term commitment

The use of fixed-term service agreements is often perceived as a benefit as well as a legally required written contract of employment. Such agreements are thought of as status symbols – signs of company commitment to its top executives which also, of course, set out the way in which directors are to be paid and the benefit entitlements they are to get. They are therefore very important in terms of the messages they provide on how remuneration can be expected to reward success.

Deferred or long-term incentives and share options are the two main ways in which remuneration policy can provide messages on the need for loyalty and commitment to the organization.

Deferred incentives are based on the setting of longer-term targets – say those which may take two or three years, sometimes more, to achieve and which are rewarded accordingly. This approach is gaining favour in the UK and is already widespread in the US. The principles covering incentive scheme design set out in Chapter 20 apply. The tax implications of the timing of payments should also be explored (see Chapter 31 on tax considerations). The lowering of top rates of tax to 40 per cent introduced and maintained since the 1988 Budget should help to make deferred incentives more appealing.

Following the 1984 Finance Act, there was an explosion of executive share option schemes in public companies and in private firms able to take advantage of the legislation. These were introduced to cover boards of directors and take maximum advantage of the Act's provisions. Few schemes have been introduced on a performance-related basis, although this pattern may now begin to change (see Chapter 17). What the introduction of this benefit has achieved is a level of commitment among directors to stay in an organization until options can be exercised on a tax effective basis and, more importantly, a very real personal sense of identity with corporate success (although prospective employers can, and do, buy them out). The introduction of these schemes has had a noticeable effect on directors' awareness of what affects their company's share price and which of its activities make City analysts report optimistically on their expectations. This does not, of course, as 'Black Monday' at the end of 1987 and its aftermath showed, prevent share prices falling rapidly, almost regardless of profitability, when a bear market supersedes a raging bull one. But although a bear market can dash the hopes of executives expecting to make a killing when they exercise their options (in practice they just do not exercise while the options are 'under water' – preferring to wait for an upturn in the market) they are good times to give out share options. The gains will be greater if they come to be exercised at a time when the market has risen again. Chapter 20 on share ownership schemes covers the detail of share options and Chapter 21 covers all-employee share schemes and profit sharing.

Individual remuneration packages

Over the last decade or so, a lot has been written about the concept of 'cafeteria' or 'menu-based' remuneration packages. Most of the work, and the practice, has occurred in the US and other countries such as Australia where the tax regime is helpful to this approach. The idea essentially is that highly paid executives should be offered the chance to select how they wish to be paid in terms of cash and benefits and so have their remuneration tailored to their personal ambitions and lifestyle. In practice, in the UK, formal schemes of this kind are a rarity. Our tax regime renders the exchange of benefits for cash unfavourable (tax experts will refer to the case of Heaton v Bell) and the main options come in the form of being able to supplement pension provisions or flexibility to take a smaller or larger car (p 413).

The story does not end there. Many remuneration packages are individually negotiated and tailored at the time of recruitment to a board level appointment. As companies find that they cannot always promote to board level from within, they face increasingly tough negotiations on remuneration packages from those they seek to recruit from outside. There are a number of reasons for this:

1. Directors, perhaps comfortably in post somewhere else and approached by executive search consultants, often feel they are in a good position to negotiate major improvements for themselves as an 'incentive' to move (they might be being enticed into a volatile and precarious environment where job security cannot be guaranteed, or one which is much more publicly exposed).
2. People are more aware than ever of market rates for top executives and see a move as an opportunity to 'catch up' to a more realistic level. People at board level probably expect something of the order of a 20 per cent improvement in earnings to make it worth their while. This makes recruiting top calibre directors from outside very expensive, unless they are working in a sector or organization where they are currently underpriced (a trick the City learned to

good effect for people with transferable skills in less well paid sectors in the rapid expansion surrounding the 'Big Bang' in 1986). Internal relativities may then be upset and cause 'knock-on' costs as other directors' pay is increased to match the new market rate.

3. Directors may employ their own specialist remuneration and sometimes pension advisers to make sure they get a good deal.
4. Being an effective director generally goes with having an ambitious and assertive personality – it is unreal to expect such people not to be shrewd negotiators and to look after their own interests. They may perceive, quite rightly, that they are being brought in to wake up a 'sleepy' organization and see a shake-up on the pay front (which usually means moving to the more competitive end of market practice), as part of a necessary process of change.
5. More rarely, they may be simply greedy, with unrealistic ideas about the remuneration they can command. These ideas are usually based on frag- mentary market data, either from contacts who may have exaggerated the package, or from the newspapers. And an exaggerated view of their worth may be reinforced by the special kind of inexperience that goes with being a high flyer who has risen too far too fast. Such individuals need tactful handling, since their potential contribution may far outweigh the drawbacks of apparent greed, and they may have powerful 'champions' already on the board.

Whatever the circumstances, personnel directors, company secretaries and indeed chief executives increasingly find themselves unable to offer just a 'stan- dard' remuneration package to new boardroom recruits. Faced with demands from an executive they may have spent a long time trying to entice, they will need to have:

■ a willingness to tailor the remuneration package to fit individual requirements;
■ a clear idea of which items of pay they are prepared to negotiate on;
■ the ability to cost out alternatives quickly;
■ a maximum total earnings cost they are prepared to go to to get the executive they are after – this can mean 'anything it takes';
■ a prepared case to defend a package which other directors or even share- holders may perceive as an unacceptable anomaly.

Guiding principles for boardroom remuneration

The following guiding principles on boardroom remuneration have been devel- oped by Hay Management Consultants.

1. Pay policies and practices for executive directors can and should be used to attract and retain executives of outstanding ability and to help focus and reward performance which results in increased sharehold value.
2. The pay of executive directors should be determined on the basis of an explicit pay philosophy and strategy which has been consciously developed to support the organization's business strategy, structure and approach to human resource management.
3. The pay of executive directors should be tailored to the organization's parti- cular culture, management style and competitive environment. Pay can help to reinforce a distinctive culture and management style. The degree to which there is a clearly agreed set of values at Board level can help to foster a desired culture throughout the organization.
4. The pay of executive directors should foster a pay-for-performance orientation

and top management focus on sustained performance and the creation of shareholder value.

5. Executive directors' pay processes should becon ɘ part of the overall management process. Performance objectives and mʳ   ɘs should be consistent with the organization's decision-making processes   d management information systems. If it is not the right measure for the ɪncentive scheme, it is probably not the right measure for making decisions.

6. The design of executive director pay packages should consider the needs of individual directors but not at the expense of underlying goals and objectives. Too many pay schemes in the UK have been developed on the basis of tax efficiency alone with little or no regard for fundamental business objectives.

7. The pay of executive directors should be determined and monitored in a manner which safeguards against self-interest and avoids impropriety. Pay philosophy, scheme design and pay levels should be approved and monitored by independent non-executive directors.

8. While the design of top pay systems can be complex, schemes should be easily understood and clearly communicated. The objective is to influence behaviour and focus efforts, not to strain for over-precise measurements. If directors do not understand the scheme, it will not work.

34

International Remuneration

The continuing development of Third World countries and improved global communications have made it essential for UK companies to compete with an international market in order to survive. UK staff in many organizations will, therefore, find themselves sent abroad to further the development of their employer's overseas interests.

Terms and conditions of employment

The terms and conditions of employment while abroad typically depend upon the nature of the work as in the following two examples:

1. *Feasibility studies:* Where an employee or team of employees visit a territory to assess the potential market for their company's goods or services. These visits rarely last longer than a month and the method of payment is usually no more sophisticated than a reimbursement of expenses.
2. *Contract work:* Construction or civil engineering companies typically recruit contract staff for specific projects. Food and accommodation is often provided on site in which case there might be no local currency payment. A lump sum for the contract, agreed in advance, is then paid in the UK.

Alternatively, or additionally, terms and conditions of employment may be determined by the type of assignment as in the following three examples:

1. *Short-term assignments:* The definition of a short-term assignment varies from company to company but often refers to a period which does not exceed six months. Some companies choose to make the break point at three months; others at twelve.

    Managers from company headquarters frequently spend periods of approximately six months in the offices of an overseas subsidiary when it is newly acquired or established and, in this capacity, are typical short-term assignees. If the assignment does not exceed three months or so, these employees are usually retained on their UK salary and given a 'daily rate' ('per diem' allowance) in local currency calculated to incorporate the likely costs of hotels, meals, taxis and sundry items such as laundry. Once an assignment exceeds three months' duration, some companies, such as those in the construction or contract software industries, would seek to reduce any per diem rate, possibly by calculating a package which acknowledged the employee as almost of expatriate status. Short-term assignees often benefit from regular trips home.
2. *Expatriate status:* Indigenization is cheap and has distinct local political advantages by comparison with expatriation, but many multinational companies adhere to a policy of mixing the local workforce with at least some

management from UK headquarters. These managers are still employees of the parent company and may be kept on the UK payroll although it is increasingly common for expatriates to be transferred to the local payroll in 'developed' countries.

In order to be operationally effective and win the co-operation of local trading partners, the expatriate is deemed to require at least two years in any territory. The typical length of a 'tour' is three years and the method of payment must, therefore, be more sophisticated than any of the three methods mentioned above. The bulk of the section 'Salary and Allowances' in this chapter deals with alternative methods of expatriate compensation.

3. *Secondment:* Secondment is frequently confused with expatriation and some companies do not distinguish between the two. However, it is generally accepted that the difference is contractual; for the duration of an assignment, a secondee is employed by the subsidiary company rather than the parent company and the source of remuneration is local.

Level of pay

How much expatriates are paid depends upon their job and status, personal commitments, the territory to which they are assigned and other variables.

An expression commonly found in the policy documents of multinational companies runs approximately thus: 'the aim of the expatriate remuneration policy is to ensure that individuals are "neither better nor worse off" as a result of their overseas tour of duty'. This is quite an understatement of the reality and many individuals actively campaign for expatriation in the hope of a substantial improvement in their bank balances.

Such discretion in the wording of policy documents does, however, safeguard the employer against massive expenditure in times of straitened circumstances. The cost of sending an employee abroad far exceeds the salary outlay. In addition, the company must consider the air fares to and from the destination which are not insignificant when individuals are accompanied by their families and may return once or twice a year for leave, or need to go to a holiday resort for rest and recuperation. Accommodation costs, relocation expenses, language training and UK boarding school fees are further financial burdens to be carried by the employer.

As Figure 34.1 (which illustrates the horrendous cost of a failed assignment) shows, many of these costs are incurred at the outset of the tour and will not be refunded if the incumbent proves unsatisfactory and returns home. On the contrary, the company will be forced to duplicate costs if the market is valuable and an immediate replacement must be sent.

The financial embarrassment of a failed expatriate assignment has led some of the major multinationals to concentrate carefully upon their expatriate selection techniques. A variety of questionnaires and psychometric tests are in use but most employers still base their decisions on interviews. Likewise, research into the stress caused by international relocation has strengthened the case for comprehensive briefing sessions prior to departure. Language tuition and independent financial counselling are often arranged for expatriates at this stage and are recognized as diminishing anxiety quite considerably.

Companies should remember that this anxiety and sense of displacement recurs when the individuals are repatriated. The problems of re-entry have been researched in some detail in recent years and good employers now recognize that

Annual gross salary	£ 52047
Recruitment costs	£ 14850
Briefing	£ 2360
Medical screening	£ 530
Medical and Repatriation Insurance (BUPA)	£ 1400
Removal costs	£ 4355
Furniture storage	£ 633
Air fares	£ 10200
Boarding schools (UK)	£ 8954
Local school	£ 4505
Outfit allowance	£ 650
Accommodation	
Agent's fee	£ 3640
Rent	£ 48474
Club	
Entrance fee	£ 2400
Annual subscription	£ 640
Utilities	£ 2262
Company car	£ 5305
Total cost	£163205

A further consideration is the employer's contribution towards national insurance for the first year of assignment.

In the example where free accomodation is given, the contributions would be:
HK$ 579802 × 0.104 = HK$ 60,299 = UK£ 5,413

Where an accommodation allowance is given, the contribution would be:
HK$ 1204865 × 0.104 = HK$ 125,306 = UK£ 11,248

Source: Information provided by Employment Conditions Abroad Limited, a leading European information and advisory service specializing in expatriate salaries and benefits worldwide, and terms and conditions of employment

Note: The assumptions about the employee's circumstances are given in Figure 34.2 on p 433.

Figure 34.1   *The effective cost of a failed assignment to Hong Kong*

the assignment does not end with the expatriate's return to the home county. Employees should be made aware that practical assistance and counselling are available to them, should they require them.

Salary and allowances

Methods of payment vary not only between companies but also between locations. There are three principal methods:

- budget system
- market rate
- balance sheet

Budget system

This payment method aims to assess the costs incurred by the expatriate, both in the home country and in the host country. These costs are then combined and expressed in a single currency – usually that of the host country – and grossed up for tax.

The major drawback of this system is that, in areas with high inflation or volatile exchange rates such as Central America, it requires constant adjustment and is therefore time-consuming and costly to administer.

UK-based companies are really the only organizations which operate the budget system, and those that do tend to be the larger, more paternalistic ones which cling to well-established but somewhat obsolete administrative procedures through laziness or sentimentality.

Market rate

Market pressure in certain industries or functions is familiar to recruitment and personnel professionals in the UK. International markets are no different. Certain territories – notably the USA and Switzerland – have a higher standard of living which is more than compensated for by high pay expectations, in relation to those of other Western countries.

In territories such as these, it is rare that a salary which would begin to compete with those offered locally could be justified by a cost-of-living survey or inducement payment. The ignominy of managers, sent abroad on perfectly adequate budget or balance sheet packages, who find that their subordinates are earning considerably more than they themselves, would prove insupportable. Consequently, the local market standards are absorbed by foreign companies in high paying countries.

Balance sheet

The balance sheet method is often referred to as the 'build-up' method and is the commonest form of expatriate remuneration package. It is preferred to the budget system for two main reasons, first, it is less cumbersome in administrative terms and is open to greater flexibility, second, it avoids the rather unrealistic expedient of combining the home country and host country commitments. Figure 34.2 shows a worked example of this method for an assignment in Hong Kong.

Its advantage over the market rate is that it is usually less expensive (although the costing-in of certain variables can make it competitive with the market rate if this is politically desirable). It is favoured by personnel departments since its 'build-up' structure is easy to communicate, both in justifying the cost to the company directors and in explaining the 'bottom line' to the outgoing expatriate.

The three components of the balance sheet system – notional home salary, spendable income, and allowances – are described below.

Notional home salary

The notional home salary is a more appropriate term for this component than the alternative 'home-base salary'. The expression 'home-base' implies an element of reality whereas this component is, in almost all organizations, hypothetical.

Its purpose is to serve as the foundation upon which the other components are built. It is used as the basis for pension contributions and is expressed in terms of the salary which the expatriate will receive upon return. It should be updated annually in line with salary increases for home-based 'peer' group staff.

Spendable income

The expression 'spendable income' is so phrased as to distinguish it from deductible income and is sometimes known as 'net disposable income'. It refers to the portion of income which remains after tax, social security, pension and, sometimes, housing and personal savings obligations have been met. It is used as a measure of expenditure levels and is a vital yardstick when ensuring that the expatriate will be 'no worse off' abroad than at home.

Certain companies deduct housing costs from the gross income, taking the view that individuals are committed to the payment of mortgages and rental in the same way as they are to tax, social security and pension contributions. However, housing has proven such an emotive issue over the years that many companies have removed it from the balance sheet altogether and treat it separately.

Allowances
Companies calculate a number of allowances in arriving at the total expatriate remuneration package. These are designed to compensate for disruption and to make the assignment attractive to the employee. Most are applied to the notional home salary but one of them, the cost of living allowance, is based on spendable income.

Cost of living allowance: The cost of living allowance is reached by applying an index to the home country spendable income. The index measures the relative cost, in the host country, of purchasing conventional 'shopping basket' items such as food and clothing.

In an effort to ensure that the expatriate maintains his or her home standard of living, indices inevitably include the pricing of items peculiar to the home country. It follows that many components of the shopping basket will be imported and it is, consequently, rare to find a cost of living index which is lower than that of the home country.

Cost of living information can be obtained from various sources such as: Employment Conditions Abroad Limited and ORC (UK) Limited (see Bibliography).

Like all indices, these should be treated with caution. Some cover diplomatic rather than commercial centres and are, therefore, based on a diplomatic lifestyle which may be very different from that adopted by an expatriate employed by an industrial concern.

Overseas premium: The 'overseas' or 'foreign service' premium is not paid by all companies since many feel that, by awarding a hardship allowance, they are providing sufficient incentive for an employee to move abroad.

Those companies which do award an overseas premium might do so in the form of a flat sum but it is more usual to find a percentage of notional home salary such as 10 per cent or 15 per cent.

The premium is designed to recognize and compensate for disruption. Being away from home, family and friends is seen as a hardship which does not vary with location and this premium is therefore available to all expatriate staff.

Hardship allowance: This allowance constitutes a financial recognition of potential discomfort and difficulty in the host country. Some of the factors to be taken into account are:

- an excessively hot or cold climate
- health hazards
- poor communications
- isolation
- language difficulties
- daily possibility of burglary, kidnap, mugging etc.
- scarcities of food
- poor amenities
- political risk
- *force majeure*, floods, typhoons, earthquakes etc.

As distinct from the overseas premium, the hardship allowance is variable and, for countries such as North America, Australia and parts of Western Europe, a zero percentage is common (although companies which build an overseas premium into their hardship allowance may have a minimum allowance of 10 per cent). Hardship allowances are usually expressed as a percentage of notional home salary. The maximum, for locations of extreme difficulty, rarely exceeds 30 per cent.

Other allowances: There are a variety of other allowances which are peculiar to locations, companies or individual circumstances. Some will be used instead of one of those listed above and some in addition. Some examples are as follows:

- Separation allowance – if personal circumstances or unpleasant conditions in the host country prevent expatriates from taking their family abroad, a separation allowance may be paid. Alternatively, additional trips home may be permitted.
- Kit allowance – a one-off payment for clothing and accessories which expatriates need to buy on account of the particular territory to which they are assigned. Tropical countries requiring light clothing are the obvious examples where kit allowances might be payable.
- Added responsibility allowance (position allowance) – occasionally applicable when the overseas job carries greater responsibility than the notional job in the home country. It is a difficult allowance to manage and, in practice, many expatriations are seen as promotions so the notional home salary is increased accordingly. The added responsibility allowance, therefore, is seldom found.
- Tax equalization allowances are often paid but company policies towards tax on expatriate emoluments are highly variable and are the subject of a separate section later in the chapter.
- Certain locations with punitive tax rates make fiscal concessions for allowances and it is common, in these countries, to find the multinational companies have developed a large portfolio of allowances – for items as far-fetched as soft furnishings – which they do not award elsewhere in the world.

Make-up of the 'balance sheet'
The 'balance sheet' is, therefore, built up in two parts: the 'local' or 'host country' component and the 'home' or 'base country' component.

The local component is calculated by applying the cost of living index to the net (home country) spendable income and converting the result at an appropriate exchange rate.

The home component consists of any other allowances added to that portion of the notional home salary which remains after deductions for home country tax, social security, pension contributions and other expenses. Where spendable income is distinct from commitments such as housing costs and savings, this, too, will be deducted. The remainder tends to represent 25–30 per cent of the notional home salary and is converted at the same exchange rate used for the local component and the two, combined, form the total net pay which is then grossed up for host country tax and social security.

The calculations in Figure 34.2 on page 433 reflect the costs to the company of expatriating a senior executive (notional UK salary £40,000) to Hong Kong. For the purpose of this exercise it has been assumed that the expatriate is married with

Senior executive. Married with two children. Non-contributory pension fund.

Index for Hong Kong   UK = 100.0
                                     Hong Kong = 141.9

Exchange Rate UK£ 1 = HK$ 11.14

UK salary	£ 40,000
Net	£ 29,267
Income	£ 19,527
Housing and savings	£ 9,740

Local spending component = UK Spendable Income × Index/100 × exchange rate

$$= 19,527 \times 4.19 \times 11.14$$
$$= HK\$ 248,400$$

Home component	: Housing and savings	£ 9,740
	: Expatriate incentive (i)	£ 6,000
	: Location allowances (ii)	£ 4,000
	: Class I contributions (iii)	£ 1,421
	Total	£ 21,161
		= HK$ 235,743

Notes (i)   Given as an incentive to be expatriated – 15% of UK notional salary.
      (ii) Specific to location of assignment ranging from 0% to 30% of UK notional salary – 10% for Hong Kong.
      (iii) Assume UK social security contributions. After the first year class 1 contributions will cease and class III contributions will be paid.

Total Hong Kong dollar requirement = HK$ 484,134 net

This figure assumes that the expatriate receives free accomodation.
Therefore the following options exist:
   (a) provide free accommodation and gross the salary up to give the expatriate sufficient to cover the extra tax liability;
   (b) give an accommodation allowance in addition to the guaranteed net salary and gross this up for Hong Kong tax.
NB At this level of salary Hong Kong tax is equivalent to 15% of gross salary.

Assume cost of accommodation = HK$ 540,000 (3 bedroom flat–midlevels)
   (a) free accommodation – taxable value 10% of gross salary

Gross	= HK$	579,802
Taxable gross	= HK$	637,782
Tax	= HK$	95,667
Net	= HK$	484,134

Accommodation allowance of HK$ 540,000 (full rental cost)

(b)	Net	= HK$	484,134
	+ Acco. Allowance	= HK$	540,000
	Total net	= HK$	1,024,134
	Gross	= HK$	1,204,865

Source: Employment Conditions Abroad Limited.

Figure 34.2 *Example of a build-up calculation for an assignment to Hong Kong*

two children, one of whom will remain in a boarding school in the UK, with the other at school in Hong Kong.

The first calculation represents the ongoing costs of a successful assignment using a build-up approach to determine the assignment salary.

One can see from this that the extra cost of providing an accommodation allowance is:

HK$ 1,204,865 – HK$ 484,134 – HK$ 540,000 = HK$ 180,731
$$= \text{\pounds}\ 16,224$$

Additional ongoing costs to company (other than salary)

Company car	HK$	59,100
Utilities	HK$	25,200
Local Education (one child)	HK$	50,200
Home Education (one child)	HK$	99,750
Club	HK$	7,150
Medical Insurance	HK$	15,600
Furniture Storage	HK$	7,050
Air fares	HK$	113,650
Accommodation	HK$	540,000
Total	HK$	917,780
Total ongoing cost	HK$	1,497,582

NB Those costs which have been incurred in sterling have been equated to HK$ at a rate of UK£1 = HK$ 11.14

Source: Employment Conditions Abroad Limited.

Method of payment

When the total earnings have been calculated and expressed in local currency, the company will opt for one of several methods of payment. Many elect to split the salary between home country and host country, particularly in countries such as Greece, Kenya or Indonesia where the home country currency is more stable than that of the host country or where the local remittance facilities are limited. The expatriate thus has the opportunity of building up some capital and is assured of a lump sum in the home country for the servicing of continuing domestic commitments such as mortgage and insurance payments.

A split salary also has political advantages in countries where the market rate is low and where marked contrasts in income and expenditure patterns would be demotivating for the local workforce. If the pay and corresponding lifestyle of the expatriate can be seen as broadly similar to those of the local business community, blind eyes may well be turned to sizeable 'offshore' payments in hard currency.

Most multinationals quote and pay a gross salary but a few guarantee net emoluments to their expatriates. Paying net throughout the world is extremely costly but it does mean that the employer rather than the employee benefits from any exchange rate fluctuations in favour of sterling.

Benefits

Housing

Housing allowances, where paid, are sometimes built into the balance sheet method of remuneration but it is more common for them to be treated as separate items. It is commoner still for accommodation to be provided free of charge although many companies place a ceiling on the annual rental costs that they are prepared to accept. Such ceilings, where enforced, tend to increase in proportion to the seniority of the expatriate. Where employers meet the total rental cost, no matter how high, it is often the case that entertainment is an essential part of the incumbent's expatriate job.

Some of the longer-established multinational companies still own houses around the world. They acquired properties in the early days of business expatriation and have never got around to disposing of them. Thus, a small family, posted to Central America, may find itself forced to live in an immense colonial-style mansion, with three or four servants per person. Relics of the past like this are, however, the exception rather than the rule.

Until recently, employer involvement in home country housing commitments was minimal. Expatriates whose companies paid for pre-departure financial counselling benefited from expert independent advice as to the disposal or otherwise of their home country residence, but few employers went so far as to offer the services of professional relocation companies to their employees.

This lack of involvement seems to be on the decline and there is evidence of a trend among certain companies to assist with home housing. The choices between selling (and risking re-entry during a property boom), letting (and risking bad tenants) and leaving the property empty (and risking squatters) are no longer regarded as decisions that can and must only be made by the home owners and their families.

Utilities

The cost of utilities can be exorbitant in certain overseas locations – particularly in hot climates where the electricity bill is distorted by the constant use of air-conditioning.

Most companies accept that it is their responsibility to make bottled gas, water, electricity and telephones available to their employees abroad but some exact a contribution from the expatriate – usually no more than 20 per cent – to discourage them from wasting power or making too many extravagant international telephone calls. Other companies put a ceiling on the total cost of reimbursing rental and utility costs.

Car

Cars are a common perquisite for expatriate staff of all grades. In many countries, for status or security reasons, a chauffeur/guard is provided by the company in addition to the car. In certain European locations, however, the company car is not as tax-efficient a benefit as it is in the UK and it is not, therefore, local custom to provide any but the most senior employees with a car – or those whose job demands it, such as salesmen. Sensible multinational companies fall in line with market practice in such territories. Likewise, although an expatriate may be entitled to a car in, for instance, Hong Kong or Tokyo, they may elect to waive the benefits on the grounds that driving in such over-populated cities is more difficult and more frustrating than using the public transport system.

Servants

Although the employment of servants may sound like a relic of a bygone century, there are still many countries in the world where it represents affluence, power and status. In such locations, expatriates – and the companies which they represent – are expected by the local populace to conform to best market practice and it is probably not unreasonable to infer that the esteem in which they are held will increase in proportion to the number of servants they employ. They will also, in many cases, be providing much-needed employment and so be contributing to the wealth of the community.

In addition, there are locations, notably African and Central American, where security poses a real threat to anyone whose affluence is notable. In such places, merely being foreign might be enough to trigger thoughts of theft, kidnap or brutality in the minds of the local criminal fraternity. It therefore goes without saying that security guards are an essential part of these remuneration packages.

Club subscriptions

Wherever appropriate, club membership fees and subscriptions are usually paid for by an expatriate's employer. The social environment is seen as an important part of the 'settling-in' process as well as a useful source of business contacts.

Sports clubs are the commonest form of benefit and, in some areas, it may be necessary to provide access to more than one club – for instance where a golf club does not have separate facilities for squash and swimming. This benefit is not to be underestimated since, in many expatriate communities, the waiting list for club membership is long and the cost of joining correspondingly high.

Education expenses

Most companies will pay for the children of expatriates to be educated in the host country. The cost is rarely as high as subsidizing home country (boarding) school fees. In many overseas territories, there may be a limited choice of foreign language schools. Where the method of instruction is, for instance, American, it may be appropriate for the children of the English expatriates to attend only for primary education, owing to UK university entrance requirements.

Many companies will take the view that it is unreasonable to expect students following one syllabus, such as GCSE, to be interrupted by a transfer to the American curriculum and will assist with UK school fees. The level of assistance varies but is commonly a percentage (such as 75 per cent) of basic boarding and tuition expenses up to a set annual maximum. It is most uncommon for companies to finance 'extras' such as fencing, tap dancing or scuba diving!

Some companies place a financial ceiling on their school fee assistance, others: age or grade minima and maxima. A few make provisions for kindergarten in the host country. In general, it is fair to say that global policies are a thing of the past. Cost conscious multinationals are now careful not to pay for UK boarding school fees unnecessarily but aim to take a flexible country-by-country approach, simultaneously assessing the individual requirements of each expatriate family.

Holiday

Annual leave

Holiday entitlement is usually in line with or slightly above home country practice, 25 or 30 working days being the norm. Comparatively ungenerous host country practice – such as the standard fortnight in the USA – tends to be over-ridden. Particularly high hardship regions may encourage companies to allow for holidays in excess of 30 working days.

Public holidays

Host country practice is usually followed with respect to public holidays although, in non-Christian countries, certain UK public holidays such as Christmas Day and Easter Day may be allowed in addition to the local festivals.

Home leave

If a norm had to be quoted, it would probably be a fair generalization to suggest that companies will pay for expatriates and their families to fly back to their home country once per year. However, the variations on this practice are too numerous to mention and are increasing all the time as the issue of home leave becomes more emotive and a matter of as much heated negotiation as the annual pay review.

Location affects the frequency of home leave; areas of extreme hardship often merit a second home trip while areas of low hardship, separated from the home country by a prohibitive air fare, such as Australia, might not even quality for an annual return trip. Indeed, it is quite common for one home trip per tour (usually three years) to be provided from the Antipodes.

Marital status, however, has the most profound effect upon the regularity of home trips. Employees on married accompanied status, particularly those with children, will, as a rule, be provided with the minimum (ie, one return trip per annum). Not surprisingly, bachelor status or married unaccompanied personnel fare rather better. Where companies distinguish between these two latter categories, the bachelor status staff tend to be provided with one extra trip per year on the grounds that it is cheaper for the employer to pay for two single fares that one family trip. In a company where this distinction is understood by the staff, it acts as an incentive for single-status employees to volunteer themselves for expatriate posts. Married unaccompanied personnel, by contrast, would be likely to benefit from three return trips per annum in an effort, on the part of the employer, to minimize their separation from their families.

Rest and recuperation

'R&R' is usually a feature of a remuneration package for an expatriate in a high hardship territory. The intention of the employer is to fly the expatriate (plus family if appropriate) to the nearest 'civilized' location where decent meals, temperate climate and good communications may be enjoyed. R&R visits rarely exceed one week and are often no more than long weekends. The advantages to the employer are twofold: the trip is relatively cheap and the employee returns to work refreshed with minimum disruption to the work schedule.

Pensions

Care should be taken to ensure that the expatriate's final pension is never adversely affected as a result of an overseas assignment. The method for maintaining home country contributions may be complex and specialist advice should be sought from a firm that specializes in this field, such as:

International Pension Plan
Unilife Assurance Group SA
5 Boulevard Joseph II
1840 Luxembourg City
Grand Duchy of Luxembourg

David Callund Esq
Hall-Godwins (Overseas) Consulting Company
Briarcliff House, Kingsmead
Farnborough
Hampshire GU14 7TE
Telephone: 0252 521701
Telex: 858241

Clarkson Puckle Overseas Limited
Ibex House
Minories
London EC3
Telephone: 071-709 0744

Health insurance

It is essential that all overseas personnel are adequately covered for private treatment by health insurance; few countries have National Health Services as sophisticated or generous as that of the UK. The cost of private medical care in the USA, for instance, is exorbitant and the national provisions are almost non-existent. The major UK schemes such as BUPA and PPP have international plans for which the premium rates will vary, depending on the country assignment and the cost of medical treatment there.

Third country nationals

The term TCN (third country national) is literal; it describes an employee, whose home country is not that of his employer, who is expatriated to a third country. They are popular animals for political and economic reasons; they appease international antagonism towards massive corporations with reputations for imposing home country culture upon an array of host countries and they render more credible the corporate claims of 'globalization'. Simultaneously, they are often cheap to employ: Filipinos, Pakistanis and Bangladeshis have proven much more willing to work on construction sites and oil rigs in the Middle East than, for instance, Americans who demand extensive financial incentives to compensate for working in regions which take a dim view of alcohol and women.

The catch phrase which is often used of TCNs is 'getting the balance right', and this can be a problem. As with any expatriate, a decision must be made as to which remuneration method to use but, once an option has been elected, there remain further decisions to be taken. For example, in the case of the balance sheet method, the moment a third country is introduced (the home country of the employee), the question arises as to which home country – that of the employer or the employee – should be used as the base country.

If the employer's home country is used as the base country, some TCNs will be worse off than if their own home country were used as the base (for instance Swiss nationals employed by a UK company) while others will be so ridiculously well-off (for instance a Portuguese national employed by an American company) as to be discontented and demotivated when repatriated to their home country.

If the employee's home country is used as the base country, and the number of TCNs employed is high, the administrative burden of calculating balance sheets from a variety of bases to a variety of hosts would be immense. Nor does this method eliminate internal inequities; it is quite possible for a company to be employing an expatriate (say, British) and a TCN (say, American) in one host country. They might be on the same grade but, owing to the contrast in their home country base, will be earning substantially different host country packages. The problem will be compounded if the host country is lower paying than either home country and their immediate superior, a local national, is earning less than either of them.

That said, the balance sheet system, using the TCN home country as base, is one of the more likely methods to succeed, if handled sensibly and sensitively. TCNs from high-paying home countries are ideal candidates for split salaries and are usually acceptable to local management if the latter are fully briefed as to the potential difficulties. It helps, of course, if the assignment is limited to two or three years. In a similar way, TCNs from low-paying home countries will be more likely to accept internal inequities if the reasons are discussed with them at the outset. Any wounded pride at being worse off, relatively, than other expatriates – and, in high-paying host countries, their local national peers – is usually counter-balanced by their being better off than their contemporaries at home. The budget system is expensive and unwieldy to administer when only two countries have to be considered. The problems multiply when third countries are introduced. It is used increasingly rarely for expatriates and almost never for TCNs.

The market rate is expensive for the employer but quite effective for TCNs when used for high-paying countries; most TCNs will be better off than at home and equity with local managers will render the assignment politically smooth. TCNs sent to low-paying countries may not maintain their home country level of income if they are from a high-paying country and offshore payments will, therefore, have to be introduced into the package. This offshore payment rarely does more than compensate for deficits in the host country market rate and the system, therefore, lacks any element of incentive.

Unfortunately, there is no perfect TCN strategy but there are companies which have applied the balance sheet or market rate successfully – and will continue to do so since the number of TCNs employed around the world is increasing all the time.

Taxation

In most cases, a UK expatriate working abroad for more than 365 days is not liable for UK tax unless his salary is paid in the UK. Local taxation rates, in host countries, however, are enormously variable. True to the policy of 'keeping the expatriate whole' (ie ensuring that they are 'no worse off' in the host country), companies may elect to safeguard them from fiscal penalization by one of the following two methods.

Tax protection

When an expatriate is paid a gross salary and working in a location where the tax rates are low, the employer need make no adjustment, but when the host country tax rates are higher than in the employee's home country, the difference is reimbursed, usually in the home country.

Tax equalization

The system of tax equalization is more equitable than that of tax protection and is therefore favoured by multinationals with large numbers of overseas employees. An expatriate who has benefited from a tax 'windfall' through the protection system, having, for instance, worked in a zero tax country such as Saudi Arabia, may, justifiably, be reluctant to be transferred to a country with rates similar to the UK where 'windfalls' and reimbursements will be equally negligible.

The tax equalization system offers a fairer global policy in that it reimburses tax excesses to those in high tax areas but makes a deduction from the total remuneration of those in low or zero-rated countries. Thus, all staff are maintained on a tax standard which reflects that of the home country.

Net payments

The payment of a net salary not only ensures expatriates throughout the world of fiscal equity but removes the onus of tax administration from the employee in countries which have no equivalent of the PAYE system. However, as mentioned above, it is extremely expensive to operate a net payment system and few companies do so. Several systems have been developed to assist companies with grossing up. Two examples are:

ECA Tax Program
Employment Conditions Abroad Limited
Anchor House
15 Britten Street
London SW3
Telephone: 071-351 7151

Sedgwick Financial Services
The International Employer Ltd
Winterton House
Nixey Close
Slough
Berkshire
Telephone: 0753 516151

35

Mergers and Acquisitions

The implications of a merger or acquisition on pay and conditions of employment do not seem to be considered seriously in most takeover battles. Employees are too often pawns in a game of chess played by remote grand masters. However, acquisitions or mergers do not always live up to expectations and one of the principal reasons for failure is the demotivation of managers and staff. This is inevitable if insufficient attention is paid to their needs and fears.

The degree to which staff are affected by a merger or acquisition does, of course, vary. At one extreme the holding company adopts a completely 'hands off' approach, leaving the acquired company to run its own business, in its own way, and with its own terms and conditions of employment, as long as it delivers the goods. At the other extreme, the acquisition is merged entirely into the parent company and all terms and conditions of employment are 'harmonized'. The employees affected, however, might have different views about the extent to which the process is harmonious.

Between these two extremes there is a measure of choice. In some cases it is only the pension scheme that is merged. In others, it is the pension scheme and all the other benefits that are harmonized, leaving separate pay structures. In making decisions about what should be done and how, the points on the following checklist should be considered jointly and in advance by the parties concerned.

Merger and acquisition check-list

Salary structure

1. *To what extent, if at all, should a common salary structure be introduced?* To answer this question information will be needed, first on the economics and strategy of each business unit to see how far they conform. Then, if the business case emerges, details will be needed on:
   (a) existing salary structures
   (b) organization structures, with salaries and grades for each job
   (c) the distribution of salaries within each grade
   (d) the method of job evaluation used
   (e) policies and procedures for grading or re-grading jobs and for fixing salaries on appointment or promotion
   (f) any terms and conditions negotiated with trade unions or staff associations
   (g) the similarities and differences between the work carried out in each company and, therefore, the type of people employed.
2. *What are the advantages and disadvantages of merging salary structures?* The advantages seem obvious. A common basis is established throughout the

group which facilitates movement and a consistent approach to salary administration. The disadvantage is the disturbance and potential cost of merging, bearing in mind the re-gradings and salary increases that might be necessary as well as the expense of job evaluation. Why go to all this trouble if the operations in the respective companies are dissimilar and they are located in entirely different parts of the country? It could even be damaging.

3. *If salary structures have to be merged, how should this be done?*
    The choice is between:
    (a) a full job evaluation exercise involving re-benchmarking which may be disturbing, time consuming and expensive but may now have to be looked at in the light of recent equal value cases; or
    (b) the arbitrary slotting of jobs into the new structure using existing job descriptions (if any). This could result in gross inequities unless very full job descriptions are available or there is already a good fit between the two salary structures; or
    (c) a compromise between (a) and (b), slotting in jobs without a full evaluation if the fit is obvious, but evaluating doubtful or marginal cases. Note that if pay is negotiated with a trade union or staff association they would have to be involved and they will obviously fight against any detrimental changes.

4. *When the merger takes place, should action be limited to the creation of a common grade structure, defining benefit levels but allowing different salary scales to reflect regional or separately negotiated variations in rates?*
    It is possible to have common grade structures with different salary levels as long as the differences can be justified by reference to market rates.

5. *What should be done about staff whose grade or salary range is changed as a result of merging pay structures?*
    To re-grade people and adjust their salaries to higher levels could be prohibitively expensive. To reduce salaries could be impossible, especially if there are trade unions in existence who carry any weight at all. It might then be necessary to 'red circle' staff affected by grade changes, that is, give them 'personal to job holder' gradings and salary brackets which they retain as long as they are in the same job.

General salary reviews

6. *Should general salary reviews be centralized and take place simultaneously in all locations?*
    The answer is clearly yes if a common salary structure exists or pay is negotiated centrally. If structures or pay levels vary or if site negotiations continue, then it may be best to maintain local arrangements.

Performance management and performance-related pay

7. *Should performance management systems and linked salary review procedures be standardized?*
    It is tempting to say that they should, in the interests of consistency and control and to facilitate career and salary planning for the new group as a whole. But there are strong arguments for maintaining the local scheme if it is operating effectively. Managers who are familiar with one system might resent change. They could be forced to accept it but reluctant appraisers are bad appraisers.

Salary administration procedures

8. *Should standardized procedures operate throughout the new group?*
   A bureaucratic centralized approach is inevitable in some organizations, but if local arrangements work well, why change them for change's sake?

Bonus schemes

9. *Should different arrangements for bonuses be allowed to continue?*
   The answer to this question again depends on how close the links between establishments are. There is much to be said for retaining effective local bonus schemes which have an immediate link to performance as long as they do not conflict too much with group policies.

Profit sharing schemes

10. *What should be done about profit sharing, assuming a scheme exists in one or other or both of the companies?*
    Clearly, if there has been a complete takeover and the merged company loses its status as a separate profit centre or can no longer issue shares under arrangements such as ADST (Approval Deferred Share Trust), then the scheme in the company which has been taken over must be discontinued and employees moved into the takeover company's scheme, if one exists. If there is no scheme in that company, consideration would have to be given to some form of compensation, which could be as high as three times the average of the last three years' payments.

Pension schemes

11. *Should the employees of the acquired firm be transferred into the acquirer's pension fund?*
    This is quite common and, obviously, there is no problem for staff if benefits are better. However, the back-funding of previous pension arrangements in order to pay for improvements can be very expensive, and it may be necessary to maintain separate schemes.
    When the pension scheme in the acquiring company is inferior, it may be possible for members to choose under which scheme they will retire in the unlikely event that both schemes can continue. This could be divisive when staff in the takeover company see that employees in the taken-over company are better off than themselves. However, many employees may leave the taken-over company before retirement and there will only be a handful of genuine anomalies reaching retiring age.
    The Government regulations on personal pensions and the development of portable pensions (see Chapter 30) would also have to be taken into account. Employees in the acquired firm should be told about their rights and given advice on what is best for them to do in their own interests.

Other benefits

12. *To what extent should employee benefits he harmonized, for example:*
    (a) company cars
    (b) free petrol for company cars
    (c) life insurance
    (d) sick pay
    (e) private medical insurance

(f)   mortgage subsidy
(g)   season ticket and other staff loans
(h)   lunch arrangements, including luncheon vouchers
(i)   educational subsidies
(j)   discount facilities?

The degree to which benefits should be harmonized is, like other areas of reward management, a policy question the answer to which depends first on the philosophy of the controlling company (the extent to which it believes in centralization and absolute consistency in the treatment of employees) and secondly, on the circumstances in each company (the degree to which their operations and their geographical locations are linked or adjacent). Considerable variations in benefits between employees in different parts of a group are undesirable, especially if there is any interaction or inter-change between establishments. But a brutal approach to harmonization which significantly reduces the total remuneration of the affected employees will damage morale – will the takeover company want its acquisition to be operated by demotivated people?

Trade unions or staff associations

13.   *If a trade union or staff association has negotiating rights, how should they be involved?*
It is desirable in these circumstances to enter into discussions as soon as possible. The two companies should already have considered the approach they want to adopt and this will provide a basis for consultation and, where negotiated terms and conditions are affected, negotiation.

Communication strategy

Apart from any discussions with bodies representing staff, it is essential to have a communication strategy which ensures that staff in *both* companies know what is going to happen and how it is going to affect them.

This strategy must be prepared in advance and this implies that the questions in the check-list will have been considered before the merger is announced.

36

Reward Policies for New and 'Start-up' Organizations

Key characteristics and influences

Designing reward systems for new organizations is often fraught with difficulty. Most new organizations start with a small group of top executives who introduce their own previous experience and prejudices with the system before anyone like an HR professional gets to look at it. The thinking of the 'start-up' cadre of top executives will typically be based on:

- reward systems from previous employers (bringing the staff handbook/salary policy with you)
- throwing out the bits of these that they found demotivating
- 'cherry picking' from reward policies they have known or liked the sound of from other employers
- selection of benefits (notably pensions) provided on a basis that suits a small high-powered cadre but can't be extended to a more balanced group of employees in a maturing organization
- failure to understand the underlying pluralism of employment – that inevitably not all employees will be fired with the same enthusiasm as top management. They are in it for different reasons, like having a job just round the corner from home, rather than wanting to make their first £1 million by 30.

Where to start

The objectives of a reward system designed to meet the needs of a business start-up are to:

- attract and keep people anxious to make the organization grow and flourish
- reward the risk of coming into a new venture with high rewards if the risk pays off – for those who have real control over development. It is more difficult and probably unrealistic to reward support and mere junior staff on a high risk basis
- provide a sensible basic salary that is reasonably competitive with the market for most staff and highly competitive if rare skills have to be brought in. This is one time to pay at the *top* of the market
- lock people in to give the business a chance – typically with generous share options for senior executives and an all-employee SAYE share scheme or profit sharing for everyone else
- minimize overheads by keeping benefits to a decent basic core until there is

some 'fat' in the system or where competitive pressure indicates additions to the various benefits

- pay out bonus or provide more cash rewards (have a party!) when key milestones in the business plan are successfully achieved
- recognize that in the early days office accommodation may be at best basic and demonstrate willingness to improve conditions as soon as practicable (fresh flowers in an aged but clean reception area – or even in the staff lavatories – can have a significant effect on the way the company is perceived).

Preparing for growth

Whatever the basic components of the reward system in a 'start-up' they should be developed with an eye to appropriateness in a larger organization. Particular attention will be needed in these areas:

- *pensions:* schemes for small partnerships/groups of professionals or the self-employed will *not* easily adapt to cover 140 to 200 employees after three years. Professional advice will be needed to achieve this
- *pay relativities:* starting on a 'spot salary' basis is logical, but internal relativities should always be defensible as the organization grows
- *share options/share schemes:* should be capable of extension – again an area for good professional advice
- *performance rewards:* need to relate to the milestones in the business plan and be based on achievement of agreed objectives/performance standards. Chief executive-driven discretionary bonuses are typically suspect unless the boss really is in the 'tough but fair' (or preferably just the fair) category.

The involvement of investors/auditors/other advisers

If the business is promising and set to grow then sooner rather than later investment will be sought from providers of venture capital. Such organizations typically take a very robust view of reward systems, requiring introduction of share options and highly geared incentives to ensure that the top management group they have entrusted with their money really are fully committed to the business. Fixed term contracts will be required and the high risk/high reward approach mentioned earlier will be what counts.

If the company decides to take itself to the market, typically the unlisted securities market (USM) in the first instance, it will have to ensure that its financial house is in order. Auditors, lawyers and others providing advice at this stage will again go over the elements of executive reward policy and the structure of payroll costs with a fine tooth comb. This is the time when beyond the fringe benefits (company yacht etc) come under scrutiny to potential institutional shareholders.

Such advisers may, or may not always, be mindful of the rationale for pay systems and the messages the individual elements can give. Sad to say, while some are very helpful and constructive, others may have a perspective that is sometimes narrow and confined to their specialism and its accomplishing prejudices – be it over-zealous cost control or a desire to pin down every last detail in fine print. This can come as a shock to a free-wheeling entrepreneurial organization. Faced with criticism about 'unorthodox' approaches to pay from such sources the important questions to ask are:

- is what we are doing illegal in any way (in terms of employment law)?
- are there tax implications we don't know about?

- is it uncompetitive for any reason?
- what messages will the symbolic act of taking it away give?
- are you mistaking 'unorthodox' on our part for real creativity in finding rewards that match our developing culture?
- what culture *should* we be aiming for as a larger/listed organization?
- where can we get advice about putting our house in order if necessary?

Reinforcing the culture of success

Much of the success of a growing organization depends on close and effective team-work. Reward systems need to support this. This means that as organizations grow they have much to gain from implementing:

- performance rewards which reflect team as well as individual achievement
- consistent and as far as possible harmonized benefits
- the beginnings of a formal approach to setting internal relativities so that a defensible 'pecking order' emerges
- management of the reward system by an individual who is a wise custodian of both policy and implementation until the organization is large enough to have a personnel/HR/remuneration professional to do the job.

This last point is, in fact, critical. Experience shows that most of the mistakes made by new business in the reward area are because the wrong person had accountability for it. If they perceive reward management as merely an administrative system, fail to take a broad view of its purpose or (at worst) incompetently develop policies that divide and cause dissent then the business is at risk. Good and promising businesses have foundered on disagreements over pay. Sensible pay policies are the oil in the works of any organization. In a small, growing organization oil can turn to grit very fast indeed.

PART 9

MANAGING REWARD PROCESSES

37

Reward Management Procedures

Reward management procedures are required to achieve and monitor the implementation of reward management policies and to budget for and control payroll costs.

The procedures will be concerned with:

- generally monitoring the implementation of pay policies concerning the pay structure and internal and external relativities;
- conducting pay reviews;
- dealing with specific procedures for fixing pay on appointment or promotion;
- dealing with anomalies;
- budgeting for pay and pay review costs;
- controlling the implementation of pay policies and budgets.

Many of the procedures required can be operated much more effectively with the aid of computer software and the use of computers is discussed at the end of this chapter.

Monitoring the implementation of pay policies and practices

The following pay policies and practices need to be monitored:

- the operation of the pay structure from the point of view of internal and external relativities, the incidence of grade drift and the degree to which the structure is appropriate as a framework for managing rewards;
- the application and impact of performance management and pay-for-performance processes and systems;
- the implementation of pay progression policies.

The check-list set out in Chapter 5 contains questions on all these aspects of reward management, and further criteria for evaluating the effectiveness of pay practices are included in the relevant chapters of this book on job evaluation, pay structures, performance management and performance pay.

There are, however, two additional methods of monitoring – compa-ratio analysis and attrition analysis – which are described below. We also discuss below approaches to monitoring internal and external relativities.

Compa-ratio analysis

A compa-ratio (short for comparative ratio) measures the relationship in a graded pay structure between actual and policy rates of pay as a percentage.

The policy value used is the reference point in the grade structure which represents the target rate for a fully competent individual in any job in the grade. This reference point is aligned to market rates in accordance with the organization's market stance policy. The reference point may be at the midpoint in a symmetrical range (say 100 per cent in a 80–120 per cent range), or the top of the scale in an incremental pay structure. Reference points need not necessarily be placed at the midpoint; organizations are increasingly positioning them at other points in the range.

Compa-ratios provide a shorthand way of answering the question: 'how high, or low, is an organization paying its employees (individually, in groups or in total) relative to its policies on pay levels?' Compa-ratios are calculated as follows:

$$\frac{\text{actual rate of pay}}{\text{reference point rate of pay}} \times 100$$

A compa-ratio of 100 per cent means that actual and policy pay are the same; less than 100 per cent means that pay is below the reference point and greater than 100 per cent means that pay exceeds the reference point.

Types of compa-ratios

There are three types of compa-ratios:

- *The individual compa-ratio* which describes the individual's position in the pay range against the pay policy reference point for the range and can be used to reposition an individual's pay in the range if it is too high or low.
- *The group compa-ratio* which quantifies the relationship between practice and policy for the whole organization or a defined population group (function, department, occupation or job family). It is a calculation of the sum of actual pay as a percentage of the sum of job reference point rates. This ratio has an important part to play in the overall pay management process. It can be used to establish how pay policy has been implemented overall and identify differences between parts of the organization which may indicate problems in the policy itself or in the way it has been implemented by managers. It can also be used to plan and control pay budgets.
- *The average compa-ratio* which is the sum of each individual's compa-ratio divided by the number of individuals. It is therefore not the same as a group compa-ratio which is based on the relationship between the sums of actual rates of pay and the sums of job reference points rates of pay. The average compa-ratio can therefore differ from the group compa-ratio according to the spread of individual compa-ratios at different job sizes. The group ratio is more frequently used.

Interpretation of compa-ratios

Compa-ratios establish differences between policy and practice. The reasons for such differences need to be established. They may be attributable to one or more of the following factors:

- differences in aggregate performance levels or performance ratings;
- differences in average job tenure – average tenure may be short when people leave the job through promotion, transfer or resignation before they have moved far through the range and this would result in a lower compa-ratio. Or a higher ratio may result if people tend to remain in the job for some time;
- the payment of higher rates within the range to people for market reasons which might require recruits to start some way up the range;
- the existence of anomalies after implementing a new pay structure;
- the rate of growth of the organization – a fast-growing organization might recruit more people towards the bottom of the range or, conversely, may be forced to recruit people at high points in the range because of market forces. In a more stable or stagnant organization, however, people may generally have progressed further up their ranges because of a lack of promotion opportunities.

Some differences may be entirely justified, others may need action such as accelerating or decelerating increases or exercising greater control over ratings and pay reviews.

Attrition

Attrition or slippage takes place when employees enter jobs at lower rates of pay than the previous incumbents. If this happens payroll costs will go down given an even flow of starters and leavers and a consistent approach to the determination of rates of pay. In theory attrition can help to finance pay increases within a range. It has been claimed that fixed incremental systems can be entirely self-financing because of attrition, but the conditions under which this can be attained are so exceptional that it probably never happens.

Attrition can be calculated by the formula: *total percentage increase to payroll arising from general or individual pay increases minus total percentage increase in average rates of pay*. If it can be proved that attrition is going to take place the amount involved can be taken into account as a means of at least partly financing individual pay increases. Attrition in a pay system with regular progression through ranges and a fairly even flow of starters and leavers is typically between two and three per cent but this should not be regarded as a norm.

Monitoring internal relativities

Internal relativities can be monitored by carrying out periodical studies of the differentials that exist vertically within departments or between categories of employees. The study should examine the differentials built into the pay structure and also analyse the differences between the average rates of pay at different levels. If it is revealed that because of changes in roles or the impact of pay reviews differentials no longer properly reflect increases in job size and/or are no longer 'felt fair', then further investigations to establish the reasons for this situation can be conducted and, if necessary, corrective action taken.

It is also useful to analyse trends in key pay ratios, eg between the pay of the chief executive and that of the lowest paid category of employee. If, for example this ratio has changed from 7:1 to 6:1 the implications will need to be considered not only for those at either end of the spectrum but also for intermediate jobs in the hierarchy.

Monitoring external relativities

One of the most important pay policy decisions an organization must make is its competitive stance – how it wants its pay levels to relate to the market. Its stance may be to pay above the market, to match the market or to pay less than the market.

Information on competitive rates and trends can be obtained by means of pay surveys, as described in Chapter 11. These can be used to establish the extent to which pay levels are generally keeping pace with the market or whether any particular groups of employees are out of line. The information can be obtained from published, specialized or 'club' surveys. Attention should be paid to trends as well as the distribution of market rates for individual jobs. Care should be taken to include in the selection of benchmark jobs chosen for comparison purposes any occupations or market groups which are particularly sensitive to competitive forces.

The information on external relativities together with general data on current pay practices can be summarized and charted as illustrated in Figure 37.1. This shows:

■ the pay practice line – the average of the actual pay of job holders in each grade;

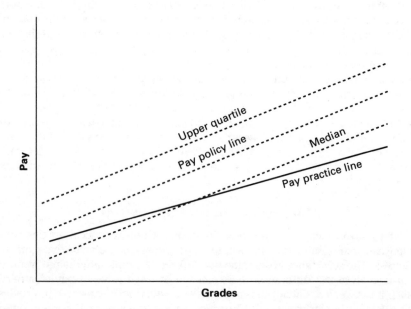

Figure 37.1 *Analysis of pay structure policy and practice in relation to market rates*

- the pay policy line – the line joining the reference points in each grade;
- the median and upper quartile market rate trend lines applicable to the benchmark jobs which are used for pay comparisons.

Particular attention should be paid to the market relativities of key jobs in the various occupations or job families.

This analysis will indicate any need for general market rate increases or a case for looking at the competitive position of particular job families or individual jobs.

Whenever any action is taken to deal with market forces by, eg setting up separate market groups, paying market rate premia or deliberately paying high in the range for some market sensitive jobs, the aim should be to make explicit and identifiable any compromises with internal equity that have been made in response to market pressures.

Market place matching

A decision has to be made on the point in the review period when the aim will be to achieve the chosen competitive stance. An organization is most competitive at the start of the review period and gradually loses ground as pay inflation inevitably takes place in the market. It is necessary for the organization to project the point in the review period where it wants to achieve its competitive position.

There are three basic approaches to making this projection:

- *Lead/lag* – project the position to half way through the review period which means that the organization will lead the projected market for the first six months and lag the projected market for the next six months.
- *Lag/lag* – select the start of the review period, in which case the organization will lag the projected market for the whole of the review period as the market pulls ahead of the policy.
- *Lead/lead* – project the position to the end of the review period so that the organization will lead the market for the full review year as the market gradually catches up with the policy.

Clearly, the lead/lead approach is the most competitive but also the most expensive.

Pay reviews

Objectives

Pay reviews are a major means of implementing the organization's reward policies for improving performance and ensuring the continued motivation and retention of employees. They are also the manifestation to employees of these reward policies.

It is important, therefore, that the way in which reviews are conducted and the outcome for employees reflect these policies and the organization's culture. So far as employees are concerned, the review should, within reason, meet the expectations the organization has created among them as to how they will be rewarded in relation to their performance and contribution. However, the extent to which this can be achieved in practice may be limited by budgetary constraints on the amount of money available for pay increases, which will ultimately be derived from the business performance of the organization, or, in the public sector, Government guidelines on pay increases. The review policy and practice will also be affected if pay is negotiated with trade unions.

When planning and conducting a pay review consideration should be given to the need to:

- provide general 'across-the-board-increases' in response to market trends, increases in the cost of living or negotiated pay settlements;
- conduct a review of the pay structure to reflect the need to respond to external pay market forces or to change differentials;
- provide individuals with performance-related pay increases;
- deal with increases in market rates affecting particular occupations or job families.

An integrated approach

We discuss these aspects of the review separately in the next four sections of this chapter. But this does not imply that they should necessarily be treated as discrete activities. There is an increasing tendency for organizations to relate pay increases entirely to the combined impact of individual performance and any changes in the individual's market worth (sometimes called performance only or merit only increases). Market worth is affected by movements in the market rate applicable to the individual's job and by the fact that the value of individuals to other organizations will increase as they gain experience and achieve higher levels of performance and competence.

An integrated approach means typically that there are no general increases, either for market rate movements or for increases in the cost of living. Everything is done on an individual basis. Clearly this is more appropriate where the type or level of jobs and the culture of the organization are in accord with the concept of individual contracts and, therefore, pay reviews. An integrated approach may be adopted for senior or highly specialized roles where performance is very much related to individual abilities and competence and more account has to be taken of market forces. It may also be appropriate in smaller and rapidly growing organizations which rely on individual endeavour and contribution. But many larger and more bureaucratic organizations are adopting this approach because it does provide them with greater flexibility in targeting pay increases where they are most likely to produce a marked impact on organizational performance.

General reviews

General reviews take place when an across-the-board increase is given to employees in response to general market rate movements, increases in the cost of living or union negotiations. The review may take place at the same time as individual reviews, in which case employees would be informed of the elements of their pay rise attributable either to general increases and/or to their performance, assuming that there is a PRP scheme.

Alternatively, the general review may be conducted separately because the organization believes that employees will be more motivated by distinct performance-related payments at a different time or because it is thought that better control can be exercised over such payments if they are dealt with separately.

Many organizations, however, have reacted against cost-of-living reviews on the grounds that the main priority is to keep their competitive position and this means responding to market rate increases. And, of course, there is no sense in giving both cost-of-living and market rate increases because movements in market rates inevitably reflect any increases that have taken place in the cost of living. So why pay twice?

A further argument against cost-of-living increases is that the organization is not in the business of protecting its employees against inflation. When rates are low this presents no problem, but no organization can cope with rates such as those prevalent in the 1970s, and it would be a hostage to fortune if any indication was made that there was a possibility of doing so in the future (inflation can go up as well as down). Yet another argument in favour of combined increases based on market rate movements and individual performance is that it provides for more flexibility to target increases, especially when financial resources are limited. Increases can be flexed more within budgets according to individual performance and market worth. High achievers can be given more and poor performers may find that their real rate of pay (ie allowing for inflation) has gone down. And there is no reason for this not to happen – why should anyone in a performance-related pay system be given the right to retain their present rate of pay irrespective of their performance?

Structural reviews

Structural reviews take place when it is necessary to make changes to pay ranges following increases in market rates or the cost of living (assuming the latter is accepted as a reason for structural changes, which we believe to be a doubtful proposition). In a graded structure a general market rate increase means that there has been a change in the pay policy line which could be represented by the percentage difference between the old and new range reference points. If existing differentials are to be maintained, this would mean the same percentage increase for all grades.

A structural review may also follow a policy decision to change the pattern of differentials to respond to changes in the organization structure or levels of responsibility. The opportunity to adjust differentials may be taken during a general market-driven structural review but care will have to be taken to avoid too much conflict between the desired pattern of internal relativities and the need to respond to market forces generally.

If it is considered that the existing range sizes should be retained, the range minima and maxima would be increased by the same percentage as the reference point. The range size could be altered by increasing or decreasing the percentage change to range maxima or minima as appropriate and this would affect the scope for pay progression within a range to reflect a decision to provide more or less room for such movement.

A structural review does not mean that individual pay increases should necessarily correspond with any general increases to range reference points or maxima.

Individual reviews

Individual reviews determine performance-related pay increases or special achievement or sustained good performance bonuses if they are allowed as additions or alternatives to base pay rate increases. They also take into account the position to which performance pay progression has brought individuals in their pay ranges or curves – this may influence the size of the performance award or a decision to give a lump sum bonus rather than a pay increase.

The reviews are conducted by reference to performance ratings as described in Chapters 15 and 17. The four main issues concerning individual reviews are timing, budgeting, guidelines for reviewing managers and control.

Timing of individual reviews

As mentioned above, individual reviews can be integrated with general reviews or conducted separately. In either case they may take place at a fixed date, typically once a year, although fast-moving organizations may prefer more frequent reviews, say twice a year. The review date can be varied to suit the circumstances of the organization. This approach can be used to advantage in rapidly growing organizations but it can also be adopted in periods of high inflation or when employee turnover is excessively high. Some organizations like to hold rolling reviews for individuals based on their birthday or starting/promotion date in order to allow more attention to be given to the individual's review. But this system is more difficult to budget for and control and it is particularly hard to give individual attention to ensuring that their pay increases reflect relevant movements in market rates.

Individual review budget

The individual performance review budget should be expressed overall in terms of the percentage increase to the payroll that can be allowed for performance-related increases. The size of the budget will be affected by the following considerations:

- The amount the organization believes it can afford to pay on the basis of budgeted revenue, profit, and payroll costs.
- What the organization thinks it ought to do to address a discrepancy between pay practice and pay policy. For example, group compa-ratio analysis may reveal that the total of actual rates of pay is less or more than the average of reference point rates of pay. If average actual rates are too low (and this is not because of a high influx of new starters) allowance may have to be made in the budget to redress the difference in full or in part, depending on how much the organization can afford to spend. Conversely, if the average of actual pay is above the policy level, the budget may be restricted.
- The organization's policies on pay progression – the size and range of performance-related increases. These policies will have influenced the design of the pay structure (see Chapter 13), and the factors affecting their development and application are considered in Chapter 17. Account should clearly be taken when budgeting, of fundamental considerations concerning how much the organization should be prepared to pay to make performance-related pay a worthwhile basis for motivating employees and awarding them according to their contribution. There is no point in having PRP unless the organization truly regards performance payments as an investment to provide for increased prosperity in the future. To skimp on them unduly in periods of temporary recession could be short-termism at its worst.

The basic budget would be set for the organization as a whole but, within that figure, departmental budgets could be flexed to reflect differences in compa-ratios or any other special circumstances.

Individual review guidelines

Guidelines for managers are necessary on how they should distribute their pay increase budget among their staff. The aim is to achieve as much consistency and equity as possible between departments while still allowing managers a reasonable degree of freedom to manage the distribution of rewards within their departments. The latter principle is in accordance with one of the fundamental tenets of human resource management (HRM) philosophy – that the performance and delivery of HRM is a line management responsibility. How can they exercise this responsibility if their freedom to act in one of the most important aspects of human resource management is unduly constrained?

There will, however, always have to be some limits to freedom, and managers generally prefer some guidance on how to distribute performance awards.

The guidance should start with rating practices – methods of helping managers to rate fairly and to achieve consistency in ratings are discussed in Chapter 15.

The main guidelines on linking pay increases to ratings are described below. In each case, ultimate control would be exercised by imposing an overall budget limit on the increase in the departmental payroll arising from performance-related payments.

Average and min/max guidelines

These indicate the average performance award – say 5 per cent (when market movement is 4–5 per cent), with restrictions on the maximum and minimum pay increases that can be awarded, eg 3 per cent minimum and 10 per cent maximum. This is the simplest form of guideline and gives a fair degree of freedom to managers. It can work well, especially in the absence of an elaborate performance rating system.

Reward/rating guidelines

These relate performance pay increases or bonuses, if they are given, to ratings by the use of a scale such as the one set out in Table 37.1.

The guidelines would also emphasise that anyone whose performance is rated as ineffective should not be eligible for an increase and, in fact, should be going through the disciplinary procedure.

This form of guideline is more directive than the min/max approach. It can help managers to achieve a more consistent relationship between the rating and the reward but it does not achieve any control over the distribution of awards between the guideline increases.

It must also be accepted that managers can and do decide in advance what increases they want to award and adjust their ratings accordingly. It is in recognition of this phenomenon that some organizations conduct pay reviews quite separately from performance reviews and use the ratings purely as a means of indicating pay increases. The ratings can simply signal an exceptional, above average, average or below average increase or no increase at all.

The problem with this approach is ensuring that pay decisions are properly and fairly linked to performance; it is, after all, a process of paying according to performance and not according to managerial whim. It is necessary to emphasize to managers that there should be a proper read-across from their performance review and they should be required to justify their recommended pay increases on this basis.

Table 37.1 *Scale for relating reward to ratings*

Rating	% Increase
Outstanding	10
Very effective	7–8
Effective	5
Developing	3

Table 37.2   *Forced choice performance pay review guidelines*

Rating	% Distribution	% Increase
Outstanding	5	10
Very effective	15	7–8
Effective	60	5
Developing	15	3
Ineffective	5	0

Forced choice distribution guidelines
These, as the name implies, indicate the way in which the different ratings and hence the awards should be distributed amongst employees by defining the percentage who should be rated at each level (see Table 37.2).

This distribution would produce an average award of about 5 per cent. It is based on the normal distribution (see Appendix B) and this could be challenged as being an unjustifiable assumption. It is certainly one that has attracted a lot of criticism when exposed in PRP evaluations. Intelligence *may* be distributed normally in large populations (although even that is not universally accepted) but there is no reason for assuming that the distribution of people according to the way in which they *apply* their intelligence follows the same pattern. In any case, can anyone be confident that the population of any single organization, let alone a department within that organization, conforms to this shape?

In recognition of this situation, organizations often skew the distribution by increasing the proportion at higher levels on the assumption, which may or may not be correct, that they employ higher than average people. Another approach, possibly with more justification, is to avoid forcing ratings into a nil award category and simply indicate that the lowest rating category should apply to, say, 10 per cent of the population. The awards in that category can be 3 per cent for developing or below average employees while ineffective employees should get nothing. The distribution between the two categories would not be forced.

Forced distribution provides the most rigid guidelines and is the easiest to control if the objective is to achieve the greatest degree of conformity. But we can not favour an approach which puts managers in straitjackets and ducks the issue of managing diversity, which is a challenge to which those responsible for reward management policies have to respond positively.

Performance matrices
Performance matrices, as described in Chapter 17, can be used to define performance-related increases according to ratings and position in the pay range. Control can be exercised over performance review costs by analysing the distribution of ratings first (preferably with the help of a computer) and then adjusting the figures in the matrix to ensure that the increase to the payroll would be within the budget. Software is available which can adopt an iterative or 'what if' approach to calculating the cost implications of different configurations of the matrix in the shape of variations in the amount and distribution of awards and/or variations in rating distributions.

Ranking
As described in Chapter 17, this is a form of forced distribution. Managers are asked to rank staff in comparable categories in order of merit (this approach is

often associated with an old fashioned system of merit rating which allocates points according to the assessed level of merit). The rank order is divided into groups and the percentage increase is dependent on the group in which individuals are placed. Thus someone in the top 10 per cent of the rank order might get a 10 per cent increase while someone in the next 10 per cent might get a 7 per cent increase and so on.

Pay modelling

The use of software packages for modelling pay systems has enabled large organizations such as building societies, government agencies and insurance companies with formal pay structures and performance or merit rating procedures to relate pay increases precisely to the ratings.

The increase may be entirely determined by a formula which allocates money according to merit points, each grade having different rates. For example, in a range of £12,000 to £15,000 with a merit scale of 200 points, anyone awarded 50 points or more would receive a merit payment of £6 per point. Thus someone with 60 points would get an increase of 3 per cent of the minimum scale rate of £12,000, ie £360. Someone with 100 points would get 5 per cent, ie £600, and so on.

The value of the points would be determined by the model on the basis of what the company is prepared to pay and the distribution of points ratings. This distribution could be forced, along the lines described above.

Choice of method

The choice between these methods depends on the degree to which the organization believes that the benefits of uniformity and consistency are more important than the benefits of giving a reasonable degree of choice to line managers. It is a matter of opinion. But as we have made plain earlier, our view is that forced distribution systems, if they are operated rigidly (and if that is not the case, the process can hardly be called one of forced distribution), go too far in the direction of constraining the rightful responsibility of managers in this important area. It is better to produce guidelines on appropriate increases for different ratings which can be varied at the discretion of managers as long as *(a)* total increases are within the pay review budget, *(b)* an upper limit for increases is not exceeded unless the circumstances are exceptional, in which case the proposed increase has to be justified, and *(c)* the distribution of awards looks sensible overall, ie it is not skewed unreasonably in either direction.

PROCEDURES FOR GRADING JOBS AND FIXING RATES OF PAY

Job grading

The procedures for grading new jobs or re-grading existing ones should lay down that grading or re-grading can only take place after a proper job evaluation study conducted by a member of the personnel department or a job evaluation panel advised and assisted by a specialist. An appeal system should be built into the procedure.

The steps which can be taken to control grade drift are discussed later in this chapter.

Fixing rates of pay on appointment

Managers should have a major say in pay offers and some freedom to negotiate when necessary but they have to take account of relevant pay policies, and the amounts should normally be confirmed by a member of the personnel function and/or a higher authority.

Policy guidelines should set out the circumstances in which pay offers above the minimum of the range can be made. It is customary to allow a reasonable degree of freedom to make offers up to a certain point, eg the 90 per cent level in an 80–120 per cent pay range. Most pay systems allow offers to be made up to the reference point depending on the extent to which the recruit has the necessary experience, skills and competences. Offers above the reference point should be exceptional because this would leave relatively little room for expansion. They are sometimes made because of market pressures, but they need to be very carefully considered because of the inevitability of grade drift unless the individual is promoted fairly soon.

Promotion increases

Promotion increases should be meaningful, say a minimum of 5 per cent but often 10 per cent or more. They should not normally take the promoted employee above the reference point in the pay range for his or her new job so that there is adequate scope for performance-related increases. One good reason for having reasonably wide differentials is to provide space for promotions.

Dealing with anomalies

Within any pay structure, however carefully monitored and maintained, anomalies will occur and they need to be addressed during a pay review. Correction of anomalies will require higher level increases for those who are under-paid relative to their performance and time in the job, and lower levels of increase for those who are correspondingly over-paid. It is worth noting that over-payment anomalies cannot be corrected in fixed incremental structures, and this is a major disadvantage of such systems.

The cost of anomaly correction should not be huge in normal circumstances if at every review managers are encouraged to 'fine tune' their pay recommendations to ensure that individuals are on the right track within their grade according to their level of performance, competence and time in the job. It is important, therefore, that managers should be given the scope to carry out such fine tuning by making adjustments to the rate of progression as necessary. Of course, they may need guidance on what they can and should do, and they also need information on the relative positions of their staff in the pay structure in relation to policy guidelines (computer printouts can be valuable for this purpose) as a basis for decision-making. The conduct of pay reviews can make a major impact, not only on motivation and commitment, but also on the perceptions of employees about the fairness of the whole process of reward management. It should not, therefore, be carried out mechanistically.

In a severely anomalous situation, which may be found at the implementation stage of a new structure or at a major review, a longer-term correction programme may be necessary either to mitigate the demotivating effects of reducing relative rates of pay or to spread costs over a number of years.

As well as individual anomaly correction there may be a need to correct an historical tendency to over-pay or under-pay whole departments, divisions or functions by applying higher or lower levels of increases over a period of time. This would involve adjustments to pay review budgets and guidelines and, obviously, it would have to be handled with great care.

Pay budgeting

The overall payroll budget is a product of the forecast number of people to be employed at different levels and in different occupations and the rates at which they will be paid during the budget period. It is therefore based on present pay roll costs adjusted for changes in the number and mix of those employed and the forecast cost of general and individual pay increases.

The pay review budget should cover the amount that will be spent on general increases, if any. This would be calculated on the basis of an analysis of trends in 'going rate' increases for particular jobs and of pay movements generally, together with predictions on the likely level of any pay settlements with trade unions.

The pay review budget should also consider the potential costs of individual performance reviews or the cost of any remaining incremental payment systems, possibly making some allowance for forecast attrition if this can be calculated reliably. The considerations affecting the formulation of individual performance review budgets are discussed earlier in this chapter.

Control

Control over the implementation of pay policies generally and pay roll costs in particular will be easier if it is based on:

- a clearly defined and understood pay structure;
- clearly defined pay review guidelines and budgets;
- well defined procedures for grading jobs and fixing rates of pay;
- clear statements of the degree of authority managers have at each level to decide on rates of pay and increases;
- a personnel (HR) function which is capable of monitoring the implementation of pay policies and providing the information and guidance managers require and has the authority and resources (including computer software) to do so;
- a systematic process for monitoring the implementation of pay policies and costs against budgets.

These aspects of control have been covered elsewhere in this book, but there are three further features of a control system which need to be considered; namely, the control of grade drift, the problem of devolving authority to managers to develop 'ownership' of the reward management processes in their departments while still retaining control, and the provision of control information.

Control of grade drift
Grade drift – the tendency for people to be upgraded without a justifiable increase in their job size – can be controlled by the following methods:

- using a strong evaluation panel trained in the job measurement methodology on a formal basis and advised as necessary by an independent expert;
- insisting on rigorous comparisons with well-established benchmark jobs – the re-evaluation of such jobs should be a major exercise;
- ensuring that panels ask pertinent questions on any claims that an increase in responsibility justifies regrading – among these questions it is useful to ask, not only what the increased responsibilities are, but also how they have arisen and what effect this will have on another job if it has lost those responsibilities;
- requiring a sponsoring manager to provide supporting justification;
- resisting demands from managers for jobs to be re-graded simply because of market rate pressures, difficulties in recruitment or threats to leave to get more

money. If these concerns are genuine there are better ways of dealing with them than upgrading by, for example, reconsidering market stance policies, market rate premiums or creating special market groups. What must not be allowed to happen is upgrading someone simply in response to threats.

Developing ownership without losing control

We have frequently referred in this book to the concept that line managers should take ownership of reward practice. This is an aspect of empowerment – devolving down the line the responsibility for making decisions on key management issues – and pay is definitely one of these issues.

Devolution does not mean abdication, and the following steps are required to ensure that freedom is exercised within the framework of generally understood guidelines on corporate pay policies and how they should be implemented:

- Discuss and agree with managers, team leaders and staff the key reward processes which will maintain standards throughout the organization – these will include processes for job evaluation, tracking market rates, performance management, performance rating and paying for performance, skill or competence.
- Ensure that all concerned thoroughly understand and appreciate the new freedoms and their associated responsibilities.
- Train managers and team leaders so that they have the level of knowledge required to make informed, business-led decisions about reward – the aim is to ensure that they are 'pay-literate'.
- Develop computerized personnel information systems which reduce all the bureaucratic reporting which has been necessary in the past. As Clive Wright, Manager, Corporate Remuneration, ICL, said at the Compensation Forum in January 1993:

  'Recording and reviewing the key business numbers at the centre, without involvement of the line operations, is essential, if you want to convince people that empowerment and reduced bureaucracy is actually happening. As long as we keep asking people to send in reports, fill out forms, and sign off changes at detailed levels, no one will believe anything has really changed'.

- Ensure that the central remuneration specialists change from a controlling to a guidance and support role.
- Spell out to all concerned that in providing this guidance and support the HR function has a duty to audit reward management processes departmentally to ensure that they are being used in the most effective way. It must be emphasized that the organization has every right to see that proper procedures are being followed and that, where appropriate, consistent policies are being applied.
- Ensure that managers understand and accept the principle that while they may have a fair degree of independence they are still interdependent with other operating units. They must therefore consider the implications of what they are doing in other parts of the business.
- Achieve, as far as possible, a reasonable balance between empowerment and control. The aim must be to give managers the maximum space and freedom to act. But it is still necessary to ensure that their actions do not contravene fundamental reward management policies and guidelines, or prejudice the

overall impact of reward processes as a means of helping the organization as a whole to move forward in accordance with its strategic plans.

Control information

The best way to generate control information is, of course, through the computer. The less form filling managers have to do the better. In principle, however, control data is required on costs against budget and the outcome of pay reviews and it can be presented – manually or as computer printouts in the formats illustrated in Figures 37.2 and 37.3.

Computerized reward management

The changing environment

The 1980s marked a significant change in the role of human resource professionals in the reward management process – from reactive administrators at the beginning of the decade to proactive decision makers at the end.

This change was helped and, to some degree, stimulated by the rapid developments in information technology that enabled the HR function to break free from the mainframe computer environment which had previously been dominant and so use the output of the technology more creatively. In most organizations the main source of pay data was the payroll system which was maintained either on an in-house mainframe computer or managed externally via a specialist bureau. As these systems were divorced from personnel and designed to meet the requirements of the finance function, they were of limited use to the reward specialist other than as a source of raw data.

With the emergence of the personal computer (PC) came the development of a range of software from databases to spreadsheets that gave managers the freedom to record and analyse data in a way that had previously been impossible. Suddenly, those responsible for reward management had the opportunity to take a much more systematic approach to the salary planning process, and it became possible to test out a range of alternative proposals in short timescales. As the development of end-user computing grew there became a greater need to integrate systems. Manually maintaining different systems which hold common data is an inefficient use of resources and inevitably leads to anomalies.

To overcome this problem the computer industry has developed industry standard file formats such as ASCII and DIF that allow data to be transferred between systems. Most software is now designed with interfacing facilities which means systems can 'talk' to each other and are no longer isolated. Thus payroll, the personnel record system and other reward management software can receive and transmit common items of data.

With the potential for information to move freely between different systems some form of verification and validation process is essential where key programs are being affected. For example, audit trails need to be incorporated into software that updates the payroll system.

Data itself is becoming more accessible. The development of multi-user software and the introduction of LANs (Local Area Networks) mean that it is now possible for several users to 'log onto' the same software simultaneously. The performance problems associated with the early networks has diminished with the introduction of 386 and 486 technology.

Most PCs are used as stand alone systems. However, it is still possible for two

SALARY REVIEW FORM

Department: Proposed by: Date: Sheet:

Date:

Name	Job title	Present salary (£)	Last increase			Assessment (Note 1)	Proposed increase (£)	Proposed salary (£)	Comments (Note 2)
			Amount (£)	Date	Reason				

Note 1: Assessment – A = outstanding, B = very effective, C = satisfactory, D = barely satisfactory, E = unsatisfactory
Note 2: Comment on any special reasons for proposed increase or for amending the proposal

Figure 37.2 *Departmental salary review form*

Department	Number employed	Payroll (£)	Number receiving increase	Proposed payroll (£)	Increase to payroll (£)

Figure 37.3 *Company salary review form*

computers to communicate with each other without the need to download files onto diskette. Over larger distances data can be transmitted over the telephone via a modem. Over short distances software, such as Laplink, allows information to be sent via a cable attached to one of the printer ports.

It is not just data that is becoming more portable, computers themselves are becoming smaller and more powerful. Only a few years ago, the term portable computer referred to a luggable beast weighing 30lbs and capable of running only off the mains. Nowadays it is possible to purchase laptop computers weighing only a few pounds that operate on batteries and yet have more storage capacity and greater processing power. As this book was being finalized the 120Mb, 4lb laptop had become a standard piece of equipment.

As the power of computers increases, it is not only the software that is becoming more sophisticated. HR professionals themselves need to adapt to this changing environment and develop more efficient management practices. Only a few years ago, it would have been difficult to imagine that a compensation manager could plan the salary review for each operating division on site, with line managers using a portable computer. Now they can 'own' the decisions as they are being made.

The computerized options

Within the increasingly complex pay environment, some sort of computer-based system is now considered essential in all but the smallest operation – and often there too! There are a number of different options available to choose from. Deciding which is the best for a particular organization depends on a number of factors, namely:

- the availability of resources – both human and financial;
- the number of employees involved;
- the complexity of the pay structure;
- the stability of the pay structure.

Defining system requirements

Any solution should allow the remuneration specialist to analyse the following:

- *Internal equity* – between individuals and across divisions/functions, (see Figure 37.4) illustrates how pay practice can be analysed using a scattergram. Using a system such as Hay's HayXpert, it is possible to highlight individuals on the scattergram by positioning the cursor on a selected data point. This will instantly provide details of the person and their salary details.
- *External comparisons* – by tracking current practice against survey and other market data.
- *Overall policy development* – testing out new pay initiatives against the employee population they are to cover to determine what the outcomes will be and decide which is the most acceptable. Figure 37.5 analyses the impact on individuals of applying a new pay policy to the existing practice.
- *Individual pay increase models* – once pay policies are agreed, reward specialists need to be able to allocate pay awards, for instance on the basis of factors such as market movements, performance, position in range, time in job and other influences on particular jobs. The system should have the facility to develop models that allow optimization of the distribution of funds based on the criteria used in that organization.

When the pay increase guidelines have been finalized the results need to be

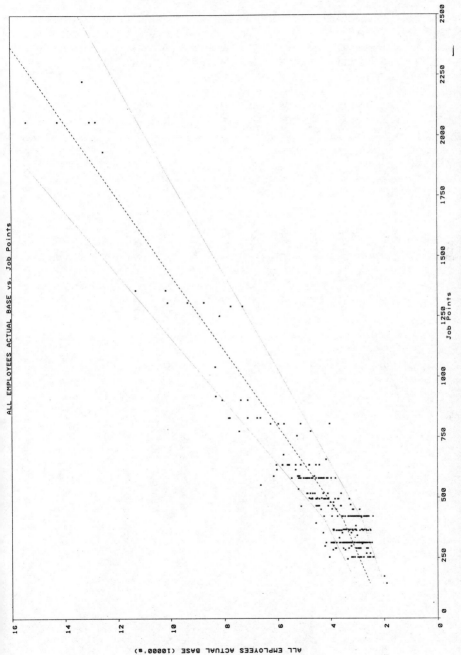

Figure 37.4 *Graphical analysis of pay practice showing lines of best fit and dispersion*

Name Job no	Init Title Job Title	PSF	Job units	Current salary	Compa ratio	80% Min	100% Midpt	120% Max
Adams 11001	AS Managing Director	1.00	2448	77186	90%	68467	85584	102701
Carrington 13001	I Operations Director	1.00	1628	41966	72%	46819	58524	70229
Williamson 12001	CJ Sales/Mkting: Director	1.00	1628	51708	88%	46819	58524	70229
Thomson 13078	W Factory Manager Nwch:	1.00	1192	33723	76%	35309	44136	52963
Johnson 15001	JG Personnel Director	1.00	1182	42759	98%	35045	43806	52567
Comben 12002	MJ Marketing Mgr: – UK	1.00	1096	38069	93%	32774	40968	49162
Cooper 13003	J Factory Manager – SOTON:	1.00	1040	30725	79%	31296	39120	46944
Smith 12003	TJ Sales Manager – UK	1.00	1040	37619	96%	31296	39120	46944

Figure 37.5 *Tabular analysis showing current pay practice against proposed policy*

Inc (£)	Proposed Salary	PIR	Inc (%)	Min	Proposed Midpt	Max	Current Salary	Curr Pos in Range
2735	30087	103 %	10	23401	29251	35101	27352	102 %
2878	26858	92 %	12	23401	29251	35101	23980	90 %
3381	24514	84 %	16	23401	29251	35101	21133	79 %
735	25240	113 %	3	17837	22296	26755	24505	120 %
1686	20421	104 %	9	15680	19600	23520	18735	104 %
2518	20503	105 %	14	15680	19600	23520	17985	100 %
1896	19132	98 %	11	15680	19600	23520	17236	96 %
1709	15948	104 %	12	12298	15373	18448	14239	101 %
1484	14973	97 %	11	12298	15373	18448	13489	96 %
1386	15250	99 %	10	12298	15373	18448	13864	98 %
600	15588	101 %	4	12298	15373	18448	14988	106 %
1335	16173	105 %	9	12298	15373	18448	14838	105 %
1484	14973	97 %	11	12298	15373	18448	13489	96 %
859	15173	111 %	6	10983	13729	16475	14314	113 %

Figure 37.6   *Salary increase report used as a basis for testing out options and costs*

communicated to managers for approval or fine-tuning. This requires the preparation of reports showing all the relevant facts about their subordinates and the funds available. A typical example is illustrated in Figure 37.6. When all the increases have been approved and signed off, employees need to be notified of their new rates of pay. This is usually communicated via a standard letter which can be produced on a proprietary wordprocessing package, using a mail merge facility to incorporate data from the database. Such letters are now commonly personalized to recognize particular achievements and performance ratings. Figure 37.7 is an example of a letter template, which contains a number of variables. The resulting output appears as per Figure 37.8 when the variables are inserted from the merge file.

In addition to the specific functional requirements outlined briefly above, an effective computer-based solution needs to be able to have some general features. These include:

Data transfer facilities
The facility to receive from, and send data to, other systems should be seen as an essential feature of any reward management system.

At the beginning of the planning process the remuneration specialist needs access to the most up-to-date information. A lot of this data, such as salaries, divisional, functional information etc. is already held on the payroll or the main personnel record system. Why reinput the data manually when it can be transferred electronically?

During the review process itself the data may need to be exported into a business graphics or spreadsheet package in order to enhance the presentation of reports and produce some *ad hoc* analyses.

Once the review process is complete relevant data needs to be output into a wordprocessing package to produce the salary notification letter, and updated salaries sent back to the payroll or personnel record system.

There are now industry standard file formats such as ASCII and DIF that enable

PERSONAL

<DATE>

<TITLE> <INITS> <SURNAME>
<DEPT>

Dear <KNOWN_AS>

I am writing to confirm that with effect from March 1st 1993
your base salary will be increased to £<SALARY>. The
attached sheet also details your revised pension and bonus
arrangements.

During the last financial year Cooper Products continued to
experience steady growth in profits and market share despite
increased levels of competition, particularly in the Far
East sector. The year end figures showed both revenue and
profits significantly ahead of budget with performance in
the final quarter exceptionally strong.

This places us in an excellent position for the coming year
and I would like to take this opportunity to thank you for
all your efforts in the last twelve months and look forward
to your continued support during 1993/1994.

Yours sincerely

A B Jones
Managing Director

Figure 37.7   *Template for salary notification letter*

data to be transferred between different computer systems.

Flexible reporting facilities
The salary review process in every organization is different and each has its own
reporting requirements. It is unlikely that these requirements will remain the same
year after year. Changes in the pay structure, for example, will result in changes to
the reporting requirements for both the compensation specialist and individual
managers. If the system is unable to respond to these changes and also any *ad hoc*
queries that may be requested from time to time, it will rapidly become redundant.

The solutions

The customized database
In the past personnel have commissioned customized programs in order to
incorporate all aspects of the salary management process into a single system.
Although the advent of 4GLs (Fourth Generation programming languages), such as

Ms R. Lawson
Marketing Dept.

Dear Rosemary

I am writing to confirm that with effect from March 1st 1993
your base salary will be increased to £25000. The attached
sheet also details your revised pension and bonus
arrangements.

During the last financial year Cooper Products continued to
experience steady growth in profits and market share despite
increased levels of competition, particularly in the Far
East sector. The year end figures showed both revenue and
profits significantly ahead of budget with performance in
the final quarter exceptionally strong.

This places us in an excellent position for the coming year
and I would like to take this opportunity to thank you for
all your efforts in the last twelve months and look forward
to your continued support during 1993/1994.

Yours sincerely

A B Jones
Managing Director

Figure 37.8 *Salary notification letter as printed after the merge routine*

DBase, Paradox and Clipper, have made systems programming quicker, this can
still be an expensive option both in terms of time and money. Besides the obvious
programming time involved, the end-user must devote a considerable amount of
time to system specification and design, testing and implementation. The customized approach tends to be valid for a set, established management process, but
this can become a straitjacket, restricting salary planning options. Building
flexibility into the system design requires a much greater degree of skill and
invariably increases both the cost and lead-time to implementation.

Spreadsheets
Spreadsheets, such as Lotus 1-2-3, Quattro and Excel, are now widely used. These
provide the user with a worksheet area, divided into cells, into which can be
inserted text numbers or formulae. This allows the user to carry out complex 'what
if' analyses, giving the flexibility to make individual or group adjustments and
accommodate policy changes or the demands of individual managers. Each set of
analyses can be saved as a separate file for future recall when final agreement or
approval is received.

Spreadsheets can be printed out in report format or as any one of a number of
different types of graph – XY, histograms, pie-charts etc. Figures 37.9–37.11
illustrate some typical examples. For enhanced presentation it is possible to use

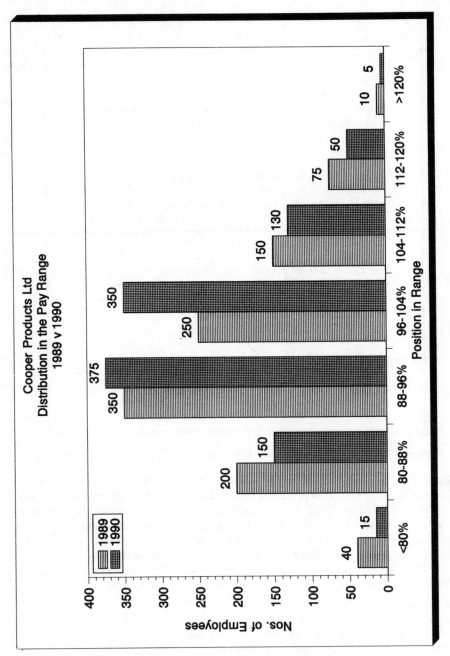

Figure 37.9   *An example of a spreadsheet printout – I*

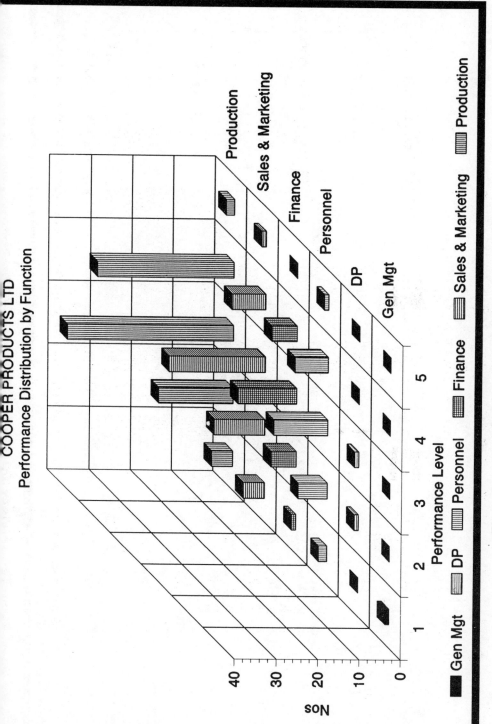

Figure 37.10 *An example of a spreadsheet printout – II*

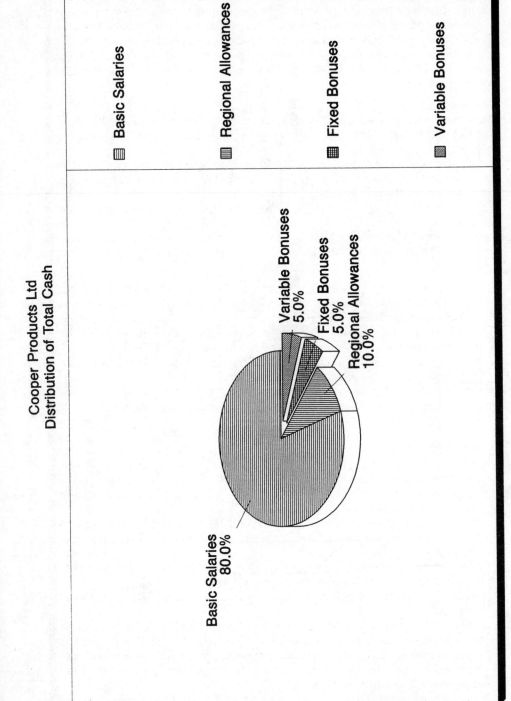

Figure 37.11   An example of a spreadsheet printout – III

specialist business graphics packages such as Harvard Graphics and Freelance.

On the whole, spreadsheets are a very powerful medium for carrying out pay analyses. However, they do have their limitations. Complex pay structures and/or medium-sized databases can become quite cumbersome to deal with and require a significant degree of skill on the part of the operator. Also, most spreadsheets will only function within the available memory on the computer. This means that the average PC is likely to run out of processing space when dealing with medium/large populations.

Proprietary software

Micro-based packages, such as Hay's HayXpert, have been designed specifically to help managers cope with the more sophisticated and flexible remuneration policies that are now emerging.

Most proprietary software of this nature is designed as a standard software shell within which there are a number of functions that allow users to customize the system according to their own requirements.

Before making any commitment, it is important to carry out a detailed evaluation of any package that might look useful to determine whether or not the system is going to meet your requirements both now and in the foreseeable future. Each organization is different but these are the basic points to consider when making your assessment.

1. Does the software do what you want it to do? This might sound obvious, but you need to consider whether the system is capable of providing the sort of outputs that will answer most of the questions that either you, managers or employees are likely to ask. It is extremely difficult to find any software that will meet all your requirements – so draw up a list of priorities.
2. Can the standard software shell be tailored to meet the requirements of your organization?
3. Can it accommodate the complexities of your pay structure and adapt to any possible future changes? Consider, for example, how easily the system would be able to handle a change in the grade structure, or a move from a single pay policy to multiple policies based on functional lines.
4. How will the system perform in your environment? Will it provide acceptable response times on existing and anticipated future volumes of data? Demonstrations on small databases provide impressive response times but enquire about the sort of performance you can expect with your hardware configuration and database size.
5. How does the system fit in with your overall strategy? You should think about how the system is going to communicate with your existing software and other systems in the pipeline.
6. What support and training does the supplier offer? Do they understand your business and the issues you are trying to address?
7. What developments are planned and does the company have a record of delivery?
8. What other resources will you have to budget for? Additional financial resources may be required to fund extra training, the upgrade of existing computer equipment, etc. Don't forget about manpower resources. The successful implementation of any new computer system requires a significant time commitment from end-users.
9. Ask for references and speak to existing users. They are a valuable source of independent advice and can help to highlight potential problems in advance.

A flexible database – some considerations

The database design is an important feature of any system as this ultimately determines the flexibility of the software and the degree to which it can be adapted to your own organization's requirements.

A proprietary system should have a user-defined database, ie the field labels should not be pre-determined. The reason for this is that organizations vary in their structure and employee groupings. Most have a number of types of employee groups each with its own characteristics. An organization must therefore be able to look at its employee groups on a global basis using those elements that are common between them. The user should specify which employee groups need to be set up in the system, the individual elements of each group and their relationships.

For example, within HayXpert, users are able to organize the database into employee groups, referred to as compensation mixes. Typically these groupings are based on the various discrete pay populations within the organization. For example, a manufacturing company may have the following employee groups.

- executives;
- management;
- technical/professional specialists;
- supervisory;
- clerical;
- manual.

Each of these groups has some element of their overall remuneration that is unique and needs to be identified separately. The executives have incentives and share options, management may have a different bonus structure, the manual level is paid on an hourly rate.

Once the different compensation mixes have been defined, the individual pay elements associated with each group must be specified. From these individual elements compensation mix aggregates can be defined. For example, the management compensation mix may contain the following discrete elements:

- basic salary;
- fixed bonus;
- variable bonus;
- paid benefits (cash equivalent).

The type of compensation mix aggregates that could be derived from these might be Total Cash (basic pay + fixed bonus + variable bonus) or Total Remuneration (basic pay + fixed bonus + variable bonus + value of benefits). Having defined all the groups the final task is to identify those global aggregates that relate all defined compensation mixes to one another on a common basis for organization-wide analysis. For example, one global aggregate may be annual base pay. To continue with our earlier example, the global aggregate may look like this:

Global Aggregate – Annual base pay

Compensation Mix	Comp. Mix Aggregate	Individual Elements
Executives	annual base	basic + fixed bonus
Management	annual base	basic + fixed bonus
Tech/Prof Spec.	annual base	basic + fixed bonus + Market Premia

Supervisors	annual base	monthly $\times$ 12 + fixed bonus
Clerical	annual base	monthly $\times$ 12
Manual	weekly wages $\times$ 52	hourly rate $\times$ 38 + bonus

This now gives us a common basis for comparing the different compensation mixes as well as a means of evaluating the organization as a whole, or in part, to the external market.

In addition to different compensation mixes, every organization has different ways of categorizing employees into certain populations by function, division, cost centre, etc. An important feature of the user-definable database is the ability to create your own code groups and definitions.

For example, you could create two code groups, location and function, with the following values:

Location	Function
A London HQ	1 Finance
B Southampton	2 Marketing
C Norwich	3 R & D

By assigning the appropriate codes to each employee you are now able to analyze populations defined by any combination of function and/or location in addition to a selected remuneration mix.

With this degree of flexibility built into the database it is possible to analyze internal equity, make external comparisons, develop new policies, and allocate individual increases for any population of employees.

Conclusions

Deciding on the best approach is very much a matter of individual choice for each organization. Invariably one has to reach some sort of compromise with any solution that is implemented but the following guidelines might be useful. For a small/medium-sized population of jobs with uncomplicated salary structures, satisfactory results can be obtained by setting up a simple database linked into a spreadsheet. This can be achieved relatively quickly and at a low cost. If you already have a suitable database, such as a personnel record system, storing the information you need to analyze, ensure that it can output data into the spreadsheet software used in your organization. For a medium/large population with more complex pay structures it is best to consider one of the commercially available alternatives, such as HayXpert. This is more cost-effective than in-house development and considerably more efficient.

Pay planning

In any pay system where progression rates vary according to performance there will be anomalies. These can arise when performance suddenly improves or gets worse and staff are either under- or over-paid because it is not possible, using the normal guidelines, to place them on the right curve immediately. In this situation these people would have to be treated individually and their salary increases adjusted to accelerate or decelerate their progression through the range, so bringing them back in line.

It is in these circumstances that managing reward processes requires judgement and a sensitive approach. Inevitably, this book has largely been about systems and procedures. But ultimately we are dealing with people who want and deserve to be treated as individuals, and this applies as equally to those who manage as to those who are being managed. Mechanistic systems of salary administration may make life easier for the personnel department but that is not the object of the exercise. No members of an organization can be really happy, well motivated and committed if they feel they are part of a machine which pays no attention to their individual needs.

Salary planning and administration must adopt the stance of thinking first of what is right for individuals in terms of their aptitudes, abilities, skills, performance and needs. Of course, this approach must always be tempered with the knowledge that the organization also has needs which demand satisfaction. But an integrated approach to reward management can optimize the needs of the organization and those of the individuals, and these should be seen as complementary, not opposed.

Salary planning therefore has to treat people as individuals who are pursuing a career. This means looking at how that career is developing and ensuring that the incentives and rewards for increasing competences and improving performance go hand in hand with progress within and through the organization.

38

Communicating the Benefits

Why communicate?

One of the prime objectives of the reward system should be to motivate people and so ensure their commitment. Hence the theme of paying for performance which has run throughout this book. But how can the system motivate if left to its own devices – if people are unsure why the system was developed, suspect that it is unfair, or are unsure about how their pay will be linked to performance, or what their future rewards are going to be as they take on greater responsibility? And how can the company get any mileage out of its logical, equitable, competitive and even creative reward system, its high level of rewards or its generous employee benefits package if it does not tell its employees all about them?

Payment systems can sometimes demotivate even more effectively than they motivate, as Herzberg established by his classic research on *The Motivation to Work*. This is because they often seem to be unfair. Pay is perceived as being either inequitable or not commensurate with performance. Elliott Jacques called this the felt-fair principle. He suggested on the basis of extensive research that people feel their pay ought to be fair in relation to their personal contribution, to what other people are being paid within the organization and to what is being paid by other organizations for similar jobs. If management wants to motivate its employees, these expectations must be satisfied. It is worth remembering that the most respected theory of motivation – the expectancy theory – states that it is what people *expect* to get, if it is worth having, which will motivate them most effectively, rather than what they have already got.

So it is important to motivate people by telling them that what they have got is worth having – if that is the case – and even more important to tell them what they can expect. This starts with the recruitment process and ends with the way in which retirement or indeed severance is handled. If they have been rewarded for doing well, that has to be communicated to them. If they are going to get higher rewards for doing even better in the future, that must also be communicated, but more forcibly.

What to communicate

The following is what you should communicate to staff in general and to individual employees:

Staff in general

1. *The company salary policy:* This will set out the principles followed in setting pay and benefit levels.
2. *The pay and benefits structure:* This will define the salary brackets for each grade and the benefits available, including details of the pension scheme.

3. *Methods of grading and re-grading jobs:* Where job evaluation exists, details will be given of the job evaluation scheme, including how evaluations are carried out and the right to appeal against gradings.
4. *Salary progression:* The method by which salaries are progressed within grades or within a salary curve system.
5. *Incentive/bonus schemes:* Details of any incentive, bonus, profit sharing or share purchase schemes including how bonuses or profit shares are calculated and distributed and the procedures for purchasing shares.
6. *Reward systems and organizational change:* How remuneration policy will be affected by mergers/takeovers, change in corporate direction and indeed the bad news of liquidation and closures.

Individual employees

1. *Job grade:* What their grade is and how it has been determined.
2. *Salary progression:* The limit to which their salary can go in their present grade and the rate at which they can progress through the grade, depending on performance.
3. *Potential:* Their potential for higher salaries following promotion, subject to meeting defined performance criteria and the availability of suitable positions. In other words, this information, plus that contained under the heading of salary progression, should create expectations of what staff can get and define the action or behaviour they have to do to get there.
4. *Performance management:* How performance and potential are focused, managed and assessed, including details of the criteria used, the method of assessment and the right of the employee to know what his or her assessment is and why it has taken that form.
5. *Salary levels:* The reasons for the level of reward they are getting or the salary increase at the last review and what the employee must do to get more.
6. *Benefit statement:* The value of the benefits the individual employee receives so that he or she appreciates the level of his or her total remuneration.

How to communicate – general information

The best way to communicate general information about salaries and benefits is to include the details in a staff handbook which is issued to all employees on joining the company and is updated regularly. This can be supplemented by brochures specially written for employees describing, for instance, the pension scheme and other profit sharing or share ownership schemes. In these publications discrete emphasis should be placed on the scale of benefits that employees enjoy and the scope provided for rewarding improved performance and loyalty to the company. Many large companies such as IBM mount continuing internal PR campaigns to explain the system and its benefits.

The written statement should be supplemented by initial briefings during the induction period. Whenever major changes are made, the information should be disseminated widely in the company magazines, or notice boards, through joint consultative committees and by means of team briefing (face-to-face briefings made by managers or supervisors to their staff).

How to communicate – individual information

Individual members of staff will, of course, receive letters of appointment which should tell them their grade and refer them to a staff handbook which gives details of the grading and performance schemes. Whenever they are upgraded or promoted they should receive another letter congratulating them on the event and providing encouragement for the future. Considerable attention should be given to the wording of these letters to ensure that they come over as warm and sincere rather than cold and bureaucratic or, worse, patronizing. They should *always* be handed over personally by the manager to ensure that the opportunity to get needed messages across is taken.

Face-to-face

The best way to communicate personal information is face-to-face. Employees should be seen regularly by their immediate superior for discussions and coaching on their performance. Personal explanations should be given to them of the reasons for the employee's rate of salary progression or most recent increase. These meetings should discuss what actions the employee has to take to progress faster or to get more next time.

Potential for promotion and salary progression in the longer term should also be discussed at these meetings. Ideally, employees should be given the opportunity to talk to their immediate supervisor's manager in order to get a broader view. People with strong potential should also meet a career planning advisor who can act as a mentor in discussing future career steps, the further training or experience they need and, without painting too glowing a picture, the glittering prizes that await them if they do really well.

Implementing communications

Considerable care will be needed in preparing handbooks, brochures and letters. They need to be clear and informative and, while they should emphasize the scale of benefits employees receive, they should not over-do it. Experts' help in preparing and presenting this information can be useful.

Individual managers and supervisors should be trained both in how to coach and review the performance of their staff and in how to convey information about assessments and rewards in a way which will motivate them. Their performance in doing this should be monitored.

Auditing communications on reward systems

Whoever is responsible for the reward system, and the messages which communications about them should convey, should regularly audit their quality, consistency and effectiveness. The key items that usually need looking at and the main questions to ask are:

- job advertisements/recruitment literature – do descriptions of the remuneration package do justice to what is on offer and what the organization is seeking to pay for?
- offer letters/contracts – is as much attention paid to highlighting the attractiveness of all elements of the package as stating the bald elements of entitlements?
- staff handbooks – is layout clear and unambiguous and is the style one that will have immediacy and meaning to the groups of employees covered? Is the information sensibly grouped?
   (*Do not* use complicated language if most of the readers left school at 16, respond better to visual presentations and have reading habits that centre on

the *Sun* and *Hello*. Remember that it *is* possible to describe share options without using arcane legal terminology and that if the way in which incentive measures are described is impenetrable this will hardly focus motivation.)

- salary increase letters – do they properly thank people for their efforts and contribution? Is delivery made an occasion of?
- policy changes – are these communicated to convey the logic and the benefits?
- severance (retirement/redundancy) – is the approach perceived as caring and concerned? If not, what is the likely effect on remaining employees?
- company videos communicating change – do these come across as sincere and provide helpful information or do they look hastily assembled and have too high a 'cringe factor' to be useful?

Major changes to reward systems

Most employers now recognize, or have learned the hard way, that major changes to reward policy not only take time to implement but that implementation has to be a carefully planned campaign. Communication is the key. The quality of communications will largely determine the acceptability of the proposed changes.

In the IDS/IPM publication *The Merit Factor – Rewarding Individual Performance*, 12 rules for Internal Communications were reproduced. As background to any communication plans we believe they have continuing value and list them below:

1. There is no such thing as a stone cold certainty in business decisions and it is important everyone in a business realizes this.
2. If a Board cannot or will not clearly spell out its business strategy, employees are entitled to assume it does not have one.
3. Assume that in an information vacuum, people will believe the worst.
4. Never take it for granted that people know what you are talking about.
5. Always take it for granted that people doing a job know more about it than you do.
6. Telling people something once is not much better than not telling them at all.
7. Never assume that people will tell you anything that reflects unfavourably upon themselves.
8. Remember that employees read newspapers, magazines and books, listen to the radio and watch television.
9. Do not be afraid to admit you were wrong; it gives people confidence that you know what you are doing.
10. Asking for help, taking advice, consulting and listening to others are signs of great strength.
11. Communicating good news is easy but even this is not often done by management; bad news is all too often left to rumours and the grapevine.
12. Changing attitudes in order to change behaviour takes years – changing behaviour changes attitudes in weeks.

Bearing these in mind (and some of the cynical, if realistic, perceptions they contain), the following means of communications media can be used to draw from, together with some of their more appropriate uses:

- poster campaigns – for creating expectations for, say, a new pay or performance management system
- staff newsletters – for explaining new policies or providing updates on how a new policy (job evaluation for instance) is being implemented

- personal letters – to explain the personal impact of policy developments
- brochures – where a major policy has to be explained, eg a PRP system or a new pension scheme
- individual meetings – where a personal, confidential or difficult message has to be got across and maximum impact is needed
- videos – where a large number of staff in distributed sites have to be reached – good if a charismatic Chief Executive can convey his or her commitment to policy changes or development
- team briefings – to inform groups of employees, consult with them and ensure they properly understand change (eg to an incentive scheme).

Whatever the chosen media, the presentation should be as professional as possible. Ill-conceived, hasty and scruffy presentations will always give employees the impression that the organization does not really care about them and that it is doing as little as it can get away with. This is not the area for penny-pinching – the price in terms of justifiable resistance and cynicism is too high.

39

Developing and Introducing Reward Management Processes – The Use of Consultants

Why use consultants?

There are four possible reasons for using management consultants:

1. They bring expertise in solving problems based on their understanding of relevant techniques and their experience in analyzing similar situations.
2. They can open closed doors, releasing ideas already developed within the organization which have been stifled by the universal habit of resisting change. The saying: 'A prophet is not without honour save in his own country and in his own house' (Matthew 57) is as true today as it was in New Testament times. Consultants can play the role of catalysts or change agents.
3. Consultants can act in an independent and disinterested way, unaffected by local politics and pressure groups.
4. Consultants have the time to concentrate on the problem they have been set. They can act as an extra pair of hands, leaving management more time to get on with the day-to-day task of running the business.

How can they help?

In reward management, the areas in which management consultants can help are:

- advising on remuneration strategy, eg following a merger or change in corporate direction
- developing and introducing tailor-made job evaluation schemes
- introducing and maintaining their own brand of job evaluation
- designing and reviewing pay structures
- conducting salary surveys
- advising on salary levels for individual jobs; for example, non-executive directors seeking information on the right remuneration for a managing director
- designing incentive bonus schemes
- developing profit sharing plans, including share ownership schemes
- advising on pension schemes

- developing total remuneration packages covering the whole range of benefits
- advising on the personal tax implications of remuneration policies.

How to choose a consultant

The golden rule in selecting consultants is to be absolutely clear in advance about what you want them to do. Objectives and terms of reference need to be defined as a basis for briefing any firms pitching for the assignment and, later, for monitoring progress.

Having defined objectives, the next step is to identify possible consultancies. The comparative advantages of large or small firms need to be considered. A large firm will have ample resources and back-up facilities. It will be able to tap a reservoir of experience and expertise. A smaller firm may be able to provide exactly the type of advice you need because it specializes in a particular area. It may also provide you with more individual attention.

Unless you are absolutely certain from personal knowledge the one firm is exactly right for you, it is always advisable to approach three or four different consultancies and get them to pitch for the job. Select firms on the basis of recommendations you can trust, or on the advice of organizations such as, in the UK, the Institute of Management Consultants and the Management Consultancy Information Service (see Bibliography).

Give the consultants your terms of reference and any further information they need to prepare a proposal. Meet them to discuss the brief – you can get some measure of their ability by the speed and accuracy with which they size up your situation and the quality of the questions they ask.

Always ask them to submit a written proposal which should set out:

(a) the terms of reference
(b) their understanding of your situation and requirements
(c) how they would carry out the assignment
(d) what they would achieve
(e) how the assignment would be staffed
(f) the proposed programme of work and who would do it
(g) the cost of their fees quoted as daily or hourly rates and as a total based on their estimate of the length of the assignment. Make sure that this specifically includes or excludes fee increases in the pipeline and ask for an estimate of expenses.

In coming to your decision on which firm to select, the following points should be taken into account:

1. The reputation of the firm.
2. The initial impression they made, ie quality of consultants.
3. The quality of their proposal with particular reference to:
    - the relevance of their proposed solutions;
    - the practicality of their proposals from the view of implementation;
    - the realism of the programme.
4. The cost of the proposals.

When you have made your choice, confirm it in writing by reference to the proposal, subject to any modifications that have been agreed. If you want to be certain about the costs of the assignment and if you believe that the length of time estimated for completing it is reasonable, it may be worth agreeing a fixed price.

Using consultants

A responsible firm of management consultants will stick to its brief, but it is natural for people with enquiring minds – and if consultants don't have those, they are in the wrong business – to identify new problems and to offer solutions to them. Even the most professional firms are not averse to drumming up more work. It is up to you to make sure that no extra time is spent on the assignment unless you agree that it is worthwhile and unless the costs are also agreed.

You have every right to expect consultants to complete their programme within their own estimate of time and costs. They could take longer if they come up against unforeseen snags and this is a joint problem if the delay has adverse effects on your business. But unless you have misled the consultants in your brief, it is their responsibility to overcome the problems and to carry the burden of any extra costs they may have incurred.

Ensure that liaison arrangements with consultants are agreed. There should be regular progress or 'milestone' meetings when you can check how the assignment is going and deal with any problems as they arise. You should expect the consultants to discuss their preliminary findings with you and to present their interim conclusions and initial recommendations. It is in everyone's interest that alternative proposals should be evaluated jointly and that the feasibility of the implementation programme should be reviewed.

The final report should include a convincing analysis of the situation and any problems that have been identified. Recommendations should be derived logically from this analysis and they should include an assessment of costs and benefits and a plan for implementation which sets out precisely who does what and when.

Working effectively with consultants is about building good working relationships, based on confidence and trust. Often this boils down to 'chemistry' – whether you believe and observe that the consultants who work with you are in sympathy with your organization and understanding what change it is able to achieve.

The best consultants rapidly build partnerships with their clients so that they can test the validity of what they are doing at several levels – from technical experts to the HR director, and as far as the chief executive when major change appears necessary. Their concern will be the overall 'health' of the organization and enabling it, and the people within it, to achieve their potential. In the reward area this will mean that technical excellence must be matched by an understanding of the business and HR strategy implications of proposed changes or improvements.

40

Issues and Trends in Reward Management

As we see them, the key issues facing reward management are:

- How can we ensure that reward management strategies support the achievement of the organization's business strategies *and* satisfy the needs and aspirations of employees for security, stability and career development?
- How can we achieve internal equity *and* external competitiveness?
- How can we respond to a fragmenting pay market *and* maintain a reasonably coherent pay structure?
- How can we concentrate on rewarding for output *and* maintain, indeed enhance, quality standards?
- How can we reward individual performance and contribution *and* promote teamwork?
- How can we introduce sophisticated performance management process *and* ensure that managers are committed and have the skills required to get the best out of them?
- How can we give high rewards to high achievers *and* motivate the core of employees upon whom we ultimately have to rely?
- How can we achieve consistency in managing reward processes *and* provide for the flexibility needed in ever-changing circumstances?
- How can we devolve power to the line managers to manage their own reward processes *and* retain sufficient control to ensure that corporate policies are implemented?
- How do we continue to provide motivation for those who have reached the top of their pay range *and* maintain the integrity of the grading system and contain costs.
- How can we introduce more powerful pay-for-performance schemes *and* ensure that we get value for money from them?
- How can we deliver the message that improved performance brings increased reward *and* cap bonus earnings to cater for windfall situations or a particularly loose incentive scheme?
- How can we operate enterprise-wide bonus schemes *and* ensure that they increase motivation and commitment?
- How do we reward people for their outputs *and* their inputs?
- How do we operate our job evaluation scheme as a means of allocating and controlling gradings in a formal hierarchy *and* cater for the role flexibility which is increasingly required in the organization?
- How can we use our formal and rigid grade structure as a basis for reward

management *and* cater for continuous career development and changing roles?

- How do we provide for a flexible remuneration and benefits system *and* ensure that there is a fair and consistent means of creating and maintaining the benefit package and controlling its cost?
- How do we justify paying vast (and some people may feel obscene) bonuses to our chief executives and directors *and* at the same time clamp down on pay increases for the rest of our employees (who also contribute)?

We have attempted in this book to provide some guidance on how these dilemmas may be dealt with. But we do not claim to have all the answers. So much depends on the particular traditions, circumstances and culture of individual organizations. All we can suggest is that the list of dilemmas we have identified are used as a basis for asking the question – are any of these our problems, and what can we do about them? You can then turn to the appropriate part of this book to find, not quick fixes, but suggestions on how reward management issues can be assessed and analysed and how alternative solutions can be evaluated.

We have expressed our own views on trends, but we also think it might be helpful to summarise the contributions of the experts who have made significant contributions to current thinking on where reward management is going.

Contributions from the experts

Michael Beer

Beer[1] expresses reservations about basing reward systems on extrinsic motivators:

> 'Tying pay and other extrinsic rewards to performance may actually *reduce* the intrinsic motivation that comes when individuals become spontaneously involved in work because they are given freedom to manage and control their jobs'.

He suggests that the design of a reward system should rarely be the place to start solving business and human resource problems, although it will always be an area that will have to be managed to complement other human resource management changes. He points out that there seems to be a contradiction between the *promise* of pay systems and the *reality* of practice. He believes that even the most sophisticated pay-for-performance systems designed specifically to motivate employees end up with significant flaws. Either they do not motivate employees, or they bring about unanticipated and dysfunctional behaviour.

He does accept, however, that pay can motivate performance provided certain conditions are met, namely: employees must believe that acceptable levels of performance can result from their efforts and that important rewards will follow achievement of these performance levels. He emphasizes that:

> 'Communication, participation and trust can have an important effect on people's perception of pay, the meaning they attach to a new pay system, and their response to that system. In short, *the process may be as important as the system*'.

He strongly supports the use of person or skill-based evaluation systems because they reward people for acquiring new skills. They also encourage management to utilize the available skills of people better because they are already being paid for those skills. Assignments are less likely to be limited because they have to be made consistent with job levels. But he appreciates that skill-based pay schemes are only capable of supporting, not leading, a change in management philosophy – one that emphasizes employee responsibility and involvement in work.

Beer notes that participation, involvement and communication are used by the Japanese in place of individual pay-for-performance to motivate their employees. He questions most performance-related pay schemes because there are few jobs which meet the conditions of individual control and independence required for success. He therefore suggests that pay should be used 'less to initiate behaviour and attitudes and more to reinforce behaviour and attitudes which are stimulated by other means: involvement in work, identity with the company, and influence over the task'.

Rosabeth Moss Kanter

Kanter[2] expresses the view that in the 'post-entrepreneurial 1990s', de-layered organizations with less hierarchical structures will have to respond more quickly to change. Pay systems will need to match remuneration more closely to the company's earnings rather than simply to reflect position or job title. She rejects merit pay as expensive, unfair, relying too much on subjective judgements, divisive and not a reliable motivator. She believes that the pay mix should include a guaranteed small amount based on level and position and a large proportion of cash from gainsharing, profit-sharing and bonus schemes, the latter being awarded for exemplary team and individual contributions.

Ed Lawler

Lawler[3] believes that 'pay practices are only as good as the impact they make on organizational effectiveness'. He rejects traditional practices as not scoring well against the kind of results a pay system should produce:

> 'They do not, for example, tend to motivate effective behaviour ... They tend to produce high fixed costs, which make organizations inflexible and non-competitive in the international market place. From a cultural point of view, they tend to produce hierarchical, rigid structures with low levels of teamwork and cooperation'.

He suggests that for a pay system to affect motivation a significant proportion of the pay package has to be performance based. Pay costs should be adjusted to match organizational performance through profit-sharing and gainsharing plans. A core principle for reward systems, especially in high technology organizations, should be that of paying individuals according to their skills, knowledge and market value. He is also in favour of egalitarian perquisites so that *all* the organization's human assets can feel valued and appreciated. He is against traditional points-factor job evaluation schemes because they depersonalize people by equating them with a set of duties rather than concentrating on what they are and what they can do. He thinks that pay should position people in the market according to their performance. Outstanding individuals should be paid above average market rates and poor individuals should be paid below market rates.

Tom Peters

Peters[4] believes in incentives for everyone, comprising:

■ pay-for-knowledge incentives to encourage employees to learn several skills;

- productivity and quality-based incentives based on team performance;
- profit distribution incentives based on profit centre performance;
- a simple and understandable bonus formula, with the incentive bonus constituting at least 20 per cent of total pay, to be distributed monthly, separate from base salary;
- an employee share ownership scheme, with the employer contributing 8–10 per cent of payroll.

Vicky Wright

Wright, Director of European Remuneration Consulting at Hay Management Consultants, suggests that the following are the key considerations affecting reward management in the 1990s:

- Remuneration can not be left within the rigid centrally administered hierarchical systems that survived, and indeed thrived, from the 1970s into the 1980s. If performance management becomes, as it should, a principal business management system, total performance pay becomes the dominant remuneration arrangement, linking to the skills, competences and outputs of individuals, the outputs of the teams and the organization as a whole.
- The issues for organizations in a competitive business environment are first, how remuneration can best be designed to ensure that it supports the achievement of organization objectives and, second, how contribution of individuals and teams to such an achievement should be reflected in pay in an environment where performance improvement is a way of life.
- Line management should not only use but also own performance management as a tool for empowerment of themselves and their teams.
- It is necessary to formulate clear plans for developing skills and competences which individuals and managers understand and are committed to, together with a framework for assessment that managers are equally committed to, so that an environment of cost-effective continuous improvement is assured.
- Reward and performance management processes should foster a management style that genuinely coaches and supports individual and team performance improvements and focuses on creating more productive relationships between the organization and its individual members.
- It is necessary to increase management understanding and ownership of pay decisions as they affect individuals and team working in their division or department. This means greater clarity about remuneration strategy, policy and practices within the discipline of budgets devolved to line managers. This inevitably leads to greater line management focus on funding pay through constant performance improvement.

Key reward management trends

The messages received from these experts and other practitioners indicate that the following are the key trends in reward management:

- Greater sensitivity to sector and functional market practice to enable more effective market positioning to help with attracting and retaining high calibre employees.
- The implementation of increasingly focused performance awards starting at the top and working down through organizations as performance orientation increases.

- The continuation of the steady move away from fixed service-related incremental payment systems.
- Pay increases linked to market worth and individual or team performance – not service and/or the cost of living.
- More attention given to achievement or success-orientated individual bonuses rather than permanent increases in base pay.
- A move towards team pay as the importance of teamwork increases.
- More flexible pay structures based on job families and using broader pay bands or pay curves.
- More integrated pay structures covering all categories of employees.
- A growing linkage between pay practice and training and development initiatives through the design and implementation of skills and competency based pay processes which reward the acquisition and use of new skills and behaviours.
- Much greater emphasis on the quality of the continuous process of performance management – often accepted as having reward value of itself.
- The development of integrated performance management systems with the emphasis on coaching development, motivation and recognition through the identification of opportunities to succeed.
- A search for simpler and more flexible approaches to job evaluation which enable a move away from the control of uniformity to the management of diversity. This will make use of techniques such as job family modelling and computer assisted job evaluation.
- Increased awareness of the need to treat job measurement as a process for managing relativities which, as necessary, has to adapt to new organizational environments and much greater role flexibility and can no longer be applied rigidly as a system for preserving existing hierarchies.
- More emphasis on the choice of benefits and 'clean cash' rather than a multiplicity of perquisites.
- Greater creativity and sensitivity in benefits practice.
- As a foundation to all this, a much more conscious alignment of pay and human resource management policies, processes and practices with overall organizational objectives and strategy.

References

1. Beer, M (1984) 'Reward systems', In M. Beer, B. Spector, P. Lawrence and D. Quinn Mills *Managing Human Assets*, The Free Press, New York
2. Kanter, R M (1989) *When Giants Learn to Dance*, Simon & Schuster, London
3. Lawler, E (1990) *Strategic Pay*, Jossey-Bass, San Francisco
4. Peters, T (1988) *Thriving on Chaos*, Macmillan, London

APPENDICES

Appendix A

Attitude Survey – Reward Policy

Objectives

This survey has been designed by xxx Consultants to help us develop a new reward policy.

The aim of this survey is to obtain your views on aspects which are relevant to this issue. All staff are being asked to complete the attached questionnaire and your response is valuable. So in order to ensure your own thoughts and opinions are represented, we ask that you take time to complete the questionnaire frankly and spontaneously.

Confidentiality

Your answers to this questionnaire will be treated as strictly confidential. No individual will be identified and no-one will see the completed questionnaire. Please complete the questionnaire as soon as possible and then send it in the attached envelope to:

xxx Consultants

_____

_____

_____

Please return by _____ , 19__ .

Feedback on the results will be given to all employees.

Thank you very much.

How to complete the questionnaire

The questionnaire will take about 20 minutes to complete. Answer the statements overleaf by placing a circle around the number which most closely matches your opinion.

For example:

	Strongly disagree	Disagree	Neutral	Agree	Strongly agree
I like my job	1	2	3	0	5

If you make an error please draw a line through the number that you have previously circled and then circle the more appropriate number.

Points about yourself

The following information will be used to make group comparisons only and your questionnaire will not be analyzed on an individual basis. Results will not be calculated for groups of less than five respondents.

Please circle *one* number for questions A to C

A. In which function do you work?

1. Finance
2. HR
3. Information Technology
4. Legal
5. Commercial
6. Marketing
7. Sales
8. Production
9. Manufacturing Services

B. Where are you located?

1.
2.
3.
4.

C. Which of the following bonus schemes are you eligible for?

1. Executive Incentive Compensation Plan
2. European Management Incentive Plan
3. Sales Incentive Plan
4. Staff Bonus Scheme

My current view is ...	strongly disagree	disagree	neutral	agree	strongly agree
1. Individual performance is adequately rewarded	1	2	3	4	5
2. Pay increases are handled fairly	1	2	3	4	5
3. Team performance is adequately rewarded	1	2	3	4	5
4. I believe my appraisal is a fair assessment of my performance	1	2	3	4	5
5. I am satisfied with the company's flexible benefits programme	1	2	3	4	5
6. Poor performance is not tolerated	1	2	3	4	5
7. The prospect of a bonus has little effect on my attitude towards work	1	2	3	4	5
8. My overall pay and benefits package is competitive (eg base pay – bonus – pension – holidays)	1	2	3	4	5
9. I feel my pay is a good reflection of my performance	1	2	3	4	5
10. Good performers get promoted first	1	2	3	4	5
11. Morale is high around here	1	2	3	4	5
12. I am clear about the end results expected of me in my job	1	2	3	4	5
13. I am kept informed about what is required for me to advance	1	2	3	4	5
14. The current appraisal system clearly differentiates on performance levels	1	2	3	4	5
15. My benefits package (eg holidays, pension etc) is competitive	1	2	3	4	5
16. I have a good understanding of how salaries and increases are determined	1	2	3	4	5
17. The size of my last bonus adequately reflected my performance	1	2	3	4	5
18. The performance results expected of me are set at realistic levels	1	2	3	4	5

My current view is ...	strongly disagree	disagree	neutral	agree	strongly agree
19. The way my bonus is determined is fair	1	2	3	4	5
20. Business strategy is clearly linked to individual roles	1	2	3	4	5
21. My manager tells me when I have not performed effectively	1	2	3	4	5
22. I feel secure in my job	1	2	3	4	5
23. I receive enough feedback on how I am performing	1	2	3	4	5
24. I have relevant skills and abilities which are not used in my present job	1	2	3	4	5
25. I understand how my role contributes to the company success	1	2	3	4	5
26. I am proud to work for the company	1	2	3	4	5
27. My manager tells me when I have done a good job	1	2	3	4	5
28. I understand the company business strategy	1	2	3	4	5
29. If I had performed poorly I would not expect a pay increase	1	2	3	4	5
30. The measures used to monitor my performance are the most approriate for my job	1	2	3	4	5
31. I have a good understanding of the company's flexible benefits programme	1	2	3	4	5
32. The pay I receive is competitive compared to other companies	1	2	3	4	5
33. Promotions and transfers are made fairly	1	2	3	4	5
34. I am clear about the behaviours I am expected to demonstrate in my job	1	2	3	4	5
35. I like my job – the kind of work I do	1	2	3	4	5
36. I have a good understanding of my potential career moves in the company	1	2	3	4	5
37. Employees who are 'better performers' receive higher pay increases than 'poor performers'	1	2	3	4	5

My current view is ...	strongly disagree	disagree	neutral	agree	strongly agree
38. Consistent performance standards are set across the organisation	1	2	3	4	5
39. I have a good understanding of how my bonus is determined	1	2	3	4	5
40. The measures used to monitor my performance are clearly linked to business objectives	1	2	3	4	5
41. I think the salary policy is overdue for review	1	2	3	4	5
42. Employees who are 'better performers' *should* receive higher pay increases than 'poor performers'	1	2	3	4	5
43. The current pay policy is flexible enough to allow my manager to use pay to motivate me	1	2	3	4	5
44. I am held accountable for the end results I produce or fail to produce	1	2	3	4	5
45. The current performance related pay system encourages better performance	1	2	3	4	5
46. My pay is fair compared to people doing similar work in the company	1	2	3	4	5

	very poor	poor	average	good	very good
47. How would you rate the company on providing each of the following benefits?					
Car	1	2	3	4	5
Holidays	1	2	3	4	5
Life Assurance	1	2	3	4	5
Long Term Disability	1	2	3	4	5
Pension	1	2	3	4	5
Private Medical Plan	1	2	3	4	5

	To a great extent			To a limited extent	Not at all
48. To what extent do you believe the following currently influences your pay:					
Cost of living	1	2	3	4	5
Company sales	1	2	3	4	5
Company profitability	1	2	3	4	5
Team performance	1	2	3	4	5
Job title	1	2	3	4	5
Skills	1	2	3	4	5

	To a great extent			To a limited extent	Not at all
Length of service	1	2	3	4	5
Performance in the job	1	2	3	4	5
The external pay market	1	2	3	4	5
Qualifications	1	2	3	4	5
Experience	1	2	3	4	5
Loyalty	1	2	3	4	5
Location	1	2	3	4	5

49. To what extent do you believe the following *should* influence your pay:

	To a great extent			To a limited extent	Not at all
Cost of living	1	2	3	4	5
Company sales	1	2	3	4	5
Company profitability	1	2	3	4	5
Team performance	1	2	3	4	5
Job title	1	2	3	4	5
Length of service	1	2	3	4	5
Performance in the job	1	2	3	4	5
The external pay market	1	2	3	4	5
Qualifications	1	2	3	4	5
Experience	1	2	3	4	5
Loyalty	1	2	3	4	5
Location	1	2	3	4	5

50. At present you are able to choose the level of many of the benefits in your flexible benefits programme. If you could extend this flexibility to cover other benefits, which benefits would you choose?

51. What do you like about the current pay and benefits policy?

52. What do you dislike about the current pay and benefits policy?

THANK YOU FOR COMPLETING THIS QUESTIONNAIRE

Statistical Terms Used in Pay Surveys and Analysis

Pay data

Most commonly used statistical methods and computer packages assume that the data under analysis is normally distributed. In such a distribution the individual items are more likely to be close to the average than far from it but are evenly distributed above and below the average. There are very few instances of data being exactly 'normal' but many are close enough to make no real difference. An example would be the heights of children at a given age; most would cluster round the average with a few extremes. Figure B.1 illustrates a normal distribution.

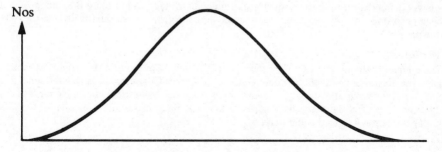

Figure B.1 *Normal distribution*

Pay data, however, tends not to be symmetrically distributed; typically there is a greater spread above the average than below it. Overall this reflects the fact that there are more people in lower paid jobs and the differences in pay between lower paid jobs is less. Pay data therefore tends to have a skewed distribution similar to that illustrated in Figure B.2. The distribution which pay typically has is known as 'lognormal'. Technically this means that the logarithm of pay is normally distributed – in simple terms it reflects the fact that an additional £1000 has a much greater impact on a salary of £10,000 than on a salary of £50,000.

Because pay is not normally distributed, most statistical methods should only be used with care.

Salary surveys

Salary and benefits surveys collect together a mass of useful, and not so useful, information. Rather than just presenting listings of the data collected, most surveys present summaries or analyzes of the data. This section provides explanations of the more usual terms used in salary surveys.

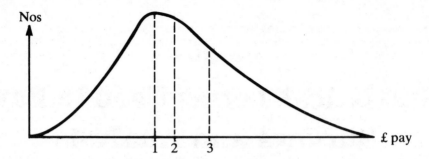

Figure B.2   *Lognormal distribution (eg pay)*

Measures of central tendency

There are three statistics that are commonly used to describe the middle or centre of a set of data, the average or mean, the median, and the mode.

Average or mean
The arithmetical average, or mean, is calculated by adding all the reported salaries together and dividing by the number reported. In salary survey data the mean can be unduly influenced by one or two extremely high (or low) values. Some surveys, therefore, also quote averages with the two highest and lowest values omitted which reduces the likelihood of the answer being distorted. If the data is lognormally distributed as in Figure B.2, the mean will be at position 3; the higher values at the top pull the mean up more than the low values pull it down.

Median
The median is the middle ranking salary, ie that which 50 per cent of the reported salaries are equal to or above and 50 per cent equal to or below. This measure is less influenced by outlying values than the average or mean and is therefore used widely in salary surveys as a measure of central tendency. In Figure B.2 it would be at position 2; this divides the area under the curve into two equal parts.

Mode
The mode is that value which appears most frequently in a given set of data. This is not always a central value and indeed in some sets of data there can be more than one modal value. Where data is clustered around a centre it can be useful to show which value(s) occur most frequently.

As salaries can vary by small amounts, they are usually grouped into ranges before a mode is derived and the range with the most reported salaries is known as the modal range. However, this is only useful if the ranges are of consistent widths. In Figure B.2 the mode is at position 1, the point where the curve is at its highest.

The mode is more commonly used in describing benefit provisions where there are often only a limited number of possible alternatives.

Relationship of mean, median and mode
As already mentioned, pay is usually lognormally distributed as in Figure B.2. If this is so then the mean will be higher than the median and the median higher than the mode. In a normal distribution as in Figure B.1, the mean, median and mode all coincide at position 1.

Measures of spread

Most surveys give some indication of the relative spread of the data as well as statistics describing its centre. The relative spread shows whether the reported salaries are close together or whether there is great variability.

Range

The range is the total spread from the highest value to the lowest value and is shown in most surveys by actually quoting the highest and lowest values. Although this is a very simple measure it can be misleading if the extremes are unrepresentative of the data as a whole.

Standard deviation

The standard deviation is of great importance in many branches of statistics, especially those linked to experiments, but has little relevance in the field of reward management. It requires a relatively complex calculation, and the main reason for its use in salary surveys is that it is available on statistical packages. Technically it is the square root of the average of the sum of the squares of the difference from the mean for each observation. If the data is normally distributed then roughly 95 per cent of all the data lie within two standard deviations each side of the mean. However, as already mentioned, pay data tends not to be normally distributed, so this approximation does not always hold good.

Quartiles

There is great confusion as to whether a quartile is a point or a range. Quartiles, in the original statistical definition, were the three points which divided the data into four equal parts; the upper quartile, the median and the lower quartile. However, in recent years it has been used increasingly to mean a range – one of the four equal parts. Indeed the confusion has spread so far that recent editions of the Oxford dictionary give both definitions.

Where salary surveys refer to upper and lower quartiles they are using the original technical sense of a point. The upper quartile is that value which 25 per cent of values exceed and 75 per cent are less than. The lower quartile is that value which 75 per cent of values exceed and 25 per cent are below. As with medians and other quantiles discussed below, the quartiles can be (and often are) equal to one or more of the values.

The quartiles, unlike the standard division or the range, are little influenced by one or two outlying values.

Inter-quartile range

This is a measure of spread between the upper and lower quartiles. It is therefore the range which covers the middle 50 per cent of values; 25 per cent of values lie below and 25 per cent above the inter-quartile range.

Deciles, percentiles and other quantiles

Other quantiles are similar to quartiles. For example the ninth decile is that value where 10 per cent of values exceed and 90 per cent are less than; the 99th percentile is that value which one per cent exceed and 99 per cent are below. These other quantiles are sometimes used in salary surveys but are more frequently used by companies to set their salary policy.

Calculation of medians, quartiles and other quantiles

When calculating quartiles and other measures the critical point is whether the sample is sufficient to support the results. In broad terms it is usually accepted that for a measure to have any validity there should be at least three observations in each part in which the sample of data is divided, and preferably more. For example medians should not be defined on less than six observations and even this can be misleading if the data included in the sample is in any way unrepresentative.

There are various formulae for calculating quantiles. The following are the most commonly used. If there are N observations and the observations are ranked in descending order:

median $\dfrac{N + 1}{2}$ observations from the top

(If there are 20 values this gives 10.5, ie the average of the 10th and 11th observations)

upper quartile $\dfrac{N + 3}{4}$ observations from the top

(If there are 20 values this gives 5.75, ie a weighted average of the 5th and 6th observations calculated by taking 3 times the 6th values and 1 times the 5th and dividing by 4)

lower quartile $\dfrac{3N + 1}{4}$ value from the top

ninth decile $\dfrac{N + 9}{10}$ value from the top

first decile $\dfrac{9N + 1}{10}$ value from the top

Pay analyses

There are three other common statistical techniques used in analyzing pay data.

Correlation

Correlation measures how closely two variables are related, for example salary and company size. Correlation coefficients vary from +1 to –1 and typically assume a straight line relationship. A value close to +1 indicates that a high value in one variable will be reflected by a high value in the other. A value close to –1 indicates that a high value in one variable will be reflected in a low value in the other, and near 0 indicates that there is no correlation and so a high value in one variable can reflect any value in the other.

For example, in low level jobs there is little correlation between pay and company size and therefore the correlation would be close to 0. For senior jobs such as managing directors there is a much stronger link and the correlation would be, say, +0.5 or +0.8. Interpreting a correlation coefficient is difficult as it depends to a certain extent on the size of the sample and the type of relationship between the variables.

Regression

Data with two variables such as pay and job size can be plotted as a scattergram (see Figure B.3). If the data is highly correlated then the data can be approximated by a (usually straight) line; this is known as a regression line. This is calculated by a complex formula, but one of the underlying assumptions is that the data is evenly distributed about the regression line. In most cases the dispersion in pay increases as the level of pay increases and so the underlying assumption is not valid. However, regression lines can be useful, especially over small variations in pay levels.

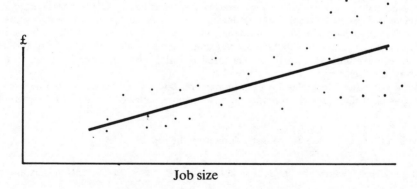

Figure B.3   *Relationship between salary and job size*

Multiple regression

This is similar to the linear regression outlined above but instead of relying on one explanatory variable it depends on two or more. For example, salary could be linked with age, experience and job size. It can be a helpful technique but the statistical assumptions underlying it assume that the explanatory variables are not correlated with each other. However, this is not always true (eg age and experience tend to go together) and therefore this method should only be used with great care.

Appendix C

Points-factor Job Evaluation Scheme: Factor and Level Definitions

Factor 1   Knowledge and skills

Factor definition

The knowledge and skills gained through education, training and experience required to achieve the overall purpose of the job by attaining the outputs and standards relating to each key result area or main task.

Level definitions

1. Ability to carry out standardized work routines and/or use simple equipment. A satisfactory standard can be achieved after a few weeks practical experience.
2. Straightforward administrative procedures are carried out such as maintaining records, dealing with routine queries and correspondence and/or operating specialized but not necessarily complex machines, eg word processors. Up to six months practical experience is required, possibly coupled with concentrated training for a few weeks.
3. Advanced administrative work is carried out which may involve the use of complex equipment, eg desk top computers. The work may involve maintaining complex records, dealing with non-routine queries, analyzing data or preparing standard reports. Up to two years practical experience may be required, probably backed up by intensive training for a few months.
4. Proficiency is required in a professional, administrative or specialist field involving the understanding and application of fairly advanced practices, procedures, concepts or principles. Five years experience may be required plus graduate level education or ability and professional/technical training of at least a year (additional years of high level experience may, however, be substituted for this training).
5. Considerable competence in a managerial or professional field required in order to understand and apply advanced policies, practices, procedures, concepts or principles. Broad experience over a number of years (five plus) is required plus, usually, appropriate academic qualifications or professional training.
6. A very high level of competence is required in directing and controlling high level activities which can only be acquired by means of deep and comprehensive experience over many years (ten plus).

Factor 2   Responsibility

Factor definition

The particular obligations assumed by job holders in terms of their accountability for results in each of the main areas of their job. The level of responsibility will be related to the impact of the job on end results, the consequence of errors and the size of the resources controlled (people, money and equipment etc).

Level definitions

1. The impact of the job and the effect of errors are limited to less important aspects of the work group, and errors can be detected almost immediately. No resources of any significance are controlled.
2. The job will impact on the performance of the work group and errors can have a short-term detrimental effect although it is quite easy to detect them. The resources controlled are limited to those personally required by the job holder to do the job.
3. The work can make a significant impact on the work of the section and although errors can be detected without too much difficulty, they can have considerable short-term detrimental effects on the department. Quite valuable equipment may be controlled and the job holder may be responsible for the routine work of up to three staff.
4. A significant impact is made on the work of the department and this will extend to other parts of the organization. Errors are not always easy to detect and can do considerable damage to departmental results. A section of four to six or so people may be controlled, together with the section's budget.
5. The job holder is expected to make a significant contribution to achieving objectives in an important aspect or area of the organization's work. Errors may be very hard to detect before they have a severe detrimental effect on the department's and, often, the organization's performance. Control may be exercised over a medium-sized department and budget.
6. The job holder is responsible for the formulation and implementation of major functional policies and plans which can make a considerable impact on the longer-term performance of the organization. Errors of judgement may not be detected for some time and can be very costly. Control may be exercised over a major department or division and a considerable budget.

Factor 3   Decisions

Factor definition

The degree to which the job involves choice of action covering the extent to which the work is routine or prescribed, the amount of supervision and guidance provided and the degree to which judgement has to be exercised.

Level definitions

1. The work is entirely routine, tasks are clearly defined, choice of action is within very narrow limits and close and continuous supervision is exercised.
2. The work is fairly routine and repetitive. Choice of action is fairly limited but there is some scope for making day-to-day decisions within well-defined limits. Other matters are referred to higher authority. Supervision is fairly close but not continuous.
3. A fair proportion of the work is standardized although there will be a number of non-routine elements. Freedom of action exists to make independent decisions but within well-established and clearly defined policy and procedural guidelines. Regular reference to higher authority is required. General supervision is exercised.
4. The work includes a large proportion of non-routine elements. To a degree, it is self-directed and carried out under general guidance only, although work plans and objectives will be spelled out in some detail. Judgement is fairly frequently exercised in deciding how to elect the most appropriate course of action within explicit policy guidelines. Reference to higher authority on matters of other than short-term significance is required.
5. The work is largely non-routine. It is mainly self-directed within the framework of

agreed work plans and objectives and policy guidelines. Judgement has frequently to be exercised without the benefit of clear policy rulings or precedents. Creative thinking is often required to reach decisions. Only occasional reference to higher authority is required.

6. The work is almost entirely non-routine. It continually requires the exercise of considerable judgement with relatively little guidance from defined policy guidelines. Creative thinking is a regular feature of the work. Only general policy direction is given.

Factor 4   Complexity

Factor definition

The variety and diversity of tasks carried out by the job holder and the range of skills used.

Level definitions

1. Highly repetitive work where the same task or group of tasks is carried out without any significant variation.
2. A fairly narrow range of tasks are carried out which tend to be closely related to one another and involve the use of a limited range of skills.
3. There is some diversity in the activities carried out although they are broadly related to one another. A fairly wide variety of skills have to be used.
4. A diverse range of broadly related tasks are carried out. A wide variety of administrative, technical or supervisory skills are used.
5. A highly diverse range of tasks are carried out, many of which are unrelated to one another. A wide variety of professional and/or managerial skills are used.
6. The work is multi-disciplinary and involves fulfilling a broad range of highly diverse responsibilities.

Factor 5   Contacts

Factor definition

The extent to which the work involves making contacts with people inside and outside the organization. In evaluating this factor consideration should be given to the extent to which the contact is concerned with routine or non-routine matters, the level and importance of the contact and the impact of the results of the contact on the reputation and performance of the organization.

Level definitions

1. Contacts limited to routine matters of exchanging information, principally within the job holder's own department.
2. Contacts of a mainly routine nature involving the exchange of information with people inside and outside the organization, but not at a senior level.
3. Contacts, sometimes on non-routine matters and involving both the exchange and interpretation of information, with people at a number of levels inside and outside the organization. Failure to relate well to the contacts may have some detrimental effects on the job holder's department but not, significantly, on the organization.
4. Contacts with a wide range of people within and outside the organization, but infrequently, if at all, at the highest level. Contacts involve making a favourable impression and the exercise of a fairly high degree of negotiating or persuasive skills or joint problem solving (although the problems are likely to be of departmental or local significance and will not significantly affect the organization as a whole). Mishandling of contacts can have some fairly short-term effects on the reputation of the organization.
5. Contacts at a high level inside and outside the organization which involve exercising a high degree of communicating, negotiating and persuasive skills and jointly solving

important problems. The impact on the organization's performance and reputation can be significant, at least in the short to medium-term.

6. Contacts at the highest level, with a particular emphasis on external relations. These involve very considerable communicating, advocacy and negotiating skills which can make a major and long-term impact on the performance and reputation of the organization.

Job Evaluation: Management Consultants' Schemes

This appendix summarizes the main features of the following most commonly used management consultants' job evaluation schemes:

- Hay Guide Chart – Profile Method
- PE International – Pay Points and Direct Consensus Method
- PA Consulting Group
- Price Waterhouse – the Profile Method
- Saville-Holdsworth – the SHL Method
- The Wyatt Company – the EPFC method
- Ernst and Young International (Employment Relations Associates) – the Decision Band Method
- Institute of Administrative Management – Office Job Evaluation
- Towers Perrin – WJQ
- KPMG Management Consulting – EQUATE

The Hay Guide Chart – Profile method of job evaluation

History and development

The Hay Guide Chart Profile Method of Job Evaluation is the most widely used single job evaluation method in the world, being used by over 7000 profit and non-profit organizations in some 40 countries. While it is perhaps best known for its application to management, professional and technical jobs, it is also extensively used for clerical and manual jobs, and when a single top-to-bottom evaluation method is required as the basis for integrated pay and grading structures.

It was initially conceived in the early 1950s, having its roots in factor comparison methods in which Edward N Hay was a pioneer, and has evolved by practical application into its present form.

Its widespread use, and the consistency of the job size numbering scale used, enables it to provide the basis for valid pay comparisons between organizations, nationally and internationally. Comprehensive pay and benefits surveys, using job-size based comparisons are conducted by the Hay Group in over 35 countries.

The method can be applied by a wide variety of processes, both manual and computer assisted, tailored to the particular requirements of the user organization.

Basis of the method

The method is based upon the following principles and observations.

- While there are many factors which could be considered in developing a job evaluation scheme, these can be grouped into three broad factors: the knowledge and skills required to do the job; the kind of thinking needed to solve the problems commonly faced; and the responsibilities assigned to the job.

■ This provides the basis of the three main factors of the Guide Chart Profile Method – Know-How, Problem Solving, and Accountability – which are common to all jobs, and which are subdivided into several elements.

■ For any given job, there will be a relationship between the three factors. Thus the output or end results expected from the job (the Accountability), will demand a certain level of input (Know-How), and processing of this Know-How (Problem Solving) to enable delivery of the output.

This can be represented by the simple model:

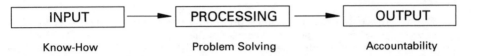

| INPUT | → | PROCESSING | → | OUTPUT |
| Know-How | | Problem Solving | | Accountability |

■ Thus jobs can be characterized not only by the size or level of each factor, but also by the balance between the factors – the Profile – which reflects the 'shape' of the job. Thus for example a research job is likely to be heavily loaded towards Know-How and Problem Solving, whereas for a sales representative or production manager, the balance will be shifted towards Accountability. In addition to evaluating each factor, evaluators also assess the profile of the job, which provides an important check on consistency of treatment.

■ The ability of evaluators to discern a difference between two jobs depends not only on the absolute difference, but on how big this difference is in relation to the size of the jobs themselves. Thus the numbering patterns used in the Guide Charts are based upon a geometric scale, each number being a constant percentage greater than the previous one. This percentage has been empirically determined at 15 per cent, as best representing the ability of experienced evaluators to discern a difference in any factor between two jobs. This 'step difference' concept provides the basic building block for the scales and for the comparisons between jobs, with one step representing a 'just discernible difference'.

■ Jobs should not be evaluated in isolation, but viewed in their organizational context, so that working relationships both vertically and horizontally throughout the organization are taken into account.

■ In order that the focus is on jobs, not the performance of jobholders, 'standard acceptable performance' is assumed. Similarly, jobs are evaluated independent of any market-driven pay conditions which may pertain, recognizing that these require addressing explicitly as pay issues, not job-size considerations.

Components of the method

The method has three main factors and eight dimensions as follows:

Know-How
The sum of every kind of knowledge, skill and experience, however acquired, needed for acceptable job performance. Its three dimensions are requirements for:

1. Practice procedures, specialized techniques and knowledge within occupational fields, commercial functions, and professional or scientific disciplines.
2. Integrating and harmonizing the diverse elements involved in managerial situations. This involves, in some combination, skills in planning, organizing, executing, controlling and evaluating and may be exercised consultatively as well as executively.
3. Active, practising person-to-person skills in work with other people, within or outside the organization.

Problem solving

The original, self-starting use of Know-How required by the job to identify, define, and resolve problems. 'You think with what you know'. This is true of even the most creative work. The raw material of any thinking is knowledge of facts, principles, and means. For that reason, Problem Solving is treated as a percentage of Know-How.

Problem Solving has two dimensions:

- the environment in which thinking takes place
- the challenge presented by the thinking to be done.

Accountability

The answerability for action and for the consequences of that action. It is the measured effect of the job on end results of the organization. It has three dimensions in the following order of importance:

1. Freedom to act: the extent of personal, procedural, or systematic guidance or control of actions in relation to the primary emphasis of the job.
2. Job impact on end results: the extent to which the job can directly affect actions necessary to produce results within its primary emphasis.
3. Magnitude: the portion of the total organization encompassed by the primary emphasis of the job. Where possible, magnitude is expressed in annual financial figures representing the area of primary emphasis of the job.

Beyond these three factors of job content, additional scales can be used to assess factors relating to the context in which the job operates; for example unpleasant working environment, hazards, physical demands, sensory attention, etc. When such factors are important for the jobs under consideration, scales are generated to enable their assessment within the context of the organization.

The Guide Charts

A Guide Chart for each factor (see Figures D.1, D.2 and D.3) contains semantic scales which reflect levels of each dimension. Each chart, except for Problem Solving, is expandable to reflect the size and complexity of the organization to which it is applied. The language of the scales, carefully evolved over many years and applied to literally millions of jobs of every kind, has remained fairly constant in recent years but is modified, as appropriate, to reflect the unique nature, character, and structure of any given organization. The numbering pattern in each chart is based upon the 15 per cent difference concept noted above.

To illustrate the use of the charts, consider the Know-How chart (1). If, for example, a job is considered to fall squarely into E Technical Know-How II Breadth of Management and 3 Human Relations Skills, then the chart indicates a Know-How value of 304 units. The 264 and 350 values are to allow for fine tuning or shading when one of the elements is considered light or heavy compared with the basic definition or with comparator jobs.

The same total Know-How score of 304 units can of course be arrived at in a variety of ways. For example, F+12 304 indicates a job which is significantly more technical, but less demanding in terms of management and human relations skills – but on balance requiring the same total volume of knowledge and skills. In addition to their primary purpose of arriving at a job size, this illustrates the way that the Guide Charts are frequently used to provide a language in which jobs can be described and characterized in a consistent way.

Use of the other two Guide Charts is similar, though in the case of Problem Solving, the chart yields a percentage value which is applied to the Know-How score to give Problem Solving units. Total job size is the sum of the three factor scores.

Consistency checks

- Profile: this is used as a powerful check for internal consistency within an evaluation. If for example the evaluation shows an Accountability score three 15 per cent steps higher than the Problem Solving score, it would be recorded as A3 (sometimes 'plus 3' or 'up to 3').

HayGroup

HAY GUIDE CHART FOR EVALUATING KNOW-HOW

DEFINITION:
Know-How is the sum of every kind of knowledge, skill and experience required for standard acceptable job performance. It is the fund of knowledge (however acquired) which is necessary for meeting:

* The requirement for know-how of practical procedures, specialised techniques and professional disciplines.
** The requirement for know-how in integrating and harmonising the diverse functions involved in managerial situations. This Know-How may be exercised in an advisory or executive way. It involves combining in some degree the elements of planning, organising, directing, controlling and evaluating, taking account of size, functional or organisational diversity, and time scale.
*** The requirement for Know-How in working with and through people (within or outside the organisation).

MEASURING KNOW-HOW:
Know-How has both breadth and depth. Thus, a job may require some knowledge about a lot of things, or a lot of knowledge about a few things. The total Know-How is the sum of both breadth and depth. This concept makes practical the comparison and weighing of the total Know-How content of different jobs in terms of 'HOW MUCH KNOWLEDGE ABOUT HOW MANY THINGS'.

*** HUMAN RELATIONS SKILLS

1. BASIC: Ordinary courtesy and effectiveness in dealing with others is required.

2. IMPORTANT: Understanding, influencing, and communicating with people are important but not overriding considerations.

3. CRITICAL: Skills in influencing, developing and/or motivating people are critical to the achievement of job objectives.

* DEPTH AND RANGE OF TECHNICAL KNOW-HOW

PRACTICAL PROCEDURES
- **A PRIMARY:** Jobs requiring Secondary education only plus some work indoctrination.
- **B ELEMENTARY VOCATIONAL:** Jobs requiring some understanding of standardised work routines and/or use of simple equipment and machines.

SPECIALISED TECHNIQUES
- **C VOCATIONAL:** Jobs requiring procedural or systematic proficiency, which may involve facility in the use of specialised equipment.
- **D ADVANCED VOCATIONAL:** Jobs requiring some specialised (generally non-theoretical) skills gained by on the job experience or through part professional qualification.

PROFESSIONAL DISCIPLINES
- **E BASIC PROFESSIONAL:** Jobs requiring a technical or specialised proficiency based on an understanding of concepts and principles normally associated with a professional or academic qualification or gained through a detailed grasp of involved practices and procedures.
- **F SEASONED PROFESSIONAL:** Jobs requiring proficiency in a technical, scientific or specialised field gained through broad and deep experience built on concepts and principles, or through wide exposure to complex practices and procedures.
- **G PROFESSIONAL MASTERY:** Jobs requiring determinative mastery of concepts, principles and practices gained through deep development in a highly specialised field or through comprehensive business experience.
- **H UNIQUE AUTHORITY:** Jobs requiring ... command of a ...

** PLANNING, ORGANISING, CONTROLLING – BREADTH OF MANAGEMENT KNOW-HOW

Column groups:
- **0. TASK:** Performance of a task (or tasks) highly specific as to objective and content and not involving the supervision of others
- **I. ACTIVITY:** Performance or supervision of work which is specific as to objective and content with appropriate awareness of related activities
- **II. HOMOGENEOUS:** Internal integration of operations which are relatively homogeneous in nature and objective, and which involve external co-ordination with associated functions
- **III. HETEROGENEOUS:** Operational or conceptual integration of functions which are diverse in nature and in objective, and which involve management area or general co-ordination of a strategic function
- **IV. (TOTAL)**

Depth	HR	0.TASK 1	0.TASK 2	0.TASK 3	I 1	I 2	I 3	II 1	II 2	II 3	III 1	III 2	III 3	IV 1	IV 2	IV 3
A	1	38	43	50	50	57	66	66	76	87	87	100	115	115	132	152
A	2	43	50	57	57	66	76	76	87	100	100	115	132	132	152	175
A	3	50	57	66	66	76	87	87	100	115	115	132	152	152	175	200
B	1	50	57	66	66	76	87	87	100	115	115	132	152	152	175	200
B	2	57	66	76	76	87	100	100	115	132	132	152	175	175	200	230
B	3	66	76	87	87	100	115	115	132	152	152	175	200	200	230	264
C	1	66	76	87	87	100	115	115	132	152	152	175	200	200	230	264
C	2	76	87	100	100	115	132	132	152	175	175	200	230	230	264	304
C	3	87	100	115	115	132	152	152	175	200	200	230	264	264	304	350
D	1	87	100	115	115	132	152	152	175	200	200	230	264	264	304	350
D	2	100	115	132	132	152	175	175	200	230	230	264	304	304	350	400
D	3	115	132	152	152	175	200	200	230	264	264	304	350	350	400	460
E	1	115	132	152	152	175	200	200	230	264	264	304	350	350	400	460
E	2	132	152	175	175	200	230	230	264	304	304	350	400	400	460	528
E	3	152	175	200	200	230	264	264	304	350	350	400	460	460	528	608
F	1	152	175	200	200	230	264	264	304	350	350	400	460	460	528	608
F	2	175	200	230	230	264	304	304	350	400	400	460	528	528	608	700
F	3	200	230	264	264	304	350	350	400	460	460	528	608	608	700	800
G	1	200	230	264	264	304	350	350	400	460	460	528	608	608	700	800
G	2	230	264	304	304	350	400	400	460	528	528	608	700	700	800	920
G	3	264	304	350	350	400	460	460	528	608	608	700	800	800	920	1056
H	1	264	304	350	350	400		460	528	608	608	700		800	920	
H	2	304	350					528	608					920	1056	

Figure D.1 *Part of the Hay Know-How Guide Chart*

HayGroup

DEFINITION: Problem Solving is the "self starting" thinking required by the job for analysing, evaluating, creating, reasoning, arriving at and drawing conclusions. To the extent that thinking is circumscribed by standards or covered by precedents, or referred to others, Problem Solving is diminished.

Problem Solving has two dimensions.

●● The environment in which the thinking takes place
●● The challenge presented by the thinking to be done

MEASURING PROBLEM SOLVING: Problem Solving measures the intensity of the mental process which employs Know-How to (1) the analysis, (2) the reasoning and (3) the arriving at conclusions. To the extent that thinking is circumscribed by standards or covered by precedents, or referred to others, thinking is knowledge of facts, principles and means, which are put together from something already there. Therefore, Problem Solving is expressed as a percentage of Know-How. (The Problem Solving score can be readily derived from the conversion table printed on the back of the Know-How Guide Chart.)

HAY GUIDE CHART FOR EVALUATING PROBLEM SOLVING

●● THINKING CHALLENGE

● THINKING ENVIRONMENT – FREEDOM TO THINK

	1. REPETITIVE Identical situations requiring solution by simple choice of things learned	2. PATTERNED Similar situations requiring solution by discriminating choice of things learned	3. VARIABLE Differing situations requiring the identification and selection of solutions through the application of acquired knowledge	4. ADAPTIVE Situations requiring analytical, interpretative, constructive thinking and evaluative judgement	5. UNCHARTED Pathfinding situations requiring creative thinking and the development of new concepts and approaches constituting significant additions to the sum of knowledge/ thought
A STRICT ROUTINE: Thinking within detailed rules, instructions and/or rigid supervision	10% 12%	14% 16%	19% 22%	25% 29%	33% 38
B ROUTINE: Thinking within standard instructions and/or continuous close supervision	12% 14%	16% 19%	22% 25%	29% 33%	38% 4
C SEMI-ROUTINE: Thinking within well defined procedures and precedents, somewhat diversified and/or supervised	14% 16%	19% 22%	25% 29%	33% 38%	43% 5
D STANDARDISED: Thinking within substantially diversified, established company procedures and standards, and general supervision	16% 19%	22% 25%	29% 33%	38% 43°	50% 5
E CLEARLY DEFINED: Thinking within clearly defined company policies, principles and specific objectives, under readily available direction	19% 22%	25% 29%	33% 38%	43% 50%	57° 66
F BROADLY DEFINED: Thinking within broad policies and objectives, under general direction	22% 25%	29% 33%	38% 43%	50% 57%	66% 76
G GENERALLY DEFINED: Thinking within general policies, principles and goals under guidance	25% 29%	33% 38%	43% 50%	57% 66%	76% 87
H ABSTRACTLY DEFINED: Thinking within business/human	29%	34%	50%	66%	87%

Figure D.2 *Part of the Hay Problem Solving Guide Chart*

HayGroup

DEFINITION: Accountability is the answerability for action and for the consequences of that action. It is the measured effect of the job on end results. It has three dimensions in the following order of importance:

● Freedom to Act – measured by the existence or absence of personal or procedural control and guidance as defined in the left-hand column below

●● Job Impact on End Results – as defined at upper right

●●● Magnitude (Area of Impact) – indicated by the general size of the area(s) most clearly affected by the job (measured on an annual money basis)

IMPACT OF JOB ON END RESULTS

INDIRECT
- REMOTE: Informational, recording, or incidental services for use by others in relation to some important end result.
- CONTRIBUTORY: Interpretative, advisory or facilitating services for use by others in taking action.

DIRECT
- SHARED: Jointly accountable with another/others (except own subordinates and superiors) within or outside the organisational unit, in taking action and exercising a controlling impact on end results
- PRIME: Controlling impact on end results, where shared accountability of others is subordinate

HAY GUIDE CHART FOR EVALUATING ACCOUNTABILITY

●●● MAGNITUDE Figures for use in 1991/92 Adjusted figures for 19 ..... (Magnitude figures for use in the following year are published each September)	AREA AND TYPE OF IMPACT (0) MINIMAL Under £33,000				(1) VERY SMALL £33,000 - £330,000				(2) SMALL £330,000 - £3.3M				(3) MEDIUM £3.3M - £33M				(4) LARGE £33M - £330M			
●● IMPACT / ● FREEDOM TO ACT	R.	C.	S.	P.	R.	C.	S.	P.	R.	C.	S.	P.	R.	C.	S.	P.	R.	C.	S.	[illegible]
A PRESCRIBED: These jobs are subject to – Direct and detailed instructions – Close supervision	8	10	14	19	10	14	19	25	14	19	25	33	19	25	33	43	25	33	43	
	9	12	16	22	12	16	22	29	16	22	29	38	22	29	38	50	29	38	50	
	10	14	19	25	14	19	25	33	19	25	33	43	25	33	43	57	33	43	57	
B CONTROLLED: These jobs are subject to – Instructions and established work routines – Close supervision	12	16	22	29	16	22	29	38	22	29	38	50	29	38	50	66	38	50	66	
	14	19	25	33	19	25	33	43	25	33	43	57	33	43	57	76	43	57	76	
	16	22	29	38	22	29	38	50	29	38	50	66	38	50	66	87	50	66	87	
C STANDARDISED: These jobs are subject, wholly or in part to – Standardised practices and procedures – General work instructions – Supervision of progress and results	19	25	33	43	25	33	43	57	33	43	57	76	43	57	76	100	57	76	100	
	22	29	38	50	29	38	50	66	38	50	66	87	50	66	87	115	66	87	115	
	25	33	43	57	33	43	57	76	43	57	76	100	57	76	100	132	76	100	132	
D REGULATED: These jobs are subject, wholly or in part to – Practices and procedures which have clear precedents or are covered by closely defined policies – Managerial control – Review of results	29	38	50	66	38	50	66	87	50	66	87	115	66	87	115	152	87	115	152	[illegible]
	33	43	57	76	43	57	76	100	57	76	100	132	76	100	132	175	100	132	175	[illegible]
	38	50	66	87	50	66	87	115	66	87	115	152	87	115	152	200	115	152	200	[illegible]
E DIRECTED: These jobs are subject to – Broad practice and procedures covered by functional precedents and policies – Achievement of a circumscribed operational activity – Managerial direction	43	57	76	100	57	76	100	132	76	100	132	175	100	132	175	230	132	175	230	[illegible]
	50	66	87	115	66	87	115	152	87	115	152	200	115	152	200	264	152	200	264	
	57	76	100	132	76	100	132	175	100	132	175	230	132	175	230	304	175	230	304	
F GENERALLY DIRECTED: These jobs by their nature or size are subject to – Functional policy objectives – General direction	66	87	115	152	87	115	152	200	115	152	200	264	152	200	264	350	200	264	350	
	76	100	132	175	100	132	175	230	132	175	230	304	175	230	304	400	230	304	[illegible]	
	87	115	152	200	115	152	200	264	152	200	264	350	200	264	350	460	264	350	[illegible]	
G GUIDED: These jobs are subject only to guidance and broad direction on orientation of policy	100	132	175	230	132	175	230	304	175	230	304	400	230	304	400	528	304	400	[illegible]	
	115	152	200	264	152	200	264	350	200	254	350	460	264	350	460	608	350	460	[illegible]	
	132	175	230	304	175	230	304	400	230	304	400	528	304	400	528	700	400	528	[illegible]	
H	152	200	264	350	200	264	350	460	264	350	460	608	350	460	608	800	460	608	800	
	175	230	304	400	230	[illegible]	[illegible]	[illegible]	304	400	528	700	400	528	[illegible]	[illegible]	528	700	920	
	[illegible]	264	350	460						[illegible]	608	800	[illegible]						1056	[illegible]

Figure D.3 *Part of the Hay Accountability Guide Chart*

- Evaluators make a separate judgement on the profile expected for the job. Thus, typically, jobs in line functions would be expected to have strongly Accountability orientated profiles, jobs in basic research would have strong Problem Solving orientation (P), while jobs in many staff functions like personnel, finance, etc are likely to have the two more in balance. If the profile which emerges from the evaluation does not agree with the evaluators' view of the appropriate profile, it indicates an inconsistency of treatment between the factors, and causes the evaluators to reconsider the evaluation.
- Rank order: Testing of rank order to identify anomalies is an important part of the process. It can be done at the level of total job size; by factor (eg total Know-How); or by individual dimension (eg freedom to act).

Application of the Guide Chart Profile method

The basic measuring instrument of the Guide Charts can be applied through a wide variety of processes, both manual and computer assisted. The choice of a particular application process depends principally on the purpose for which the job evaluation is being undertaken, the size and diversity of the job population under consideration, and the time and resource constraints which exist. Thus traditional processes, based upon multi-functional evaluation committees, can provide great sensitivity to a wide diversity of jobs, and can generate valuable output in terms of organizational analysis and clarification, though they are demanding in terms of time and resources. Computer assisted processes reduce the time and resource demands, particularly for large populations, but may reduce the opportunity for organizational debate and analysis. Hay consultants advise client organizations on the most appropriate process to meet particular needs and circumstances. The range of processes is illustrated in the following examples.

Committee based process

In this, the most commonly applied traditional process, evaluation judgements are made by a committee (or committees), trained in the use of the Guide Charts, and using job information in the form of job descriptions.

The process usually starts with the selection of a benchmark of jobs, to reflect the range of job types and levels in the population, and to enable basic evaluation standards and interpretations to be set.

Job descriptions for the benchmark jobs may be prepared by trained analysts, by jobholders or their managers – depending on circumstances. In most cases, approval of the final document by both jobholder and manager is adopted, whoever has prepared the description. A variety of job description formats may be used, but an important feature of Hay job descriptions is an emphasis on the results expected from a job – the principal accountabilities – which assists clarity and conciseness, and can provide links into related processes such as organizational analysis and performance management.

The benchmark committee is selected, usually including members from a range of functions, not purely HR specialists, so as to provide a range of inputs and perspectives, and foster ownership of the results. Depending on the organization's needs, the committee may be a management group, or may include peer group members and/or trade union representatives.

The committee is trained and guided by a Hay consultant, and evaluates the benchmark sample to provide clear reference points, and standards and principles to assist evaluation of non-benchmark jobs.

An important component of this process is the establishment of evaluation interpretations which reflect the organization's values and emphases, within the Guide Chart framework.

For a small population or in a highly centralized organization, the same committee may proceed to evaluate the remaining jobs. Otherwise, additional committees are selected and trained (for example divisional committees in a diversified business), and processes established to ensure application of common standards.

Computer based administrative support is available to assist this process, in the form of the QED Chart component of the HayXpert® suite of software. This enables recording and storage of job evaluation data, evaluation rationales and, if required, job descriptions, for rapid sorting and access when comparisons or rank order checks are being made.

Comparison and classification methods

The Guide Chart Profile method can also be used to underpin a variety of comparison or classification approaches, particularly for large and relatively homogeneous populations.

These processes normally start with committee evaluation of a benchmark sample, using the Guide Charts in the conventional way.

Based on the results of this sampling and standard setting, a classification or 'slotting' framework can be established, to facilitate evaluation of remaining jobs by direct comparison. This can be presented in written 'workbook' form, or as a computer based framework in HayXpert® software.

Such methods can achieve very rapid evaluation of large populations and provide for significant devolution of responsibility for evaluation, with relatively low training requirements.

Computer assisted evaluation processes

In these processes, the use of job descriptions and committees for the bulk of the job population is replaced by structured questionnaires, processed by computer to generate evaluations directly, using an algorithm which has been established from full evaluation of a benchmark sample.

Where a single approach is required to cover all (or most) of the jobs in an organization, a single, comprehensive questionnaire is constructed. A benchmark sample of jobs is evaluated conventionally, using the Guide Charts, to provide the basic standards to underpin the process. The same jobs are also rated on the questionnaire and an algorithm built to replicate Hay job unit results from the questionnaire responses and programmed into HayXpert® software. For non-benchmark jobs, questionnaires are completed and processed through the computer (batch or interactive) to yield comparative evaluations. Quality checks are built in, both to the software and processes to ensure consistency.

An alternative approach, for a more tightly defined job group, is the job family questionnaire. This provides a shorter, more focused questionnaire which is typically developed in conjunction with members of the family in question to reflect quite explicitly the key differentiating factors which affect job size in that family, expressed in their language. It is often used when relationships between job evaluation, career development and competency analysis are important. The process for its implementation is similar to that described for the 'universal' questionnaire.

Mixed processes

Since all these application processes are underpinned by the same Guide Chart principles and numbering scales, they yield comparable results and so different processes can be applied to different job groups without loss of compatibility.

PE International Pay Points

History and development

PE International Pay Points was developed in 1979 based upon the experience and developmental work undertaken by Inbucon Management Consultants over some 30 years. It can be applied to determine market-related salaries for senior executives and middle management jobs and as an analytical method of job evaluation extending to clerical and manual jobs. The system has the advantage of an automatic link to PE International's salary database derived from their regular surveys of executive salaries and fringe benefits.

The evaluation process

Concise job descriptions are prepared and points are awarded against levels under five factors in the traditional analytical points rating manner. The factors cover:

- knowledge and experience
- complexity and creativity
- judgements and decisions
- operational responsibility
- contacts and communications.

A sixth factor (working environment) is often adopted for particular job populations.

Depending on the number of jobs to be considered, the system may be applied to a sample of jobs first which can then be used as benchmarks or reference jobs for evaluating others. Jobs can be left individually scored or put into a grading structure with each grade having a specific range of points. Job scores are converted into market-related salaries by the application of two multipliers derived from PE International's own extensive database. The first multiplier called 'company factor' takes account of the size and characteristics of the particular company or operating unit in which the job is situated. The second multiplier called 'salary factor' simply converts points scored into an assessed market salary for the job which then becomes the mid-point of a salary range. There is provision in the system for taking account of industry and regional salary differentials and of specific job premiums where a market scarcity applies. Salary ranges can also be pitched at market median, upper quartile or other intermediate values depending on a particular company's salary policy. The system has been extensively applied in both public and private sectors in the UK and Europe.

PE International Direct Consensus Method (DCM)

History and development

DCM was first developed by PE International some 25 years ago, and uses job ranking by paired comparisons. Jobs are compared within a number of different factors to develop a factor plan. The system is highly flexible and is suitable for both large and small organizations. It can cover senior management, as well as clerical and manual jobs. DCM can be applied with full employee participation, or purely as a management exercise.

The evaluation process

For job populations above 70–80, a series of jobs, typically 40–60, would be selected for ranking as benchmarks. In the case of a participative exercise, employees whose jobs will be covered by the evaluation are first of all briefed on the project, and a judging panel of 6–16 panelists is chosen to represent a cross section of the organization by level, function and sex. The panel then decides the factors which will be used in the evaluation.

There is complete flexibility as to the factors chosen. The main criteria are that they need to suit the jobs which are being evaluated. Thus, it may be expedient to use different factors for managerial, clerical and manual jobs, although otherwise the approach is the same. Care must be taken to ensure that the selected factors are free from sex bias. If job descriptions do not already exist, these must be prepared with due prominence being given to each of the selected factors. Jobs are then arranged in pairs on a ranking form with each job paired with every other job against each of the chosen factors.

Although job descriptions are available the judges are required to familiarize themselves with the jobs to be ranked. They then record their decisions on the ranking forms provided, by marking the job with the greatest demands in each pair of jobs against each factor. After individual factor assessments have been completed, each pair of jobs is separately compared on a 'total factor' basis.

Analyzing the results and providing weightings

The judging panel's decisions are processed by computer, which prints out the rank orders of jobs as decided by the panel, both for each factor and also on a 'total factor' basis. The program also produces decision matrices, which highlight judgements contrary to the general consensus so that these can be examined and resolved. The implied factor weights are then calculated by computer, based on the judges' decisions in ranking jobs against individual factors and on a total factor basis. In this way, a factor plan is prepared which is unique to the organization and the evaluated jobs. The ranking is divided into a number of grades and the remaining jobs, ie those not ranked, are then fitted into grades by the application of the factor plan. The development of a factor plan as described above readily facilitates the development of a unique factor points system of job evaluation and meets the particular requirements of an organization and job population being evaluated.

Using the concepts of DCM outlined above, tailor-made analytical factor points systems are also developed and applied.

PA Consulting Group

History and development

The factor based approach to job evaluation developed by the PA Consulting Group gives greater prominence to internal relativities than external comparisons. PA emphasize that their experience has shown people at work place a relatively higher importance on pay comparisons with colleagues than with those doing similar work in other organizations. Each scheme is therefore developed to meet the client's own needs, particularly in the selection of factors. The approach utilizes the advantages of the traditional paired comparison method in developing the system parameters by using cross ranking, allowing a line of best fit between results obtained from the paired comparison and the factor plan. All jobs are finally ranked by their weighted factor scores alone.

Particular care is taken throughout the process, both at the stage of factor choice and definition and during evaluation meetings, to avoid any bias and this applies particularly to sex bias, in line with the spirit of the Equal Pay (Amendment) Regulations.

Recent developments include:

- the availability of a 'standard PA system' which encapsulates PA's job evaluation experience in six pre-defined factors, each with two dimensions;
- the 'PA/Monitor' expert system, which enables consistent and reliable evaluation of jobs through direct entry by jobholder and manager to a PC based questionnaire, eliminating all paperwork and panel meetings.

Scheme development

There are three broad stages involved in developing a client-tailored scheme:

- factor selection and definition
- evaluation of benchmark jobs
- analysis and review of results and development and testing of the final structure.

Plus, increasingly

- tailoring the PA/Monitor system to replicate the benchmark panel's decision processes.

The end of the development phase results in a unique, validated scheme for each client.

Basis of the scheme

For those clients looking for a tailored scheme, factors are selected and defined uniquely for each client and, typically, between six and ten factors are chosen. These will normally be developed from the six standard PA factors including for example 'judgement'; job impact; communication and theoretical knowledge and application. But it is up to the client organization to select which factors it considers important. Each factor will normally be divided into two logically linked dimensions, both having levels or degrees, with narrative descriptions using client terminology.

The evaluation process

The client is encouraged to set up a steering group to oversee the process. That group will select 30 to 40 benchmark jobs which are representative of both senior and junior levels in the organization and of all functions. The steering group will appoint a panel including a wide cross section of people in the company, to evaluate the jobs.

Company job descriptions are completed, either by the job holder or by an analyst, depending on time and cost constraints. As well as a traditional job description, a factor based questionnaire is also completed. These are reviewed for consistency prior to the panel meeting.

At the evaluation meeting, each job is considered in turn, separately from the other jobs. The chairman of the panel introduces the job and ensures there is sufficient discussion to enable each panel member to examine the scope and responsibilities of the job. Factors are considered one at a time and the appropriate degree finally selected by a majority vote. At least a two-thirds majority is required and discussion continues until there is this level of consensus.

Each panel member then separately completes the paired comparison exercise. This involves comparing each job with each other job on paired comparison sheets. This process of course involves subjective judgement, but panel members will have gained an up-to-date knowledge of the scope of these jobs during their discussion in the factor analysis process. Again stress is placed on the need to avoid sex discrimination, and to think to the future rather than to justify the status quo.

Analysis, development and validation of the scheme

All results are processed by computer, using PA's own software. First, the paired comparison results are checked for consistency between judges and the average rank order then compared with the factor analysis scores. Weightings are produced which give the closest fit between the paired comparison results and the factor analysis.

These results are then carefully reviewed with the client to ensure that the scheme which has been developed is the optimum scheme for that client. Thus the parameters of the system are tested and refined before proceeding to the application stage.

Application and use of the scheme – manual system

The remaining jobs are evaluated using the factors; weightings are developed in the previous phase. (The benchmark jobs, having been evaluated during the development phase, do not need re-evaluation.)

Participation and disclosure: There is potential for this system to be highly participative at every stage. A manual is produced for use by the job evaluation panel at its meetings, containing all the information necessary to conduct future evaluations and to deal with new jobs as they are created. The information disclosed to employees will typically include a summary of the purpose, processes and results of the scheme but will usually exclude factor weightings.

When the results are announced, employees are normally allowed to appeal against the grading, following a procedure recommended by the consultant. Once these appeals have been considered and settled, the scheme is in full operation. New and changed jobs are evaluated as necessary.

Maintenance: To ensure the scheme keeps up to date and is responsive to changes in the clients' situation, various levels of maintenance are recommended, and detailed in the manual. In the short term, annual job content reviews are recommended, in the longer term (three to five years), factor and weighting audits.

Application and use of the scheme – computerized system

Following the validation of the tailored system by the evaluation panel, the PA/Monitor system will itself be tailored to reflect the client's new system. This involves modifying and adding to the question library (the standard system has over 200 questions) the answer options and the 'evaluation rules' which the system will use to replicate the decision processes of the benchmark panel re-evaluating the jobs on the system.

The remaining jobs are then evaluated by the jobholder and manager following the questioning sequence presented to them on the PC. (The system runs in 'Windows' and 'help' screens are available throughout so that the ability to operate a 'mouse' is all that is required.) The evaluation of any one job will typically trigger a route through about 50 relevant questions (selected by the system on the basis of previous responses). Automatic validation is built in and after the final question has been answered a 'job overview' is produced which describes the job in terms directly related to the evaluation factors and provides a detailed rationale for the evaluations produced.

PA claims that the system is truly 'paperless' and user-friendly, being open for any jobholder to 'appeal' by re-evaluating their own job. The evaluation process is devolved to line management with the Personnel Department retaining only the overall audit, validation and control functions.

Price Waterhouse: The Profile Method

The Profile Method is based on an approach developed by Urwick Orr and Partners, who merged with Price Waterhouse in 1985. The method is designed to help organizations develop tailored schemes to meet their own needs quickly and easily. In recent years it has been developed to cover all jobs ranging from board level to the shop floor, across a wide range of industries and sectors. Profile Method schemes are robust in equal value terms, and can also be developed as 'expert system' applications.

Main components of the system

The Profile Method builds schemes around a tailored set of factors, termed 'characteristics', which are selected to meet an individual client's needs. Similarly, weightings developed for the characteristics are specific to each client company. Price Waterhouse stress the difficulty in consistently evaluating jobs when the rating scale comprises too many levels. Typically, their Profile Method uses only between four and eight levels within each characteristic.

As experience is gained during the design and operation of the scheme, guidelines are drawn up for ensuring consistency. Typical characteristics cover the areas of responsibility, knowledge, social skills and mental skills.

Benchmark jobs are selected by a steering committee, and job descriptions completed. Where possible, in-house analysts are trained to minimize dependency on external consultants.

The benchmark jobs are looked at in two ways. First, they are compared analytically, characteristic by characteristic, to produce 'profiles' of the jobs. Second, they are compared on a whole-job basis, to place them in a simple felt-fair rank order. These two sets of data are compared statistically to produce a set of weightings that enable the 'profiles' to be converted into an evaluation score. The weighting computation is carried out using a specially developed computer program designed to place greatest weighting on those characteristics that are most highly correlated with the felt-fair rank order.

The remaining jobs are then also profiled and scored using the weighted characteristics, to provide detailed evaluations of all jobs. Alternatively, a grading structure can be developed around the benchmark job results, with the remaining jobs slotted into grades by comparing them with the grades of benchmarks.

Throughout each assignment, consultants encourage full participation and discussion. Evaluation teams may be wholly management led, or include employees from a range of levels. The atmosphere in which the evaluations are conducted is important, and in-house involvement in the development of the scheme ensures greater acceptability. It also prolongs the life of the scheme by achieving high consistency in assessment.

Saville and Holdsworth – The SHL approach to job evaluation

History and development

An integral feature of the SHL approach to job evaluation is the linkage with the Work Profiling System of job analysis, which provides a comprehensive range of human resource management applications.

The WPS is a standardized job analysis questionnaire which is normally completed by the jobholder and is then read by an optical scanner. The computer produces both a detailed technical report and a short summary report on the job. It is possible for a number of jobholders in the same job to complete the questionnaire and produce a combined report showing the mean and standard deviation for up to 99 jobholders.

The WPS has been developed over four years and was sponsored by 21 major UK organizations.

More than 1000 jobs were submitted to quantitative scaled questionnaires (critical component questionnaires) as well as qualitative research via repertory grid, critical incidents and paired comparisons techniques. This led to three structured trial questionnaires with over 800 questions between them and the generation of a human attribute model covering over 200 attributes.

Main components of the scheme

The use of the WPS allows information to be collected about a job in a structured way using either paper and pencil or computer administration. The expert aspect of the WPS computer system is in the:

- 800 plus equations used to predict human attributes from job task and context information
- linking assessment methods to the human attribute model
- matching procedure for individuals to jobs
- standardized guidance in setting interview questions and personality link caveats.

For job evaluation purposes organizations have the choice of selecting relevant factors from the 28 sections in Part II of the WPS questionnaire or if necessary the 32 sections in Part I of the WPS. Thus each organization may develop a unique job evaluation system from the same menu of variables.

The scheme is introduced by means of the following eight steps:

Step one: steering committee appointed

The steering committee, comprising management and staff representatives, has three main tasks:

- agreeing the principles of the job evaluation scheme
- helping in the smooth introduction of the scheme
- monitoring the long-term performance.

Ideally, the steering committee should collectively have knowledge of all the jobs covered by the scheme. This helps in the various decisions that need to be made and provides confidence to staff that the scheme will be administered fairly.

It is important that all members of the steering committee have a basic understanding of the job evaluation process and the Work Profiling System. The first meeting will be largely devoted to these two objectives.

It is desirable for the appeals procedure to be defined at an early stage. This is likely to take the form of a sub-committee of the steering committee. Time periods should be set for the receipt of appeals following the announcement of the results of job evaluation.

A sample of benchmark jobs need to be selected which reflect a clearly perceived hierarchy within the current pay structure. Benchmark jobs are chosen to represent the full range of job values and are jobs about which there is substantial agreement on current relative value. Being selected as a benchmark does not mean that a job will necessarily remain on the same grade once the exercise has been completed. Those jobs selected as benchmarks would then be analyzed using the Work Profiling System.

Step two: job analyst training

Validating the Work Profiling System questionnaires will be a key element in the job evaluation process. Job analysts will require comprehensive knowledge of the WPS and specific training in the validation interview. This will help to develop the skill and expertise of the organization's own job analyst team.

Step three: selection of evaluation dimensions

From approximately 30 main sections in Part I of the WPS and the 21 sectors in Part II the steering committee selects those dimensions which reflect the needs of the organization. At this stage it is possible to attach additional items that may not appear in the WPS, and yet be of importance to the organization and relevant to the jobs under review. Having identified the key dimensions for the scheme it is then required to allocate weightings to them for inclusion in the WPS analysis. SHL provides guidance on the various ways of doing this.

Step four: evaluation of benchmark jobs by steering committee

Using job objectives and key job tasks produced via the WPS, the steering committee evaluates the benchmark jobs on a 'felt-fair' basis, and creates a metric derived from the rank order of jobs. Paired comparison technique can be used for this procedure, although other methods are available.

Step five: evaluation of benchmark jobs by WPS

The benchmark jobs are put through the WPS and evaluation scores generated as weighted aggregates. These are then validated by correlating against the felt-fair metric. If the degree of correlation is inadequate, a review of differences is undertaken. This could result in a revision of weights and re-validation.

Step six: preparation of explanatory documentation

To keep staff informed of the scheme, a general explanatory document and technical manual will need to be prepared. These documents may well be supported by other activities – for example, staff meetings to introduce the evaluation method.

Critical monitoring of the job analysis process will be required on an ongoing basis, including the validation interviews.

Step seven: data preparation

Once all the jobs have been analyzed using the WPS it will be necessary to collate the scattergram of scores and present this to the steering committee to aid their decision on relating points to salary grades.

Step eight: review of appeals

Due to the thoroughness of the WPS as a means of analyzing jobs it is unlikely that many appeals will arise on the grounds of an inadequate job description. However, some appeals may occur where jobholders feel there is inequity in the grading of their own job compared with that of another staff member perceived to be performing similar duties.

Wyatt – The Employee Points Factor Comparison Method (EPFC)

History and development

This variation on points rating was developed in 1978–79 by the Wyatt Company UK Ltd. It is the product of a search for a method which is quantifiable and avoids the problem encountered in some factor schemes of scoring jobs twice on the same factor, and yet which arrives at an integrated evaluation of jobs at all levels. Since such a scheme would provide an acceptable framework for the collection of comparative pay information, Wyatt devised the EPFC as a necessary preliminary to the establishment of their Remuneration Data

Services (RDS). At that stage the scheme was not primarily intended for use by companies as a method of in-house job evaluation. Company in-house adoption of the scheme came at the request of individual participants and is not a condition of membership of the RDS.

Current components of the scheme

The EPFC approach is essentially a factor based points rating scheme. It is based on the premise that since jobs cannot be carried out without people, why not measure them by reference to the demands the job makes on the people doing them? Employees have two attributes to offer in fulfilling the requirements of any job: knowledge and personal skills. Wyatt therefore base their scheme on a detailed analysis of these two dimensions as follows.

Knowledge

Knowledge is measured by the combination of formal learning (education) and practical application (experience). The education breakdown measures the jobholders' required store of knowledge that can only be gained by formal education or training. The experience analysis measures the knowledge and skills which cannot be gained by formal education or training but which are essential for satisfactory job performance. A section illustrating the knowledge chart is shown below. The full chart contains eight degrees of education and seven degrees of experience (see Figure D.4).

Skills

The axes for the chart measuring skills are mental aptitude, human relations skills and physical skills. The mental 'aptitude' elements define the range of mental skills required and start from simple observance of limited rules governing basic tasks through various levels of analysis, decision-making and original thought. The human relations breakdowns define the levels of influence required for effective job performance. Physical skills are scored against three levels from no special skills to highly developed skills. A section of the skills chart is illustrated below. The full chart contains six degrees for human relations and seven degrees for mental aptitude. This chart appears to be more complex than the knowledge chart, because it has to represent three factors rather than just two.

For the purposes of comparison with the RDS the scheme divides into level or grades from 1, eg cleaner/janitor, to 24, eg international chief executive. Company structures vary from this pattern but are carefully cross checked by Wyatt for the purpose of salary comparisons on the data bank (see Figure D.5).

Within each chart there is an opportunity to distinguish jobs further by shading the levels (+ or –).

In addition to overall sorethumbing, the EPFC system allows for 'profiling' jobs by assessing the balance between the knowledge and skills requirements. A very high profile would suggest a highly skilled job with a low amount of knowledge supporting it and a negative profile would indicate the reverse – an over specification of knowledge with limited application in terms of skills.

Both these situations would highlight either inconsistent evaluations or poor job design.

The evaluation process

Wyatt recommend that evaluations are based wherever possible on up-to-date job descriptions, although it is recognized that the design of these will in each case need to be consistent with the needs, goals and culture of the organization. Jobs should be evaluated where practicable by panels of four to six members (although larger groups may be necessary where wider representation is required) including representatives of different areas of the organization. All evaluation decisions should be recorded formally with a written justification of the score allotted to each job. Within this framework it is understood and accepted that no two organizations will want their job evaluation system to be implemented in the same way, and Wyatt's approach is appropriately flexible. Wyatt prefer to use the method most suitable to an organization's culture. However, they insist that good

EDUCATION	I. Experience is limited to basic exposure to the routines of life. Little or no previous work experience required.			II. Jobs requiring work related experience to gain limited but specialised knowledge of equipment, procedures and work routines.			III. Jobs requiring experience of a range of business procedures, specialised experience of complex equations or processes, or technical sufficiency in a specialised subject.	
A. No formal requirements other than basic numeracy and literacy, eg an ability to communicate with others and perform elementary arithmetic calculations.	23	27	32	32	38	44	44	52
	27	32	38	38	44	52	52	61
	32	38	44	44	52	61	61	72
B. Job requires basic proficiency in a number of specific practical or academic subjects.	32	38	44	44	52	61	61	72
	38	44	52	52	61	72	72	85
	44	52	61	61	72	85	85	100
C. Job requires proficiency in a range of techniques in one or more craft(s)/vocational subject(s).	44	52	61	61	72	85	85	100
	52	61	72	72	85	100	100	115
	61	72	85	85	100	115	115	132
D. Job requires an understanding of principles and techniques in one or more academic or vocational subject(s).	61	72	85	85	100	115	115	132
	72	85	100	100	115	132	132	152
	85	100	115	115	132	152	152	175
E. Job requires an understanding of theories, principles and techniques in one or more advanced vocational/technical subject(s).	85	100	115	115	132	152	152	175
	100	115	132	132	152	175	175	201
	115	132	152	152	175	201	201	231
F. Job requires an understanding of concepts, theories and principles in an academic or professional discipline.	115	132	152	152	175	201	201	231
	132	152	175	175	201	231	231	266
	152	175	201	201	231	266	266	306
G. Job requires an advanced and comprehensive understanding of concepts, theories and principles in an academic or professional discipline, or an understanding at a conceptual level in more than one related discipline.	152	175	201	201	231	266	266	306
	175	201	231	231	266	306	306	352
	201	231	266	266	306	352	352	405
H. Job requires total mastery of a profound discipline at a 'pathfinding' level of expertise.	201	231	266	266	306	352	352	405
	231	266	306	306	352	405	405	465
	266	306	352	352	405	465	465	535

Figure D.4 *Section of a knowledge chart – Wyatt EPFC Method*

PHYSICAL SKILLS

1. Jobs requiring no special physical skills, little or no physical effort and which are performed in reasonably pleasant and safe surroundings.

2. Jobs requiring highly specialised physical skills *or* considerable sustained exertion *or* which are performed in extremely unpleasant or hazardous surroundings. Alternatively, jobs with a combination of physical requirements at a less demanding level under at least two of the above categories.

3. Jobs simultaneously requiring highly specialised physical skills, considerable sustained exertion *and* which are performed in extremely unpleasant and hazardous surroundings.

MENTAL APTITUDE	PHYSICAL SKILLS	I. No more than ordinary courtesy required.			II. Jobs with a basic service element, perhaps in answering queries from the public, explaining instructions, supervising a team on routine work or in circumstances requiring tact and diplomacy.		
A. Simple repetitive duties requiring no special mental skills. All activities are guided by detailed instructions and/or continuously available supervision. All non-routine matters are referred to others.	1	61	72	85	85	100	115
	2	85	100	115	115	132	152
	3	115	132	152	152	175	201
B. Straightforward duties requiring concentration, attention to detail or simple analysis. Judgements are uninvolved and are based upon standard procedures. Supervision is generally available and unusual matters are referred to others.	1	85	100	115	115	132	152
	2	115	132	152	152	175	201
	3	152	175	201	201	231	266
C. Activities require the exercise of discretion in making judgements involving specific commitments based on well-defined procedures and clear precedents. Job holder deals with most situations but advice is readily available in handling complex cases or in making more sensitive judgements/decisions.	1	115	132	152	152	175	201
	2	152	175	201	201	231	266
	3	201	231	266	266	306	352
D. Analytical skills are required in making decisions or more complicated judgements, within general operating guidelines and precedents, which may involve some commitment or allocation of resources. Specialist advice or access to management guidance is generally available as required	1	152	175	201	201	231	266
	2	201	231	266	266	306	352
	3	266	306	352	352	405	465
E. Decisions concerning operating methods or processes, involving the commitment or allocation or significant resources, or highly complex judgements requiring advanced innovative or analytical abilities. A broadly defined frame of reference and expert advice or general managerial direction are available.	1	201	231	266	266	306	352
	2	266	306	352	352	405	465
	3	352	405	465	465	535	615
F. Decisions concerning operational policy, involving the commitment of large-scale resources, or the handling of unique problems or novel situations involving highly complex analysis or conceptualisation of solutions. Guidance is available from broad terms of reference and general direction and 'expert' advice may be available on specific technical issues.	1	266	306	352	352	405	465
	2	352	405	465	465	535	615
	3	465	535	615	615	708	814
G. Decisions have a critical impact on the organisation's strategy and survival, and require a profound understanding of fundamental business and commercial principles. Little guidance is available except the broadest corporate goals, although peers and subordinates may be available to discuss issues and concepts.	1	352	405	465	465	535	615
	2	465	535	615	615	708	814
	3	615	708	814	814	936	1076

Figure D.5 *Section of a skills chart – Wyatt EPFC Method*

records are the key to a fully supported job evaluation programme and full notes of both job details and the evaluations are kept as part of the programme.

The scheme has been used in a variety of environments, including both staff and union representatives.

The EPFC process can also be introduced in a computerized form. This approach involves a closed-ended questionnaire designed around the EPFC factors. The information gathered via the questionnaire is then analyzed against a statistical model in order to produce 'evaluated' scores.

This adaptation allows for an organization to introduce a more rapid evaluation process while continuing to be supported by the robust EPFC methodology.

Wyatt-MULTICOMP

Basis of the system

MULTICOMP was developed in the United States and is available in the UK from the Wyatt Company. It is described by them as a computerized, multiple-regression-based job evaluation system.

Components of the system

MULTICOMP uses a questionnaire, specially tailored to the needs of the organization, which is filled out by incumbents or their supervisors to create a comprehensive company database which measures how each job reflects the key factors which are specific to the organization.

Benchmark positions are selected and, using multiple regression analysis, MULTICOMP then evaluates questionnaire responses to develop a statistical model for each benchmark position. Mathematical relationships are then established between benchmark data and grades which enable benchmark jobs to be slotted into a grade structure.

Using what Wyatt calls the 'Electronic Devil's Advocate' feature, the reasonableness of employee questionnaire responses is monitored by the computer against the benchmark jobs. Every answer is verified and invalid responses are flagged for further investigation. If the response in a questionnaire is verified as falling within acceptable limits, MULTICOMP calculates the grade appropriate to the job responsibilities.

Employment Relations: the decision band method (DBM)

History and development

DBM was devised by Dr T T Paterson who applied it in Africa and Europe. It has been applied extensively in the USA and Canada by Arthur Young Management Consultants. In 1981, Arthur Young acquired the world rights to implement DBM. DBM is available in the UK through Employment Relations Associates Ltd. DBM is a registered trademark.

DBM is derived from Dr Paterson's work on organizational theory and practice. As such it is an aid to organizational analysis as well as a job evaluation and pay determination method.

In common with many other job evaluation methods, DBM requires three stages: analysis of jobs, grading of jobs and pricing of jobs. DBM is a relatively simple method to implement.

Components of the scheme

A common characteristic of all jobs is that they are required to make and/or advise those making decisions. As such, decision-making/advising can be used as a means of comparing jobs in an organization. The nature of the decision ranges from the most far-reaching decisions on policies to simpler decisions such as how fast to clean an area or key in data. Dr Paterson observed that there are six levels (termed bands) of decision-making/advice present within organizations. The bands form an end–means continuum, ie the higher band sets the end for the next band, etc. These six bands form the basic framework of the grading approach and incorporate various aspects of decision-making which are treated as separate factors in some other methods. Other factors such as skill are also considered as explained below.

The six bands are summarized below.

Band F – corporate policy-making decisions

Decisions that determine the scope, the direction, the overall goals of the total enterprise, subject to few constraints other than those imposed by law and/or economic conditions. These decisions take into consideration the functions of the enterprise. Such decisions also set the goals of the major functions and set the limits of the funds available to each and to the extent of their intended programmes. Band F decisions are of the kind made at Board or chief executive level.

Band E – programming decisions

Decisions on the means of achieving the goals (ends) established by Band F decisions – specifying goals for the constituent functions of these major functions, and allocating resources (facilities, people, money, materials) among these constituent functions in order to achieve the goals.

Band D – interpretive decisions

Decisions on the means of achieving the goals (ends) established by Band E decisions specifying what is to be done in lower bands, and deploying the allocated resources. If circumstances change, involving uncertainty of information or outcome, a Band D decision is required to establish what is to be done in similar circumstances in the future.

Band C – process decisions

Decisions on the means (selection of a process) of achieving the goals (ends) established by Band D decisions, subject to the limits imposed by the available technology and resources, and the constraints set at Band D. The selection of the process is a decision that must precede the carrying out of the operations that constitute the process. That is, the process decision specifies what is to be done at Band B.

Band B – operational decisions

Decisions on the carrying out of the operations of a process specified by a Band C decision. There is, within the limits set by the specific process, a choice as to how the operations are carried out, but not as to what operations constitute the process.

Band A – defined decisions

Decisions on the manner and speed of performing the elements of an operation. There is, within the limits set by the prescribed operation, a choice as to how the elements are performed, but not as to what elements constitute the operation.

The grading method

When each job has been analyzed, the jobs are then banded, graded and sub-graded, if appropriate. The need and the extent of sub-grading depends upon the nature and requirements of the organization. The three steps are:

1. *Banding:* Each job is placed in an appropriate band.
2. *Grading:* Each band has an upper and lower division (termed grades). If a job has a coordinating responsibility for other jobs in the same band as itself, it is placed in the upper division, if not, it is placed in the lower division.
3. *Sub-grading:* Degrees of job difficulty can be distinguished within the grades by comparing jobs on aspects such as diversity and complexity of tasks, need for special alertness, precision, technical or professional skills.

The grading steps are illustrated in Figure D.6. It does not mean that posts must appear in all the bands and grades. This will depend on the organization, eg Band E tasks are often undertaken by Band F postholders in small/medium-size organizations. In practice, it is

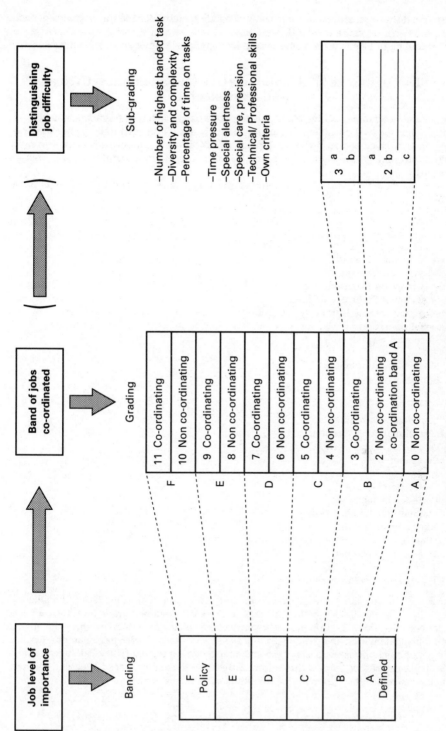

Figure D.6 *Decision banding method*

often found that a maximum of three sub-grades are required for the lower grades of each band and two sub-grades for the higher grade.

The grading of jobs is usually undertaken by a group of managers and employees.

The Institute of Administrative Management – Office Job Evaluation

The Institute of Administrative Management's (IAM) approach to job grading was born in 1942 but has evolved considerably since those early days. It is essentially a job classification scheme developed to cover all aspects of office work. The classification currently divides into nine grades (Grades A–F and M1–M3). These Grade Definitions are given in Figure D.7.

For each of the following office activities, typical tasks are described and defined in some detail:

- Audit
- Computers
  - Computer analysis
  - Computer operators
  - Personal Computers
  - Computer Programming
  - Systems Control and Management
  - Visual Display Unit (VDU) operating
- Depot operation
- Document reproduction
- Filing
- Financial accountancy
- Foreign exchange
- Insurance
- Libraries
- Management accounting
- Marketing and advertising
- Organization and methods
- Personnel
- Post
- Production control
- Facilities management
- Purchasing administration
- Sales administration
- Statistics
- Telecommunications
- Travel
- Typing and secretarial duties

These tasks have each been allocated a grade level. Job grading is achieved by matching actual tasks against graded definitions and deciding the dominant grade level for each job under consideration. The IAM manual gives detailed guidance on this, together with advice on the implementation and maintenance of the scheme and broader pay related issues.

This approach forms the basis of job matching for IAM's regular Office Salaries Analysis. It is supported and developed through the Office Job Evaluation User Group and through training courses and certification of practitioners.

Towers Perrin – WJQ (Weighted Job Questionnaire)

This computer assisted approach to analytical factor/points based job evaluation can either be based on five 'core' job factors or applied in the 'WJQ Custom' form which allows for

Grade definitions

A
Jobs or duties that require no previous work experience and are:
1. simple enough to require very limited training;
2. closely controlled by supervision or self-checking procedures.

B
Jobs or duties which remain simple but require a short period of training. Duties consist of standard routines following well defined rules less closely controlled.

C
Jobs or duties which require some experience or special aptitude. The duties are generally standardized with regular control but there is a little scope for initiative to be developed.

D
Jobs or duties requiring considerable experience and a limited degree of initiative but remaining mostly within predetermined procedures. Routines may vary and be without close supervisory control.

E
Jobs or duties which require either or both of the following:
1. a technical or specialist knowledge at a basic level applied where the occasional use of discretion and initiative is necessary;
2. work supervision normally of up to five lower grade staff.

F
Jobs or duties which require the application of both knowledge and experience in one or more of the following:
1. technical or professional operations at intermediate qualification level of an appropriate professional institute;
2. performance or control complex work whether secretarial, technical or adminstrative where judgement and initiative is called for;
3. supervision requiring leadership, guidance on work procedures, training of others and motivation covering a team where control of work alone is delegated to a lower level grade.

M1
Jobs or duties require one or more of the following:
1. professional or specialized knowledge beyond the intermediate level examination of an appropriate professional institute but not necessarily to a final qualification of such institutes;
2. performance or control of work of wide complexity including non-routine decisions and regular use of judgement and initiative within determined policy;
3. management of sufficient numbers of staff to require grade F level activities to be carried out by more than one subordinate.

M2
Jobs requiring one or more of the following:
1. the final qualification of an appropriate professional institute or a University degree with some experience;
2. performance or control of work of significant complexity and importance requiring regular non-routine decisions, using initiative and judgement, and assistance in the development of policy changes;
3. management of specialist functions where more than one level of supervision is necessary to control the range of activities involved (eg with responsibility for one or more M1 level staff).

M3
Jobs requiring one or more of the following:
1. in addition to final qualification and/or equivalant University degree (first or higher), a period of typically several years experience consistent with the level of authority;
2. performance or control of work over several functions demanding general as well as specialist expertise and involvement in policy making at the highest level;
3. management of a series of specialist functions where management level jobs report in for guidance, control and monitoring.

Figure D.7 *Institute of Administrative Management – Office Job Evaluation*

tailor-made factors or skills/competencies. Both are described below and are subject to continuing support and development.

Core WJQ

At the heart of this approach is a questionnaire designed to gather accurate and specific job data. The questionnaire contains 13 measurement sections representing the different dimensions of the five core job factors contained in the WJQ. These are:

1. *Skill and knowledge*
   - level of formal/academic training
   - technical complexity
   - craft, athletic or artistic talent
   - level of proficiency.
2. *Problem solving*
   - fact-finding and analysis
   - originality and creativity
3. *Contacts*
   - internal/external contacts
4. *Scope of responsibility*
   - organizational authority level
   - scope of people management responsibility
   - impact of errors
   - scope and degree of monetary responsibility
5. *Working conditions*
   - physical activity
   - work environment.

Each section of the questionnaire contains one or more 'items' requiring a response and in total there are 65 items requiring responses. These may be either numeric responses such as number of subordinates or responses selected from multiple choice 'response tables'.

'Core' WJQ allows for customization to client needs both through tailoring of the factors, responses and questions to reflect an organization's culture, values and language and through customized factor weighting and scoring routines.

WJQ – Custom

This is a highly flexible approach accommodating job evaluation or skills based pay. Essentially the factors and questionnaire are created specifically for the client, while all the benefits of established WJQ software routines can be used, eg

■ Challenger	checking the consistency of a given job's responses
■ Up/down comparator	comparing a job profile with those of the positions above and below it
■ Inter-rater	comparing multiple responses for the same job and reporting on any deviates
■ Factor comparisons	providing a hierarchy of predicted factor levels
■ Levels summary	lines of predicted factor levels by all factors used
■ Points summary	displaying the points hierarchy for each factor as well as total points and grade assignments for selected jobs.

WJQ is well established around the world and is now quite widely used in the UK in both the public and private sectors. The software, which can operate in a 'Windows' environment, also contains modules for additional salary management applications. These include job description production, salary survey analysis and remuneration planning.

KPMG Management Consulting – EQUATE

A relative newcomer to the UK computer assisted job evaluation scene, EQUATE was initially developed by Link Consultants with whom KPMG entered into a joint agreement a few years ago. Essentially it is an expert system shell-software environment which has been designed to accept and help manage and audit any analytical factor based points rating job evaluation system. It can, therefore, be used as a means of managing existing 'manual' schemes, as a basis for auditing and restructuring schemes subject to decay and drift as well as the implementation of newly designed schemes.

Its main features are as follows:

- flexibility over factor selection and definition
- a customized questionnaire design and validation process for job data collection
- an algorithm building process to programme in the evaluation rules into the system shell
- a weighting process designed to reflect the needs and values of the organization
- a series of software routines for checking the validity of job data, comparing and validating factor scores
- salary management software.

EQUATE links into an integrated job information system (currently under development) so that the job database derived from questionnaires can be used to build:

- a salary management process
- a job evaluation module
- a selection module aimed at giving recruitment specifications and selection test criteria
- a competency specification module aimed at delivering job performance criteria
- a training module which links in training needs analysis.

A version of EQUATE-MEDEQUATE has been developed to service clients in the health services sector.

Other job evaluation approaches are available from:

- Mercer Fraser – Compmaster
- Hewitts
- Many smaller HR/personnel consultancies are able to develop 'tailor-made' approaches.

Appendix E

Weighting Factors

If a points evaluation scheme has four factors, such as those mentioned in Chapter 9, and if it is decided that the maximum number of points is 100, the decision on how these points should be distributed between the factors – how they should be weighted – is a critical one. It could be decided that factors are equally important and that the maximum number of points for each factor should be the same. But it might be thought that one factor is much more important than another. If, in these circumstances, it were decided that resources controlled should be allocated, say, 80 points and the remaining 20 points distributed between the other three factors, then the scheme is obviously going to favour staff with large budgets or numbers of people under them rather than the high powered specialist advisers. Either of these alternatives could be right, but it would be unwise to make such an assumption without testing it. This is why standard schemes with predetermined weightings should be used with care.

Weightings can be tested by trial and error. An initial assumption is made about the weighting based upon the preliminary analysis of the jobs, and the jobs are evaluated accordingly by the points method. A separate paired comparison exercise is carried out to produce an overall ranking of the jobs. This overall ranking is compared with the ranking produced by the points scheme to determine the degree of correlation between them. The degree of correlation is a measure of the validity of the values or weightings assigned to the factors. Thus, if the paired comparison ranking list is replicated by the points score ranking list, it could be assumed that the factor values are probably right. If there is little correlation between the two lists, the values are probably wrong. The degree to which the two lists match can be established by calculating the coefficient of correlation – a statistical formula which if it produces a result of +1 indicates a completely positive correlation, while a result of –1 indicates a completely negative correlation. Values between these extremes indicate the degree of positive or negative correlation. Experience of using this technique has shown that a correlation of +0.75 is acceptable, given the inevitable limitations of the original data, although a result of +0.8 or more would be better. If the initial trial produces an unsatisfactory correlation, the weightings are readjusted until an acceptable figure is obtained.

This approach is clumsy and time consuming, especially if the initial assumptions are seriously out of line. A more sophisticated approach is to use the multiple regression analysis technique. Multiple regression analysis is defined as the statistical method for investigating the relationships between independent and dependent variables and obtaining a 'regression equation' for predicting the latter in terms of the former. In a factor weighting exercise the different factors are the independent variables for which points are assessed and added up for each of the jobs to produce the dependent variable of the overall rank order. A multiple regression analysis exercise consists of the following steps:

1. The whole jobs are ranked by paired comparisons. A computer can be used to calculate the rankings, especially if it is decided to increase the accuracy or acceptability of the results by using a number of different judges and reconciling their views for the final ranking.
2. Each factor is ranked separately for all the jobs by paired comparisons, again with the help of a computer.

3. The multiple regression analysis computer program then:
    (a) establishes the degree of correlation between each of the independent variables (the factors) and the dependent variable (the overall rank order)
    (b) ranks each factor in turn (starting with the factor with the highest correlation and finishing with the factor with the least correlation) and reconstructs the whole job ranking order by applying weightings to the ranking orders within the factors
    (c) tests the independent variables by measuring the correlations between them to establish the degree to which they separately contribute to producing the overall rank order (a very high correlation between two factors would suggest a high degree of overlap and might result in one of the factors being eliminated).

Thus multiple regression analysis can indicate which are the most significant factors and weight the degree to which they are significant. As a result, unnecessary factors can be dispensed with.

This is a sophisticated technique which will produce better results than relying on trial and error, as long as the initial assumptions about the overall rank order are correct. In this respect, the approach is somewhat specious. If the subjectively established overall rank order is wrong, what degree of confidence can be attached to the factor weightings? The method has a circular look about it, but it all depends on the degree to which care has been exercised in choosing and analyzing the benchmark jobs. This has to be done thoroughly to ensure that a soundly based scheme is developed for future use.

Appendix F

Computerized Job Evaluation

The need

Whatever basic measuring instrument is used, conventional job evaluation is usually carried out by a process involving:

- collection of data about jobs, typically in the form of job descriptions
- evaluation of jobs, using the selected method, by a group or committee of evaluators. The first stage is frequently the evaluation of a benchmark of jobs to enable the committee to set standards and reference points, against which to test further evaluations
- review of the overall relativities emerging from the evaluations.

Depending on the particular methodology chosen, this can give great sensitivity to individual job design, and thus enable the process to deal with a wide variety of job types. In addition it can yield additional benefits from the evaluation debate, such as input to organizational understanding and clarification.

The conventional process does, however, have a number of disadvantages which are being perceived with increasing acuteness as organizations become more restricted in the resources that they are able, and willing, to devote to the process. These include:

- the time and resource needed for conventional job description preparation and committee evaluation
- the need for significant training of evaluators to enable them to operate effectively
- the difficulty in achieving consistency of standards when evaluation is devolved to multiple committees, and the extensive training and control processes which are needed to maintain consistency between committees.

These difficulties have led to the increasing perception that job evaluation is a bureaucratic and time-consuming activity – though it is important to recognize that the degree to which this is justified is a function of the process adopted for evaluation, not of the basic method of measurement itself.

Over the years, many attempts have been made to address these criticisms by more structured approaches to job evaluation. Thus, particularly for large job populations, a variety of techniques such as job matching to generic descriptions, and classification approaches have been used. While these methods gain significantly in speed over 'conventional' committee evaluation where each job is considered individually, they lose sensitivity to job differences because of the degree of 'force-fitting' which is inherent in them, as well as raising questions about equal value from which standpoint a fully analytical method is to be preferred.

In recent years, much effort has been devoted to developing computer-based systems aimed at combining high speed with high sensitivity, and thus addressing directly the criticisms of conventional job evaluation processes. Figure F.1 illustrates the balance between speed and sensitivity for alternative evaluation processes.

534

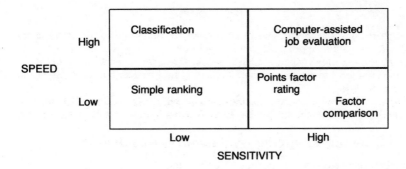

Figure F.1   *Alternative evaluation processes – the balance between speed and sensitivity*

Type of computer assistance

Ways in which computers can assist the process of job evaluation fall into two broad categories:

1. Software systems which support and improve the efficiency and consistency of conventional evaluation processes.
2. Approaches in which evaluations are computer-generated from questionnaire responses.

Within each of these categories, a number of possible approaches exist.

As with conventional job evaluation, a single 'packaged' process solution cannot satisfy the wide range of requirements of different organizations – nor in many cases the diverse needs of different job groups within an organization.

Factors influencing the choice of process include:

■ The purpose of the exercise, and the use to which the results are to be put, for example, whether the requirement is purely for a simple grading result, or whether additional outputs or linkages are demanded.
■ The scale and diversity of the job population to be covered.
■ The resources and time constraints applying both to initial implementation and to maintenance.
■ The requirements for communication of, or participation in the process, and the degree of devolution/decentralization needed.

Even within a single organization, consideration of these factors may well indicate the need for different processes to be applied to various job groups.

Thus for example there may be a large clerical and manual job population where the requirement is mainly for an efficient grading process: a group of professional specialists where pay and grading considerations are intimately linked to issues of competency and career development; and a small group of senior managers where a process is required which assists in the clarification of objectives and performance criteria.

For these reasons, computer assisted processes should:

■ be capable of being designed to fit the specific organization and job group requirements;
■ yield results which are compatible, whatever process options are selected;
■ use flexible software capable of supporting, in an integrated way, a variety of processes.

These are the basic design principles which have guided the development and introduction of HayXpert by Hay Management Consultants.

HayXpert

HayXpert provides a powerful and flexible computer environment, in which a range of related and compatible approaches can be operated.

It is built around a high capacity, high speed database, which enables the storage, sorting and retrieval of job and related information, and is equipped with a full range of reporting and output facilities.

Within this environment, specific facilities enable both the provision of computer support to conventional job evaluation, and the use of questionnaire-based CAJE approaches.

Computer support to conventional job evaluation

Within this broad category, two facilities are provided:

1. QED Chart

This is an efficient on-line support tool for conventional evaluation processes using the Guide-Chart Profile technique. It provides a number of 'notepad' screens for recording evaluations, job information, evaluation notes and rationales, and if required, full job descriptions, enabling a 'paperless' evaluation process.

Computerized Guide Charts are incorporated with ratings matrix and logic built in.

During an evaluation, information on any comparator job which is in the database can be called up on to overlay screens, contributing greatly to consistency of standards. Similarly, listings of jobs and evaluations can be called up, sorted by evaluation factor, by job size, function, department, etc – depending on whatever code structure has been put in – enabling rapid 'sore-thumbing' and evaluation reviews. Figure F.2 illustrates a typical screen showing comparator job information.

A flexible report generator enables data to output in whatever form is required, including the facility to produce organization charts. It is used by organizations who wish to retain the conventional evaluation process, but improve its speed, efficiency and consistency.

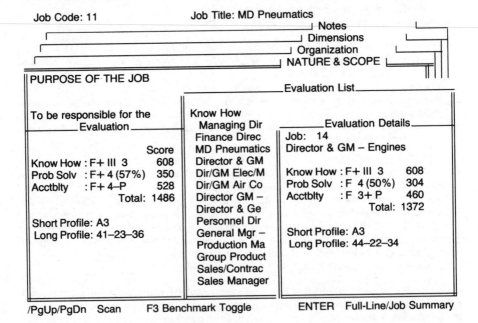

Figure F.2   *Screen from QED Chart showing overlays with comparator job information and listing*

2. QED Comparison

This facility is to enable the rapid 'slotting' of large numbers of jobs into a pre-defined framework of benchmark jobs and factor level definitions. The first stage in its use is the evaluation of a benchmark of jobs in the conventional way.

The pattern of results which emerges is carefully analyzed to determine the way that some jobs and evaluations group together, while others are distinguished. From this, a framework of simplified 'slotting' factors and levels can be isolated, enabling rapid evaluation of all remaining jobs by direct comparison with both the slotting factors and the original benchmarks.

The software provides a split-screen facility, in which the factor levels are displayed on one side, with the corresponding benchmark jobs on the other, thus providing the user with the information needed to 'slot' other jobs by direct comparison. That is illustrated in Figure F.3.

Overlay screens can be called up to give more detailed information on the factor level definitions when needed. Similarly, because all the facilities of QED Chart are incorporated, full data on any bench-mark job (or any other job in the database) can be called up to test the slotting, and all the sorethumbing and reporting facilities can be used.

Because the slotting factors can be expressed in plain English rather than evaluation jargon, and can be made highly specific to the organization, it enables extensive devolution of the process to involve line managers with little job evaluation knowledge, but detailed job knowledge.

QED Comparison is typically used for relatively large populations of jobs where the main reason for evaluation is grading, and where a very rapid, simple process is required.

Questionnaire-based techniques

While the above techniques provide computer support and assistance to the evaluation process, questionnaire-based CAJE techniques take this a stage further by:

Job code: 00030   Job title: SR PROJECT ENG

O Manager of a more complex dept. An advanced professional with sufficient technical expertise to be called upon as consultant or for very complex assignments.	00029 00030 00031 00033 00034	BUSINESS SYSTEMS MGR SR PROJECT ENGR MIS MGR FINANCIAL REPORT MGR QUALITY STANDARDS MGR
N Basic level manager of a department. A professional with a thorough knowledge of a technical or specialized area.	00032 00035 00036 00037 00038	SR TECH SLS REP PRODUCTION MGR MATERIALS MANAGER SENIOR CHEMIST SENIOR RES CHEMIST
M Basic level manager of a specialized skill. A journey level professional (i.e. fully qualified) in a non-technical area.	00041 00045 00047 00048 00049	TERRITORY SALES MGR TECH SERV ENGINEER TECH SALES REP MGR DIST COST CONTROL TERRITORY SALES MGR

GRADE: 11   FACTOR: Know-How   304
      ESCAbort   F2 Slot Change   F6 Confirm   F8 Zoom   F10 Menu
PgUp, DgDnMove   F3 Benchmark   F7 Exit   F9 Evaluation Status

Figure F.3 *Screen from QED Comparison showing part of a slotting factor scale with reference jobs for each level*

- gathering job data in structured, quantitative form through a questionnaire
- processing the questionnaire data through a computer-based algorithm to yield, directly, an evaluation result.

Clearly, such approaches offer major advantages over conventional evaluation in terms of process efficiency, because they:

- eliminate the need for the time-consuming process of job description preparation
- replace the evaluation committee for the bulk of its work by computer processing
- yield high consistency of results, enabling devolution of the process without the need for heavyweight bureaucratic control mechanisms, or extensive training programmes.

HayXpert provides for two different approaches to questionnaire techniques, designed to satisfy differing requirements.

Universal questionnaire

This is the approach designed for the evaluation of most jobs in an organization quickly and efficiently, using a single instrument in questionnaire format. The questionnaire is tailored to meet the specific needs of the organization and/or job group, and the algorithm is specifically built to reproduce the value standards of the organization. This is accomplished through the following process stages:

1. Having defined the job population to be covered, a representative benchmark sample of jobs is selected.
2. The benchmark jobs are then evaluated, using the Guide Chart Profile Method, in the conventional way. This step enables the organization to set its value standards and relativities, on which to base the computer algorithm.
3. An appropriate questionnaire is then developed, selecting and devising questions to elicit the necessary information about jobs, and building level descriptions for each question. A typical extract from a questionnaire is shown in Figure F.4.
4. The questionnaire is completed for each benchmark job, and a mathematical algorithm built to relate the questionnaire responses to the evaluated job size.
5. Following testing and refinement, the algorithm is then programmed in HayXpert.
6. Evaluations for subsequent jobs can then be generated by completing the questionnaire and processing through the computer – either interactively or by batch processing from paper questionnaires.

While the above sequence describes the main 'technical' steps involved, the application process needs careful design to meet the organization's requirements and yield high quality results. Issues requiring particular attention are listed below:

IMPACT ON EXTERNAL CONTACTS. To what degree is the job accountable for establishing and/or maintaining (customers, suppliers, consultants, public administrators, etc.).

> 2. . . .
> 3. collecting/exchanging information, making or responding to inquiries.
> 4. . . .
> 5. ensuring or controlling the delivery of standard or well-defined products or services (for example, follow up of orders, collecting receivables, reordering of supplies or raw material, providing maintenance services, inside sales, etc.).
> 6. . . .

F1-Help   F2-Comments   F3-Goto   F4-Previous   F5-Next   F7-Quit   F9-Footer
F10-Header

Figure F.4   *Part of a typical Questionnaire factor on screen*

- What is the process for completing and reviewing the questionnaire – job holder, supervisor, HR specialist, or a combination of these?
- What is the application process? Is the computer to be used as a tool by evaluators, or is it to be the primary process, subject only to quality assurance reviews?
- Quality Assurance (QA) checks. The software itself contains sophisticated checking procedures for flagging up apparent inconsistencies within a questionnaire as illustrated in Figure F.5, but no electronic checks can identify consistent over- or under-stating of a job. QA processes for the review of input data and of output results need to be designed and implemented
- Communication and participation. Universal Questionnaire offers the potential for much greater devolution and involvement in the process than conventional evaluation, but this opportunity can be lost if it is seen as a 'black box', mechanistic approach. Careful design of the development and implementation processes is needed to ensure that full advantage is taken of this potential.

Job family questionnaire

Within many organizations there exist significant groups of jobs which are linked by a commonality of purpose or nature, and where a much more focused approach is required, tailored to the specific needs of that group.

Such groups – job families – may be linked by the nature of work undertaken (eg a clerical family), by a professional or technical discipline (eg scientists, engineers), by a common function (eg production management), or may be essentially the same job existing at different levels (eg branch bank managers).

Within such a family, there will be many common factors – these are what make them a family – but jobs will be distinguished by quite specific differentiating factors.

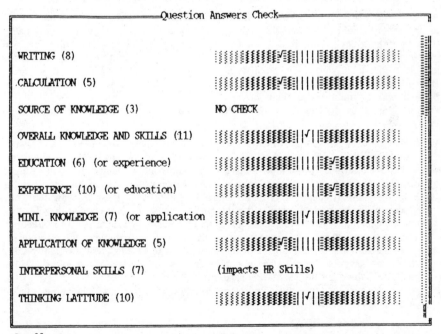

:Scroll

Figure F.5   *QA validation screen showing variance of question responses from expected*

The process of Job Family Modelling concentrates on identifying these differentiating factors and basing questionnaires directly upon them.

In this way, questionnaires can be developed which are short, output oriented and sharply focused on the particular jobs in question. They can be developed in conjunction with members of the family itself, and the questionnaire can be expressed in language familiar to the family.

The technique provides clear links between job evaluation and related HR processes such as career development, performance management and competency analysis, and for these reasons is particularly valuable in environments where the traditional job/person separation is a difficult one – for example, technical/professional hierarchies.

In outline, the process involves the following steps:

1. Definition of the scope of the family and understanding of the range and levels of jobs to be covered.
2. Evaluation of a representative sample of jobs, using conventional Guide Chart process.
3. Identification, in conjunction with members of the family, of the critical differentiating factors.
4. Building of scales and level descriptions for each factor, and presentation of these in questionnaire form.
5. Rating of the benchmark jobs against the factor scales.
6. Development, testing and refinement of an algorithm to enable job size to be predicted from questionnaire responses.
7. Programming into HayXpert.
8. Designing the implementation process, involving similar considerations to those described for Universal Questionnaire.

Particular characteristics of the HayXpert approach

All the facilities described above are contained within the same computer environment, and all are underpinned by the same basic scale of job measurement ratings. Hence evaluation process options can be combined to meet the diverse needs of complex organizations, with consistent results. For example, a Job Family Questionnaire might be applied to a major group of core jobs, with a Universal Questionnaire for the bulk of jobs in other areas. Benchmarks for both of these could be stored in the QED database, while one-off jobs might be dealt with by traditional evaluation.

Underpinning by the Hay Guide Chart Profile Method has two further important implications:

1. It is acknowledged as the world's leading job measurement methodology, and is sufficiently flexible to enable the organization's values to be fully reflected in the algorithms which are built. All questionnaire-based CAJE approaches require an initial rating or ranking of jobs in order to provide the basic values on which to base the algorithm: this is known as the dependent variable. There are major advantages in using the Guide Chart Profile Method to provide the dependent variable when compared with alternatives which are proxies for job size, for example current grade or pay, or market pay. There are clear weaknesses inherent in these alternatives: using current grade or pay presents difficulties if the object of the exercise is to develop new pay and grading structures because the old ones are deficient; use of market pay requires periodic changes to the algorithm as market relativities change.
2. It provides access to the extensive Hay remuneration databases, which use Hay job size as the basis for analysis and comparison.

Additional features of HayXpert

This description has concentrated on the job evaluation capabilities of HayXpert, but the software also includes facilities for job pricing and salary administration, and for job competency analysis questionnaires, thus enabling much greater integration between these related HR processes than was previously possible.

Computer-assisted job evaluation and HayXpert – summary

For job evaluation to serve its purpose within an organization, it must reflect that organization's values and requirements, and must be seen to do so by both managers and employees. CAJE approaches which are viewed as a 'black box' will not achieve this objective. It is sometimes claimed that CAJE methods eliminate the need for human judgement in the evaluation process. They do not, neither should they seek to. What they do provide is the means of capturing and clarifying the organization's judgements and values about jobs, and reproducing these in a consistent way. Viewed in this light, it is clear that they can provide enormous advances in terms of the efficiency of the job evaluation process and the reduction in the bureaucracy so often associated with traditional processes.

But as with traditional methods, the process must be designed to meet the particular demands and constraints of the user organization. HayXpert has been designed to provide the flexibility and range of approaches needed to satisfy this requirement.

Link Group Consultants Limited – The George computerized job evaluation system

The operation and maintenance of a job evaluation scheme embraces a number of important activities, ie:

- scoring and grading of jobs
- maintenance of an up-to-date rank order
- maintenance of accurate evaluation records
- regular audit of job description within grades
- comparative audits of the grade distribution of jobs within various functions or divisions
- monitoring of the structure for grade drift
- consistency checks on evaluation by different analysts or assessment teams.

Without regular monitoring and audits, inconsistencies creep in and the scheme starts to decay. Such tasks, however, are time consuming and require the allocation of scarce personnel resources to keep on top of them. The George computer program is designed to make job evaluation maintenance simple, quick and highly efficient and gives management the initiative in controlling its job evaluation schemes.

System overview

The system is designed so that users can configure it for their own job evaluation scheme without any outside help. It will accommodate any type of factor based scheme, no matter how complicated the scoring system or grading structure.

As well as job evaluation information, other relevant information about the job can be included, eg department, division, function, location, salary etc.

Entry of job evaluation data is simplified by using predefined entries. For example, all the department titles or site locations can be pre-entered. Once entered, the system scores the job under each factor, applies weights if appropriate, determines the total job score, grades it and displays it at the correct point in the rank order.

If at some later point in time it is felt necessary to change the number of grade lines or the factor weights, this can be performed through the set-up program.

Features of the system

1. Interrogation
Full details of any job, together with its evaluation line, grade and score can be found and displayed instantly, with print-outs available if required.

2. Search and sort

Any group of jobs can be searched for and sorted depending on specified criteria, eg all the accounting jobs within a salary range of £15,000 to £30,000 based in London, Birmingham and Bristol.

Alternatively, the search and sort facilities can be used to monitor consistency of assessment, eg display all jobs which were placed in Factor Level 4 for Responsibility.

3. Audits

Because the job evaluation rank order is up to date and all information is instantly accessible, it is possible to carry out any form of audit the user wishes, eg distribution of jobs and people across the grade structure, comparative spread of jobs by function, location or division.

It is possible to check on whether one analyst assesses more tightly than another.

In a decentralized scheme the consistency with which one division assesses its jobs compared with others can be monitored.

4. Statistics

A range of statistics is available, such as the number of jobs in each grade, spread of jobs above and below the mid-point, average salary in grade, spread of salaries within grade.

5. Salary information

Salary information about each job holder can be entered and either displayed or kept hidden as required. Based on this, the salary structure can be interrogated and analyzed using the search and sort facilities.

A further feature is the facility to transport data to a spreadsheet program and produce a salary curve for all or any part of the job population. This is a useful monitoring tool and can be used when making market comparisons.

6. Job details

George provides five standard fields common to all job populations – job title, date, salary, benchmark and number in job. An additional seven fields can then be defined to capture the information relevant to the scheme.

In addition to the fields described, three lines of text are available to record comments.

7. Job profiles

George can accommodate schemes with up to 15 different factors. For each factor of the scheme the accepted values are defined, whether they be:

- levels (1, 2, 3 etc)
- pre-weighted point scores (15, 25, 55 etc)
- a range (1–200).

In addition, the weights to be applied to factor values can be specified to achieve a weighted points score. Once defined, George allows the user to enter job profiles quickly and accurately.

Sample screens

Figure F.6 shows examples of four screens.

Link Group Consultants Ltd: The 'Jeeves' computerized system

The Jeeves system is tailor-made to assist in the whole process of evaluating jobs rather than simply administering the evaluation scheme, which is what George does.

Jeeves is an expert system shell which can be tailored to any analytical job evaluation scheme. An expert system shell is a form of computer program into which can be entered a body of expertise in the form of 'rules' which enable decisions to be made on the basis of factual information presented to the computer.

Jeeves assumes that each scheme will have:

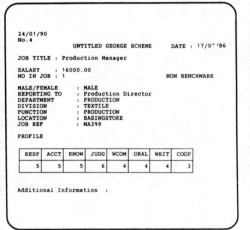

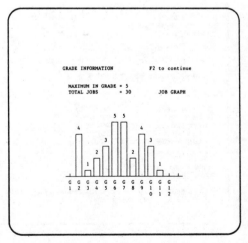

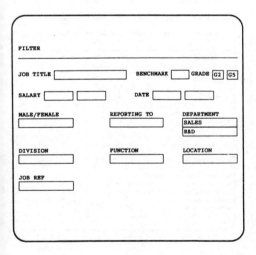

Figure F.6   *Four sample 'George' screens*

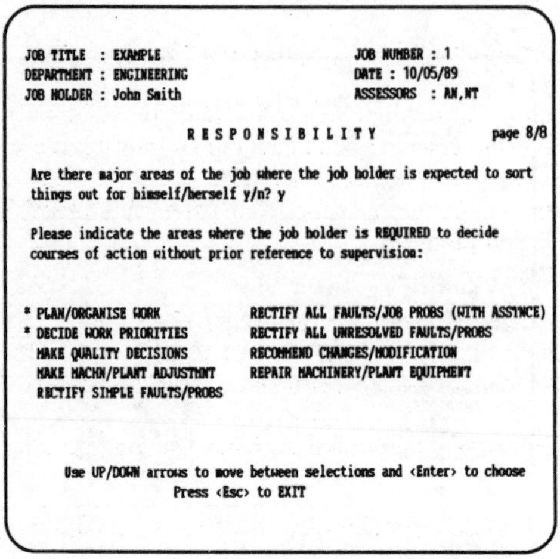

JOB TITLE : EXAMPLE JOB NUMBER : 1
DEPARTMENT : ENGINEERING DATE : 10/05/89
JOB HOLDER : John Smith ASSESSORS : AN,NT

RESPONSIBILITY page 8/8

Are there major areas of the job where the job holder is expected to sort things out for himself/herself y/n? y

Please indicate the areas where the job holder is REQUIRED to decide courses of action without prior reference to supervision:

* PLAN/ORGANISE WORK
* DECIDE WORK PRIORITIES
MAKE QUALITY DECISIONS
MAKE MACHN/PLANT ADJUSTMNT
RECTIFY SIMPLE FAULTS/PROBS
RECTIFY ALL FAULTS/JOB PROBS (WITH ASSTNCE)
RECTIFY ALL UNRESOLVED FAULTS/PROBS
RECOMMEND CHANGES/MODIFICATION
REPAIR MACHINERY/PLANT EQUIPMENT

Use UP/DOWN arrows to move between selections and <Enter> to choose
Press <Esc> to EXIT

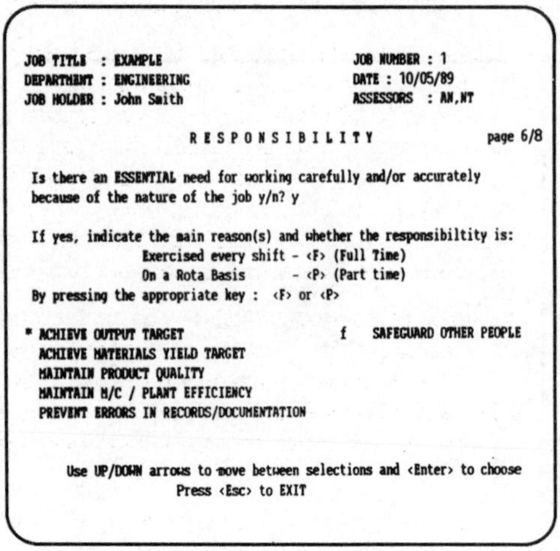

JOB TITLE : EXAMPLE JOB NUMBER : 1
DEPARTMENT : ENGINEERING DATE : 10/05/89
JOB HOLDER : John Smith ASSESSORS : AN,NT

RESPONSIBILITY page 6/8

Is there an ESSENTIAL need for working carefully and/or accurately because of the nature of the job y/n? y

If yes, indicate the main reason(s) and whether the responsibiltity is:
Exercised every shift - <F> (Full Time)
On a Rota Basis - <P> (Part time)
By pressing the appropriate key : <F> or <P>

* ACHIEVE OUTPUT TARGET f SAFEGUARD OTHER PEOPLE
ACHIEVE MATERIALS YIELD TARGET
MAINTAIN PRODUCT QUALITY
MAINTAIN M/C / PLANT EFFICIENCY
PREVENT ERRORS IN RECORDS/DOCUMENTATION

Use UP/DOWN arrows to move between selections and <Enter> to choose
Press <Esc> to EXIT

1. Typical Information Input Screens

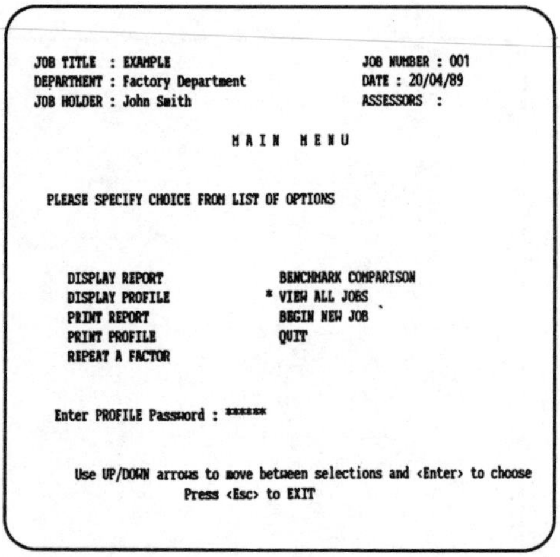

JOB TITLE : EXAMPLE JOB NUMBER : 001
DEPARTMENT : Factory Department DATE : 20/04/89
JOB HOLDER : John Smith ASSESSORS :

MAIN MENU

PLEASE SPECIFY CHOICE FROM LIST OF OPTIONS

DISPLAY REPORT
DISPLAY PROFILE
PRINT REPORT
PRINT PROFILE
REPEAT A FACTOR
BENCHMARK COMPARISON
* VIEW ALL JOBS
BEGIN NEW JOB
QUIT

Enter PROFILE Password : ******

Use UP/DOWN arrows to move between selections and <Enter> to choose
Press <Esc> to EXIT

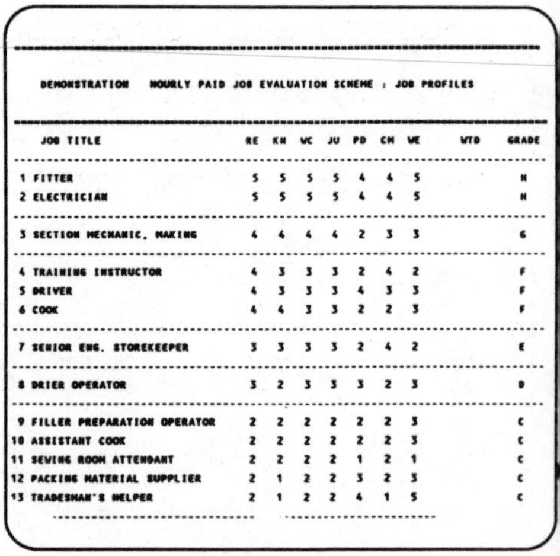

DEMONSTRATION HOURLY PAID JOB EVALUATION SCHEME : JOB PROFILES

JOB TITLE	RE	KN	WC	JU	PD	CM	WE	WTD	GRADE
1 FITTER	5	5	5	5	4	4	5		H
2 ELECTRICIAN	5	5	5	5	4	4	5		H
3 SECTION MECHANIC, MAKING	4	4	4	4	2	3	3		G
4 TRAINING INSTRUCTOR	4	3	3	3	2	4	2		F
5 DRIVER	4	3	3	3	4	3	3		F
6 COOK	4	4	3	3	2	2	3		F
7 SENIOR ENG. STOREKEEPER	3	3	3	3	2	4	2		E
8 DRIER OPERATOR	3	2	3	3	3	2	3		D
9 FILLER PREPARATION OPERATOR	2	2	2	2	2	2	3		C
10 ASSISTANT COOK	2	2	2	2	2	2	3		C
11 SEWING ROOM ATTENDANT	2	2	2	2	1	2	1		C
12 PACKING MATERIAL SUPPLIER	2	1	2	2	3	2	3		C
13 TRADESMAN'S HELPER	2	1	2	2	4	1	5		C

2. Main Menu showing JEEVES facilities **3. Printout of Rank Order by Grade**

Figure F.7 *Three sample 'Jeeves' screens*

- weighted factors
- a demand scale or a matrix for each factor, eg points, levels, degrees
- assessment standards for each factor which guide evaluators to the correct rating of jobs; these may take the form of benchmark jobs and/or level definitions.

It also requires that there will be adequate information available on benchmark jobs in the form of job descriptions and factor information.

The rationale behind the Jeeves system is that in every analytical job evaluation scheme there must be clear and discernible reasons why jobs have been placed in the various degree or demand levels of each factor. Indeed if there were no apparent reasons or 'rules', the job evaluation system could not function in a consistent manner. At the same time the system recognizes that the 'rules' may be both detailed and complex.

In essence Jeeves has been so constructed that:

1. the evaluation 'rules' can be defined both qualitatively and/or quantitatively;
2. the rules can be enshrined in the system shell;
3. the computer can be programmed to ask sufficient questions about each factor to enable it to apply the evaluation rules;
4. when the job information has been entered, the computer can apply the rules and determine the factor score.

Once the system has been set up Jeeves will therefore consistently apply the rules each time and produce an evaluated score for a factor.

By also entering factor weights and grade line positions to the system, Jeeves can go on to:

- score the job
- grade the job
- sort it into position in the rank order
- store the job information entered in the form of a factor analysis

Sample screens for Jeeves are given in Figure F.7.

Other major market contenders in the area of CAJE are:

- WJQ from Towers Perrin Forster and Crosby
- Compmaster from Mercer Fraser
- Equate and Medequate from KPMG Peat Marwick human resources consultants
- Multicomp from Wyatt.

For contact addresses see Bibliography.

Appendix G

Equal Pay Considerations

The impact of equal pay legislation

The Equal Pay Act of 1970 provided that a woman was entitled to equal pay with a man (or vice versa) working for the same employer at the same establishment where her work was 'like' to his, or where their work had been rated equivalent on a job evaluation study.

The Act was amended with effect from 1 January 1984, following a European Court ruling which found the provisions insufficient to meet the requirements of the European Economic Community's Directive on Equal Pay.

Under the Equal Value Amendment, women are entitled to equal pay with men (and vice versa) where the work is of equal value in terms of the demands made under various headings, to quote: 'for instance, effort, skill, decision'. Claims can cut across job families, occupational groups and bargaining units. Women can claim equal pay with men employed on work quite dissimilar in nature – and they have. The legal provisions are especially important in instances where there is separation of men's jobs and women's jobs, and where methods of pay determination vary within the organizations. The legislation forces comparison of the content of jobs where neither employers nor union pressure would have demanded it.

The implications for job evaluation

Job evaluation has become central to equal value because the jobs concerned must, by definition, be evaluated by some method in order to determine their relative value. Employees can base claims on the results of a job evaluation scheme. Employers can seek to have a claim set aside at an early stage if the work of both the applicant and comparator has been rated differently under a common job evaluation scheme.

Claims for equal pay can be made whether or not a job evaluation scheme is in existence in the organization concerned. If a defence to a claim is based on an existing scheme, the onus is on the employer to prove that this scheme is analytical in nature and free from sex bias both in design and implementation.

Unless the tribunal can dismiss a claim at this early stage, it must commission a report by an 'independent expert'. The independent expert is drawn from a list appointed by the Advisory Conciliation and Arbitration Service (ACAS) and is required to assess the equality of value between the applicant and comparator. The method and basis of assessment is decided by each individual independent expert although, again, it must be an analytical approach.

Case law affecting job evaluation

Case law affecting job evaluation is limited, but there have been three major decisions, which are summarized below.

Hayward v Cammell Laird (House of Lords 1988)
The first successful case under the Equal Value Amendment was that of a cook, Julie Hayward, claiming equal value with three male comparators – a painter, a joiner, and a thermal insulation engineer.

An independent expert was appointed to examine the relative 'value' of the work and concluded that the cook's work was of equal value to the male comparators. The tribunal accepted this conclusion and ordered the employers to raise Hayward's pay in line with the pay of the comparators.

The company argued that a variety of benefits to which Hayward was entitled should be offset in the difference in base pay levels. When the case reached the House of Lords, it was ruled that the proper interpretation of the law, as written, was that 'term' meant any specific element of the remuneration package. Hayward therefore gained equal basic pay and retained the additional benefits which were applicable to her job, but not to the jobs of the male comparators.

Pickstone v Freemans (House of Lords 1988)

The significant ruling of this case was that the female applicants were not precluded from claiming Equal Pay for Work of Equal Value with higher paid men performing different work just because a small percentage of those performing the same work as the applicants were men.

Bromley and others v H & J Quick (Court of Appeal 1988)

Although the detailed anatomy of the job evaluation system was not the issue on which this case turned, it did serve to establish that a job evaluation system can only provide a defence if it is analytical in nature.

This case also established that the onus rests with the employer to demonstrate absence of sex bias in any common job evaluation system which is to be relied on as a defence.

The need was indicated for careful attention to procedures for slotting jobs against bench-marks. Since the jobs of applicant and comparators had neither been fully evaluated using the factors, nor were identical to the bench-mark jobs, it was ruled that they were not, for the purposes of law, 'covered' by the job evaluation system common to all. The system could, therefore, not be relied upon to set aside the claim and the report of an independent expert had to be obtained.

Example of discriminatory job factors

Factors	Maintenance fitter	Company nurse
(each factor is scored on a scale from 1 to 10)		
(for simplicity no weights have been applied)		
Skill		
Experience in job	10	1
Training	5	7
Responsibility		
For money	0	0
For equipment and machinery	8	3
For safety	3	6
For work done by others	3	0
Effort		
Lifting requirement	4	2
Strength required	7	2
Sustained physical effort	5	1
Conditions		
Physical environment	6	0
Working position	7	0
Hazards	7	0
TOTAL	64	22

This set of factors is discriminatory because it contains many aspects of the male job and very few relating to the female job. There is also double counting, for example 'strength required' and 'lifting required' would frequently have similar scores, either high or low. The example below shows what in the opinion of the Equal Opportunities Commission are less biased job evaluation factors.

Example of non-discriminatory job factors

Factors	Maintenance fitter	Company nurse
(each factor is scored on a scale from 1 to 10)		
(for simplicity no weights have been applied)		
Basic knowledge	6	8
Complexity of task	6	7
Training	5	7
Responsibility for people	3	8
Responsibility for materials and equipment	8	6
Mental effort	5	6
Visual attention	6	6
Physical activity	8	5
Working conditions	6	1
TOTAL	53	54

Factor weighting

A scheme may also discriminate in the factor weightings used. Bias will creep in if the factors on which a male job scores highly are given higher weights than the factors on which a female job scores highest (or vice versa).

The EOC example in Table G.1 shows how discriminatory factor weights produce a biased evaluation of the two jobs.

Table G.1 *The EOC's example of discriminatory factor weighting*

Factors	Unweighted scores		Biased weights	Weighted scores		Unbiased weights	Weighted scores	
	Fitter	Nurse		Fitter	Nurse		Fitter	Nurse
Basic knowledge	6	8	7%	0.42	0.56	5%	0.30	0.40
Complexity of task	6	7	8%	0.48	0.56	15%	0.90	1.05
Training	5	7	7%	0.35	0.49	15%	0.75	1.05
Responsibility for people	3	8	15%	0.45	1.20	15%	0.45	1.20
Responsibility for materials and equipment	8	6	15%	1.20	0.90	15%	1.20	0.90
Mental effort	5	6	8%	0.40	0.48	10%	0.50	0.60
Visual attention	6	6	10%	0.60	0.60	10%	0.60	0.60
Physical activity	8	5	15%	1.20	0.75	10%	0.80	0.50
Working conditions	6	1	15%	0.90	0.15	5%	0.30	0.05

Appendix H

Examples of Job Descriptions

Example of a job description in narrative format

Job description

Job Title: Marketing Director

Reports To: Managing Director

Date:

Purpose

To develop and, after agreement, direct the implementation of short- and long-term sales and marketing plans which will provide for the achievement of the Company's objectives of growth and profitability.

Dimensions

Annual Turnover:	£78 million
Staff:	46
Overseas Sales Companies	9

Principal accountabilities

1. Develop short- and long-term sales and marketing plans which will provide for the realization of the Company's strategic objectives.
2. Direct and control the Company's sales and marketing operations to ensure the achievement of agreed profit and turnover objectives.
3. Review, develop and maintain an organization which will maximize the effectiveness of the Company's sales and marketing operations.
4. Recruit, motivate and develop senior sales and marketing managers to ensure commitment and consistently high performance.
5. Develop and guide overseas sales companies to ensure profitable operation and growth in line with established corporate objectives.
6. Effectively represent the interests of the Company to major customers and lead negotiations for major contracts.
7. Identify new markets and liaise with Production Director to ensure product development which will increase the Company's market penetration and growth.
8. Contribute, as an executive director, to the identification and formulation of strategic objectives for the Company.

Nature and scope of position

The Marketing Director reports directly to the Managing Director of the company along with the Finance Director and the Operations Director. Under the leadership of the MD, these four posts make up the executive board which is the main policy making body within the Company. Together they provide the direction necessary to the achievement of agreed strategic objectives and coordination between them is achieved primarily through a weekly meeting, chaired by the MD. In addition to discussing plans and monitoring their implementation, this meeting provides a regular forum in which sales achievement can be translated into production activity.

The jobholder is responsible for the development and, after agreement, implementation of sales and marketing plans. While the largest single market remains the UK, only 25 per cent of the Company's production is sold in the home market. 25 per cent is sold direct into overseas markets with territory sales managers selling primarily to approved agents and distributors. The remaining 50 per cent is sold into overseas markets through nine overseas subsidiaries, established to market and sell the Company's products. Two of these subsidiary companies have been established in the USA while the remaining seven are concentrated on particular European countries or countries which form part of the old Commonwealth. The Managing Director of each of the nine companies reports direct to the Marketing Director along with:

- Sales Manager – There are four territory sales managers covering in broad terms all those countries where there is no overseas subsidiary. The four territories are the UK, Europe, Australia and Asia and the Middle East and Africa. Their activities are coordinated by the sales manager who is also responsible for market research, sales publicity and promotion and after sales service.
- Commercial Manager – Advice and support on the form of contract is provided by this manager who is also responsible for a team of contract managers who are the main point of customer contact and liaison during the product process. In addition the Commercial Manager is also responsible for the distribution and storage of the company's products and the sale of spares.

The Marketing Director sees the development of strategy as very much a personal responsibility and works closely with the MD in the formulation of sales plans and the assessment of market priorities. There is little scope for fundamental innovation in the form of product the company is offering and little can be achieved by any significant diversification. The development of the company and continued growth of turnover, therefore, very much depends upon which markets are developed, the optimal timing for their development and the way in which the market is entered.

Information and intelligence to enable the development of the marketing strategy are gathered through the territory Sales Managers and the Sales Manager with specialist support from the Market Research Manager and the Technical Services Manager. The Technical Services Manager's contribution in this area is largely related to monitoring developments with regard to prime movers (the diesel engines which drive the generators). The Marketing Director also liaises closely with the Finance Director in considering the most appropriate forms of market entry.

Plans are produced on a one plus five year basis and once approved are translated into targets for the territory Sales Managers. This translation process is largely carried out by the Sales Manager subject to the approval of the Marketing Director. The Marketing Director works directly with the Managers of the overseas companies setting targets in terms of volume, turnover, profit and sales costs.

The market for the company's product is fairly well established and most potential customers are readily identifiable.

Field sales effort is, therefore, largely one of establishing and maintaining contact with likely users. Once real sales potential has been identified initial contact and negotiation is carried out by Territory Sales Managers operating within price and contract norms, determined by the Marketing Director. Price norms are reviewed regularly in the light of the company's business circumstances and the jobholder will expect to discuss changes to these with other Executive Directors. Most of the contracts carried out by the Company are of sufficient business significance to warrant senior management involvements and many of the major contracts would be handled personally either by the Marketing Director or indeed on occasions by the MD.

The Marketing Director has a brief weekly meeting with the Sales Manager and the Commercial Manager which is essentially a pre-briefing prior to meeting with the MD and other Executive Directors. The jobholder expects, however, to be kept closely in touch with the sales situation. The jobholder endeavours to see the overseas subsidiary managers between two and four times per annum depending upon the confidence placed in the individuals, and monitors the activities of these subsidiary companies largely through the receipt of monthly reports.

Example of a short-form job description

Job description

Job Title:	Management Accountant
Reports To:	Financial Controller
Business:	Food and Speciality Chemicals
Location:	
Jobholder:	AN Other
Date:	
Job Ref:	17

Purpose

Maintain and develop the company's management information and product costing systems to aid the decision making process.

Dimensions

Turnover	£50 million
Payroll Costs	£7.0 million
Manufacturing Costs	£10 million
Staff	3

Organization chart

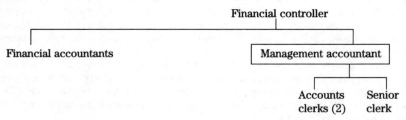

Principal accountabilities

1. Collate and prepare the information required for the Company budget which meets the corporate objectives and which provides the basis for management decision-making.
2. Provide accurate and up-to-date product cost information so that product prices can be maintained at levels which will ensure that Company profit targets are achieved.
3. Prepare accurate, timely and cost effective management accounts and highlight variances so that management can take effective action to improve operating performance.

4. Evaluate stock holdings and determine valuations which reflect current costs and conform to accounting standards.
5. Plan and control the day-to-day activities of the department to ensure that the information provided is accurate and punctual.
6. Liaise with Directors and Senior Managers regarding the establishment of effective information systems, recommending changes and developments to the Financial Controller and I.T. Manager.

Special features

The jobholder is responsible for keeping track of product costs accurately, and regularly updates the records to keep pace with cost increases. The jobholder is also responsible for the evaluation of all stocks, the organization of physical counts and the evaluation of their accuracy. Being able to monitor profit margins and derive the best possible pricing structure is an important component in improving the business performance.

The jobholder works with the Financial Accountant in the preparation of company statutory accounts, and liaises with the external auditors when required. All budget preparation and planning is managed by the jobholder, working with various department heads to produce balanced and accurate figures.

The IT systems are now rather old and inappropriate for the current business complexity and the jobholder is working with the systems people to develop new ways of dealing with the financial information for costing and forecasting purposes.

Performance Management Check-lists and Forms

Manager's preparation check-list

The check-list of questions in this form is designed to provide you with an aide-mémoire for use during the main review. It should be completed by reference to the objectives and plans agreed at the previous main review meeting including any subsequent amendments which may have been agreed. A note should be made of any changes affecting the individual's job since the last main review.

1. How well do you think the individual has done in achieving his/her objectives during the review period?
2. How well have any improvement, development or training plans as agreed at the last review meeting been put into effect?
3. What objectives relating to the individual's key tasks would you like to agree with him/her for the next review period?
4. Has the individual had any problems in carrying out his/her work? If so, what sort of problems and what can be done about them?
5. Are you satisfied that you have given the individual sufficient guidance or help on what he/she is expected to do? If not, what extra help/guidance could you provide?
6. Is the best use being made of the individual's skills and abilities? If not, what should be done?
7. Is the individual ready to take on additional responsibilities in his/her present job? if so, what?
8. Do you think the individual and the company would benefit if he/she were provided with further experience in other areas of work?
9. What direction do you think the individual's career could take within the company?
10. What development or training does the individual need to help in his/her work and/or to further his/her career with the company?

Individual's preparation form

The check-list of questions in this form is designed to provide you with an aide-mémoire for use during the main review. It should be completed by reference to the objectives and plans agreed at the previous main review meeting including any subsequent amendments which may have been agreed.A note should be made of any changes affecting your job which have taken place since the last review.

1. How well do you think you have done in achieving your objectives during the review period?
2. How well have any improvement, development or training plans as agreed at your last review meeting been put into effect?
3. What objectives relating to the key tasks in your present job would you like to agree with your manager for the next review period?

4. Have you met any problems in carrying out your work? If so, what sort of problems and what can be done about them?
5. Do you think your manager could provide you with more guidance or help in what he or she expects you to do? If so, what guidance or help do you need?
6. Do you think the best use is being made of your skills and abilities? If not, what needs to be done about it?
7. Do you feel you are ready to take on additional responsibilities in your present job? If so, what would you like to do?
8. Would you like to gain further experience in other related areas of work? If so, what?
9. What direction would you like your future career to take with the company?
10. What development or training would you like to help you in your job and/or further your career with the company?

Review and agreement checklist

Review

1. How well have the agreed objectives, improvement and development plans been achieved?
2. What factors have contributed to the results obtained?
3. What other matters were discussed at the meeting?

Agreement

1. Objectives agreed for the next review period:
2. Action plans agreed for the next review period:
3. Specific development and training needs:

PERFORMANCE AGREEMENT FORM

Name:	Job title
Department	Review period From: To:

Agreed performance objectives (state performance measures)

Agreed competency requirements

Agreed development/training plan

Signed	Individual	Date
	Reviewer	Date

PERFORMANCE REVIEW FORM

Name:	Job title
Department	Review period From: To:

Comments on achievement of objectives

Comments on achievement of competency levels

Comments on progress in meeting development/training plan

REVIEWER'S SUMMARY

Overall level of achievement   [ ] VE = very effective   E = effective   D = developing   B = basic
Comments on achievements during review period

Individual's comments

Comments on any points arising from review

Reviewer's manager's comments

Signed	Reviewer	Date
	Individual	Date
	Reviewer's manager	Date

Appendix J

Examples of Incentive Schemes

To illustrate in more detail the principles set out in Chapter 18, we give here examples of the following forms of incentive scheme:

A   a scheme for main board directors of a public company
B   a scheme for directors of a subsidiary company of a diversified UK parent multinational
C   a senior/middle management incentive plan in a subsidiary of a US multinational in high technology
D   a long-term incentive scheme.

They are presented in the form of case studies to give greater insight into the way in which such schemes are introduced. Although fictionalized, the details are drawn from actual practice in a range of UK employers. They illustrate what can be done, but we cannot emphasize too strongly the need for companies to tailor incentives to meet their own needs and business plants.

Example A – an incentive scheme for main board directors of a public company

The company

A reasonably successful and profitable manufacturer with an annual sales turnover of £50 million. Profit before tax in the year prior to introduction of the incentive scheme was £3.5 million. Although it was operating in a highly competitive market, the directors believed that there was considerable growth potential. The board consisted of five executive and three non-executive directors:

- a non-executive chairman
- managing director
- finance director
- production director
- sales and marketing director
- personnel director
- two non-executive directors.

The chairman and non-executive directors formed the remuneration committee of the board, taking advice on current pay issues from the personnel director. Until 1987 there were no bonus or incentive schemes and directors' pay increased at the chief executive's discretion.

Shortly after a new managing director was appointed in 1986, he proposed introducing an executive incentive plan for full-time directors. His objectives in doing so were:

- to focus the board on the need to improve company profitability
- to provide a 'group reward' to consolidate team-working at board level – the previous

managing director had resigned after a boardroom row and the production director had only recently been recruited following the voluntary early retirement of his predecessor
- to match competitive practice in the industry – the managing director felt that despite reasonably competitive basic salaries, the company was slipping behind on the pay front because it did not provide incentives for directors. His previous employer in the same industry had operated an incentive scheme that paid out quite well in response to improved profitability
- to provide further evidence to shareholders and City analysts that this was a forward looking organization, prepared to set itself challenging growth targets and reward success.

The incentive scheme

The board decided to opt for a simple scheme in the first instance. The Remuneration Committee therefore recommended the adoption of a plan linked to the achievement of a target based on growth in profit before tax. The inclusion of targets based on improvements in earnings per share and return on capital employed were also considered, but rejected at least for the first year of the scheme's operation. Instead, the company opted for four non-financial targets – one for each of the executive directors. These were closely related to the business plan which had as the key objective the improvement and updating of existing systems in production, sales and the finance function and the introduction of appraisal and succession planning for the first time by the personnel function.

For the 1987/88 financial year the directors therefore set themselves the following targets:

- an improvement in profit before tax of 10 per cent
- the introduction of a quality management programme based on quality circles in the production area with the objective of reducing 'rejects' from 5 per cent of finished articles down to $2\frac{1}{2}$ per cent or less
- the introduction of a performance appraisal scheme for all management and supervisory staff together with the development of a succession plan
- reorganization of the field salesforce to deal with developing markets and completion of a training programme covering the latest thinking in the area of customer care
- the introduction of an improved computer system for producing management accounts to replace one introduced four years ago.

The 1986/87 increase in profit before tax was 7 per cent. The 10 per cent target was therefore considered reasonably stretching. The remuneration committee decided to start paying incentive payments once a 7 per cent increase was achieved (ie once last year's figure was matched) and to increase payments on the following basis:

% profit increase	% incentive payment
7	10
8	12
9	14
10	16
11	19
12	22
13	25
14	28
15	31
16	35
17	39
18	43
19	47
20	51

This incentive plan was based on a 2 per cent increase in incentive payment for each 1 per cent profit improvement between last year's figure and the 10 per cent improvement target, and a 3 per cent increase between the target and 15 per cent. As an additional reward for exceptional performance, a 4 per cent increase for each percentage improvement between 16 and 20 per cent would be given. A 'cap' on bonus payments was set at 51 per cent of salary. This was competitive for the industry. The directors also believed that an increase much in excess of 15 per cent over the year was extremely unlikely and would, if it occurred, be almost certainly due to 'windfall' factors beyond the directors' collective control.

The remuneration committee drew up a set of rules covering the scheme. This set out the basic rules affecting payments and included worked examples for each director to show the amounts payable as cash lump sums in relation to the gearing set out above. It decided that incentive payments would not be pensionable but could be 'sacrificed' into the pension scheme as additional voluntary contributions. Progress towards the achievement of non-financial targets would be monitored quarterly. Only if these were met would the full amount of bonus payable in relation to profit improvement be paid.

The scheme was formally introduced following acceptance by shareholders at the annual general meeting. It was launched at a full board meeting at which the chairman gave a presentation explaining how it would work and how it linked in to the achievement of the business plan.

The scheme was to run for one year in the first instance, then to be reviewed with a view to adding in financial targets, setting new non-financial targets related to the business plan and providing greater rewards for success.

In the 1987/88 financial year the company achieved a 12 per cent improvement in profit before tax and the directors' non-financial targets were met. They therefore each received lump sum payments of 22 per cent ie:

Title	Basic salary	Incentive
Managing Director	£75,000	£16,500
Finance Director	£61,000	£13,420
Production Director	£54,000	£11,880
Sales and Marketing Director	£60,000	£13,200
Personnel Director	£55,000	£12,100

Profit improvement = £420,000
Additional cost of incentive plan = £67,150

Example B – an incentive plan for directors of a subsidiary

The company

A subsidiary of a diversified major multinational with a £40 million annual sales turnover and well developed and sophisticated reporting systems. The objective in introducing an incentive plan was to pay all directors of subsidiaries on a basis which reflected their contribution to the business and focused their activities on agreed business targets. It was also introduced as a retention factor because several able directors who were being groomed for main board responsibilities had recently been headhunted by rival organizations.

The incentive plan

Each subsidiary is set annual targets by the parent board related to its business plan. These are drawn from the following list of both quantitative and non-quantitative factors. The actual targets are agreed with the subsidiary board at the beginning of the financial year.

- profit before tax
- return on capital employed
- sales turnover
- operating costs
- market share
- new product profitability

- employee turnover
- special project completion
- inventory levels
- company image
- employee relations climate
- succession planning.

The targets set for this organization in 1987/88 were:

- a 15 per cent improvement in profit before tax
- return on capital employed of 20 per cent
- annual sales turnover of £47 million
- a reduction in employee turnover from 12 per cent to 10 per cent
- settlement of the annual shopfloor wage negotiations without industrial action and within six weeks of the annual settlement date
- redesign and successful relaunch of an existing product to boost sales by 20 per cent.

Provided all these targets were met, a maximum pensionable incentive of 25 per cent of basic salary would be paid to all directors. Lower achievement would be less well rewarded at the discretion of the parent company board. If none of the targets were met then no incentive payments would be given. To preserve and foster team working, directors would each be paid the same percentage of their basic salary as an incentive payment.

Because of a downturn in the market for the company's products the outcome for the 1987/88 financial year was somewhat disappointing. Performance in relation to targets was as follows:

- an increase in profit before tax of only 12 per cent
- return on capital employed of 17 per cent
- annual sales turnover of £44 million
- employee turnover reduced to nine per cent (exceeding target)
- wage negotiations completed without problems in time for implementation on the settlement date
- the product/package re-launch happened on schedule but only achieved an increase in sales of 12 per cent.

In view of the partial achievement of the targets, the parent company board decided to pay an incentive payment reflecting reward for reasonable achievement in a difficult market. It was still concerned about executive retention and aware that without the sustained effort of the current directors, the situation would have been much worse. An incentive payment of 12.5 per cent of basic salary was therefore paid, ie half the maximum amount due for full target achievement.

Example C – A senior and middle management incentive plan

The company

This organization is a subsidiary of a US multinational employing about 1500 people in the UK. Its activities are selling and servicing products manufactured elsewhere in the world. Incentives are paid to senior and some middle managers as part of the company's long-term philosophy of tying rewards to the achievements of the business plan. Management information systems are very sophisticated and the achievement of targets can be closely monitored in all areas. The company pays very competitive basic salaries in relation to its market. All its remuneration practices have a strong US 'flavour' but have been adapted to the UK market.

The incentive plan

There is a separate management plan for sales executives. This plan therefore covers managers across all functions of the business except direct sales. Each year, managers agree between five and eight objectives from the list given below plus others particularly relevant to their activities. The closer they are to the customer, the more emphasis there is on revenue earnings.

Examples of target areas are:

- sales revenue
- sales bookings
- consultancy revenue
- contribution
- control of discretionary expenses
- credit control (reducing debtor days)
- cash collection
- discretionary (short term) goals
- staff development
- employee satisfaction.

Factors are divided into quarterly and annual targets. Quarterly targets are measured cumulatively throughout the year, so the quarterly incentive payments made are called 'advances' and, to deal with under- or over-payment, these are balanced out in the final payments at the end of the year.

Because the company recognizes the importance of individual control over results, factors are weighted to favour those elements over which each manager has most personal control. Staff development is measured by the number of training days actually undertaken against those required. Employee satisfaction is measured by the use of mandatory employee attitude surveys which provide indicators of subordinates' views of their boss.

To prevent individuals achieving their own goals at the expense of others and to promote team working, the company also has a system of 'shared goals'.

Incentive targets typically range from payment triggered at around 97 per cent of target to a cut off at 105 per cent. On target performance attracts around 75 per cent of the maximum amount payable.

Payments are made on a flat rate basis for each factor irrespective of individual salary. Maximum payments range from 10 to 50 per cent of basic salary. Payments are non-pensionable but can be sacrificed to purchase additional pension.

This system clearly depends on very sensitive performance measurements and excellent management information systems. The use of attitude surveys to measure employee satisfaction is innovative in the UK but reflects a more widespread practice in the US.

Example D – A long-term incentive scheme

(*Source:* Monks Guide to performance related incentives for senior managers.)

The company wishes to emphasize the need for growth in earnings per share (EPS). At a time when inflation is rising at about 7 per cent, it decides upon an absolute minimum level of acceptable achievement in EPS growth of 10 per cent compound per year. Bonus may start to be earned at this level.

The company also concludes that growth in excess of 25 per cent compound over three years is a realistic maximum, having regard to the industry in which the company operates. Growth in excess of 25 per cent in any year is likely to be due to a substantial measure of good luck, so 25 per cent compound will be the upper limit for bonus. The company concludes that, in its circumstances, a payment of 0.75 per cent salary for every 1p increase in EPS between these two thresholds will be paid out at the end of year 3.

In reaching its decision to offer 0.75 per cent for every 1p increase, it assumes a second longer term plan will start at the end of year 3 so that there is some overlap. It would like to see the four participating executives receive a lump sum of about 75 per cent of salary once the accounts are approved by shareholders for year 3, if compound growth of 25 per cent EPS is achieved. The longer term plan complements an annual plan with an upper limit of 40 per cent of salary, plus options over shares worth 4 × salary.

The bonus potential is illustrated in the table below. The percentage of salary which can be earned in each year increases, with most weight attached to year 3. The base EPS is 100 pence per share. If the maximum bonus is earned, EPS nearly doubles in 3 years.

Bonus scale – Base Year 100p

End of Year	Min EPS p	Max EPS p	Max EPS Increase for Bonus p	Max Bonus in Year at 0.75% of salary per p
Year 1	110	125	15	11.25%
Year 2	121	156	35	26.25%
Year 3	133	195	62	46.50%
		Maximum Total Bonus		84%

The participants have to stay until the accounts for year 3 are approved before they can receive any bonus, so the plan acts as a tie. At the end of year 2 a new plan will start so the participants should have something more 'under their belt' by the time bonus is paid out in year 3. The new plan may take a different form if objectives have changed.

A UK Share Option Pricing Model

Increasingly, use is being made of option pricing models to communicate to executives the value of share options at the time they are granted. This is because it is typically hard for them to understand the worth of the options they are being given and assess their value in terms of capital accumulation.

Option pricing is a contentious area and only recently have real studies been made in the pricing of executive options. The IDS Top Pay Unit, in their Personal Tax Guide 1986/87, published an option valuation matrix, based on forecast share price growth. The Black–Scholes model which is used by short-term options and financial futures traders is widely used in the US but assumes an economist's world of no taxes. Neither of these has proved particularly satisfactory.

On 2 August 1990 Accountancy Age published an article by Alan M Judes, a director of Cockman, Consultants & Partners Limited setting out a model specifically catering for UK tax rates and practices. This appendix explains the Judes model.

The Judes model is based on treating the option to acquire shares as an alternative to a purchase of a similar number of shares at current market value. It treats the option grant as a prelude to share ownership and not as a method of financial speculation. Instead of buying shares now, the option holder who intends to purchase shares in the future would be willing to pay a lesser amount for an option to acquire shares at today's price at a future time, and make an alternative investment with the balance of his funds.

The main information needed to value such an option is the long-term rate of return available to the option holder.

This information can be used to determine the value of an option to subscribe for a share at current market value. Assume a share which pays no dividends and has a market value of £1.00. One way to place a minimum value on the option to buy that share in 5 years' time at £1.00 is to subtract from the current market value the amount needed to accumulate the £1.00 exercise price over the 5-year period. The remaining amount is what the option is worth. In the simple example in Chart 1, it is assumed that the investment can roll up tax free and that rates of interest over the 5-year period are 10 per cent.

Chart 1	
Share value (exercise price)	£1.00
less investment needed to produce £1.00 in 5 years' time	.62p
Value of option	.38p

In the simple world of Chart 1, the option holder would always be in the same position as, or better off than, the actual shareholder. Contrast the position of an investor who bought the share at £1.00 (Investor S) and an option holder who bought the option at 38p (Investor O). The details are set out in Chart 2. The conclusion is surprising.

Chart 2

Investor S paid for a share	£1.00
Investor O paid for an option	38p
made an investment of	62p
Outlays of S and O are identical	£1.00

If in 5 years' time the share price has increased say to £3.00.

Investor S has a share worth	£3.00
Investor O has investment worth	£1.00
has an option 'gain' of	£2.00
	£3.00

If the share price has not moved and is still £1.00

Investor S has 1 share worth	£1.00
Investor O has investment worth	£1.00

If the value of the share has fallen to say 50p.

Investor S has 1 share worth	50p
Investor O has investment worth	£1.00

The option holder is better off than the shareholder!

Clearly the real world has dividends paid on shares, tax due on transactions and volatility of share prices. Consequently a much more sophisticated option pricing model for equities has been developed by two Americans, Black and Scholes, in 1973, and is appropriately known as the Black–Scholes model. The Black–Scholes model is complex mathematically and takes into account the price of the underlying share, the exercise price of the option, the time to maturity, the price volatility of the asset, the risk free rate of interest and the expected level of dividends. It is used by traders of options on the London markets, typically for very short-term transactions. However, it assumes a world without any tax charges.

Judes identified the need for an alternative to the Black–Scholes model which addresses UK taxation issues and UK market practice for much longer term option granting. Chart 3 sets out an option pricing model for UK equities. All of the variables can be altered to meet specific circumstances and to calculate a value for an option. The key determinants of the option price are:

1. the after-tax return that an investor can get on a specific gilt to fund the option exercise;
2. the dividend yield of the share and the assumed price growth;
3. the value of shares placed under option, typically as a multiple of salary in the UK context;
4. the risk-free rate of interest available to investors at the time of the option grant.

Chart 4 provides the model's calculation in the same way that Chart 2 demonstrates the simplistic approach.

Two developments have taken place that are relevant for companies granting options. First is the draft proposed by the US Financial Accounting Standards Board which is suggesting that a model much as Black–Scholes is used to price options and that, in 1994,

Option pricing model for UK equities   *Chart 3*

Copyright: Cockman, Consultants & Partners Limited 1990

Variables

8.026%	given after tax yield to redemption for gilt
100p	share price at time of option grant
3.00%	dividend yield
5.00%	assumed future share price growth
7	year life of option (maximum 15)
£25,000	salary of employee at time of option grant
2	multiple of salary placed under option (maximum 4)
40%	marginal rate of income tax
10.00%	risk free rate of interest
140.71p	future value of share at end of option period

Calculation

Value of shares under option	£50,000
Number of shares under option	50,000
After tax yield to redemption	8.026%

Value of option	for holding for	1 share
		£.p
Initial option value	20,875	0.42
less present value of future dividends	(8,338)	(0.17)
Option value	12,537	0.25

Option pricing model for UK equities   *Chart 4*

Demonstration of calculation

	for holding for	1 share
S buys shares worth	50,000	1.00
Total expense of S	50,000	1.00
O purchases future dividends for	8,338	0.17
O invests in gilt described above	29,125	0.58
O purchases option for option value	12,537	0.25
Total expense of O	50,000	1.00
at end of option period		
S has holding worth	70,355	1.41
O receives proceeds from gilt	50,000	1.00
O has option gain of	20,355	0.41
O's holding is worth	70,355	1.41

S and O have received similar income streams

footnote disclosure of the values is given and, from 1997, expense be recognized in the income statement of the company. Secondly, Judes is now using the developments in the derivatives markets and obtaining actual quotes from brokers and futures traders as to what they would be prepared to spend to buy an option from the company. This gives a real value rather than a theoretical one, and larger companies can benefit from such reach values.

One way or another the subject is not going to go away and companies should develop a strategy now for dealing with these issues in the future.

Bibliography and Sources of Information

The section on information sources is divided into four sections:

- Books/reports on salary administration
- Articles
- Salary surveys and sources of information – UK
- International surveys and data on living costs.

It is intended as a guide to the main sources and is therefore selective rather than exhaustive. The fact that a particular source or organization is listed here does not imply the author's recommendation – readers are referred to Chapter 11 and Appendix B for how best to use and interpret remuneration data.

Books/reports on salary administration

This section contains the main recent books and sources of research into pay and benefits practice in the UK. We are indebted to both Incomes Data Services and the Institute of Personnel Management for permission to quote from their bibliographies and directories of sources.

General

Armstrong, M (1993) *Managing Reward Systems*, Open University Press, Buckingham
Beer, M 'Reward systems', In M Beer, B Spector, P Lawrence and D Quinn Mills (1984) *Managing Human Assets*, The Free Press, New York
Bowey, A (1989) *Managing Salary and Wage Systems*, Gower Press, Aldershot
Dunn, B (1993) 'Executive compensation: a matter of alignment', *Benefits and Compensation International* March
Incomes Data Services – Top Pay Unit (1990) *Putting Pay Philosophies into Practice*, London
Kanter, R (1987) 'The attack on pay', *Harvard Business Review* March–April
Lawler, E (1990) *Strategic Pay*, Jossey-Bass, San Francisco
Lawler, E (1971) *Pay and Organizational Effectiveness*, McGraw-Hill, New York
Lupton, T and Bowey, A (1983) *Wages and Salaries*, Gower, Aldershot
Murlis, H and Wright, V (1993) 'Decentralising pay decisions: empowerment or abdication?' *Personnel Management* March
Murlis, H and Wright, V (1993) 'Remuneration' in Report from the UK, Benefits and Compensation International, January/February
Rock, M and Berger, L (Eds.) (1991) *The Compensation Handbook*, McGraw-Hill, New York
Schuster, J and Zingheim, P (1992) *The New Pay*, Lexington Books, Boston, Mass

Job evaluation

Grayson, D (1987) *Job Evaluation in Transition*, Work Research Unit, London
Incomes Data Services (1991) *IDS Focus No. 60*, September

569

Incomes Data Services – Top Pay Unit (1986) *Job Evaluation Review*, London
Industrial Relations Services (1993) 'Job Evaluation in the 1990s', October
Lawler, E (1986) 'What's wrong with points-factor job evaluation', *Compensation and Benefits Review* March–April
Pritchard, D and Murlis, H (1992) *Jobs, Roles and People: The New World of Job Evaluation*, Nicholas Brealey, London

Market pay surveys

Incomes Data Services – Top Pay Unit (1990) *Understanding Salary Surveys*, London
Incomes Data Services – Management Pay Review (1993) Directory of Salary Surveys, London

Performance management

Bevan, S and Thompson, M (1991) 'Performance management at the cross roads', *Personnel Management* November
Fletcher, C and Williams, R (1992) 'The route to performance management', *Personnel Management* October
Fletcher, C (1993) 'Appraisal: an idea whose time has gone?' *Personnel Management* September
Fletcher, C (1993) *Appraisal*, Institute of Personnel Management, London
Wright, V and Brading, L (1992) 'A balanced performance', *Total Quality Magazine* October

Performance pay

Berlet, K and Cravens, D (1991) *Performance Pay as a Competitive Weapon*, Wiley, New York
Binder, A (1990) *Paying for Productivity*, Brookings, Washington, DC
Cannell, M and Wood, S (1992) *Incentive Pay: Impact and Evolution*, Institute of Personnel Management, London
Greenhill, R (1990) *Performance-Related Pay for the 1990s*, Director Books, London
Income Data Services (1989) *Pay and Bonuses in Sales*, London
Incomes Data Services (1988) *Paying for Performance*, London
Incomes Data Services – Top Pay Unit and Institute of Personnel Management (1987) *Executive Bonus Schemes*, London
Kohn, A (1993) 'Why incentive plans cannot work', *Harvard Business Review*, Sept/Oct, pp 54–63
Marsden, D and Richardson, R (1991) *Does Performance Pay Motivate? A Study of Inland Revenue Staff*, London School of Economics, London
Murlis, H (1990) 'Just rewards' *Pensions and Employee Benefits* February
Murlis, H (1992) 'Payment by Results: The Search for Performance Improvement', Public Finance and Accountancy, February
Nalbantian, H (1987) *Incentives, Cooperation and Risk Sharing*, Rowan and Littlefield, Totowa, NJ
Smith, I (1993) *Incentive Schemes*, Croner, Kingston-upon-Thames
Smith, I (1991) *Incentive Schemes, People and Profits*, Croner, Kingston-upon-Thames
Smith, I (1983) *The Management of Remuneration: Paying for Effectiveness*, Institute of Personnel Management, London
Vernon-Harcourt, A (1989) *Performance-Related Bonuses for Senior Management*, Monks Publications, Saffron Walden
Vernon-Harcourt, A, Shoebridge, J and Tulloch, C (1991) *Employee Share Schemes in Practice*, Monks Publications, Saffron Walden
Wright, V (1991) 'Performance-related pay', In F Neale (Ed.), *The Handbook of Performance Management*, Institute of Personnel Management, London

Skill-based pay

Cross, M (1992) *Skill-based Pay: a Guide for Practitioners*, Institute of Personnel Management, London

Lawler, E and Ledford, G (1987) 'Skill-based pay: an idea that's catching on', *Management Review*, February

Salary surveys and sources of information – UK

The listing given below covers all the main producers of published salary and survey data. Space does not permit us to include all the consultants in this area who run small, closed 'participant only' surveys. Further information on these can be obtained from the Management Consultants Association, The Institute of Management Consultants and from the Management Consultancy Information Service who regularly produce a Directory of Management Consultants (enquiries to):

MCIS
38, Blenheim Avenue
Ilford Essex IG2 6JQ
Tel: 081-554 4695

Regular commentary on and trend data from salary and benefits surveys are given by:

Incomes Data Services
Management Pay Review
193, St John Street
London EC1V 4LS
Tel: 071-250 3434

Industrial Relations Services
Pay and Benefits Bulletin
18–20 Highbury Place
London N5 1QP
Tel: 071-354 5858

Personnel Management and PM Plus
17 Britton Street
London EC1M 5NQ
Tel: 071-336 7646

Further information on sources can also be obtained from the library and information services of:

The Institute of Personnel Management
IPM House
Camp Road
Wimbledon
London SW19 4UW
Tel: 081–946 9100

The Institute of Management
Cottingham Road
Corby
Northants NN17 1TT
Tel: 0536-204222

Major published surveys
Note: * = available to participants only

The Institute of Management
National Management Salary Survey – Produced in association with
Remuneration Economics (see below)

Charterhouse Group Ltd
Top Management Remuneration – UK
Published by Monks Publications Ltd (see below)

Computer Economics Ltd
Computer Staff Salary Surveys
Survey House
51, Portland Road
Kingston upon Thames
Surrey KT1 2SH
Tel: 081-549 8726

Cromer Pay and Benefits Briefing
Cromer Publications
Cromer House
London Road
Kingston upon Thames
Surrey KT2 6SR
Tel: 081-547 3333

Department of Employment
New Earnings Survey
Her Majesty's Stationery Office
49, Holborn
London WC1V 6HB
(and other Government bookshops)

Hay Management Consultants
Main surveys:

Hay Remuneration Comparison*
Boardroom Pay Survey*
Data Processing Survey*
Survey of Employee Benefits*

Functional Surveys of:

Accountants*
Architects/Surveyors*
Data Processing*
Engineers*
HR/Personnel*
Investment Fund Managers
Retail*
Salesforce*
Solicitors/Legal*
Taxation*
Treasury*
Health Authorities*
Local Authorities

52, Grosvenor Gardens
London SW1W 0AU
Tel: 071-730 0833

PE-International
Survey of Executive Salaries and Fringe Benefits
Salary Research Unit
Park House
Wick Road
Egham
Surrey PW20 0HW
Tel: 0784 43411

Korn/Ferry International
Boards of Directors Study
12 Buckingham Street
London WC2N 6DF
071-930 4334

Monks Partnership

UK Studies
Management Remuneration in the UK
Board and Senior Management Remuneration
UK Board Earnings
Board Earnings in FT-SE 100 Companies

European Studies
Management Moves in Europe
Incentives and Benefits in Europe
Czech Republic Wage Survey

Specialist Topics
Incentives for Management
Company Car Policy in the UK
Disclosing Board Earnings
Debden Green
Saffron Walden
Essex CB11 3LX
Tel: 0371-830939

National Computing Centre
Salaries and Staff Issues in Computing
Oxford Road
Manchester M1 7ED
Tel: 061-228 6333

Office of Manpower Economics
Review Body on Senior Salaries Report
Her Majesty's Stationery Office
(see address above)

PA Consulting Group
Graduate Salaries and Recruitment Trends
International Pay and Benefits Survey
Sales Salary and Benefits Survey
123 Buckingham Palace Road
London SW1W 9SR
Tel: 071-730 9000

Remuneration Economics Ltd

Main surveys:
REL/BIM National Management Salary Survey (see above)
Financial Functions
Engineering Functions
Personnel Functions
Qualified Actuaries and Actuarial Students
Sales and Marketing

Survey House
51, Portland Road
Kingston upon Thames
Surrey KT1 2SH
Tel: 081-549 8726

Reward Group

Main Surveys
Local Salary and Wage Surveys
Research and Development Salary Survey
Salary and Cost of Living Report
Directors Rewards (in association with the Institute of Directors)
Sales and Marketing Rewards (in association with the Institute of Marketing)

Reward House
Diamond Way
Stone Business Park
Staffordshire ST15 0SD
Tel: 0785 813566

Towers Perrin (formerly TPF&C)

Main Surveys:
Executive Pay in the Electronics Industry*
Executive Pay in UK Subsidiaries of US Companies*
Top Executive Remuneration Survey*

Castlewood House
77–91 New Oxford Street
London WC1A 1PX
Tel: 071-379 3311

The Wyatt Company (UK) Ltd

Main Surveys:
Remuneration Data Service*
Compensation Survey for Electronics Companies*
Survey of Total Compensation for the Insurance Industry*
Survey of Total Compensation for Investment Staff*
Office and Business Automation Data Bank*

Park Gate
21, Tothill Street
London SW1H 9LL
Tel: 071-222 8033

William M Mercer Ltd

Main Surveys:
Company Secretariat Legal and Corporate Affairs
Facility Management Pay and Benefits
Finance Directors, Managers and Accountants
National Pay Planning Survey

Dexter House
2 Royal Mint Court
London EC3 4NH
Tel: 071-488 4949

Major professional institutions producing salary surveys:

Bar Association for Commerce Finance and Industry
The Engineering Council
Institute of Directors
Institute of Marketing
Institute of Physics
Institution of Chemical Engineers
Institution of Civil Engineers
Institution of Electrical and Electronics Incorporated Engineers
The Institution of Electrical Engineers
Institution of Geologists
Institution of Mechanical Engineers
Royal Institute of British Architects
Royal Society of Chemistry

International surveys and data on living costs

Employment Conditions Abroad Ltd
Anchor House
15, Britten Street
London SW3
Tel: 071-351 7151

Executive Compensation Service Inc
(A Member of the Wyatt Company)
273 Avenue de Tervuren (Box 4)
1150 Brussels, Belgium
Tel: Brussels 771 99 10

PE-International Salary Research Unit (see previous section)
Hay Management Consultants (see previous sections)

Organization Resources Counsellors Inc
78, Buckingham Gate
London SW1E 6PE
Tel: 071-222 9231

PA Consulting Group (see previous section)
Towers Perrin Forster and Crosby (see previous section)
Articles and commentaries on various aspects of international remuneration and benefits appear in:

Benefits and Compensation International
Pension Publications Ltd
East Wing
4th Floor
45 Great Peter Street
London SW1P 3LT
Tel: 071-222 0288

Incomes Data Services – European Report (see previous section)
Industrial Relations Services – European Industrial Relations Review
William M Mercer
(see previous section)

KPMG Peat Marwick (Equate)
PO Box 695
8, Salisbury Square
London EC4Y 8BB
Tel: 071 236 8000

Index